WILEY

GAAP for Governments 2019

Subscriber
Update
Service

BECOME A SUBSCRIBER!

Did you purchase this product from a bookstore?

If you did, it's important for you to become a subscriber. John Wiley & Sons, Inc. may publish, on a periodic basis, supplements and new editions to reflect the latest changes in the subject matter that you ***need to know*** in order stay competitive in this everchanging industry. By contacting the Wiley office nearest you, you'll receive any current update at no additional charge. In addition, you'll receive future updates and revised or related volumes on a thirty-day examination review.

If you purchased this product directly from John Wiley & Sons, Inc., we have already recorded your subscription for this update service.

To become a subscriber, please call **1-877-762-2974** or send your name, company name (if applicable), address, and the title of the product to

mailing address: **Supplement Department**
John Wiley & Sons, Inc.
One Wiley Drive
Somerset, NJ 08875
e-mail: subscriber@wiley.com
fax: **1-732-302-2300**
online: www.wiley.com

For customers outside the United States, please contact the Wiley office nearest you:

Professional & Reference Division
John Wiley & Sons Canada, Ltd.
22 Worcester Road Southern Gate,
Etobicoke, Ontario M9W 1L1
CANADA
416-236-4433
Phone: 1-800-567-4797
Fax: 416-236-4447
Email: canada@jwiley.com

John Wiley & Sons, Ltd.
The Atrium
Chichester
West Sussex, PO19 8SQ
ENGLAND
Phone: 44-1243-779777
Fax: 44-1243-775878
Email: customer@wiley.co.uk

John Wiley & Sons Australia, Ltd.
33 Park Road
P.O. Box 1226
Milton, Queensland 4064
AUSTRALIA
Phone: 61-7-3859-9755
Fax: 61-7-3859-9715
Email: brisbane@johnwiley.com.au

John Wiley & Sons (Asia) Pte. Ltd.
2 Clementi Loop #02-01
SINGAPORE 129809
Phone: 65-64632400
Fax: 65-64634604/5/6
Customer Service: 65-64604280
Email: enquiry@wiley.com.sg

WILEY

GAAP for Governments 2019

Interpretation and Application of
GENERALLY ACCEPTED
ACCOUNTING PRINCIPLES
for State and Local Governments

Warren Ruppel

WILEY

Published by John Wiley & Sons, Inc., Hoboken, New Jersey.
Published simultaneously in Canada.

For general information on our other products and services or for technical support, please contact our Customer Care Department within the United States at (800) 762–2974, outside the United States at (317) 572–3993, or fax (317) 572–4002.

Wiley publishes in a variety of print and electronic formats and by print-on-demand. Some material included with standard print versions of this book may not be included in e-books or in print-on-demand. If this book refers to media such as a CD or DVD that is not included in the version you purchased, you may download this material at http://booksupport.wiley.com. For more information about Wiley products, visit www.wiley.com.

Library of Congress Cataloging-in-Publication Data is Available:

ISBN 978-1-119-51168-7 (paperback)
ISBN 978-1-119-51158-8 (ePDF)
ISBN 978-1-119-51167-0 (ePub)

Cover Design and Image: Wiley

Printed in the United States of America

V10015026_102619

CONTENTS

PREFACE

Governmental accounting is a specialized area that has undergone significant changes over the past few decades. As governmental accounting standards have developed, the complexities of preparing financial statements for governmental entities have greatly increased. Providing meaningful financial information to a wide range of users is not an easy task. Adding to these challenges, the Governmental Accounting Standards Board (GASB) brought sweeping changes to the governmental financial reporting model and is now continuing the process of addressing many important accounting areas related to that model.

Given this rapidly changing environment, the financial statement preparer needs a technical resource that provides more than accurate, competent technical information. The resource needs to be written to fit today's governmental accounting environment. It needs to take a fresh look at some of the long-standing accounting questions faced by governments and to provide meaningful up-to-date information on recently issued and soon-to-be-issued accounting pronouncements.

The purpose of this book is to meet these needs by providing a useful, complete, and practical guide to governmental accounting principles and financial reporting. Throughout, the book will provide the reader with:

- An understanding of the concepts and theories underlying each topic discussed.
- A complete, authoritative reference source to assure the reader that all aspects of a particular topic are covered.
- Practical guidance to allow financial statement preparers and auditors to meet the requirements of generally accepted accounting principles for governments and to efficiently and effectively implement new requirements.

The approach used in this book is to provide the reader with useful information in a usable format. Accounting theory must correspond with practical examples to be useful, because theory seldom matches the specific situation. For technical information to be usable, it must be clearly presented without clutter and unnecessary repetition. The substance of accounting requirements must also be understood in order for them to be properly applied. Understanding the reasons why technical requirements exist is an important ingredient in properly applying accounting standards.

The 2019 edition of this book begins with an overview of governmental accounting principles and a description of the various types of funds currently in use by governmental entities. It then describes basic financial statements and provides guidance for reporting various assets, liabilities, revenues, and expenses/expenditures. Finally, it examines the accounting and financial reporting requirements for several specific types of governmental entities. The book also includes a "Disclosure Checklist," which should prove very helpful in determining the completeness of a governmental entity's financial statement disclosures.

This book would not have come to fruition without the hard work and perseverance of a number of individuals. John DeRemigis of John Wiley & Sons had the confidence to work with me in developing the original concept for the book and in ensuring its continuing quality and success. Pam Reh's efforts in producing past editions of the book are greatly appreciated, as are the current members of the Wiley team.

Of course, the time and effort needed to write and maintain this book would not be possible without a supportive family, for which I am grateful to my wife, Marie, and my sons, Christopher and Gregory.

Warren Ruppel, CPA
Woodcliff Lake, NJ
May 2019

ABOUT THE AUTHOR

Warren Ruppel, CPA, is a Partner at Marks Paneth LLP, New York, in the firm's Nonprofit, Government and Healthcare Group, where he serves as the Practice Leader for Government Services. He formerly was the assistant comptroller for accounting of the City of New York, where he was responsible for all aspects of the City's accounting and financial reporting. He has over 35 years of experience in governmental and not-for-profit accounting and financial reporting. He began his career at KPMG after graduating from St. John's University, New York. His involvement with governmental accounting and auditing began with his first audit assignment—the second audit ever performed of the financial statements of the City of New York. From that time he served many governmental and commercial clients until he joined Deloitte & Touche in 1989 to specialize in audits of governments and not-for-profit organizations. Mr. Ruppel has also served as the chief financial officer of an international not-for-profit organization.

Mr. Ruppel has served as an instructor for many training courses, including specialized governmental and not-for-profit programs and seminars. He has also been an adjunct lecturer of accounting at the Bernard M. Baruch College of the City University of New York. He is the author of five other books, *OMB Circular A-133 Audits, Not-for-Profit Organization Audits, Not-for-Profit Accounting Made Easy, Government Accounting Made Easy,* and *Not-for-Profit Audit Committee Best Practices*. He is also the government specialist for SmartPros online CPA Report, in which he appears quarterly to provide a governmental accounting and auditing update.

Mr. Ruppel is a member of the American Institute of Certified Public Accountants as well as the New York State Society of Certified Public Accountants, where he served on the board of directors and chaired its Audit Committee. He also serves on the Governmental Accounting and Auditing Committee and is a past president of the Foundation for Accounting Education. He is a past president of the New York Chapter of the Institute of Management Accountants. Mr. Ruppel is a member of the New York State Government Finance Officers Association, where he serves on its Accounting, Auditing and Financial Reporting Committee. He also serves on the Special Review Committee of the national Government Finance Officers Association. In addition, he is a member of the Executive Advisory Board to the Department of Accounting and Taxation of St. John's University.

1 NEW DEVELOPMENTS

INTRODUCTION

The 2019 Governmental GAAP Guide incorporates all of the pronouncements issued by the Governmental Accounting Standards Board (GASB) through December 2018. This chapter is designed to keep the reader up to date on all pronouncements recently issued by the GASB and their effective dates, as well as to report on the Exposure Drafts, Preliminary Views, and Invitations to Comment (ITCs) for proposed new statements or interpretations that are currently outstanding. This chapter also includes relevant information on the GASB's Technical Agenda for the upcoming year to give readers information as to potential areas for future GASB requirements.

RECENTLY ISSUED GASB STATEMENTS AND THEIR EFFECTIVE DATES

	GASB Statement	*Effective Date*	*Where in This Book*
74	Financial Reporting for Postemployment Benefit Plans Other Than Pension Plans	Fiscal years beginning after June 15, 2016	Chapter 22
75	Accounting and Financial Reporting for Postemployment Benefits Other Than Pensions	Fiscal years beginning after June 15, 2017	Chapter 17
76	The Hierarchy of Generally Accepted Accounting Principles for State and Local Governments	Periods beginning after June 15, 2015	Chapter 2
77	Tax Abatement Disclosures	Periods beginning after December 15, 2015	Chapter 9
78	Pensions Provided through Certain Multi-Employer Defined Benefit Plans	Periods beginning after December 15, 2015	Chapter 17
79	Certain External Investment Pools	Periods beginning after June 15, 2015	Chapter 12

80	Blending Requirements for Certain Component Units—An Amendment of GASB Statement No. 14	Periods beginning after June 15, 2016	Chapter 11
81	Irrevocable Split-Interest Agreements	Periods beginning after December 15, 2016	Chapter 12
82	Pension Issues—An Amendment of GASB Statements No. 67, No. 68, and No. 73	Periods beginning after June 15, 2016	Chapter 17
83	Certain Asset Retirement Obligations	Periods beginning after June 15, 2018	Chapter 14
84	Fiduciary Activities	Periods beginning after December 15, 2018	Chapter 8
85	Omnibus 2017	Periods beginning after June 15, 2017	Chapters 11, 12, 14, 17
86	Certain Debt Extinguishment Issues	Periods beginning after June 15, 2017	Chapter 15
87	Leases	Periods beginning after December 15, 2019	Chapter 19
88	Certain Disclosures Related to Debt, Including Direct Borrowings and Direct Placements	Periods beginning after June 15, 2018	Chapter 15
89	Accounting for Interest Costs Incurred before the End of a Construction Period	Periods beginning after December 15, 2019	Chapter 15
90	Majority Equity Interests—An Amendment of GASB Statements No. 14 and No. 61	Periods beginning after December 15, 2018	Chapter 11

The GASB has a number of Exposure Drafts, Preliminary Views, and Invitations to Comment that it has issued, which will affect future accounting and financial reporting requirements when final standards are developed. The following provides a brief synopsis of what is being covered by each Exposure Draft and Invitation to Comment document. Readers should always be aware that the GASB often modifies proposal stage literature based upon its continuing deliberations and consideration of comments that it receives on each Exposure Draft and Invitation to Comment document.

EXPOSURE DRAFTS

Exposure Drafts—Implementation Guide

The GASB issued an Exposure Draft of an Implementation Guide for Leases, which will address issues relating to GASBS 87 on Leases. The requirements of a final Implementation Guide would be effective for reporting periods beginning after December 15, 2019, with earlier application encouraged if GASBS 87 has been implemented.

GASB Implementation Guides are considered authoritative GAAP for governments and consist of a series of very specific questions and answers that are designed to assist financial statement preparers and auditors to implement GASB Statements. In some cases, they address practice questions that arise; in another case, they address questions that the GASB chose not to specifically address in a GASB Statement itself.

PRELIMINARY VIEWS

Financial Reporting Model Improvements

In September 2018 the GASB issued this PV to address the accounting used by governmental funds, currently the modified accrual basis of accounting and the current financial resources measurement focus. This PV follows the Invitation to Comment on the same topic. The GASB has reached a preliminary view that the current financial resources measurement focus will be replaced by a short-term financial resource model, where short-term is defined as one year.

The PV also addresses other issues including the format of the resource flows statement for the governmental funds, communication of major component unit information, a schedule of government-wide expenses by natural classification, and budgetary comparison reporting.

INVITATION TO COMMENT

Revenue and Expense Recognition

In January 2018 the GASB issued this ITC related to a project to develop a comprehensive revenue and expense model. According to the ITC, the GASB believes this is necessary because:

- Existing guidance for exchange revenue and expense transactions is limited, resulting in inconsistent reporting of information by governments.
- Existing guidance for nonexchange revenue and expense transactions, though generally effective, could be clarified and improved.
- Other accounting standards setters are considering or implementing a "performance obligation" approach for revenue recognition.
- A comprehensive model is expected to result in more robust, principles-based guidance for addressing a wide range of transactions that will improve comparability and provide more useful information.

As stated, the GASB will be considering whether it would be appropriate to adopt a "performance obligation" approach for revenue recognition, which is the basis used in a recent FASB standard on revenue recognition. Clearly, this project is broader that the FASB's standard in that it also addresses expense recognition.

GASB PROJECT PLAN

The GASB has a number of additional important projects on its agenda that will likely affect governmental accounting and financial reporting in the future. Some of the more significant projects are as follows.

Financial reporting model. The PV discussed earlier in this chapter is part of this project, which is taking a fresh look at the basic financial reporting model required by GASBS 34, as amended, to determine if it is working effectively and whether any changes to the model need to be made.

Conduit debt. This project will address the accounting and financial reporting for entities that issue debt on behalf of other organizations, such as industrial development agencies. In most cases, these entities do not report the debt on their financial statements. This project will address whether that continues to be the appropriate accounting treatment and whether there would be any circumstance in which the debt would be reported by the issuing entity.

Public-private partnerships. The growing use and diversity of these relationships has prompted the GASB to address this area and determine whether additional guidance or modifications to the guidance already provided for service concession agreements would be appropriate.

Deferred compensation plans. This is an area that the GASB has not looked at for a long period of time and has begun a project to reexamine the accounting and financial reporting for these plans.

SUMMARY

The GASB, as always, maintains an active agenda, and the accounting and financial reporting standards for governments are consistently evolving. Financial statement preparers need to keep an eye on emerging new GASB pronouncements to ensure that they have adequate time to plan for their implementation, as well as to inform financial statement users about their potential impacts.

2 FOUNDATIONS OF GOVERNMENTAL ACCOUNTING

INTRODUCTION

The field of governmental accounting and financial reporting has undergone significant growth and development over the last 30 years. Generally accepted accounting principles for governments were once a loosely defined set of guidelines followed by some governments and governmental entities, but now have developed into highly specialized standards used in financial reporting by an increasing number of these entities. Because of this standardization, users are able to place additional reliance on these entities' financial statements. The Governmental Accounting Standards Board (GASB) has designed a model for financial reporting by governments that results in a significantly different look to governmental financial statements from those of the past, as well as from those of commercial organizations. There have also been substantive changes in the accounting principles used by governments. Governmental financial statement preparers, auditors, and users must have a complete understanding of these requirements to fulfill their financial reporting obligations.

CHAPTER OVERVIEW

This chapter provides a background on the development and purpose of governmental accounting standards. The topics in this chapter follow.

- Entities covered by governmental accounting principles.
- Overview of the history of governmental accounting standards setting.
- Objectives of governmental accounting and financial reporting.
- Communication methods.
- Elements of financial statements.
- Hierarchy of governmental accounting standards.

ENTITIES COVERED BY GOVERNMENTAL ACCOUNTING PRINCIPLES

This book addresses this topic in much more detail throughout its later chapters as specific types of entities are discussed. However, in general, the following entities are covered by governmental generally accepted accounting principles:

- State governments.
- Local governments such as cities, towns, counties, and villages.
- Public authorities such as economic development, parking, housing, water and sewer, and airport authorities.
- Governmental colleges and universities.
- School districts.
- Public employee retirement systems.
- Public hospitals and other health care providers.

Throughout this book, when "governmental entities" or "governments" are mentioned, the reference is to these types of entities. Governments covered by governmental accounting principles are sometimes distinguished as general-purpose governments (which include states, cities, towns, counties, and villages) and special-purpose governments (which is a term used in GASBS 34, *Basic Financial Statements—and Management's Discussion and Analyses*, to refer to governments and governmental entities other than general-purpose governments). Both general-purpose and special-purpose governments are covered by governmental generally accepted accounting principles and by this book.

Not-for-profit organizations are not included within the scope of governmental accounting standards unless they are considered governmental not-for-profit organizations (discussed in detail below), nor are the federal government and its various agencies and departments. Not-for-profit organizations and the federal government are sometimes confused with the governments that this book is addressing when they are homogenized into something commonly referred to as the "public sector." Not all public-sector entities (as described above) are subject to governmental accounting principles and standards.

Distinguishing a Governmental Entity from a Not-for-Profit Organization

Some organizations are difficult to categorize as either a governmental entity or not-for-profit organization. For example, local governments may set up economic development corporations that have many characteristics of not-for-profit organizations, including federal tax-exempt status under Section 501(c)(3) of the Internal Revenue Code. However, these organizations are usually considered governmental not-for-profit organizations that should follow generally accepted accounting principles for governments. A definition of a governmental not-for-profit organization (subject to the accounting standards promulgated by the GASB) is found in the AICPA Audit and Accounting Guide *State and Local Governments* (the Guide). The Guide defines governmental organizations as "public corporations and bodies corporate and politic." Other organizations are governmental organizations under the Guide's definition if they have one or more of the following characteristics:

- Popular election of officers or appointment (or approval) of a controlling majority of the members of the organization's governing body by officials in one or more state or local governments.
- The potential for unilateral dissolution by a government with the net assets reverting to a government.
- The power to enact or enforce a tax levy.

In applying the above definitions, a public corporation is described in the Guide as an artificial person, such as a municipality or a governmental corporation, created for the administration of public affairs. Unlike a private corporation, it has no protection against legislative acts altering or even repealing its charter. Public corporations include instrumentalities created by the state, formed and owned in the public interest, supported in whole or part by public funds, and governed by managers deriving their authority from the state. Exhibit 1 provides some consensus examples of public corporations often found at the state and local government level.

Furthermore, entities are presumed to be governmental if they have the ability to issue directly (rather than through a state or municipal authority) debt that pays interest exempt from federal taxation. However, entities possessing only that ability (to issue tax-exempt debt) and none of the other governmental characteristics may rebut the presumption that they are governmental if their determination is supported by compelling, relevant evidence.

The Guide provides that entities are governmental or nongovernmental for accounting, financial reporting, and auditing purposes based solely on the application of the preceding criteria and that other factors are not determinative. As an example the Guide provides that the fact that an entity is incorporated as a not-for-profit organization and exempt from federal income taxation under the provisions of Section 501 of the Internal Revenue Code is not a criterion in determining whether an entity is governmental or nongovernmental for accounting, financial reporting, and auditing purposes.

NOTE: GASBS 34 eliminated some of the apparent inconsistencies that existed in the past about financial reporting for governmental not-for-profit organizations. Under GASBS 34, they are special-purpose governments that should follow the accounting guidance as delineated under GASBS 34 and all other applicable GASB pronouncements.

Exhibit 1: Examples of public corporations

The following are examples of "public corporations" that are often found at the state and local government level. These organizations would usually be considered governmental entities when the definition provided in the Guide is applied.

- Public hospital.
- Public college or university.
- Economic development corporation.
- Housing authority.
- Water and sewer utility.

- Electric or gas utility.
- Industrial development authority.
- Educational construction authority.

Typically, these organizations are created by acts of state legislatures. Their continued existence and legal authority to operate can generally be changed at the discretion of the state legislature.

GASBS 39, Determining Whether Certain Organizations Are Component Units—An Amendment of GASB Statement No. 14, resulted in more not-for-profit organizations being included within the financial reporting entity of a government or governmental entity. In these cases, GASBS 39 does not require that these not-for-profit organizations comply with the financial reporting requirements for governments. Despite their inclusion within a government's reporting entity, many of these types of organizations (such as fundraising foundations) would not be considered governmental organizations and would still report their separately issued financial statements using the standards of the Financial Accounting Standards Board (FASB). The financial statement preparer should incorporate the not-for-profit organization's financial statements (reported using FASB principles) within the governmental reporting model (using GASB principles) which may require that the not-for-profit organization actually be reported somewhat separately from the primary government, such as on a separate page. Appendix E of GASBS 39 provides an illustration of including a not-for-profit organization foundation with a governmental university. GASBS 39 is more fully discussed in Chapter 11.

OVERVIEW OF THE HISTORY OF GOVERNMENTAL ACCOUNTING STANDARDS SETTING

Understanding how governmental accounting standards were developed appears difficult at first because it seems that so many different entities and organizations were involved in the standards-setting process. Working from the current process through history is the easiest way to understand the interrelationships of the various entities involved. Currently, governmental accounting standards are established by the GASB. The GASB is a "sister" organization to the Financial Accounting Standards Board (FASB). The FASB establishes accounting standards for private-sector entities, including both commercial entities and not-for-profit organizations. Both the FASB and the GASB are overseen by the Financial Accounting Foundation (FAF), an independent, private-sector organization that among other things is responsible for the oversight, administration, and finances of the GASB and FASB.

NOTE: One significant difference between the GASB and the FASB is the FASB's role in setting accounting principles for public companies. Under the Sarbanes-Oxley Act of 2002, accounting standards for public companies are the responsibility of the US Securities and Exchange Commission (SEC). The SEC continues to recognize accounting standards promulgated by the FASB.

Prior to the formation of the GASB, governmental accounting standards were promulgated by the National Council on Governmental Accounting (NCGA). The NCGA was an outgrowth of a group called the National Committee on Governmental Accounting, which itself was an outgrowth of a group called the National Committee on Municipal Accounting (NCMA). These groups were sponsored by the Government Finance Officers Association (GFOA), originally known as the Municipal Finance Officers Association (MFOA).

The first of several collections of municipal accounting standards issued by the NCGA in 1934 became known as the "blue book." Subsequently, a second blue book was issued by the NCGA in 1951, and a third was issued in 1968, entitled *Governmental Accounting, Auditing, and Financial Reporting* (GAAFR). Subsequent versions of this book were issued in 1980, 1988, and 1994. In 2001, the GFOA issued a major revision of the GAAFR to incorporate the changes to governmental financial reporting as a result of GASBS 34. Another update was published in 2005 to include the new standards for accounting and reporting for postemployment benefits other than pensions established by GASBS 43 and 45. A 2012 update includes reporting deferred inflows and outflows of resources under GASBS 63 and 65. However, these later blue books were different from the 1968 and prior blue books in that they were not meant to be authoritative sources of governmental accounting standards. None of the 1988 through 2012 blue books would be an authoritative source of accounting standards, since the GASB was created in 1984 to serve this purpose; thus the GFOA no longer has the ability to issue authoritative accounting standards. Even with the issuance of the 1980 blue book, the GFOA (then known as the MFOA) decided not to use the blue book as a means of promulgating new accounting standards. Rather, the focus of the blue book was changed to provide financial statement preparers (and their auditors) with detailed and practical guidance to implement authoritative accounting standards. The blue book continues to be used by the GFOA to set the requirements for its "Certificate of Achievement for Excellence in Financial Reporting" program, covered in Chapter 9.

NOTE: The FASB world of accounting standards has been impacted by a move to "converge" standards with International Financial Reporting Standards (IFRS) as promulgated by the International Accounting Standards Board. The reader may wonder if there is an equivalent process in place in the world of government accounting standards. The answer is yes, although there is not nearly the same momentum to converge the US standards with the international standards. Rather, the International Public Sector Accounting Standards Board (IPSASB) has a strategy to converge its International Public Sector Accounting Standards (IPSAS) with IFRS, which are issued by the International Accounting Standards Board. As part of this strategy, IPSASB has developed guidelines for modifying IFRS for application by public sector entities. As discussed later in this chapter, the hierarchy of accounting principles for governments includes IPSAS standards as "other accounting literature." The FAF, along with the GASB and FASB, has developed a strategic plan which mentions increased involvement of the GASB in international standards as a goal.

OBJECTIVES OF GOVERNMENTAL ACCOUNTING AND FINANCIAL REPORTING

In describing the history of the governmental accounting standards development process, one could logically ask the question, "Why were separate accounting and financial reporting standards needed for governments?" The answer to this depends on the identities of the groups of readers and users of the financial statements of state and local governments, the objectives of these readers and users, and the overall objectives of governmental financial reporting.

GASB Concepts Statement 1

The GASB addressed this basic question relatively soon after it was created to serve as an underpinning for all of its future standards-setting work. The GASB issued Concepts Statement 1, Objectives of Financial Reporting (GASBCS 1), which identifies the primary users of the financial statements of state and local governments and their main objectives.

To determine the objectives of governmental financial reporting, the GASB first set forth the significant characteristics of the governmental environment. These characteristics are listed in Exhibit 2.

Exhibit 2: Characteristics of the governmental environment under GASB Concepts Statement 1

- Primary characteristics of a government's structure and the services it provides.
- Control characteristics resulting from a government's structure.
- Use of fund accounting for control purposes.
- Dissimilarities between similarly designated governments.
- Significant investment in non-revenue-producing capital assets.
- Nature of the political process.
- Users of financial reporting.
- Uses of financial reporting.
- Business-type activities.

Primary Characteristics of a Government's Structure and the Services It Provides

- **The representative form of government and the separation of powers.** This emphasizes that the ultimate power of governments is derived from the citizenry. The most common forms of government used in the United States are based on a separation of power among three branches of government: executive, legislative, and judiciary.
- **The federal system of government and the prevalence of intergovernmental revenues.** This characteristic describes the three primary levels of government: federal, state, and local. Because of differences in abilities to raise revenues through taxes and other means, many intergovernmental grants result in revenues passing from one level to another. For example, federal funds for the Temporary Assistance for Needy Families (TANF) program start at the federal level and flow through the states to local governments, where the program is actually administered.
- **The relationship of taxpayers to service receivers.** In terms of impact on the objectives of financial reporting, this characteristic of governments may be the most significant. Following are some interesting points that the GASB included in GASBCS 1 that may affect financial reporting objectives:
  - Taxpayers are involuntary resource providers. They cannot choose whether to pay their taxes.
  - Taxes paid by an individual taxpayer generally are based on the value of property owned or income earned and seldom have a proportional relationship to the cost or value of the services received by the individual taxpayer.
  - There is no exchange relationship between resources provided and services received. Most individual taxes do not pay for specific services.
  - The government generally has a monopoly on the services that it provides.
  - It is difficult to measure optimal quality or quantity for many of the services provided by governments. Those receiving the services cannot decide the quantity or quality of a particular service of the government.

Control Characteristics Resulting from a Government's Structure

- **The budget as an expression of public policy and financial intent and a method of providing control.** In the commercial world, revenues exceeding budget and expenses under budget would almost always be considered good things. In the governmental environment, higher revenues might indicate that taxes are set too high. Even more problematic, expenditures below budget might indicate that levels of spending for public purposes are not achieved because the budgeted funding level is a matter of public policy. Politically speaking, expenditures below budget might not be a good thing, unless the reductions were achieved by unanticipated efficiencies.

- **The budget is a financial plan or expression of financial intent.** This is a similar concept to the public policy question, but also brings into consideration the fact that the budgets of governments generally need to be balanced; for instance, revenues should equal expenditures, highlighting the concept that governments need to live within their means.
- **The budget is a form of control that has the force of law.** Since governments' budgets generally are subject to approval of both executive and legislative branches (similar to the process for other forms of legislation), violation of the budget's spending authority can be construed as a violation of the law.
- **The budget may be used as a mechanism to evaluate performance.** This characteristic is generally less useful in the government environment than in the commercial environment, since performance evaluation is not viewed as the primary purpose of the budget. To be effective, comparison of budgeted to actual results over time would have to be made, as well as consideration of the government's service efforts and accomplishments.

Use of fund accounting for control purposes. Most governments are required by law to use a fund accounting structure as a means to control use of resources. In some cases, bond indentures may require establishing and maintaining funds. In other cases, the government may decide to use fund accounting not because it is required, but simply because it can provide a useful control mechanism for distinguishing various components of its operation.

Regardless of the reason for the use of fund accounting, when examining the objectives of financial reporting for governments, the predominant use of fund accounting must be considered to properly recognize the potential needs of financial statement users.

Dissimilarities between similarly designated governments. GASBCS 1 concludes that the differences in the organization of governmental entities, the services they provide, and their sources of revenues all need to be considered when developing financial reporting objectives. For example, different governments at the same level (for example, county governments) may provide significantly different services to their constituents. The levels and types of services provided by county governments depend on the services provided by the cities, towns, villages, and so forth, within the county, as well as by the state government under which the counties exist. In other unique examples, such as the city of New York, there are five county governments located within the city. Beyond boundary differences, the level of provision of services (such as human services and public safety) varies from county to county. In addition, counties also derive their primary revenues from different sources. Some counties may rely primarily on a county tax on real property within the county. Other counties may rely more heavily on a portion of a sales tax. The important point is that there is a high degree of variability among governments that are at comparable levels.

NOTE: This dissimilarity, while an important characteristic to consider when determining financial reporting objectives, is not unlike that encountered in the commercial environment. A financial statement reader of commercial entities encounters many dissimilarities among the nature of the operations of companies in seemingly identical industries.

Significant investment in non-revenue-producing capital assets. Governments do not determine their capital spending plans based strictly upon return-on-investment criteria. In fact, governments invest in large, non-revenue-producing capital assets, such as government office buildings, highways, bridges, sidewalks, and other infrastructure assets. In many cases, these assets are built or purchased for public policy purposes. Along with this capital investment is a capital maintenance assumption that governments have an obligation to maintain their capital assets. A government's implicit commitment to maintain its assets and its ability to delay maintenance and rehabilitation expenditures (particularly for non-revenue-producing capital assets) were important considerations in GASBCS 1.

Uncertain return on investment is considered. Where governments engage in fee-for-service activities, these considerations are not unlike those found in commercial company accounting. For example, should the public water utility invest in a new piece of equipment that will reduce its costs by $XX or enable it to serve XX number of new customers and generate more revenue? In addition to the business-type decisions, however, governments also make cost/benefit decisions in other seemingly non-revenue-producing activities. For example, a town may decide to invest in new sidewalks and street lighting in its shopping district to raise property values of the businesses in this district, as well as the overall appeal of the town itself. While this investment is non-revenue-producing in the strictest sense, the long-term strategy of the town is the maintenance and enhancement of its property values, and accordingly, its property tax revenues. At the same time, the government may reduce its judgments and claims costs as the number of trip-and-fall lawsuits decreases because of the improved infrastructures.

Nature of the political process. Governments must reconcile the conflict between the services desired by the citizens and the citizens' desire to provide resources to pay for those services. The objectives of the citizenry are to obtain the maximum amount of service with a minimum amount of taxes. These conflicts are handled by politicians whose relatively short terms in public office encourage the use of short-term solutions to long-term problems. Accordingly, governments are susceptible to adopting the practices of satisfying some service needs by deferring others, paying for an increased level of services with nonrecurring revenues, and deferring the cash effect of events, transactions, and circumstances that occur in a particular period. GASBCS 1 concludes that to help fulfill a government's duty to be accountable, financial reporting should enable the user to assess the extent to which operations were funded by nonrecurring revenues or long-term liabilities were incurred to satisfy current operating needs.

Users of financial reporting. GASBCS 1 identifies three primary groups as the users of governmental financial reports:

- The citizenry (including taxpayers, voters, and service recipients), the media, advocate groups, and public finance researchers.
- Legislative and oversight officials, including members of state legislatures, county commissions, city councils, boards of trustees, school boards, and executive branch officials.
- Investors and creditors, including individual and institutional, municipal security underwriters, bond rating agencies, bond insurers, and financial institutions.

While these three user groups have some overlap with the commercial environment, clearly the citizenry and legislative users are somewhat unique to governments.

NOTE: As will be further examined in Chapter 10, which examines the governmental budgeting process, the budget to actual reporting that is considered by many as inherently necessary in governmental financial reporting is designed to meet the needs of the citizenry and legislative users. These groups are somewhat unique to governments as users of financial reporting. This is why budget to actual financial reporting is included where budgets are legally adopted by governments, whereas this reporting has no counterpart in the commercial accounting (or even the not-for-profit accounting) environment.

For example, the expenditures budgeted in a government's general fund represent the amounts that the citizens/taxpayers have authorized the government (through their legislators) to spend from that fund. In order for the government to demonstrate its financial accountability to the citizens and legislators, information is needed within governmental financial reporting that compares the amounts actually spent with the amounts that were legally authorized to be spent.

Uses of financial reporting. The uses of financial reporting by governments center upon economic, political, and social decisions, as well as assessing accountability. These uses are accomplished by the following means:

- **Comparing actual financial results with the legally adopted budget.** Spending in excess of budget may indicate poor financial management, weak budgetary practices, or uncontrollable, unforeseen circumstances. Underspending may indicate effective cost containment or that the quality or quantity of services provided by the government could have been increased without going over budget.
- **Assessing financial condition and results of operations.** Each of the three user groups described above has a different primary reason for assessing a government's financial condition and results of operations. For example, investors and creditors are interested in the financial condition of a government in order to assess whether the government will be able to continue to pay its obligations and meet its debt service requirements. Similarly, these users look to a government's results of operations and cash flows for indications of whether the financial condition of the government is likely to improve or worsen. As another example, the citizenry is interested in the financial condition and operating results of a government as indications of the need to change the rate of tax levies or increase or decrease the levels of services provided in the future.
- **Assisting in determining compliance with finance-related laws, rules, and regulations.** Governmental financial reports can demonstrate compliance with legally mandated budgetary controls and controls accomplished through the use of fund accounting. For example, if the government is legally required to have a debt service fund, and the existence and use of such a fund is clear from a financial statement presentation, compliance is demonstrated. Similarly, compliance with debt covenants, bond indentures, grants, contracts, and taxing and debt limits can also be demonstrated by governmental financial reporting.
- **Assisting in evaluating efficiency and effectiveness.** Governmental financial reporting may be used to obtain information about service efforts, costs, and accomplishments.

Users of this information are interested in the economy, effectiveness, and efficiency of a government. This information may form the basis of their funding or voting decisions.

NOTE: In the governmental financial reporting model promulgated by GASBS 34, the GASB concluded that both government-wide and fund financial statements were necessary in order for the financial reporting model to meet the financial reporting objectives and needs of users as described in GASBCS 1. The objectives described in GASBCS 1, including the needs of the various user groups described above, were driving forces in determining how the financial reporting model promulgated by GASBS 34 took shape.

Business-type activities. In addition to the general governmental characteristics that must be considered in determining the appropriate objectives of financial reporting, circumstances in which governments perform business-type activities must also be examined. Activities are considered "business-type" not solely because they resemble those performed by the private sector but because there is an exchange involved between the receiver and provider of the service; for instance, the receiver or consumer of the services is charged for those services.

The environment for the provision of business-type activities has some overlap with the traditional governmental environment described above. However, the elements of customer and service provider bring different characteristics into the environment that must be considered in determining financial reporting objectives. The following list describes those characteristics that were considered by the GASB in GASBCS 1:

- **Relationship between services received and resources provided by the consumer.** For business-type activities, there is frequently a direct relationship between the charge for the service and the service itself. This exchange relationship causes users of financial information to focus on the costs of providing the service, the revenues obtained from the service, and the difference between the two.

NOTE: The fact that a charge is assessed for a service does not imply that the charge covers all of the costs of a service. There may be a conscious decision on the part of the government to subsidize the costs of particular services with revenues from other sources that are not part of the exchange transaction. Less frequently, the government may also decide to charge more than the cost of the service to provide a "profit" to be used for some other non-business-type or governmental activity.

- **Revenue-producing capital assets.** Many of the capital assets purchased or constructed by governments for business-type activities are revenue-producing. Many business-type activities are capital intensive, and the need for information concerning those assets must be considered when developing financial reporting objectives for governments.
- **Similarly designated activities and potential for comparison.** There is generally a greater potential for comparability among business-type activities performing similar functions than there is among governmental-type activities. Governmental business-type activities generally only perform a single function, such as supplying water. The problems, procedures, and cost components of obtaining, treating, and delivering water are similar, regardless of whether the function is performed by a commercial enterprise, a public authority, an enterprise fund, or as part of a government's basic operations.

NOTE: More information to help the reader distinguish among these differences is provided in Chapter 7. These similarities facilitate comparison of financial reporting among entities (or parts of entities) providing similar services.

- **Nature of the political process.** Business-type activities are generally regarded as less influenced by the political process because their fee-for-service operations take them out of the budgetary debate to which governmental activities are subject. However, in many cases, the business-type activities are subsidized by the government in order to keep the fees lower than cost or market values. The rate-setting process then ensues and subjects the business-type activities to pressures from the political process experienced by general governmental activities. Similar influences from the political process develop when the general government furnishes capital funds, even when there is no direct operating subsidy.

- **Budgets and fund accounting.** Business-type activities generally do not have legally adopted budgets. Budgets are more likely to be used as internal management tools rather than as a revenue and spending plan with the force of law. In addition, since business-type activities are generally found to perform only single functions, the use of fund accounting is far less common than with general governmental activities.

In addition to the characteristics of governments, including those characteristics relating to general government activities and business-type activities described above, the GASB considered three factors in determining the financial reporting objectives for governments. These three factors are:

1. Accountability and interperiod equity.
2. Characteristics of information in financial reporting.
3. Limitations of financial reporting.

The following paragraphs describe why these are important factors in determining the objectives of financial reporting for governments.

Accountability and interperiod equity. ASBCS 1 describes accountability as the "cornerstone" of all financial reporting in governments. Accountability requires that governments answer to the citizenry in order to justify the raising of public resources and the purposes for those resources. Accountability is based on the general belief that the citizenry has a right to know financial information and a right to receive openly declared facts that may lead to public debate by the citizens and their elected representatives.

Interperiod equity is the concept underlying many of the balanced budget legal requirements found in governments, which intend that the current generation of citizens should not be able to shift the burden of paying for current-year services to future-year taxpayers. GASBCS 1 states that interperiod equity is a significant part of accountability and is fundamental to public administration. As such, it needs to be considered when establishing financial reporting objectives. Financial reporting should help users assess whether current-year revenues are sufficient to pay for the services provided that year and whether future taxpayers will be required to assume burdens for services previously provided.

Note that the concept of a "balanced budget" for a government's governmental funds, particularly the main operating fund, which is called the general fund, falls short of providing true interperiod equity. This is because providing for long-term liabilities (such as pensions and retiree health benefits) are often not funded at appropriate levels currently to provide for benefits to be paid in the future.

Characteristics of information in financial reporting. In order for financial information to be an effective method of communication, it must possess certain characteristics that improve its effectiveness. These are described in Exhibit 3.

Exhibit 3: Characteristics of effective financial reporting

- **Understandable** Governmental financial reporting should be expressed as simply as possible so that financial reports can be understood by those who may not have detailed knowledge of accounting principles. This does not mean, however, that information should be excluded from financial reports merely because it is difficult to understand.

- **Reliable** The information presented in financial reports should be verifiable, free from bias, and should faithfully represent what it purports to represent. This requires that financial reporting be comprehensive; for instance, nothing significant or material is left out from the information to faithfully represent the underlying events and conditions. Reliability is affected by the amount of estimation in the measurement process and by uncertainties inherent in the item being measured. To this end, financial reporting may need to include narrative explanations about the underlying assumptions and uncertainties inherent in the process.
- **Relevant** Relevancy implies that there is a close logical connection between the information provided in financial reporting and its purpose. Information should be considered relevant if it can make a difference in a user's assessment of a problem, condition, or event.
- **Timely** If financial reports are to be useful, they must be issued soon enough after the reported events to affect decisions. Timeliness in some circumstances may be so essential that it may be worth sacrificing some degree of precision or detail in the information presented.
- **Consistent** Presumably, once an accounting principle or reporting method is adopted, it will be used for all similar transactions and events. Consistency should extend to all areas of financial reporting, including valuation methods, basis of accounting, and determination of the financial reporting entity.
- **Comparable** Financial reporting should facilitate comparisons between governments, such as comparing costs of specific functions or components of revenue. Comparability implies that differences between financial reports should be due to substantive differences in the underlying transactions or the governmental structure, rather than selection among different alternatives in accounting procedures or practices.

Limitations of financial reporting. GASBCS 1 acknowledges that in setting objectives of financial reporting for governments, the limitations of financial reporting must be taken into consideration. All financial reporting has certain inherent limitations, such as including approximations and estimates of transactions or events. The primary limitation, however, is the cost/benefit relationship that exists in determining whether financial information should be required. On one hand, since accountability is identified as a cornerstone of financial reporting, an almost unlimited amount of information and detail could be required. On the other hand, too much detail may inhibit a clear understanding of the overall financial picture of a government and its operations. In addition, the needs of every potential reader and user of a government's financial statements could never be realistically identified and never practically met.

The GASB determined that in setting financial reporting standards, it should focus its attention on the common needs of users. More importantly, the GASB acknowledged that it must strike a balance between the almost unlimited financial reporting that could be required to demonstrate accountability and the costs that would be incurred by governments in obtaining and reporting the required information. The GASB also stated that it will consider factors such as the ability of certain classes of financial statement users to obtain information by special request, the intensity of the needs of all of the groups of users, the risks or costs to users of not having certain types of information, and the relative costs and benefits, considering the size or type of governmental entities involved.

The GASB issued GASB Concepts Statement 5, *Service Efforts and Accomplishments Reporting—An Amendment of GASB Concepts Statement No. 2* (GASBCS 5), to provide an update to the service efforts and accomplishment reporting concepts contained in GASB Concepts Statement 2, *Service Efforts and Accomplishments Reporting* (GASBCS 2).

The GASB has made clear that service efforts and accomplishments reporting (SEA) is not required by generally accepted accounting principles for governments and is outside the scope of this book. SEA reporting is more currently referred to as performance measurement. The GASB's role in promulgating SEA (or performance measurement reporting) concepts has been quite controversial. GASBCS 5 makes it clear that it is beyond the scope of GASB to establish the goals and objectives of state and local governmental services, specific nonfinancial measures or indicators of service performance, or standards or benchmarks for service performance.

Nevertheless, the GASB issued GASBCS 5 to update GASBSCS 2 based upon the significant amount of research performed by the GASB in SEA reporting. It identifies elements of SEA performance measures for reporting purposes that focus on three different types of SEA performance measures:

- Measures of service efforts.
- Measures of service accomplishments.
- Measures that relate service efforts to service accomplishments.

GASBCS 5 also addresses the limitations of SEA performance information and comments on the usefulness of SEA performance information.

Since there is no requirement to consider the concepts in GASBSCS 5 for reporting in accordance with generally accepted accounting principles, there is no effective date for these concepts.

OBJECTIVES OF FINANCIAL REPORTING

With all of the above factors taken into consideration, GASBCS 1 describes what the GASB set forth as the financial reporting objectives for governments. All of the financial reporting objectives listed and described below flow from what the GASB believes to be the most important objective of financial reporting for governments: accountability. The GASB concluded that the same objectives apply to governmental-type activities as to business-type activities, since the business-type activities are really part of the government and are publicly accountable.

The following are the financial reporting objectives contained in GASBCS 1:

- Financial reporting should assist in fulfilling government's duty to be publicly accountable and should enable users to assess that accountability. Financial reporting should provide information to help determine whether current year revenues were sufficient to pay for current year services.
- Financial reporting should demonstrate whether resources were obtained and used in accordance with the entity's legally adopted budget. It should also demonstrate compliance with other finance-related legal or contractual requirements.
- Financial reporting should provide information to assist users in assessing the service efforts, costs, and accomplishments of the governmental entity.

NOTE: These objectives demonstrate the GASB's interest in using financial reporting to demonstrate a government's progress in achieving interperiod equity, described above, and as a means to compare actual performance with the legally adopted budgeted performance. In addition, service efforts and accomplishments reporting, which is the concept of financial performance indicators used in conjunction with nonfinancial indicators, is another means to measure performance. For example, how many miles of road did the government repave in the past year? How did this compare with what it planned to repave, and what it did repave in the prior year? How much did it cost per mile to repave the road? How much did it budget per mile to repave the road? How much did it cost per mile to repave the road last year?

- Financial reporting should assist users in evaluating the operating results of the governmental entity for the year. Financial reporting should provide information about origins and uses of financial resources.
  - Financial reporting should provide information about how the governmental entity financed its activities and met its cash requirements.
  - Financial reporting should provide information necessary to determine whether the entity's financial position improved or deteriorated as a result of the year's operations.

NOTE: These objectives are fundamental to basic financial accounting and reporting and would be appropriate as part of the objectives for financial reporting for commercial entities as well.

- Financial reporting should assist users in assessing the level of services that can be provided by the governmental entity and its ability to meet its obligations as they become due. Financial reporting should provide information about the financial position and condition of a governmental entity.
  - Financial reporting should provide information about a governmental entity's physical and other nonfinancial resources having useful lives that extend beyond the current year, including information that can be used to assess the service potential for those resources.
  - Financial reporting should disclose legal or contractual restrictions on resources and risks of potential loss of resources.

NOTE: These financial reporting objectives are meant to provide the user of the financial statements with information as to how financially capable the government is to continue to provide services to its constituents. For example, can the government continue to collect sufficient tax revenues to support its current level of service? Has the government made significant investments in capital resources that are available to benefit future generations of citizens and taxpayers?

At a time when the GASB is significantly changing the financial accounting and reporting model of governments, it is important to understand and keep in mind the underlying objectives of governmental financial reporting described in GASBCS 1.

The preparer or auditor of a governmental entity's financial statements must also understand these objectives as part of the framework used to determine the appropriate accounting treatment for the many types of transactions that fall within a "gray" area. Many times, the precise accounting treatment for a particular transaction or type of transaction is unclear from the promulgated standards. Understanding the financial reporting objectives and the conceptual framework with which these objectives were developed provides additional input in attempting to record these types of gray-area transactions within the spirit and intent of the promulgated accounting standards.

As mentioned earlier in this chapter, GASBCS 1 was issued in 1987 and the reader may be wondering whether these concepts and ideas are still relevant given all of the recent changes that have been made to governmental accounting and financial reporting since its issuance. The GASB published a whitepaper entitled "Why Governmental Accounting and Financial Reporting Is—and Should Be—Different," which, as its title suggests, makes a case to reinforce the need to have separate accounting and financial reporting standards for governments and governmental entities. (The whitepaper is available for download on the GASB website—www.gasb.org.) It is remarkable that in making this case, the whitepaper looks back on and affirms many of the concepts contained in GASBCS 1, which are still very relevant in today's financial reporting environment. The whitepaper concludes (and the author agrees) that distinctive accounting and financial reporting rules for governments are made necessary by government's uniqueness relative to other types of organizations—including not-for-profit organizations.

COMMUNICATION METHODS

Concepts Statement 3—Communication Methods in General-Purpose External Financial Reports that Contain Basic Financial Statements

The GASB issued GASBCS 3 on communication methods to provide conceptual guidance on the placement of information within general-purpose external financial reports. GASBCS 3 addresses when information should be communicated in one of the following methods:

- Recognition in the basic financial statements.
- Disclosure in the notes to the financial statements.
- Presentation as required supplementary information.
- Presentation as supplementary information.

The principal user of the concepts contained in GASBCS 3 is the GASB, which will use these concepts in determining the communication methods to be used for information resulting from future Standards. However, financial statement preparers would also use the concepts in determining how to communicate information that is not specifically covered by a GASB pronouncement. The following briefly describes the intended uses for each of these communications methods as contained in the Concept Statement.

- **Recognition in the basic financial statements.** Items recorded in the financial statements are intended to provide reliable representations of the effects of transactions and other events. Items that are elements of financial statements and are measurable with sufficient reliability are recognized in the financial statements. Disclosure in the notes to financial statements or presentation as supporting information is not an adequate substitute.
- **Disclosure in the notes to the financial statements.** Notes are essential to a user's understanding of the financial statements, meaning that they are so important as to be indispensable to a user (1) with a reasonable understanding of government and public finance activities and of the fundamentals of government financial reporting and (2) with a willingness to study the information with reasonable diligence. Notes may include management's objective explanation of recognized amounts and related known facts, contingencies, certain risks that affect financial statements, subsequent events, measurement methods, accounting policies, and other information essential to understanding the financial

statements. Notes do not include subjective assessments of the effects of reported information on the reporting unit's financial position or predictions about the effects of future events on financial position.

- **Presentation as required supplementary information.** Required supplementary information (RSI) is supporting information that the GASB has concluded is essential for placing the basic financial statements and notes in an appropriate operational, economic, or historical context. RSI may include explanations of known amounts, analysis of known facts or conditions, or information for placing the basic financial statements or notes in proper context. RSI would not include subjective assessments of the effects of reported information on the reporting unit's future financial position, predictions about the effects of future events on future financial position, or information unrelated to the financial statements.
- **Presentation as supplementary information.** Supplementary information (SI) is supporting information that is useful for placing the basic financial statements and notes in appropriate operational, economic, or historical context. Presentation of SI is voluntary; however, any applicable standards regarding content and format of the information should be followed.

ELEMENTS OF FINANCIAL STATEMENTS

The GASB issued Concepts Statement 4, *Elements of Financial Statements* (GASBCS 4), which is a component of the conceptual framework of objectives and fundamental concepts that can be used as a basis for establishing consistent financial reporting standards.

GASBCS 4 establishes definitions for the seven elements of historically based financial statements of state and local governments as follows:

- *Assets* are resources with present service capacity that the entity controls.
- *Liabilities* are present obligations to sacrifice resources that the government has little or no discretion to avoid.
- *A deferred outflow of resources* is a consumption of net assets by the government that is applicable to a future reporting period.
- *A deferred inflow of resources* is an acquisition of net assets by the government that is applicable to a future reporting period.
- *Net position* is the residual of all other elements presented in a statement of financial position.
- An *outflow of resources* is a consumption of net assets by the government that is applicable to the reporting period.
- An *inflow of resources* is an acquisition of net assets by the government that is applicable to the reporting period.

Clearly, GASBCS 4's definitions all hinge on the concept of "resources." A resource is defined as an item that can be drawn upon to provide services to the citizenry.

OBSERVATION: The definitions of deferred inflows and outflows of resources described above became the foundation for GASB Statement No. 63, Financial Reporting of Deferred Outflows of Resources, Deferred Inflows of Resources, and Net Position, which is discussed in Chapter 9.

Measurement of Elements of Financial Statements

In March 2014 the GASB issued Concepts Statement No. 6—*Measurement of Elements of Financial Statements* (GASBCS 6). This Concepts Statement addresses both measurement approaches and measurement attributes for elements of financial statements. As described in GASBCS 6, a measurement approach determines whether an asset or liability presented in a financial statement should be (1) reported at an amount that reflects a value at the date that the asset was acquired or the liability was incurred or (2) remeasured and reported at an amount that reflects a value at the date of the financial statements. A measurement attribute is the feature or characteristic of the asset or liability that is measured.

GASBCS 6 establishes the two measurement approaches that would be used in financial statements, as follows:

- **Initial-transaction-date-based measurement (initial amount).** The transaction price or amount assigned when an asset was acquired or a liability was incurred, including subsequent modifications to that price or amount, such as through depreciation or impairment.
- **Current-financial-statement-date-based measurement (remeasured amount).** The amount assigned when an asset or liability is remeasured as of the financial statement date.

GASBCS 6 establishes the four measurement attributes that would be used in financial statements, as follows:

- Historical cost is the price paid to acquire an asset or the amount received pursuant to the incurrence of a liability in an actual exchange transaction.
- Fair value is the price that would be received to sell an asset or paid to transfer a liability in an orderly transaction between market participants at the measurement date.
- Replacement cost is the price that would be paid to acquire an asset with equivalent service potential in an orderly market transaction at the measurement date.
- Settlement amount is the amount at which an asset could be realized or a liability could be liquidated with the counterparty, other than in an active market.

NOTE: Concepts Statements themselves do not change existing GAAP; rather, they form a basis on which the GASB will likely issue a new statement, which will then change existing GAAP. Essentially, it represents a reexamination of the accounting basis (historical cost or fair value) of the various components of the financial statements.

Concepts Statements are used by the GASB in its standards-setting process. There is nothing that a financial statement preparer needs to implement relative to a Concepts Statement. However, when a financial statement preparer is faced with an accounting issue for which no clear standards or practices exist, Concepts Statements can be a useful resource in selecting an appropriate accounting treatment.

HIERARCHY OF GOVERNMENTAL ACCOUNTING STANDARDS

The GASB is responsible for promulgating accounting principles for governments. The manner in which the GASB promulgates accounting principles depends somewhat on the pervasiveness and the degree of impact that a new accounting principle is anticipated to have. Generally, an issue or topic will be brought to the GASB's attention for consideration from any of a number of sources, including governments themselves, independent auditors, the GASB board members, or GASB staff. In addition, advisory committees, such as the Governmental Accounting Standards Advisory Council, may also bring matters to the GASB's attention for consideration. Based on the input of these individuals, organizations, and groups regarding important technical issues that need to be addressed, the GASB will determine its formal technical agenda. Once a matter is placed on the GASB's technical agenda, staff resources are devoted to the issue to study and evaluate various alternatives to address it. After the initial research is completed, the GASB staff may issue an Invitation to Comment (ITC) or a Discussion Memorandum (DM) to solicit comments from the constituent groups regarding the advantages and disadvantages of the various alternatives available. Upon receipt and analysis of the feedback from an ITC or a DM, the GASB may be able to reach some initial conclusions about the contents of a final accounting standard. If this is the case, the GASB will issue an Exposure Draft (ED) for public comment. If the GASB still has remaining questions or feels that additional feedback is needed from the constituent community, it may issue a Preliminary Views document (PV). The PV sets forth preliminary views on an accounting matter, but also poses additional questions to the constituent community with the hope of soliciting additional input to be included in the next stage in the due process procedure, the ED.

For issues that are not very pervasive or complex, or where the alternatives are limited, the GASB will decide not to issue an ITC or a DM and move directly to issue an ED. This is the most frequently used approach. ITCs and DMs are reserved for the more important and complex issues. The GASB evaluates and considers the feedback obtained from an ED and then issues a final Statement. If significant changes result from the feedback obtained from the ED, the GASB may choose to issue a second ED before it proceeds to the final Statement.

The process described above would apply whether the GASB is issuing a new Statement or an Interpretation of an existing Statement. In addition to Statements and Interpretations, the GASB issues Technical Bulletins (TBs) and Implementation Guides (usually called "Q&As" because of their question-and-answer format). These two documents are not subject to the same due process procedures described above for new Statements and Interpretations. TBs and Q&As are actually issued by the GASB staff, but they may not be issued if, after review, a majority of the GASB board objects to their issuance.

GAAP Hierarchy for Governments

The GASB issued Statement No. 76, *The Hierarchy of Generally Accepted Accounting Principles for State and Local Governments (GASBS 76)*. GASBS 76 superseded Statement No. 55, *The Hierarchy of Generally Accepted Accounting Principles for State and Local Governments (GASBS 55)*. The objective of setting a GAAP hierarchy is to identify the sources of accounting principles used to prepare financial statements of state and local governmental entities in conformity with GAAP and the framework for selecting those principles. GASBS 76 reduced the GAAP to two categories, as follows:

Category A Officially established accounting principles, which consist of GASB Statements.

Category B GASB Technical Bulletins: GASB Implementation Guides, and literature of the AICPA that has been cleared by the GASB.

GASBS 76 provides that if the accounting treatment for a transaction or other event is not specified by a pronouncement in Category A, a governmental entity should then consider whether the accounting treatment is specified by a source in Category B.

If the accounting treatment for a transaction or other event is not specified in Category A or Category B, a government should first consider accounting principles for similar transactions within Categories A and B. If the accounting treatment cannot be determined from this consideration, then nonauthoritative accounting literature from other sources, described below, may be considered provided the other source does not conflict with or contradict the authoritative GAAP of Categories A and B.

In addition, GASBS 76 specifies that a governmental entity should not apply the accounting principles in authoritative GAAP to similar transactions or events if those accounting principles prohibit the application of the accounting treatment to the particular transaction or event or indicate that the accounting treatment should not be applied by analogy.

Sources of nonauthoritative accounting literature. GASBS 76 provides that the sources of nonauthoritative accounting literature include:

- GASB Concepts Statements.
- Pronouncements and other literature of the:
  - Financial Accounting Standards Board.
  - Federal Accounting Standards Advisory Board.
  - International Public Sector Accounting Standards Board.
- AICPA literature not cleared by the GASB.
- Practices that are widely recognized and prevalent in state and local government.
- Literature of other professional associations or regulatory agencies: Accounting textbooks, handbooks, and articles.

In evaluating the appropriateness of nonauthoritative literature, GASBS 76 provides that a governmental entity should consider the consistency of the literature with GASB Concepts Statements, the relevance of the literature to the particular circumstances, the specifics of the literature, and the general recognition of the issuer or author as an authority.

CODIFICATION OF CERTAIN FASB AND AICPA ACCOUNTING AND FINANCIAL REPORTING GUIDANCE

The GASB issued Statement No. 62 (GASBS 62), *Codification of Accounting and Financial Reporting Guidance Contained in Pre–November 30, 1989 FASB and AICPA Pronouncements*, which incorporates into the GASB standards certain accounting and financial reporting guidance that is included in pronouncements of the FASB and AICPA issued on or before November 30, 1989, which do not conflict with or contradict GASB pronouncements.

Previously, GASB Statement No. 20 (GASBS 20), *Accounting and Financial Reporting for Proprietary Funds and Other Governmental Entities That Use Proprietary Fund Accounting*, required funds and other governmental entities that use proprietary accounting (which would also include government-wide financial statements) to apply all applicable GASB pronouncements, as well as the following pronouncements of the FASB and AICPA issued on or before November 30, 1989, unless those pronouncements conflict with or contradict GASB pronouncements:

- FASB Statements.
- FASB Interpretations.
- Accounting Principles Board Opinions.
- Accounting Research Bulletins.

As all authoritative GAAP for private sector organizations is now contained solely in the FASB's Accounting Standards Codification, these FASB and AICPA pronouncements technically no longer exist. Accordingly, the GASB addressed this issue by including in the GASB standards (by means of GASBS 62) all of the applicable pre–November 30, 1989, FASB and AICPA standards.

GASBS 62 addresses the following general accounting topics:

- Capitalization of Interest Cost.
- Revenue Recognition for Exchange Transactions.
- Revenue Recognition when Right of Return Exists.
- Statement of Net Assets Classification.
- Special and Extraordinary Items.
- Comparative Financial Statements.
- Related Parties.
- Prior Period Adjustments.
- Accounting Changes and Error Corrections.
- Disclosure of Accounting Policies.
- Contingencies.
- Construction-Type Contracts—Long Term.
- Extinguishments of Debt.
- Troubled Debt Restructuring.
- Foreign Currency Transactions.
- Interest Costs—Imputation.
- Inventory.
- Investments in Common Stock.
- Leases.
- Nonmonetary Transactions.
- Sales of Real Estate.
- Costs and Initial Rental Operations of Real Estate Projects.
- Research and Development Arrangements.

GASBS 62 also addresses the following industry-specific standards:

- Broadcasters.
- Cable Television Systems.
- Insurance Entities—Other Than Public Entity Risk Pools.
- Lending Activities.
- Mortgage Banking Activities.
- Regulated Operations.
- Rights of Offset.

While substance of the above content is onerous (GASBS 62 is hundreds of pages long), the GASB used the approach of adopting the accounting and reporting requirements essentially as they existed in the applicable pre–November 30, 1989, FASB and AICPA pronouncements, modifying the language as appropriate to recognize the effects of the governmental environment without affecting the substance of the provisions. Accordingly, GASBS 62 is not intended to establish new financial reporting requirements or modify existing requirements. Rather, it incorporates FASB and AICPA accounting and reporting guidance applicable to governments and governmental entities into the GASB literature. While the GASB's intent was not to change accounting of financial reporting requirements, in the Basis for Conclusions of GASBS 62 the GASB does state that it recognizes that practitioners in exercising professional judgment may have reached different conclusions in applying the hierarchy without specific guidance. This Guide incorporates the significant general guidance areas of GASBS 62.

The GASB issued Statement No. 66 (GASBS 66), *Technical Corrections—2012, an Amendment of GASB Statements No. 10 and 62*, to make some minor corrections/clarifications to these two GASB Statements. As pertains to GASBS 66, the technical corrections are as follows:

Operating Leases—GASBS 62, paragraphs 222 and 227(b), is amended to delete what could be perceived as a prohibition of the use of the fair value method that is permitted in paragraph 6(b) of FASB Statement No. 13.

Purchase of a Loan or Group of Loans—GASBS 62, paragraph 442, is amended to clarify that the purchase of a loan or group of loans should be reported at its purchase price. The initial investment in a purchased loan or group of loans should include the amount paid to the seller plus any fees paid or less any fees received.

Service Fees—GASBS 62, paragraph 460 is deleted to remove the provision that the same price should be adjusted, for purposes of determining any gain or loss on the sale, to provide for the recognition of a normal servicing fee in each subsequent year.

SUMMARY

This chapter provides a basic foundation for the governmental accounting and financial reporting environment. Understanding this environment will help the reader understand and apply the details of the accounting and financial reporting principles discussed throughout the rest of this book.

3 FUND ACCOUNTING FUNDAMENTALS

INTRODUCTION

To fully understand the accounting and financial reporting principles of state and local governments, financial statement preparers and auditors must be familiar with two key concepts: fund accounting and the basis of accounting and measurement focus used by funds. This chapter discusses the following information:

- A definition of *fund* and the purposes of fund accounting.
- A synopsis of the various types of funds used by governments for accounting and financial reporting.
- A definition of *basis of accounting* and *measurement focus*.
- Recognition and measurement of certain fund liabilities and expenditures.
- A description of which basis of accounting and measurement focus are used by each type of fund.

These concepts are key components of the fundamental differences between the accounting and financial reporting for governments and private enterprises. Financial statement preparers and their auditors will need to understand these concepts in understanding the differences between government-wide and fund financial statements. This chapter includes some summarized information to give the reader an overview of the governmental accounting and financial reporting structure. More detailed information is contained in later chapters, which examine not only the accounting for, but also the uses of, the various types of funds and how typical transactions of these funds are reflected in the accounting records. Chapter 9 describes the accounting treatment of various types of transactions that can occur between funds.

DEFINITION OF *FUND* AND THE PURPOSE OF FUND ACCOUNTING

Fund was defined by Statement 1 of the National Council on Governmental Accounting (NCGAS 1), entitled *Governmental Accounting and Financial Reporting Principles*, as follows:

> *A fund is defined as a fiscal and accounting entity with a self-balancing set of accounts recording cash and other financial resources, together with all related liabilities and residual equities or balances, and changes therein, which are segregated for the purpose of carrying on specific activities or attaining certain objectives in accordance with special regulations, restrictions, or limitations.*

This definition requires some explanation and clarification to be useful.

First, a fund is a separate entity for accounting and financial reporting purposes. A fund in itself is not a separate legal entity, although it may be established to comply with laws that require that certain transactions be segregated and accounted for as a separate "fund."

Second, a fund has a self-balancing set of accounts that record assets, liabilities, fund balance, and the operating activities of the fund. In other words, a balance sheet and operating statement can be prepared for individual funds. A fund's financial statements would not necessarily include all of the accounts for assets and liabilities that one would expect to find in a commercial enterprise's financial statements. As will be discussed later in this chapter, fixed assets or long-term liabilities are not recorded in the financial statements of funds classified as "governmental." Rather, governmental fixed assets, now referred to as capital assets, and long-term liabilities are reported only on the government-wide financial statements under the GASBS 34 financial reporting model. Thus, *self-balancing* should not be taken to mean a complete picture. It should indicate that the transactions that are supposed to be recorded in a fund are self-balancing; for instance, the debits equal the credits (its trial balances), and that assets less liabilities equals the fund's residual (or, stated differently, its equity or fund balance).

NOTE: One common mistake that is often made by those not familiar with fund accounting is to assume that a fund is synonymous with a "pot of money" available to spend. This is not the case. A fund's "fund balance" represents the difference between the fund's assets and the fund's liabilities (as well as any deferred inflows and outflows of resources). Many of a fund's assets may not be in the form of currency, such as a receivable. Therefore, it is important to keep in mind that a "fund" is an accounting convention for control and financial reporting purposes, and is not the same as a bank account.

Why Do Governments Use Fund Accounting?

Fund accounting for governments was developed in response to the need for state and local governments to be fully accountable for their collection and use of public resources. The use of funds is an important tool for governments to demonstrate their compliance with the lawfully permitted use of resources. A predecessor to fund accounting was the use of separate bank accounts for separate purposes. The finer the degree of financial reporting, management, accountability, and segregation of resources, the less likely it is that governments would overspend budgets or not be as candid in financial reporting as they should be. Clearly, maintaining separate bank accounts for all of the different revenue sources and types of expenditures for the complex governments of today is not practical. Thus, separate bank accounts were replaced by the use of separate funds.

Fund Accounting under the GASBS 34 Reporting Model

Fund accounting remains an important aspect of financial reporting for governments. GASBS 34 includes within its financial reporting model fund financial statements. Fund financial statements enable governments to continue to demonstrate legal compliance as described above. Since the overwhelming number of general-purpose governments have legally adopted budgets at the fund level, demonstration of compliance with budgets is an important component of fund reporting under the GASBS 34 reporting model. However, under the GASBS 34 reporting model, information about a government's overall financial condition and activities is presented in government-wide financial statements that do not provide fund information and in fact are prepared using different accounting methods than the fund financial statements. Reading the government-wide financial statements provides additional information to the user of a government's financial statements that was not previously available from the prior reporting model, which relied exclusively on fund and account group reporting.

NOTE: While fund accounting is an important part of the GASBS 34 reporting model, a review of the more significant accounting pronouncements of the GASB issued after implementation of the GASBS 34 reporting model reveals an emphasis on the accounting used in the government-wide financial statements (and proprietary funds) rather than the governmental fund financial statements (with some notable exceptions). This doesn't necessarily signal that the GASB deemphasizes the importance of governmental funds, but they are clearly, at least to the author, not a high priority for new accounting pronouncements. That said, the GASB's project related to financial reporting model improvements in governmental funds will very likely result in a change to the current financial resources measurement focus and modified accrual basis of accounting used by these funds.

How Is the Number of Funds to Be Established Determined?

The number of separate funds to be established should be based on either legal requirements or management judgment for sound financial administration. In other words, where statute or law requires the establishment of particular funds, certainly these funds must be established by the government. Similarly, establishment of separate funds may be required by contracts into which the government enters, such as bond indentures.

Beyond these legal and contractual requirements, management should determine how many funds should be established to segregate the activities related to carrying on specific activities or attaining certain objectives in accordance with special regulations, restrictions, or limitations.

As discussed below, there are different fund types, and most governments will find that they have at least one fund in each fund type.

NOTE: Under the GASBS 34 financial reporting model, distinctions of fund types became somewhat less important, since financial reporting is driven by whether a fund is a major or nonmajor fund, rather than its fund type. The concept of fund type, however, is useful in understanding the purposes for different funds. While reporting by all fund types is not a component of GASBS 34, distinguishing between governmental and business-type activities remains important. In addition, presentation of funds in the fund financial statements grouped by their fund type within the major and nonmajor fund categories can be useful to the financial statement reader. Determination of major funds is discussed later in this chapter. GASBS 54, Fund Balance Reporting and Governmental Fund Type Definitions, fine-tunes the definitions of the fund types. The specific new definitions are discussed in later chapters that discuss the specific fund types.

However, other governments have multiple funds in each fund type. These governments could easily find that they have over 100 funds that "roll up" or combine into one fund type. The financial management of these governments should consider, however, that the establishment of too many funds is likely to result in cumbersome accounting and financial reporting procedures. The development of more sophisticated accounting software, with increasingly greater capability to segregate transactions within expanding account code structures, is likely to encourage governments to use fewer funds. Accountability may be achieved with better account coding, rather than with the establishment of many funds (see Exhibit 1).

Exhibit 1: Size of government's operations versus number of funds

The size of a government's operations does not necessarily coincide with the number of funds that it establishes. For example, excluding component units, the city of New York uses one general fund (a government can have only one general fund), one special revenue fund, one capital projects fund, and one debt service fund to account for its governmental activities. These four funds (in addition to blended component units) are used to account for total revenues in excess of $75 billion. Many smaller governments have dozens of special revenue, capital projects, and debt service funds to account for a far lower volume of activity.

The number of funds is influenced not only by legal requirements, but also by the reliance on fiscal controls built into financial accounting systems. The number of funds established is also affected by the political forces that shape the financial functioning of the government. Some executive branches (mayors, governors, etc.) and legislatures (city councils, state legislatures, etc.) believe financial accountability is increased by using many funds. The result is a wide disparity in the number of funds found at all levels of government.

A SYNOPSIS OF THE VARIOUS TYPES OF FUNDS USED BY GOVERNMENTS FOR ACCOUNTING AND FINANCIAL REPORTING

The following paragraphs introduce the various types of funds that a government may have. This is only a brief introduction to each of these fund types. Each fund type is more fully discussed in later chapters.

The fund types are categorized into three different activities: governmental, business-type, and fiduciary.

1. Governmental:
   (a) General fund.
   (b) Special revenue funds.
   (c) Capital projects funds.
   (d) Debt service funds.
   (e) Permanent funds.
2. Proprietary (business-type):
   (a) Enterprise funds.
   (b) Internal service funds.
3. Fiduciary:
   (a) Pension and other employee benefit trust funds.
   (b) Investment trust funds.
   (c) Agency funds.
   (d) Private-purpose trust funds.

NOTE: As discussed in Chapter 8, the GASB issued Statement No. 84 Fiduciary Activities that will impact the accounting and financial reporting for certain fiduciary funds.

Following is a summary of the basic characteristics of each of these fund types and funds. Later chapters provide more detailed information.

Governmental Funds

General Fund

The general fund is used to account for all of the financial resources of the government, except those required to be accounted for in another fund. It is the primary operating fund of the government. It should account for all activities of the government unless there is a compelling reason to account for the activities in another fund type, including the legal and contractual requirements discussed previously. In addition, circumstances in which funds need to be segregated to carry on specific activities or attain certain objectives in accordance with special regulations, restrictions, or limitations are reasons for using another fund type. The latter require the judgment of management to determine whether the activities will be accounted for in the general fund or in other fund types.

Special Revenue Funds

Special revenue funds are used to account for the proceeds of specific revenue sources legally restricted to expenditures for specific purposes. The legal restriction on the expenditures does not mean that there is a legal requirement to establish a special revenue fund. If there is a legal or contractual requirement to establish a special revenue fund to account for these ear-marked revenues, the government should establish the mandated fund. If there is no legal or contractual requirement, the use of special revenue funds is optional. GAAP does not require the use of special revenue funds (with one small exception relating to blended component units, described below). The activities normally recorded in special revenue funds are frequently accounted for by governments in their general fund. If the government decides to set up special revenue funds, the government also needs to determine how many to establish—for instance, one for all special revenues or numerous funds to account for a variety of types of special revenue. However, given that the purpose of special revenue funds is basically to account for restricted revenues, it is unlikely that using one special revenue fund for many types of special revenues would be helpful in demonstrating legal compliance.

A common example of earmarked revenues that governments may choose to account for in a special revenue fund are the proceeds from grants or other aid programs. Generally, these grant or aid program revenues must be used for specific types of expenditures, and accordingly, accountability for the expenditure may be facilitated by using a special revenue fund. In addition, if not accounted for in the general fund, states should use a special revenue fund to account for the administration of the federal food stamp program.

Certain revenues are precluded by GAAP from being recorded in special revenue funds. Revenues that are earmarked for expenditures for major capital projects should not be recorded in special revenue funds.

The instance in which GAAP requires the use of special revenue funds involves the reporting of component units. As more fully described in Chapter 6, certain legally separate entities may be included in a government's financial reporting entity. Some of these entities may have governmental activities that are blended with the reporting government's own governmental funds, as if the component unit were part of the reporting government. In cases where these blended component units have general funds, these general funds should not be combined with the general fund of the reporting government, but should be reported as special revenue funds.

Capital Projects Funds

Capital projects funds may be used to account for financial resources to be used for acquisition or construction of major capital facilities other than those financed by proprietary or trust funds. As with special revenue funds, the use of capital projects funds (with one exception, described below) is optional to the government, absent any legal or contractual requirement. Again, if the government elects to use capital projects funds, it must also decide whether to establish one fund to account for all capital projects or separate capital projects funds for each capital project or group of projects.

The exception, the situation in which a government is required to establish a capital projects fund under GAAP, relates to when grants or shared revenues are received for capital projects. NCGAS 2, *Grant, Entitlement, and Shared Revenue Accounting by State and Local Governments*, states that capital grants and shared revenues restricted for capital acquisitions or construction (other than those associated with enterprise and internal service funds) should be accounted for in a capital projects fund.

Debt Service Funds

A government may use debt service funds to account for accumulation of resources for and payment of general long-term debt principal and interest. The use of debt service funds is generally optional for a government, absent any legal or contractual requirement. (Before deciding not to establish debt service funds, financial managers of governments should ensure that these funds are not required by any of the government's bond indentures.)

NCGAS 1 states, "Debt service funds are required when they are legally mandated and/or if financial resources are being accumulated for principal and interest payments maturing in future years." The second part of this statement requires some clarification. The phrase has been interpreted to mean that the government is regularly setting aside resources to pay more than one year's debt service (principal and interest payments). In other words, the government is using a mechanism similar to a sinking fund to accumulate resources to pay debt service in the future. In this case, the government would be required by GAAP to establish a debt service fund. On the other hand, if the government only sets aside resources to pay the next year's debt service, it is not interpreted to be "accumulating" resources, and a debt service fund would not be required. In this latter case, the government may still establish a debt service fund if it facilitates financial management of these resources.

There is a second instance in which GAAP would require the establishment of a debt service fund. NCGAS 2 states that grants, entitlements, or shared revenues received for the payment of principal and/or interest on general long-term debt should be accounted for in a debt service fund.

Permanent Funds

GASBS 34 created a new type of governmental fund known as a permanent fund. A permanent fund is used to report resources that are legally restricted to the extent that only earnings, and not principal, may be used for purposes that support the reporting government's programs, meaning that the earnings are for the benefit of the government or its citizenry. Types of arrangements that would often be accounted for in a permanent fund are sometimes called "endowments." Permanent funds are not the same as a private-purpose trust fund (a fiduciary fund also created by GASBS 34 that is described later), which is used to report situations in which the government is required to use the principal or earnings for the benefit of individuals, private organizations, or other governments and not for the support of its own programs.

Proprietary (Business-Type) Funds

Proprietary funds, as the name implies, are used to account for the proprietary or business-type activities of a government. GASBS 34 established requirements for when enterprise and internal service funds should be used. The requirements are discussed later in this section as they apply separately to enterprise and internal service funds.

Enterprise Funds

NCGAS 1 defines the purpose of enterprise funds as:

> *to account for operations (a) that are financed and operated in a manner similar to private business enterprises—where the intent of the governing body is that the costs (expenses, including depreciation) of providing goods or services to the general public on a continuing basis be financed or recovered primarily through user charges; or (b) where the governing body has decided that periodic determination of revenues earned, expenses incurred, and/or net income is appropriate for capital maintenance, public policy, management control, accountability, or other purposes.*

A government may use an enterprise fund to account for activities if the criteria of either (a) or (b) are met. In most cases, governments use enterprise funds because there are certain activities performed by governments for the public that closely resemble the characteristic described in (a) above. For example, the government may operate a water and sewer utility that charges its customers for the services rendered. The net results of operations for this particular activity are determined using accounting similar to that used by a commercial enterprise, generally providing the most relevant information to the financial statement user. The government's intent does not have to be to recover all of the costs of the particular activity. However, even if only partial cost recoupment is intended, it is still likely to be desirable to use an enterprise fund to determine the extent of the government's subsidy of a particular activity.

While the criterion under (a) above provides the most common reason to establish enterprise funds, the criterion in (b) certainly provides the government's management with latitude to determine whether to account for certain activities in an enterprise fund.

As will be more fully described in later chapters, there are two activities that GAAP requires to be accounted for in enterprise funds. These activities are a government-operated hospital (Chapter 25) and a government public entity risk pool (Chapter 24).

Governments may use enterprise funds to report any activity for which a fee is charged to external users for goods or services. Accordingly, a government may report as enterprise funds those activities in which a fee is charged to external users of goods or services. The significant change made by GASBS 34 was to establish conditions when the use of an enterprise fund would actually be required.

Activities are required to be reported in an enterprise fund if any one of the following criteria is met. The criteria are to be applied in the context of the activity's principal revenue sources. This means that if the criteria are met for a revenue other than the principal revenue for an activity, the use of an enterprise fund would not be required. In addition, the criteria are applied to activities, which is different from applying them to a fund. In other words, if an activity presently accounted for in the general fund meets any of the criteria, the use of an enterprise fund is required, despite the fact that the activity is not presently accounted for in a separate fund. (These criteria are not meant to require that insignificant activities of governments be reported as enterprise funds simply because a fee or charge is levied. If that fee or charge is not the activity's principal revenue source, the use of an enterprise fund is not required.) The criteria are as follows:

- The activity is financed with debt that is secured solely by a pledge of the net revenues from the fees and charges of the activity, with two additional clarifications:
    - If the debt is secured in part by a portion of its own proceeds, it would still be considered as payable solely from the revenues of the activities. In other words, if some of the proceeds from the debt from an activity were placed in debt service reserve accounts, this would not exempt the activity from being reported as an enterprise fund if it would otherwise meet this criterion.
    - Debt that is secured by a pledge of revenues from fees and charges and the full faith and credit of a related primary government or component unit is not payable solely from the fees and charges of the activity, and the activity would not be required to be reported as an enterprise fund. (The primary government or the component unit does not have to be expected to make any payments—the pledge of its full faith and credit is sufficient to avoid the requirement to account for the activity using an enterprise fund.)
- Laws and regulations require that the activity's costs of providing services, including capital costs (such as depreciation and debt service), be recovered with fees and charges, rather than taxes or similar revenues.
- The pricing policies of the activity establish fees and charges designed to recover its costs, including capital costs (such as depreciation and debt service).

Under GASBS 34, state unemployment insurance funds and public entity risk pools are required to be accounted for in enterprise funds. GASBS 34 did not affect the accounting for special assessment projects because there is no activity for which external users are charged a fee for goods or services. In the case of special assessments, capital assets are constructed and the property owners reimburse the government for amounts necessary to pay principal and interest on bonds.

Internal Service Funds

NCGAS 1 states that internal service funds may be used "to account for the financing of goods or services provided by one department or agency to other departments or agencies of the governmental unit, or to other governmental units, on a cost-reimbursement basis." In other words, these are activities that are not performed for the general public (as with enterprise funds), but are performed for other parts of the government itself, hence the term *internal* service funds (Exhibit 2). Governments decide to establish internal service funds if they believe that the cost management of a particular activity can be improved by first identifying the costs of the activity or service and then charging the cost of the activity or service to the recipient agencies or departments.

Exhibit 2: Internal service fund example

Understanding the use of an internal service fund can best be explained by the use of an example.

The city of Anywhere uses an internal service fund to account for the operations of its motor vehicles, commonly referred to as a motor pool. Many of the city's agencies and departments use cars and trucks, such as the police department, fire department, social services administration, as well as the executive and administrative functions of the city.

The motor pool internal service fund maintains the city's fleet of vehicles, including purchasing and servicing the vehicles. The total of the costs of the motor pool is estimated and "charged" to the departments that use the vehicles on some equitable basis, such as the number of vehicles used by the various departments. In charging the departments, consideration may also be given to the type of vehicle, since the costs of maintaining a compact car are quite different from those of a large truck.

The motor pool sets its charges so that it breaks even on its operations. The city benefits from the economies of scale of maintaining all or most of its vehicles by a centralized source. In addition, the user agencies and departments save their own time and effort in not having to handle the details of purchasing and maintaining their own individual fleets of vehicles.

Establishing an internal service fund is completely at the discretion of the government. There are no instances in which GAAP requires internal service funds.

GASBS 34, however, established one circumstance when an internal service fund should not be used. Internal service funds should be used only if the reporting government is the predominant participant in the activity. If it is not, the activity should be reported as an enterprise fund.

Fiduciary Funds

Fiduciary funds are used if the government has a fiduciary or custodial responsibility for assets. Fiduciary funds should be established when there is a legal restriction of the resources, such as with a pension plan or when there is a written trust agreement. Governments may choose to establish fiduciary funds based on the government's own unilateral actions, solely to improve the government's own accountability. In these discretionary instances (absent a legal or other reason), the government should keep in mind that the transactions accounted for in fiduciary funds may be just as easily accounted for in the general fund or a special revenue fund.

The types of fiduciary funds are described briefly below.

Pension and Other Employee Benefit Trust Funds

Many governments sponsor pension plans that provide benefits to their employees and to other governmental employers. In cases in which the government manages the pension plans, or when the pension plans are part of the reporting entity of the government, they are accounted for as pension trust funds. Accounting rules for pension plans are somewhat unique and are covered more fully in Chapter 24. Governments that report deferred compensation plans under Sections 457 and 401(k) of the Internal Revenue Code within their reporting entity would account for these plans within this fund type.

Investment Trust Funds

Investment funds are used by governments to report the external portion of separate investment pools that are sponsored by governmental entities. This type of fiduciary fund was created by GASB Statement 31, *Accounting and Financial Reporting for Certain Investments and for External Investment Pools*, and is discussed in Chapter 12. The accounting for investment trust funds matches that used by proprietary funds.

Agency Funds

Agency funds are used to account for situations in which the government receives and disburses resources in an *agency* capacity. Because all of the assets of agency funds are associated with third parties, agency funds have no equity. Their assets equal their liabilities. Accordingly, they have no *operations*, either, which means that no operating statement is prepared for agency funds, since they have no revenues or expenditures.

Private-Purpose Trust Funds

GASBS 34 created a type of fiduciary fund that is referred to as a private-purpose trust fund. This fund should be used to report all other trust arrangements (that is, those that otherwise wouldn't be accounted for as another type of fiduciary fund or as a permanent fund) under which principal and income benefit individuals, private organizations, or other governments.

Major Funds

As mentioned above, when reporting fund financial statements, the focus of the reporting is on major funds. Consideration of fund financial reporting is dependent upon the proper identification of major and nonmajor funds. GASBS 34 provides the following guidance for determining what is a major fund:

- The main operating fund (the general fund or its equivalent) is always considered a major fund.
- Other individual governmental and enterprise funds should be reported as major funds based on the following criteria:

- Total assets, liabilities, revenues, or expenditures/expenses of that individual fund are at least 10% of the corresponding total (assets, liabilities, revenues or expenditures/expenses) for all funds of that category or type (i.e., total governmental or total enterprise funds); and
- Total assets, liabilities, revenues, or expenditures/expenses of the individual fund are at least 5% of the corresponding total for all governmental and enterprise funds combined.

- In applying the 5% and 10% criteria above to governmental funds, it should be noted that revenues do not include other financing sources, and expenditures do not include other financing uses. This serves to avoid wide year-to-year variances in major fund determinations that may be caused by activities such as bond issuances. In applying the 5% and 10% criteria above to enterprise funds, it should be noted that both operating and nonoperating revenues and expenses should be considered as well as gains, losses, capital contributions, additions to permanent endowments, and special items.

In addition, if a government has only governmental funds and no enterprise funds, only the 10% criteria need be applied. In other words, if an individual governmental fund failed the 10% test, the government should not then subject this fund, in this example, to the 5% test. This fund would not be reported as a major fund.

- In addition to these criteria, if the government believes that a particular fund not meeting the above criteria is important to financial statement readers, it may be reported as a major fund. (In other words, nonmajor funds are reported in a single column. If a government desires to break out a nonmajor fund separately, it should treat that fund as a major fund.)
- Blended component units of the component unit should be evaluated to determine whether they must be reported as major funds.
- The major fund determination is done using the combined fund type amounts, regardless of any reconciling items to the government-wide financial statements. In addition, the analysis is done using amounts as reported under generally accepted accounting principles—the budgetary basis of accounting (if different from generally accepted accounting principles) should not be used.
- The calculations provided above represent the minimum requirements for government and proprietary funds that must be considered major funds. If a fund of these fund types does not meet the monetary criteria described above, the government is permitted to report that fund as a major fund, if it so chooses. A government may do this because a fund that may be smaller in size may be of particular interest to financial statement readers.

A DEFINITION OF *BASIS OF ACCOUNTING* AND *MEASUREMENT FOCUS*

Two of the most important distinguishing features of governmental accounting and financial reporting are the basis of accounting and measurement focus used. Additionally, as discussed in the next section, not all of the funds of a government use the same basis of accounting and measurement focus, further distinguishing and complicating governmental accounting and financial reporting. A simple rule of thumb to help clarify the difference between the two concepts is that the basis of accounting determines *when* transactions will be recorded and the measurement focus determines *what* transactions will be recorded.

Basis of Accounting

Basis of accounting refers to when revenues, expenditures, expenses, and transfers (and the related assets and liabilities) are recognized and reported in the financial statements. Most accountants are familiar with the cash and accrual bases of accounting. Commercial enterprises generally use the accrual basis of accounting. There are exceptions to this general rule, however. Small businesses may use the cash basis of accounting. Other businesses, such as real estate tax-shelter partnerships, may prepare financial statements on an income-tax basis, and still other commercial enterprises, such as utilities, may prepare special reports on a regulatory basis of accounting.

For governmental accounting, an additional basis of accounting, the modified accrual basis, is used by certain funds of a government. To understand the modified accrual basis of accounting, the accountant first needs to understand the cash and accrual bases of accounting.

Cash Basis of Accounting

Under the cash basis of accounting, revenues and expenditures are recorded when cash is received or paid. For example, an entity purchases goods that are received and used by the entity. However, the bill for the goods is not paid until two months after the goods were received. Under the cash basis of accounting, the expense for the purchased goods is not recognized in the financial statements until the bill is actually paid, regardless of when the goods were received or consumed by the entity. Using a strict interpretation of the cash basis of accounting, an entity's balance sheet would have two accounts: cash and equity. The statement of activities under the pure cash basis consists solely of a listing of cash receipts and cash disbursements for the period. As a practical matter, entities using the cash basis of accounting often record some transactions not strictly in accordance with the cash basis, such as inventory, fixed assets, and debt. When these types of assets and liabilities are recorded in financial statements that are otherwise on a cash basis, the accounting basis is often referred to as the modified cash basis of accounting.

Accrual Basis of Accounting

The accrual basis of accounting is generally recognized as a better method than the cash basis for accounting for the economic resources of an organization, both commercial and governmental. The accrual basis of accounting presents a better presentation of the financial condition and results of operations of organizations, including governments. The accrual basis accounts for transactions when they occur. Revenues are recorded when *earned* or when the organization has a right to receive the revenues. Expenses are recorded when incurred. Unlike the cash basis, revenues and expenses are recorded when they occur, regardless of when the related cash is received or disbursed.

Modified Accrual Basis of Accounting

As will be discussed throughout this book, governmental funds use the modified accrual basis of accounting. The modified accrual basis of accounting can be categorized as falling somewhere between the cash basis of accounting and the accrual basis of accounting. This accounting basis was promulgated in NCGAS 1, which stated that while the accrual basis of accounting was recommended for use to the *fullest extent possible* in the governmental environment, there were differences in the environment and in the accounting measurement objectives for governmental funds that justified a divergence from the full accrual to the modified accrual basis. NCGAS 1 noted that these modifications to the accrual basis were both practical and appropriate for governmental funds to use.

The most important feature of the modified accrual basis of accounting involves the recognition of revenue in the financial statements. NCGAS 1 specifies that revenues (and other governmental fund financial resource increments) are recognized in the accounting period in which they become *susceptible to accrual*, that is, when they become both *measurable* and *available* to finance expenditures of the current period. In determining whether revenues are measurable, the government does not have to know the precise amount of the revenue in order for it to be subject to accrual. Reasonable calculations of revenues based on cash collections subsequent to the end of the fiscal year are the most likely way in which revenues become measurable. Governments are not precluded, however, from using other means to measure revenues, including historical collection patterns. In addition, a government may be able to measure revenues under cost-reimbursable grants and programs based on the amount of the expenditures claimed as revenue under each grant or program.

Determining whether revenues are available to finance expenditures of the current period is a unique consideration for governments in deciding whether revenues are subject to accrual. *Available* means that the revenue is collectible within the current period or soon enough thereafter to pay liabilities of the current period. Since governmental funds generally only record current liabilities, the availability criteria result in governmental funds only recording revenues related to the current fiscal year and received after year-end to be received within a relatively short period after the end of the fiscal year to meet the availability criteria. Assessing the criteria for the various types of revenues typically found in governments is described in later chapters.

Recording expenditures and liabilities under the modified accrual basis of accounting more closely approximates the accrual basis of accounting for other than long-term liabilities than does the recording of revenues. Expenditures in governmental funds recorded using the modified accrual basis of accounting are recorded when the related liability is incurred. Expenditures for goods and services received prior to a governmental fund's fiscal year-end are recorded in the year received, just as under the accrual basis of accounting. However, in applying this general principle, there are several important distinctions to keep in mind, as follows:

- The basis of accounting describes when transactions are recorded, not what transactions are recorded. Accordingly, as described below concerning measurement focus, allocations such as depreciation and amortization are not recorded as expenditures of governmental funds, nor are long-term liabilities.
- The most significant exception to the liability-incurred criterion for expenditure recognition involves payments of debt service on general long-term obligations. Debt service is recognized as an expenditure in the accounting period in which it is paid. There is no expenditure accrual, for example, for accrued interest on debt service up to the date of the fiscal year-end. Rather, both principal and interest are recognized as expenditures at the time that they are paid. (Chapter 9 describes an exception to the general rule when resources for debt service are accumulated in the current year and paid early in the subsequent year. It also describes the impact of GASBI 6 on this exception.)
- A second exception for expenditure recognition on the modified accrual basis of accounting involves inventory items, such as materials and supplies. Inventory may either be considered to be an expenditure when purchased (known as the *purchase method*) or may be recorded as an asset and recognized as an expenditure when consumed (known as the *consumption method*).

- Finally, the expenditures for insurance and similar services extending over more than one fiscal year do not have to be allocated between or among the fiscal years to which they relate. Rather, insurance and similar services may be recognized as expenditures in the period during which they were acquired.

More detailed information on the modified accrual basis of accounting and its application to various types of revenues and expenditures is contained in the following chapters, which cover the different types of governmental funds.

RECOGNITION AND MEASUREMENT OF CERTAIN FUND LIABILITIES AND EXPENDITURES

In the course of deliberations on GASBS 34, the GASB discussed areas where there were divergences in practice in the application of the modified accrual basis of accounting and current financial resources measurement focus. Because this basis of accounting and measurement focus continues to be used by governmental funds in the fund financial statements, GASB Interpretation 6 (GASBI 6), *Recognition and Measurement of Certain Fund Liabilities and Expenditures in Governmental Fund Financial Statements*, clarifies the recording of certain fund liabilities and expenditures.

GASBI 6 applies to funds that use the modified accrual basis of accounting and the current financial resources measurement focus and applies to the fund financial statements of governmental funds. It addresses when certain liabilities should be recorded as fund liabilities of governmental funds. Specifically, it includes within its scope liabilities that fall within the following categories:

- Those that are generally required to be recognized when due (debt service on formal debt issues, such as bonds and capital leases).
- Those that are required to be recognized to the extent that they are normally expected to be liquidated with expendable available financial resources (such as compensated absences, judgments and claims, landfill closure and postclosure care costs, and special termination benefits).
- Those for which no specific accrual modification has been established.

GASBI 6 does not address whether, when, or the amount that a government should recognize as a liability, but rather clarifies the standards for distinguishing the parts of certain liabilities that should be reported as governmental fund liabilities. It also does not address the financial reporting for liabilities associated with capital leases with scheduled rent increases, employer contributions to pension plans, or postemployment health care plans. Each of these liabilities has been addressed by GASB standards subsequent to GASBI 6.

Governmental funds should report matured liabilities as fund liabilities. Matured liabilities include:

- Liabilities that normally are due and payable in full when incurred.
- The matured portion of general long-term debt (i.e., the portion that has come due for payment).

In the absence of an explicit requirement (i.e., the absence of an applicable modification, discussed below) a government should accrue a governmental fund liability and expenditure in the period in which the government incurs the liability. Examples of these types of expenditures include salaries, supplies, utilities, professional services, and so forth. These types of liabilities generally represent claims against current financial resources to the extent that they are not paid.

As described in GASBI 6, there is a series of specific accrual modifications that have been established in generally accepted accounting principles for reporting certain forms of long-term indebtedness, such as:

- Debt service on formal debt issues (bonds and capital leases) should be reported as a governmental fund liability and expenditure when due (i.e., matured). An optional additional accrual method (described below) may be used in certain limited circumstances.
- Liabilities for compensated absences, claims and judgments, special termination benefits, and landfill closure and postclosure care costs should be recognized as governmental fund liabilities and expenditures to the extent that they are normally expected to be liquidated with expendable available resources. Governments are normally expected to liquidate liabilities with expendable available resources to the extent that they mature (i.e., come due for payment). In other words, if the liability hasn't come due, the governmental fund should not record a liability and expenditure.
    - For example, consider an employee who terminates employment with a government and is owed accrued vacation time. A liability for the employee's unused vacation leave does not become due until the employee terminates employment. A fund liability and expenditure is not recorded until the employee actually terminates employment and the amounts are due him or her. Accordingly, if a government's fiscal year ends on June 30, and the employee terminates employment on July 1 and is paid for unused vacation time on July 20, no liability or expenditure would be recorded for the June 30 financial statements of the governmental fund. On the other hand, if the employee terminates employment on June 29 and is paid on July 20, a fund liability and expenditure would be recognized in the June 30 fund financial statements because the amount is due the employee as of June 30.
- GASBI 6 specifies that the accumulation of net assets in a governmental fund for the eventual payment of unmatured long-term indebtedness does not constitute an outflow of current financial resources and should not result in the recognition of an additional fund liability or expenditure. Accumulated net assets should be reported as part of fund balance.

As mentioned above, an additional accrual of a liability and expenditure for debt service is permitted under generally accepted accounting principles if a government has provided financial resources to a debt service fund for payment of liabilities that will mature early in the following period. GASBI 6 specifies that a government has provided financial resources to a debt service fund if it has deposited in or transferred to that fund financial resources that are dedicated for the payment of debt service. In addition, "early in the following year" is defined as a short period of time, usually one or several days, but not more than one month. In addition, accrual of an additional liability and expenditure is not permitted for financial resources that are held in another government or that are nondedicated financial resources transferred to a debt service fund at the discretion of management.

Measurement Focus

In addition to the basis of accounting used, the other term that is key to having a full understanding of governmental accounting is *measurement focus*. As mentioned earlier, measurement focus determines what transactions will be reported in the various funds' operating statements.

Governmental funds use a measurement focus known as the *flow of current financial resources*. The operating statement of a governmental fund reflects changes in the amount of financial resources available in the near future as a result of transactions and events of the fiscal period reported. Increases in spendable resources are reported as *revenues* or *other financing sources* and decreases in spendable resources are reported as *expenditures* or *other financing uses*.

Since the focus is on the financial resources available in the near future, the operating statements and balance sheets of governmental funds reflect transactions and events that involved current financial resources, for instance, those assets that will be turned into cash and spent and those liabilities that will be satisfied with those current financial resource assets. In other words, long-term assets and those assets that will not be turned into cash to satisfy current liabilities will not be reflected on the balance sheets of governmental funds. At the same time, long-term liabilities (those that will not require the use of current financial resources to pay them) will not be recorded on the balance sheets of governmental funds.

Proprietary funds use the flow of economic resources measurement focus. This measurement focus, which is generally the same as that used by commercial enterprises, focuses on whether the proprietary fund is economically better off as a result of the events and transactions that have occurred during the fiscal period reported. Transactions and events that improve the economic position of proprietary funds are reported as *revenues* or *gains*, and transactions and events that diminish the economic position of proprietary funds are reported as *expenses* or *losses*. In other words, proprietary funds reflect transactions and events regardless of whether there are current financial resources. This results in reporting both long-term assets and liabilities on the balance sheets of proprietary funds.

NOTE: The following examples use the proprietary fund to demonstrate the accrual basis of accounting and the economic resources measurement focus. The government-wide financial statements are prepared using the accrual basis of accounting and the economic resources measurement focus, which are demonstrated in the following proprietary fund examples. In other words, the entries that are recorded in the governmental fund are simultaneously reflected in the government-wide financial statements in a manner that is essentially the same as demonstrated for the proprietary fund.

The following examples illustrate how the various transactions are recorded by governmental and proprietary funds when a government issues debt for capital projects, pays the debt service on the debt, and constructs a capital asset. (For purposes of this example, we will treat *governmental funds* as a generic term to avoid too many details about transfers from the general fund to and from the debt service and capital projects funds. These issues will be addressed in later chapters.)

Example: Government issues $100,000 in debt to be used for capital projects

Governmental Fund

When debt is issued for any purpose, a governmental fund records the transaction in its operating statement as an increase in current financial resources. The governmental fund has more current financial resources to spend, and its operating statement reflects this increase as follows:

Cash	100,000	
Other financing source		100,000

To record the receipt of proceeds from the sale of bonds

Proprietary Fund

When a proprietary fund issues debt, there is no real change in its economic resources, and accordingly, the transaction has no effect on the operating statement. While the proprietary fund has incurred a liability, it has also received an equivalent amount of cash, which conceptually is available to pay that liability. The proprietary fund would record the issuance of debt on its balance sheet only, as follows:

Cash	100,000	
Bonds payable		100,000

To record the receipt of cash from the issuance of bonds

Example: Government pays debt service ($2,500 interest, $5,000 principal)

Governmental Fund

When a governmental fund pays debt service, it reflects the decrease in its current financial resources by making the debt service payment. The following entry is recorded:

Expenditures—debt service	7,500	
Cash		7,500

To record principal and interest payment on outstanding debt

Notice that both the principal and interest payment were reflected as expenditures in the governmental fund.

Proprietary Fund

The proprietary fund will reflect that the only economic resource being used is for the payment of interest. The principal portion of the debt service payment merely results in a decrease in cash and a decrease in a liability, thus having no effect on economic resources. The following entry is recorded:

Bonds payable	5,000	
Interest expense	2,500	
Cash		7,500

To record a debt service payment of both principal and interest

If a debt service payment was not made at the end of a financial reporting period, interest expense would be accrued by the proprietary fund. The following entry would be recorded:

Interest expense	2,500	
Interest payable		2,500

To record the accrual of interest on proprietary fund debt

Assuming that the debt service payment was made the following day (that is, the amount of interest paid is the same as the amount accrued), the following entry would be recorded to reflect the debt service payment:

Bonds payable	5,000	
Interest expense	2,500	
Cash		7,500

To record a debt service payment of both principal and accrued interest

Example: Government pays $100,000 to a contractor after purchasing a building (a capital asset)

Governmental Fund

Again, governmental funds will recognize that current financial resources have decreased by $100,000 and will record the following entry:

Expenditures—capital projects	100,000	
Cash		100,000

To record the purchase of a capital asset

Proprietary Fund

The proprietary fund would record the following entry to record the purchase of the building:

Building	100,000	
Cash		100,000

To record the purchase of a building

Again, there is no effect on net economic resources; since one asset (a building) is being substituted for another (cash), there is no effect on the statement of operations.

Example: Building has been in use for one year of its 20-year useful life

Governmental Fund

The governmental fund does not record any depreciation on the building since no current financial resources are depleted by the aging of the building.

Proprietary Fund

The proprietary fund reflects the fact that some of its economic resources have been depleted by the building's use for one year. It would reflect the following entry, which would affect its statement of operations:

Depreciation expense	5,000	
Accumulated depreciation—buildings		5,000

To record the first year's depreciation on the building

The depreciation entries would be repeated in subsequent years by the proprietary funds, and (if recording accumulated depreciation is elected by the government) in subsequent years in the general fixed asset account group.

Example: After five years, the government sells the building to a not-for-profit organization for $20,000

Governmental Fund

The governmental fund would record the $20,000 as an increase in its current financial resources, as follows:

Cash	20,000	
Miscellaneous revenues (or "Other financing sources" if the amount is material)		20,000

To record sale of building

Proprietary Fund

A proprietary fund would reflect the economic loss from the sale for $20,000 of an asset with a book value of $75,000. A proprietary fund would record the following entry:

Cash	20,000	
Accumulated depreciation	25,000	
Loss on sale of building	55,000	
Building		100,000

To record the sale of a building

The above examples and journal entries were simplified to highlight the differences in measurement focus between governmental and proprietary funds; however, they demonstrate how the same transaction can have significantly different accounting treatments. The measurement focus of proprietary funds is familiar to most accountants because of its similarity to that used by commercial enterprises. The current financial resources measurement focus used by governmental funds generally is more difficult for accountants just becoming familiar with governmental accounting, since there is virtually no comparable measurement focus used outside of government. Accountants must take care in applying the principles of the current financial resources focus to ensure that all facets of recording a particular transaction and event are considered and properly recorded.

A SYNOPSIS OF BASIS OF ACCOUNTING AND MEASUREMENT FOCUS USED BY EACH TYPE OF FUND

Exhibit 3 serves as a reference for determining the basis of accounting and measurement focus used by the different fund types used in governmental accounting and financial reporting. For specific information on how the common transactions found in each particular fund type are treated under the particular fund's measurement focus, government financial statement preparers and auditors should refer to the specific chapters covering each of the fund types.

Exhibit 3: Reference for determining the basis of accounting and measurement focus

Fund	*Measurement focus*	*Basis of accounting*
Funds (current GAAP):		
General	Flow of current financial resources	Modified accrual
Special revenue	Flow of current financial resources	Modified accrual
Capital projects	Flow of current financial resources	Modified accrual
Debt service	Flow of current financial resources	Modified accrual
Permanent	Flow of current financial resources	Modified accrual
Enterprise	Flow of economic resources	Accrual
Internal service	Flow of economic resources	Accrual
Pension and other employee benefit trust	Flow of economic resources	Accrual
Investment trust	Flow of economic resources	Accrual
Agency	Not applicable	Modified accrual
Private-purpose trust	Flow of economic resources	Accrual

SUMMARY

Understanding the concepts of basis of accounting and measurement focus is important to understanding the nuances of governmental accounting. The differences in basis of accounting and measurement focus found in governmental accounting represent attempts by standards setters to better attain the financial reporting objectives discussed in Chapter 2.

4 GENERAL FUND AND SPECIAL REVENUE FUNDS

INTRODUCTION

The general fund and special revenue funds are distinct. This chapter examines them together because many of the accounting and reporting aspects of these two fund types are the same. The financial reporting of a general fund is often used as an important indication of a government's financial performance. When a state or municipality reports that it has a "surplus" or a "deficit," what it is often referring to is the financial performance reported by the general fund. To enable the financial statement preparer to understand how and when these funds should be used, this chapter examines the following topics:

- Basis of accounting and measurement focus.
- Nature and use of the general fund.
- Nature and use of special revenue funds.
- Accounting for certain revenues and expenditures of general and special revenue funds.
- Accounting for assets, liabilities, and fund balances of general and special revenue funds.

Additional information regarding the budgets and display of these types of funds in a government's financial statements is found in Chapters 9 and 10, respectively.

BASIS OF ACCOUNTING AND MEASUREMENT FOCUS

The general and special revenue funds are governmental funds. As such, they use the modified accrual basis of accounting and the current financial resources measurement focus.

Under the modified accrual basis of accounting, revenues and other general and special revenue fund revenues are recognized in the accounting period in which they become susceptible to accrual. *Susceptible to accrual* means that the revenues are both measurable and available. *Available* means that the revenues are collectible within the current period or soon enough thereafter to be used to pay liabilities of the current period. In applying the susceptibility to accrual criterion, judgment must be used to determine materiality of the revenues involved, the practicality of determining the accrual, and the consistency in application of accounting principles.

Under the modified accrual basis of accounting, expenditures are recognized when the liability is incurred and payment is due. Goods and services received prior to the end of the fiscal year of the government are recognized in the period that a liability for the goods or services is incurred, generally when the goods and services are received. (As described later in this chapter, an exception to the general rule is that inventories and prepaid items may be recognized as expenditures when they are used instead of when they are received.)

The general fund and the special revenue funds use the current financial resources measurement focus. The measurement focus determines what transactions are recognized in the funds, in contrast to the basis of accounting, which determines when transactions are recognized in the funds.

Under the current financial resources measurement focus, the emphasis is on increases and decreases in the amount of spendable resources during the reporting period. Thus, as a generalization, long-term assets and liabilities are not recorded in general and special revenue funds. Rather, these long-term assets and liabilities are recorded in the government-wide financial statements, along with all of the other long-term assets and liabilities of the primary government and its component units.

NOTE: The reader should refer to Chapter 9, which describes changes to the reporting of amounts related to revenue recognition in governmental funds upon the effectiveness of GASB Statement No. 65, Items Previously Reported as Assets and Liabilities. Revenue and other governmental fund financial resources should be recognized in the accounting period in which they become both measurable and available. When an asset is recorded in governmental fund financial statements but the revenue is not available, the government should report a deferred inflow of resources until such time as the revenue becomes available.

NATURE AND USE OF THE GENERAL FUND

The general fund is the chief operating fund of a government. A government is permitted by GAAP to report only one general fund. GASBS 54, *Fund Balance Reporting and Governmental Fund Definitions*, provides that the general fund "…should be used to account for all financial resources not accounted for and reported in another fund." This definition is consistent with current practices and should not result in a change in what has historically been reported in the general fund. There should be a compelling reason for a government to account for financial resources in a fund other than the general fund. The GAAFR provides three examples of compelling reasons that might justify accounting for resources in a fund other than the general fund. These reasons are

1. In certain circumstances, GAAP specifically requires the use of another fund. For example, a capital projects fund is required to account for capital grants or shared revenues restricted for capital acquisition or construction. (This requirement does not apply to grants and shared revenues associated with enterprise and internal service funds, which would be accounted for in these funds.)

2. There may be legal requirements that a certain fund type be used to account for a given activity. For example, some governments require that all repayments of general obligation debt be accumulated in a debt service fund.
3. The requirements to exercise sound financial administration may require the use of a fund other than the general fund. Governments, for example, typically use an enterprise fund to account for the activities of a public utility that they operate. This not only segregates the activities of the public utility; it also permits the public utility to use the accrual basis of accounting and the economic resources measurement focus, which more appropriately reports the activity of a profit-oriented operation.

NOTE: The above example of a public utility's operation being set up in an enterprise fund is an excellent example of using a separate fund for sound financial administration. However, governments should be careful not to overuse the "sound financial administration" justification. Less sophisticated, manual accounting systems of the past may have used fund accounting to promote sound financial administration. However, even the simplest accounting software package today generally allows users to set up numerous agencies, cost centers, departments, or other tracking mechanisms that can facilitate financial management, thereby not requiring separate funds to promote sound financial administration.

Since the general fund is a "catchall" fund, it would make no sense for a government to have more than one general fund. As mentioned earlier, a government is prohibited from having multiple general funds for accounting and financial reporting. However, two situations require special treatment.

1. If a state or local law or other requirement specifies that a government should have more than one general fund, these "multiple general funds" should be treated as components of a single general fund.
2. A blended component unit may have its own general fund. When the financial information of the component unit is blended with that of the primary government, it would logically result in more than one general fund reported in the "general fund" column. In this case, the general fund of each component unit should be reported as a special revenue fund when the financial information of the component unit is blended. In this way, the general fund for the reporting entity represents the single general fund of the primary government.

NATURE AND USE OF SPECIAL REVENUE FUNDS

GASBS 54 provides that special revenue funds "...are used to account for and report the proceeds of specific revenue sources that are restricted or committed to expenditure for specific purposes other than debt service or capital projects." Restricted and committed resources are discussed in Chapter 9 with regard to fund balance reporting. Generally:

- Restricted resources are amounts restricted to specific purposes (consistent with the definition of "restricted" in GASBS 34) when the constraints on the use of resources are either:
  - Externally imposed by creditors (such as through debt covenants), grantors, contributors, or laws or regulations of other governments; or
  - Imposed by law through constitutional provisions or enabling legislation.
- Committed resources are amounts that can only be used for specific purposes resulting from constraints imposed by the formal action of the government's highest level of decision-making authority.

It is important to note that special revenue funds should not be used to account for resources that are only assigned or unassigned. Assigned resources are those amounts constrained by the government's intent to those amounts for specific purposes but are neither restricted nor committed. Unassigned resources are resources that are not restricted, committed, or assigned. Thus, in practice, implementation of GASBS 54 may result in resources currently being accounted for in special revenue funds no longer qualifying for reporting in a special revenue fund, in which case their accounting would be moved to the general fund.

Second, it is important to note that GASB 54 does not require that resources that are restricted or committed be reported in a special revenue fund. The use of special revenue funds remains optional.

Several other points on special revenue funds are worth noting from GASBS 54:

- The phrase "proceeds of specific resources" used above in defining what resources may be reported in a special revenue fund means that one or more specific restricted or committed revenues should be the foundation for a special revenue fund. In other words, special revenue funds should be driven more by their revenue sources rather than their activities.
- If restricted or committed resources are initially received in another fund and subsequently distributed to a special revenue fund, those amounts should not be recognized as revenue in the fund initially receiving the resources. Rather, the inflow of these resources should be recognized as revenue in the special revenue fund in which they will be expended in accordance with specific purposes.
- Special revenue funds should not be used to account for resources held in trust for individuals, private organizations, or other governments.

GASBS 54 also provides that the restricted or committed proceeds of specific revenue sources should be expected to continue to comprise a substantial portion of the inflows reported in the fund. Other resources (such as investment earnings and transfers from other funds) also may be reported in the fund if those resources are restricted, committed, or assigned to the specified purpose of the fund. For revolving loan arrangements that are initially funded with restricted grant revenues, the consideration may be whether those restricted resources continue to comprise a substantial portion of the fund balance in the fund's balance sheet.

GASBS 54 specifies that governments should discontinue reporting a special revenue fund, and instead report the fund's remaining resources in the general fund, if the government no longer expects that a substantial portion of the inflows will derive from restricted or committed revenue sources.

In addition, GASBS 54 requires governments to disclose in the notes to the financial statements the purpose for each major special revenue fund—identifying which revenues and other resources are reported in each of those funds.

NOTE: The accountability concern described above is often cited as a reason for establishing special revenue funds and should be easy to address in terms of budget and other controls on accounts that are maintained in a government's general fund. As long as the specially designated revenue and related expenditures can be specifically identified in the accounts of the general ledger, accountability should be demonstrable without the use of special revenue funds.

Similarly, the conceptual issue of including restricted revenues and expenditures in the general fund, thus masking the restriction, should not preclude governments from accounting for these revenues and expenditures in their general fund. The restriction of revenues and expenditures is part of the budget process. Continuing the gasoline tax example, if a government budgets its gasoline tax revenues at a certain amount, it needs to budget its road repair expenditures based on the budgeted revenues available for use. It must do this whether the gasoline tax and the road repair expenditures are accounted for in the general fund or in a special revenue fund.

In practice, the gasoline tax may not actually pay for all of the road repairs that a government desires to make during a reporting period, and the government may elect to incur expenditures for road repairs in an amount greater than the amount of the gasoline tax revenue. This excess would be made up from other nonrestricted revenues of the general fund. In this case, it would seem to report all road repair expenditures in the same fund—the general fund.

NOTE: When revenues are derived from new or increased taxes that are specifically restricted for a particular use, it is often simply a mechanism to mask a new or increased tax. In the example, taxpayers are assumed to be more willing to pay a new or increased gasoline tax if it is restricted for road repairs. Nevertheless, the government probably would have incurred the same level of expenditures for road repair whether a gasoline tax was imposed or increased. Therefore, is this "restriction" of revenue or a specific type of expenditure more form-over-substance and not worthy of its own special revenue fund? It is arguable that this is exactly the case and a special revenue fund should not be established.

When a government decides that it will use special revenue funds, it must then decide how many special revenue funds it should create. On one hand, particularly when the government is electing on its own to establish special revenue funds, only one special revenue fund may be established. This would then account for all of the types of special revenues and their related expenditures.

On the other hand, if there are laws, regulations, or contractual agreements that require that particular designated revenues and their expenditures be accounted for in their own funds, the government will need to establish as many separate special revenue funds as it is legally or otherwise required to have. Exhibit 1 provides an example of the process that a government may use to determine how many special revenue funds to establish.

Exhibit 1: Determining number of special revenue funds

Consider the following example for a government determining how many special revenue funds it should establish and use. Assume that the only specially restricted revenues that the government receives are categorical grants. There is no legal or contractual requirement to account for these funds as special revenue funds. The government may choose to establish one special revenue fund to account for all of its categorical aid revenues and expenditures. On the other hand, the government may choose to classify categorical aid in special revenue funds based on funding source or type of aid. For example, separate special revenue funds might be established for federal, state, county, or other local government categorical aid. Similarly, separate special revenue funds may be established for categorical education aid, social service program aid, or public safety grants. At the extreme level, a government may choose to establish a separate special revenue fund for each categorical aid grant or contract that it receives. It may even segregate these further by establishing new special revenue funds for each grant or contract year. Keep in mind that the governments may also establish no special revenue funds for categorical aid, accounting for all of these revenues and expenditures in the general fund.

ACCOUNTING FOR CERTAIN REVENUE AND EXPENDITURES OF GENERAL AND SPECIAL REVENUE FUNDS

The following pages review in detail the types of revenue transactions typically accounted for by both the general fund and special revenue funds. Many of the revenues recorded by the general and special revenue funds are derived from nonexchange transactions that are described in Chapter 20.

Special program considerations—food stamps. Specific guidance on accounting and financial reporting for food stamps was provided by GASBS 24. State governments should recognize distributions of food stamp benefits (now referred to as the Supplemental Nutrition Assistance Program, or "SNAP") as revenues and expenditures in the general fund or in a special revenue fund, whether the state government distributes the benefits directly or through agents, to the ultimate individual recipients regardless of whether the benefits are in paper or electronic form. Expenditures should be recognized when the benefits are distributed to the individual state government or its agents. Revenue should be recognized at the same time. When food stamps are distributed using an electronic benefit transfer system, distribution (and accordingly, expenditure and revenue recognition) takes place when the individual recipients use the benefits.

State governments should report food stamp balances held by them or by their agents at the balance sheet date as an asset offset by deferred revenue. Revenues, expenditures, and balances of food stamps should be measured based on the face value of the food stamps.

NOTE: GASBS 24's requirements for recording revenues and expenditures for food stamps apply to state governments because of the substance of their administrative requirements for this program. The GASB did not require local governments to report revenues and expenditures for food stamp coupons or vouchers that another entity redeems from a retailer. The GASB noted that local government involvement in the administration of the food stamp program will decrease as the use of electronic benefit transfer systems increases. In addition, the GASB did not impose any disclosure requirements on local governments relative to their involvement in the food stamp program.

Special program considerations—on-behalf payments for fringe benefits and salaries. On-behalf payments for fringe benefits and salaries are direct payments made by one entity (the paying entity or paying government) to a third-party recipient for the employees of another, legally separate entity (the employer entity or employer government). On-behalf payments include pension plan contributions, employee health and life insurance premiums, and salary supplements or stipends. For example, a state government may make contributions directly to a pension plan for elementary and secondary school teachers employed in public school districts within the state. For purposes of this discussion, on-behalf payments do not include contributed services, such as office space or utilities.

On-behalf payments include payments made by governmental entities on behalf of nongovernmental entities and payments made by nongovernmental entities on behalf of governmental entities. (For example, a nongovernmental fundraising foundation affiliated with a governmental college or university may supplement salaries of certain university faculty. Those payments constitute on-behalf payments for purposes of reporting by the university if they are made to the faculty members in their capacity as employees of the college or university.)

On-behalf payments may be made not only for paid employees of the employer entity, but may also be for volunteers, such as state government pension contributions for volunteer firefighters who work with a city fire department.

An employer government should recognize revenue and expenditures for on-behalf payments for fringe benefits and salaries. The employer government should recognize revenue equal to the amounts that third-party recipients of the payments received and that are receivable at year-end for the current fiscal year.

GASBS 24 provides the following guidance:

- If the employer government is not legally responsible for the payment, it should recognize expenditures (or expenses if paid out of a fund using proprietary fund–type accounting) equal to the amount recognized as revenue.
- If the employer government is legally responsible for the payment, it should follow accounting standards for that type of transaction to recognize expenditures and related assets or liabilities. For example, expenditures for on-behalf payments for contributions to a pension plan should be recognized and measured using pension plan accounting standards for state and local governmental employers. A legally responsible entity is the entity required by legal or contractual provisions to make the payment. For example, for a state government's payments to pension plans that cover local government employees, state laws generally provide that either the state government or the local government employer shall make the current payment.

GASBS 24 also includes disclosure requirements for on-behalf payments. Employer governments should disclose in the notes to the financial statements the amounts recognized for on-behalf payments for fringe benefits and salaries. For on-behalf payments that are contributions to pension plans for which an employer government is not legally responsible, the employer government should disclose the name of the plan that covers its employees and the name of the entity that makes the contributions.

Special Considerations—Component Units

In some cases, legally separate entities that are part of the same governmental reporting entity may make pass-through payments and on-behalf payments to and from each other. These payments should be reclassified for purposes of the presentation in the governmental fund financial statements as operating transfers in and out, rather than as revenues and expenditures.

Special Assessments

Some capital improvements or services provided by local governments are intended to benefit a particular property owner or group of property owners rather than the general citizenry. Special assessments for capital improvements are discussed in Chapter 5. Special assessments for special services, however, are generally accounted for in the general fund or in a special revenue fund, and therefore are included in this chapter.

Service-type special assessment projects are for operating activities and do not result in the purchase or construction of fixed assets. The assessments are often for services that are normally provided to the public as general governmental functions that are otherwise financed by the general fund or a special revenue fund. Examples of these services include street lighting, street cleaning, and snow plowing. Financing for these routine services typically comes from general revenues. However, when routine services are extended to property owners outside the normal service area of the government or are provided at a higher level or more frequent intervals than for the general public, a government sometimes levies a special assessment on those property owners who are the recipients of the higher level of service.

GASB Statement 6 (GASBS 6), *Accounting and Financial Reporting for Special Assessments*, eliminated a separate fund type for special assessments and directed that these arrangements be accounted for in a general fund, special revenue fund, capital projects fund, or debt service fund, depending on the nature of the special assessment.

The general fund or special revenue funds should be used to account for special service-type assessments. Without special legal restrictions to create a separate fund, the general fund is usually a good choice to account for these activities and the related revenue. Service-type special assessment revenues should be treated in a manner similar to user fees and should be recorded in accordance with the modified accrual basis of accounting. The related expenditures should also be accounted for similarly to other expenditures of the general fund and special revenue fund. Accounting for expenditures of these funds is discussed in a later section of this chapter.

Miscellaneous Revenues

In addition to the major categories of revenues described above, the general and special revenue funds are used to account for various miscellaneous revenues that the government receives. Examples of these miscellaneous revenues include fines and forfeitures, golf and swimming fees, inspection charges, parking fees, and parking meter receipts. These miscellaneous revenues should theoretically be accounted for using the modified accrual basis of accounting in the funds and the accrual basis of accounting in the government-wide financial statements. However, sometimes these are de minimis amounts and recording these types of revenues on the cash basis may be acceptable since the difference between the cash basis and the modified accrual and accrual basis would be very small.

Expenditures

The measurement focus of governmental fund accounting is on expenditures rather than expenses. Expenditures in the general and special revenue funds result in net decreases in financial resources. Since most expenditures and transfers out of the fund are measurable, they should be recorded when the related liability is incurred.

General and special revenue funds should therefore generally record expenditures when a liability is incurred and payment is due. In the simplest example, goods and services received prior to the end of the fiscal year should be accrued as expenditures because the liability for the goods or services has been incurred and the payment is due to the vendor that provided the goods and services. The special nature of the current financial resources measurement focus used by governmental funds results in eight different types of expenditures to not be recognized when the liability is incurred. These types of expenditures (and the chapter in which they are addressed) are as follows:

- Compensated absences (Chapter 18).
- Judgments and claims (Chapter 21).
- Unfunded pension contributions (Chapter 17).
- Special termination benefits (Chapter 17).
- Landfill closure and postclosure costs (Chapter 16).
- Debt service (Chapter 6).
- Supplies inventories and prepaids (discussed below).
- Operating leases with scheduled rent increases (Chapter 19).

The exceptions referred to above arise because governmental funds such as the general fund and special revenue funds record expenditures when a liability is incurred, but only record the liability for the fund when the liability will be liquidated with expendable available financial resources. In addition, the focus on current financial resources means that the accounting for the purchase of long-term assets is different than that encountered in commercial organizations. These concepts are more fully discussed below and in Chapter 3.

NOTE: For governments that have fundraising activities, readers should be aware of the guidance of AICPA Statement of Position 98-2, Accounting for Costs of Activity of Not-for-Profit Organizations and State and Local Governmental Entities That Include Fundraising. This SOP, now included in the FASB Accounting Standards Codification at 958–720, is discussed more fully in Chapter 23. This SOP was cleared by the GASB and includes governmental entities in its scope, and thus is category guidance for governmental entities.

ACCOUNTING FOR ASSETS, LIABILITIES, AND FUND BALANCES OF GENERAL AND SPECIAL REVENUE FUNDS

The balance sheets of the general fund and special revenue funds should contain only assets that are current financial resources and the liabilities that those current financial resources will be used to pay.

On the asset side of the balance sheet, the following are the typical assets normally found on general and special revenue fund balance sheets, along with the location in this Guide where the accounting and financial reporting requirements are discussed:

- Cash and investments (Chapter 12).
- Receivables (discussed with related revenue accounts in this chapter and Chapter 20).
- Interfund receivables (Chapter 9).
- Inventories and prepaids (discussed below).

On the liability side of the balance sheet, the following are the typical liabilities normally found on general and special revenue fund balance sheets, along with the location in this Guide where the accounting and financial reporting requirements are discussed:

- Accounts payable and accrued expenses (addressed with related expenditure recognition in this chapter).
- Interfund payables (Chapter 9).
- Deferred revenues (discussed with the related revenue accounts in this chapter).
- Revenue anticipation notes and tax anticipation notes (Chapter 7).

As can be seen from the previous paragraphs, there are limited accounts and balances that are reported on the balance sheets of the general fund and special revenue funds. Two areas that are not covered elsewhere in this guide relating to the balance sheets of these fund types are the accounting and financial reporting for inventories and prepaids and the classification of fund balances. These two topics are discussed in the following sections.

Inventories and Prepaids

There are alternative expenditure and asset recognition methods at the final financial statement level for materials and supplies and prepaids.

- Inventory items, such as materials and supplies, may be considered expenditures when purchased (referred to as the *purchase method*) or when used (referred to as the *consumption method*). (Exhibit 2 provides an example of the journal entries resulting from the use of the consumption method.) However, when a government has significant amounts of inventory, it should be reported on the balance sheet. The credit amount that offsets the debit recorded on the balance sheet for inventories is "reserved fund balance," discussed in the following section on fund balance reservations. A similar reservation of fund balance is recorded when prepaid items are recorded as assets on the balance sheet.

- Expenditures for insurance and similar services extending over more than one accounting period need not be allocated between or among accounting periods but may be accounted for as expenditures in the period of acquisition.

Exhibit 2: Journal entries from use of consumption method

The following journal entries illustrate the use of the consumption method of accounting for supplies inventory. Assume that the city of Anywhere purchases $50,000 of supplies inventory during the fiscal year. It began the fiscal year with $25,000 of supplies inventory on hand (that is, an asset was recorded for $25,000 and a reservation of fund balance was recorded for $25,000 at the beginning of the year). All of these beginning-of-the-year supplies were consumed. At the end of the fiscal year, $10,000 of supplies remain on hand.

The following journal entries would be recorded during this fiscal year.

	Debit	Credit
1. Expenditures—Supplies	25,000	
Supplies		25,000

To record the consumption of supplies on hand at the beginning of the year

	Debit	Credit
2. Fund balance—Reserved for supplies	25,000	
Fund balance		25,000

To record the removal of the reservation of the beginning-of-the-year fund balance for supplies consumed

	Debit	Credit
3. Supplies	50,000	
Cash (or accounts payable)		50,000

To record the purchase of supplies during the year

	Debit	Credit
4. Expenditures—Supplies	40,000	
Supplies		40,000

To record the consumption of supplies that were purchased during the current year

	Debit	Credit
5. Fund balance	10,000	
Fund balance—Reserved for supplies		10,000

To record a reservation of fund balance for supplies on hand at the end of the fiscal year

Thus, at the end of the year, the balance sheet will reflect an asset for the $10,000 of supplies remaining on hand, along with a reservation of fund balance for an equal amount. Expenditures for the year for supplies will be $65,000, which reflects consumption of the $25,000 of supplies on hand at the beginning of the year in addition to the consumption of $40,000 of supplies that were purchased during the year.

For accounting for inventories at the government-wide financial statement level, the consumption method would be used. In addition, there would be no restriction on net position to correspond to the reservation of fund balance recorded above.

Fund Balances

The equity (assets less liabilities) of the general fund and any special revenue funds is reported as fund balance. GASBS 54, *Fund Balance Reporting and Governmental Fund Definitions*, resulted in significant changes to the way that fund balance information is disclosed in fund financial statements. Fund balances are reported as restricted, committed, assigned, and unassigned. These distinctions are more fully described in Chapter 9. Note, however, that only a general fund would report a positive amount of its fund balance as "unassigned" under GASBS 54.

SUMMARY

This chapter discussed appropriate uses of the general fund and special revenue funds, when the government is required or elects to establish special revenue funds. It also addressed some of the more common types of revenues, expenditures, assets, and liabilities found in the general fund and special revenue funds. This guidance should be used in conjunction with the other specialized accounting treatments for various types of transactions and balances discussed throughout this guide.

5 CAPITAL PROJECTS FUNDS

INTRODUCTION

Governments often use the capital projects fund type to account for and report major capital acquisition and construction activities. GASBS 54, *Fund Balance Reporting and Governmental Fund Definitions*, provides that capital projects funds should be used to "...account for and report financial resources that are restricted, committed, or assigned to expenditure for capital outlays, including the acquisition of construction of capital facilities and other capital assets." GASBS 54 further provides that capital projects funds should exclude those types of capital related outflows financed by proprietary funds or for assets that will be held in trust for individuals, private organizations, or other governments.

This is actually a broader definition of the use of capital projects funds than previously existed under GAAP, which provided that capital projects funds be used to account for the acquisitions or construction of *major capital facilities*. Despite the previous GAAP definition, many governments in practice used capital projects funds to account for the acquisitions of all capital assets, not just major capital facilities. The GASB had originally proposed keeping the existing definition essentially unchanged. As current practice had evolved away from promulgated GAAP, the new standard would have ironically resulted in many governments having to change what they accounted for in capital projects funds, despite the definition not changing. The GASB responded to this inconsistency and broadened the definition that was adopted by GASBS 54 so that there should have been little, if any, change in practice upon implementation of GASBS 54.

BASIS OF ACCOUNTING

As a governmental fund type, capital projects funds use the modified accrual basis of accounting. Revenues are recorded when they are susceptible to accrual (that is, they are accrued when they become measurable and available). Expenditures are recorded when the liability is incurred. The expenditure recognition exceptions (inventories, prepaid items, judgments and claims, etc.) described in Chapter 4 relating to general and special revenue funds would also apply to capital projects funds.

MEASUREMENT FOCUS

As a governmental fund type, capital projects funds use the current financial resources measurement focus. The operating statement of the capital projects fund reports increases and decreases in spendable resources. Increases in spendable resources are reported in the operating statement as "revenues" and "other financing sources" while decreases in spendable resources are reported as "expenditures" or "other financing uses." As such, it is worthy to note that while capital projects funds are used to account for resources used in major acquisition or construction projects, the resulting assets are not reported as assets of the capital projects fund. Rather, these assets are reported only in the government-wide financial statements. The capital projects fund accounts for the acquisition and construction of assets as expenditures.

NOTE: The reader should refer to Chapter 9, which describes changes to the reporting of amounts related to revenue recognition in governmental funds upon the effectiveness of GASB Statement No. 65, Items Previously Reported as Assets and Liabilities. Revenue and other governmental fund financial resources should be recognized in the accounting period in which they become both measurable and available. When an asset is recorded in governmental fund financial statements but the revenue is not available, the government should report a deferred inflow of resources until such time as the revenue becomes available.

WHEN ARE CAPITAL PROJECTS FUNDS USED?

In most cases, governments are permitted, but not required, to establish capital projects funds to account for resources used for major acquisition and construction of assets. The majority of governments use one or more capital projects funds to account for these activities. As seen in the following discussion, the significance of the dollar amounts that flow through the capital projects fund to the general fund might well result in an overshadowing of the general governmental activities reported in the general fund. Capital projects funds are also used to account for special revenues that relate to capital projects as well as capital improvements financed by special assessments. A later section of this chapter describes the accounting and financial reporting when special assessment debt is issued to finance capital projects.

While GAAP does not require the use of capital projects funds, their use may sometimes be required by particular grants, contracts (including debt covenants), or local laws. They are often used when debt proceeds are required to be used for capital projects.

Once a government determines that it desires to establish a capital projects fund, the government needs to decide how many capital projects funds should be established. A government may well determine that it can adequately account for and manage its capital projects with one capital projects fund. This serves to simplify financial reporting and provide the government with the opportunity to utilize its accounting system to track and manage individual projects within its capital projects funds.

On the other hand, a government may decide that establishing a number of capital projects funds will better serve its accountability and financial management needs. While governmental financial statement preparers will certainly have their own views on when using multiple capital projects funds is appropriate, it would seem that when there are two to five major capital projects that dominate the major asset acquisition or construction activities of the government, using an individual capital projects fund for each of these few significant capital projects would be appropriate.

REVENUES AND OTHER FINANCING SOURCES

The number of categories and types of revenues and other financing sources that are typically found in capital projects funds are usually far fewer than those found in the general and special revenue funds. Since governments typically finance major acquisitions and construction of capital assets through the use of debt, the issuance of debt is typically the most significant source of resources for capital projects funds, and it is reported as an "other financing" source. In addition, capital projects funds may account for receipt of resources in the form of nonexchange transactions from federal, state, or other aid programs, transfers from other funds, such as the general fund, and capital leases. The following paragraphs describe some of the accounting issues that governments may encounter in accounting for these resources in capital projects funds.

Proceeds from Debt Issuance

This section describes the appropriate accounting for the proceeds from debt issuance. In addition to the general concept of accounting for debt proceeds in the capital projects fund, specific guidance that relates to bond anticipation notes, demand bonds, special assessment debt, and arbitrage rebate considerations is discussed.

Basic journal entries to record the issuance of debt. As mentioned above, proceeds from the sale of debt to finance projects accounted for by the capital projects funds should be recorded as an other financing source of the capital projects fund. To illustrate the proper accounting within the capital projects fund, assume that a government issues debt with a face amount of $100,000. The basic journal entry that would be recorded is

Cash	100,000	
Other financing sources—proceeds from the sale of bonds		100,000

To record the sale of bonds

However, the simplicity of this journal entry is rarely encountered in practice. For example, when bonds are issued, there are underwriter fees, attorney fees, and other costs that are typically deducted from the proceeds of the bonds. Assume in the above example that such fees are $5,000. A government has two ways to account for these fees. It can record the proceeds from the bonds net of the issuance costs and fees, or it can record the proceeds of the debt at the gross amount and record an expenditure for the issuance fees and costs. The GAAFR recommends that the latter method be used, in which an expenditure is recorded for the issuance fees and costs. Using this recommended approach, the following journal entry would be recorded:

Cash	95,000	
Expenditures—bond issuance costs	5,000	
Other financing sources—proceeds from the sale of bonds		100,000

To record the issuance of bonds and the payment of bond issuance costs

If the government were to record the proceeds of the bond issuance net of applicable issuance costs and expenses, the following entry would be recorded:

Cash	95,000	
Other financing sources—proceeds from the sale of bonds		95,000

To record the proceeds from the sale of bonds, net of issuance costs

There are two other instances that represent a departure from the simplified first journal entry provided above. These instances are when bonds are issued at a premium or a discount.

Bonds are issued at a discount when the prevailing market interest rate at the time of issuance is higher than the stated or coupon rate of interest for the particular bonds being issued. If the $100,000 of face-amount bonds were actually sold for $97,500 and there was still $5,000 of issuance costs, the recommended journal entry is

Cash	92,500	
Expenditures—bond issuance costs	5,000	
Other financing sources—proceeds from the sale of bonds		97,500

To record the sale of bonds at a discount, net of issuance costs and fees

If the prevailing market rate of interest is lower than the stated or coupon rate of interest of the specific bonds being issued, the bonds would be sold at a premium. Assuming the same facts as in the previous journal entry, except that the bonds were sold at a $2,500 premium instead of a $2,500 discount, the following journal entry would be recorded:

Cash	97,500	
Expenditures—bond issuance costs	5,000	
Other financing sources—proceeds from the sale of bonds		102,500

To record the sale of $100,000 face-amount bonds at a premium, net of bond issuance costs and fees

Note that no further journal entries to amortize the premium or discount would be required by the capital projects fund. Because the measurement focus of the capital projects fund is on current financial resources, the fund simply records the bond proceeds (that is, the current financial resources received) which will likely reflect premium or discount. Since the debt is not recorded in the capital projects fund, there is no need to record amortization of the premium or discount. Amortization of premium or discount (as well as issuance costs) would be recorded in the government-wide financial statements.

Bond Anticipation Notes

Bond anticipation notes are a mechanism for state and local governments to obtain financing in the form of a short-term note that the government intends to pay off with the proceeds of a long-term bond. Revenue and tax anticipation notes are also sources of short-term financing for governments. However, these short-term notes are not anticipated to be repaid from bond proceeds. They are expected to be paid from future collections of tax revenues, often real estate taxes, or other sources of revenue, often federal or state categorical aid. The accounting for transactions of the capital projects fund is most concerned with bond anticipation notes, since bonds are the most likely source of proceeds to finance the capital projects accounted for by the capital projects fund. The accounting question for bond anticipation notes is whether the notes should be recorded as a short-term liability and recorded in the fund, or whether certain prescribed conditions are met to enable the notes to be treated as long-term obligations and recorded only in the government-wide financial statements.

NCGA Interpretation 9 (NCGAI 9), *Certain Fund Classifications and Balance Sheet Accounts,* addresses the question of how bond, revenue, and tax anticipation notes should be reflected in the financial statements of a government, particularly how they should be accounted for by governmental funds. This guidance is particularly relevant for the capital projects funds because these are the funds that usually receive the proceeds of bonds issued to finance major asset acquisitions or construction.

NCGAI 9 prescribes that if all legal steps have been taken to refinance the bond anticipation notes and the interest is supported by an ability to consummate refinancing the short-term notes on a long-term basis in accordance with the criteria originally set forth in FASB Statement 6 (SFAS 6), *Classification of Short-Term Obligations Expected to Be Refinanced* (now at FASB Accounting Standards Codification Topic 470), they should not be shown as a fund liability, although they would be recorded as a liability on the government-wide statement of net position. However, if the necessary legal steps and the ability to consummate refinancing criteria have not been met, then the bond anticipation notes should be reported as a fund liability in the fund receiving the proceeds.

The requirements (referred to above) are as follows:

The enterprise's intent to refinance the short-term obligation on a long-term basis is supported by an ability to consummate the refinancing demonstrated in either of the following ways:

(a) Post-balance-sheet date issuance of long-term obligation or equity securities. After the date of an enterprise's balance sheet, but before that balance sheet is issued, a long-term obligation…has been issued for the purpose of refinancing the short-term obligation on a long-term basis; or

(b) Financing agreement. Before the balance sheet is issued, the enterprise entered into a financing agreement that clearly permits the enterprise to refinance the short-term obligation on a long-term basis on terms that are readily determinable, and all of the following conditions are met:

  (i) The agreement does not expire within one year (or operating cycle) from the date of the enterprise's balance sheet and during that period the agreement is not cancelable by the lender or the prospective lender or investor (and obligations incurred under the agreement are not callable during that period) except for the violation of a provision with which compliance is objectively determinable or measurable.

  (ii) No violation of any provision of the financing agreement exists at the balance sheet date and no available information indicates that a violation has occurred thereafter but prior to the issuance of the balance sheet, or, if one exists at the balance sheet date or has occurred thereafter, a waiver has been obtained.

  (iii) The lender or the prospective lender or investor with which the enterprise has entered into the financing agreement is expected to be financially capable of honoring the agreement.

For purposes of applying the above provisions, a "violation of a provision" is a failure to meet a condition set forth in the agreement or breach or violation of a provision such as a restrictive covenant, representation, or warranty, whether or not a grace period is allowed or the lender is required to give notice. In addition, when a financing agreement is cancelable for violation of a provision that can be evaluated differently by the parties to the agreement (for instance, when compliance with the provision is not objectively determinable or measurable), it does not comply with the condition of b(ii) above.

NOTE: To meet the above-described conditions to not record short-term bond anticipation notes as a fund liability, a government has to either have completed the financing after the balance sheet date but before the financial statements are issued, or has to have a solid agreement in place to obtain the long-term financing after the financial statements are issued. This appears to be a fairly narrow opening to avoid recording the financing as a long-term liability in the general long-term debt account group. However, the chances of complying with these conditions may be better than they appear, since the requirements of the bond anticipation notes themselves will likely require that concrete agreements to issue the long-term bonds are in place before the lenders provide the short-term financing through the bond anticipation notes.

If bond anticipation notes are not recorded as a liability of the fund because the criteria have been satisfied, the notes to the financial statements should include a general description of the financing agreement and the terms of any new obligation incurred or expected to be incurred as a result of a refinancing. Exhibits 1 and 2 illustrate the journal entries that should be recorded for bond anticipation notes.

NOTE: For a further understanding of the entries of the debt service fund and the government-wide financial statements, readers should refer to Chapters 6 and 8, respectively.

Exhibit 1: Journal entries for bond anticipation notes

The following journal entries demonstrate the accounting for bond anticipation notes.

Assume that the city of Anywhere issues $1,000,000 of bond anticipation notes. The criteria established by FASB ASC 740 have been satisfied so that the liability for the debt is included in the government-wide statement of net position, rather than the capital projects fund. When the bond anticipation notes are issued, the following journal entries are recorded:

Capital projects fund

Cash	1,000,000	
Other financing sources—proceeds from the issuance of bond anticipation notes		1,000,000

To record the receipt of funds from the issuance of bond anticipation notes

Government-wide financial statements:

Cash	1,000,000	
Bond anticipation notes payable		1,000,000

To record the issuance of bond anticipation notes

When the city of Anywhere issues the long-term debt that is "anticipated" by the bond anticipation notes, the following journal entries are recorded. (Assume that the long-term debt is issued the next day and that there are no interest payments.)

General fund

Cash	1,000,000	
Other financing sources—proceeds from sale of long-term bonds		1,000,000

To record the issuance of long-term bonds

Other financing sources—transfer to the debt service fund	1,000,000	
Cash		1,000,000

To record the transfer to the debt service fund

(Note that a government may record the proceeds of the long-term debt in the debt service fund, if that coincides with the facts of the actual transaction.)

Debt service fund

Cash	1,000,000	
Other financing sources—transfer from the general fund		1,000,000

To record receipt of a transfer from the general fund

Other financing uses—repayment of bond anticipation notes	1,000,000	
Cash		1,000,000

To record the repayment of bond anticipation notes
Government-wide financial statements:

Bond anticipation notes	1,000,000	
Bonds payable		1,000,000

To record the issuance of long-term bonds

Exhibit 2: Journal entries for bond anticipation notes as fund liability

Assume the same facts as in Exhibit 1, except that the city of Anywhere has not satisfied the criteria and must record the bond anticipation notes as a fund liability.

The following journal entries would be recorded at the time that the bond anticipation notes are issued:

Capital projects fund

Cash	1,000,000	
Bond anticipation notes payable		1,000,000

To record the issuance of bond anticipation notes

Government-wide financial statements

Same entry as above. Assume that the city of Anywhere then issues long-term bonds (assume that the proceeds are received directly by the capital projects fund) and pays off the bond anticipation notes.

Capital projects fund

Cash	1,000,000	
Other financing sources—proceeds from sale of bonds		1,000,000

To record the issuance of long-term bonds

Bond anticipation notes payable	1,000,000	
Cash		1,000,000

To record the repayment of bond anticipation notes

Government-wide financial statements

Bond anticipation notes payable	1,000,000	
Bonds payable		1,000,000

To record the issuance of long-term bonds

Demand Bonds

Demand bonds are financial instruments that create a potential call on a state or local government's current financial resources. A similar accounting question arises in relation to demand bonds as for bond anticipation notes: Should the debt be recorded as a liability of the capital projects fund (assuming the most typical case where the debt is used to finance major acquisitions or construction of capital projects) or only on the government-wide statement of net position? The GASB issued guidance through GASB Interpretation 1 (GASBI 1), *Demand Bonds Issued by State and Local Governmental Entities*, discussed below.

Demand bonds are debt issuances that have demand provisions (termed *put* provisions) as one of their features that gives the bondholder the right to require that the issuer redeem the bonds within a certain period, after giving some agreed-upon period of notice, usually 30 days or less. In some cases, the demand provisions are exercisable immediately after the bonds have been issued. In other cases, there is a waiting period of, for example, five years, until the put provisions of the bonds may be exercised by the bondholder. These provisions mean that the bondholder is less subject to risks caused by rising interest rates. Because the bondholder is assured that he or she can receive the par value of the bond at some future date, a demand bond has some features and advantages of a short-term investment for the bondholder in addition to being a potential long-term investment. Accordingly, depending on the current market conditions, governments can issue these types of bonds at a lower interest rate than would be possible with bonds that did not have the demand bonds' put provision.

Because the issuance of demand bonds represents significant potential cash outlays by governments, steps are usually taken to protect the government from having to fund, from its own cash reserves, demand bonds redeemed by bondholders. First, governments usually appoint remarketing agents whose function is to resell bonds that have been redeemed by bondholders. In addition, governments usually obtain letters of credit or other arrangements that would make funds available sufficient to cover redeemed bonds.

To provide for long-term financing in the event that the remarketing agents are unable to sell the redeemed bonds within a specified period (such as three to six months), the government issuing demand bonds generally enters into an agreement with a financial institution to convert the bonds to an installment loan repayable over a specified period. This type of arrangement is known as a "take-out" agreement and may be part of the letter of credit agreement or a separate agreement.

As addressed by GASBI 1, demand bonds are those that by their terms have demand provisions that are exercisable at the balance sheet date or within one year from the date of the balance sheet. These bonds should be reported by governments in the capital projects fund unless all of the following conditions delineated in GASBI 1 are met:

- Before the financial statements are issued, the issuer has entered into an arm's-length financing (take-out) agreement (an arm's-length agreement is an agreement with an unrelated third party, with each party acting in his or her own behalf) to convert bonds put (but not resold) into some other form of long-term obligation.
- The take-out agreement does not expire within one year from the date of the issuer's balance sheet.
- The take-out agreement is not cancelable by the lender or the prospective lender during that year, and obligations incurred under the take-out agreement are not callable during that year.
- The lender, prospective lender, or investor is expected to be financially capable of honoring the take-out agreement.

Regarding the conditions above, if the take-out agreement is cancelable or callable because of violations that can be objectively verified by both parties and no violations have occurred prior to issuance of the financial statements, the demand bonds should be classified and recorded as long-term debt in the government-wide financial statements and not a liability of the fund. If violations have occurred and a waiver has been obtained before issuance of the financial statements, the bonds should also be classified and recorded as long-term debt in the government-wide financial statements and not a liability of the fund. Otherwise, the demand bonds should be classified and recorded as liabilities of the governmental fund and included as a current liability in the government-wide financial statements.

If the take-out agreement is cancelable or callable because of violations that cannot be objectively verified by both parties, the take-out agreement does not provide sufficient assurance of long-term financing capabilities, and the bonds should be classified as liabilities of the fund and as a current liability in the government-wide financial statements.

If a government exercises a take-out agreement to convert demand bonds that have been redeemed into an installment loan, the installment loan should be reported as a long-term liability in the government-wide statement of net position.

If the above conditions are not met, the demand bonds should be recorded as a liability of a governmental fund, such as the capital projects fund. The selection of the fund to record the liability is determined by which fund receives the bond proceeds from the issuance of the demand bonds. Most often, this is the capital projects fund.

In addition, if a take-out agreement expires while its related demand bonds are still outstanding, the government should report a fund liability in the fund for the demand bonds that were not previously reported as a liability of the fund. The liability is reported as a liability of the fund that originally reported the proceeds of the bond. A corresponding debit to "Other financing uses" should be made at this time to record the fund liability.

In addition to the accounting requirements relative to demand bonds, GASBI 1 requires that a number of disclosures be made about this type of bond and the related agreements. These disclosures are in addition to the normal disclosures required about debt and include the following:

- General description of the demand bond program.
- Terms of any letters of credit or other standby liquidity agreements outstanding.
- Commitment fees to obtain the letters of credit and any amounts drawn on them outstanding as of the balance sheet date.
- A description of the take-out agreement, including its expiration date, commitment fees to obtain that agreement, and the terms of any new obligation under the take-out agreement.
- The debt service requirements that would result if the take-out agreement were to be exercised.

Special Assessment Debt

The capital projects fund typically accounts for capital projects financed with the proceeds of special assessment debt. (Service-type special assessments are described in Chapter 4.) More often than not, special assessments projects are capital in nature and are designed to enhance the utility, accessibility, or aesthetic value of the affected properties. The projects may also provide improvements or additions to a government's capital assets, including infrastructure. Some of the more common types of capital special assessments include streets, sidewalks, parking facilities, and curbs and gutters.

The cost of a capital improvement special assessment project is usually greater than the amount the affected property owners can or are willing to pay in one year. To finance the project, the affected property owners effectively mortgage their property by allowing the government to attach a lien on their property so that the property owners can pay their pro rata share of the improvement costs in installments. To actually obtain funds for the project, the government usually issues long-term debt. Ordinarily, the assessed property owners pay the assessments in installments, which are timed to be due based on the debt service requirements of the debt that was issued to fund the projects. The assessed property owners may also elect to pay for the assessment immediately or at any time thereafter, but prior to the installment due dates. When the assessed property owners satisfy their obligations, the government removes the liens from the respective properties.

GASB Statement 6 (GASBS 6), *Accounting and Reporting for Special Assessments,* defines *special assessment debt* as those long-term obligations that are secured by a lien on the assessed properties, for which the primary source of repayment is the assessments levied against the benefiting properties. Often, however, the government will be obligated in some manner to provide resources for repayment of special assessment debt in the event of default by the assessed property owners. It is also not uncommon for a local government to finance an improvement entirely with the proceeds of a general obligation debt and to levy special assessments against the benefiting property owners to provide some of the resources needed to repay the debt.

The primary source of funds for the repayment of special assessment debt is the assessments against the benefiting property owners. The government's role and responsibility for the debt may vary. The government may be directly responsible for paying a portion of the project cost, either as a public benefit or as a property owner benefiting from the improvement. General government resources repay the portion of the debt related to the government's share of the project cost. These costs of capital projects would be expenditures of the capital projects fund. On the other hand, the government may have no liability for special assessment debt issues. Between these two extremes, the government may pledge its full faith and credit as security for the entire special assessment bond issue, including the portion of the bond issue to be paid by assessments against the benefiting property owners.

GASBS 6 states that the special assessment fund type previously used in governmental accounting should no longer be used. Legal or other requirements to account for special assessment transactions in accounts or funds separate from other accounts or funds of the government can usually be satisfied by maintaining separate special revenue, capital projects, and debt service funds for the individual special assessment projects.

Government obligation for special assessment debt. The manner in which capital projects financed with special assessment debt recorded in the capital projects fund is affected by whether the government is obligated in some manner for the special assessment debt. If the government is obligated in some manner to assume the payment of related debt service in the event of default by the property owners, all transactions related to capital improvements financed by special assessments should be reported in the same manner, and on the same basis of accounting, as any other capital improvement and financing; that is, transactions of the construction phase of the project should be reported in a capital projects fund (or other appropriate fund), and transactions of the debt service phase should be reported in a debt service fund, if a separate debt service fund is being used.

At the time of the levy of a special assessment, special assessments receivable should be recorded in the capital projects fund, offset by the same amount recorded as deferred revenue. The government should consider the collectibility of the special assessment receivables and determine whether the receivable should be offset by a valuation allowance. The deferred revenue amount should then be decreased because revenues are recognized when they become measurable and available. On the government-wide financial statements the same receivable would be recorded but revenue would be recognized and described as "contributions from property owners" or some similar title.

Further information on accounting for the debt portion of the special assessment debt when the government is obligated in some manner is provided in Chapters 6 and 15 on debt service funds and the general long-term debt account group.

There is one aspect of the determination of whether the government is obligated for special assessment debt that affects the capital projects fund, and this effect is principally in the source of funds and the terminology used to record the source of funds. The debt service transactions of a special assessment issue for which the government is not obligated in any manner should be reported in an agency fund, rather than a debt service fund, to reflect the fact that the government's duties are limited to acting as an agent for the assessed property owners and the bondholders. When a government is not obligated for special assessment debt, the construction phase should, however, be reported like other capital improvements—in a capital projects fund or other appropriate fund. The source of funds in the capital projects fund, however, should be identified by a description other than "bond proceeds," such as "contributions from property owners." The capital assets constructed or acquired with this debt for which the government is not obligated in any manner should be reported in the government-wide statement of net position.

Arbitrage Rebate Accounting

The interest paid by state and local governments on debt issued for public purposes is generally not subject to federal taxation. Since this interest is not subject to federal taxes, the interest rate at which the government is able to issue debt is generally lower than the interest rate required for comparable debt whose interest payments are taxable to the debt holder.

Accordingly, a government has the opportunity for "arbitrage" earnings on the spread between its tax-exempt interest rate and the rate that it is able to earn on taxable investments purchased in the open market. Subject to certain safe-harbor requirements in which the bond proceeds are disbursed within a limited period, the state or local government is required to "rebate" these arbitrage earnings to the federal government. Typically, arbitrage rebate payments must be made to the federal government every five years and within 60 days of the related debt's financial maturity.

Although a government may not be required to remit the arbitrage rebate payments until several years have passed, the government should recognize a liability for rebatable arbitrage as soon as it is both probable and measurable that a liability has been incurred. In determining the amount of the liability, it must be considered that the excess arbitrage earnings earned in one year may be offset by lesser earnings in a subsequent year. Therefore, the liability recognized for the year should be only that portion of the estimated future payment that is attributable to earnings of the current period. In other words, the government should take into consideration whether its earnings on the same investments in subsequent years will offset excess earnings in the first year, for example, so that it is not necessarily required to record a liability for the full amount of any excess earnings in the first or beginning years of a debt issue.

All interest income, regardless of whether it is rebatable, should be reported as revenue of the capital projects fund. The liability for the arbitrage rebate is then reported only in the government-wide statement of net position. However, when the amounts become due and payable to the federal government, they would be reported as a fund liability. This approach is the only one permitted by the GAAFR.

SUMMARY

Governments often establish capital projects funds to account for the major acquisition and construction of capital assets. This chapter focused on the basic accounting for the typical transactions of the capital projects fund and also on some unique areas of accounting, which primarily involve the issuance of debt providing the funds for capital projects. The reader should also consider the information in Chapters 6, 14, and 15, which describe the accounting and reporting for debt service funds, capital assets, and the general long-term debt for additional information on transactions that affect the accounts of the capital projects fund.

6 DEBT SERVICE FUNDS

INTRODUCTION

Governments often issue long-term debt to finance various governmental projects. Generally, this long-term debt is repaid from a governmental fund called a debt service fund. In some cases, although not legally required, a government may choose to establish a debt service fund to account for the accumulation of resources that will be used for debt service.

This chapter discusses the following topics in relation to the establishment and use of debt service funds:

- Situations in which a debt service fund is required or desirable.
- Basis of accounting and measurement focus.
- Expenditure recognition for debt service payments.
- Accounting for the advance refunding of long-term debt.

In addition to the above topics, useful information relative to a government's issuance and repayment of long-term debt is provided in Chapters 8 and 11.

SITUATIONS WHEN A DEBT SERVICE FUND IS REQUIRED OR DESIRABLE

GASB Statement No. 54 (GASBS 54), *Fund Balance Reporting and Governmental Fund Type Definitions*, describes the purpose of a debt service fund as to account for and report financial resources that are restricted, committed, or assigned to expenditure for principal or interest. GASBS 54 provides that debt service funds should be used to report resources if legally mandated. In addition, financial resources that are being accumulated for principal and interest maturing in future years should be reported in debt service funds. This definition and requirements for use are generally consistent with preexisting GAAP.

In deciding to establish one or more debt service funds, a government should first determine whether it is required to establish such a fund or funds. The first requirement to consider is whether there are any laws that require the government to use a debt service fund. In addition to any legal requirements that might be established through the legislative process of the government, another potential source of legal requirement is the bond indenture agreements executed when long-term obligations are issued and sold. These agreements may require that debt service funds be used for the protection of the bondholders. The requirement to establish debt service funds as an accounting and financial reporting mechanism is different from the requirement in many bond indentures or similar agreements that establish reserve funds or other financial requirements. These other requirements may well be met through other mechanisms, such as restricted cash accounts, rather than the establishment of a debt service fund. Financial statement preparers should review these legal requirements carefully to ensure compliance with the requirements, which does not automatically lead to the use of a debt service fund.

In addition to the legal requirements described above, GAAP requires the use of a debt service fund if financial resources are being accumulated for principal and interest payments maturing in future years. This requirement might be interpreted to mean that if a government has resources at the end of a fiscal year to use to pay debt service in the following year, a debt service fund would be required. This would result in almost all governments with long-term debt outstanding to be required to establish a debt service fund. In practice this requirement is interpreted more narrowly. An accumulation is only deemed to have occurred for determining whether a debt service fund is required if the government has accumulated resources for debt service payments in excess of one year's worth of principal and interest payments.

As is consistent with GAAP, the number of funds established should be kept to the minimum either required to be established by law or considered necessary by the government for the appropriate financial management of its resources. When considering these two instances, the government also needs to determine whether it is required to establish one or more debt service funds. Ideally, in keeping with the goal of minimizing the number of funds that a government uses, a government would establish one debt service fund. This one fund should provide an adequate mechanism for the government to use to account for the accumulation of resources and payment of long-term debt. However, the legal requirements of the government itself or the bond indentures mentioned above may actually result in more than one debt service fund, perhaps even a separate debt service fund for bond issues of the government.

It should be noted that the debt service fund should be used to account for the accumulation and payment of debt service. There are other long-term obligations, such as those for capital leases, judgments and claims, and compensated absences, considered to be nondebt long-term obligations. The payments of these obligations should be reported in the fund that budgets for their payment, which is most often the general fund. The debt service fund should be used only for the accumulation of resources and payment of debt service for long-term obligations that are considered to be debt, and not for other nondebt long-term obligations.

BASIS OF ACCOUNTING AND MEASUREMENT FOCUS

As a governmental fund, the debt service fund should use the modified accrual basis of accounting and the current financial resources measurement focus. Revenues are recorded when they are susceptible to accrual. That is, they are accrued when they become measurable and available. Expenditures are recorded when the liability is incurred. However, recognition criteria of expenditures for debt service principal and interest payments are unique for debt service funds. The recognition criteria for debt service payments are discussed in the following section of this chapter.

As a governmental fund type, the debt service fund uses the current financial resources measurement focus. The operating statement of the debt service fund reports increases and decreases in spendable resources. Increases in spendable resources are reported in the operating statement as "revenues" and "other financing sources" while decreases in spendable resources are reported as "expenditures" or "other financing uses."

In applying these accounting principles to debt service funds, the financial statement preparer may encounter the situation where a specific revenue source, such as property taxes or sales taxes, is restricted for debt service on general long-term debt. Assuming that the government has established a debt service fund, the government must determine whether these restricted tax revenues should be recorded directly into the debt service fund, or whether they should be recorded as revenues of the general fund, and then recorded as a transfer to the debt service fund.

When taxes are specifically restricted for debt service, generally they should be reported directly in the debt service fund, rather than as a transfer from the general fund to the debt service fund. However, circumstances such as a legal requirement to account for all of the restricted taxes in the general fund may sometimes require that restricted taxes be reported first in the general fund. In this case, an operating transfer from the general fund to the debt service fund would be recorded for the amount of the specific tax.

NOTE: In many cases, the taxes that are restricted to debt service may present only a portion of the total of the particular tax reported as revenue for the reporting entity as a whole. For example, a city may collect $100 million of property taxes, required to be pledged to cover the city's annual debt service payments of $40 million. Once the $40 million of debt service requirements are collected, the balance of the property tax revenue, or $60 million, is available for the government's general use. It may be that the government's full $100 million of property tax revenue is budgeted in the general fund, along with a transfer of $40 million to the debt service fund for debt service. In this case, it may be more appropriate to record the $100 million of property tax revenue in the general fund and then record an operating transfer of $40 million from the general fund to the debt service fund to reflect the transfer for debt service.

EXPENDITURE RECOGNITION FOR DEBT SERVICE PAYMENTS

As stated above, debt service funds should use the modified accrual basis of accounting and recognize expenditures when the liability is incurred. NCGAS 1, as subsequently amended by GASBS 6, provides a significant exception to this recognition criterion for debt service payments. The exception relates to unmatured principal and interest payments on general long-term debt, including special assessment debt for which the government is obligated in some manner.

Financial resources are usually appropriated in other funds for transfer to a debt service fund in the period in which maturing debt principal and interest must be paid. Theoretically, these amounts are not current liabilities of the debt service fund because their settlement will not require expenditure of existing resources of the debt service fund. If the debt service fund accrued an expenditure and liability in one period but recorded the transfer of financial resources for debt service payments in a later period, it would result in an understatement of the fund balance of the debt service fund.

Thus, the NCGA and the GASB concluded that debt service payments are usually appropriately accounted for as expenditures in the year of payment. Therefore, there is no accrual of interest or principal payments prior to the actual payments. Principal and interest expenditures are essentially recognized in the debt service fund on a cash basis, with only disclosure of subsequent-year debt service requirements. The cash basis is a practical way to consider recognition of debt service expenditures, although there is an assumption that debt is paid when it is due. Technically, debt service expenditures are actually recognized when the expenditure is due. Therefore, if there is a default on the payment of debt service (or if debt service is not paid because a payee cannot be located), an expenditure and corresponding liability would be recorded in the debt service fund.

The above discussion is based on the premise that the resources to actually make the debt service payment are not transferred into the debt service fund until the time that the debt service payment is actually going to be made. There is an additional consideration that must be made when the government has transferred or provided the resources for debt service payments that are due in a subsequent period. Under GAAP, if the debt service fund has been provided the resources during the current year for the payment of principal and interest due early in the following year, the expenditure and the related liability may be recognized in the debt service fund. This consideration often arises when resources are provided to a paying agent before year-end for debt due very early in the next fiscal year, such as when a fiscal year ends on June 30, and debt holders are entitled to an interest payment on July 1. In addition, the debt principal amount may be removed from the long-term debt account group.

It is important to note that the recognition of expenditures in the debt service fund for unmatured debt service principal and interest is optional for the government. Governments are not required to recognize debt service expenditures in debt service funds until they are due.

In instances where the government has an option to accrue debt service payment expenditures for unmatured debt service payments because resources have been provided in the current year for payments to be made early in the subsequent year, the GAAFR addresses the requirements that must be met in order to use this option. If a government elects to follow the early recognition option described in the preceding paragraph, the GAAFR provides that the following three conditions are met:

- The government uses a debt service fund to account for debt service payments.
- The advance provision of resources to the debt service fund is mandatory rather than discretionary.
- Payment is due within a short time period, usually one to several days and not more than one month.

These conditions reflect those promulgated by GASB Interpretation 6, *Recognition and Measurement of Certain Liabilities and Expenditures in Governmental Fund Financial Statements*.

The following are illustrative journal entries that would be recorded by a typical debt service fund that obtains the resources for debt service payments from transfers from the general fund:

1. The government transfers $10,000 from the general fund to the debt service fund for annual debt service payments.

Cash	10,000	
Other financing sources—operating transfers in—general fund		10,000

To record the receipt of $10,000 from the general fund.

2. The government invests $6,000 of the cash transfer from the general fund that will not be needed until the next semiannual debt service payment is due.

Investments	6,000	
Cash		6,000

To record the investment of cash not immediately needed for debt service

3. The government transfers $4,000 to its fiscal agent, which will disburse interest and principal payments to individual bondholders.

Cash with fiscal agent	4,000	
Cash		4,000

To record the transfer of cash for the immediately due semiannual debt service payment

4. The principal and interest payments on debt service reach the maturity date.

Expenditures—debt service	4,000	
Matured debt service payable		4,000

To record an expenditure and liability for matured debt service requirements

5. The fiscal agent disburses the cash to the individual bondholders for matured interest and principal payments.

Matured debt service payable	4,000	
Cash with fiscal agent		4,000

To record the debt service payment to bondholders by the fiscal agent

6. The government accrues interest on the balance of the operating transfer that it holds.

Interest receivable on investments	500	
Revenues—interest		500

To record accrued interest receivable on investments

7. Entry 6 demonstrates that interest on investments should follow the usual revenue accrual procedures using the modified accrual basis of accounting. If, in addition to the accrued interest recorded above, the debt service fund received $100 of interest during the fiscal year, the following entry would be recorded:

Cash	100	
Revenues—interest income		100

To record the receipt of $100 of interest on investments

NOTE: The reader should refer to Chapter 9, which describes changes to the reporting of amounts related to revenue recognition in governmental funds upon the effectiveness of GASB Statement No. 65, Items Previously Reported as Assets and Liabilities. Revenue and other governmental fund financial resources should be recognized in the accounting period in which they become both measurable and available. When an asset is recorded in governmental fund financial statements but the revenue is not available, the government should report a deferred inflow of resources until such time as the revenue becomes available.

ACCOUNTING FOR THE ADVANCE REFUNDING OF LONG-TERM DEBT

One of the more unique accounting transactions likely to be accounted for in a debt service fund is the advance refunding of long-term debt. While this topic is closely related to the requirements of GAAP as to when the refunded debt can be removed from the government-wide statement of net position, it has an effect on the debt service fund as well, because it is the most likely place where refundings, including advance refundings, of long-term debt are reported. GASB Statement 7 (GASBS 7), *Advance Refundings Resulting in Defeasance of Debt*, provides significant background and accounting guidance for determining the appropriate accounting for these activities.

There are several reasons why a government might desire to refund its debt in advance of the debt's maturity date. Three of these reasons are:

1. Most frequently, governments refinance debt to take advantage of more favorable interest rates. If interest rates have declined for similar securities, it is likely that the government can realize savings by refunding its older debt in advance.
2. Governments may also refinance debt to change the structure of debt service payments, such as by shortening or lengthening the period of debt service.
3. Governments might also refinance debt to escape from unfavorable bond covenants, such as restrictions on issuing additional debt.

NOTE: The Tax Cuts and Jobs Act of 2017 provided that interest on bonds issued as part of an advance refunding of debt would essentially no longer be tax exempt for federal tax purposes. This will likely significantly reduce the number of advance refunding transactions. Note that refunding bonds (used to pay off bonds that have reached a callable date and are actually paid off) are not impacted.

NOTE: Another reason that governments refund debt in advance is related to the second reason listed above. Debt may be refinanced to change the period that debt service payments are due. For example, assume that a government's fiscal year ends on June 30, and in refinancing the debt the government changes the maturity and interest payment date from June 30 to July 1 for the debt issued to refinance the original debt. Because debt service payments are recognized essentially on the cash basis, the government might effectively skip a debt service payment, which, assuming these payments are originally funded by the general fund, can provide an immediate savings in the general fund. Alternatively, the government may effectively capitalize a debt service payment by obtaining the resources for the payment from the proceeds of the new debt issued to refinance the old debt. The variations of these themes are limited only by the imagination of the bond underwriters proposing these types of transactions.

Because the benefits a government may realize from the above reasons are likely to be available before the debt is actually due or redeemable, it is necessary for a government to advance refund the debt. A government accomplishes an advance refunding by taking the proceeds of a new debt that is issued to refinance the old debt by placing the proceeds of the new debt in an escrow account that is subsequently used to provide funds to do the following, at minimum:

- Meet periodic principal and interest payments of the old debt until the call or maturity date.
- Pay the call premium, if redemption is at the call date.
- Redeem the debt at the call date or the maturity date.

Most advance refunding transactions result in a defeasance of the debt, enabling the government to remove the amount of the old debt from the general long-term debt account group. A defeasance can be either legal or in-substance.

- A legal defeasance occurs when debt is legally satisfied based on certain provisions in the instrument, even though the debt is not actually repaid.
- An in-substance defeasance is the far more common type of defeasance. An in-substance defeasance occurs when debt is considered defeased for accounting purposes even though a legal defeasance has not occurred.

GASBS 7 prescribes the criteria that must be met before debt is considered defeased in substance for accounting and reporting purposes. The government must irrevocably place cash or assets with an escrow agent in a trust to be used solely for satisfying scheduled payments of both interest and principal of the defeased debt, and the possibility that the debtor will be required to make future payments on that debt is remote. The trust is restricted to owning only monetary assets that are essentially risk-free as to the amount, timing, and collection of interest and principal. The monetary assets should be denominated in the currency in which the debt is payable. GASBS 7 also prescribes that for debt denominated in US dollars, risk-free monetary assets are essentially limited to

- Direct obligations of the US government (including State and Local Government Series securities [SLGS] that the US Treasury issues specifically to provide state and local governments with required cash flows at yields that do not exceed the Internal Revenue Service's arbitrage limits).
- Obligations guaranteed by the US government.
- Securities backed by US government obligations as collateral and for which interest and principal payments generally flow immediately through to the security holder.

The following describes the accounting treatment for advance refundings of debt in the debt service fund. Chapter 7 provides a significantly different model for accounting for advance refundings of the debt of proprietary funds. In addition, disclosure requirements for advance refundings are included in Chapter 15.

For advance refundings that result in defeasance of debt reported in the government-wide statement of net position, the proceeds from the new debt should be reported as "other financing source—proceeds of refunding bonds" in the fund receiving the proceeds, which, for purposes of this guide, is assumed to be the debt service fund. Payments to the escrow agent from resources provided by the new debt should be reported as "other financing use—payment to the refunded bond escrow agent." Payments to the escrow agent made from other resources of the entity should be reported as debt service expenditures. Exhibit 1 provides an example, and the related journal entries will help to clarify this accounting.

Exhibit 1: Example of advance refunding of debt in debt service fund

Assume that the city of Anywhere has $10,000 of general long-term debt bonds outstanding that it wishes to advance refund, resulting in an in-substance defeasance. To accomplish this, the city of Anywhere needs to put $13,000 in an escrow account, of which it already has $1,000 available in the debt service fund and will issue new bonds with proceeds set to be $12,000. The city of Anywhere will record the following journal entries:

1. The city of Anywhere issues the $12,000 of new debt, the proceeds of which are immediately placed in the escrow account.

Other financing uses—payment to refunded bond fiscal agent	12,000	
Other financing source—proceeds of refunding bonds		12,000

To record issuance of refunding bonds and their payment to the escrow account

2. The $1,000 already available in the debt service fund is paid to the escrow account.

Expenditures—debt service—advance refunding escrow	1,000	
Cash		1,000

To record debt service fund cash paid to the escrow account

The above journal entries would be different if the refunding either was not a legal defeasance or did not meet all of the requirements for the transaction to be considered an in-substance defeasance.

Crossover Transaction and Refunding Bonds

A crossover refunding transaction is a transaction in which there is no legal or in-substance defeasance and the debt is not removed from the general long-term debt account group. In fact, both the new bonds that were issued and the original bonds that were refunded appear in the long-term debt account group. In a crossover refunding transaction, the escrow account is not immediately dedicated to debt service principal and interest payments on the refunded debt. Instead, the resources in the escrow account are used to temporarily meet the debt service requirements on the refunding bonds themselves. At a later date, called the crossover date, the resources in the escrow account are dedicated exclusively to the payment of principal and interest on the refunded debt. While an in-substance defeasance does not occur when the refunding bonds are issued, an in-substance defeasance may occur at the crossover date if the in-substance defeasance requirements of GASBS 7 are met.

There are circumstances when refunding bonds are issued in a transaction that is not immediately accounted for as an in-substance or legal defeasance. In these circumstances, the assets in the escrow account would be accounted for in the debt service fund. In addition, the liability for the debt that is eventually refunded is not removed from the government-wide statement of net position until the debt is actually repaid or defeased legally or in substance. Assuming the same facts as in Exhibit 1, the following journal entry would be recorded in the debt service fund:

Cash with fiscal agent—escrow account	13,000	
Other financing source—refunding bonds		12,000
Cash		1,000

To record the establishment of an escrow account for refunded debt

SUMMARY

Debt service funds provide a useful mechanism for governments to account for transactions relating to the payment of principal and interest on long-term debt. Governments should consider both their legal and financial management requirements in determining whether to use a debt service fund and how many funds are to be established.

In determining the proper accounting for debt service transactions, governments also need to consider transactions accounted for in the general fund and the government-wide statement of net position.

7 PROPRIETARY FUNDS

INTRODUCTION

Proprietary funds are used to account for a government's ongoing organizations and activities that are similar to those found in the private sector. In other words, these activities resemble commercial activities performed by governments, and the basis of accounting and measurement focus of these funds reflect this resemblance. There are two types of proprietary funds—enterprise funds and internal service funds.

This chapter describes the basic characteristics and accounting for proprietary funds, both enterprise and internal service funds. The following specific topics are addressed:

- Basis of accounting and measurement focus for proprietary funds.
- Enterprise funds: Background and uses.
- Specific accounting issues:
  - Restricted assets.
  - Debt.
  - Contributed capital.
  - Advance refundings of debt.
  - Tap fees.
  - Regulated industries.
  - Fixed assets—Infrastructure and contributions of general fixed assets.
- Internal service funds: Background and uses.
- Specific accounting issues: Duplications of revenues and expenses.
- Surpluses and deficits.
- Risk financing activities.

While GASBS 34 did not affect the basis of accounting and measurement focus of proprietary funds (the same are used in both the government-wide and fund financial statements), it did affect certain aspects of how and when these funds are used. These points will be highlighted throughout the chapter.

BASIS OF ACCOUNTING AND MEASUREMENT FOCUS FOR PROPRIETARY FUNDS

In general terms, proprietary funds use the same basis of accounting and measurement focus as commercial enterprises. Proprietary funds use the accrual basis of accounting and the economic resources measurement focus. Accordingly, proprietary funds recognize revenues when they are earned and recognize expenses when a liability is incurred. Revenue recognition is sometimes difficult to determine in the commercial accounting arena. However, the types of goods and services typically provided by governmental units through proprietary funds should make this difficulty rare.

For example, a municipal water utility would recognize revenue for water provided to customers at the time that it actually provides the water to the customers. In contrast to the modified accrual basis of accounting, the timing of the billing of the water customers does not enter into the revenue recognition criteria. Under the accrual basis of accounting, even if a water customer does not pay his or her bill for a year, the revenue is still recognized by the proprietary fund. Under the modified accrual basis of accounting, revenue not collected for a year after its billing will likely be determined not to meet the "available" criterion for revenue recognition.

For expenses recognition, the timing of the recognition of expenses (i.e., when the liability is incurred) is a common element under the modified accrual basis of accounting. However, expenditures under the modified accrual basis of accounting are not recognized unless they are due, a significant departure from expense recognition. In addition, the difference between "expenses" recognized by proprietary funds and "expenditures" recognized by governmental funds is in what "costs" are included in expenses and expenditures. This is determined by the different measurement focuses used by proprietary funds and governmental funds. Proprietary funds use the flow of economic resources measurement focus. Governmental funds use the current financial resources measurement focus, which recognizes as expenditures those costs that result in a decrease in current financial resources. Under the flow of economic resources measurement focus, costs are recognized when the related liability is incurred, including the recognition of depreciation expense. In addition to depreciation, the most significant differences in recognizing expenses in proprietary funds (compared with expenditures in governmental funds) are related to the recognition of the liability and expense for the longer-term portions of liabilities for vacation and sick leave, judgments and claims, landfill liabilities, and accrued interest expense. The accounting for these activities is specifically described either later in this chapter or in separate chapters of this guide; however, at this point it is important to understand the conceptual difference between the two. For example, a proprietary fund that incurs costs for vacation and sick leave will recognize an expense for these costs as it accrues a liability for vacation and sick leave pay, regardless of when these amounts will be paid. In contrast, a governmental fund would not record an expenditure for vacation and sick leave costs that will not be paid from current financial resources. Accordingly, governmental funds generally record expenditures for vacation and sick leave costs when these amounts are actually paid to the employees.

In addition to the long-term liabilities described above, a proprietary fund records long-term bonded debt and other notes as a fund liability. On the other side of the balance sheet, assets that are capitalized are recorded as long-term assets of the proprietary fund (net of accumulated depreciation), which would not be the case for governmental funds.

The equity section of a proprietary fund's balance sheet also differs significantly from that of a governmental fund. A proprietary fund's net position is categorized as invested in capital assets, net of related debt, restricted, and unrestricted. Designation of unrestricted net position should not be reported by proprietary funds on the face of the financial statements. Capital contributions are not shown separately as a component of net position.

NOTE: Under GASBS 34, there are no "retained earnings" to report as reserved, so this concept is essentially replaced by the restricted versus unrestricted presentation. Furthermore, GASBS 34 states that there should be no "designations" of unrestricted net position reported by proprietary funds on the face of the financial statements.

Accounting Requirements under GASBS 62

It is conceptually simple to state that proprietary funds should use the commercial accounting model. However, the actual application of this concept is much more difficult because some accounting principles and standards promulgated by the FASB for commercial enterprises may conflict with pronouncements promulgated by the GASB. A proprietary fund attempting to apply accounting principles applicable to commercial enterprises would be unclear as to which of the conflicting accounting principles should be applied.

As also discussed in Chapter 2 the GASB issued Statement No. 62 (GASBS 62), *Codification of Accounting and Financial Reporting Guidance Contained in Pre–November 30, 1989 FASB and AICPA Pronouncements,* which incorporates into the GASB standards certain accounting and financial reporting guidance that is included in pronouncements of the FASB and AICPA issued on or before November 30, 1989, which do not conflict with or contradict GASB pronouncements.

GASBS 62 includes the accounting and financial reporting requirements previously contained in FASB and AICPA pronouncements applicable to proprietary funds and governmental entities that use proprietary accounting in governmental GAAP.

GASBS 62 addressed the following general accounting topics:

- Capitalization of Interest Cost.
- Revenue Recognition for Exchange Transactions.
- Revenue Recognition When Right of Return Exists.
- Statement of Net Position Classification.
- Special and Extraordinary Items.
- Comparative Financial Statements.
- Related Parties.
- Prior Period Adjustments.
- Accounting Changes and Error Corrections.
- Disclosure of Accounting Policies.
- Contingencies.
- Construction-Type Contracts—Long-Term.
- Extinguishments of Debt.
- Troubled Debt Restructuring.

- Foreign Currency Transactions.
- Interest Costs—Imputation.
- Inventory.
- Investments in Common Stock.
- Leases.
- Nonmonetary Transactions.
- Sales of Real Estate.
- Costs and Initial Rental Operations of Real Estate Projects.
- Research and Development Arrangements.

GASBS 62 also addresses the following industry-specific standards:

- Broadcasters.
- Cable Television Systems.
- Insurance Entities—Other Than Public Entity Risk Pools.
- Lending Activities.
- Mortgage Banking Activities.
- Regulated Operations.
- Right of Offset.

While substance of the above content is onerous (GASBS 62 is hundreds of pages long), the GASB used the approach of adopting the accounting and reporting requirements essentially as they existed in the applicable pre–November 30, 1989, FASB and AICPA pronouncements, modifying the language as appropriate to recognize the effects of the governmental environment without affecting the substance of the provisions. Accordingly, GASBS 62 is not intended to establish new financial reporting requirements or modify existing requirements. Rather, it incorporates FASB and AICPA accounting and reporting guidance applicable to governments and governmental entities into the GASB literature. While the GASB's intent was not to change accounting of financial reporting requirements, in the Basis for Conclusions of GASBS 62, the GASB does state that it recognizes that practitioners in exercising professional judgment may have reached different conclusions in applying the hierarchy without specific guidance.

After the issuance of GASBS 62, some of its accounting guidance was amended by subsequent GASB Statements. For example, interest capitalization (discussed in Chapter 14) was significantly modified by a subsequent GASB Statement.

ENTERPRISE FUNDS

Background and Uses

Enterprise funds are used to account for operations that fall within two basic categories:

1. Operations that are financed and operated in a manner similar to private business enterprises, where the intent of the governing body is to finance or recover costs (expenses, including depreciation) of providing goods and services to the general public on a continuing basis primarily through user charges.
2. Operations where the governing body has decided that periodic determination of revenues earned, expenses incurred, and/or net income is appropriate for capital maintenance, public policy, management control, accountability, or other purposes.

Enterprise funds are primarily used to account for activities that are financed through user charges. However, the total cost of the activity does not have to be paid for by the user charges. The government (or other governmental entity) may subsidize a significant portion of the costs of the enterprise fund.

For example, a government may establish a water authority to provide water to its residential and commercial water users. In this case, the water rates are generally set to recover the full cost of the water authority's operations. On the other hand, there may be circumstances where public policy determinations result in the user charges not covering the total costs of the operations. For example, a transit authority might be established to provide public transportation by buses, trains, or subways. Often, fares charged to the customers of the transit means provided by transit authorities do not cover the full cost of operation of the transit authority. Usually, the local government would subsidize the transit authority's operations. In addition, there may be state and federal mass transportation grants that help to subsidize the operations of the transit authority. These subsidies sometimes result in the transit fares covering a relatively small percentage of the total cost of the transit authority.

The decision to account for a particular operation as an enterprise fund is based both on whether the cost recovery through user charges is fundamental to the enterprise fund, and on whether the government finds it useful to have information on the total cost of providing a service to the government's citizens. This decision disregards the degree to which the charges to the users of the service cover the total cost of providing the service.

GASBS 34 continued the previous practice that an enterprise fund may be used to report any activity for which a fee is charged to external users as goods and services. However, GASBS 34 also specifies three situations where the use of an enterprise fund is required. The criteria are to be applied to the activity's principal revenue sources, meaning that insignificant activities where fees are charged would not automatically require the use of an enterprise fund. An enterprise fund is required to be used if one of the following criteria is met:

1. The activity is financed with debt that is secured solely by a pledge of the revenues from fees and charges of the activity. If the debt is secured in part from its own proceeds, it is still considered to be payable solely from the revenues of the activity. In other words, if a portion of the proceeds of a revenue bond issued is placed in a debt service reserve account, yet the revenue bond is payable solely from the revenues of the activity with the exception of the potential use of the reserve funds, this criterion is still met and the use of an enterprise fund would be required. On the other hand, if the debt is secured by a pledge of the revenues of the activity and the full faith and credit of a related primary government or component unit, it is not considered payable solely from the fees of the activity, even if it is not expected that the primary government or other component unit would actually make any payments on the debt. In this case, the criterion is not met and the use of an enterprise fund would not be required. In addition, this criterion would not apply to special assessment debt for which a government is not obligated in any manner.
2. Laws or regulations require that the activity's costs of providing services (including capital costs such as depreciation or debt service) be recorded from fees and charges, rather than taxes or similar revenues.
3. The pricing policies of the activity establish fees and charges designed to recover its costs, including capital costs such as depreciation or debt service.

Specific Accounting Issues

Restricted Assets

Typically, enterprise funds are used to issue long-term bonds to provide financing for their activities. The benefit of issuing bonds by the enterprise fund, rather than by the general government, is that there is typically a dedicated revenue stream in the enterprise fund that can be pledged to the service of the related debt. Often, this dedicated and pledged revenue results in a higher rating on the enterprise fund's long-term debt, resulting in a lower interest cost for the government. For example, a water utility may issue long-term debt to finance investments in water and sewer infrastructure, such as water filtration plants or sewage treatment plants. Water and sewer charges may represent a fairly constant source of revenue that may be judged by the investment community to be more reliable than general tax revenues. Accordingly, if the enterprise fund pledges its receipts for water and sewer charges to debt service, the related debt, commonly referred to as a revenue bond, will probably carry a lower interest rate than the government's general long-term debt.

As a result of the high level of debt issuance typically found in enterprise funds, these funds can often be found to have restricted assets. These restricted assets normally represent cash and investments whose availability to the enterprise fund is restricted by bond covenant. The following are examples of commonly found restricted assets:

- Revenue bond construction (such as cash, investments, and accrued interest segregated by the bond indenture for construction).
- Revenue bond operations and maintenance (such as accumulations of resources equal to operating costs for a specified period).
- Revenue bond current debt service (such as accumulations of resources for principal and interest payments due within one year).
- Revenue bond future debt service (such as accumulations of resources for principal and interest payments beyond the subsequent 12 months).
- Revenue bond renewal and replacement (such as accumulations of resources for unforeseen repairs and maintenance of assets originally acquired from bond proceeds).

One other form of restricted assets results from the enterprise fund holding deposits from its customers. Typically, the cash and investments related to these deposits are recorded as a restricted asset with a related offsetting liability that reflects the fact that the enterprise fund must return the deposits to its customers.

Debt

As stated earlier in this chapter, long-term debt applicable to the financing of the activities of proprietary funds is recorded in the funds as a fund liability. Some enterprise debt may be backed by the full faith and credit of the government. Even though the debt may be a general obligation of the government, it should be reported as a liability of the enterprise fund if the debt was issued for enterprise fund purposes and is expected to be repaid from enterprise fund resources. Therefore, it is the expected source of repayment for the debt (rather than the security interest for the debt) that is the primary factor in determining whether a liability for debt is recorded as a liability of the enterprise fund.

An additional consideration relating to the issuance of long-term debt that will be repaid from the resources of an enterprise fund concerns the accounting for arbitrage rebate. As more fully described in Chapter 8, governments that earn excess interest on the proceeds resulting from the issuance of tax-exempt debt must rebate these arbitrage earnings after a period of time to the federal government.

Contributed Capital

Because enterprise funds use an accounting and financial reporting model that resembles in many aspects the commercial accounting and reporting model, the concept of *capital*, or how the funds obtain their resources for operations (other than the issuance of debt), must be addressed.

Under GASBS 34, the accounting for capital contributions to proprietary funds changed significantly. There is no "contributed capital" classification of net position for proprietary funds as there had been in prior practice. Net position is categorized as invested in capital assets, net of related debt (which would include within it the resulting net position from capital contributions), restricted and unrestricted. Contributed capital is not displayed separately on the face of the financial statements.

The more significant change under the new financial reporting model, however, was that capital contributions are not recorded directly as an increase in the net assets (now net position) of the proprietary fund. Instead they flow through the statement of revenues, expenses, and changes in net position, where they are reported separately from operating revenues and expenses. The following presents an example of an abbreviated operating statement that reflects how capital contributions would be reported under the new financial reporting model:

Operating revenues:	
(Details of operating revenues)	xxx
Operating expenses:	
(Details of operating expenses, including depreciation on all depreciable fixed assets)	xxx
Operating income (loss)	xxx
Nonoperating revenues/expenses	
(Details of nonoperating revenues)	xxx
Income (loss) before other revenues (expenses, gains, losses, and transfers, if applicable)	xxx
Capital contributions	xxx
Increase (decrease) in net position	xxx
Net position—beginning of period	xxx
Net position—end of period	xxx

Refundings of Debt

The underlying background and general principles of refundings of debt for governments are fully described in Chapters 6 and 15. Statement 23 (GASBS 23), *Accounting and Financial Reporting for Refundings of Debt Reported by Proprietary Activities*, addresses the accounting issues related to advance refundings of debt for proprietary funds. Because these funds have an income determination focus, previous guidance resulted in the entire amount of the gain or loss being recognized for financial reporting purposes in the year of the advance refunding.

GASBS 23 applies to both current refundings and advance refundings of debt resulting in defeasance of debt reported by proprietary activities, which includes proprietary funds and other governmental entities that use proprietary fund accounting, such as public benefit corporations and authorities, utilities, and hospitals and other health care providers.

Refundings involve the issuance of new debt whose proceeds are used to repay previously issued, or old, debt. The new debt proceeds may be used to repay the old debt immediately, which is a current refunding. The new debt proceeds may also be placed with an escrow agent and invested until they are used to pay principal and interest on the old debt in the future, which is an advance refunding. An advance refunding of debt may result in the in-substance defeasance, provided that certain criteria (described in Chapter 13) are met. GASBS 23 applies to both current refundings and advance refundings that result in a defeasance of debt.

GASBS 23 requires that for current refundings and advance refundings resulting in a defeasance of debt reported by proprietary activities, the difference between the reacquisition price and the net carrying amount of the old debt should be deferred and amortized as a component of interest expense in a systematic and rational manner over the life of the old or new debt, whichever is shorter.

In applying the guidance of GASBS 23, two special terms need to be defined:

1. Reacquisition price. The reacquisition price is the amount required to repay previously issued debt in a refunding transaction. In a current refunding, this amount includes the principal of the old debt and any call premium incurred. In an advance refunding, the reacquisition price is the amount placed in escrow that, together with interest earnings, is necessary to pay interest and principal on the old debt and any call premium incurred. Any premium or discount and issuance costs pertaining to the new debt are not considered part of the reacquisition price. Instead, this premium or discount should be accounted for as a separate item relating to the new debt and amortized over the life of the new debt.
2. Net carrying amount. The net carrying amount of the old debt is the amount due at maturity, adjusted for any unamortized premium or discount and issuance costs related to the old debt.

On the balance sheet of the proprietary fund, the amount deferred should be reported as a deduction from or an addition to the new debt liability. The new debt may be reported net with either parenthetical or note disclosure of the deferred amount on refunding. The new debt may also be reported gross with both the debt liability and the related deferred amount present.

Two other situations involving prior refundings are also addressed by GASBS 23. For current refundings of prior refundings and for advance refundings of prior refundings resulting in the defeasance of debt, the difference between the reacquisition price and the net carrying amount of the old debt, together with any unamortized difference from prior refundings, should be deferred and amortized over the shorter of the original amortization period remaining from the prior refundings, or the life of the latest refunding debt. In other words, for a subsequent refunding of debt that was originally used to refund some other debt, add (or subtract) the remaining deferred gain or loss to the new gain or loss that would normally be calculated for the new refunding transaction. Amortize this combined amount over the shorter of the previous deferred amount's amortization period or the life of the new debt resulting from the new refunding transaction.

NOTE: The reader should refer to Chapter 9, which describes changes to the reporting of amounts related to debt refunding upon the effectiveness of GASB Statement No. 65, Items Previously Reported as Assets and Liabilities.

For current refundings and advance refundings resulting in a defeasance of debt reported by governmental activities, business-type activities, and proprietary funds, the difference between the reacquisition price and the net carrying amount of old debt should be reported as a deferred outflow of resources or a deferred inflow of resources and recognized as a component of interest expense in a systematic and rational manner over the remaining life of the old debt or the life of the new debt, whichever is shorter.

Prior to the expiration of the lease term, if a change in the provisions of a lease results from a refunding by the lessor of tax-exempt debt, including an advance refunding, in which (1) the perceived economic advantages of the refunding are passed through to the lessee and (2) the revised agreement is classified as a capital lease by the lessee, then the lessee should adjust the lease obligation to the present value of the future minimum lease payments under the revised lease. The adjustment of the lease obligation to present value should be made using the effective interest rate applicable to the revised agreement. The resulting difference should be reported as a deferred outflow of resources or a deferred inflow of resources. The deferred outflow of resources or the deferred inflow of resources should be recognized as a component of interest expense in a systematic and rational manner over the remaining life of the old debt or the life of the new debt, whichever is shorter.

In addition, under GASBS 65 issuance costs for debt are no longer reported as assets in the government-wide or proprietary fund financial statements.

Tap Fees

Tap fees refer to fees that new customers pay to a governmental utility to "tap into" or connect to the utility's existing system. They are also sometimes referred to as *connection fees* or *systems development fees*. The amount of the fee usually exceeds the actual cost to the utility to physically connect the new customer to the system. The excess profit that is built into tap fees is conceptually a charge to the new customers for their share of the costs of the existing infrastructure and systems of the governmental utility or a charge to offset a portion of the cost of upgrading the system.

The accounting issue relates to the treatment of the excess of the tap fee over the actual cost to the governmental utility to connect the new customer, which is considered an imposed nonexchange transaction. The GAAFR recommends that the portion of the tap fee that equals the cost of physically connecting the new customer be reported as operating revenue. This operating revenue then matches the operating expenses incurred in connecting the new customer. The amount charged in excess of the actual cost of physically connecting the new customer should be recorded by the governmental utility as nonoperating revenue as soon as the government has established an enforceable legal claim to the payment, usually upon connection. Prior to implementation of GASBS 34, these excess amounts were treated as contributed capital.

Customer and Developer Deposits

Utility-type and similar enterprise funds often require customers to pay a deposit to the enterprise fund to assure the timely payment for services. These deposits should be recorded by the enterprise fund as a current liability, until such time as the enterprise fund returns the deposit to the customers (such as when the service is terminated) or applies the deposit to an unpaid bill.

In some cases, land developers may also be required to make "good-faith" deposits to finance the cost of the enterprise fund to extend utility service to the new development. These developer deposits are also recorded as current liabilities of the enterprise fund until such time as they are no longer returnable to the developer, at which time they should be recorded as revenue. The subsequent use of these resources is legally restricted to capital acquisition or related debt service and should be reflected as a restriction of net position rather than as unearned revenue.

Fixed Assets—Infrastructure and Contribution of General Fixed Assets

Infrastructure assets are assets that are not movable and are of value only to the government. Proprietary funds are required to capitalize all of their assets, including infrastructure, even prior to the adoption of GASBS 34. For example, a water and sewer authority might have a grid of pipes and other connections that deliver water and collect waste water. The proprietary fund would be required to record these assets at their historical cost and depreciate them over their estimated useful lives.

When general fixed assets are contributed to a proprietary fund from another fund within the government, the contributed asset should be valued by the proprietary fund as though it had originally been acquired by that fund and subsequently depreciated. For example, assume that a general fixed asset with an original cost of $10,000 and a useful life of ten years is contributed to a proprietary fund at the end of four years. Assuming that straight-line depreciation is being used, the proprietary fund would either record the equipment on a net basis at $6,000, or would record the asset at $10,000, with a corresponding accumulated depreciation amount of $4,000. The proprietary fund would then continue to depreciate the asset at $1,000 per year for its remaining six-year life. This situation applies only when an existing asset of the government is transferred to a proprietary fund. Under GASBS 34, the accounting is similar, but the asset would be recorded at the net book value of the asset as reported in the government-wide statement of net position. Contributions of fixed assets from parties outside the government are valued at fair value and depreciation is recorded when the asset is placed in service, similar to when a new asset is acquired.

INTERNAL SERVICE FUNDS

Background and Uses

Internal service funds are used to account for the financing of goods or services provided by one department or agency of a governmental unit to other departments or agencies of the same governmental unit on a cost-reimbursement basis. In some cases, blended component units are reported as internal service funds.

Because internal service funds use the flow of economic resources measurement focus and accrual basis of accounting (as discussed below), they allow the full cost of providing goods or services to other departments or agencies to be charged to the receiving department or agency. Were these activities to be accounted for using a governmental fund, the full cost of the goods or services would not be determinable because the governmental fund would focus on the effect on current financial resources, rather than the full cost of the goods or services.

As the main purpose of internal service funds is to identify and allocate costs of goods or services to other departments, it is generally recommended that governments use separate internal service funds for different activities. Although the use of internal service funds is not required by GAAP, it is logical that disparate activities be accounted for in separate internal service funds to more accurately determine the costs of the goods and services. It should be noted that GAAP does not require that internal service funds include the full cost of services that are provided. A government may choose to leave some of the related costs out of the internal service fund, such as a rent charge or utility charge.

For example, internal service funds are often used to determine and allocate the costs for activities as diverse as the following:

- Duplicating and printing services.
- Central garages.
- Motor pools.

- Data processing.
- Purchasing.
- Central stores and warehousing.

Clearly, combining the costs of providing motor pool services with the costs of providing data processing services in the same internal service fund will not result in a very useful basis on which to allocate costs. Establishing separate funds will result in a more effective cost-allocation process.

Governments generally use internal service funds to determine and allocate costs of goods and services to other agencies and departments within the governmental unit, but they may also be used for other purposes. For example, internal service funds may be used for goods and services provided on a cost-reimbursement basis to other governmental entities within the reporting entity of the primary government. In some cases, internal service funds are used for goods and services provided on a cost-reimbursement basis to quasigovernmental organizations and not-for-profit organizations. In these circumstances, the government may find it more appropriate to classify these activities as enterprise funds, rather than internal service funds, depending on the individual circumstances. In fact, GASBS 34 specifies that if the reporting government is not the predominant participant in the activity, the activity should be reported as an enterprise fund.

Specific Accounting Issues

The accounting issues described above for enterprise funds also generally pertain to internal service funds, and the accounting and financial reporting guidance described above should be used as required in accounting for internal service funds.

Duplications of Revenues and Expenses

Many of the transactions between internal service funds and other funds take the form of quasiexternal transactions. The funds receiving the goods or services from the internal service fund report an expenditure or an expense while the internal service fund reports revenue. The consequence of this approach is that there is duplicate reporting of expenditures and expenses with the financial reporting entity of the government. For example, an internal service fund records an expense to recognize the cost of providing goods or services to another fund. This same expense is then duplicated in the other funds when the funds that received the goods or services are charged for their share of the cost. Revenue is also recognized in the internal service fund, based entirely on a transaction involving the funds of the government—in other words, an internal transaction. GASBS 34 specifies that eliminations should be made in the statement of activities to remove the "doubling-up" effect of internal service activities.

Surpluses and Deficits

Surpluses or deficits in internal service funds are likely to indicate that the other funds were not properly charged for the goods and services that they received. However, the government should take the view that internal service funds should operate on a breakeven basis over time. Surpluses or deficits in individual reporting periods may not necessarily indicate the need to adjust the basis on which other funds are charged for the goods or services provided by the internal service fund. It is only when internal service funds consistently report significant surpluses or deficits that the adequacy or inadequacy of charges made to other funds must be reassessed.

If it is determined that the charges made to other funds are either more or less than is needed to recover cost over a reasonable period, the excess or deficiency should be charged back to the participating individual funds. The GAAFR prescribes that it is not appropriate to report a material deficit in an internal service fund with the demonstrable intent and ability to recover that amount through future charges to other funds over a reasonable period.

In some cases, internal service funds use a higher amount of depreciation in determining charges to other funds than would ordinarily be calculated using acceptable depreciation methods in conjunction with historical cost. This is done so that the internal service fund accumulates enough resources from the other funds to provide for replacement of depreciable assets at what is likely to be a higher cost at the time of replacement. In this case, the surpluses recorded from the higher fees will eventually be offset by higher depreciation expense once the asset is replaced at a higher cost, and the higher cost is used in the depreciation expense calculation.

GASBS 34 has an interesting twist for reporting internal service fund asset and liability balances on the government-wide statement of net position. Any asset or liability balances that are not eliminated would be reported in the governmental activities column. While one would expect that internal service fund balances would be reported in the business-type activities column, the rationale used by GASBS 34 is that the activities accounted for in internal service funds are usually more governmental than business-type in nature. However, if enterprise funds are the predominant or only participant in an internal service fund, the government would report the internal service fund's residual assets and liabilities within the business-type activities column in the statements of net position.

Risk Financing Activities

Governments are required to use either the general fund or an internal service fund if they desire to use a single fund to account for all of their risk financing activities. Risk financing activities are fully described in Chapter 21. However, for purposes of understanding the use of internal service funds, the following brief discussion is provided.

If a government elects to use an internal service fund to account for its risk financing activities, interfund premiums are treated as quasiexternal transactions, similar to external insurance premiums. In other words, the internal service fund would record an expense and a liability for the judgments and claims that are probable and measurable for the reporting period. However, it may charge a higher premium to the other funds (and record the higher amount as revenue). Because interfund premiums paid to external service funds are treated as quasiexternal transactions rather than as reimbursements, their amounts are not limited by the amount recognized as expense in the internal service fund, provided that:

- The excess represents a reasonable provision for anticipated catastrophe losses; or
- The excess is the result of a systematic funding method designed to match revenues and expenses over a reasonable period, for example, an actuarial funding method or a funding method based on historical cost.

As will be more fully described in Chapter 21, deficits in risk-financing internal service funds must be charged back as expenditures or expenses to other funds if they are not recovered over a reasonable period. In addition, surplus retained earnings resulting from premiums charged for future catastrophe losses should be reported as a designation of retained earnings. This designation should be reported in the notes to the financial statements, rather than on the face of the financial statements. This is the sole instance where a designation of retained earnings is required by generally accepted accounting principles for a proprietary fund, although other designations are permitted and appropriate.

SUMMARY

The accounting and financial reporting for proprietary funds closely follows the accounting and financial reporting for commercial activities. However, there are some important differences and some unique accounting applications described in this chapter that distinguish this accounting from true commercial accounting. These differences must be understood by financial statement preparers to provide appropriate financial reports for proprietary activities.

8 FIDUCIARY FUNDS

INTRODUCTION

Governments are often required to hold or manage assets on behalf of others. NCGAS 1 recognized the need for fiduciary funds (known as *trust and agency funds* prior to GASBS 34), "to account for assets held by a governmental unit in a trustee capacity or as an agent for individuals, private organizations, other governmental units, and/or other funds."

GASBS 34 updated the types of fiduciary funds to include the following:

1. Pension (and other employee benefit) trust funds.
2. Investment trust funds.
3. Private-purpose trust funds.
4. Agency funds.

The funds are reported under GASBS 34 only in fiduciary fund financial statements. They are not reported as part of the government-wide financial statements.

Each of these fund types is described below. In addition, Chapter 22 describes the accounting and financial reporting principles used by pension trust funds.

NOTE: As discussed later in this chapter, the GASB issued Statement No. 84, Fiduciary Activities, which will impact the accounting and financial reporting for certain fiduciary funds.

AGENCY FUNDS

Agency funds are used to account for assets held solely in a custodial capacity. As a result, assets in agency funds are always matched by liabilities to the owners of the assets.

The accounting and financial reporting for agency funds are unique and do not really follow those of governmental funds or proprietary funds. Agency funds use the modified accrual basis of accounting for purposes of recognizing assets and liabilities, such as receivables and payables. However, agency funds do not have or report operations, and accordingly are said to not have a measurement focus.

In determining whether an agency fund or a trust fund is used to account for various types of transactions, there are no clear-cut distinctions for selecting the proper fund to account for a particular transaction. The degree of the government's management involvement and discretion over assets is generally much greater over trust fund assets than over agency fund assets. Private-purpose trust funds, for example, may require that a government's management identify eligible recipients, invest funds long- or short-term, or monitor compliance with regulations. Agency funds, on the other hand, typically involve only the receipt, temporary investment, and remittance of assets to their respective owners.

Agency funds are often used by school districts to account for student activity funds that are held by the school district but whose assets legally belong to the students. Another common use of agency funds is to account for taxes collected by one government on behalf of other governments. The collecting government has virtually no discretion on how the funds in the agency fund are to be spent. They are simply collected and then remitted to the government on whose behalf they were collected. In addition to this example, there are three instances where the use of an agency fund is mandated. These mandated uses are described in the following paragraphs.

Pass-Through Grants

GASB Statement 24 (GASBS 24), *Accounting and Financial Reporting for Certain Grants and Other Financial Assistance*, states that as a general rule, cash pass-through grants should be recognized as revenue and expenditures or expenses in a governmental, proprietary, or trust fund. GASBS 24 provides, however, that in those infrequent cases where a recipient government only serves as a cash conduit, the grant should be reported in an agency fund. The GAAFR, using the guidance of GASBS 24, states that an agency fund should only be used to account for grants if the government has no administrative involvement with the program and has no direct financial involvement with the program. Examples provided are as follows:

Administrative requirements:

- The government functions solely as an agent for some other government in collecting and forwarding funds.
- The government undertakes no responsibility for subrecipient monitoring for specific requirements.
- The government is not responsible for determining the eligibility of recipients.

Direct financial involvement:

- The government has no matching requirements; and
- The government is not liable for grant repayments.

If a grant does not meet these criteria, it is required that the revenues and expenditures or expenses of the grant be accounted for and reported in one of the other fund types.

Special Assessments

The accounting and financial reporting for special assessments is described in Chapter 4.

The use of an agency fund for special assessments is required when a government is not obligated in any manner for capital improvements financed by special assessment debt. GASBS 6 requires that "the debt service transactions of a special assessment issue for which the government is not obligated in any manner should be reported in an agency fund rather than a debt service fund, to reflect the fact that the government's duties are limited to acting as an agent for the assessed property owners and the bondholders."

When an agency fund is used for this purpose, any cash on hand from the special assessment would be shown on the agency fund's balance sheet. In addition, receivables would be reported for delinquent assessments. Only delinquent receivables would be reported as receivables on the agency fund's balance sheet, however. If the total receivables relating to the special assessment were shown, they would be offset by a liability that would essentially represent the special assessment debt. This would violate the requirement that special assessment debt for which the government is not obligated in any manner should not be displayed in the government's financial statements.

NOTE: In practice, agency funds are used by governments for the activities described above that are either repetitive or long-term. For infrequent transactions that will be settled within one or two years (for example, the asset will be received and the liability paid), many governments choose to simply use asset and liability accounts of the fund actually receiving the assets and paying the obligations rather than setting up a separate agency fund. Typically, these asset and liability accounts are set up in the government's general fund. The reason for using this approach, instead of setting up a large number of agency funds, is to avoid the administrative work involved in using a large number of agency funds.

PENSION (AND OTHER EMPLOYEE BENEFIT) TRUST FUNDS

Governments almost always offer pension benefits to their employees. The pension plans related to these benefits are reported as pension trust funds in the government's financial statements if either of the following criteria is met:

- The pension plan qualifies as a component unit of the government.
- The pension plan does not qualify as a component unit of the government, but the plan's assets are administered by the government.

Pension (and other employee benefit) trust funds are used to account for other employee benefit funds held in trust by a government, such as an Internal Revenue Code Section 457 deferred compensation plan, discussed below. This type of fund would also be used for trust funds established to fund postemployment benefits other than pensions (i.e., other postemployment benefits [OPEBs]).

Pension (and other employee benefit) trust funds use the flow of economic resources measurement focus and the full accrual basis of accounting, similar to nonexpendable trust funds and proprietary funds. A separate pension (and other employee benefit) trust fund should be used for each separate plan. Separate pension (and other employee benefit) trust funds are also sometimes established to account for supplemental pension benefits.

Governmental pension plans are usually administered by a public employee retirement system (PERS). The GASB has specific pronouncements governing the accounting and financial reporting for both governmental employers that offer pension plans and the accounting and financial reporting of the plans themselves. Chapter 18 addresses the governmental employer accounting questions, and Chapter 24 addresses the accounting for the plans themselves.

Deferred Compensation Plans

Many governments establish and offer participation to their employees in deferred compensation plans established under Section 457 of the Internal Revenue Code. These plans are often referred to as *Section 457 plans*. The laws governing these plans were changed so that as of August 20, 1996, new deferred compensation plans would not be considered eligible under Internal Revenue Code Section 457 unless all assets and income of the plan are held in trust for the exclusive benefit of the plan participants and their beneficiaries. For existing plans to remain eligible under Internal Revenue Code Section 457, this requirement was required to be met by January 1, 1999. Thus, the entire nature of the access to the assets of deferred compensation plans changed under the new requirements. The assets (and their related earnings) are no longer to be accessible to the governmental entity and its creditors. They are held in trust for the exclusive benefit of the plan participants and their beneficiaries. Governments also sometimes offer employees similar deferred compensation plans established under Section 401(k) of the Internal Revenue Code. The accounting guidance discussed in this section would apply to the Section 401(k) plans as well.

In applying the requirements of GASBS 32, the first step for governments is to determine whether the Internal Revenue Code Section 457 plan should be included as a fiduciary fund of the reporting government. If the plan meets the criteria of NCGAS 1 for inclusion as a fiduciary fund, the plan would be reported under GASBS 32 as part of pension (and other employee benefit) trust funds. If the criteria of NCGAS 1 are not met, then the plan would not be included as a fiduciary fund of the reporting government.

NCGAS 1 defines fiduciary funds as "Trust and Agency funds to account for assets held by a governmental unit in a trustee capacity or as an agent for individuals, private organizations, other governmental units, and/or other funds." No additional guidance on when to report Internal Revenue Code Section 457 plans is provided by GASBS 32. The basis for conclusions of GASBS 32 indicates that the GASB's research indicated at the time of the statement issuance that most governments had little administrative involvement with their plans and did not perform the investing function for those plans. This is consistent with the practice that has emerged upon adoption of GASBS 32 of many governments not reporting their plans as fiduciary funds.

However, whether the plan is reported is a matter of professional judgment, and the extent of the government's activities relating to the plan, particularly in selecting investment alternatives and holding the assets in a trustee capacity, needs to be evaluated.

Governments that report Internal Revenue Code Section 457 deferred compensation plans should apply the valuation provisions of GASB Statement 31 (GASBS 31), *Accounting and Financial Reporting for Certain Investments and for External Investment Pools*. In addition, all other plan investments should be reported at fair value. Thus, all of the investments of the plan will be reported at fair value.

GASBS 32 further provides that if it is impractical to obtain investment information from the plan administrator as of the reporting government's balance sheet date, the most recent report of the administrator should be used—for example, reports ending within the reporting government's fiscal year or shortly thereafter, adjusted for interim contributions and withdrawals.

INVESTMENT TRUST FUNDS

A special type of trust fund, the investment trust fund, is used by governments that sponsor external investment pools and that provide individual investment accounts to other legally separate entities that are not part of the same financial reporting entity. The investment trust fund is required to be used in these circumstances by GASBS 31, *Accounting and Financial Reporting for Certain Investments and for External Investment Pools*. The accounting for these funds is unchanged by GASBS 34.

Investment trust funds report transaction balances using the flow of economic resources measurement focus and the accrual basis of accounting. Accordingly, the accounting and financial reporting for investment trust funds is similar to that used by nonexpendable trust funds (and proprietary funds).

The two instances where GASBS 31 specifies that investment trust funds be used are as follows:

External portion of external investment pools. An external investment pool commingles the funds of more than one legally separate entity and invests on the participants' behalf in an investment portfolio. GASBS 31 specifies that the external portion of each pool should be reported as a separate investment trust fund. The external portion of an external investment pool is the portion of the pool that belongs to legally separate entities that are not part of the sponsoring government's financial reporting entity.

In its financial statements, the sponsoring government should present for each investment trust fund a statement of net position and a statement of changes in net position. The difference between the external pool assets and liabilities should be captioned "net position held in trust for pool participants." In the combined financial statements, investment trust funds should be presented in the balance sheet along with the other trust and agency funds. A separate statement of changes in net position should be presented for the combined investment trust funds, although GASBS 31 permits that statement to be presented with similar trust funds, such as pension trust funds.

Individual investment accounts. GASBS 31 requires that governmental entities that provide individual investment accounts to other legally separate entities that are not part of the same financial reporting entity should report those investments in one or more separate investment trust funds. Given the way that individual investment accounts function, specific investments are acquired for individual entities and the income from and changes in the value of those investments affect only the entity for which they were acquired.

The manner of presentation should be consistent with that described above for the external portion of external investment pools.

PRIVATE-PURPOSE TRUST FUNDS

Private-purpose trust funds are a type of fiduciary fund introduced by GASBS 34. They are used to report all trust arrangements (other than pension and other employee benefit, and investment trust funds), under which principal and income benefit individuals, private organizations, or other governments. Similar to other fiduciary funds, private-purpose trust funds cannot be used to support a government's own programs. It is important, therefore, to make sure that an activity is absent any public purpose of the government before it is accounted for as a private-purpose trust fund, even if individuals, private organizations, or other governments receive direct or indirect benefits from the activity. The distinction that a private-purpose trust fund should not be used to account for a grant program that supports a government's own programs is an important one. If a donor provides a government with a grant for the government to use to support its own programs, that grant should be recorded in the government's general fund as grant revenue. The expenditures for this example program then become subject to the budgetary appropriations of the government's general fund. However, if the grant does not directly benefit the government or go to support its own programs, then the grant is properly accounted for as a private-purpose trust fund. Generally because of their nature, there are no legal budgetary appropriations for these types of fiduciary funds and the program is administered essentially only in accordance with the grant agreement.

GASB Statement 84 Fiduciary Activities

In January 2017 the GASB issued Statement No. 84, *Fiduciary Activities* (GASBS 84), which provides some clarifications and changes to fiduciary fund accounting. GASBS 84 establishes specific criteria for identifying activities that should be reported as fiduciary activities and clarifies whether and how business-type activities should report their fiduciary activities.

Identifying Fiduciary Activities

GASBS 84 notes that a primary government or its component units may be engaged in fiduciary activities. GASBS 84 first describes component units that are engaged in fiduciary activities. A component unit is a fiduciary activity (a fiduciary component unit) if it meets the criteria described below, as applicable.

Fiduciary Component Units

GASBS 84 provides that an organization that meets the component unit criteria in GASBS 14, *The Financial Reporting Entity*, as amended, is a fiduciary activity if it is one of the following arrangements:

(a) A pension plan that is administered through a trust that meets the criteria in GASBS 67, *Financial Reporting for Pension Plans—An Amendment of GASB Statement No. 25.*
(b) Another postemployment benefit (OPEB) plan that is administered through a trust that meets the criteria in GASBS 74, *Financial Reporting for Postemployment Benefit Plans Other Than Pension Plan.*
(c) A circumstance in which assets from entities that are *not* part of the reporting entity are accumulated for pensions as described in GASBS 73, *Accounting and Financial Reporting for Pensions and Related Assets That Are Not within the Scope of GASB Statement 68, and Amendments to Certain Provisions of GASB Statements 67 and 68*, in paragraph 116.
(d) A circumstance in which assets from entities that are *not* part of the reporting entity are accumulated for OPEB as described in GASBS 74, paragraph 59.

GASBS 84 notes that, in general, pension plans that are administered through trusts under GASBS 68 and GASBS 74 are legally separate entities. In determining whether those legally separate entities are component units, a primary government is considered to have a financial burden if it is legally obligated or has otherwise assumed the obligation to make contributions to the pension plan or OPEB plan. As such, most pension and OPEB plans administered through trusts would be expected to be reported as fiduciary component units.

GASBS 84 further provides that a component unit that is not a pension arrangement or OPEB arrangement as described above is a fiduciary activity if the assets associated with the activity have one or more of the following characteristics:

(a) The assets are (1) administered through a trust agreement or equivalent arrangement (hereafter referred to as a trust) in which the government itself is not a beneficiary, (2) dedicated to providing benefits to recipients in accordance with the benefit terms, and (3) legally protected from the creditors of the government.
(b) The assets are for the benefit of individuals, and the government does *not* have administrative involvement with the assets or direct financial involvement with the assets. In addition, the assets are *not* derived from the government's provision of goods or services to those individuals.
(c) The assets are for the benefit of organizations or other governments that are *not* part of the financial reporting entity. In addition, the assets are *not* derived from the government's provision of goods or services to those organizations or other governments.

In determining whether a component unit is a fiduciary component unit, control of the assets of the component unit by the primary government (as discussed below) is *not* a factor to be considered.

Pension and OPEB Arrangements That Are Not Component Units

GASBS 84 specifies that, if they are not component units, the following pension and OPEB arrangements are fiduciary activities if the government controls (as described below) the assets of the arrangement:

(a) A pension plan that is administered through a trust that meets the criteria in GASBS 67.
(b) An OPEB plan that is administered through a trust that meets the criteria in GASBS 74.
(c) A circumstance in which assets from entities that are not part of the reporting entity are accumulated for pensions as described in GASBS 73.
(d) A circumstance in which assets from entities that are not part of the reporting entity are accumulated for OPEB as described in GASBS 74.

In applying the criteria listed above, a government has administrative involvement with the assets under GASBS 84 if, for example, it (a) monitors compliance with the requirements of the activity that are established by the government or by a resource provider that does not receive the direct benefits of the activity, (b) determines eligible expenditures that are established by the government or by a resource provider that does not receive the direct benefits of the activity, or (c) has the ability to exercise discretion over how assets are allocated. A government has direct financial involvement with the assets if, for example, it provides matching resources for the activities.

Other Fiduciary Activities

For activities not addressed above, GASBS 84 provides that the activity is a fiduciary activity if all of the following criteria are met:

(a) The assets associated with the activity are controlled by the government (as described below).

(b) The assets associated with the activity are not derived either:

1. Solely from the government's own-source revenues (also described below) or
2. From government-mandated nonexchange transactions or voluntary nonexchange transactions with the exception of pass-through grants for which the government does not have administrative involvement or direct financial involvement.

(c) The assets associated with the activity have one or more of the following characteristics:

1. The assets are (a) administered through a trust in which the government itself is not a beneficiary, (b) dedicated to providing benefits to recipients in accordance with the benefit terms, and (c) legally protected from the creditors of the government.
2. The assets are for the benefit of individuals and the government does not have administrative involvement with the assets or direct financial involvement with the assets. In addition, the assets are not derived from the government's provision of goods or services to those individuals.
3. The assets are for the benefit of organizations or other governments that are *not* part of the financial reporting entity. In addition, the assets are *not* derived from the government's provision of goods or services to those organizations or other governments.

Control of Assets

GASBS 84 provides that a government controls the assets of an activity if the government (a) holds the assets or (b) has the ability to direct the use, exchange, or employment of the assets in a manner that provides benefits to the specified or intended recipients. However, restrictions from legal or other external restraints that stipulate the assets can be used only for a specific purpose do not negate a government's control of the assets.

Own-Source Revenues

In applying the above criteria, GASBS 84 considers own-source revenues to be revenues that are generated by a government itself. They include exchange and exchange-like revenues (for example, water and sewer charges) and investment earnings. Derived tax revenues (such as sales and income taxes) and imposed nonexchange revenues (such as property taxes) also are included.

Reporting Fiduciary Activities in Fiduciary Funds

GASBS 84 provides that governments should report fiduciary activities in the fiduciary fund financial statements of the basic financial statements. The fiduciary fund used to report the activities should be based on the requirements below.

Pension (and other employee benefit) trust funds are used to report fiduciary activities for the following:

- Pension plans and OPEB plans that are administered through trusts that meet the criteria in GASBS 67 and 74.
- Other employee benefit plans for which (1) resources are held in a trust that meets the criteria described above and (2) contributions to the trust and earnings on those contributions are irrevocable.

Investment trust funds are used to report fiduciary activities from the external portion of investment pools and individual investment accounts that are held in a trust that meets the criteria described above in item c (3).

Private-purpose trust funds are used to report all fiduciary activities that (a) are *not* required to be reported in pension (and other employee benefit) trust funds or investment trust funds and (b) are held in a trust that meets the criteria described above in item c (3).

Custodial funds are used to report fiduciary activities that are *not* required to be reported in pension (and other employee benefit) trust funds, investment trust funds, or private-purpose trust funds. The external portion of investment pools that are not held in a trust that meets the criteria described above in item c (3) should be reported in a separate *external investment pool fund* column, under the custodial funds classification.

NOTE: The most significant change in these types of fiduciary funds is that agency funds have been replaced with custodial funds. As will be described below, custodial funds will also present their activities for the reporting period.

As to business-type activities, including enterprise funds, GASBS 84 provides that they may report assets with a corresponding liability that otherwise should be reported in a custodial fund in the statement of net position of the business-type activity if those assets, upon receipt, are normally expected to be held for three months or less. A business-type activity that chooses to report such assets and liabilities in its statement of net position should separately report additions and deductions, if significant, as cash inflows and cash outflows, respectively, in the operating activities category of its statement of cash flows.

Statement of Fiduciary Net Position

The statement of fiduciary net position is used to report the assets, deferred outflows of resources, liabilities, deferred inflows of resources, and fiduciary net position of pension (and other employee benefit) trust funds, investment trust funds, private-purpose trust funds, and custodial funds.

Except for pension and OPEB entities discussed below, GASBS 84 provides that a liability to the beneficiaries of a fiduciary activity should be recognized in a fiduciary fund when an event has occurred that compels the government to disburse fiduciary resources.

Events that compel a government to disburse fiduciary resources occur when a demand for the resources has been made or when no further action, approval, or condition is required to be taken or met by the beneficiary to release the assets. GASBS 84 provides the example that a county government should recognize a liability when it collects taxes for other governments, even though it may not be required to distribute the taxes to those governments until a specified time in the future. Liabilities other than those to beneficiaries should be recognized in accordance with existing accounting standards using the economic resources measurement focus.

GASBS 84 further provides that a government that reports a pension plan or an OPEB plan in a pension (or other employee benefit) trust fund should report the plan's assets, deferred outflows of resources, liabilities, deferred inflows of resources, and fiduciary net position in accordance with GASBS 67 or 74, as applicable.

Statement of Changes in Fiduciary Net Position

The statement of changes in fiduciary net position is used to report additions to and deductions from pension (and other employee benefit) trust funds, investment trust funds, private-purpose trust funds, and custodial funds.

Except for pension and OPEB entities discussed above, or custodial funds discussed below, GASBS 84 provides that the statement of changes in fiduciary net position should disaggregate additions by source including, if applicable, separate display of:

(a) Investment earnings.
(b) Investment costs (including investment management fees, custodial fees, and all other significant investment-related costs).
(c) Net investment earnings (investment earnings minus investment costs).

Investment-related costs are reported as investment costs if they are separable from (a) investment earnings and (b) administrative costs. The statement of changes in fiduciary net position should disaggregate deductions by type and, if applicable, should separately display administrative costs.

GASBS 84 provides that a government may report a single aggregated total for additions and a single aggregated total for deductions of custodial funds in which resources, upon receipt, are normally expected to be held for three months or less. The descriptions of the aggregated totals of additions and deductions should indicate the nature of the resource flows. The example provided is that of a custodial fund addition description, *property taxes collected for other governments*. An example of a custodial fund deduction description is *property taxes distributed to other governments*.

In addition, GASBS 84 provides that a government that reports a pension plan or OPEB plan in a pension (or other employee benefit) trust fund should report changes in the plan's fiduciary net position in accordance with GASBS 67 and 74, as applicable.

Reporting Fiduciary Component Units

When reported in the fiduciary fund financial statements of a primary government, a fiduciary component unit should include the combined information of its own component units that are fiduciary component units. That combined information should be aggregated with the primary government's fiduciary funds based on the classifications of the various types of fiduciary funds described earlier.

Effective Date

GASBS 84 is effective for reporting periods beginning after December 15, 2018. Earlier application is encouraged. Changes adopted to conform to the provisions of this Statement should be applied retroactively by restating financial statements, if practicable, for all prior periods presented. If restatement for prior periods is not practicable, the cumulative effect, if any, of applying GASBS 84 should be reported as a restatement of beginning net position (or fund balance or fund net position, as applicable) for the earliest period restated. In the first period that this Statement is applied, the notes to the financial statements should disclose the nature of the restatement and its effect.

SUMMARY

Governments frequently hold assets in a fiduciary capacity and should use the appropriate fiduciary fund to account for the assets and liabilities relating to these fiduciary responsibilities. The use of fiduciary funds provides the capability to improve accountability and control over these assets.

9 FINANCIAL STATEMENTS PREPARED BY GOVERNMENTS

INTRODUCTION

This chapter describes some of the unique aspects of the financial statements prepared by governments. The information presented in this chapter is consistent with the financial reporting model promulgated by GASBS 34, as amended. This information also incorporates the more important guidance provided by GASB staff through the use of Question and Answer Implementation Guides concerning the financial reporting model. While the basic financial statement elements of a balance sheet, operating statement, and in some cases cash flow statement exist in a significantly modified way for governments, there are many concepts unique to financial reporting for governments. These financial reporting concepts are discussed throughout this chapter.

This chapter also provides information and discussion on the following topics:

- Basic financial statements (BFS).
- Interfund and intra-entity transactions.
- Reporting deferred inflows and outflows of resources.
- Comprehensive annual financial report (CAFR).
- Cash flow statement preparation and reporting.

This chapter focuses on the overall financial reporting for governments. There are a number of specific reporting and presentation issues that relate to specific fund types. These issues are discussed in later chapters.

BASIC FINANCIAL STATEMENTS

The basic financial statements used for a governmental entity's fair presentation in accordance with generally accepted accounting principles (GAAP) include both information reported on a government-wide basis and information presented on a fund basis. Certain budget-to-actual comparisons may also be required. Specifically, components of the basic financial reporting for the governmental entities included in the scope of the financial reporting model are as follows:

- Management's discussion and analysis (MD&A).
- Basic financial statements (BFS):
  - Government-wide financial statements.
  - Fund financial statements.
- Notes to the financial statements.
- Required supplementary information (RSI).

Each of the elements is described more fully below.

Management's Discussion and Analysis

Management's discussion and analysis (MD&A) is an introduction to the financial statements that provides readers with a brief, objective, and easily readable analysis of the government's financial performance for the year and its financial position at year-end. The analysis included in MD&A should be based on currently known facts, decisions, or conditions. For a fact to be currently known, it should be based on events or decisions that have already occurred, or have been enacted, adopted, agreed upon, or contracted. This means that governments should not include discussions about the possible effects of events that might happen. (Discussion of possible events that might happen in the future may be discussed in the letter of transmittal that is prepared as part of a comprehensive annual financial report.) MD&A should contain a comparison of current year results with those of the prior year.

GASBS 34 provides a listing of very specific topics to be included in MD&A, although governments are encouraged to be creative in presenting the information using graphs, charts, and tables. The GASB would like MD&A to be a useful analysis that is prepared with thought and insight, rather than boilerplate material prepared by rote every year. However, the phrase "the minimum is the maximum" applies. This means that MD&A should address all of the applicable topics listed in GASBS 34, but MD&A should address *only* these topics. Of course, governments preparing comprehensive annual financial reports can include in the letter of transmittal any topic that would be precluded from being included in MD&A.

NOTE: In the author's experience, one thing has unfortunately become clear—many MD&A presentations have become somewhat boilerplate and often do not provide any real insight into a government's performance or financial position. In some instances, the analysis consists only of a computation of an increase or decrease in a financial statement line item, along with a corresponding percentage.

The requirements of GASBS 34 call for an analysis of performance and financial position. To accomplish this, the reasons for significant increases and decreases in certain financial statement amounts should be provided to assist the reader in understanding why these fluctuations occurred (or perhaps did not occur). Financial statement preparers should take care that MD&A provides sufficient information to the reader to meet the requirements of GASBS 34. This would include providing information beyond simple fluctuation calculations that readers of the financial statements would otherwise be able to calculate on their own.

Current year information is to be addressed in comparison with the prior year, although the current year information should be the focus of the discussion. If the government is presenting comparative financial data with the prior year in the current year financial statements, the requirements for MD&A apply to only the current year. However, if the government is presenting comparative financial statements, that is, a complete set of financial statements for each year of a two-year period, then the requirements of MD&A must be met for each of the years presented. The requirements may be met by including all of the required information in the same presentation, meaning that two completely separate MD&As for comparative financial statements are not required, provided that all of the requirements relating to each of the years are met in the one discussion.

In addition, MD&A should focus on the primary government. For fund information, the analysis of balances and transactions of individual funds would normally be confined to major funds, although discussion of nonmajor fund information is not precluded. Governments must use judgment in determining whether discussion and analysis of discretely presented component unit information is included in MD&A. The judgment should be based upon an individual component unit's significance to the total of all discretely presented component units, as well as its significance to the primary government.

The minimum requirements for MD&A are as follows:

1. Brief discussion of the basic financial statements, including the relationships of the statements to each other and the significant differences in the information that they provide. (This is where governments should explain the differences in results and measurements in the government-wide financial statements and the fund financial statements. This discussion provides the reporting government an opportunity to help the financial

statement reader understand the financial statements and understand the differences between the fund financial statements and the government-wide financial statements.)

2. Condensed financial information derived from the government-wide financial statements, comparing the current year to the prior year. GASBS 34 specifies that the following elements are included:
   (a) Total assets, distinguishing between capital assets and other assets.
   (b) Total liabilities, distinguishing between long-term liabilities and other liabilities.
   (c) Total net position, distinguishing among amounts invested in capital assets, net of related debt; restricted amounts; and unrestricted amounts.
   (d) Program revenues, by major source.
   (e) General revenues, by major source.
   (f) Total revenues.
   (g) Program expenses, at a minimum by function.
   (h) Total expenses.
   (i) The excess or deficiency before contributions to term and permanent endowments or permanent fund principal, special and extraordinary items.
   (j) Contributions.
   (k) Special and extraordinary items.
   (l) Transfers.
   (m) Change in net position.
   (n) Ending net position.

   Although charts and graphs may be used to supplement or elaborate on information contained in the condensed financial information, they cannot be used in place of the condensed financial information.
3. Analysis of the government's overall financial position and results of operations. This information should assist users in determining whether financial position has improved or deteriorated as a result of the current year's operations. Both governmental and business-type activities should be discussed. The reasons for significant changes from the prior year should be described, not simply the computation of percentage changes.
4. Analysis of the balances and transactions of individual funds.
5. Analysis of significant variations between original and final budgeted amounts and between financial budget amounts and actual budget results for the general fund (or its equivalent). MD&A should discuss the reasons for significant budget variances, such as why the significant variance occurred.
6. Description of significant capital asset and long-term debt activity during the year. Note that special assessment debt for which the government is not obligated in any manner should not be part of this discussion.
7. For governments that use the modified approach to report some or all of their infrastructure assets, the following should be discussed:
   (a) Significant changes in the assessed condition of eligible infrastructure assets.
   (b) How the current assessed condition compares with the condition level the government has established.
   (c) Significant differences from the estimated annual amount to maintain/preserve eligible infrastructure assets compared with the actual amounts spent during the year.
8. Description of currently known facts, decisions, or conditions that are expected to have a significant effect on financial position or results of operations.

NOTE: In meeting the MD&A requirements of GASB 34, two matters should be considered:

- *First, the relationship between MD&A and the letter of transmittal presented as part of a CAFR must be addressed. Including any information required in MD&A in a letter of transmittal does not fulfill any of the requirements for MD&A since MD&A is a required supplement to the basic financial statements of a government and the letter of transmittal of a CAFR is not. On the other hand, certain information that is required in MD&A may formerly have been included in the letter of transmittal. This information may be moved from the transmittal letter to MD&A. However, the Governmental Accounting, Auditing, and Financial Reporting (GAAFR) of the Government Finance Officers Association (GFOA) includes guidance for the requirements of the letter of transmittal for its Certificate of Achievement for Excellence in Financial Reporting program upon adoption of GASBS 34. Governments that intend to apply for the GFOA Certificate of Achievement should make sure that they do not remove information from the letter of transmittal that is required by the Certificate program.*
- *MD&A is a required supplement to the basic financial statements of a government. These statements are frequently included in Official Statements prepared by governments when the governments are selling debt to the public. Official Statements generally include a significant amount of analytical information about the financial condition and financial performance of the government. Care must be taken that analytical information included in MD&A about currently known facts, decisions, and conditions is consistent with statements made in the Official Statement, after taking into consideration the passage of time between the issuance of financial statements and the issuance of an Official Statement.*

Government-Wide Financial Statements

Government-wide financial statements include two basic financial statements—a statement of net position and a statement of activities. These statements should include the primary government and its discretely presented component units (presented separately), although they would not include the fiduciary activities or component units that are fiduciary in nature. The statements would distinguish between governmental activities (which are those financed through taxes, inter-governmental revenues, and other nonexchange revenues) and business-type activities (which are those primarily financed through specified user fees or similar charges). Presentation of prior year data on the government-wide financial statements is optional. Presenting full prior year financial statements on the same pages as the current year financial statements may be cumbersome because of the number of columns that might need to be presented. Accordingly, a government may wish to present summarized prior year data. On the other hand, if full prior year statements are desired (for presentation in an Official Statement for a bond offering, for example), the prior year statements may be reproduced and included with the current year statements. In this case, footnote disclosure should also be reviewed to make sure that both years are addressed.

Basis of accounting and measurement focus. The government-wide financial statements are prepared using the economic resources measurement focus and the accrual basis of accounting for all activities. Presentation of financial statement balances in the government-wide financial statements is discussed throughout the various specific topics covered in this guide. The following pages address the more important financial statement display issues when reporting under the new financial reporting model.

The government-wide financial statements should present information about the primary government's governmental activities and business-type activities in separate columns, with a total column that represents the total primary government. Governmental activities generally include those activities financed through taxes, intergovernmental revenues, and other nonexchange revenues. Business-type activities are those activities financed in whole or part by fees charged to external parties for goods or services (i.e., enterprise fund activities). Discretely presented component units are presented in a separate column. A column that totals the primary government and the discretely presented component units to represent the entire reporting entity is optional, as is prior year data.

Reporting for governmental and business-type activities should be based on all applicable GASB pronouncements, including the standards promulgated by GASB Statement No. 62 (GASBS 62), *Codification of Accounting and Financial Reporting Guidance Contained in Pre–November 30, 1989 FASB and AICPA Pronouncements*, which incorporates into the GASB standards certain accounting and financial reporting guidance that was included in pronouncements of the FASB and AICPA issued on or before November 30, 1989, which do not conflict with or contradict GASB pronouncements.

Statement of Net Position

GASBS 34 provides several examples of how the statement of net position may be presented. There are several key presentation issues that must be considered in implementing this statement. These are summarized as follows:

- The net of assets plus deferred outflows of resources and liabilities plus deferred inflows of resources is labeled "net position." This difference should not be labeled as equity or fund balance.
- Governments are encouraged to present assets and liabilities in order of their relative liquidity but may instead use a classified format that distinguishes between current and long-term assets and liabilities. An asset's liquidity is determined by how readily it is expected to be converted to cash and whether there are restrictions on the use of the asset. A liability's liquidity is based on its maturity or when cash is expected to be used to liquidate it. GASBS 34 allows that the liquidity of classes of assets and liabilities may be assessed using their average liquidity, even if some particular assets or liabilities are more or less liquid than others within the same class. Liabilities whose average maturities are greater than one year should be reported in two components—the amount due within one year and the amount due in more than one year.

Net position is comprised of three components:

- Invested in capital assets, net of related debt.
- Restricted net position (distinguishing among major categories of restrictions).
- Unrestricted net position.

The net position components listed require some additional explanation and analysis.

Invested in capital assets, net of related debt. This amount represents capital assets (including any restricted capital assets), net of accumulated depreciation, and reduced by the outstanding bonds, mortgages, notes, or other borrowings that are attributable to the acquisition, construction, or improvement of those assets. If there are significant unspent debt proceeds that are restricted for use for capital projects, the portion of the debt attributable to the unspent proceeds should not be included in the calculation of net position invested in capital assets, net of related debt. Instead, that portion of the debt would be included in the same net asset component as the unspent proceeds, which would likely be net position restricted for capital purposes. This net asset category would then have both the asset (proceeds) and the liability (the portion of the debt) recorded in the same net asset component. Note that if the amount of debt issued for capital purposes exceeds the amount of the net book value of capital assets, this number will be reported as a negative amount. For example, if a Phase 3 government that elected not to retroactively record infrastructure assets used debt to finance its infrastructure costs, it will have the debt issued for these assets recorded, but will have no corresponding asset recorded.

NOTE: Ongoing experience with determining the invested in capital assets net of related debt amount confirms that its computation can be difficult. For governments that have active capital programs that are financed with debt, the calculation of this amount can be very problematic. Often capital assets can be specifically identified with the debt that paid for them at the time that they are purchased or constructed. Over time, however, this linkage becomes difficult to maintain. The capital assets, in most cases, are being depreciated over various useful lives and, perhaps, using various depreciation methods. At the same time, the related debt is impacted by normal principal repayments and may also be impacted by call features, premium or discount amortization, and refundings. Matching the book value of capital assets with the remaining outstanding balance of the debt that paid for them can result in a painstaking process to develop the financial statement amount. Amounts related to outstanding debt, particularly bond issuance costs, may also be impacted by the implementation of GASBS 65, Items Previously Reported as Assets and Liabilities.

Restricted net position. This amount represents those net positions that should be reported as restricted because constraints are placed on the net asset use that are either:

- Externally imposed by creditors (such as those imposed through debt covenants), grantors, contributors, or laws or regulations of other governments, or
- Imposed by law through constitutional provisions or enabling legislation.

Basically, restrictions are not unilaterally established by the reporting government itself and cannot be removed without the consent of those imposing the restrictions or through formal due process. Restrictions can be broad or narrow, provided that the purpose is narrower than that of the reporting unit in which it is reported. In addition, the GASB Implementation Guide clarifies that legislation that "earmarks" that a portion of a tax be used for a specific purpose does not constitute "enabling legislation" that would result in those assets being reported as restricted. In addition, the GASB Implementation Guide provides the example of a general state statute pertaining to local governments that provides that revenues derived from a fee or charge not be used for any purpose other than that for which the fee or charge was imposed. In this case, the general statute applies to all jurisdictions in the state and creates a legally enforceable restriction on the use of the resources raised through fees and charges.

The GASB Implementation Guide also addresses two other common issues in determining restricted net position. First, when assets in a restricted fund exceed the amounts required to be restricted by the external parties or the enabling legislation, the excess over the required amounts would be classified as unrestricted for financial reporting purposes. The second question addresses which component of net position should be used to report unamortized debt issuance costs and deferred amounts from refundings. Basically, these amounts should "follow the debt." For example, if the debt is capital-related, the net proceeds of the debt would be used in the calculation of invested in capital assets, net of related debt.

The GASB issued Statement No. 46 (GASBS 46), *Net Assets Restricted and Enabling Legislation—An Amendment of GASB Statement 34*, addressing a specific issue as to classification of net assets (now net position) into one of its three categories.

GASBS 46 addresses only the issue of net positions that are restricted by enabling legislation. The basic issue is how to interpret whether enabling legislation of a government imposes a restriction on net position. In some jurisdictions, for example, a legislature cannot bind a future legislature. If the current legislature passes a law imposing a new tax that is restricted to a particular use, are net positions arising from that tax restricted or not? In this example, the subsequent legislature not only cannot be bound, but arguably, the current legislature has the ability to pass new legislation to remove the restriction.

GASBS 46 does not allow governments to make a blanket assessment that enabling legislation does not impose a restriction on net position. GASBS 34 requires that net position be reported as restricted when constraints are placed on the assets externally (creditors, grantors, etc.) or imposed by law through constitutional provisions or enabling legislation. Enabling legislation is that which authorizes the government to assess, levy, charge, or otherwise mandate payment of resources and includes a legally enforceable requirement that those resources be used only for the specific purpose stipulated in the legislation.

GASBS 46 provides a definition of *legally enforceable* to mean that a government can be compelled by an external party, such as citizens, public interest groups, or the judiciary, to use resources created by the enabling legislation only for the purposes specified in the legislation. It provides that generally the enforceability of an enabling legislation restriction is determined by professional judgment, which may be based on actions such as analyzing the legislation to determine if it meets the qualifying criteria for enabling legislation, reviewing determinations made for similar legislation of the government or other governments, or obtaining the opinion of legal counsel. Enforceability cannot ultimately be proven unless tested through the judicial process, which may never occur. In addition, the determination that a particular restriction is not legally enforceable may lead a government to reevaluate the legal enforceability of similar enabling legislation restrictions, but should not necessarily lead a government to conclude that all enabling legislation restrictions are unenforceable.

GASBS 46 provides that if a government passes new enabling legislation that replaces the original enabling legislation by establishing new legally enforceable restrictions on the resources raised by the original enabling legislation, then from that period forward, the resources accumulated under the new enabling legislation should be reported as restricted to the purpose specified by the new enabling legislation. Professional judgment should be used to determine if remaining balances accumulated under the original enabling legislation should continue to be reported as restricted for the original purpose, restricted to the purpose specified in the new legislation, or unrestricted.

GASBS 46 further provides that if resources are used for a purpose other than those stipulated in the enabling legislation or if there is other cause for reconsideration, governments should reevaluate the legal enforceability of the restrictions to determine if the resources should continue to be reported as restricted. If reevaluation results in a determination that a particular restriction is no longer legally enforceable, then from the beginning of that period forward the resources should be reported as unrestricted. If it is determined that the restrictions continue to be legally enforceable, then for financial reporting purposes the restricted net position should not reflect any reduction for resources used for purposes not stipulated in the enabling legislation.

GASBS 46 requires that a net position at the end of the reporting period that is restricted by enabling legislation be disclosed in the notes to the financial statements.

When permanent endowments or permanent fund principal amounts are included in restricted net position, restricted net position should be displayed in two additional components—expendable and nonexpendable. Nonexpendable net positions are those that are required to be retained in perpetuity.

Unrestricted net position. This amount consists of net positions that do not meet the definition of restricted net position or net position invested in capital assets, net of related debt.

NOTE: As discussed later in the chapter, governmental funds also report restricted assets on their statement of financial position. GASBS 54, Fund Balance Reporting and Governmental Fund Definitions, adopted the same basic definition of restricted net asset used in government-wide and proprietary fund reporting to governmental fund reporting. This results in consistency between the government-wide financial statements and the governmental fund financial statements. GASBS 54 is more fully described later in this chapter.

Exhibit 1 presents a sample classified statement of net position, based on the examples provided in GASBS 34.

Exhibit 1: Sample classified statement of net position

City of Anywhere
Statement of Net Position
June 30, 20XX

		Primary Government		
	Governmental Activities	***Business-Type Activities***	***Total***	***Component Units***
Assets				
Current assets:				
Cash and cash equivalents	$ xx,xxx	$ xx,xxx	$ xx,xxx	$ xx,xxx
Investments	xx,xxx	xx,xxx	xx,xxx	xx,xxx
Receivables (net)	xx,xxx	xx,xxx	xx,xxx	xx,xxx
Internal balances	xx,xxx	(xx,xxx)	–	–
Inventories	xx,xxx	xx,xxx	xx,xxx	xx,xxx
Total current assets	xxx,xxx	xxx,xxx	xxx,xxx	xxx,xxx
Noncurrent assets:				
Restricted cash and cash equivalents	xx,xxx	xx,xxx	xx,xxx	–
Capital assets				
Land and infrastructure	xx,xxx	xx,xxx	xx,xxx	xx,xxx
Depreciable buildings, property, and equipment, net	xx,xxx	xx,xxx	xx,xxx	xx,xxx
Total noncurrent assets	xxx,xxx	xxx,xxx	xxx,xxx	xxx,xxx
Total assets	$xxx,xxx	$xxx,xxx	$xxx,xxx	$xxx,xxx
Liabilities				
Current liabilities:				
Accounts payable	$ xx,xxx	$ xx,xxx	$ xx,xxx	$ xx,xxx
Deferred revenue	xx,xxx	xx,xxx	xx,xxx	xx,xxx
Current portion of long-term obligations	xx,xxx	xx,xxx	xx,xxx	xx,xxx
Total current liabilities	xxx,xxx	xxx,xxx	xxx,xxx	xxx,xxx
Noncurrent liabilities:				
Noncurrent portion of long-term obligations	xx,xxx	xx,xxx	xx,xxx	xx,xxx
Total liabilities	xxx,xxx	xxx,xxx	xxx,xxx	xxx,xxx

Net Position				
Invested in capital assets, net of related debt	xx,xxx	xx,xxx	xx,xxx	xx,xxx
Restricted for:				
Capital projects	xx,xxx	–	xx,xxx	xx,xxx
Debt service	xx,xxx	xx,xxx	xx,xxx	–
Community development projects	xx,xxx	–	xx,xxx	–
Other purposes	xx,xxx	–	xx,xxx	–
Unrestricted	xx,xxx	xx,xxx	xx,xxx	xx,xxx
Total net position	xxx,xxx	xxx,xxx	xxx,xxx	xxx,xxx
Total liabilities and net position	$xxx,xxx	$xxx,xxx	$xxx,xxx	$xxx,xxx

Statement of Activities

GASBS 34 adopts the net (expense) revenue format, which is easier to view than describe. See Exhibit 2 for an example of a statement of activities based on the examples provided in GASBS 34.

The objective of this format is to report the relative financial burden of each of the reporting government's functions on its taxpayers. The format identifies the extent to which each function of the government draws from the general revenues of the government or is self-financing through fees or intergovernmental aid.

The statement of activities presents governmental activities by function (similar to the current requirements) and business-type activities at least by segment. Segments are identifiable activities reported as or within an enterprise fund or another stand-alone entity for which one or more revenue bonds or other revenue-backed debt instrument are outstanding.

Expense Presentation

The statement of activities should present expenses of governmental activities by function in at least the level of detail required in the governmental fund statement of revenues, expenditures, and changes in fund balances. Categorization and level of detail are basically the same for governmental activities by function in pre–GASBS 34 financial statements. Expenses for business-type activities are reported in at least the level of detail as by segment, which is defined as "an identifiable activity reported as or within an enterprise fund or another stand-alone entity for which one or more revenue bonds or other revenue-backed debt instruments are outstanding. A segment has a specific identifiable revenue stream pledged in support of revenue bonds or other revenue-backed debt, and business-related expenses, gains and losses, assets, and liabilities that can be identified."

Governments should report all expenses by function except for those expenses that meet the definitions of special items or extraordinary items, discussed later in this chapter. Governments are required, at a minimum, to report the direct expenses for each function. Direct expenses are those that are specifically associated with a service, program, or department, and, accordingly, can be clearly identified with a particular function.

There are numerous government functions—such as the general government, support services, and administration—that are actually indirect expenses of the other functions. For example, the police department of a city reports to the mayor. The direct expenses of the police

Exhibit 2: Sample statement of activities

City of Anywhere Statement of Activities for the Fiscal Year Ended June 30, 20XX

		Program Revenues			*Net (Expense) Revenue and Changes in Net Position Primary Government*			
Functions/Programs	***Expenses***	***Charges for Services***	***Operating Grants and Contributions***	***Capital Grants and Contributions***	***Governmental Activities***	***Business-Type Activities***	***Total***	***Component Units***
Primary government:								
Governmental activities:								
General government	$ xx,xxx	$ xx,xxx	$ xx,xxx	$–	$ (xx,xxx)	$–	$(xx,xxx)	$–
Public safety	xx,xxx	xx,xxx	xx,xxx	xx,xxx	(xx,xxx)	–	(xx,xxx)	–
Public works	xx,xxx	xx,xxx	–	xx,xxx	(xx,xxx)	–	(xx,xxx)	–
Health and sanitation	xx,xxx	xx,xxx	xx,xxx	–	(xx,xxx)	–	(xx,xxx)	–
Community development	xx,xxx	–		xx,xxx	(xx,xxx)	–	(xx,xxx)	–
Education	xx,xxx	–		–	(xx,xxx)	–	(xx,xxx)	–
Interest on long-term debt	xx,xxx	–		–	(xx,xxx)	–	(xx,xxx)	–
Total governmental activities	xxx,xxx	xxx,xxx	xxx,xxx	xxx,xxx	(xxx,xxx)	~	(xxx,xxx)	~
Business-type activities:								
Water and sewer	xx,xxx	xx,xxx	–	xx,xxx	–	xx,xxx	xx,xxx	–
Parking facilities	xx,xxx	xx,xxx		–		(xx,xxx)	(xx,xxx)	–
Total business-type activities	xxx,xxx	xxx,xxx	–	xxx,xxx	–	xxx,xxx	xxx,xxx	–
Total primary government	$xxx,xxx	$xxx,xxx	$xxx,xxx	$ xxx,xxx	xxx,xxx	xxx,xxx	(xxx,xxx)	–
Component units:								
Landfill	$ xx,xxx	$ xx,xxx	–	$ xx,xxx	–	–	–	$ xx,xxx
Public school system	xx,xxx	xx,xxx	$ xx,xxx	–	–	–	–	(xx,xxx)
Total component units	$ xxx,xxx	$ xxx,xxx	$xxx,xxx	$ xx,xxx		–	–	$(xx,xxx)
	General revenues:							
	Taxes:							

(Continued)

		Program Revenues			Net (Expense) Revenue and Changes in Net Position Primary Government			
		City of Anywhere Statement of Activities for the Fiscal Year Ended June 30, 20XX						
Functions/Programs	***Expenses***	***Charges for Services***	***Operating Grants and Contributions***	***Capital Grants and Contributions***	***Governmental Activities***	***Business-Type Activities***	***Total***	***Component Units***
	Property taxes		xx,xxx	–	xx,xxx	–		
	Franchise taxes	xx,xxx	–	xx,xxx	–			
	Payment from city of Anywhere					xx,xxx		
	Grants and contributions not restricted to specific programs		xx,xxx		xx,xxx	xx,xxx		
	Investment earnings		xx,xxx	xx,xxx	xx,xxx	xx,xxx		
	Miscellaneous		xx,xxx	xx,xxx	xx,xxx	xx,xxx		
	Special item— Gain on sale of baseball stadium		xx,xxx		xx,xxx			
	Transfers		xx,xxx	(xx,xxx)	–			
	Total general revenues, special items, and transfers		xxx,xxx	xxx,xxx	xxx,xxx	xxx,xxx		
	Change in net position		(xxx,xxx)	xxx,xxx	xxx,xxx	xxx,xxx		
	Net position—beginning		xxx,xxx	xxx,xxx	xxx,xxx	xxx,xxx		
	Net position—ending		$xxx,xxx	$xxx,xxx	$xxx,xxx	$xxx,xxx		

department would likely be reported under the function "public safety" in the statement of activities. However, the mayor's office (along with payroll, personnel, and other departments) supports the activities of the police department although they are not direct expenses of the police department. Governments are permitted, but not required, to allocate these indirect expenses to other functions. Governments may allocate some but not all indirect expenses, or they may use a full-cost allocation approach and allocate all indirect expenses to other functions. If indirect expenses are allocated, they must be displayed in a column separate from the direct expenses of the functions to which they are allocated. Governments that allocate central expenses to funds or programs, such as through the use of internal service funds, are not required to eliminate these administrative charges when preparing the statement of activities, but should disclose in the summary of significant accounting policies that these charges are included in direct expenses.

The reporting of depreciation expense in the statement of activities requires some careful analysis. Depreciation expense for the following types of capital assets is required to be included in the direct expenses of functions or programs:

- Capital assets that can be specifically identified with a function or program.
- Capital assets that are shared by more than one function or program, such as a building in which several functions or programs share office space.

Some capital assets of a government may essentially serve all of the functions of a government, such as a city hall or county administrative office building. There are several options for presenting depreciation expense on these capital assets. These options are:

- Include the depreciation expense in an indirect expense allocation to the various functions or programs.
- Report the depreciation expense as a separate line item in the statement of activities (labeled in such a way as to make clear to the reader of the financial statements that not all of the government's depreciation expense is included on this line).
- Report the depreciation expense as part of the general government (or its equivalent) function.

Depreciation expense for infrastructure assets associated with governmental activities should be reported in one of the following ways:

- Report the depreciation expenses as a direct expense of the function that is normally used for capital outlays for and maintenance of infrastructure assets.
- Report the depreciation expense as a separate line item in the statement of activities (labeled in such a way as to make clear to the reader of the financial statements that not all of the government's depreciation expense is included on this line).

Interest expense on general long-term liabilities should be reported as an indirect expense. In the vast majority of circumstances, interest expense will be displayed as a separate line item on the statement of activities. In certain limited circumstances where the borrowing is essential to the creation or continuing existence of a program or function and it would be misleading to exclude interest from that program or function's direct expenses, GASBS 34 would permit that interest expense to be reported as a direct expense. The GASBS 34 Implementation Guide also prescribes that interest on capital leases or interest expense from vendor financing arrangements should not be reported as direct expenses of specific programs.

Revenue Presentation

Revenues on the statement of activities are distinguished between program revenues and general revenues.

- **Program revenues** are those derived directly from the program itself or from parties outside the government's taxpayers or citizens, as a whole. Program revenues reduce the net cost of the program that is to be financed from the government's general revenues. On the statement of activities, these revenues are deducted from the expenses of the functions and programs discussed in the previous section. The GASB Implementation Guide provides that separate columns may be presented under a particular revenue category heading. For example, if fines are a significant part of charges for services (defined below), a government may elect (but is not required) to have a separate column under the charges for services heading that breaks out fines as a separate column. There are three categories into which program revenues should be distinguished.
  - **Charges for services.** These are revenues based on exchange or exchange-like transactions. This type of program revenues arises from charges to customers or applicants who purchase, use, or directly benefit from the goods, services, or privileges provided. Examples include water use charges, garbage collection fees, licenses and permits such as dog licenses or building permits, and operating assessments, such as for street cleaning or street lighting.
  - **Program-specific operating grants and contributions.** (See the following discussion on program-specific capital grants and contributions.)
  - **Program-specific capital grants and contributions.** Both program-specific operating and capital grants and contributions include revenues arising from mandatory and voluntary nonexchange transactions with other governments, organizations, or individuals, that are restricted for use in a particular program. Some grants and contributions consist of capital assets or resources that are restricted for capital purposes, such as purchasing, constructing, or renovating capital assets associated with a particular program. These revenues should be reported separately from grants and contributions that may be used for either operating expenses or capital expenditures from a program, at the discretion of the government receiving the grant or contribution. The GASB Implementation Guide addresses the question of the accounting for revenues that meet the definition of program revenues, but the grants specify amounts for specific programs that are spread in the statement of activities over several functions. If a grant meets the definition of program revenue, it should be recorded as such. If the grant is detailed by program and the statement of activities is detailed by function, a reasonable allocation method should be used to assign the program revenues to the appropriate functions. This issue, however, is different from when a government has the discretion to use a particular grant for more than one program or function. In this case, the grant would be considered a general revenue instead of a program revenue because of the discretion that the government can exert in how the grant amounts are used.
- **General revenues** are all those revenues that are not required to be reported as program revenues. All taxes, regardless of whether they are levied for a specific purpose, should be reported as general revenues. Taxes should be reported by type of tax, such as real estate taxes, sales tax, income tax, franchise tax, and so on. (Although operating special assessments are derived from property owners, they are not considered taxes and are properly reported as program revenues.) General revenues are reported after total net expense of the government's functions on the statement of activities.

Extraordinary and special items. GASBS 34 provides that a government's statement of activities may have extraordinary and special items. Extraordinary items are those that are unusual in nature and infrequent in occurrence. This tracks the private sector accounting definition of this term.

Special items are a concept introduced by GASBS 34. They are defined as "significant transactions or other events within the control of management that are either unusual in nature or infrequent in occurrence." Special items are reported separately in the statement of activities before any extraordinary items.

The GASBS 34 Implementation Guide cites the following events or transactions that may qualify as extraordinary or special items:

Extraordinary items:

- Costs related to an environmental disaster caused by a large chemical spill from a train derailment in a small city.
- Significant damage to the community or destruction of government facilities by a natural disaster or terrorist act. However, geographic location of the government may determine if a weather-related natural disaster is infrequent.
- A large bequest to a small government by a private citizen.

Special items:

- Sales of certain general government capital assets.
- Special termination benefits resulting from workforce reductions due to sale of the government's utility operations.
- Early-retirement program offered to all employees.
- Significant forgiveness of debt.

Eliminations and reclassifications. GASBS 34 requires that eliminations of transactions within the governmental business-type activities be made so that these amounts are not "grossed up" on the statement of net position and statement of activities. Where internal service funds are used, their activities are eliminated where their transactions would cause a double recording of revenues and expenses.

Fund Financial Statements

There are many similarities between the way in which fund financial statements under the new financial reporting model are prepared and the way in which they were previously prepared. One of the most notable similarities is that governmental funds continue to use the modified accrual basis of accounting and the current financial resources measurement focus in the fund financial statements. However, there are also many important differences in the way these statements are prepared. The following discussion highlights these differences.

Fund financial statements are prepared only for the primary government. They are designed to provide focus on the major funds within each fund type. Fund financial statements include financial statements for fiduciary funds, but they do not include financial statements for discretely presented component units. The following are the types of funds included in fund-type financial statements:

- Governmental funds:
  - General fund.
  - Special revenue funds.
  - Capital projects funds.

    - Debt service funds.
    - Permanent funds.
- Proprietary funds:
    - Enterprise funds.
    - Internal service funds.
- Fiduciary funds and similar component units:
    - Pension (and other employee benefit) trust funds.
    - Investment trust funds.
    - Private-purpose trust funds.
    - Agency funds.

The following are the required financial statements for the various fund types. A reference to each exhibit that provides a sample of each of these statements is also provided.

Governmental funds:

- Balance sheet (Exhibit 3).
- Statement of revenues, expenditures, and changes in fund balances (Exhibit 4).

Proprietary funds:

- Statement of net position or balance sheet (Exhibit 5).
- Statement of revenues, expenses, and changes in fund net position or fund equity (Exhibit 6).
- Statement of cash flows (Exhibit 7).

Fiduciary funds:

- Statement of fiduciary net position (Exhibit 8).
- Statement of changes in fiduciary assets (Exhibit 9).

In preparing these fund financial statements, the following significant guidance of GASBS 34 should be considered:

- A reconciliation of the governmental fund activities in the government-wide financial statements with the governmental fund financial statements should be prepared. A summary reconciliation to the government-wide financial statements should be presented at the bottom of the fund financial statements or in an accompanying schedule. If the aggregation of reconciling information obscures the nature of the individual elements of a particular reconciling item, a more detailed explanation should be provided in the notes to the financial statements. Exhibits 10 and 11 provide examples of these reconciliations presented as a separate schedule.
- General capital assets and general long-term debt are not reported in the fund financial statements. (Note that capital assets and long-term debt are reported in proprietary funds, however.)
- GASBS 34 requires activities to be reported as enterprise funds if any one of the following criteria is met:
    - The activity is financed with debt that is secured solely by a pledge of the net revenues from fees and charges of the activity.
    - Laws or regulations require that the activity's costs of providing services, including capital costs, be recovered with fees and charges, rather than with taxes or similar revenues.
- The pricing policies of the activity establish fees and charges designed to recover its costs, including capital costs.

Exhibit 3: Governmental funds balance sheet

City of Anywhere
Governmental Funds
Balance Sheet June 30, 20XX

	General	*Capital Projects*	*Debt Service*	*Nonmajor Governmental Funds*	*Total Governmental Funds*
Assets					
Cash and cash equivalents	$xx,xxx	$xx,xxx	$xx,xxx	$xx,xxx	$xx,xxx
Investments	xx,xxx	–	xx,xxx	xx,xxx	xx,xxx
Receivables					
Real estate taxes	xx,xxx		–		xx,xxx
Federal, state, and other aid	xx,xxx	xx,xxx	–		xx,xxx
Taxes other than real estate	xx,xxx	–	–	xx,xxx	xx,xxx
Other	xx,xxx		–		xx,xxx
Due from other funds	xx,xxx	xx,xxx	xx,xxx	xx,xxx	xx,xxx
Due from component units	xx,xxx	xx,xxx	–	xx,xxx	xx,xxx
Restricted cash and investments	–	xx,xxx	–	xx,xxx	xx,xxx
Total assets	$xx,xxx	$xx,xxx	$xx,xxx	$xx,xxx	$xx,xxx
Liabilities and Fund Balances					
Liabilities:					
Accounts payable and accrued liabilities	$xx,xxx	$xx,xxx	$xx,xxx	$xx,xxx	$xx,xxx
Bond anticipation notes payable	–	–	–	xx,xxx	xx,xxx
Accrued tax refunds:					
Real estate taxes	xx,xxx		–		xx,xxx
Other	xx,xxx		–		xx,xxx
Accrued judgments and claims	xx,xxx	xx,xxx	–		xx,xxx
Deferred revenues:					
Prepaid real estate taxes	xx,xxx		–		xx,xxx
Uncollected real estate taxes	xx,xxx		–		xx,xxx
Taxes other than real estate	xx,xxx	–	–	xx,xxx	xx,xxx
Other	xx,xxx	xx,xxx	–	xx,xxx	xx,xxx
Due to other funds	xx,xxx	xx,xxx	xx,xxx	xx,xxx	xx,xxx
Due to component units	xx,xxx		–		xx,xxx
Total liabilities	xx,xxx	xx,xxx	xx,xxx	xx,xxx	xx,xxx

Fund Balances					
Reserved for:					
Debt service	–	–	xx,xxx	xx,xxx	xx,xxx
Noncurrent mortgage loans	–	–	–	xx,xxx	xx,xxx
Unreserved reported in:					
General fund	xx,xxx		–		xx,xxx
Capital Projects Fund	–	xx,xxx	–		xx,xxx
Nonmajor funds	–	–	–	xx,xxx	xx,xxx
Total fund balances (deficit)	xx,xxx	xx,xxx	xx,xxx	xx,xxx	xx,xxx
Total liabilities and fund balances	$xx,xxx	$xx,xxx	$xx,xxx	$xx,xxx	$xx,xxx

The reconciliation of the fund balances of governmental funds to the net position of governmental activities in the statement of net position is presented in an accompanying schedule.

Governmental Fund Balance Reporting

GASBS 54, *Fund Balance Reporting and Governmental Fund Definitions*, provides guidance as to how governmental funds report their fund balances. Total fund balance is still the residual between a fund's assets and liabilities and its deferred inflows and outflows of resources. Under GASBS 54, fund balance is classified into these categories, as applicable:

- Nonspendable fund balance.
- Restricted fund balance.
- Committed fund balance.
- Assigned fund balance.
- Unassigned fund balance.

As might be gleaned from this list, the classification hierarchy is based on the extent to which the government is bound to honor constraints on the specific purposes for which amounts in those funds can be spent.

The following pages describe the definition of these classifications as promulgated by GASBS 54, certain specific accounting treatments relating to stabilization agreements, and disclosure requirements.

Nonspendable Fund Balance

GASBS 54 provides that the nonspendable fund balance classification includes amounts that cannot be spent because they are either:

1. Not in spendable form; or
2. Legally or contractually required to be maintained intact.

The "not in spendable form" criterion includes items that are not expected to be converted to cash—for example, inventories and prepaid amounts. (In existing GAAP, these amounts were usually reported as "reserved.")

This category also includes the long-term amount of loans and notes receivable, as well as property acquired for resale. However, if the use of the proceeds from the collection of those receivables or from the sale of those properties is restricted, committed, or assigned, then they should be included in the appropriate fund balance classification (restricted, committed, or assigned), rather than nonspendable fund balance.

The corpus (or principal) of a permanent fund is an example of an amount that is legally or contractually required to be maintained intact. Permanent funds are used to account for and report resources that are restricted to the extent that only earnings, and not principal, may be used for purposes that support the government's programs (i.e., for the benefit of the government and its citizenry). For readers familiar with not-for-profit accounting, the equivalent concept in that financial reporting model is referred to as permanently restricted net assets or, the more common terminology, an endowment fund.

NOTE: One slight difference in reporting restricted net position on the government-wide financial statements and restricted fund balance under GASBS 54 relates to nonspendable resources. In the government-wide statements, resources that are required to be retained in perpetuity are reported as a subcategory of restricted net position. In the fund financial statements under GASBS 54, such nonspendable resources are reported in their own classification—nonspendable resources.

Restricted Fund Balance

Amounts that are restricted to specific purposes, pursuant to the definition of *restricted* in GASBS 34 and 46 (as described previously in this chapter), should be reported as restricted fund balance, with the slight exception of the matter described in the preceding Note. Accordingly, under GASBS 54, fund balance should be reported as restricted when constraints placed on the use of resources are either:

1. Externally imposed by creditors (such as through debt covenants), grantors, contributors, or laws or regulations of other governments; or
2. Imposed by law through constitutional provisions or enabling legislation.

Enabling legislation, as the term is used in GASBS 54, authorizes the government to assess, levy, charge, or otherwise mandate payment of resources (from external resource providers) and includes a legally enforceable requirement that those resources be used only for the specific purposes stipulated in the legislation. Legal enforceability means that a government can be compelled by an external party—such as citizens, public interest groups, or the judiciary—to use resources created by enabling legislation only for the purposes specified by the legislation.

Committed Fund Balance

The concepts of nonspendable and restricted described above are readily understandable and have precedents in existing GAAP. Accordingly, their implementation should not result in significant implementation difficulties. However, the concepts of committed and assigned fund balances (discussed in this and the following section) are new, so implementation of GASBS 54 for these classifications may be a bit more challenging.

GASBS 54 provides that amounts that can only be used for specific purposes pursuant to constraints imposed by formal action of the government's highest level of decision-making authority should be reported as committed fund balance. Those committed amounts cannot be used for any other purpose unless the government removes or changes the specified use by taking the same type of action (for example, legislation, resolution, ordinance) it employed to previously commit those amounts. The authorization specifying the purposes for which amounts can be used should have the consent of both the legislative and the executive branches of the government, if applicable. Committed fund balance also should incorporate contractual obligations to the extent that existing resources in the fund have been specifically committed for use in satisfying those contractual requirements.

NOTE: The language used in GASBS 54 for committed fund balance may seem vague, as it does not specify what specific formal action of the decision-making body would result in committed resources (i.e., resolution, ordinance, etc.). As a practical matter, governments operate very differently from each other, and different powers may be indicated by different types of actions. Committed fund balance represents resources that are subject to a self-imposed constraint at a level high enough to represent the consensus objective of the governing body as a whole, meaning they come from the highest level of decision-making authority.

In contrast to fund balance that is restricted by enabling legislation, as discussed above, GASBS 54 states that amounts in the committed fund balance classification may be redeployed for other purposes with appropriate due process. Constraints imposed on the use of committed amounts are imposed by the government, separately from the authorization to raise the underlying revenue. Therefore, compliance with constraints imposed by the government that commit amounts to specific purposes is not considered to be legally enforceable.

GASBS 54 also provides that the formal action of the government's highest level of decision-making authority that commits fund balance to a specific purpose should occur prior to the end of the reporting period, but the amount, if any, that will be subject to the constraint may be determined in the subsequent period.

Assigned Fund Balance

GASBS 54 provides that amounts that are constrained by the government's intent to be used for specific purposes, but are neither restricted nor committed, should be reported as assigned fund balance, except for stabilization arrangements, as discussed below. GASBS 54 states that intent should be expressed by (1) the governing body itself or (2) a body (a budget or finance committee, for example) or official to which the governing body has delegated the authority to assign amounts to be used for specific purposes.

In other words, assigned fund balance represents resources where the constraint is less binding than that for committed resources, but not so available to the government that they would be considered unassigned.

Both the committed and assigned fund balance classifications include amounts that have been constrained to being used for specific purposes by actions taken by the government itself. However, the authority for making an assignment is not required to be the government's highest level of decision-making authority. Furthermore, the actions necessary to remove or modify an assignment are not as difficult to accomplish as they are for the committed fund balance classification. GASBS 54 notes that some governments may not have both committed and assigned fund balances, as not all governments have multiple levels of decision-making authority.

Applying the logic of the four classifications described above, GASBS notes that assigned fund balance includes:

1. All remaining amounts (except for negative balances) that are reported in governmental funds, other than the general fund, that are not classified as nonspendable and are neither restricted nor committed.

2. Amounts in the general fund that are intended to be used for a specific purpose in accordance with the definition of assigned fund balance discussed above.

Why is item 1 always true? By reporting particular amounts that are not restricted or committed in a special revenue, capital projects, debt service, or permanent fund, the government has effectively assigned those amounts to the purposes of the respective funds. By reporting resources in a governmental fund other than the general fund, the government is at least assigning those resources to the purposes for which those funds exist.

GASBS 54 does provide, however, that governments should not report an assignment for an amount to a specific purpose if the assignment would result in a deficit in unassigned fund balance. It also notes that an appropriation of existing fund balance to eliminate a projected budgetary deficit in the subsequent year's budget in an amount no greater than the projected excess of expected expenditures over expected revenues satisfies the criteria to be classified as an assignment of fund balance. However, again, assignments should not cause a deficit in unassigned fund balance to occur.

Unassigned Fund Balance

Unassigned fund balance is the residual classification for the general fund. This classification represents fund balance that has not been assigned to other funds and that has not been restricted, committed, or assigned to specific purposes within the general fund. The general fund should be the only fund that reports a positive unassigned fund balance amount.

GASBS 54 provides, however, that in other governmental funds, if expenditures incurred for specific purposes exceeded the amounts restricted, committed, or assigned to those purposes, it may be necessary to report a negative unassigned fund balance, as discussed below.

Fund Balance Classifications

Sometimes, a government has expenditures for purposes for which both restricted and unrestricted (including committed, assigned, and unassigned) resources exist. Which resources should the government consider to have been expended first? The government may adopt an accounting policy that states which resources it considers to have been spent in this case. In addition, the government may adopt an accounting policy that states which unrestricted classification of resources is considered to have been spent in a similar case where more than one classification of unrestricted resources is available. GASBS 54 permits the adoption and consistent application of these policies. If a government does not establish a policy for its use of unrestricted fund balance amounts, it should consider that committed amounts would be reduced first, followed by assigned amounts, and then unassigned amounts when expenditures are incurred for purposes for which amounts in any of those unrestricted fund balance classifications could be used.

GASBS 54 notes that, in a governmental fund other than the general fund, expenditures incurred for a specific purpose might exceed the amounts in the fund that are restricted, committed, and assigned to that purpose, and a negative residual balance for that purpose may result. If that occurs, amounts assigned to other purposes in that fund should be reduced to eliminate the deficit. If the remaining deficit eliminates all other assigned amounts in the fund, or if there are no amounts assigned to other purposes, the negative residual amount should be classified as unassigned fund balance. In the general fund, a similar negative residual amount would have been eliminated by reducing unassigned fund balance pursuant to the policy described above. A negative residual amount should not be reported for restricted, committed, or assigned fund balances in any fund.

Stabilization Agreements

GASBS 54 has special requirements pertaining to stabilization agreements. These types of agreements sometimes are referred to as "rainy day funds," as they are meant to set aside resources in favorable times to provide resources in times that are less favorable.

GASBS 54's requirements relate to those agreements which are formal arrangements for amounts that are subject to controls that dictate the circumstances under which they can be spent. Many governments have formal arrangements to maintain amounts for budget or revenue stabilization, working capital needs, contingencies or emergencies, and other similarly titled purposes. The authority to set aside those amounts generally comes from statute, ordinance, resolution, charter, or constitution. Stabilization amounts may be expended only when certain specific circumstances exist. The formal action that imposes the parameters for spending should identify and describe the specific circumstances under which a need for stabilization arises. Those circumstances should be such that they would not be expected to occur routinely.

GASBS 54 provides the example of a stabilization amount that can be accessed "in an emergency" as not qualifying to be classified within the committed category because the circumstances or conditions that constitute an emergency are not sufficiently detailed, and it is not unlikely that an emergency of some nature would routinely occur. In addition, GASBS 54 provides that a stabilization amount that can be accessed to offset an "anticipated revenue shortfall" would not qualify unless the shortfall was quantified and was of a magnitude that would distinguish it from other revenue shortfalls that occur during the normal course of governmental operations.

For the purposes of reporting fund balance, GASBS 54 considers stabilization a *specific purpose*, as discussed above. Stabilization amounts should be reported in the general fund as restricted or committed if they meet the criteria for those classifications, based on the source of the constraint on their use. Stabilization arrangements that do not meet the criteria to be reported within the restricted or committed fund balance classifications should be reported as unassigned in the general fund. Further, a stabilization arrangement would satisfy the criteria to be reported as a separate special revenue fund only if the resources derive from a specific restricted or committed *revenue* source.

Fund Balance Display on the Balance Sheet

GASBS 54 provides that amounts for the two components of nonspendable fund balance—(1) not in spendable form and (2) legally or contractually required to be maintained intact—may be presented separately, or nonspendable fund balance may be presented in the aggregate. Restricted fund balance may be displayed in a manner that distinguishes between the major restricted purposes, or it may be displayed in the aggregate. Similarly, specific purposes information for committed and assigned fund balances may be displayed in sufficient detail so that the major commitments and assignments are evident to the financial statement user, or each classification may be displayed in the aggregate. Where aggregate disclosures are displayed, note disclosure of details will be required, as described in the next section.

Disclosures

1. GASBS 54 requires governments to disclose the following about their fund balance classification policies and procedures in the notes to the financial statements: For *committed* fund balance: (1) the government's highest level of decision-making authority and (2) the

formal action that is required to be taken to establish (and modify or rescind) a fund balance commitment.

2. For *assigned* fund balance: (1) the body or official authorized to assign amounts to a specific purpose and (2) the policy established by the governing body pursuant to which that authorization is given.
3. For the classification of fund balances:
   (a) Whether the government considers restricted or unrestricted amounts to have been spent when an expenditure is incurred for purposes for which both restricted and unrestricted fund balance is available; and
   (b) Whether committed, assigned, or unassigned amounts are considered to have been spent when an expenditure is incurred for purposes for which amounts in any of those unrestricted fund balance classifications could be used.

The following additional disclosures are also required, where applicable:

1. For governments that use encumbrance accounting, significant encumbrances should be disclosed in the notes to the financial statements by major funds and nonmajor funds in the aggregate in conjunction with required disclosures about other significant commitments. Encumbered amounts for specific purposes for which resources already have been restricted, committed, or assigned should not result in separate display of the encumbered amounts within those classifications. Encumbered amounts for specific purposes for which amounts have not been previously restricted, committed, or assigned should not be classified as unassigned, but rather should be included within committed or assigned fund balance, as appropriate, based on the definitions and criteria described above.
2. If nonspendable fund balance is displayed in the aggregate on the face of the balance sheet, amounts for the two nonspendable components should be disclosed in the notes to the financial statements. If restricted, committed, or assigned fund balances are displayed in the aggregate, specific purposes information, as required in paragraph 22, should be disclosed in the notes to the financial statements. Governments may display the specific purpose details for some classifications on the face of the balance sheet and disclose the details for other classifications in the notes to the financial statements.
3. For stabilization agreements, even if an arrangement does not meet the criteria to be classified as restricted or committed, the following information should be disclosed in the notes to the financial statements:
   (a) The authority for establishing stabilization arrangements (for example, by statute or ordinance).
   (b) The requirements for additions to the stabilization amount.
   (c) The conditions under which stabilization amounts may be spent.
   (d) The stabilization balance, if not apparent on the face of the financial statements.
4. If a governing body has formally adopted a minimum fund balance policy (for example, in lieu of separately setting aside stabilization amounts), the government should describe in the notes to its financial statements the policy established by the government that sets forth the minimum amount.

Exhibit 4: Government funds statement of revenues, expenditures, and changes in fund balances

City of Anywhere
Governmental Funds
Statement of Revenues, Expenditures, and Changes in Fund Balances
for the Year Ended June 30, 20XX

	General	*Capital Projects*	*Debt Service*	*Nonmajor Governmental Funds*	*Total Governmental Funds*
Revenues					
Real estate taxes	$xx,xxx	$–	$–	$–	$xx,xxx
Sales and use taxes	xx,xxx		–		xx,xxx
Other taxes	xx,xxx		–		xx,xxx
Federal, state, and other categorical aid	xx,xxx	xx,xxx	–	xx,xxx	xx,xxx
Unrestricted federal and state aid	xx,xxx		–		xx,xxx
Charges for services	xx,xxx		–		xx,xxx
Investment income	xx,xxx	–	xx,xxx	xx,xxx	xx,xxx
Other revenues	xx,xxx	xx,xxx	xx,xxx	xx,xxx	xx,xxx
Total revenues	xx,xxx	xx,xxx	xx,xxx	xx,xxx	xx,xxx
Expenditures					
Current operations:					
General government	xx,xxx	xx,xxx	–	xx,xxx	xx,xxx
Public safety and judicial	xx,xxx	xx,xxx			xx,xxx
Education	xx,xxx	xx,xxx	–	xx,xxx	xx,xxx
Social services	xx,xxx	xx,xxx	–		xx,xxx
Environmental protection	xx,xxx	xx,xxx	—		xx,xxx
Transportation services	xx,xxx	xx,xxx	–		xx,xxx
Parks, recreational, and cultural activities	xx,xxx	xx,xxx	—		xx,xxx
Housing	xx,xxx	xx,xxx	–		xx,xxx
Health (including payments to Health and Hospitals Corporation)	xx,xxx	xx,xxx			xx,xxx
Pensions	xx,xxx		–		xx,xxx
Debt service:					
Interest	–	–	xx,xxx	xx,xxx	xx,xxx
Redemptions	–	–	xx,xxx	xx,xxx	xx,xxx
Total expenditures	xx,xxx	xx,xxx	xx,xxx	xx,xxx	xx,xxx
Excess (deficiency) or revenues over expenditures	xx,xxx	(xx,xxx)	(xx,xxx)	(xx,xxx)	(xx,xxx)
Other Financing Sources (Uses)					
Transfers from (to) general fund	–	–	xx,xxx	(xx,xxx)	xx,xxx
Proceeds from sale of bonds	–	xx,xxx	–	xx,xxx	xx,xxx
Capitalized leases	–	xx,xxx	–		xx,xxx
Transfer from capital projects fund	–	–	–	(xx,xxx)	–
Transfer to debt service fund	(xx,xxx)		–		(xx,xxx)

Transfer to component units for debt service	(xx,xxx)		–		(xx,xxx)
Transfers to nonmajor debt service fund	–	–	–	(xx,xxx)	(xx,xxx)
Total other financing sources (uses)	(xx,xxx)	xx,xxx	xx,xxx	(xx,xxx)	xx,xxx
Net change in fund balances	xx,xxx	xx,xxx	xx,xxx	(xx,xxx)	(xx,xxx)
Fund Balances at Beginning of Year	xx,xxx	xx,xxx	xx,xxx	xx,xxx	xx,xxx
Fund Balances at End of Year	$xx,xxx	$xx,xxx	$xx,xxx	$(xx,xxx)	$(xx,xxx)

The reconciliation of the change in fund balances of governmental funds to the change in net position of governmental activities in the statement of net position is presented in an accompanying schedule.

Exhibit 5: Proprietary funds classified statement of net position

City of Anywhere
Statement of Net Position
Proprietary Funds June 30, 20XX

	Enterprise Funds			
	Water and Sewer	*Electric Utility*	*Total*	*Internal Service Funds*
Assets				
Current assets:				
Cash and cash equivalents	$xx,xxx	$xx,xxx	$xx,xxx	$xx,xxx
Investments	–	–	–	xx,xxx
Receivables, net	xx,xxx	xx,xxx	xx,xxx	xx,xxx
Due from other governments	xx,xxx	–	xx,xxx	–
Inventories	xx,xxx	–	xx,xxx	xx,xxx
Total current assets	xx,xxx	xx,xxx	xx,xxx	xx,xxx
Noncurrent assets:				
Restricted cash and cash equivalents	–	xx,xxx	xx,xxx	–
Capital assets:				
Land and improvements	xx,xxx	xx,xxx	xx,xxx	–
Construction in progress	xx,xxx	–	xx,xxx	–
Distribution and collection systems	xx,xxx	–	xx,xxx	–
Buildings and equipment	xx,xxx	xx,xxx	xx,xxx	xx,xxx
Less accumulated depreciation	(xx,xxx)	(xx,xxx)	(xx,xxx)	(xx,xxx)
Total noncurrent assets	xx,xxx	xx,xxx	xx,xxx	xx,xxx
Total assets	xx,xxx	xx,xxx	xx,xxx	xx,xxx
Liabilities				
Current liabilities:				
Accounts payable	xx,xxx	xx,xxx	xx,xxx	xx,xxx
Due to other funds	xx,xxx	–	xx,xxx	xx,xxx
Compensated absences	xx,xxx	xx,xxx	xx,xxx	xx,xxx
Claims and judgments	–	–	–	xx,xxx

(*Continued*)

City of Anywhere
Statement of Net Position
Proprietary Funds June 30, 20XX

	Enterprise Funds			
	Water and Sewer	***Electric Utility***	***Total***	***Internal Service Funds***
Bonds, notes, and loans payable	xx,xxx	xx,xxx	xx,xxx	xx,xxx
Total current liabilities	xx,xxx	xx,xxx	xx,xxx	xx,xxx
Noncurrent liabilities:				
Compensated absences	xx,xxx	xx,xxx	xx,xxx	–
Claims and judgments	xx,xxx	xx,xxx	xx,xxx	xx,xxx
Bonds, notes, and loans payable	xx,xxx	xx,xxx	xx,xxx	–
Total noncurrent liabilities	xx,xxx	xx,xxx	xx,xxx	xx,xxx
Total liabilities	xx,xxx	xx,xxx	xx,xxx	xx,xxx
Net Position				
Invested in capital assets, net of related debt	xx,xxx	xx,xxx	xx,xxx	xx,xxx
Restricted for debt service	–	xx,xxx	xx,xxx	–
Unrestricted	xx,xxx	xx,xxx	xx,xxx	xx,xxx
Total net position	$xx,xxx	$xx,xxx	$xx,xxx	$xx,xxx

Exhibit 6: Proprietary funds statement of revenues, expenses, and changes in fund net position

City of Anywhere
Statement of Revenues, Expenses, and
Changes in Fund Net Position Proprietary Funds
for the Year Ended June 30, 20XX
Enterprise Funds

	Water and Sewer	***Electric Utility***	***Total***	***Internal Service Funds***
Operating Revenues				
Charges for services	$xx,xxx	$xx,xxx	$xx,xxx	$xx,xxx
Miscellaneous	–	xx,xxx	xx,xxx	xx,xxx
Total operating revenues	xx,xxx	xx,xxx	xx,xxx	xx,xxx
Operating Expenses				
Personal services	xx,xxx	xx,xxx	xx,xxx	xx,xxx
Contractual services	xx,xxx	xx,xxx	xx,xxx	xx,xxx
Utilities	xx,xxx	xx,xxx	xx,xxx	xx,xxx
Repairs and maintenance	xx,xxx	xx,xxx	xx,xxx	xx,xxx
Other supplies and expenses	xx,xxx	xx,xxx	xx,xxx	xx,xxx
Insurance claims and expenses	–	–	–	xx,xxx
Depreciation	xx,xxx	xx,xxx	xx,xxx	xx,xxx
Total operating expenses	xx,xxx	xx,xxx	xx,xxx	xx,xxx

(Continued)

City of Anywhere
Statement of Revenues, Expenses, and
Changes in Fund Net Position Proprietary Funds
for the Year Ended June 30, 20XX
Enterprise Funds

	Water and Sewer	*Electric Utility*	*Total*	*Internal Service Funds*
Operating income (loss)	xx,xxx	(xx,xxx)	xx,xxx	(xx,xxx)
Nonoperating Revenues (Expenses)				
Interest and investment revenue	xx,xxx	xx,xxx	xx,xxx	xx,xxx
Miscellaneous revenue	–	xx,xxx	xx,xxx	xx,xxx
Interest expense	(xx,xxx)	(xx,xxx)	(xx,xxx)	(xx,xxx)
Miscellaneous expense	–	(xx,xxx)	(xx,xxx)	(xx,xxx)
Total nonoperating revenue (expenses)	(xx,xxx)	(xx,xxx)	(xx,xxx)	(xx,xxx)
Income (loss) before contributions and transfers	xx,xxx	(xx,xxx)	xx,xxx	(xx,xxx)
Capital contributions	xx,xxx	–	xx,xxx	xx,xxx
Transfers in	–	–	–	xx,xxx
Transfers out	(xx,xxx)	(xx,xxx)	(xx,xxx)	(xx,xxx)
Change in net position	xx,xxx	(xx,xxx)	xx,xxx	(xx,xxx)
Total net position—beginning	xx,xxx	xx,xxx	xx,xxx	xx,xxx
Total net position—ending	$xx,xxx	$xx,xxx	$xx,xxx	$xx,xxx

Exhibit 7: Proprietary funds statement of cash flows

City of Anywhere
Statement of Cash Flows
Proprietary Funds
for the Year Ended June 30, 20XX

	Enterprise Funds			
	Water and Sewer	*Electric Utility*	*Total*	*Internal Service Funds*
Cash Flows from Operating Activities				
Receipts from customers	$xx,xxx	$xx,xxx	$xx,xxx	$xx,xxx
Payments to suppliers	(xx,xxx)	(xx,xxx)	(xx,xxx)	(xx,xxx)
Payments to employees	(xx,xxx)	(xx,xxx)	(xx,xxx)	(xx,xxx)
Internal activity—payments to other funds	(xx,xxx)	–	(xx,xxx)	(xx,xxx)
Claims paid	–	–	–	(xx,xxx)
Other receipts (payments)	(xx,xxx)	–	(xx,xxx)	xx,xxx
Net cash provided by operating activities	xx,xxx	xx,xxx	xx,xxx	xx,xxx

(*Continued*)

City of Anywhere
Statement of Cash Flows
Proprietary Funds
for the Year Ended June 30, 20XX

	Enterprise Funds			
	Water and Sewer	*Electric Utility*	*Total*	*Internal Service Funds*
Cash Flows from Noncapital Financing Activities				
Operating subsidies and transfers to other funds	(xx,xxx)	(xx,xxx)	(xx,xxx)	xx,xxx
Cash Flows from Capital and Related Financing Activities				
Proceeds from capital debt	xx,xxx	xx,xxx	xx,xxx	–
Capital contributions	xx,xxx	–	xx,xxx	–
Purchases of capital assets	(xx,xxx)	(xx,xxx)	(xx,xxx)	(xx,xxx)
Principal paid on capital debt	(xx,xxx)	(xx,xxx)	(xx,xxx)	(xx,xxx)
Interest paid on capital debt	(xx,xxx)	(xx,xxx)	(xx,xxx)	(xx,xxx)
Other receipts (payments)	–	xx,xxx	xx,xxx	xx,xxx
Net cash (used) by capital and related financing activities	(xx,xxx)	(xx,xxx)	(xx,xxx)	(xx,xxx)
Cash Flows from Investing Activities				
Proceeds from sales of investments	–	–	–	xx,xxx
Interest and dividends	xx,xxx	xx,xxx	xx,xxx	xx,xxx
Net cash provided by investing activities	xx,xxx	xx,xxx	xx,xxx	xx,xxx
Net (decrease) in cash and cash equivalents	(xx,xxx)	(xx,xxx)	(xx,xxx)	(xx,xxx)
Balances—beginning of the year	xx,xxx	xx,xxx	xx,xxx	xx,xxx
Balances—end of the year	$xx,xxx	$xx,xxx	$xx,xxx	$xx,xxx
Reconciliation of operating income (loss) to net cash provided by operating activities:				
Operating income (loss)	$xx,xxx	$(xx,xxx)	$xx,xxx	$(xx,xxx)
Adjustments to reconcile operating income to net cash provided by operating activities:				
Depreciation expense	xx,xxx	xx,xxx	xx,xxx	xx,xxx
Change in assets and liabilities:				
Receivables, net	xx,xxx	xx,xxx	xx,xxx	xx,xxx
Inventories	xx,xxx	–	xx,xxx	xx,xxx
Accounts and other payables	(xx,xxx)	(xx,xxx)	(xx,xxx)	xx,xxx
Accrued expenses	(xx,xxx)	xx,xxx	(xx,xxx)	(xx,xxx)
Net cash provided by operating activities	$xx,xxx	$xx,xxx	$xx,xxx	$xx,xxx
Noncash capital financing activities:				
Capital assets of $xx,xxx were acquired through contributions from developers.				

Exhibit 8: Statement of fiduciary net position

City of Anywhere Fiduciary Funds
Statement of Fiduciary Funds
June 30, 20XX (in thousands)

	Pension and Other Employee Benefit Trust Funds	*Agency Fund*
Assets		
Cash and cash equivalents	$xx,xxx	$xx,xxx
Receivables:		
Receivable for investment securities sold	xx,xxx	–
Accrued interest and dividend receivable	xx,xxx	–
Investments:		
Other short-term investments	xx,xxx	–
Debt securities	xx,xxx	xx,xxx
Equity securities	xx,xxx	–
Guaranteed investment contracts	xx,xxx	–
Mutual funds	xx,xxx	–
Collateral from securities lending transactions	xx,xxx	–
Due from other funds	xx,xxx	–
Other	xx,xxx	xx,xxx
Total assets	xx,xxx	xx,xxx
Liabilities		
Accounts payable and accrued liabilities	xx,xxx	xx,xxx
Payable for investment securities purchased	xx,xxx	–
Accrued benefits payable	xx,xxx	–
Due to other funds	xx,xxx	–
Securities lending transactions	xx,xxx	–
Other	xx,xxx	xx,xxx
Total liabilities	xx,xxx	xx,xxx
Net position		
Held in trust for benefit payments	$xx,xxx	$–

Exhibit 9: Fiduciary funds statement of changes in fiduciary net position

City of Anywhere Fiduciary Funds Statement of Changes in Fiduciary Net Position for the Year Ended June 30, 20XX

	Pension and Other Employee Benefit Trust Funds
Additions	
Contributions:	
Member contributions	$xx,xxx
Employer contributions	xx,xxx
Total contributions	xx,xxx

(*Continued*)

City of Anywhere Fiduciary Funds Statement of Changes in Fiduciary Net Position for the Year Ended June 30, 20XX

	Pension and Other Employee Benefit Trust Funds
Investment income:	
Interest income	xx,xxx
Dividend income	xx,xxx
Net depreciation in fair value of investments	(xx,xxx)
Less investment expenses	xx,xxx
Investment loss, net	(xx,xxx)
Payments from other funds	xx,xxx
Other	xx,xxx
Total additions	(xx,xxx)
Deductions	
Benefit payments and withdrawals	xx,xxx
Payments to other funds	xx,xxx
Administrative expenses	xx,xxx
Total deductions	xx,xxx
Decrease in plan net position	(xx,xxx)
Net position	
Held in trust for benefit payments	
Beginning of year	xx,xxx
End of year	$xx,xxx

Exhibit 10: Reconciliation of the fund balances of governmental funds to the net position of governmental activities

City of Anywhere Reconciliation of the Balance Sheet of Governmental Funds to the Statement of Net Position June 30, 20XX

Amounts reported for *governmental activities* in the statement of net position are different because:	
Total fund balances—governmental funds	$(xx,xxx)
Inventories recorded in the statement of net position are recorded as expenditures in the governmental funds	xx,xxx
Capital assets used in governmental activities are not financial resources and therefore are not reported in the funds	xx,xxx
Other long-term assets are not available to pay for current period expenditures and therefore are deferred in the funds	xx,xxx
Long-term liabilities are not due and payable in the current period and accordingly are not reported in the funds:	
Bonds and notes payable	(xx,xxx)
Accrued interest payable	(xx,xxx)
Other long-term liabilities	(xx,xxx)
Net position (deficit) of governmental activities	$(xx,xxx)

Exhibit 11: Reconciliation of the net change in governmental fund balances with the change in net position of governmental activities

City of Anywhere Reconciliation of the Statement of Revenues, Expenditures, and Changes in Fund Balances of Governmental Funds to the Statement of Activities for the Year Ended June 30, 20XX

Amounts reported for *governmental activities* in the statement of activities are different because:		
Net change in fund balances—total governmental funds		$(xx,xxx)
Governmental funds report capital outlays as expenditures.		
However, in the statement of activities the cost of those assets is allocated over their estimated useful lives and reported as depreciation expense. This is the amount by which capital outlays exceeded depreciation in the current period.		
Purchases of fixed assets	$xx,xxx	
Depreciation expense	(xx,xxx)	xx,xxx
The net effect of various miscellaneous transactions involving capital assets and other (i.e., sales, trade-ins, and donations) is to decrease net position.		(xx,xxx)
The issuance of long-term debt (e.g., bonds, leases) provides current financial resources to governmental funds while the repayment of the principal of long-term debt consumes the current financial resources of governmental funds. Neither transaction, however, has any effect on net position. Also, governmental funds report the effect of issuance costs, premiums, discounts, and similar items when debt is first issued, whereas these amounts are deferred and amortized in the statement of activities. This amount is the net effect of these differences in the treatment of long-term debt and related items.		
Proceeds from sales of bonds	(xx,xxx)	
Principal payments of bonds	xx,xxx	
Other	(xx,xxx)	(xx,xxx)
Some expenses reported in the statement of activities do not require the use of current financial resource and therefore are not reported as expenditures in governmental funds.		(xx,xxx)
Revenues in the statement of activities that do not provide current financial resources are not reported as revenues in the funds.		(xx,xxx)
Change in net position—governmental activities		$(xx,xxx)

Budgetary Comparison Schedules

GASBS 34 requires that certain budgetary comparison schedules be presented in required supplementary information (RSI). This information is required only for the general fund and each major special revenue fund that has a legally adopted annual budget. Governments may elect to report the budgetary comparison information in a budgetary comparison statement as part of the basic financial statements, rather than as RSI.

The budgetary comparison schedules must include the originally adopted budget, as well as the final budget. The government is given certain flexibility in the format in which this information is present. For example, the comparisons may be made in a format that resembles the budget document instead of being made in a way that resembles the financial statement presentation. Of important note, the actual information presented is to be presented on the budgetary basis of accounting, which for many governments differs from GAAP. Regardless of the format used, the financial results reported in the budgetary comparison schedules must be reconciled to GAAP-based fund financial statements.

The GASB issued Statement No. 41 (GASBS 41), *Budgetary Comparison Schedules—Perspective Differences*, to address the issue of governments which have significant budgetary perspective differences that result in their not being able to present budgetary comparison information for their general fund and major special revenue funds. This new statement does not address instances where there are minor budgetary fund structures that have minor perspective differences from their fund structure used for reporting under GAAP. These differences are usually readily handled in the required reconciliation between the budgetary perspective and the GAAP perspective. GASBS 41 addresses situations where there are significant perspective differences where budgetary structures prevent governments from associating their estimated revenues and appropriations from their legally adopted budget to the major revenue sources and functional expenditures that are reported in the general fund and major special revenue funds.

GASBS 41 requires that governments with significant budgetary perspective differences that result in a government's not being able to present budgetary comparisons for the general fund and major special revenue funds present budgetary comparison schedules based on the fund, organization, or program structure that the government uses for its legally adopted budget. This comparison schedule must be presented as part of required supplementary information (RSI).

GASBS 41 essentially has two main points. First, if there are significant perspective differences between the budgetary perspective and the GAAP perspective, governments are still required to present budgetary comparison information for the general fund and major special revenue funds. The comparison should be presented in accordance with the format in which the budget is legally adopted. Second, where such perspective differences exist, governments do not have the option to present the budgetary comparison schedule as part of the basic financial statements. It must be presented as part of RSI.

Notes and Other Disclosures

The notes to the financial statements are an integral part of the basic financial statements. Because the basic financial statements and required supplemental information must be "liftable" from the CAFR (i.e., have the ability to function as freestanding financial statements), the notes to the financial statements should always be considered to be part of the "liftable" basic financial statements.

This section provides an overview of certain required disclosures in the notes and the various areas that the financial statement preparer should consider for disclosure in the notes. Almost every new accounting pronouncement issued by the GASB, however, contains some additional disclosures that must be included in the notes. Therefore, to use this book to properly prepare notes for a state or local government, the reader should consider the following broad outline of the financial statement notes described below, review each chapter that addresses specific unique accounting and financial reporting guidance on required disclosures, and consider the "Disclosure Checklist" included in this guide.

The notes to the financial statements are essential to the fair presentation of the financial position, results of operations, and, where applicable, cash flows. Notes considered to be essential to the fair presentation of the financial statements contained in the basic financial statements include individual discretely presented component units, considering the particular component unit's significance to all discretely presented component units, and the nature and significance of the individual unit's relationship to the primary government. The notes prepared under the new financial reporting model should focus on the primary government, which includes blended component units.

Determining which discretely presented component unit financial statements should be included in the notes to the financial statements requires that the financial statement preparer exercise professional judgment. These judgments should be made on a case-by-case basis. Certain disclosures that may be required and appropriate for one component unit may not be required for another. As stated above, these considerations should be made based on the relative significance of a particular discretely presented component unit to all of the discretely presented component units and the significance of the individual discretely presented component unit to the primary government.

The GASB issued GASBS 38 as a result of its project to review financial statement note disclosures. A need to reevaluate note disclosures in the context of the new financial reporting model established by GASBS 34 provided the impetus for the GASB to issue this statement before most governments begin implementing the new financial reporting model.

The GASB reevaluated note disclosures that have been in existence since 1994 and not been under reevaluation under some other project. As a result of this evaluation, several new note disclosures have been added while relief from previous disclosure requirements was rare. While the effect of the potential changes will vary from government to government, it appears that disclosures relating to interfund balances and transfers appear to be the most significant.

The Codification of Governmental Accounting and Financial Reporting Standards published by the GASB (GASB Codification) identifies the more common note disclosures required of state and local governments. The broad categories of notes that would normally be included in the financial statements of a state or local government would include the following:

- Summary of significant accounting policies, including:
  - A description of the government-wide financial statements, noting that neither fiduciary funds nor component units that are fiduciary in nature are included.
  - The measurement focus and basis of accounting used in the government-wide statements.
  - The policy for eliminating internal activity in the statement of activities.
  - The policy for capitalizing assets and for estimating the useful lives of those assets (used to calculate depreciation expense).
  - Governments that choose to use the modified approach for reporting eligible infrastructure assets should describe that approach.
  - A description of the types of transactions included in program revenues and the policy for allocating indirect expenses to functions in the statement of activities.
  - The government's policy for defining operating and nonoperating revenues of proprietary funds.
  - The government's fund balance classification policies and procedures.
  - The government's policy regarding whether to first apply restricted or unrestricted resources when an expense is incurred for purposes for which both restricted and unrestricted net position are available.
  - Descriptions of the activities accounted for in each of the following columns (major funds, internal service funds, and fiduciary fund types) presented in the financial statements.
  - A brief description of the component units of the overall governmental reporting entity and the units' relationships to the primary government. This should include a discussion of the criteria for including component units in the financial reporting

  entity and how the component units are reported. (The determination of the reporting entity is more fully described in Chapter 11.) The notes should also indicate how the separate financial statements of the component units may be obtained.
  - Revenue recognition policies.
  - The period of availability used for revenue recognition in governmental fund financial statements.
  - Policy on capitalization of interest costs on fixed assets.
  - Definition of *cash* and *cash equivalents* used in the statement of cash flows for proprietary and nonexpendable trust funds.
- Cash deposits with financial institutions.
- Investments.
- Significant contingent liabilities.
- Significant effects of subsequent events.
- Pension plan and other postemployment benefit (OPEB) costs and obligations.
- Significant violations of finance-related legal and contractual requirements and actions to address these violations.
- Debt service requirements to maturity, as follows:
  - Principal and interest requirements to maturity, presented separately for each of the five succeeding fiscal years and in five-year increments thereafter. Interest requirements for variable-rate debt should be made using the interest rate in effect at the financial statement date.
  - The terms by which interest rates change for variable-rate debt.
  - For capital and noncancelable operating leases, the future minimum payments for each of the five succeeding fiscal years and in five-year increments thereafter should be disclosed.
  - Details of short-term debt should be disclosed, even if no short-term debt exists at the financial statement date. Short-term debt results from borrowings characterized by anticipation notes, uses of lines of credit, and similar loans. A schedule of changes in short-term debt, disclosing beginning- and end-of-year balances, increases, decreases, and the purpose for which short-term debt was issued.
- Commitments under noncapitalized (operating) leases.
- Construction and other significant commitments:
  - Required disclosures about capital assets.
  - Required disclosures about long-term liabilities.
  - Required disclosures about leases.
  - Interfund balances and transfers.
  - For each major component unit, the nature and amount of significant transactions with other discretely presented component units.
  - Disclosures about donor-restricted endowments.
- Any excess of expenditures over appropriations in individual funds.
- Deficit fund balances or net position of individual funds.
- Balances of receivables and payables reported on the statement of net position and balance sheet may be aggregations of different components, such as balances due to or from taxpayers, other governments, vendors, beneficiaries, employees, and others. When the aggregation of balances on the statement of net position obscures the nature of significant individual accounts, the governments should provide details in the notes to the financial statements. Significant receivable balances not expected to be collected within one year of the date of the financial statements should be disclosed.

- For interfund balances reported in the fund financial statements, disclose the following:
  - Identification of amounts due from other funds by individual major fund, nonmajor funds in the aggregate, internal service funds in the aggregate, and fiduciary fund type.
  - A description of the purpose for interfund balances.
  - Interfund balances that are not expected to be repaid within one year from the date of the financial statements.
- For interfund transfers reported in the fund financial statements, disclose the following:
  - Identification of the amounts transferred from other funds by individual major fund, nonmajor funds in the aggregate, internal service funds in the aggregate, and fiduciary fund type.
- A general description of the principal purposes for interfund transfers.
- A general description and the amount of significant transfers that:
  - Are not expected to occur on a routine basis; and/or
  - Are inconsistent with the activities of the fund making the transfer—for example, a transfer from a capital projects fund to the general fund.

The GASB Codification identifies the following additional disclosures that may apply to state and local governments:

- Entity risk management activities.
- Property taxes.
- Segment information for enterprise funds.
- Condensed financial statements for major discretely presented component units.
- Differences between the budget basis of accounting and GAAP not otherwise reconciled in the basic financial statements.
- Short-term debt instruments and liquidity.
- Related-party transactions.
- The nature of the primary government's accountability for related organizations.
- Capital leases.
- Joint ventures and jointly governed organizations.
- Debt extinguishments and troubled debt restructurings.
- Nonexchange transactions, including grants, taxes, and contributions, that are not recognized because they are not measurable.
- Fund balance classification details.
- Interfund eliminations in the combined financial statements that are not apparent from financial statement headings.
- Pension plans in both separately issued plan financial statements and employer statements.
- Postemployment benefit plans other than pensions—both in separately issued plan financial statements and in employer statements.
- Bond, tax, or revenue anticipation notes excluded from fund or current liabilities.
- Nature and amount of any inconsistencies in the financial statements caused by transactions between component units having different fiscal year-ends or changes in component unit year-ends.
- In component unit separate reports, identification of the primary government in whose financial report the component unit is included and a description of its relationship to the primary government.
- Deferred compensation plans.
- Reverse repurchase and dollar reverse repurchase agreements.
- Securities lending transactions.

- Special assessment debt and related activities.
- Demand bonds.
- Landfill closure and postclosure care.
- Pollution remediation obligations.
- On-behalf payments to fringe benefits and salaries.
- Entity involvement in conduit debt obligations.
- Sponsoring government disclosures about external investment pools reported as investment trust funds.
- The amount of interest expense included in direct expenses in the government-wide statement of activities.
- Significant transactions or other events that are either unusual or infrequent but not within the control of management.
- Nature of individual elements of a particular reconciling item, if obscured in the aggregated information in the summary reconciliation of the fund financial statements to the government-wide statements.
- Discounts and allowances that reduce gross revenues, when not reported on the face of the financial statements.
- Disaggregation of receivable and payable balances.
- Impairment losses, idle impaired capital assets, and insurance recoveries, when not otherwise apparent from the face of the financial statements.
- The amount of the primary government's net position at the end of the reporting period that are restricted by enabling legislation.
- Termination benefits.
- Future revenues that are pledged or sold.
- Derivative instruments.
- Conditions and events giving rise to substantial doubt about the government's ability to continue as a going concern.
- Required disclosures about bankruptcies.
- Stabilization agreements.
- Minimum fund balance policies.
- Information about major special revenue funds.
- Changes in the manner of or basis for presenting corresponding items for two or more periods in comparative financial statements.
- Asset valuation allowances.
- Short-term obligations.
- Long-term construction-type contracts.
- Effects of prior-period adjustments on the change in net position of prior periods.
- Accounting changes and error corrections.
- Investments in common stock.
- Description of receivables and payables that represent contractual rights to receive money or contractual obligations to pay money on fixed or determinable dates, whether or not there is any stated provision for interest, including the effective interest rate and face amount.
- Nonmonetary transactions.
- Foreign currency transactions.
- Insurance enterprises.
- Lending and mortgage banking activities.
- Retail land sales operations.
- Research and development arrangements.

- Regulated business-type activities.
- Information about deferred outflows and deferred inflows of resources and the effect on net position.
- Service concession arrangements.

The GASB Codification reiterates that the above list of areas to be considered for note disclosure is not meant to be all-inclusive, nor is it meant to replace professional judgment in determining the disclosures necessary for fair presentation in the financial statements. The notes to the financial statements, on the other hand, should not be cluttered with unnecessary or immaterial disclosures. The individual circumstances and materiality must be considered in assessing the propriety of the disclosures in the notes to the financial statements. Notes to the financial statements provide necessary disclosure of material items, the omission of which would cause the financial statements to be misleading.

GASBS 34 requires governments to provide additional information in the notes to the financial statements about the capital assets and long-term liabilities. The disclosures should provide information that is divided into the major classes of capital assets and long-term liabilities as well as those pertaining to governmental activities and those pertaining to business-type activities. In addition, information about capital assets that are not being depreciated should be disclosed separately from those that are being depreciated.

Required disclosures about major classes of capital assets include:

- Beginning- and end-of-year balances (regardless of whether beginning-of-year balances are presented on the face of the government-wide financial statements), with accumulated depreciation presented separately from historical cost.
- Capital acquisitions.
- Sales or other dispositions.
- Current period depreciation expense, with disclosure of the amounts charged to each of the functions in the statement of activities.

Required disclosures about long-term liabilities (for both debt and other long-term liabilities) include:

- Beginning- and end-of-year balances (regardless of whether prior year data are presented on the face of the government-wide financial statements).
- Increases and decreases (separately presented).
- The portions of each item that are due within one year of the statement date.
- Which governmental funds typically have been used to liquidate other long-term liabilities (such as compensated absences and pension liabilities) in prior years.

NOTE: Providing required disclosures about increases and decreases to certain long-term liability amounts can be challenging. The best example of these challenges can be demonstrated using the long-term liability for compensated absences as an example. Most governments can calculate this liability as of the end of each fiscal year, using basic assumptions for vesting of sick leave and vacation time to compute the net change in this liability for a fiscal year. Conceptually, the increase in the compensated absences liability represents all of the vacation and sick leave time earned by employees that becomes vested during the year. The decrease in the compensated absences liability represents vested time used by employees, paid to employees who have left the government, or lost to employees because of other circumstances or employer requirements. Few governments are likely to have systems in place to capture the increases and decreases in this liability, particularly in terms of amounts of dollars rather than numbers of hours. These governments will need to devise methodologies to estimate these amounts, focusing on how employees typically accumulate and use vacation and sick leave time. Sampling individual employees across the government, perhaps using separate samples for different types of employees such as civilian and uniformed employees, may provide sufficient support for estimated amounts of additions and deletions to the long-term compensated absence liability.

The GASB Implementation Guide notes that for governments reporting a net pension obligation as a long-term liability, no amount due within one year should be presented for the net pension obligation liability.

In addition, GASBS 34 requires governments that report enterprise funds or that use enterprise fund accounting and financial reporting report certain segment information for those activities in the notes to the financial statements. A segment for these disclosure purposes is defined as "… an identifiable activity reported as or within an enterprise fund or another stand-alone entity for which one or more revenue bonds or other revenue-backed debt instruments (such as certificates of participation) are outstanding. A segment has a specific identifiable revenue stream pledged in support of revenue bonds or other revenue-backed debt, and business-related expenses, gains and losses, assets, and liabilities that can be identified." GASBS 34 specifies that disclosure requirements be met by providing condensed financial statements and other disclosures as follows in the notes to the financial statements:

1. Type of goods or services provided by the segment.
2. Condensed statement of net position:
   (a) Total assets—distinguishing among current assets, capital assets, and other assets. Amounts receivable from other funds or component units should be reported separately.
   (b) Total liabilities—distinguishing between current and long-term amounts. Amounts payable to other funds or component units should be reported separately.
   (c) Total net position—distinguishing among restricted amounts (separately reporting expendable and nonexpendable components), unrestricted amounts, and amounts invested in capital assets, net of related debt.
3. Condensed statement of revenues, expenses, and changes in net position:
   (a) Operating revenues (by major source).
   (b) Operating expenses. Depreciation (including any amortization) should be identified separately.
   (c) Operating income (or loss).
   (d) Nonoperating revenues (or expenses)—with separate reporting of major revenues and expenses.
   (e) Capital contributions and additions to permanent and term endowments.
   (f) Special and extraordinary items.
   (g) Transfers.
   (h) Change in net position.
   (i) Beginning net position.
   (j) Ending net position.
4. Condensed statement of cash flows:
   (a) Net cash provided (or used) by:
      1. Operating activities.
      2. Noncapital financing activities.
      3. Capital and related financing activities.
      4. Investing activities.
   (b) Beginning cash and cash equivalent balances.
   (c) Ending cash and cash equivalent balances.

One accounting area of special interest to governments is that of interfund transactions. While the terminology used to refer to these transactions makes them appear more complicated than they actually are, the financial statement preparer and auditor must be familiar with the accounting for these transactions to properly reflect the financial position and results of operations of governmental entities. In addition, GASBS 34 provides guidance for certain transactions occurring between entities within the financial reporting entity, and low interfund balances and transactions should be presented.

The following sections describe the nature of and the accounting and reporting requirements for each of these types of interfund transactions. While this section addresses interfund transactions, consideration must also be given to transactions between a primary government and its component units. Transfers between the primary government and its blended component units and receivables and payables between the primary government and its blended component units are reported as described for interfund transactions by this chapter. However, for discretely presented component units, the amounts of balances and transfers between the primary government and its discretely presented component units should be reported separately from interfund balances and transfers from other funds. In addition, due to and due from amounts between the same two funds are allowed to be netted when a right of offset exists. Since component units are legally separate entities, it is not likely that a right of offset will exist for receivables and payables between one fund and a blended component unit. Care must be taken to ensure that amounts are not netted for blended component units when there is no right of offset.

Disclosure Requirements for Tax Abatements

The GASB issued Statement No. 77 (GASBS 77), *Tax Abatement Disclosures*, to provide disclosure requirements for certain types of tax abatements. Many governments use tax abatements, particularly to spur economic development. The GASB believes that the financial statements should provide information about these tax abatements, particularly the impact on reducing or limiting tax revenues. GASBS 77 provides a number of disclosure requirements for the types of tax abatements that are within its scope.

The disclosure requirements of GASBS 77 encompass tax abatements that result from both of the following:

(a) Agreements that are entered into by the reporting government.
(b) Agreements that are entered into by other governments and that reduce the reporting government's tax revenues.

For financial reporting purposes, GASBS 77 defines a tax abatement as:

A reduction in tax revenues that results from an agreement between one or more governments and an individual or entity in which (a) one or more governments promise to forgo tax revenues to which they are otherwise entitled and (b) the individual or entity promises to take a specific action after the agreement has been entered into that contributes to economic development or otherwise benefits the governments or the citizens of those governments.

In determining whether a particular transaction meets this definition, GASBS 77 provides that the transaction's substance, not its form or title, is a key factor in determining whether the transaction meets the definition of a tax abatement for the purposes of determining whether it is subject to these disclosure requirements.

NOTE: There are a number of other circumstances where taxes are forgone by a government but are not considered tax abatements under GASBS 77. Using real estate taxes as an example, certain types of organizations, such as not-for-profit organizations or other governmental entities, may be exempt from the tax. Other taxpayers, such as senior citizens or veterans, may pay a reduced rate. While some might conceptualize that these situations are a form of "tax abatement," they are clearly outside the scope of GASBS 77.

GASBS 77 provides the following general principles with regard to tax abatement disclosures:

(a) Disclosures should distinguish between tax abatements resulting from:
  1. Agreements that are entered into by the reporting government; and
  2. Agreements that are entered into by other governments and that reduce the reporting government's tax revenues.

(b) Disclosure information for tax abatements may be provided individually or may be aggregated.

(c) Disclosure information for tax abatements resulting from agreements entered into by the reporting government (whether presented individually or in the aggregate) should be organized by each major tax abatement program, such as an economic development program or a television and film production incentive program.

(d) Disclosure information for tax abatements resulting from agreements entered into by other governments (whether presented individually or in the aggregate) should be organized by the government that entered into the tax abatement agreement and the specific tax being abated.

(e) Disclosure should commence in the period in which a tax abatement agreement is entered into and continue until the tax abatement agreement expires, except as specified in item (d) below.

GASBS 77 provides that a government that chooses to disclose information about individual tax abatement agreements should present individually only those that meet or surpass a quantitative threshold selected by the government. Those agreements should be presented as set forth in items (c) and (d) above.

The specific disclosure requirements related to tax abatement agreements required by GASBS 77 are as follows:

(a) Brief descriptive information, including:
  1. Names, if applicable, and purposes of the tax abatement programs.
  2. The specific taxes being abated.
  3. The authority under which tax abatement agreements are entered into.
  4. The criteria that make a recipient eligible to receive a tax abatement.
  5. The mechanism by which the taxes are abated, including:
    (a) How the tax abatement recipient's taxes are reduced, such as through a reduction of assessed value.
    (b) How the amount of the tax abatement is determined, such as a specific dollar amount or a specific percentage of taxes owed.
  6. Provisions for recapturing abated taxes, if any, including the conditions under which abated taxes become eligible for recapture.
  7. The types of commitments made by the recipients of the tax abatements.

(b) The gross dollar amount, on an accrual basis, by which the government's tax revenues were reduced during the reporting period as a result of tax abatement agreements.

(c) If amounts are received or are receivable from other governments in association with the forgone tax revenue:
   1. The names of the governments.
   2. The authority under which the amounts were or will be paid.
   3. The dollar amounts received or receivable from other governments.

(d) If the government made commitments other than to reduce taxes as part of a tax abatement agreement, a description of:
   1. The types of commitments made.
   2. The most significant individual commitments made. Information about a commitment other than to reduce taxes should be disclosed until the government has fulfilled the commitment.

(e) If tax abatement agreements are disclosed individually, a brief description of the quantitative threshold the government used to determine which agreements to disclose individually.

(f) If a government omits specific information required by this Statement because the information is legally prohibited from being disclosed, a description of the general nature of the tax abatement information omitted and the specific source of the legal prohibition.

As mentioned above, GASBS 77 also applies to tax abatement agreements that are entered into by other governments and that reduce the reporting government's tax revenues. In these circumstances, GASBS 77 requires reporting governments to disclose the following in the notes to the financial statements:

(a) Brief descriptive information, including the names of the governments entering into the tax abatement agreement and the specific taxes being abated.

(b) The gross dollar amounts, on an accrual basis, by which the reporting government's tax revenues were reduced during the reporting period as a result of tax abatement agreements.

(c) If amounts are received or are receivable from other governments in association with the forgone tax revenue:
   1. The names of the governments.
   2. The authority under which the amounts were or will be paid.
   3. The dollar amount received or receivable from other governments.

(d) If tax abatement agreements are disclosed individually, a brief description of the quantitative threshold the reporting government used to determine which agreements to disclose individually.

(e) If a government omits specific information required by this Statement because the information is legally prohibited from being disclosed, a description of the general nature of the tax abatement information omitted and the specific source of the legal prohibition.

GASBS 77 provides that governments that are legally prohibited from disclosing specific information that would otherwise be required to be disclosed may omit that information, subject to the disclosure requirements for these circumstances noted above.

Tax abatement agreements that are entered into by a government's discretely presented component units and that reduce the government's tax revenues should be disclosed as if they were granted by the reporting government (i.e., the fuller disclosures) if the government concludes that the information is essential for fair presentation (based on the application of Statement No. 14, *The Financial Reporting Entity*, as amended). Otherwise, such tax abatements should be disclosed as if they were part of a tax abatement agreement entered into by another government.

NOTE: The reference to GASBS 14 in the preceding paragraph seems a bit out of place, but is explained in the Basis for Conclusions of GASBS 77. The example provided is where a government may have an economic development corporation that is reported as a discretely presented component unit that enters into a tax abatement agreement that results in the reporting government's taxes being abated. The Basis for Conclusions suggests that in these cases, the reduced disclosure requirements for circumstances in which the tax abatement agreement is entered into by another government may not be sufficient and the fuller disclosure requirements may be required for a fair presentation of the financial statements. Some judgment will be required by the financial statement preparer in making this determination.

Loans

Loans may be the easiest of the interfund transactions to understand and record. Loans between funds are treated as balance sheet transactions; the borrowing fund reports a liability and increase in cash, and the loaning fund reports a receivable and a decrease in cash. There is no effect on the operating statement for loans between funds.

In addition, these loans should be reported as fund assets or liabilities regardless of whether the loan will be repaid currently or noncurrently. Accordingly, governmental funds should report all interfund loans in the fund itself, rather than in the government-wide financial statements. For the funds that record a receivable as a result of an interfund loan, if the receivable is not considered an expendable available resource, a reservation of fund balance should be recorded.

Example

Assume that the general fund loans the capital projects fund $10,000 to cover a cash shortage in the capital projects fund, which will be repaid by the capital projects fund immediately after the end of the fiscal year. The following journal entries are recorded:

General Fund		
Due from capital projects fund	10,000	
Cash		10,000
To record a loan to the capital projects fund		
Capital Projects Fund		
Cash	10,000	
Due to general fund		10,000
To record a loan from the general fund		

The above example makes clear that the operating statements of the two funds that enter into a loan transaction are not affected. However, the substance of the transaction should also be considered. In a loan transaction, there should be an intent to actually repay the amount to the loaning fund. Without an intent to repay, the transaction might be more appropriately accounted for as a transfer, which is described more fully later in this chapter.

Reimbursements

A reimbursement is an expenditure or expense that is made in one fund, but is properly attributable to another fund. Many times, the general fund will pay for goods or services (such as a utility bill or rent bill) and is then reimbursed in whole or in part by other funds that benefit from the purchase. The proper accounting for reimbursements is to record an expenditure (or an expense) in the reimbursing fund and a reduction of expenditure (or expense) in the fund that is reimbursed.

Example

Assume that the general fund pays a telephone bill that includes telephone calls made by individuals who work for the government's water utility, which is accounted for as an enterprise fund of the primary government. Further assume that of the $5,000 total telephone bill, $1,000 can specifically be identified as related to the water utility, which will reimburse the general fund for these calls. The following journal entries are recorded:

General Fund

Expenditures—telephone	5,000	
Cash		5,000

To record payment of telephone bill

Due from water utility fund	1,000	
Expenditures—telephone		1,000

To record receivable for reimbursement for telephone bill

Alternatively, the receivable could be established at the same time the bill is paid, as follows. (This is a less likely approach, since determination of the cost allocation for expenditures or expenses usually takes longer than the time until the bill is paid.)

Expenditures—telephone	4,000	
Due from water utility fund	1,000	
Cash		5,000

To record payment of telephone bill and reimbursement owed by the water utility fund

Water Utility Fund

The water utility would record the following journal entry to reflect the reimbursement of the general fund:

Expenses—telephone	1,000	
Cash (or due to general fund)		1,000

To record payment (or amount owed) to the general fund to reimburse it for telephone expenses

INTERFUND TRANSACTIONS—FUND FINANCIAL STATEMENTS

GASBS 34 redefined reporting of interfund transactions, which it describes as follows:

Interfund activity within and among the three fund categories (governmental, proprietary, and fiduciary) should be classified and reported as follows:

(a) **Reciprocal interfund activity** is the internal counterpart to exchange and exchange-like transactions. It includes:

1. **Interfund loans**—amounts provided with a requirement for repayment. Interfund loans should be reported as interfund receivables in lender funds and interfund payables in borrower funds. This activity should not be reported as other financing sources or uses in the fund financial statements. If repayment is not expected within a reasonable time, the interfund balances should be reduced and the amount that is not expected to be repaid should be reported as a transfer from the fund that made the loan to the fund that received the loan.
2. **Interfund services provided and used**—sales and purchases of goods and services between funds for a price approximating their external exchange value. Interfund services provided and used should be reported as revenues in seller funds and expenditures or expenses in purchaser funds. Unpaid amounts should be reported as interfund receivables and payables in the fund balance sheets or fund statements of activities.

(b) **Nonreciprocal interfund activity** is the internal counterpart to nonexchange transactions. It includes:

1. **Interfund transfers**—flows of assets (such as cash or goods) without equivalent flows of assets in return and without a requirement for repayment. This category includes payments in lieu of taxes that are not payments for, and are not reasonably equivalent in value to, services provided. In governmental funds, transfers should be reported as other financing uses in the funds making transfers and as other financing sources in the funds receiving transfers. In proprietary funds, transfers should be reported after nonoperating revenues and expenses.
2. **Interfund reimbursements**—repayments from the funds responsible for particular expenditures or expenses to the funds that initially paid for them. Reimbursements should not be displayed in the financial statements.

INTRA-ENTITY TRANSACTIONS—GOVERNMENT-WIDE FINANCIAL STATEMENTS

GASBS 34 provides guidance for handling internal balances and transactions when preparing the government-wide financial statements. The following paragraphs summarize this guidance.

Statement of Net Position

Eliminations should be made in the statement of activities to minimize the grossing-up effect on assets and liabilities within the governmental and business-type activities columns of the primary government. Amounts reported as interfund receivables and payables should be eliminated within the governmental and business-type activities columns of the statement of net position, except for residual amounts due between the governmental and business-type activities, which should be presented as internal balances. Amounts reported in the funds as receivable from or payable to fiduciary funds should be included in the statement of net position as receivable from or payable to external parties. This is consistent with the nature of fiduciary funds as more external than internal. All internal balances should be eliminated in the total primary government column.

Statement of Activities

Eliminations should also be made in the statement of activities to remove the doubling-up effect of internal service fund activity. The effect of similar internal events that are in effect allocations of overhead expenses from one function to another or within the same function should also be eliminated.

The effect of interfund services provided and used between functions should not be eliminated in the statement of activities because doing so would misstate the expenses of the purchasing function and the program revenues of the selling function.

Intra-Entity Activity

Resource flows between the primary government and blended component units should be reclassified as internal activity of the reporting entity and treated as interfund activity is treated. Resource flows (except those that affect only the balance sheet) between a primary government and its discretely presented component units should be reported as if they were external transactions. Amounts payable and receivable between the primary government and its discretely presented component units or among those component units should be reported on a separate line.

REPORTING DEFERRED INFLOWS AND OUTFLOWS OF RESOURCES

GASB issued Statement No. 63 (GASBS 63), *Financial Reporting of Deferred Outflows of Resources, Deferred Inflows of Resources, and Net Position*, which describes how deferred inflows and outflows of resources are reported in a government's financial statements.

GASB Concepts Statement No. 4 (GASBCS 4), *Elements of Financial Statements*, defined deferred outflows and deferred inflows of resources separately from assets and liabilities. They result from transactions that result in the consumption or acquisition of net assets in one period that are applicable to future periods. Accountants generally refer to the nature of these types of items as deferred charges or deferred credits; however, this terminology will no longer apply in the realm of GAAP for governments.

To be considered a "deferred outflow" or "deferred inflow" of resources, the transaction must be specifically identified as such by a GASB Statement. For example, in GASB Statement No. 53, *Accounting and Financial Reporting for Derivative Instruments*, the changes in fair values of hedging derivative instruments are reported as either deferred inflows or deferred outflows in the statement of net position. In addition, GASB Statement No. 60, *Accounting and Financial Reporting for Service Concession Arrangements*, includes instances where accounting for service concession arrangements results in the recording of deferred inflows and outflows of resources. However, as described below, the GASB issued Statement No. 65 (GASBS 65), *Items Previously Reported as Assets and Liabilities*, which defines a number of transactions that previously were reported as assets and liabilities that will be reported as deferred outflows and inflows of resources (and in some cases, as an expense) when GASBS 65 is implemented.

Display Requirements

GASBS 63 provides that amounts that are required to be reported as deferred outflows of resources should be reported in a statement of financial position in a separate section following assets. Similarly, amounts that are required to be reported as deferred inflows of resources should be reported in a separate section following liabilities. The total for deferred outflows of resources may be added to the total for assets, and the total for deferred inflows of resources may be added to the total for liabilities to provide subtotals.

Statement of Net Position

GASBS 63 replaces the statement of net assets with the statement of net position, which reports all assets, deferred outflows of resources, liabilities, deferred inflows of resources, and net position. Since what still effectively remains as the government's "balance sheet" now reports items other than assets and liabilities, the term *net assets* is no longer appropriate and has been replaced with *net position*. GASBS 63 encourages governments to present the statement of net position in a format that displays assets, plus deferred outflows of resources, less liabilities, less deferred inflows of resources, equals net position, although a balance sheet format (assets plus deferred outflows of resources equals liabilities plus deferred inflows of resources, plus net position) may be used.

Regardless of the format used, the statement of net position should report the residual amount as *net position*, rather than net assets, proprietary or fiduciary fund balance, or equity. Net position represents the difference between all other elements in a statement of financial position and should be displayed in three components—*net investment in capital assets, restricted* (distinguishing among major categories of restrictions), and *unrestricted.*

Net Investment in Capital Assets Component of Net Position

The *net investment in capital assets* component of net position consists of capital assets, net of accumulated depreciation, reduced by the outstanding balances of bonds, mortgages, notes, or other borrowings that are attributable to the acquisition, construction, or improvement of those assets. GASBS 63 provides that deferred outflows of resources and deferred inflows of resources that are attributable to the acquisition, construction, or improvement of those assets or related debt also should be included in this component of net position. If there are significant unspent related debt proceeds or deferred inflows of resources at the end of the reporting period, the portion of the debt or deferred inflows of resources attributable to the unspent amount should not be included in the calculation of net investment in capital assets. Instead, that portion of the debt or deferred inflows of resources should be included in the same net position component (restricted or unrestricted) as the unspent amount.

Restricted and Unrestricted Components of Net Position

GASBS 63 provides that the restricted component of net position consists of restricted assets reduced by liabilities and deferred inflows of resources related to those assets. Generally, a liability relates to restricted assets if the asset results from a resource flow that also results in the recognition of a liability or if the liability will be liquidated with the restricted assets reported.

The unrestricted component of net position is the net amount of the assets, deferred outflows of resources, liabilities, and deferred inflows of resources that are not included in the determination of net investment in capital assets or the restricted component of net position.

Financial Reporting for Governmental Funds

GASBS 63 provides that deferred outflows of resources and deferred inflows of resources that are required to be reported in a governmental fund balance sheet should be presented in a format that displays *assets plus deferred outflows of resources equals liabilities plus deferred inflows of resources plus fund balance.*

Disclosures

GASBS 63 notes that balances of deferred outflows of resources and deferred inflows of resources reported in a statement of net position or a governmental fund balance sheet may be aggregations of different types of deferred amounts. Accordingly, GASBS 63 requires that governments provide details of the different types of deferred amounts in the notes to the financial statements if significant components of the total deferred amounts are obscured by aggregation. Disclosure in the notes to the financial statements is required only if the information is not displayed on the face of the financial statements.

In addition, in some situations, the amount reported for a component of net position (net investment in capital assets, restricted, and unrestricted) may be significantly affected by a transaction that has resulted in recognition of a deferred outflow of resources or deferred inflow of resources. If the difference between a deferred outflow of resources or deferred inflow of resources and the balance of the related asset or liability is significant, a government should provide an explanation of that effect on its net position in the notes to the financial statements.

Items Previously Reported as Assets and Liabilities

In order to identify all of the financial statement items that meet the definition of deferred inflows and outflows of resources, in March 2012 the GASB issued Statement No. 65 (GASBS 65), *Items Previously Reported as Assets and Liabilities*. GASBS 65 identifies all of the items previously reported as assets and liabilities that will need to be reported as deferred outflows and deferred inflows of resources upon GASBS 65's effective date.

The following are the items that would be impacted by implementation of GASBS 65.

Refundings of Debt

For current refundings and advance refundings resulting in a defeasance of debt reported by governmental activities, business-type activities, and proprietary funds, the difference between the reacquisition price and the net carrying amount of old debt should be reported as a deferred outflow of resources or a deferred inflow of resources and recognized as a component of interest expense in a systematic and rational manner over the remaining life of the old debt or the life of the new debt, whichever is shorter.

Prior to the expiration of the lease term, if a change in the provisions of a lease results from a refunding by the lessor of tax-exempt debt, including an advance refunding, in which (1) the perceived economic advantages of the refunding are passed through to the lessee and (2) the revised agreement is classified as a capital lease by the lessee, then the lessee should adjust the lease obligation to the present value of the future minimum lease payments under the revised lease. The adjustment of the lease obligation to present value should be made using the effective interest rate applicable to the revised agreement. The resulting difference should be reported as a deferred outflow of resources or a deferred inflow of resources. The deferred outflow of resources or the deferred inflow of resources should be recognized as a component of interest expense in a systematic and rational manner over the remaining life of the old debt or the life of the new debt, whichever is shorter.

Nonexchange Transactions

Imposed nonexchange revenue transactions. Deferred inflows of resources should be recognized when resources are received or recognized as a receivable before (1) the period for which property taxes are levied or (2) the period when resources are required to be used or when use is first permitted for all other imposed nonexchange revenues in which the enabling legislation includes time requirements.

Government-mandated nonexchange transactions and voluntary nonexchange transactions. Resources transmitted before the eligibility requirements are met (excluding time requirements) should be reported as assets by the provider and as liabilities by the recipient. Resources received or recognized as receivable before time requirements are met, but after all other eligibility requirements have been met, should be reported as a deferred outflow of resources by the provider and a deferred inflow of resources by the recipient. GASBS 65 points out that recognition of assets and revenues should not be delayed pending completion of purely routine requirements, such as the filing of clients for allowable costs under a reimbursement program.

Sales of Future Revenues and Intra-Entity Transfers of Future Revenues

Sales of future revenues. In a sale of future revenues, the transferor government should report the proceeds as a deferred inflow of resources in both the government-wide and fund financial statements except for instances wherein recognition as revenue in the period of sale is appropriate.

Intra-entity transfers of future revenues. When accounting for intra-entity transfers of future revenues, a transferee government should not recognize an asset and related revenue until recognition criteria appropriate to that type of revenue are met. Instead, the transferee government should report the amount paid as a deferred outflow of resources to be recognized over the duration of the transfer agreement. The transferor government should report the amount received from the intra-entity transfer as a deferred inflow of resources in its government-wide and fund financial statements and recognize the amount as revenue over the duration of the transfer agreement.

Deferred inflows of resources and deferred outflows of resources resulting from intra-entity transfers of future revenues and the periodic recognition of those balances as revenue and expense/expenditure should be accounted for similarly to internal balances and intra-entity activity within the financial reporting entity.

Debt Issuance Costs

Debt issuance costs include all costs incurred to issue the bonds, including but not limited to insurance costs (net of rebates from the old debt, if any); financing costs (such as rating agency fees); and other related costs (such as printing, legal, administrative, and trustee expenses). Debt issuance costs, except any portion related to prepaid insurance costs (net of any rebates from the old debt), should be recognized as an expense in the period incurred. Prepaid insurance costs should be reported as an asset and recognized as an expense in a systematic and rational manner over the life of the related debt.

NOTE: This provision of GASBS 65 has resulted in many governments that previously (and correctly) reported debt issuance costs as assets and then amortized them to expense now having to restate their prior year financial statements to reflect these costs as if they had been expensed in the year incurred. While much of GASBS 63 and GASBS 65 involved display issues of presenting deferred inflows and outflows separately from assets and liabilities, this particular requirement for debt issuance costs actually impacts net position. The caution is that GASBS 65 not only requires certain former assets and liabilities to be recorded as deferred outflows and inflows of resources, but also requires some former assets and liabilities to be treated as expenses or revenue in the period incurred or earned.

Leases

Initial direct costs of operating leases. The lessor should recognize initial direct costs of an operating lease as expense/expenditure in the period incurred.

Sale-leaseback transactions. The gain or loss on the sale of property that is accompanied by a leaseback of all or any part of the property for all or part of its remaining economic life should be recorded as a deferred inflow of resources or a deferred outflow of resources, respectively, and recognized in a systematic and rational manner over the arrangement in proportion to the recognition of the lease asset if a capital lease, or in proportion to the related gross rental charged to expense/expenditure over the lease term if an operating lease, subject to certain exceptions.

Acquisition Costs Related to Insurance Activities

Acquisition costs related to insurance activities should be recognized as expense in the period incurred.

Lending Activities

Lending, committing to lend, refinancing or restructuring loans, arranging standby letters of credit, and leasing activities are lending activities for the purpose of applying these requirements.

Loan origination fees and costs. Loan origination fees, except any portion related to points, should be recognized as revenue in the period received. Points received by a lender in relation to a loan origination should be reported as a deferred inflow of resources and recognized as revenue in a systematic and rational manner. Direct loan origination costs should be recognized as expense in the period incurred.

Commitment fees. Except as set forth in items 1 and 2 below, fees received for a commitment to originate or purchase a loan or group of loans should be recorded as a liability and, if the commitment is exercised, recognized as revenue in the period of exercise. If the commitment expires unexercised, the commitment fees should be recognized as revenue upon expiration of the commitment.

1. If the government's experience with similar arrangements indicates that the likelihood that the commitment will be exercised is remote, the commitment fee should be recognized as revenue in the period received.
2. If the amount of the commitment fee is determined retrospectively as a percentage of the line of credit available but unused in a previous period, and if that percentage is nominal in relation to the state interest rate on any related borrowing, and, finally, if that borrowing will bear a market interest rate at the date the loan is made, the commitment fee should be recognized as revenue as of the determination date.

Purchase of a loan or group of loans. Any fees paid or any fees received related to this purchase should be recognized as expense or revenue, respectively, in the period that the loan(s) was/were purchased.

Mortgage Banking Activities

Similar to lending activities, mortgage banking activities may include the receipt or payment of nonrefundable loan and commitment fees representing compensation for a variety of services.

Loan origination fees and costs. If the loan is held for investment, loan origination fees, except any portion related to points, and the direct loan origination costs should be recognized as revenue or expense, respectively, in the period the loan is originated. Points received by a lender in relation to a loan held for investment should be reported as a deferred inflow of resources and recognized as revenue, in a systematic and rational manner. If the loan is held for sale, origination fees, including any portion related to points, and direct loan origination costs should be recorded as a deferred inflow of resources and a deferred outflow of resources, respectively, until the related loan is sold. Once the related loan is sold, the amount reported as a deferred inflow of resources related to the loan origination fees, including any portion related to points, and the amount reported as a deferred outflow of resources related to the direct loan origination costs should be recognized as revenue and expense, respectively, in the period of sale.

Fees relating to loans held for sale. Fees received for guaranteeing the funding of mortgage loans to borrowers, builders, or developers should be accounted for as described above for commitment fees. Fees paid to permanent investors to ensure the ultimate sale of the loans (residential or commercial loan commitment fees) should be recognized as expense in the period when the loans are sold to permanent investors or when it becomes evident the commitment will not be used. Prior to the sale of the loans, the fees paid to permanent investors should be recorded as a deferred outflow of resources until the sale of the loan occurs.

Regulated Operations

General standards of accounting for the effects of regulation. The result of rate actions of a regulator can result in a liability or a deferred inflow of resources being imposed on a regulated business-type activity. Liabilities are usually obligations to the regulated business-type activity and its customers, and deferred inflows of resources represent an acquisition of net position from the regulated business-type activity's customers that are applicable to a future reporting period. The usual ways in which a transaction results in a liability or a deferred inflow of resources and the resulting accounting are as follows:

1. A regulator may require refunds to customers. Refunds that meet the criteria for accrual of loss contingencies should be recorded as liabilities and as reductions of revenue or as expenses of the regulated business-type activity.
2. A regulator can establish current rates intended to recover costs that are expected to be incurred in the future with the understanding that if those costs are not incurred, future rates will be reduced by corresponding amounts. If current rates are intended to recover such costs and the regulator requires the regulated business-type activity to remain accountable for any amounts charged pursuant to such rates and not yet expended for the intended purpose, the regulated business-type activity should not recognize as revenues amounts charged pursuant to such rates. Those amounts should be recorded as a deferred inflow of resources and recognized as revenue when the associated costs are incurred.
3. A regulator can require that a gain or other reduction of net allowable costs be given to customers over future periods. That would be accomplished, for rate-making purposes, by allocating, in a systematic and rational manner, the gain or other reduction of net allowable costs over those future periods and adjusting rates to reduce revenues in approximately the amount of the allocation. If a gain or other reduction of net allowable costs is to be allocated over future periods for rate-making purposes, the regulated business-type activity should not recognize that gain or other reduction of net allowable costs in the current period. Instead, it should be recorded as a deferred inflow of resources for future reductions of charges to customers that are expected to result.

Revenue Recognition in Governmental Funds

Revenue and other governmental fund financial resources should be recognized in the accounting period in which they become both measurable and available. When an asset is recorded in governmental fund financial statements but the revenue is not available, the government should report a deferred inflow of resources until such time as the revenue becomes available.

NOTE: This will likely be a common instance for many general-purpose governments. For example, for real estate tax receivables that are not expected to be received within the 60-day "available" window, a corresponding deferred revenue (liability) was recorded. Under GASBS 65, the corresponding amount will not be a deferred revenue (liability); rather, it will be a deferred inflow of resources. There are likely to be other revenue streams that will have a similar treatment as well.

In addition to the guidance on specific items above, GASBS 65 also provides the following more general guidance.

Use of the term *deferred*. The use of the term *deferred* should be limited to deferred outflows of resources or deferred inflows of resources.

Major fund criteria. Assets should be combined with deferred outflows of resources, and liabilities should be combined with deferred inflows of resources for the purpose of determining which elements meet the criteria for major fund determination as set forth in Statement 34, as amended.

COMPREHENSIVE ANNUAL FINANCIAL REPORT

As described in the beginning section of this chapter, the basic financial statements (BFS) and required supplementary information (RSI) under GASBS 34 constitute a significant component of a state or local government's comprehensive annual financial report (CAFR). The BFS and RSI, however, represent only one part of the CAFR. The CAFR contains additional sections that are important components of a government's external financial reporting.

One of the more challenging aspects of preparing a CAFR can be to distinguish the requirements of GAAP and the requirements of the GFOA's Certificate of Achievement for Excellence in Financial Reporting Program (Certificate of Achievement). As described in Chapter 2 detailing the history of accounting standards setting for governments, the GFOA and its predecessor organizations were at one time the accounting standards-setting bodies. When this role was assumed by the GASB, the GFOA refocused its issuance of documents to set the requirements for its Certificate of Achievement program. The Certificate of Achievement program has a number of detailed requirements for the CAFR that are not requirements of the GASB and GAAP. The Certificate of Achievement requirements for financial statements are included in the GFOA's *Governmental Accounting, Auditing, and Financial Reporting* (GAAFR) and subsequent revisions.

The GASB has updated the requirements of a CAFR prepared in accordance with GAAP through GASB Statement No. 44, *Economic Condition Reporting: The Statistical Section—An Amendment of NCGA Statement 1*, that will change the requirements for CAFR's statistical section upon implementation. GASBS 44's requirements are included in this chapter.

A government desiring to meet only the requirements of GAAP need only meet the requirements for the CAFR specified by the GASB. In this case, the government might still use the guidance of the GAAFR as Level 4 guidance in the hierarchy of GAAP for governments. The

GAAFR presents many instances and examples that constitute industry practices that are widely recognized as acceptable and are often the prevalent practice of an accounting or disclosure treatment used by state or local governments.

A government desiring to meet the requirements of the Certificate of Achievement program will need to prepare a CAFR in compliance with both GASB and GAAFR standards.

This book describes the characteristics and contents of a CAFR as required by GAAP as promulgated by the GASB. This guidance is supplemented with more substantive suggestions contained in the GAAFR. Where possible, a distinction is made between the requirements of GAAP and those of the Certificate of Achievement program.

CAFR Requirements

What should constitute a government's annual financial report—a CAFR or that part of the CAFR known as the basic financial statements? The GASB concludes that, while no governmental financial statements are actually *required*, the annual financial report of a government should be presented as a comprehensive annual financial report—a CAFR.

The GASB does not preclude a government, however, from issuing basic financial statements separately from the CAFR. Basic financial statements are often issued for inclusion in official statements on bond offerings and are sometimes used for wide distribution to users who require less detailed information about a government's finances than is contained in the CAFR. A transmittal letter from the government accompanying the separately issued BFS should inform users of the availability of the CAFR for those requiring more detailed information.

The CAFR should encompass all funds of the primary government, including its blended component units. The CAFR also encompasses all of the discretely presented component units of the reporting entity.

The CAFR should contain:

- The BFS, including any RSI.
- Combining statements for the nonmajor funds of the primary government, including its blended component units. For GAAFR purposes, the combining statements present information for nonmajor funds and component units, since information on the major funds and major component units is presented in the BFS.
- Individual fund statements and schedules for the funds of the primary government, including its blended component units.
- Introductory, supplementary, and statistical information.
- Schedules needed to demonstrate compliance with finance-related legal and contractual provisions.

The general outline and minimum content of the CAFR specified by the GASB Codification are as follows:

(I) Introductory section—includes table of contents, letter of transmittal, and other material deemed appropriate by management.

(II) Financial section—includes the following:
- Auditor's report.
- BFS, including any RSI.
- Combining nonmajor fund or component unit statements and schedules.

(III) Statistical tables.

The GAAFR provides much more detailed information on each of these sections of the CAFR. The following pages use the more substantive guidance of the GAAFR to assist the reader in understanding the detailed information included in the three main sections of the CAFR listed above.

NOTE: Not all of the detailed requirements for the Certificate of Achievement program are included in the following discussion; only the more substantive requirements are included. For example, the GAAFR specifies the contents of the title page of the CAFR. The following discussion does not include these detailed comments, because they can easily be obtained directly from the GAAFR or from the checklist used to qualify CAFRs that received the Certificate of Achievement. On the other hand, the GAAFR describes what should be included, at a minimum, in the letter of transmittal. This is a substantive contribution to the contents of the CAFR and is included in the following discussion.

Introductory section. The introductory section is generally excluded from the scope of the independent audit. This section includes the following:

- Report cover and title page.
- Table of contents. This table should list the various statements and schedules included in the CAFR, broken down by location in the introductory, financial, and statistical sections. In addition, the table of contents should clearly indicate which financial statements constitute the BFS and should also make clear that the notes to the financial statements are a part of the BFS.
- Letter of transmittal. The GASB requires that the introductory section include a letter of transmittal, but the GAAFR provides significant guidance on the topics to include in the letter of transmittal.

The letter of transmittal requirements in the GAAFR are significantly different from those of the previous GAAFR because a fair amount of the content that was previously required in the letter of transmittal is now part of MD&A, and the GFOA suggests that duplication of information in the letter of transmittal and MD&A must be avoided. Accordingly, the following are the basic requirements for the letter of transmittal as contained in the GAAFR:

- Formal transmittal of the CAFR. This section is the actual communication of the CAFR to its intended users. For example, the letter of transmittal might cite the legal requirements for preparing the CAFR and then indicate that the submission of the CAFR is in fulfillment of those requirements. Other topics that are suggested for inclusion are:
  - Management's framework of internal controls.
  - Independent audit of the financial statements, including limitations inherent in a financial statement audit.
  - Reference to other independent auditor reports, such as those resulting from a single audit of federal awards programs.
  - Direction of readers' attention to the MD&A contained in the financial section of the CAFR.
- Profile of the government. This would include a brief description of the government's structure and the types of services it provides. This section might also briefly discuss the inclusion of component units and the budget process.
- Information useful in assessing the government's financial position. The GAAFR distinguishes financial condition from financial position in that financial condition focuses on both existing and future resources and claims on those resources. Because this

future-looking information is generally precluded from inclusion in the MD&A, the letter of transmittal should serve as a vehicle to discuss these subjective factors affecting financial condition. The GAAFR specifically lists the following subtopics that would be included in this section of the transmittal letter:

- Local economy.
- Long-term financial planning.
- Cash management and investments.
- Risk financing.
- Pension benefits.
- Postemployment benefits.

- Awards and acknowledgments. This would include any Certificate of Achievement from the GFOA received by the previous year's CAFR, as well as other awards and acknowledgments of those contributing to the preparation of the CAFR.

NOTE: Letters of transmittal for governments can be made more useful if the "cookbook" approach of taking wording directly out of the GAAFR is avoided. While the sample transmittal letter contained in the GAAFR is a useful guide for governments, the writer of the actual transmittal letter should customize the letter to the actual circumstances of the government. This is particularly true if there are topics of unique importance to a particular government that are not included in the GAAFR's sample transmittal letter. Reporting on these topics in the transmittal letter is likely to improve the reader's understanding of the government and its finances.

The GASB encourages governments to include "other material deemed appropriate by management" in the introductory section. The GAAFR includes the following suggestions:

- A reproduction of the Certificate of Achievement on the prior year's financial statements, if this award was in fact obtained.
- A list of the principal officials of the government.
- An organizational chart of the government showing the assignment of responsibilities of personnel.
- Audit committee letter that may be issued by a government's audit committee.

Financial section. The financial section of the CAFR is composed of these main components:

- The independent auditor's report.
- Management's discussion and analysis (MD&A).
- The basic financial statements (BFS).
- Required supplementary information (RSI).
- The combining and individual nonmajor fund and component unit financial statements and schedules.

The following discussion provides additional detail on the independent auditor's report and the combining and individual fund financial statements and schedules. The contents of the general-purpose and basic financial statements and MD&A were described in detail in the previous sections of this chapter, and RSI is discussed in other chapters of this book.

Independent auditor's report. The independent auditor's report should be the first item included in the financial section of the CAFR preceding MD&A. The independent auditor should report on whether the financial statements are fairly presented in accordance with GAAP. The auditor may also provide an opinion on the combining financial statements and schedules "in relation to" the financial statements (this "in relation to" coverage of the combining is required for the Certificate of Achievement program). The auditor should also indicate whether he or she has audited the other financial information in the CAFR. The independent auditor generally indicates that the information in the statistical section of the CAFR has not been audited.

Combining and individual nonmajor fund and nonmajor component unit financial statements and schedules. As mentioned earlier, the combining and individual fund financial information prepared in a CAFR after implementation of GASBS 34 focuses on information about nonmajor fund and nonmajor component unit financial information, rather than information about fund types that was previously reported. Since the basic financial statements provide information about major funds, the GAAFR uses the combining and individual fund presentation to complete the financial reporting picture by providing information about nonmajor funds and nonmajor component units. A government with a full range of fund types and component units would conceivably have the following sets of combining statements:

- Nonmajor governmental funds.
- Nonmajor enterprise funds.
- Internal service funds.
- Private-purpose trust funds.
- Pension (and other employee benefit) trust funds.
- Investment trust funds.
- Agency funds.
- Nonmajor discretely presented component units.

Note that using these combining statements of nonmajor funds—for example, nonmajor governmental funds—combines nonmajor funds of more than one fund type. The GAAFR suggests that columnar headings be used on these combining statements to identify the fund type of each individual fund presented in that statement. In addition, when there are too many nonmajor funds to fit on a particular combining statement, subcombining statements can be used, with the totals of the subcombining statements carrying forward to the combining statements. Note that if subcombining statements are used, breaking the subcombining statements into fund types would appear to be a good way to preserve some of the nonmajor fund-type information within the combining statement section.

The GAAFR presents the following examples of situations where individual fund financial presentations would need to be included in this section:

- Budgetary comparisons not required in connection with the basic financial statements. While budgetary comparisons statements are required in the basic financial statements for the general fund and major special revenue funds that adopt budgets, CAFR budgetary comparisons are required for any other individual governmental fund for which annual appropriated budgets have been adopted.
- Detailed budgetary comparisons for the general fund and major individual funds. Governments that prepare CAFRS are required to present budgetary comparisons at a level of detail sufficient to demonstrate legal compliance. Additional individual fund financial presentations would be included in this section to meet this requirement.
- Comparative data. Individual fund presentations in the financial section of the CAFR are often used by governments to present comparative financial data.
- Greater detail. Governments may use the individual fund presentations to present information about individual funds.

The GAAFR also specifies that governments may also present supplementary information that is believed to be useful to financial statement readers, such as cash receipt and disbursements information for the general fund, and this information should be included in the financial section if so desired by the government.

Statistical tables. The third section of the CAFR is the statistical section. The statistical section provides both financial and nonfinancial information that is often very useful to investors, creditors, and other CAFR users. The statistical section presents certain information on a trend basis; that is, summary information is provided for each year in a ten-year period.

The GASB issued GASBS 44 to address the schedules and other disclosures that are contained in the statistical section of the CAFR prepared by governments. GASBS 44 addresses only disclosures that are required when a government prepares a CAFR.

The GASB addressed the statistical section to consider and incorporate information relating to the government-wide financial statements. In addition, the requirements for the statistical section had not been addressed for a long period of time and were in need of refreshing.

Some of the schedules that are described below are the same as those previously required in statistical sections of CAFRs. One important feature of GASBS 44, however, is that there are more specific requirements for each schedule than had existed in the past. For example, a government may be currently providing a schedule of property tax levies and collections. GASBS 44 has specific instructions for preparing this schedule, which a government's previous schedule may not meet. The GASB deliberately included these specific instructions and requirements to facilitate the comparability of reports among different governments.

As will be described later, GASBS 44 also requires narrative explanations to be included in the statistical section. The requirements are very general as to when an explanation is required and will require a fair amount of judgment on the part of a government to implement.

From an implementation perspective, GASBS 44 has many requirements that will take a fair level of effort to interpret and implement. It encourages, but very importantly does not require, any retroactive restatement of information from years prior to implementation.

GASBS 44 describes five categories of information in which ten-year trend information is to be presented. The information should focus on the primary government, including blended component units. However, GASBS 44 acknowledges that providing additional information about individual discretely presented component units may be advantageous in providing information about the economic condition of a government.

The following summarizes the five categories of information and lists the statistical tables that would be required for each:

1. **Financial trends information.** This category is intended to help in understanding and assessing how a government's financial position has changed over time. The required schedules are:

    - Information about net position, presented for each of the three categories of net position (invested in capital assets net of related debt, restricted and unrestricted) for governmental activities, business-type activities, and the total primary government.
    - Information about changes in net position that includes expenses, program revenues, and net (expense) revenue by function or program, general revenues, and other changes in net position, along with a total change in net position. The most significant charges for services revenue should also be presented, categorized by function, program, or identifiable activity.
    - Information about governmental funds, including:

- Reserved and unreserved fund balances for both the general fund and all other governmental funds in the aggregate.
- For total governmental funds, the following should be presented:
  - Revenues by source.
  - Expenditures by function.
  - Other financing sources and uses, and other changes in fund balance.
  - Total change in fund balances.

  Interest and principal components of debt service expenditures should be shown separately.

2. **Revenue capacity information.** This information is intended to help in understanding and assessing the factors affecting a government's ability to generate its own-source revenues by providing information about a government's most significant own-source revenue. The required schedules are:
   - Information about revenue bases shown by major component, such as real and personal property, including the total direct rate applied to the revenue base.
   - Information about revenue rates applied by the government to the revenue base.
   - Information about principal revenue payers.
   - Information about property tax levies and collections, including:
     - The amount levied for the period.
     - The amount collected prior to the end of that period and the percentage of the total levy that amount represents.
     - The amount of the levy collected in subsequent years, the total amount collected to date, and the percentage of the total levy that has been collected year to date.
3. **Debt capacity information.** This information is intended to help in understanding and assessing a government's debt burden and its ability to issue additional debt. The required schedules are:
   - Information about ratios of outstanding debt for each type of debt and divided between debt for governmental activities and business-type activities. The ratio of outstanding debt to total personal income should also be presented.
   - Information about ratios of general bonded debt. The ratio of general bonded debt to the total estimated value of property should be presented if the debt is to be repaid with property taxes. An alternative revenue base should be used when bonded debt is not repaid with property taxes.
   - Information about direct and overlapping debt.
   - Information about debt limitations, including the relevant revenue base, debt limit amount, debt applicable to the limit, and legal debt margin amount.
   - Information about pledged-revenue coverage for nongeneral obligation debt that is secured by a pledge of a specific revenue stream. Government should present gross revenues, principal and interest requirements, and a coverage ratio.
4. **Demographic and economic information.** This information is intended to help in understanding the socioeconomic environment within which a government operates and to provide information that enables comparisons of financial statement information over time and among governments. The required schedules are:
   - Demographic and economic information, including population, personal income, per capita personal income, and unemployment rates.
   - Information about principal employers for the current year and the period nine years prior.

5. **Operating information.** This is intended to provide information about a government's operations and resources to assist in understanding a government's economic condition. The required schedules are:
   - Information about government employees, including the number of persons employed by function, program, or identifiable activity.
   - Information about operating indicators by function, program, or identifiable activity that presents indicators of the demand for services or the level of services provided.
   - Information about capital assets, including indicators of the volume, usage, or nature of capital assets by function, program, or identifiable activity.

Operating information for each individual pension and other postemployment benefit (OPEB) plan should be presented that includes:

- Information about retired members by type of benefit for the current year.
- Information about the average monthly benefit, average final salary, and number of retired members.
- For multiemployer plans, information about the principal participating employers, the number of covered employees each has, and the percentage of total covered employees that each represents.

Narrative Explanations

One of the more important changes resulting from GASBS 44 is the requirement to include narrative explanations in the statistical section. Explanations should be analytical in nature, but may be data explanations as well. GASBS 44 states that judgment should be used in deciding whether to present narrative explanations and, if so, what types of explanations and their extent. The four types of explanations listed in GASBS 44 are:

- Explanations of the objects of statistical information in general and the five categories of statistical information, as well as individual schedules, if appropriate.
- Explanations of basic concepts that may be unfamiliar to users of the statements.
- Explanations that identify relationships between items of information in various statistical schedules, as well as between the statistical schedule and information in other sections of the report.
- Explanations of atypical trends and anomalous data that users of the report would not otherwise understand.

CASH FLOW STATEMENT PREPARATION AND REPORTING

The cash flow statement prepared by governments differs from those of a commercial enterprise in three basic ways:

- Not all of the fund types that are reported by the governmental entity are required to prepare a cash flow statement. A cash flow statement of a commercial enterprise would include all of the operations of the enterprise.
- Differences exist in the categorization of cash receipts and cash disbursements and in some of the related disclosure requirements.
- Governmental entities that are required by GASBS 34 to present a cash flow statement must use the direct method, which is explained later in this chapter.

The following paragraphs provide detailed guidance on when a cash flow statement is required and how a cash flow statement for a governmental entity is prepared.

When Is a Cash Flow Statement Required?

Generally, a cash flow statement is required for each period that an operating statement is presented in the government's financial statements. However, not all of the fund types must be included in the statement of cash flows. Statements of cash flows must be prepared for proprietary funds and special-purpose governments that are engaged in business-type activities, such as public benefit corporations and authorities, governmental utilities, governmental hospitals and other health care providers, and governmental colleges and universities. Public employee retirement systems (PERS) and pension and other employee benefit trust funds are exempt from the requirement to present a statement of cash flows. PERS and pension trust funds are not precluded, however, from presenting a statement of cash flows. A government-wide cash flow statement is not required by GASBS 34.

For purposes of this book, the entities that are required to prepare a statement of cash flows will be referred to as *governmental enterprises*. This is for convenience, but also for consistency with GASBS 9, *Reporting Cash Flows of Proprietary and Nonexpendable Trust Funds and Governmental Entities That Use Proprietary Fund Accounting*.

Objectives of the Statement of Cash Flows

In presenting a statement of cash flows, the preparer of the government's financial statements should keep in mind the purpose of the statement of cash flows. GASBS 9 highlights that the information about cash receipts and disbursements presented in a statement of cash flows is designed to help the reader of the financial statements assess (1) an entity's ability to generate future net cash flows; (2) its ability to meet its obligations as they come due; (3) its needs for external financing; (4) the reasons for differences between operating income or net income, if operating income is not separately identified on the operating statement; and (5) the effects of the entity's financial position on both its cash and its noncash investing, capital, and financing transactions during the period.

***Cash* and *Cash Equivalents* Definitions**

While a statement of cash flows refers to and focuses on cash, included in the definition of the term *cash* for purposes of preparing the statement are cash equivalents. Cash equivalents are short-term, liquid investments that are so close to cash in characteristics that, for the purposes of preparing the statement of cash flows, they should be treated as if they were cash.

GASBS 9 provides specific guidance as to what financial instruments should be considered cash equivalents for the purposes of preparing a statement of cash flows. *Cash equivalents* are defined as short-term, highly liquid investments that are:

- Readily convertible to known amounts of cash.
- So near their maturity that they present insignificant risk of changes in value because of changes in interest rates.

In general, only those investments with original maturities of three months or less are considered in GASBS 9 to meet this definition. *Original maturity* means the maturity to the entity holding the investment. Under GASBS 9, both a three-month U.S. Treasury bill and a three-year Treasury note purchased three months from maturity qualify as cash equivalents. If the three-year Treasury note was purchased three years ago, it does not become a cash equivalent as time passes and it has only three months left until maturity.

Common examples of cash equivalents are Treasury bills, commercial paper, certificates of deposit, money market funds, and cash management pools. When these cash equivalents are purchased and sold during the year as part of the entity's cash management practices, these purchases and sales are not reported as cash inflows or outflows on the statement of cash flows. To do so would artificially inflate inflows and outflows of cash that are reported.

The total amount of cash and cash equivalents at the beginning and end of the period shown in the statement of cash flows should be easily traceable to similarly titled line items or subtotals shown in the statement of financial position as of the same dates. Cash and cash equivalents are included in the statement of cash flows regardless of whether there are restrictions on their use. Accordingly, when comparing the cash and cash equivalents on the statement of financial position with the statement of cash flows, both restricted and unrestricted cash and cash equivalents on the statement of financial position must be considered.

The governmental enterprise should establish an accounting policy on which securities will be considered cash equivalents within the boundaries established above. In other words, a governmental entity may establish an accounting policy that is more restrictive than that permitted by GASBS 9 regarding what is considered a cash equivalent. The accounting policy should be disclosed in the notes to the financial statements.

NOTE: Given that transactions involving purchases and sales of cash equivalents are not reported as cash inflows and outflows on the statement of cash flows, a more restrictive policy on the definition of a cash equivalent under GASBS 9 will result in more transactions being reported in the statement of cash flows as purchases and sales of securities. This "inflation" of the amounts on the statement of cash flows should be considered by the governmental entity when establishing its accounting policy for defining cash equivalents.

Classification of Cash Receipts and Cash Disbursements

A statement of cash flows should classify cash receipts and disbursements into the following categories:

- Cash flows from operating activities.
- Cash flows from noncapital financing activities.
- Cash flows from capital and related financing activities.
- Cash flows from investing activities.

Gross and net cash flows. In applying the categorization of cash flows into these classifications, governmental enterprises should consider that the GASB concluded that reporting gross cash receipts and payments during a period is more relevant than information about the net amount of cash receipts and payments. However, the net amount of cash receipts and disbursements provides sufficient information in certain instances that GASBS 9 permits "net" reporting rather than displaying the gross amounts of cash receipts and cash payments. These specific instances are as follows:

- Transactions for the purchase and sale of cash equivalents as part of the cash management activities of the governmental enterprise may be reported as net amounts.

- Items that qualify for net reporting because of their quick turnovers, large amounts, and short maturities are cash receipts and disbursements relating to investments (other than cash equivalents), loans receivable, and debt, provided that the original maturity of the asset or liability is three months or less. (Amounts that are due on demand meet the requirement of having a maturity of three months or less.)
- In certain circumstances, governmental enterprises may report the net purchases and sales of their highly liquid investments rather than report the gross amounts. These requirements are somewhat onerous, and one would not expect many governmental enterprises to meet this circumstance when net reporting would be permitted. Such net reporting is allowed if both of the following conditions are met:
  - During the period, substantially all of the governmental enterprise's assets were highly liquid investments, such as marketable securities and other assets for which a market is readily determinable.
  - The government enterprise had little or no debt, based on average debt outstanding during the period, in relation to average total assets.

The following paragraphs provide guidance on classifying transactions into these categories and provide examples of the types of cash inflows and outflows that should be classified.

Cash flows from operating activities. Operating activities generally result from providing services and producing and delivering goods. On the other hand, operating activities include all transactions and other events that are not defined as capital and related financing, noncapital financing, or investing activities, and therefore could be viewed as a catchall for transactions that don't meet the definition of the other cash flow classifications. Cash flows from operating activities are generally the cash effects of transactions and other events that enter into the determination of operating income. Although *operating income* is not defined in the literature for governments, it is generally agreed to represent operating revenues less operating expenses.

GASBS 9 provides the following examples of cash inflows from operating activities:

- Cash inflows from sales of goods and services, including receipts from collection of accounts receivable and both short- and long-term notes receivable arising from those sales.
- Cash receipts from quasi-external operating activities with other funds.
- Cash receipts from grants for specific activities considered to be operating activities of the grantor government. (A grant agreement of this type is considered to be essentially the same as a contract for services.)
- Cash receipts from other funds for reimbursement of operating transactions.
- All other cash receipts that do not result from transactions defined as capital and related financing, noncapital financing, or investing activities.

Some examples of cash outflows from operating activities are the following:

- Cash payments to acquire materials for providing services and manufacturing goods for resale, including principal payments on accounts payable and both short- and long-term notes payable to suppliers for those materials or goods.
- Cash payments to other suppliers for other goods or services.
- Cash payments to employees for services.
- Cash payments for grants to other governments or organizations for specific activities considered to be operating activities of the grantor government.

- Cash payments for taxes, duties, fines, and other fees or penalties.
- Cash payments for quasi-external operating transactions with other funds, including payments in lieu of taxes.
- All other cash payments that do not result from transactions defined as capital and related financing, noncapital financing, or investing activities.

In addition to the cash flows described above, the government may also need to consider some of its loan programs as having cash flows from operations if the loan programs themselves are considered part of the operating activities of the governmental enterprise. For example, program-type loans such as low-income housing mortgages or student loans are considered part of a governmental enterprise's program in that they are undertaken to fulfill a governmental enterprise's responsibility. Accordingly, the cash flows from these types of loan activities would be considered operating activities, rather than investing activities, the category in which loan cash flows are included.

Cash flows from noncapital financing activities. As its title indicates, cash flows from noncapital financing activities include borrowing money for purposes other than to acquire, construct, or improve capital assets and repaying those amounts borrowed, including interest. This category should include proceeds from all borrowings, including revenue anticipation notes not clearly attributable to the acquisition, construction, or improvement of capital assets, regardless of the form of the borrowing. In addition, this classification of cash flows should include certain other interfund and intergovernmental receipts and payments.

GASBS 9 provides the following examples of cash inflows from noncapital financing activities:

- Proceeds from bonds, notes, and other short- or long-term borrowing not clearly attributable to the acquisition, construction, or improvement of capital assets.
- Cash receipts from grants or subsidies (such as those provided to finance operating deficits), except those specifically restricted for capital purposes and specific activities that are considered to be operating activities of the grantor government.
- Cash received from other funds except (1) those amounts that are clearly attributable to acquisition, construction, or improvement of capital assets; (2) quasi-external operating transactions; and (3) reimbursement for operating transactions.
- Cash received from property and other taxes collected for the governmental enterprise and not specifically restricted for capital purposes.

Examples of cash outflows for noncapital purposes include the following:

- Repayments of amounts borrowed for purposes other than acquiring, constructing, or improving capital assets.
- Interest payments to lenders and other creditors on amounts borrowed or credit extended for purposes other than acquiring, constructing, or improving capital assets.
- Cash paid as grants or subsidies to other governments or organizations, except those for specific activities that are considered to be operating activities for the grantor government.
- Cash paid to other funds, except for quasi-external operating transactions.

Special considerations are needed to properly classify grants made by a governmental enterprise (the grantor). For the grantor's classification purposes, it is irrelevant whether the grantee uses the grant as an operating subsidy or for capital purposes. The grantor should classify all grants as noncapital financing activities, unless the grant is specifically considered to be part of the operating activities of the grantor governmental enterprise.

Cash flows from capital and related financing activities. This classification of cash flows includes those cash flows for (1) acquiring and disposing of capital assets used in providing services or producing goods; (2) borrowing money for acquiring, constructing, or improving capital assets and repaying the amounts borrowed, including interest; and (3) paying for capital assets obtained from vendors on credit.

GASBS 9 includes the following examples of cash inflows from capital and related financing activities:

- Proceeds from issuing or refunding bonds, mortgages, notes, and other short- or long-term borrowing clearly attributable to the acquisition, construction, or improvement of capital assets.
- Receipts from capital grants awarded to the governmental enterprise.
- Receipts from contributions made by other funds, other governments, and the cost of acquiring, constructing, or improving capital assets.
- Receipts from sales of capital assets and the proceeds from insurance on capital assets that are stolen or destroyed.
- Receipts from special assessments or property and other taxes levied specifically to finance the construction, acquisition, or improvement of capital assets.

Examples of cash outflows for capital and related financing activities include the following:

- Payments to acquire, construct, or improve capital assets.
- Repayments or refundings of amounts borrowed specifically to acquire, construct, or improve capital assets.
- Other principal payments to vendors that have extended credit to the governmental enterprise directly for purposes of acquiring, constructing, or improving capital assets.
- Cash payments to lenders and other creditors for interest directly related to acquiring, constructing, or improving capital assets.

NOTE: In determining whether cash flows are related to capital or noncapital activities, the financial statement preparer should look to the substance of the transaction to determine proper classification. The classification of the transaction in the balance sheet and statement of operations should indicate classification in the statement of cash flows. (Is the asset capitalized on the balance sheet?) In addition, GASBS 9 provides specific guidance to assist in making this determination, discussed below.

Determining whether cash flows represent capital or noncapital activities. The classification of cash flows as capital or noncapital activities is an important difference between the statements of cash flows prepared by commercial organizations and those prepared by governmental enterprises. In most cases, distinguishing between "capital and related financing" and "noncapital financing" is relatively simple. For example, when a governmental enterprise uses mortgages, capital improvement bonds, or time-payment arrangements to construct a capital asset, these financing activities clearly fall within the category of capital and related financing activities. However, in some cases, the distinction is not clear, and GASBS 9 provides limited guidance on making this determination. For example:

- Debt that is clearly attributable to capital construction, acquisition, or improvement should be considered capital debt, and the debt proceeds should be classified as capital and related financing.

- Debt that is not clearly attributable to capital construction, acquisition, or improvement should be considered noncapital debt, and the debt proceeds and subsequent payments of principal and interest should be classified as noncapital financing.
- Principal and interest payments on debt that was issued to acquire, construct, or improve capital assets that have been sold or otherwise disposed of should remain classified as capital and related financing.
- In a defeasance of debt, the proceeds of a debt issue used to provide proceeds that will be set aside in a trust to pay the debt service on an existing issue of capital debt should be reported as a cash inflow in the capital and related financing category, and the payment to defease the existing capital debt should be reported as an outflow in that category. Chapter 15 provides additional information on refundings and defeasances. Subsequent principal and interest payments on the refunding debt should also be reported as cash outflows in the capital category. An exception arises when the refunding issue is in excess of the amount needed to refund the existing capital debt. In this situation, the total proceeds and the subsequent principal and interest payments should be allocated between the capital financing category and the noncapital financing category based on the amounts used for capital and noncapital purposes.

Cash flows from investing activities. The final category of cash flows is cash flows from investing activities. Investing activities include buying and selling debt and equity instruments and making and collecting loans (except loans considered part of the governmental enterprise's operating activities, as described above).

GASBS 9 provides the following examples of cash inflows from investing activities:

- Receipts from collections of loans (except program loans) made by the governmental enterprise and sales of the debt instruments of other entities (other than cash equivalents) that were purchased by the governmental enterprise.
- Receipts from sales of equity instruments and from returns on the investments in those instruments.
- Interest and dividends received as returns on loans (except program loans), debt instruments of other entities, equity securities, and cash management or investment pools.
- Withdrawals from investment pools that the governmental enterprise is not using as demand accounts.

Examples of cash outflows that should be categorized as cash flows from investing activities include the following:

- Disbursements for making loans (except program loans) made by the governmental enterprise and payments to acquire debt instruments of other entities (other than cash equivalents).
- Payments to acquire equity instruments.
- Deposits into investment pools that the governmental enterprise is not using as demand accounts.

Direct Method of Reporting Cash Flows from Operating Activities

GASBS 34 requires the direct method of reporting cash flows from operating activities to be used. The direct method reports the major classes of gross cash receipts and gross cash payments; the sum (the total receipts less the total payments) equals the net cash provided by operating activities. The term *net cash* used by operating activities should be used if the total of the gross cash payments exceeds the amount of gross cash receipts. Governmental enterprises that use the direct method should report separately, at a minimum, the following classes of operating cash receipts and payments, where applicable:

- Cash receipts from customers.
- Cash receipts from interfund services provided.
- Other operating cash receipts, if any.
- Cash payments to employees for services.
- Cash payments to other suppliers of goods or services.
- Cash payments for interfund services used, including payments in lieu of taxes that are payments for, and reasonably equivalent in value to, services provided.
- Other operating cash payments, if any.

In addition to the minimum classes listed above, the GASB encourages governmental enterprises to provide further detail of operating cash receipts and cash payments if it is considered useful to do so.

When governmental enterprises use the direct method as described above, the statement of cash flows should also present a reconciliation between the net cash flows provided or used by operations with the amount of net operating income. This reconciliation requires adjusting operating income to remove the effects of depreciation, amortization, or other deferrals of past operating cash receipts and payments, such as changes during the period in inventory, deferred revenue, and similar accounts. In addition, accruals of expected future operating cash receipts and payments must be reflected, including changes in receivables and payables.

The governmental enterprise may also present a reconciliation of net cash flows provided by or used by operations to net income if an amount for operating income is not separately identified on the statement of operations.

Format of the Statement of Cash Flows

The statement of cash flows should report net cash provided or used by each of the four categories described above. The total of the net effects of each of the four categories should reconcile the beginning and ending cash balances reported in the statement of financial position. The following paragraphs describe some additional formatting and disclosure requirements that the financial statement preparer should consider when preparing a statement of cash flows.

- Cash inflows and outflows in the capital financing, noncapital financing, and investing activities categories should be shown in the statement of cash flows on a gross, not a net, basis. In other words, payments for purchases of capital assets would be shown separately from the proceeds of the sales of capital assets. The statement of cash flows should report the two gross amounts, not a line such as "net increase in capital assets." Similarly, the amounts of repayments of debt should be reported separately from the amounts of new borrowings.
- Statements of cash flows for individual funds should report the gross amounts of interfund transfers in the appropriate categories using the guidance described above. However, interfund transfers may be eliminated in the combined and combining statements of cash flows for all proprietary funds if the interfund transfers are also eliminated in the combining process for other financial statements.

- Disclosures of information about noncash activities. GASBS 9 requires that information about all investing, capital, and financing activities of a governmental enterprise during a period that affect recognized assets or liabilities but do not result in cash receipts or cash payments in the period should be disclosed. The information should be presented in a separate schedule that may be in either narrative or tabular format, and should clearly describe the cash and noncash aspects of the transactions involving similar items. Examples of noncash transactions are the acquisition of assets by assuming directly related liabilities, obtaining an asset by entering into a capital lease, and exchanging noncash assets or liabilities for other noncash assets or liabilities. If some transactions are part cash and part noncash, the cash portion should be included in the statement of cash flows. The noncash portion should be reported in the separate schedule described in this paragraph.

SUMMARY

This chapter provided a broad summary of the financial reporting requirements of governments. The level and extent of the detailed reporting requirements included in governments' CAFRs is extensive and presents a challenge to financial statement preparers and auditors. Specific information about accounting and reporting for individual funds is provided in Chapters 4 through 8 and should be used in conjunction with the overview requirements presented in this chapter.

10 THE IMPORTANCE OF BUDGETS TO GOVERNMENTS

INTRODUCTION

Almost all organizations—governmental, commercial, or not-for-profit—operate using some form of budgeting to ensure that resources are used in accordance with management's intentions and to facilitate obtaining results of operations consistent with management's plans. In the governmental environment, budgets take on greater importance, because they provide the framework in which public resources are spent. From an accounting and financial reporting viewpoint, budgets in government are a key component in achieving the accountability objective described in Chapter 2. Budgets in government generally represent adopted law, which is far more significant than simply a financial planning tool. Because many governments do not follow GAAP to prepare their budgets, achieving the accountability objective by comparing a non-GAAP-based budget with GAAP-based results presents some unique challenges. GASBS 34 affirmed the importance of budgetary reporting by governments by incorporating such reporting, in certain circumstances, into the financial reporting model of governments. These requirements are described in this chapter.

This chapter provides an overview of the budgeting process in governments and highlights the important areas in which budget information is incorporated into the financial statements of governments. It's important to note that there is a fair amount of disparity in how governments manage their budget-making processes, which are based upon their own legal requirements. While the budget process described in this chapter may be typical, there are likely to be differences encountered in actual practice.

BUDGET BACKGROUND

NCGAS 1, *Governmental Accounting and Financial Reporting Principles,* and NCGA Interpretation 10 (NCGAI 10), *State and Local Government Budgetary Reporting,* provide useful background information on the budgeting process typically found in state and local governments. One of the difficulties in understanding the budgeting process is the definition of a *typical* budgetary process, because it is the result of legislative actions, and accordingly, many governmental units are far from typical. However, the following discussion provides sufficient general information on the subject to enable governmental accountants and auditors to handle any budgeting situation encountered in any particular state or local governmental unit.

There are various components of a governmental budget:

- Executive budget.
- Appropriated budget.
- Nonappropriated budget.

Executive Budget

The budgetary process typically begins with the preparation of an executive budget by the executive branch of the government (for example, the governor, mayor, or county executive) for submission to the legislature. NCGAI 10 defines the *executive budget* as "the aggregate of information, proposals, and estimates prepared and submitted to the legislative body by the chief executive and the budget office." This budget represents the efforts of the chief executive to accumulate and filter all of the budget requests for spending authority submitted by the various agencies and departments of the government. It also includes estimates of the expected revenues and other financing sources that will be used to pay for that spending authority. In addition to specific agency requests, the executive budget should also reflect the executive branch's calculations of expenditures for required payments. For example, expenditures for debt service are seldom at the discretion of the government in terms of amounts to be paid or whether the payments will be made. Pension contributions are another example of expenditures that are usually determined centrally by the executive branch.

Appropriated Budget

The executive branch usually submits the executive budget to the legislative branch of the government. After discussion and negotiation between the executive branch and the legislature, the legislature will pass the budget for signature by the executive branch. At this point, the budget is known as an *appropriated budget*. NCGAI 10 defines an appropriated budget as "the expenditure authority created by the appropriation bills or ordinances which are signed into law and related estimated revenues. The appropriated budget would include all reserves, transfers, allocations, supplemental appropriations, and other legally authorized legislative and executive changes." The importance of the appropriated budget is that it contains the legally authorized level of expenditures (the appropriations) that the government cannot legally exceed.

Nonappropriated Budget

Certain aspects of the government may operate under a financial plan that does not need to go through the formal appropriations process described above. This type of budget is referred to as a *nonappropriated budget*. A nonappropriated budget is defined by NCGAI 10 as "a financial plan for an organization, program, activity, or function approved in a manner authorized by constitution, charter, statute, or ordinance but not subject to appropriation and therefore outside the boundaries of the definition of the appropriated budget." The extent to which governments use nonappropriated budgets depends on the extent to which these types of expenditures are specifically authorized (as described in the definition).

Budgetary Execution and Management

NCGAI 10 defines budgetary execution and management as "all other suballocation, contingency reserves, rescission, deferrals, transfers, conversions of language appropriations, encumbrance controls, and allotments established by the executive branch, without formal legislative enactment. These transactions may be relevant for various accounting control and internal reporting purposes, but are not part of the appropriated budget." Budget execution and management are the link between the higher-level appropriated budget described above and the more detailed budget that enables management of the government and its various agencies and departments to use the budget as a management and resource allocation tool. (See Exhibit 1.)

Exhibit 1: Budget setting example

The following example should help clarify some of the components of the budget setting process. Assume for this example that the only agency of a city government is the community development agency. The agency commissioner (or equivalent title) submits a detailed spending request to the mayor for the next fiscal year. The budget request is for $3 million for 50 staff members and managers, $2 million for other-than-personal-service overhead expenses, and $5 million for program activities to be performed by not-for-profit neighborhood organizations under contract with the city. This executive budget request is submitted to the legislature, which adopts the budget as proposed. In this example, the appropriated budget consists of the three amounts: $3 million for personal service expenditures, $2 million for overheads, and $5 million for contracts, representing the "legal level of control" that cannot be exceeded. The community development agency must then subdivide these amounts. For example, what positions will the $3 million personal service expenditures cover? How many managers? How many staff members? To what sublevels are managers and staff broken down? What are their salaries and scheduled salary increases during the next fiscal year? Similar questions must be asked about the overhead authorization. Also, how much of the $2 million will be spent for rent, utilities, supplies, transportation, training, and so forth? Similarly, the $5 million of authorized contract expenditures must be further broken down. What types of programs will be purchased? In what neighborhoods of the city will the programs be offered? These breakdowns of the three amounts that constitute the legal level of control are what is meant by budget execution and management. A sub-coding system is usually set up with what are sometimes called *budget codes*, or objects that can be summed to equal the legal level of control. The agency usually has discretion over transferring appropriations among these budget codes. The agency would be precluded, however, from moving any of the authorized appropriations among any of the three amounts that constitute the legal level of control. Approval of the legislative branch (which effectively means an amendment of the law that adopted the budget) would be required to transfer appropriations from one legal level of control to another.

NOTE: The importance of effective budgeting is highlighted by the existence of the Government Finance Officers' Association's Distinguished Budget Presentation Awards Program. Interested governments can submit budgetary documents to the GFOA under this program for consideration of the award, similar to the way that Comprehensive Annual Financial Statements (discussed in Chapter 9) can be submitted to the GFOA for consideration for its Certificate of Achievement for Excellence in Financial Reporting Award.

Budget Amendments

After adoption of a budget for a government's fiscal year, it often becomes necessary to make changes in the budget during the fiscal year. There are any number of reasons why budgets of governments might need to be amended. For example:

- Tax revenues may fall short of expectations, requiring the approved level of expenditures to be decreased.
- Unusual weather circumstances (above-normal snowfalls, hurricanes, floods, etc.) may result in the unforeseen use of significant amounts of a government's resources.
- Policy issues developing during the year may result in a government desiring to shift spending authority to new or different programs.
- Overtime and employee benefit costs may be more or less than expected.

When budgets are legally adopted, the budget modification process will be dictated by the local laws of the government. Frequently, government agencies are given the ability to shift budgetary funds for relatively small amounts among their various budget categories. In addition, there may be limits as to shifting funds between budget amounts for personal-service expenditures and other-than-personal-service expenditures. When budgetary changes are for other than insignificant amounts, the legislative body will usually be required to adopt a budget amendment to formally amend the budget.

As part of the local requirements mentioned above, the period of time during which the budget may be modified will vary among governments. For example, a budget amendment adopted on the last day of the government's fiscal year provides no control over the use of governmental resources, but may be used by a government to disguise large variances from an originally budgeted amount. Local laws may prevent this type of manipulation, although some governments actually have the ability to modify their budgets months after the end of their fiscal year.

Budgetary Reporting

GASBS 34 requires governments to include in required supplementary information (RSI) a budgetary comparison schedule containing original budget amounts, final budget amounts, and actual amounts for the general fund and for each major special revenue fund for which a budget is legally adopted. Instead of presenting their information as RSI, a government may elect to report the budgetary comparison information in a budgetary comparison statement as part of the basic financial statements. The actual amounts presented should be on the same basis of accounting that is used for the budgeted amounts. Variance columns are encouraged, but not required. GASBS 37 requires disclosure of excesses of expenditure over appropriations in the general fund and for each major special revenue fund that has a legally adopted annual budget.

The following definitions are provided in GASBS 34 to distinguish the original budget from the final budget:

- The original budget is the first complete appropriated budget. The original budget may be adjusted by reserves, transfers, allocations, supplemental appropriations, and other legally authorized legislative and executive changes before the beginning of the fiscal year. The original budget should also include actual appropriation amounts automatically carried over from prior years by law. For example, a legal provision may require the automatic rolling forward of appropriations to cover prior year encumbrances.
- The final budget is the original budget adjusted by all reserves, transfers, allocations, supplemental appropriations, and other legally authorized legislative and executive changes applicable to the fiscal year, whenever signed into law or otherwise legally authorized.

In addition, Management's Discussion and Analysis is required to include an analysis of significant variations between original and final budget amounts, and between final budget amounts and actual budget results for the general fund, or its equivalent. The analysis should contain any currently known reasons for those variations that are expected to have a significant effect on future services or liquidity.

GASB Statement 41, *Budgetary Comparison Schedules—Perspective Differences* (GASBS 41), addresses the issue of when significant budgetary differences result in a government's being unable to present budgetary comparison information for the general fund and major special revenue funds. Governments are required to present budgetary comparison schedules as RSI based on the fund, organization, or program structure that the government uses for its legally adopted budget. Basically, GASBS 41 provides that when there are significant perspective differences (perspective differences are described later in this chapter), the government is still required to present a budgetary comparison schedule. The schedule should use the perspective used in the legally adopted budget. However, this schedule must be reported as RSI. The government in this situation does not have the option to present the budgetary comparison information in a budgetary comparison statement that is part of the basic financial statements.

WHICH FUNDS OF THE GOVERNMENT ADOPT BUDGETS?

NCGAS 1 states that an annual budget should be adopted by every governmental unit. However, the adoption of budgets may be different for governmental and proprietary activities. In practice, the extent to which budgets are adopted for all funds varies significantly among governments, and there is equal variability in the extent to which there are legally adopted (appropriated) budgets. The following paragraphs summarize some of the common considerations about the budgets for the various governmental funds.

General Fund

Almost universally, a budget is legally adopted for the general fund. Because the most significant operating activities of the government are normally found in the general fund, there is also usually a great deal of budget management in the general fund. This budget management means that the legally adopted budget is broken down into smaller allocations that enable the government's management to manage the finances of the government's general fund.

Special Revenue Funds

Budgets are usually legally adopted for special revenue funds. However, to the extent that special revenue funds are used to account for grants and other expenditure-driven revenues, governments may choose not to legally adopt budgets for special revenue funds that account for these activities. In these cases, the rationale is that the particular grants or contracts provide sufficient controls over expenditures (and their related revenues) so that a legally adopted budget is not considered necessary.

Capital Projects Funds

Budgets for capital projects funds differ from budgets for other funds because capital projects generally span more than one year. Therefore, governments are likely to adopt budgets on a multiyear project basis, rather than having annual appropriations for all capital projects.

These multiyear project budgets may or may not be subject to approval of the legislature, based on the legal and operating environment of the particular government.

Debt Service Funds

Debt service funds adopt legal budgets infrequently. Debt service payments are determined under bond and note indentures and seldom require additional controls. In addition, governments normally transfer the annual debt service requirements of the debt service funds from the general fund to the debt service funds. The amount transferred from the general fund is already included in the legally adopted budget of the general fund. Governments should ensure, however, that they have in place a plan for debt service payments throughout the year so that as principal and interest payments or debt retirements occur, the debt service funds have sufficient resources to meet these obligations.

Proprietary Funds

Budgets are seldom legally adopted by proprietary funds. Proprietary funds often use budgeting in a manner similar to commercial enterprises. Budgets help proprietary funds determine whether their costs will be recovered or to estimate the amount of subsidy needed from the government if costs are not meant to be recovered. Proprietary fund budgets are sometimes referred to as "variable" or "flexible," because the expense budgets fluctuate with the volume of the revenue-generating activities.

Fiduciary Funds

Budgets are infrequently adopted for fiduciary funds. Trust funds and agency funds are controlled by the specific contracts or agreements that cause these funds to be established. Control over these assets by a legal process outside of these contracts or agreements would lessen the validity of the contracts or agreements. For example, government employees often contribute to deferred compensation plans established under Section 457 of the Internal Revenue Code, which are accounted for as fiduciary funds. It would not be appropriate for the government to have to legally adopt a budget of the amount of estimated account withdrawals to be made during the upcoming fiscal year.

DIFFERENCES BETWEEN THE BUDGET AND GAAP

As previously mentioned, there may be differences between budgetary accounting and reporting and GAAP-based accounting and reporting. As will be described in Chapter 9, a government's financial statements will include a financial statement that is actually prepared on the budgetary basis of accounting. NCGAI 10 describes the most significant categories that might give rise to these differences. These categories follow.

Basis of Accounting Differences

A government may choose to prepare its budget on a different basis of accounting than that required by GAAP. For example, while GAAP requires that the general fund use the modified accrual basis of accounting, a government may prepare its general fund budget on a different basis, such as the cash basis. Alternatively, a government may prepare its general fund budget on the modified accrual basis, with the exception of certain items that it elects to budget on a different basis, such as the cash basis.

Timing Differences

Budgets may be prepared using different time frames than the funds to which they relate use for financial reporting purposes. In addition, certain items (such as carryovers of appropriations) may be treated differently for budget purposes than for GAAP accounting and reporting. In some infrequent cases, governments adopt biennial budgets. One of the more common instances occurs when there are long-term projects that are budgeted for several years while the fund that accounts for the construction activities (such as the capital projects fund) prepares an annual budget.

Perspective Differences

Differences sometimes arise because the fund structure that governs the way in which transactions are reported under GAAP may differ from an organizational or program structure used for budgeting purposes. NCGAI 10 defines the *organizational structure* as "the perspective of a government that follows from the formal, usually statutory, patterns of authority and responsibility granted to actually carry out the functions of the government." In other words, it reflects the organizational chart and the superior/subordinate relationships that exist in actually running the government. These relationships may be different than those that would be reported for GAAP purposes within the fund structure. The program structure is defined by NCGAI 10 as "the grouping of the activities, assignments of personnel, uses of expenditure authority, facilities, and equipment all intended to achieve a common purpose." In other words, budgeting may be performed on a project basis while there may be various funds that pay for (1) the personnel assigned to the project (such as the general fund), (2) construction of the assets that the project personnel are using (such as the capital projects fund), and (3) the debt service on the money borrowed to construct the assets that the project personnel are using (such as the debt service fund).

Entity Differences

A government's appropriated budget may not include all of the entities included in its reporting entity. This is particularly important when component units are "blended" with the funds that make up the primary government. (More information is provided on the reporting entity in Chapter 11.) Governments may also legally adopt budgets for some funds, but not for all funds of a particular type of fund. These other funds would fall within the "nonappropriation budget" described earlier in this chapter.

The question naturally arises of what to do when budgetary reporting differs from reporting under GAAP. NCGAI 10 affirms that differences between the government's budget practices and GAAP not otherwise reconciled in the general-purpose financial statements that are attributable to basis, timing, perspective, and entity differences should be reconciled in the footnotes. Exhibit 2 provides an example of a reconciliation of a budget basis of accounting to a GAAP basis of accounting. It illustrates how this reconciliation may be shown in the notes to the financial statements.

Exhibit 2: Reconciling budget basis of accounting to GAAP basis of accounting

The city's budgetary basis of accounting used for budget versus actual reporting differs from GAAP. For budgetary purposes, encumbrances are recorded as expenditures, but are reflected as reservations of fund balance for GAAP purposes. Expenditures are recorded when paid in cash or encumbered for budgetary purposes, as opposed to when goods or services are received in accordance with GAAP. For budgetary purposes, property taxes are recognized as revenue in the year in which they become an enforceable lien. A reconciliation of the different bases of revenue and expenditure recognition for the year ended June 30, 20X1, is as follows:

General Fund	
Revenues, GAAP basis	$100,000
Add:	
Current year property tax levy	20,000
Deduct:	
Prior year property tax levy	(19,000)
Revenues, budgetary basis	$101,000
Expenditures, GAAP basis	$95,000
Add:	
Current year encumbrances	5,000
Prior year accrued liabilities recognized in the current year budget	15,000
Deduct:	
Payments on prior year encumbrances	(4,000)
Current year accrued liabilities not recognized in current year budget	(10,000)
Expenditures, budget basis	$101,000

BUDGETARY CONTROL

One of the primary purposes of budgeting is to provide control over the revenues and expenditures of the government. To achieve an appropriately high level of control, budgets must be integrated with the government's accounting system. This is particularly relevant for expenditures. To control and limit expenditures by the accounting system, it must have mechanisms and controls in place to ensure that budgets are not exceeded.

The accounting system budgetary controls reflect the fact that budgets include various levels of detail. For example, expenditures may be budgeted on a fundwide basis. The fundwide basis may be further divided into governmental functions. The budget for each governmental function may be further refined into budgets for several departments or agencies that perform the function. Each department's or agency's budget may be divided into several activities. For each activity, there may be further divisions into specific expenditure objects (such as for the type of expenditures: personal services, postage, rent, utilities, and so forth). Objects may be divided into subjects (for example, full- and part-time personnel and managerial and nonmanagerial personnel).

One of the important concepts in understanding how these controls should be designed and implemented is the legal level of control. The legal level of control represents the lowest budgetary level at which a government's management may not reassign resources without special approval. For an appropriated budget passed by a legislature, this special approval would encompass going back to the legislature to effectively have this body amend the law that adopted the original budget. The legal level of control can vary greatly from one government to another.

Although budgets are usually prepared at the level of detail described above, management often has the latitude to shift budget appropriations. This latitude is defined by each government. The accounting system must be able to accommodate this latitude, while at the same time ensuring that it is used only within the previously authorized parameters.

The budgetary controls used in an accounting system are more complicated than simply comparing actual expenditures to the total budget. Encumbrances must be considered, as well as any difference in the basis of accounting between the budget and GAAP. (Encumbrances represent commitments related to unfilled purchase orders or unfulfilled contracts. In other words, the government is committed or intends to spend the funds, but the actual goods or services have not been received. The encumbrance represents a "placeholder" that helps ensure that the budgeted funds for these commitments are not spent elsewhere.) Typically, a comparison of the expenditures authorized by appropriation is made with the sum of the following:

- Liquidated expenditures (goods and services have been received and the bill has been paid).
- Unliquidated expenditures (goods and services have been received, but the bill has not as yet been paid).
- Encumbrances (goods and services have not been received, but the government has committed to purchase [ordered] them).
- Preencumbrances (used by some governments when the government has not committed to purchase goods and services, but plans to in the future and wants to reserve the budget appropriation for these anticipated commitments).

The accounting system should consider all of these categories to effectively make budgetary comparisons, although many systems do not distinguish between liquidated and unliquidated expenditures. Most governments use at least some form of automated system designed to integrate these budgetary control comparisons. In "classical" governmental accounting, a budget entry is recorded on the books of the government to reflect the budget amounts. Often governments don't actually record this entry on their books and rely on the automated controls instead. However, since this is a complete and comprehensive guide to governmental accounting and financial reporting, the following examples walk through the journal entries of a government to record its budget. Exhibit 3 provides examples of journal entries that would be recorded by a government to record a budget.

Exhibit 3: Journal entry examples for recording a budget

Example 1

The following entry would be made to record the annual appropriated budget. Note that since the budget entries are meant to offset the actual amounts to arrive at budget-to-actual differences, the normal use of debits and credits is reversed. In other words, estimated revenues are recorded as a debit and expenditure appropriations are recorded as a credit.

Estimated revenues	1,000,000	
Appropriations		1,000,000

To record the annual appropriated budget

Example 2

While the above entry would reflect the situation in which the government expects the budget to be perfectly balanced, the government may budget to increase (or decrease) its fund balance. If the government expected revenues to be more than expenditures, it would record the following journal entry:

Estimated revenues	1,000,000	
Appropriations		950,000
Budgetary fund balance		50,000

To record the annual appropriated budget

These budget entries would stay on the books of the government throughout the fiscal year. At the end of the fiscal year, the budget entry would be reversed as follows, for each of the two examples described above:

Example 1

Appropriations	1,000,000	
Estimated revenues		1,000,000

To close the annual appropriated budget

Example 2

Appropriations	950,000	
Budgetary fund balance	50,000	
Estimated revenues		1,000,000

To close the annual appropriated budget

During the fiscal year, the government would theoretically record journal entries to record encumbrances as follows:

Encumbrances	100,000	
Budgetary fund balance—Reserved for encumbrances		100,000

To record an encumbrance related to a purchase order issued

When the goods or services bought with the purchase order are received by the government, the actual cost is $95,000. The following entries would be recorded:

Budgetary fund balance—Reserved for encumbrances	100,000	
Encumbrances		100,000

To reverse an encumbrance for goods and services received

Expenditures	95,000	
Vouchers/accounts payable		95,000

To record the liability relative to the receipt of goods and services

At the end of the fiscal year, there may be encumbrances still outstanding. Assume that $10,000 of encumbrances are outstanding at the end of the fiscal year. First, the government needs to remove the budgetary accounts from the books relating to the outstanding encumbrances. The following journal entry would be recorded:

Budgetary fund balance—Reserved for encumbrances	10,000	
Encumbrances		10,000

To remove budgetary accounts relating to outstanding encumbrances at the end of the fiscal year

If the government intends to honor the encumbrances in the following fiscal year, the government should record a reservation of fund balance to indicate that a portion of the fund balance will not be available for the following year because it already has been encumbered in the prior fiscal year. The following journal entry would be recorded:

Unrestricted fund balance	10,000	
Fund balance—Reserved for encumbrances		10,000

To establish a reserve of fund balance for encumbrances outstanding at year-end that the government will honor in subsequent fiscal years

At the beginning of the next fiscal year, to honor encumbrances of the prior fiscal year, the government would record the following two entries. First, the amount of the encumbrances should be reestablished for the next fiscal year by recording the following journal entry:

Encumbrances	10,000	
Budgetary fund balance—Reserved for encumbrances		10,000

To record encumbrances carried forward from the prior fiscal year

Second, a journal entry would be recorded to reflect the removal of the reservation of the prior year's ending fund balance. The following journal entry would be recorded:

Fund balance—Reserved for encumbrances	10,000	
Unreserved fund balance		10,000

To eliminate the reservation of fund balance relating to prior year encumbrances

In recording journal entries for budgets, it's important to keep in mind that at the close of the fiscal year, all budgetary journal entries should be removed from the books. Where encumbrances will be honored in following fiscal years, the effect on the books is solely the reservation of fund balance, which is not part of the "budgetary" journal entries that record and remove the budget from the books.

SUMMARY

As mentioned at the beginning of this chapter, budgets are an important part of maintaining control of a government's finances and are a means of achieving the financial reporting objective of accountability. Careful attention and reporting of budget-related matters are an important consideration in governmental accounting and financial reporting.

11 DEFINITION OF THE REPORTING ENTITY

INTRODUCTION

One of the challenges facing the preparer of financial statements for a governmental entity is to determine what entities should be included in the reporting entity of the government. Governments typically have related governmental entities and not-for-profit organizations that are so closely related to the government that their financial position and results of operations should be included with those of the government. These may also be for-profit organizations that should be included in the reporting entity of a government.

Unlike the consolidation principles used by private enterprises, there are no generally no "ownership" percentages in the governmental and not-for-profit environments that the accountant can examine to determine what entities should be consolidated with that of the government. GASB Statement No. 14 (GASBS 14), *The Financial Reporting Entity*, provides guidance on inclusion in the government's reporting entity. While GASBS 14's guidance has proven effective in helping governments determine the proper reporting entity, there is still a significant degree of judgment needed to define a government's reporting entity. The guidance for determining the reporting entity is not affected by the implementation of GASBS 34.

This chapter provides a discussion of the detailed requirements of GASBS 14 and includes some practical guidance on applying its principles. It also describes the provision of GASB Statement No. 39 (GASBS 39), *Determining Whether Certain Organizations Are Component Units—An Amendment of GASB Statement No. 14*. GASBS 39 provides that certain organizations for which a primary government is not financially accountable nevertheless warrant inclusion as part of the financial reporting entity because of the nature and significance of their relationship with the primary government, including their ongoing financial support of the primary government and its other component units.

This chapter also addresses GASB Statement No. 80 (GASBS 80), *Blending Requirements for Certain Component Units—An Amendment of GASB Statement No. 14* as well as GASB Statement No. 90 (GASBS 90), *Majority Equity Interests—An Amendment of GASB Statements No. 14 and No. 61*.

In addition, this chapter provides guidance on the accounting and financial reporting for government mergers, acquisitions, and transfers of operations of GASB Statement No. 69 (GASBS 69), *Government Combinations and Disposals of Government Operations*.

BACKGROUND

Governments often create separate legal entities to perform some of the functions normally associated with or performed by government. These separate entities may themselves be governmental entities or they may be not-for-profit or for-profit organizations. Sometimes these separate organizations are created to enhance revenues or reduce debt service costs of governments. Other times, these separate organizations are created to circumvent restrictions to which the state or local government would be subject. The following are some examples of these other organizations that are commonly created by a government:

- A separate public authority that operates as a utility, such as a water and sewer authority, may be created as a separate legal entity. Because a utility such as the water and sewer authority has a predictable revenue stream (the water and sewer charges to its customers), the utility will likely be able to sell debt in the form of revenue bonds, pledging the water and sewer charge revenues to the debt service on the revenue bonds. Because of this identification of a specific revenue stream, it is likely that the revenue bonds issued by the authority will carry a lower interest rate than general obligation bonds issued by the local government.
- A housing finance authority may be created to finance the construction of affordable housing. The rental income on the constructed rental units can be correlated with the

debt of the housing finance authority, again resulting in a lower interest cost to the government. The debt issued by the housing finance authority is likely to be issued without requiring a bond resolution approved by the voters of the jurisdiction. The existence of the housing finance authority expedites (or circumvents, in some minds) the government's flexibility as to when and how much debt it issues. In a related use of a financing agency, the state or local government may be approaching its statutory limit on its ability to issue debt. If the housing finance authority's debt is not included in the state or local government's debt limit calculation, the state or local government avoids having the debt issued by the housing finance authority count against its debt limit, even though the state or local government may have chosen to issue the debt itself.

- In some instances, a not-for-profit organization can be invested with powers that might require a constitution or charter amendment. For example, an economic development authority may be established to buy, sell, or lease land and facilities, assist businesses within the jurisdiction, or negotiate and facilitate tax rate reductions to encourage businesses to remain in or relocate to the jurisdiction. Usually this separately incorporated entity is able to assume more powers and operate with greater flexibility than the state or local government itself.

The types and purposes of these entities continue to expand as governments seek to facilitate operations and to enter new service areas needed by their constituents. The above are but a few examples of the types of entities and areas of responsibility that the financial statement preparer and auditor are likely to encounter.

ACCOUNTABILITY FOCUS

In developing new accounting principles relative to defining the reporting entity for state and local governments, the GASB focused on the concept of "accountability." As described in Chapter 2, the GASB has defined *accountability* as the cornerstone of governmental financial reporting, because the GASB believes that financial reporting plays a major role in fulfilling government's responsibility to the public.

Despite the outward appearance of autonomy, the organizations described above are usually administered by governing bodies appointed by the elected officials of the state or local government or by the government's officials serving in ex officio capacities of the created entities. These officials of the state or local government are accountable to the citizens of the government. These officials are accountable to the citizens for their public policy decisions, regardless of whether they are carried out by the state or local government itself or by the specially created entity. This broad-based notion of the accountability of government officials led the GASB to the underlying concept of the governmental financial reporting entity. GASBS 14 states that "governmental organizations are responsible to elected governing officials at the federal, state, or local level; therefore, financial reporting by a state or local government should report the elected officials' accountability for those organizations."

Because one of the key objectives of financial reporting as defined by the GASB is accountability, it became logical for the GASB to define the financial reporting entity in terms of the accountability of the government officials (and ultimately to the elected officials that appointed these government officials). The GASB also concluded that the users of financial statements should be able to distinguish between the financial information of the primary government and its component units (these terms are discussed in more detail below).

To accomplish the objectives and goals described above, the reporting entity's financial statements should present the fund types and account groups of the primary government (including certain component units whose financial information is blended with that of the primary government, because, in substance, they are part of the primary government) and provide an overview of the other component units, referred to as discretely presented component units.

FINANCIAL REPORTING ENTITY DEFINED

The GASBS 14 definition of the *financial reporting entity* is as follows:

> *... the financial reporting entity consists of (a) the primary government, (b) organizations for which the primary government is financially accountable, and (c) other organizations for which the nature and significance of their relationship with the primary government are such that exclusion would cause the reporting entity's financial statements to be misleading or incomplete.*

Primary Government

The *primary government* is defined as a separately elected governing body—that is, one that is elected by the citizens in a general, popular election. A primary government is any state or local government (such as a municipality or county). A primary government may also be a special-purpose government, such as a department of parks and recreation or a school district, if it meets all of the following criteria:

- It has a separately elected governing body.
- It is legally separate (defined below).
- It is fiscally independent of other state and local governments (defined below).

A primary government consists of all of the organizations that make up its legal entity. This would include all funds, organizations, institutions, agencies, departments, and offices that are not legally separate. If an organization is determined to be part of the primary government, its financial information should be included with the financial information of the primary government.

It is important to note that a governmental organization that is not a primary government (including component units, joint ventures, jointly governed organizations, or other stand-alone governments) will still be the nucleus of its own reporting entity when it issues separate financial statements. Although GASBS 14 addresses reporting issues for primary governments, these other organizations should apply the guidance of GASBS 14 as if they were a primary government when issuing separate financial statements.

NOTE: An example of this latter point of an entity other than a primary government being the nucleus of its own reporting entity might clarify this situation.

Assume that a city located on a major river establishes a separate legal entity to manage its port operations and foster shipping and other riverfront activities. The port authority is a separate legal entity, although its governing board is appointed by the city's mayor; that is, the governing board is not elected. The port authority is not a primary government.

However, assume the port authority itself sets up two additional separate legal entities: an economic development authority (to promote economic activity on the riverfront) and a souvenir shop (to raise funds as well as to publicize the riverfront activities). If these two separate entities meet the tests described in the chapter to be considered component units of the port authority, they would be included in the port authority's reporting entity, even though the port authority is not a primary government.

Separate legal standing. GASBS 14 provides specific guidance to determine whether a special-purpose government qualifies as legally separate, which is one of the three criteria for consideration as a primary government.

An organization has separate legal standing if it is created as a body corporate or a body corporate and politic, or if it otherwise possesses the corporate powers that would distinguish it as being legally separate from the primary government. Corporate powers generally give an organization the capacity to, among other things:

- Have a name.
- Have the right to sue or be sued in its own name and without recourse to a state or local governmental unit.
- Have the right to buy, sell, lease, and mortgage property in its own name.

Financial statement preparers should look to the organization's charter or the enabling legislation that created the organization to determine what its corporate powers are. A special-purpose government (or other organization) that is not legally separate should be considered for financial reporting purposes as part of the primary government that holds the corporate powers described above.

Determining fiscal independence or dependence. A special-purpose government must also demonstrate that it is fiscally independent of other state or local governments to be considered a primary government. A special-purpose government is considered to be fiscally independent if it has the ability to complete certain essential fiscal events without substantive approval by a primary government. A special-purpose government is fiscally independent if it has the authority to do all of the following:

- Determine its budget without another government's having the authority to approve and modify that budget.
- Levy taxes or set rates or charges without approval by another government.
- Issue bonded debt without the approval of another government.

The approvals included in these three criteria refer to substantive approval and not mere ministerial or compliance approvals. GASBS 14 offers the following examples of approvals that are likely to be ministerial or compliance oriented rather than substantive:

- A requirement for a state agency to approve local government debt after review for compliance with certain limitations, such as a debt margin calculation based on a percentage of assessed valuation.
- A requirement for a state agency such as a department of education to review a local government's budget in evaluating qualifications for state funding.
- A requirement for a county government official such as a county clerk to approve tax rates and levy amounts after review for compliance with tax rate and levy limitations.

A special-purpose government subject to substantive approvals should not be considered a primary government. An example of a substantive approval is if a government has the authority to modify a special-purpose government's budget.

In determining fiscal independence using the criteria listed above, the financial statement preparer must be careful in determining whether approval is required or the special-purpose government is legally authorized to enter into a transaction. For example, consider a special-purpose government that would otherwise meet the criteria for fiscal independence, but is statutorily prohibited from issuing debt. In this case, a special-purpose government's fiscal independence is not precluded because its issuance of debt is not subject to the approval of another government. Rather, it is simply prohibited from issuing debt by statute.

Another situation may be encountered in which a primary government is temporarily placed under the fiscal control of another government. A common example of this would be when a state government temporarily takes over the fiscal oversight of a school district. A primary government temporarily under the fiscal control of another government is still considered fiscally independent for purposes of preparing its financial statements as a primary government under the criteria of GASBS 14. The reason is that the control of the primary government is only temporary and fiscal independence will be restored in the future.

Component units. Component units are organizations that are legally separate from the primary government for which the elected officials of the primary government are financially accountable. A component unit may be a governmental organization (except a governmental organization that meets the definition of a primary government), a not-for-profit organization, or even a for-profit organization. In addition to qualifying organizations that meet the "financial accountability" criteria (described more fully below), a component unit can be another type of organization whose relationship with the primary government requires its inclusion in the reporting entity's financial statements. As will be more fully described later in this chapter, once it is determined that the organization is a component unit included in the reporting entity, the financial statement preparer decides whether the component unit's financial information should be "blended" with that of the primary government or "discretely presented." Exhibit 1 presents a decision-tree flowchart adapted from GASBS 14 that will assist the reader in applying the tests to determine whether a related entity is a component unit.

Financial accountability. The GASB is careful to distinguish accountability from financial accountability. Elected officials are accountable for an organization if they appoint a voting majority of the organization's governing board. However, these appointments are sometimes not substantive because other governments, usually at a lower level, may have oversight responsibility for those officials. GASBS 14 uses the term *financial accountability* to describe the relationship that is substantive enough to warrant the inclusion of the legally separate organization in the reporting entity of another government. The criteria for determining whether a legally separate organization is financially accountable to a government, and therefore must be considered a component unit of the government's reporting entity, are:

- The primary government is financially accountable if it appoints a voting majority of the organization's governing body, and (1) it is able to impose its will on that organization or (2) there is a potential for the organization to provide specific financial benefits to, or impose specific financial burdens on, the primary government. (In determining whether the primary government appoints a majority of the organization's board, the situation may be encountered where the members of the organization's governing body consist of the primary government's officials serving as required by law, that is, as ex officio members.

Exhibit 1: Flowchart to determine whether a related entity is a component unit

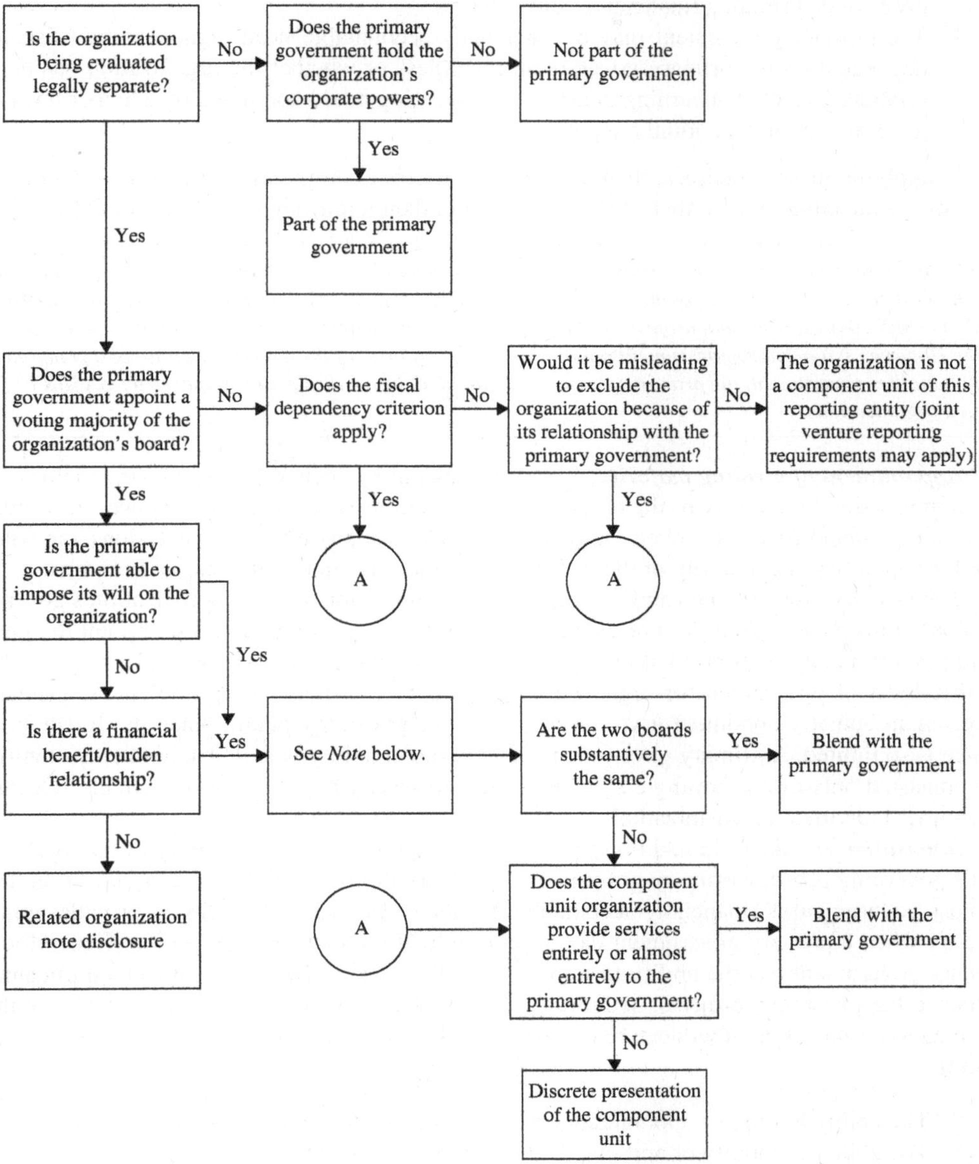

Source: This flowchart is adapted from a similar flowchart contained in Appendix C of GASBS 14. It should be used as a guide in applying the detailed component unit criteria described in this chapter.

While not technically "appointed" [because the individuals serve on the organization's board because their positions make them board members by law], this situation should be treated as if the individuals were actually appointed by the primary government for purposes of determining financial accountability.)

- The primary government may be financially accountable if an organization is fiscally dependent on the primary government regardless of whether the organization has (1) a separately elected governing board, (2) a governing board appointed by a higher level of government, or (3) a jointly appointed board.

In applying these principles, there are several matters to define more carefully. GASBS 14 clarifies the meaning of a number of terms to assist in their application, as shown in Exhibit 1.

NOTE: An organization for which a primary government is financially accountable may be fiscally dependent on another government. An organization should be included as a component unit of only one reporting entity. GASBS 14 prescribes that professional judgment be used to determine the most appropriate reporting entity. However, if a primary government appoints a voting majority of the governing board of a component unit of another government, the primary government should make the disclosures required by GASBS 14 for related organizations.

Appointment of a voting majority. A primary government generally has a voting majority if it appoints a simple majority of the organization's governing board members. However, if more than a simple majority of the governing board is needed to approve financial decisions, the criterion for appointing the majority of the board to determine accountability has not been met.

The primary government's ability to appoint a voting majority of the organization's governing board must have substance. For example, if the primary government must appoint the governing board members from a list or slate of candidates that is very narrow and controlled by another level of government or organization, it would be difficult to argue that the primary government actually appointed a voting majority of a governing board, since the freedom of choice is so limited. A primary government's appointment ability would also not be substantive if it consisted only of confirming candidates to the governing board that were actually selected by another individual or organization.

Imposition of will. If, in addition to its ability to appoint a voting majority of an organization's governing board, a primary government is able to impose its will on the organization, the primary government is financially accountable for the organization. GASBS 14 provides guidance on when a primary government can impose its will on another organization. Generally, a primary government has the ability to impose its will on an organization if it can significantly influence the programs, projects, activities, or level of services performed or provided by the organization. Imposition of will can be demonstrated by the existence of any one of the following conditions:

- The ability to remove appointed members of the organization's governing board.
- The ability to modify or approve the budget of the organization.
- The ability to modify or approve rate or fee changes affecting revenues, such as water usage rate increases.
- The ability to veto, overrule, or modify the decisions (other than the budget and rates or fee changes listed above) of the organization's governing body.
- The ability to appoint, hire, reassign, or dismiss those persons responsible for the day-to-day operations or management of the organization.

GASBS 14 acknowledges that there are other conditions that may exist that also indicate that the primary government has the capability to impose its will on another organization. As with the previously described tests, the focus should be on substantive instances where the primary government's will can be imposed, rather than on insignificant or ministerial approvals.

Financial benefit to or burden on the primary government. As described above, financial accountability for another organization can be demonstrated by a primary government if the primary government appoints a majority of the organization's governing board and imposes its will on the organization. In addition to these tests, there is another test that a government can use to demonstrate financial accountability for another organization. If the primary government appoints a voting majority of the organization's governing board and there is a potential for the organization to either provide specific financial benefits to or impose specific financial burdens on the primary government, the primary government is financially accountable for the organization.

The benefit or burden to the primary government may be demonstrated in several ways, such as legal entitlements or obligations or reflection of the benefit or burden in decisions made by the primary government or agreements between the primary government and the organization.

GASBS 14 lists the following conditions, any one of which could demonstrate that the primary government and the organization have a financial burden or benefit relationship:

- The primary government is legally entitled to or can otherwise access the organization's resources.
- The primary government is legally obligated or has otherwise assumed the obligation to finance the deficits of, or provide financial support to, the organization.
- The primary government is obligated in some manner for the debt of the organization.

The above conditions would not include exchange transactions, in which a primary government purchases or sells goods or services to or from the organization. In exchange transactions, both parties give something up and receive something in return whose values are approximately the same. Therefore, an exchange transaction would not demonstrate the financial burden or benefit relationship contemplated by this aspect of financial accountability contained in GASBS 14. In evaluating whether there is a financial burden or benefit relationship, the financial statement preparer should recognize that the financial burden or benefit may be direct or indirect. A direct financial burden or benefit occurs when the primary government is entitled to the resources or is obligated for the deficits or debts of the organization. An indirect benefit or burden exists if one or more of the primary government's component units is entitled to the resources or is obligated for the deficits or debts of the organization. For purposes of applying the financial burden or benefit provision, if the primary government is either directly or indirectly entitled to the resources or directly or indirectly obligated for the deficits or debts of the organization, then the financial benefit or burden test has been met.

GASBS 14 provides additional guidance in applying the financial benefit and burden provisions listed above. The following paragraphs describe this guidance and highlight some considerations for the financial statement preparer.

- **Legally entitled to or can otherwise access the organization's resources**. To meet this test, the important factor to consider is whether the primary government has the ability to access the resources of the organization, not whether the primary government has actually exercised this ability by extracting resources from the organization in the past. In determining whether this ability exists, it is necessary to evaluate whether the organization would continue to exist as a going concern. In other words, if the primary government can only access the organization's assets in the event of the liquidation of the organization, it would not be considered an ability to access the resources of the organization for purposes of applying this test.

In some cases, the ability to access the assets of the organization is fairly obvious. For example, if an organization is established to administer a lottery for a state or local primary government, the primary government is likely to have easy access to the assets of the lottery authority. In fact, there are likely to be daily, weekly, or monthly transfers of revenues from the lottery authority to the primary government. However, sometimes the access to assets is less clear. For example, a state government may be able to access excess funds held by a state housing finance authority that are not needed for the authority's operations. While there may be no strong precedent for the state to take the excess funds from the housing finance authority, and such an event might be rare, the state's right to do so would be adequate to meet the test.

- **Legally obligated or has otherwise assumed the obligation to finance the deficits of, or provide financial support to, the organization.** If a primary government appoints a voting majority of an organization's board and has legally or otherwise assumed the obligation to finance the deficits of, or provide financial support to, that organization, the primary government is financially accountable for that organization. It is important to note that the primary government may either be legally obligated to provide the financial support, or it may choose to be obligated to provide the financial support, for a variety of reasons. GASBS 14 provides two examples of when a primary government assumes the obligation to financially support another organization.
- Organizations are sometimes established to provide public services financed by user charges that are not expected to be sufficient to sustain their operations. Typical examples include higher education, mass transportation, and health care services. In these cases, a public policy decision is made to require a state or local government to provide financial support to the organization to increase the availability and affordability of the service to a broader segment of citizens. The support from the primary government may take a number of forms, including annual appropriations to meet operating costs, periodic capital grants, or payments of debt service on behalf of the organization.
- A primary government may also assume the obligation to finance the deficits of an organization. These deficits may or may not be expected to recur annually. A financial burden exists, for the purposes of applying this test, regardless of whether the primary government has ever actually financed the organization's deficit, or even if the organization has never actually had a deficit. The key is the *obligation* to finance the deficit, not whether it has actually occurred.

In other cases, an organization's operations are funded fully or partially by revenues generated through tax increment financing. Legally separate development or redevelopment authorities sometimes receive the incremental taxes resulting from tax increment financing arrangements. In this case, a taxing government temporarily waives its right to receive the incremental taxes from its own levy. The incremental taxes instead are remitted to the separate organization. This type of tax increment financing should be considered evidence of an obligation to provide financial support to an organization (that is, a financial burden), regardless of whether the primary government collects the taxes and remits them to the organization or the incremental taxes are paid directly to the organization.

- **Obligated in some manner for the debt of the organization.** The concept of a primary government being obligated in some manner for the debt of the organization is similar to that of the primary government being responsible for operating deficits in determining whether the organization should be included in the reporting entity of the primary government. The obligation on the part of the primary government for the debt of the organization can be either expressed or implied. A primary government is considered to be obligated in some manner for the debt of an organization if:
  - It is legally obligated to assume all or part of the debt in the event of default by the organization on the debt; or
  - It may take certain actions to assume secondary liability for all or part of the debt, and the primary government takes (or has given indications that it will take) those actions.

GASBS 14 notes the following conditions that would indicate that the primary government is obligated in some manner for the debt of the organization:

- The primary government is legally obligated to honor deficiencies to the extent that proceeds from other default remedies are insufficient.
- The primary government is required to temporarily cover deficiencies with its own resources until funds from the primary repayment source or other default remedies are available.
- The primary government is required to provide funding for reserves maintained by the debtor organization, or to establish its own reserve or guarantee fund for the debt.
- The primary government is authorized to provide funding for reserves maintained by the debtor organization or to establish its own reserve or guarantee fund and the primary government establishes such a fund. (If the fund is not established, the considerations of the conditions listed below in which the government "may" cover the deficiencies nevertheless provide evidence that the primary government is obligated in some manner.)
- The primary government is authorized to provide financing for a fund maintained by the debtor organization for the purpose of purchasing or redeeming the organization's debt, or to establish a similar fund of its own, and the primary government establishes such a fund. (As in the preceding example, if such a fund is not established, the intentions or probability of the primary government to cover the debt may nevertheless provide evidence that the primary government is obligated in some manner.)
- The debtor government explicitly indicates by contract, such as a bond agreement or offering statement, that in the event of a default, the primary government may cover deficiencies, although it has no legal obligation to do so. The bond offering statement may specifically refer to a law that authorizes the primary government to include an appropriation in its budget to provide funds, if necessary, to honor the debt of the organization.
- Legal decisions within the state or previous actions by the primary government related to actual or potential defaults on another organization's debt make it probable that the primary government will assume responsibility for the debt in the event of default.

If the primary government appoints a voting majority of the organization's governing body and is obligated in some manner for the debt of the organization, the primary government is financially accountable for that organization.

Concept of fiscal dependency. A primary government may be fiscally accountable for another organization regardless of whether the other organization has a separately elected governing board, a board appointed by another government, or a jointly appointed board. The fiscal accountability in these cases results from the organization's fiscal dependency on the primary government. GASBS 14 describes the circumstances for each of the three examples of the origins of the governing board listed above.

1. **Special-purpose governments with separately elected governing boards.** Special-purpose governmental entities with separately elected governments may be fiscally dependent on a primary government. The best example of a fiscally dependent special-purpose government is a school district. For example, a school board may be separately elected; however, if the primary government approves the school board's budgets and levies taxes to fund the school district, the school district is fiscally dependent on the primary government and should be included as a component unit in the primary government's reporting entity.
2. **Governmental organizations with boards appointed by another government.** Fiscal dependency may also exist even when the organization's governing board is appointed by a higher-level government. Continuing with the school district example, the local school board may be appointed by state officials, although the local primary government approves the school board's budgets, authorizes the school board's issuance of debt, and levies property taxes on the citizens of the primary government to financially support the school board. In this case, the school board would usually be included as a component unit of the local primary government. The school board is fiscally dependent on the local primary government, even though it does not appoint a voting majority of the members of the school board.
3. **Governmental organizations with jointly appointed boards.** The type of governmental entity with a jointly appointed board is often a port authority, river authority, transportation authority, or other regional government that adjoins several governments. Sometimes these governmental organizations are governed by boards in which none of the participating primary governments appoints a majority of the voting board members. If this type of governmental organization is fiscally dependent on only one of the participating primary governments, it should be included as a component unit of the reporting entity of that primary government. For example, if a port authority serves two states and is governed by a board appointed equally by the two states, and is empowered to issue debt with the substantive approval of only one of the states, the port authority should be included in the reporting entity of that state government.

GASB STATEMENT NO. 61 (GASBS 61), *THE FINANCIAL REPORTING ENTITY—AN AMENDMENT OF GASB STATEMENTS NO. 14 AND NO. 34*

The accounting guidance for determining what entities should be included in a government's financial reporting entity and how those entities should be presented had not been addressed by the GASB since implementation of the financial reporting model promulgated by GASBS 34. Accordingly, GASBS 61 addresses these issues. A fine-tuning of the requirements has resulted, rather than a massive change in reporting entities and presentation.

GASBS 61 changes certain requirements for inclusion of component units in the financial reporting entity. Specifically:

- For organizations that were previously required to be included as component units by meeting the fiscal dependency criterion, a financial benefit or burden relationship would also have to be present between the primary government and the organization for it to be included as a component unit.
- For organizations that do not meet the financial accountability criteria for inclusion but that should be included because the primary government's management determines that it would be misleading to exclude them, the proposed statement clarifies the manner in which that determination should be made and the types of relationships that generally should be considered in making that determination.

GASBS 61 also amends the criteria for reporting component units as blended component units (i.e., as if they were part of the primary government). Specifically:

- For component units that are currently blended based upon the "substantively the same governing body" criterion, GASBS 61 requires that:
- The primary government and the component unit have a financial benefit or burden relationship; or
- Management below the level of elected officials of the primary government have the operational responsibility (as defined) for the activities of the component unit.
- Blending is required for component units whose total debt outstanding is expected to be repaid entirely or almost entirely with resources of the primary government.
- Funds of a blended component unit have the same characteristics and the same reporting options as a fund of a primary government. The general fund of a blended component unit should be reported as a special revenue fund.
- Additional reporting guidance would be provided for blending a component unit if the primary government is a business-type activity that uses a single-column presentation for financial reporting. The component unit may be blended by consolidating its financial statement data within the single column of the primary government and presenting combining information in the notes to the financial statements.

GASBS 61 also requires a primary government to report its equity interest in a component unit as an asset, with the asset being eliminated in the blending process if the component unit meets the blending criteria.

DETERMINING WHETHER CERTAIN FUNDRAISING ORGANIZATIONS ARE COMPONENT UNITS—*AMENDMENT OF GASB STATEMENT NO. 14*

The GASB issued GASBS 39, which provides that certain organizations for which a primary government is not financially accountable nevertheless warrant inclusion as part of the financial reporting entity because of the nature and significance of their relationship with the primary government, including their ongoing financial support of the primary government and its other component units.

A legally separate, tax-exempt organization should be reported as a component unit of a reporting entity if all of the following criteria are met:

- The economic resources received or held by the separate organization are entirely or almost entirely for the direct benefit of the primary government, its component units, or its constituents.

- The primary government, or its component units, is entitled to, or has the ability to otherwise access, a majority of the economic resources received or held by the separate organization.
- The economic resources received or held by an individual organization that the specific primary government, or its component units, is entitled to, or has the ability to otherwise access, are significant to that primary government.

In addition, GASBS 39 states that other organizations should be evaluated as potential component units if they are closely related to, or financially integrated with, the primary government. It is a matter of professional judgment to determine whether the nature and the significance of a potential component unit's relationship with the primary government warrant inclusion in the reporting entity.

NOTE: The rules promulgated by GASBS 39 in the first two bullets above qualify many organizations that raise funds that are used by governmental entities for inclusion in the government's reporting entity. This would include foundations for public colleges or universities as well as public health care facilities. Even parent associations that raise money for school districts would meet these first two criteria in many cases, of course dependent upon how the not-for-profit organizations are actually set up. However, the third bullet, wherein the number of resources that the primary government has access to or is entitled to should be significant to the primary government, will likely cause fewer of these types of not-for-profit organizations to be included within a primary government's reporting entity.

Reporting of Component Units

GASBS 39 prescribes that organizations that meet all three criteria described above and are to be included in the reporting entity as component units should be treated as discretely presented component units. In other words, the financial statements of these component units should not be blended with those of the primary government. However, the other organizations described above that are reported as component units because they are closely related to, or financially integrated with, the primary government may be presented as either blended or discretely presented component units, depending upon how they meet the criteria for each specified in GASBS 14. (The financial statement display requirements of GASBS 14 are discussed later in this chapter.)

Other Organizations That Are Included in the Reporting Entity

In applying the criteria and conditions that indicate financial accountability, a significant amount of judgment is required on the part of the financial statement preparer, because the breadth of variation in the "typical" governmental reporting entity is wide. In addition, GASBS 14 specifies that certain organizations should be included in the reporting entity of a primary government even if the financial accountability test is not met. These organizations should be included as component units if the nature and significance of their relationships with the primary government are such that exclusion from the financial reporting entity of the primary government would make the primary government's financial statements incomplete or misleading. Clearly, a significant amount of judgment is required for compliance with this provision by the primary government. GASBS 14 provides some guidance and examples on applying this provision.

Organizations should be evaluated as potential component units if they are closely related to the primary government. Organizations affiliated with governmental units, agencies, colleges, universities, hospitals, and other entities may need to be included based on the closeness of their relationships. For example, a not-for-profit organization whose purpose is to raise funds for a governmental university may have such a close relationship with the governmental university that it should be included in the reporting entity. Issues such as these have been further addressed by the GASB in GASBS 39.

As another example, authorities with state-appointed boards may be created to provide temporary fiscal assistance to a local government. The authority should be evaluated as a potential component unit of the local government. If the authority issues debt on behalf of the local government and serves as a conduit for receiving dedicated revenues of the local government designated for repayment of the debt, the nature and significance of the relationship between the authority and the local government would warrant including it as a component unit. The temporary nature of the state authority emphasizes that the debt and revenues are, in substance, the debt and revenues of the local government.

NOTE: The larger the governmental organization, the more difficult it will be to identify all potential component units and to analyze whether each potential component unit should actually be included in the reporting entity. As will be discussed in the following section, once a decision is made to include a component unit in the reporting entity, an additional decision must be made as to whether its financial information will be blended with the primary government or presented discretely. One of the best ways to perform this analysis is to use a questionnaire to be completed by the reporting entity's potential component units. While this was particularly important during the implementation of GASBS 14, a questionnaire is still very useful to periodically review the status of all component units, because events and legal structures may change the initial determination. The questionnaire is also useful when new entities are created. These new entities should be asked to complete the questionnaire as a basis for their consideration as potential component units. (A sample questionnaire is provided at the end of this chapter.) This questionnaire should be tailored to the particular needs of the government. The replies to the questionnaire should be used as the initial step in determining the status as a component unit. While the responses to the questionnaire include some organizations that should clearly be component units and some that should not, there will be many responses that require additional research to fine-tune and clarify responses and to identify areas in which substance and form may be different.

GASB STATEMENT NO. 90 (GASBS 90), *MAJORITY EQUITY INTERESTS—AN AMENDMENT OF GASB STATEMENTS NO. 14 AND NO. 61*

In August 2018, the GASB issued GASBS 90 that modifies previous guidance for reporting a government's majority equity interest in a legally separate organization. It also provides guidance for reporting a component unit if a government acquires a 100 percent equity interest in that component unit.

For purposes of applying GASBS 90, an equity interest is a financial interest in a legally separate organization evidenced by ownership of shares of the organization's stock or by otherwise having an explicit, measurable right to the net resources of the organization that is usually based on an investment of financial or capital resources of the government. An equity interest is explicit and measurable under GASBS 90 if the government has a present or future claim to the net resources of the entity and the method for measuring the government's share of the entity's resources is determinable.

The basic guidance of GASBS 90 provides guidance for how to account for a majority equity interested as an investment and as a component unit.

Investment Accounting

GASBS 90 notes that a government can own or acquire a majority of the equity interest in a legally separate organization (such as by acquiring voting stock or a corporation or acquiring an interest in a partnership). If the holding of that equity interest meets the definition of an investment under GASBS Statement No. 72, Fair Value Measurement and Application (GASBS 72), the equity interest should be reported as an investment and measured using the equity method of accounting, with the following exception. If a special-purpose government engaged only in fiduciary activities, a fiduciary fund, or an endowment or permanent fund holds a majority equity interest in a legally separate organization that meets the definition of an investment, that majority equity interest should be measured at fair value. This exception might be commonly encountered in the financial statements of pension plans.

Component Unit Accounting

If the majority equity interest as described above does not meet the definition of an investment, GASBS 90 concludes that holding the majority equity interest results in the government being financially accountable for the organization, and therefore the government should report the legally separate organization as a component unit.

GASBS 90 provides that the majority equity interest reported as a component unit should be reported as an asset of the government that holds the equity interest measured using the equity method of accounting. However, if the component unit is blended, the asset and net position should be eliminated in the blending process. In financial statements prepared using the current financial resources measurement focus, GASBS 90 provides that the asset representing the government's equity interest should be limited to amounts appropriately reported under the current financial resources measurement focus.

If a government acquires a 100 percent equity interest that is reported as a component unit in accordance with the provisions discussed above, GASBS 90 provides that the provisions of GASBS 69 (discussed later in this chapter) should be applied at the date on which the government acquires the 100 percent equity interest. In applying that guidance, GASBS 90 provides that the consideration provided should include the net resources exchanged to complete the acquisition of the 100 percent equity interest plus the balances of any equity interest asset and deferred outflow of resources recognized prior to the completion of the 100 percent equity interest. The net position acquired should be equal to the net position of the component unit after measuring assets, deferred outflows of resources, liabilities, and deferred inflows of resources. The flows statements should include only those transactions that occurred subsequent to the acquisition of the 100 percent equity interest.

Effective Date

GASBS 90 is effective for reporting periods beginning after December 15, 2018, with earlier application encouraged. The provisions for reporting a majority interest as a component unit should be applied prospectively. The other provisions should be applied retroactively by restating financial statements, if practicable, for all periods presented. If not practicable, the cumulative effect of applying GASBS 90 should be reported as a restatement of beginning net position for the earliest period presented.

GASB TECHNICAL BULLETIN 2004-1 (GASBTB 2004-1), *TOBACCO SETTLEMENT RECOGNITION AND FINANCIAL REPORTING ENTITY ISSUES*

The GASB issued GASBTB 2004-1 to address certain financial accounting and reporting issues relating to revenues received by state and local governments as a result of the settlement of tobacco-related claims. In 1998 the U.S. tobacco industry reached an agreement with state governments releasing tobacco companies from present and future smoking-related claims that had been, or potentially could be, filed by states. The tobacco companies agreed to make annual payments in perpetuity to the states, subject to certain conditions and adjustments. The agreement is commonly referred to as the Master Settlement Agreement, or MSA. The states of California and New York entered into additional agreements with their county governments and certain major cities to allocate a specific portion of their ongoing annual settlement payments to those local governments. Some of the governments receiving revenues under these agreements have created separate legal entities (which GASBTB 2004-1 calls tobacco settlement authorities, or TSAs) to issue debt and to obtain the rights to all or a portion of the settling governments' future tobacco settlement revenues (or, as referred to in GASBTB 2004-1, TSRs).

GASBTB 2004-1, through a series of six questions and answers, addresses two primary issues. The first is whether a TSA would be part of the reporting entity of a primary government, and, if so, whether it should be presented as a blended or discretely presented component unit. The second issue is whether future anticipated revenues under the MSA should be recognized as a receivable and in the financial statements. The following are three of the six questions addressed by GASBTB 2004-1 along with a synopsis of the answers. Note that the answers address the common manner in which TSAs have been created.

Question 1—Is a TSA that is created by a settling government to obtain the rights to all or a portion of the government's TSRs a component unit of that government?

The requirements of GASB Statement 14 (GASBS 14), *The Financial Reporting Entity*, provide the foundation for the response to this question. Similar structures have been used by governments in creating separate organizations for the purpose of selling bonds and using the proceeds to obtain the government's TSRs. Generally, the government appoints a voting majority of the TSA's governing board. TSA boards are usually comprised of certain of the government's officials (by virtue of their office or title), by appointees of the government, or by a combination of the two. Accordingly, the GASBS 14 criterion for financial accountability by the appointment of a voting majority of the governing board would be met.

Generally, the settling government is ultimately entitled to the proceeds of any future bond issuances by the TSA and any TSRs not needed for debt service or to pay the operating expenses of the TSA. By virtue of the TSA's unequivocal right to future TSRs and the government's right to the potential excess resources of the TSA, GASBTB 2004-1 concludes that the government is entitled to the resources of the TSA. When this entitlement is combined with the appointment of the voting majority of the TSA's governing board, the financial accountability criteria are met and the TSA should be reported as a component unit of the settling government.

Question 2—Should a component unit TSA be included in the settling government's financial reporting entity through blending or discrete presentation?

GASBTB 2004-1 provides that the terms of legislation creating a TSA and the provisions of the agreement between the TSA and the settling government establish a relationship that would generally require the TSA component unit to be blended. This conclusion is based on GASBS 14, which provides that blending is required for component units that exclusively provide benefits to the primary government, including financing services provided solely to the primary government.

Question 3—Should a settling government recognize an asset and related revenue for future MSA payments?

The most significant factor affecting the annual payments under the MSA is a volume adjustment, which creates a direct relationship between domestic shipment of cigarettes and the annual payments. Based on the MSA, the tobacco companies have no obligation to make settlement payments until cigarettes are shipped.

Because annual TSR payments are based on cigarette sales from the preceding calendar year, governments should estimate accrued TSRs that derive from sales from January 1 to their respective fiscal year-ends. Under the modified accrual basis of accounting, revenue should be recognized to the extent that the event occurs and the resources become available.

NOTE: Chapter 15 describes the provisions of GASB Statement No. 48 (GASBS 48), Sales and Pledges of Receivables and Future Revenues and Intra-Entity Transfers of Assets and Future Revenues. While GASBS 48 does not address the reporting entity issues addressed by GASBTB 2004-1, its guidance should be used for accounting purposes for recording these types of transactions.

DISPLAY OF COMPONENT UNITS

The issue of which organizations should be included in the financial reporting entity of a state or local government is the first of a two-step process in addressing the financial statements of a state or local government. After determining which component units to include in the financial reporting entity of the government, the second step is to determine how the financial information of those component units (and their related disclosures) will be presented. This section addresses this second step of presenting the financial information of the component units as part of the financial statements of the reporting entity of the state or local government.

Overview of Reporting Component Units

An objective of the financial statements of the reporting entity should be to provide an overview of the entity based on financial accountability while at the same time allowing financial statement users to distinguish among the financial information of the primary government and the financial information of the component units. As will be more fully described later in this chapter, some component units are so closely related to the primary government that their information is blended with that of the primary government. Other component units, which generally comprise the majority of component units, should be presented discretely from the primary government.

One other factor to consider in this overview of financial reporting is that a component unit of a reporting entity may itself have component units. To further an example presented earlier, a not-for-profit organization that raises funds for a governmental university may be a component unit of that governmental university. At the same time, the governmental university may be a component unit of the state government to which it is financially accountable. While the not-for-profit organization is not a component unit of the state, its financial information will be included in the state's reporting entity, because in treating the governmental university as a component unit of the state, all of the component units of the governmental university are included with the financial information of the governmental university included in the state's reporting entity.

In addition, the determination of whether an organization is a component unit and whether it should be blended or discretely presented is a process independent of the considerations that governments make in reporting fiduciary funds. There may be organizations that do not meet the definition for inclusion in the financial reporting entity. These organizations should be reported as fiduciary funds of the primary government if the primary government has a fiduciary responsibility for them. For example, pension funds or deferred compensation plans are not evaluated as component units. Rather, they are included in a government's reporting entity because of the government's fiduciary role and responsibility.

Discrete Presentation of Component Units

Most component units will be included in the financial statements of the reporting entity using discrete presentation. GASBS 14 defines *discrete presentation* as "the method of reporting financial data of component units in a column(s) separate from the financial data of the primary government." An integral part of this method of presentation is that individual component unit supporting information is required to be provided either in condensed financial statements within the notes to the reporting entity's financial statements, or in combining statements in the general purpose financial statements (GPFS).

Government-wide financial statements. The reporting entity's government-wide statement of net position should include a column to display the combined balance sheet of the discretely presented component units. Similarly, the reporting entity's government-wide statement of activities should include a column to display the activities for discretely presented component units. GASBS 34 also requires that separate information about major component units be presented in the government-wide financial statements. Separate columns for major component units may be displayed on the face of the government-wide financial statements. Alternatively, a combining schedule of major component units (including a column that combines all nonmajor component units) may be presented as part of the basic financial statements. This is further discussed later in this chapter. Discretely presented component units are presented only in the government-wide financial statements. There is no reporting of discretely presented component units at the fund level under GASBS 34.

Required disclosures. GASBS 34's requirements for providing information in the basic financial statements about component units of a reporting entity government can be met in one of three ways (note that these requirements do not apply to component units that are fiduciary in nature). These options are discussed later in this chapter.

Blended Component Units

The preceding discussion focused on the presentation and disclosures required for discretely presented component units. This section will focus first on the determination of whether a component unit's financial information should be "blended" with that of the primary government. Then, the presentation and disclosure requirements for component units that are determined to be blended component units are discussed.

Why blend some component units? One of the objectives of the financial reporting for the reporting entity described earlier was to be able to distinguish the financial information of the primary government from its component units. A question arises of why this objective seems to be abandoned in order to blend certain component units so that they are less distinguishable from the primary government. The answer to this is that the GASB concluded that there are component units that, despite being legally separate from the primary government, are so intertwined with the primary government that they are, in substance, the same as the primary government. It is more useful to report these component units as part of the primary government. These component units should be reported in a manner similar to the balances and transactions of the primary government itself, a method known as "blending." This view was reinforced by GASBS 34, which made the primary government, including blended component units, the focus of financial reporting in the basic financial statements and required supplementary information.

Determination of blended component units. GASBS 14 describes two circumstances in which a component unit should be blended, as follows:

- The component unit's governing board is substantively the same as the governing body of the primary government. S*ubstantively the same* means that there is sufficient representation of the primary government's entire governing body on the component unit's governing body to allow complete control of the component unit's activities. For example, the board of a city redevelopment authority may be composed entirely of the city council and the mayor, serving in an ex officio capacity. The primary government is, essentially, serving as the governing body of the component unit. On the other hand, if the mayor and city council have three seats on the governing board of a public housing authority that has a governing board of ten seats, the housing authority's governing board would not be substantively the same as the primary government's. GASBS 14 also states that this criterion will rarely, if ever, apply to a state government because of the impracticality of providing sufficient representation of the state's entire governing body.
- The component unit provides services entirely (or almost entirely) to the primary government, or otherwise exclusively (or almost exclusively) benefits the primary government even though it does not provide services directly to it. The nature of this type of arrangement is similar to that of an internal service fund. The goods and services are provided to the government itself, rather than to the individual citizens. GASBS 14 provides the example of a building authority created to finance the construction of office buildings for the primary government. If the component unit provides services to more than just the primary government, it should still be blended if the services provided to others are insignificant to the overall activities of the component unit. Other component units that should be blended are those that exclusively (or almost exclusively) benefit the primary government by providing services indirectly. GASBS 14 provides the example of a primary government that establishes a component unit to administer its employee benefit programs. In this case, the component unit exclusively benefits the primary government, even though the component unit provides services to the employees of the primary government, rather than to the primary government itself.

In some cases, the component units that are to be blended with the primary government have funds of different fund types. For example, a component unit may have a general fund and a capital projects fund. If they meet the definition of major funds, they would be reported as such. If they are nonmajor funds, they would be blended with those of the primary government by including them in the appropriate nonmajor fund combining statements of the primary government. In addition, since the primary government's general fund is usually the main operating fund of the reporting entity and is a focal point for users of the financial statements, the primary government's general fund should be the only general fund for the reporting entity. The general fund of a blended component unit should be reported as a special revenue fund.

NOTE: In January 2016 the GASB issued Statement No. 80 (GASBS 80), Blending Requirements for Certain Component Units—An Amendment of GASB Statement No. 14. GASBS 80 adds an additional criterion for when blending of a component unit is required. The additional criterion requires blending of a component unit incorporated as a not-for-profit corporation in which the primary government is the sole corporate member. This criterion does not apply to component units included in the financial reporting entity pursuant to the provisions of GASBS 39. GASBS 80 is effective for reporting periods beginning after June 15, 2016, with earlier application encouraged.

NOTE: In March 2017 the GASB issued Statement No. 85 (GASBS 85), Omnibus 2017, which includes a specific requirement for a primary government that is a business-type activity and uses a single column for financial statement presentation of its business-type activities. In this case, a component unit may be blended only if the component unit meets the criterion for blending in GASBS 14. This addressed a question in practice as to whether GASBS 61 provided an option to blend any component unit in this circumstance. GASBS 85 makes it clear that in this circumstance, a component unit must meet the criterion for blending in order to be permitted to be blended.

GASBS 85 is effective for reporting periods beginning after June 15, 2017. Earlier application is permitted by topic to the extent that all of the requirements associated with a single topic are implemented simultaneously. The blending requirement discussed above is a single topic and can be implemented early by itself, if so desired by a reporting government.

Other reporting entity issues. In addition to the basic issues of determining a state or local government's reporting entity and providing guidance on presenting blended and discretely presented component units, GASBS 14 addresses several other issues related to the government's reporting entity, including:

- Investments in for-profit corporations.
- Reporting discretely presented component units.
- Budgetary presentations.
- Intra-entity transactions and balances.
- Reporting periods.
- Note disclosures.
- Separate and standalone financial statements.
- Reporting organizations other than component units.

The following section discusses each of these reporting entity issues that should be understood by financial statement preparers.

Investments in for-profit corporations. Sometimes governments own a majority of the voting stock of a for-profit corporation. The government should account for an investment in a for-profit corporation based on the government's intent for holding the stock. For example, GASBS 14 uses the example of a government that buys all of the outstanding voting stock of a major supplier of concrete so that it can control the operations of the corporation as a source of supply. In this case, the government has bought the stock for something other than an investment—it bought the stock to ensure the supply of concrete that the government needs for capital projects. In this case, the for-profit subsidiary should be considered a component unit of the government because the intent of the government in obtaining the company is to directly enhance its ability to provide governmental services. The criteria for determining whether the component unit should be blended with the primary government or discretely presented should be determined using the criteria described in this chapter. On the other hand, if the government purchases the stock of a for-profit corporation as an investment, rather than to directly aid in providing government services, the government should report the stock as an investment and not treat the corporation as a component unit.

Reporting discretely presented component units. GASBS 34 quotes GASBS 14's requirement for presenting information about discretely presented component units as follows: "… the reporting entity's financial statements should … provide an overview of the discretely presented component units." The term *overview* perhaps best describes the approach to discretely presented component units taken by GASBS 34. (Note that this discussion does not apply to blended component units, which are presented as if part of the primary government, and component units that are fiduciary in nature, which are included only in the fund financial statements with the primary government's fiduciary funds.)

GASBS 34 requires information about each major component unit to be presented. Information about nonmajor component units should be aggregated in one column; however, the government may choose to display a nonmajor component unit as if it were a major component unit, if it desires. The requirements of GASBS 34 can be accomplished by one of three alternatives:

- Reporting each major component unit in a separate column in the reporting entity's government-wide statement of net position and statement of activities.
- Including combining statements of major component units in the reporting entity's basic statements after the fund financial statements. Aggregate totals would then be included in the government-wide financial statements for component units, supported by this combining schedule.
- Presenting condensed financial statements in the notes to the reporting entity's financial statements.

If the government selects the alternative to present component unit information in the notes, GASBS 34 specifies that the following details be provided:

1. Condensed statement of net position:
   (a) Total assets—distinguishing between capital assets and other assets. Amounts receivable from the primary government or other component units should be reported separately.
   (b) Total liabilities—distinguishing between long-term debt outstanding and other liabilities. Amounts payable to the primary government or to other component units should be reported separately.
   (c) Total net position—distinguishing between restricted, unrestricted, and amounts invested in capital assets, net of related debt.

2. Condensed statement of activities:
   (a) Expenses (by major functions and for depreciation expense, if separately reported).
   (b) Program revenues by type.
   (c) Net program (expense) revenue.
   (d) Tax revenues.
   (e) Other nontax general revenues.
   (f) Contributions to endowments and permanent fund principals.
   (g) Special and extraordinary items.
   (h) Change in net position.
   (i) Beginning net position.
   (j) Ending net position.

Budgetary presentations. As described in Chapter 5, a government's basic financial statements must include a budgetary comparison (on the budget basis) for the general and special revenue for which annual budgets have been legally adopted either as part of the basic financial statements or as required supplementary information. This requirement would apply to blended component units as well. Budgetary data for the discretely presented component units that use governmental accounting are not required to be presented.

Intra-entity transactions and balances. Special attention is required for transactions between and among the primary government, its blended component units, and its discretely presented component units. The following table can be used as guidance for recording and displaying certain of these intra-entity transactions and balances in the fund financial stateents.

Transaction/balance	*Accounting treatment*
Transfers between primary government and its blended component units.	Recorded as an interfund transfer.
Transfers between blended component units.	Recorded as an interfund transfer.
Receivables/payables between primary government and blended component units or between blended component units.	Reported as amounts due to and due from other funds.
Transactions and balances between primary government and discretely presented component units.	Report as external transactions, although receivables and payables should be presented on a separate line.

For government-wide financial statements prepared under GASBS 34, resource flows between a primary government and a blended component unit should be reclassified as an internal activity in the financial statements of the reporting entity. Resource flows between a primary government and its discretely presented component units should be reported as if they were external transactions. However, receivable and payable balances between a primary government and a discretely presented component unit should be displayed on a separate line. See Chapter 20 for additional information on reporting internal activity.

Capital lease agreements between the primary government and its blended component units (or between blended component units) should not be reported as capital leases in the reporting entity's financial statements. The blended component unit's debt and assets related to the lease should be reported as a form of the primary government's debt and assets. For example, in a lease of general fixed assets, the leased general fixed assets would be reported in the general fixed asset account group and the related debt would be reported in the general long-term debt account group.

Capital lease agreements between the primary government and its discretely presented component units should be treated as any other capital lease agreement entered into by the government. However, the related receivables and payables should not be combined with other amounts due to/from component units or with capital lease receivables and payables outside the reporting entity. Rather, these receivables and payables should be separately displayed. Eliminations of assets and liabilities resulting from capital lease transactions may be made to avoid the duplicate recording of assets and liabilities.

Reporting periods. The primary government and its component units are likely to have different fiscal year-ends. GASBS 14 encourages a common fiscal year-end for the primary government and its component units, although full compliance with this is difficult, particularly when there are a large number of component units that have existed for a long time. The financial statement preparers of the primary government should encourage new component units to adopt the same fiscal year-end as the primary government.

If a common fiscal year-end cannot be achieved, the reporting entity (which uses the same fiscal year-end as the primary government) should incorporate the financial statements for the component unit's fiscal year ending during the reporting entity's fiscal year. If the component unit's fiscal year ends within the first quarter of the reporting entity's subsequent year, it is acceptable to incorporate that fiscal year of the component unit, rather than the fiscal year ending during the reporting entity's fiscal period. Of course, this should be done only if timely and accurate presentation of the financial statements of the reporting entity is not adversely affected.

NOTE: The reporting entity should not delay the issuance of its financial statements or incorporate draft or otherwise inaccurate information from a component unit in order to utilize this first quarter following year-end exception. Generally, the reporting entity is better served by consistently applying the rule that includes the component units with year-ends that fall within the reporting entity's year-end.

Another problem arises when there are transactions between the primary government and its component units or between component units that have different year-ends. These different year-ends may result in inconsistencies in amounts reported as due to or from, transfer to or from, and so forth. The nature and amount of those transactions should be disclosed in the notes to the financial statements. The fiscal year of the component units included in the reporting entity should be consistent from year to year, and changes in fiscal years should be disclosed.

Note disclosures. The notes to the financial statements of a financial reporting entity that includes many component units may be significantly expanded because of the need and requirements to disclose information about major component units.

The notes to the financial statements of the reporting entity should include a brief description of the component units of the financial reporting entity and their relationship to the primary government. The notes should include a discussion of the criteria for including the component units in the financial reporting entity and how the component units are reported. The note should also include information about how the separate financial statements of the individual component units may be obtained.

NOTE: As an alternative to providing a large listing of names and addresses where the individual financial statements may be obtained, the department responsible for preparing the reporting entity's financial statements may take responsibility for making the reports available, so that only the address of this department would be necessary. This is clearly not the approach to take if it is anticipated that the volume of requests for individual financial statements will be high. GASBS 34 also requires that the notes to the financial statements should disclose, for each major component unit, the nature and amount of significant transactions with the primary government and other component units.

GASBS 14 emphasizes that the financial statements of a reporting entity that includes component units should enable the user of the financial statements to distinguish between the financial information of the primary government and the financial information of the component units. Therefore, because the notes to the financial statements and required supplementary information are integral parts of the financial statements, they should distinguish between information pertaining to the primary government (including its blended component units) and that of its discretely presented component units.

GASBS 14 specifies the following as the notes essential to a fair presentation in the reporting entity GPFS:

- The fund types of the primary government, including its blended component units.
- Individual discretely presented component units that are considered major component units.

Exhibit 2 provides illustrative language that would be included in the notes to the financial statements to describe the primary government's relationship with its component units.

Exhibit 2: Illustrative reporting entity note to the financial statements

The city of Anywhere is a municipal corporation government governed by a mayor and a 15-member city council.

As required by generally accepted accounting principles, these financial statements present the city and its component units, which are entities for which the city is financially accountable.

The city is financially accountable for all organizations that make up its legal entity. In addition, the city is financially accountable for legally separate organizations if its officials appoint a voting majority of an organization's governing body, and either it is able to impose its will on that organization or there is a potential for the organization to provide specific financial benefits to, or to impose specific burdens on, the city. The city may also be financially accountable for governmental organizations that are fiscally dependent on it.

There are two methods of presentation of component units.

1. Blended component units, although legally separate entities from the city, are, in substance, part of the city's operations and so data from these component units are combined with data of the city.

The following entity is reported by the city as a blended component unit.

The Anywhere City Electric Utility Authority (the authority) serves all of the citizens of the city and is governed by a board comprised of the city's elected city council. The rates for user charges and bond issuance authorizations are approved by the city council and the legal obligation for the general obligation portion of the authority's debt remains with the city. The authority is reported as an enterprise fund. The authority's fiscal year-end is June 30, and its separately issued financial statements may be obtained at:

Anywhere City Electric Utility Authority
1234 Shocking Lane
Anywhere, SW 99999

2. Discretely presented component units are reported in a separate column(s) in the combined financial statements to emphasize that they are legally separate from the city.

The following entity is presented by the city as a discretely presented component unit:

The Anywhere School District (the district) provides elementary and secondary education for residents within the city's legal boundaries. The members of the board of education, which governs the district, are elected by the voters. However, the district is fiscally dependent upon the city. The city council approves the district's budget, levies taxes to support the district's budget, and is required to approve any district debt issuances. The district is presented as a governmental fund type. The district's fiscal year-end is June 30, and its separately issued financial statements may be obtained at:

Anywhere School District
9876 Learning Lane
Anywhere, SW 99999

NOTE: There is a high level of judgment needed in determining the note disclosures to include in the financial statements of the reporting entity relating to component units. The guidance from GASBS 14 is rather vague even after amendment by GASBS 34. Interestingly, many governments err on the side of including too much disclosure about component units rather than too little. It is easier and less risky to simply include most of the footnote disclosures from the component units' financial statements rather than to be selective about information presented. Financial statement preparers should keep in mind that sometimes too much information hinders the process of communication to the financial statement reader, and they should critically review the disclosures that are made in the financial statements relative to component units. GASBS 34 makes clear that the emphasis in the financial statements should be on the primary government.

Separate and stand-alone financial statements. A primary government may find it necessary or useful to prepare financial statements that do not include the financial information of its component units. When these primary government-only statements are issued, the statements should acknowledge that they do not include the financial data of the component units necessary for a fair presentation of the financial statements in accordance with GAAP.

In addition, component units themselves may issue separate financial statements. These separate financial statements should use a title that indicates that the entity is a component unit of a primary government. Unlike those of the primary government, the separate financial statements of the component unit can be issued in accordance with GAAP, provided that the component unit's financial reporting entity includes all of its own component units. The component unit itself can serve as a financial reporting "nucleus" and itself be considered a primary government that includes its own component units. The notes to the separately issued financial statements should identify the primary government in whose financial reporting entity it is included and describe the component unit's relationship with the primary government.

GASBS 14 also addresses "other stand-alone government financial statements." Other stand-alone governments are legally separate governmental organizations that do not have a separately elected governing body and do not meet the definition of a component unit of a primary government. These types of governments might include special-purpose governments, joint ventures, jointly governed organizations, and pools. Although the nucleus of a financial reporting entity is usually a primary government, another stand-alone government serves as the nucleus of its reporting entity when it issues financial statements. The financial reporting entity in this case consists of the stand-alone government and all component units for which it is financially accountable, and other organizations for which the nature and significance of their relationship with the stand-alone government are such that exclusion would cause the reporting entity's financial statements to be misleading or incomplete. In addition, any stand-alone government with a voting majority of its governing board appointed by another government should disclose that accountability relationship in its financial statements.

Reporting organizations other than component units. Sometimes primary government officials may appoint some or all of the governing board members of organizations that are not included as component units in a primary government's reporting entity. These organizations can fall into one of the following three categories:

1. Related organizations.
2. Joint ventures and jointly governed organizations.
3. Component units of another government with characteristics of a joint venture or jointly governed organization.

The following paragraph describes the proper treatment of related organizations, followed by the accounting and financial reporting for joint ventures and jointly governed organizations.

Related organizations. Organizations for which a primary government is accountable because that government appoints a voting majority of the governing board but is not financially accountable are termed *related organizations*. The primary government should disclose the nature of its accountability for related organizations in the notes to its financial statements. Groups of related organizations with similar relationships with the primary government may be summarized for the purposes of the disclosures. Therefore, related organizations are not considered component units. Their financial information is not included with that of the primary government. The only requirement is footnote disclosure of the relationship with the related organization that is described above. In addition, the related organization should disclose its relationship with the primary government in its own financial statements.

Joint ventures and jointly governed organizations. As mentioned above, a primary government may appoint some or all of the governing board members of organizations that are not included as component units of the primary government's reporting entity. Two classifications for these organizations are joint ventures and jointly governed organizations. (Jointly governed organizations are discussed later in this chapter.) This section describes the accounting and financial reporting requirements for organizations that fall into these categories.

Joint ventures. A *joint venture* is defined by GASBS 14 as:

> *A legal entity or other organization that results from a contractual arrangement and that is owned, operated, or governed by two or more participants as a separate and specific activity subject to joint control, in which the participants retain (a) an ongoing financial interest or (b) an ongoing financial responsibility.*

Joint ventures are generally established to pool resources and share the costs, risks, and rewards of providing goods or services to the joint venture participants directly, or for the benefit of the general public or specific recipients of service. What distinguishes a joint venture from a "jointly governed organization" is that a jointly governed organization is jointly controlled by the participants, but the participants do not have an ongoing financial interest or ongoing financial responsibility for it.

The "joint control" of a jointly governed organization means that no single participant has the ability to unilaterally control the financial or operating policies of the joint venture.

In determining whether a relationship is a joint venture, the concepts of ongoing financial interest and ongoing responsibilities are important to understand. The following sections examine these terms as they relate to joint ventures.

Ongoing financial interest. An ongoing financial interest in a joint venture involves any arrangement that causes a participating government to have access to the joint venture's resources, including an equity interest.

Access to a joint venture's resources can occur directly, such as when the joint venture pays its surpluses directly to the participants. Access to the joint venture's resources can also occur indirectly, such as when the joint venture undertakes projects of interest to the participants. Indirect access would occur when the participating governments can influence the management of the joint venture to take on special projects that benefit the citizens of the participating governments.

Ongoing financial responsibility. A participating government has an ongoing financial responsibility for a joint venture if it is obligated in some manner for the debts of the joint venture. The tests to determine this obligation are the same as those used in determining whether a primary government is responsible in some manner for the debts of an organization being evaluated as a component unit. In addition, a participating government has an ongoing financial interest in a joint venture if the continued existence of the joint venture depends on the continued funding by the participating government.

Ongoing financial responsibility might also be evidenced by the nature of the joint venture established. For example, assume that a joint venture is created by participating governments to provide goods or services to the participating governments or to provide goods or services directly to the constituents of the governments. The participating governments are financially responsible for the joint venture because they are responsible for financing operations either by purchasing the goods and services from the joint venture or by subsidizing the provisions of the goods or services to the constituents.

Financial reporting for joint ventures. The financial accounting and reporting for joint ventures is determined by whether the participating governments have an equity interest in the joint venture. An equity interest in a joint venture may be in the form of ownership of shares of joint venture stock or otherwise having an explicit, measurable right to the net resources of a joint venture (usually based on an investment of financial or capital resources by a participating government). The equity interest may or may not change over time as a result of an interest in the net income or losses of the joint venture. An equity interest in a joint venture is explicit and measurable if the joint venture agreement stipulates that the participants have present or future claim to the net resources of the joint venture and sets forth the method to determine the participant's shares of the joint venture's net resources.

The definition of an equity interest in a joint venture should not be interpreted to mean that it is the same as a government's residual interest in assets that may revert to the government on dissolution for lack of another equitable claimant. GASBS 14 relates this type of interest to an escheat interest, in which the reversion of property to a state results from the absence of any known, rightful inheritors to the property.

If it is determined that a participating government has an equity interest in a joint venture, that equity interest should be reported as an asset of the fund that has the equity interest. Differences in reporting this asset of a fund will result depending on whether the fund holding the equity interest in the joint venture is a proprietary fund or a governmental fund.

- **Proprietary funds and presentation in the government-wide financial statements.** A proprietary fund that has an equity interest in a joint venture would record the investment as an asset in an account usually entitled "Investment in joint venture." The initial investment in the joint venture should be recorded at cost. If the joint venture agreement provides that the participating governments share in the net income or loss of the joint venture, the investment account should be adjusted for the participating governments' share of the net income or loss of the joint venture. This adjustment would be similar to what a commercial enterprise would record for an investment accounted for by the equity method. In recording this adjustment, the financial statement preparer should determine whether there are any operating profits or losses recorded by the joint venture on transactions between the proprietary fund and the joint venture. If there are operating profits or losses on transactions between the fund and the joint venture, these amounts should be eliminated before recording the adjustment for the share of the profits and losses of the joint venture. For financial statement display purposes, the investment in the joint venture and the fund's share of the joint venture's net income or loss should be reported as single amounts in the balance sheet and operating statement. In other words, the participating government does not record pro rata shares of each of the joint venture's assets, liabilities, revenues, and expenses. The accounting methodology described in this paragraph would also be used for presentation in the government-wide financial statements.

- **Governmental funds.** The accounting for investments in joint ventures for governmental funds is different from that of proprietary funds because the equity interest in the joint venture does not meet the definition of a financial resource and would not be recorded as an asset of the fund. However, the general fund may report an amount payable to or receivable from the joint venture. Differences also arise in a governmental fund's recording of the operating activities of a joint venture. Governmental fund operating statements should report changes in joint venture equity interests only to the extent that the amounts received or receivable from the joint venture or the amounts paid or payable to the joint venture satisfy the revenue or expenditure recognition criteria for governmental funds. For amounts receivable from the joint venture, while the "measurable" criteria for revenue recognition may be readily met, the "available" criteria will generally be met only if the joint venture distributes the fund's share of the joint venture's net income soon after the fund's fiscal year-end so that the fund has the cash available to pay for its current obligations.

Exhibit 3 provides a sample note disclosure for a joint venture.

Exhibit 3: Sample note disclosure for a joint venture

The City of Anywhere participates in a joint venture that provides emergency medical services to its citizenry. The Emergency Medical Services Authority (EMSA) provides these services to participating jurisdictions, which are the city of Anywhere and the city of Somewhere. The EMSA Board of Trustees is comprised of four trustees appointed by the city of Anywhere and four trustees appointed by the city of Somewhere. EMSA has established capital accounts for each beneficiary jurisdiction. These capital accounts record the economic activity of the jurisdiction and represent an equity interest.

Summarized information for EMSA's fiscal years ending June 30, 20XY, and June 30, 20XX, is included in the following table (in thousands):

Summarized totals for EMSA:	**June 30, 20XY**	**June 30, 20XX**
Assets	xxx	xxx
Liabilities	xxx	xxx
Total equity	xxx	xxx
Joint venture debt consists of the following:		
Short-term	xxx	xxx
Long-term	xxx	xxx
Capital interests:		
July 1, 20XX, capital	xxx	xxx
Contributions		xx
Net income (loss)	xx	xx
June 30, 20XY, capital	xxx	xxx

Debt as of June 30, 20XX, is collateralized by assets and revenues of EMSA.
EMSA issues separate financial statements, which are available from:
Emergency Medical Services Authority
1234 Ambulance Lane
Anywhere, SW 99999

Disclosure requirements—equity interest and nonequity interests. While GASBS 14 only requires the recording of amounts for joint ventures in the financial statements of participating governments when they have an equity interest in the joint venture, it does prescribe disclosure requirements for joint ventures regardless of whether there is an equity interest. These disclosure requirements are as follows:

- A general description of each joint venture, including:
- Description of the participating government's ongoing financial interest (including its equity interest, if applicable) or ongoing financial responsibility. This disclosure should also include information to allow the reader to evaluate whether the joint venture is accumulating significant financial resources or is experiencing fiscal stress that may cause an additional financial benefit to or burden on the participating government in the future.
- Information about the availability of separate financial statements of the joint venture.
- The participating governments should also disclose any other information relevant to the joint venture from the broad prospective of the participating governments' overall footnote presentation.

Other joint organization issues. In addition to the common joint venture–type agreement that is discussed above, there are any number of additional joint relationships that may have to be evaluated by a government in determining its reporting entity and the proper accounting for joint ventures. GASBS 14 addresses several of these unique cases that provide additional guidance to the financial statement preparer. These cases also provide examples whose concepts can be used in evaluating situations similar to, but not the same as, the situations specifically addressed by GASBS 14.

Joint building or finance authorities. Some governments create a building, urban development, or economic development authority whose sole purpose is to construct or acquire capital assets for the participating governments and then subsequently lease the facilities to the governments. In accounting for these capital lease agreements, the participating governments already should have reported their respective shares of the assets, liabilities, and operations of the joint venture. Accordingly, it is unnecessary to calculate and report a participant's equity interest (if any) in the joint building, urban development, or economic authority. In addition, the disclosures filed above are not required because they would duplicate the usual disclosures required for capital leases.

Jointly governed organizations. Some states and other jurisdictions allow for the creation of regional governments or other multigovernmental arrangements that are governed by representatives from each of the governments that created the regional organization. These organizations have certain characteristics that make them appear to be joint ventures. For example, they often provide goods or services to the citizenry of the participating governments. However, many of these regional organizations do not meet the definition of a joint venture because there is no ongoing financial interest or responsibility by the participating governments. If a participating government does not retain an ongoing financial interest or responsibility, the relationship should be considered for general footnote disclosure; however, there are no specific joint venture disclosures that are required.

Component units and related organizations with component joint venture characteristics. An organization may be established and composed of several participating governments. If one of the participating governments appoints a voting majority of the organization's governing board and joint control is precluded because that participating government has the power to make decisions unilaterally, the organization is either a component unit or a related organization and should be reported in the participating government's financial statements. The other minority participating governments, however, should report their participation in the organization in accordance with the requirements described above for joint ventures. The organization itself, when included as a component unit in the majority participating government's financial statements, should report any equity interests of the minority participants as fund balance or retained earnings "reserved for minority interests." In addition, there may be instances where a jointly controlled organization, such as a regional government, is considered a component unit of one of the participating governments because it is fiscally dependent on that participating government. This type of organization should be reported by all participants in the same way described for majority and minority interests.

Pools. A *pool* is defined by GASBS 14 as "another multijurisdictional arrangement that has the characteristics of a joint venture, but has additional features that distinguish it, for financial reporting purposes, from the traditional joint venture ...." An investment pool generally has open membership. Governments are free to join, resign from, and increase or decrease their participation in the pool without the knowledge or consent of the other participants. A participant's equity in a pool (such as a share in an investment pool) should already be recognized in its financial statements. Accordingly, calculating and reporting an equity interest in a joint venture would be redundant. Because of the broad-based, constantly changing membership shares typically found in a pool, the disclosures normally required of a joint venture are not mandatory. The financial statement preparer should be aware that entities participating in public entity risk pools are covered by separate accounting and reporting guidance, more fully discussed in Chapter 21.

Undivided interests. An undivided interest is an arrangement that resembles a joint venture, but no entity or organization is created by the participants. This arrangement is sometimes referred to as a joint operation. An *undivided interest* is an ownership arrangement in which two or more parties own property whose title is held individually to the extent of each party's interest. Also implied in the definition is that identifiable obligations of the operation would also be the liability of each participant. In an undivided interest, there is no entity created that has assets, liabilities, and equity that can be allocated to the participating entities. A government that participates in this type of arrangement should report its assets, liabilities, revenues, and expenditures associated with the joint operation. The disclosures required for a joint venture are not required for an undivided interest.

Some joint venture arrangements result in hybrid agreements. They create separate organizations but also provide for undivided interests in specific assets, liabilities, and equity interests in the other net resources of the organizations. For these hybrid types of arrangements, the government should report the portion of the arrangement that involves an undivided interest in accordance with the requirements described in this section. The portion of the agreement that represents an equity interest in a joint venture should be accounted for in the same manner as accounting for the equity interests of joint ventures.

Cost-sharing arrangements. GASBS 14 describes several types of agreements that may have some of the characteristics of a joint venture, but that are not joint ventures for various overriding reasons. For example:

- Cost-sharing projects (such as highway projects financed by federal, state, and local governments) should not be considered joint ventures because the participating governments do not retain an ongoing financial interest or responsibility for the projects.

- Joint purchasing agreements, in which a group of governments agree to purchase a commodity or service over a specified period and in specified amounts, should not be considered joint ventures.
- Multi-employer public employee retirement systems should also not be considered joint ventures.
- Investment pools should not be considered joint ventures.

NOTE: The GASB has a project on its agenda to evaluate the effectiveness of GASBS 14 and determine whether any changes in determining the reporting entity and how component units are displayed in the financial statements should be made. Included in the project is a look at when to include or exclude fiduciary activities from the financial statements. As of this writing, the GASB was still deliberating several issues and had not issued an Exposure Draft of a new Statement relating to the reporting entity.

GOVERNMENT COMBINATIONS AND DISPOSALS OF GOVERNMENT OPERATIONS

The GASB issued Statement No. 69 (GASBS 69), *Government Combinations and Disposals of Government Operations*, to address accounting and financial reporting issues related to government combinations and disposals of government operations. As used in GASBS 69, the term *government combinations* refers to a variety of transactions referred to as mergers, acquisitions, and transfers of operations. Transfers of operations may be present in shared service arrangements, reorganizations, redistricting, annexations, and arrangements in which an operation is transferred to a new government created to provide these services. In addition, GASBS 69 defines an *operation* as an integrated set of activities conducted and managed for the purpose of providing identifiable services with associated assets and liabilities. The example provided is that of a fire department within a general purpose government, which would be considered an operation. On the other hand, fire engines donated to or acquired by the fire department would not be considered an operation.

Identifying Government Combinations

To be considered a government combination under GASBS 69, an arrangement should result in the continuation of a substantial portion of the services provided by the previously separate entities or their operations after the transaction has occurred. Generally, the terms and conditions of an arrangement establish whether service continuation was intended. However, there may be uncertainty about whether a service continuation was intended or whether a government has acquired a group of assets and related liabilities. GASBS 69 provides that service continuation means that the new or continuing government intends to provide services similar to the formerly separate governments, organizations, or operations. If the specific provisions of an arrangement do not indicate the extent to which services will continue to be provided, professional judgment should be used to determine whether a government combination, subject to the requirements of this Statement, has occurred.

Types of Government Combinations

GASBS 69 defines a *government merger* as a government combination of legally separate entities in which no significant consideration is exchanged and either:

- Two or more governments (or one or more governments and one or more nongovernmental entities) cease to exist as legally separate entities and are combined to form one or more new governments; or

- One or more legally separate governments or nongovernmental entities cease to exist and their operations are absorbed into, and provided by, one or more continuing governments.

GASBS 69 defines a *government acquisition* as a government combination in which a government acquires another entity, or the operations of another entity, in exchange for significant consideration. In addition, the consideration provided should be significant in relation to the assets and liabilities acquired. The acquired entity or operation becomes part of the acquiring government's legally separate entity.

GASBS 69 defines a *transfer of operations* as a government combination involving the operations (as defined above) of a government or nongovernmental entity, rather than a combination of legally separate entities, in which no significant consideration is exchanged.

Operations may be transferred to another existing entity or to a new entity. GASBS 69 describes each of these scenarios as follows:

- A transfer of operations to an existing entity occurs when a government transfers operations, for example, a public safety function, to another existing government. A transfer of operations to an existing entity also may result from arrangements such as reorganizations, redistricting, and annexations, in which operations are combined through jurisdictional changes in boundaries. Similarly, a transfer of operations to an existing entity may be present in shared service arrangements in which governments agree to combine operations.
- A transfer of operations to a new government occurs in shared service arrangements in which governments agree to combine operations and transfer assets and liabilities to a new government. Similarly, the transfer of operations to a new government occurs when an operation of a single government is reorganized as a new government created to provide those services, for example, the formation of a library district that was formerly a department of a general purpose government.

NOTE: It's important to properly categorize a transaction as a merger, acquisition, or transfer of operations to ensure that the appropriate accounting guidance, described below, is used, as the accounting is specific for each type of transaction.

NOTE: As many local governments, particularly smaller ones, face continuing cost pressures, they are reevaluating the need to provide services (such as police, public works, even education) separately from neighboring towns, villages, or other municipalities. Accordingly, shared services arrangements and transfers of operations are becoming increasingly common. It may be that GASBS 69's accounting requirements are applied more frequently in these types of transactions than they are in actual mergers and acquisitions. There may be a tendency to assume that GASBS 69 applies only to mergers and acquisitions, which is clearly not the case.

Government Mergers

GASBS 69's accounting and reporting guidance for government mergers is dependent upon whether a new government results from the merger or whether the merging entity is absorbed into a continuing government, as described above.

New Governments

GASBS 69 specifies that for a government merger where a new government results the merger date is the date on which the combination becomes effective. The initial reporting period of the new government begins on the merger date. The combined assets, deferred outflows of resources, liabilities, and deferred inflows of resources of the merging entities should be recognized and measured in the statement of net position as of the beginning of that initial reporting period.

Recognition. As of the merger date, GASBS 69 provides that a new government should recognize the assets, deferred outflows of resources, liabilities, or deferred inflows of resources of the merging entities. If financial statements are not prepared for a dissolved entity as of the merger date, the assets, deferred outflows of resources, liabilities, or deferred inflows of resources as of the merger date should be recognized based on the accounting principles applied in the most recent financial statements (subject to the provisions of the following paragraph).

GASBS 69 specifies that the new government should not recognize additional assets, deferred outflows of resources, liabilities, or deferred inflows of resources that authoritative guidance for state and local governments does not require or permit the merging governments to recognize (for example, intangible assets that were not required to be reported). If the assets, deferred outflows of resources, liabilities, or deferred inflows of resources of one or more of the merging entities are not recognized in conformity with authoritative guidance for state and local governments, those elements should be adjusted to bring them into conformity with that guidance before the merged government recognizes the combined assets, deferred outflows of resources, liabilities, and deferred inflows of resources.

Measurement. Under GASBS 69, the new government measures the assets, deferred outflows of resources, liabilities, or deferred inflows of resources as of the merger date at the *carrying values* as reported in the separate financial statements of the merging entities. If financial statements are not prepared for a dissolved entity as of the merger date, the assets, deferred outflows of resources, liabilities, or deferred inflows of resources as of the merger date are measured based on the accounting principles applicable to state and local governments applied in the most recent financial statements (subject to the provisions of the preceding paragraph).

The beginning net position of the merged government results from combining the carrying values of the assets, deferred outflows of resources, liabilities, or deferred inflows of resources of the separate entities. However, GASBS 69 permits the new government to adjust some carrying values to bring the accounting principles of the merging entities into alignment. Certain carrying values may also need to be adjusted for the impairment of capital assets as described below.

The merging entities may have measured assets, deferred outflows of resources, liabilities, or deferred inflows of resources by applying different, but acceptable, methods of accounting in their separate financial statements. GASBS 69 allows the new government to adjust the amounts of those elements to reflect a consistent method of accounting as long as those methods comply with the accounting and financial reporting requirements for state and local governments. If such adjustments are made, they should be applied to the opening balances carried forward into the merged government's financial statements and an explanation provided in the notes to the financial statements. One caveat is that financial statement amounts that are based on accounting estimates should be carried forward into the opening balances of a new government's financial statements without modifications. If changes in accounting estimates are made, they should be recognized in the flows statements of the new government.

Impairment. GASBS 69 provides that if the merging entities decide before the merger date to dispose of capital assets and the new government will use those capital assets until the disposal occurs, those capital assets should be measured and reported at their carrying values by the new government. On the other hand, if the new government will not use capital assets that have been identified for disposal, those assets should be evaluated for impairment by the new government in accordance with the provisions of GASB Statement No. 42, *Accounting and Financial*

Reporting for Impairment of Capital Assets and for Insurance Recoveries, as amended (see Chapter 14), to determine whether their carrying values should be adjusted. Similarly, if the merging entities decide before the merger date that the manner or duration of use of specific capital assets that will not be disposed of will change, the new government should evaluate those capital assets for impairment.

Continuing Governments. Under GASBS 69, for a continuing government merger as described earlier, the merger date is the beginning of the reporting period in which the combination occurs, regardless of the actual date of the merger. Continuing governments should recognize and measure the combined assets, deferred outflows of resources, liabilities, and deferred inflows of resources, results of operations, and cash flows, if applicable, of the merging entities for the reporting period in which the combination occurs as though the entities had been combined at the beginning of the continuing government's reporting period.

Recognition. GASBS 69 provides that the continuing government, as of the merger date, should recognize the assets, deferred outflows of resources, liabilities, or deferred inflows of resources of the merging entities. If financial statements are not prepared for a dissolved entity as of the merger date, the assets, deferred outflows of resources, liabilities, or deferred inflows of resources as of the merger date should be recognized based on the accounting principles applied in the most recent financial statements (except as described in the following paragraph).

The continuing government should not recognize additional assets, deferred outflows of resources, liabilities, or deferred inflows of resources that authoritative guidance for state and local governments do not require or permit the merging governments to recognize (for example, intangible assets that were not required to be reported). If the assets, deferred outflows of resources, liabilities, or deferred inflows of resources of one or more of the merging entities are not recognized in conformity with authoritative guidance for state and local governments, those elements should be adjusted to bring them into conformity with that guidance before the continuing government recognizes the combined assets, deferred outflows of resources, liabilities, and deferred inflows of resources.

Measurement. GASBS 69 provides that the continuing government should measure the assets, deferred outflows of resources, liabilities, or deferred inflows of resources as of the merger date at the carrying values as reported in the separate financial statements of the merging entities. If financial statements are not prepared for a dissolved entity as of the merger date, the assets, deferred outflows of resources, liabilities, or deferred inflows of resources as of the merger date should be measured based on the accounting principles applicable to state and local governments applied in the most recent financial statements (subject to the provisions of the previous paragraph).

Thus, under GASBS 69 the beginning net position of the merged government results from combining the carrying values of the assets, deferred outflows of resources, liabilities, and deferred inflows of resources of the separate entities. However, the guidance related to conforming accounting principles, accounting estimates, and impairment described above for new governments would also apply where there is a continuing government.

NOTE: The principal difference in accounting for a government merger between when a new government is created and when a continuing government is involved is the date the financial statements recognize the transaction. For new governments, the initial reporting period begins on the merger date. For continuing governments, the combination is reflected as if it occurred at the beginning of the continuing government's reporting period. In both cases, carrying values are used, subject to certain adjustments that may be made (or in the case of estimates, prohibited to be adjusted as part of recording the merger).

Eliminations. GASBS 69 provides that transactions between the merging entities that occur before the combination should be eliminated in the combination process except for the effect of interfund services provided and used. Receivables and payables between the merging entities should be eliminated.

Reporting Government Mergers in Governmental Fund Financial Statements

In a government merger, the assets, deferred outflows of resources, liabilities, and deferred inflows of resources that will be reported in governmental funds should be recognized pursuant to the financial reporting requirements for governmental funds.

Recognition and Measurement of Government Acquisitions

In a government acquisition, GASBS 69 provides that the date on which the acquiring government obtains control of the assets and becomes obligated for the liabilities of an acquiree entity or its operations is the acquisition date. Generally, the acquisition date coincides with the date on which the acquiring government provides consideration—the closing date. However, the parties may have designated another date as the acquisition date.

Under GASBS 69, the acquiring government recognizes the assets, deferred outflows of resources, liabilities, or deferred inflows of resources acquired or assumed at the acquisition date. The acquiring government's application of recognition principles may result in recognizing assets, deferred outflows of resources, liabilities, or deferred inflows of resources that the acquired organization was not required to recognize.

If the acquired entity had recognized deferred outflows of resources (or goodwill, by a nongovernmental entity) from previous acquisition transactions, the acquiring government should not recognize such deferred outflows of resources (or goodwill).

GASBS 69 provides that the acquiring government should measure the acquired assets, deferred outflows of resources, liabilities, or deferred inflows of resources (except as noted in the previous paragraph and the following paragraphs) at acquisition value as of the acquisition date. For purposes of GASBS 69, *acquisition value* is defined as a market-based entry price. An entry price is assumed to be based on an orderly transaction entered into on the acquisition date. Acquisition value represents the price that would be paid for acquiring similar assets, having similar service capacity, or discharging the liabilities assumed as of the acquisition date.

Exceptions to the use of acquisition value. GASBS 69 provides the following exceptions to the use of acquisition value (in addition to the deferred outflows of resources or goodwill from previous acquisitions, as described above):

- The acquiring government should measure assets, deferred outflows of resources, liabilities, or deferred inflows of resources related to the acquired entity's employment benefit arrangements, such as compensated absences, pensions, other postemployment benefits, or termination benefits, using the accounting and financial reporting requirements for state and local governments that are applicable to those transactions to the extent such benefits are not terminated.
- The acquiring government should measure liabilities (and assets, if any) related to the acquired entity's municipal solid waste landfill closure and postclosure care costs or obligations for pollution remediation using the accounting and financial reporting requirements for state and local governments that are applicable to those transactions.
- The acquiring government should measure investments, including derivatives that are required to be reported at fair value, using the accounting and financial reporting requirements for state and local governments that are applicable to those transactions.

- Deferred outflows of resources and deferred inflows of resources should be measured at the carrying values previously reported by the acquired government, except for those that relate to effective hedging arrangements as provided for in GASB Statement No. 53 (GASBS 53), *Accounting and Financial Reporting for Derivative Instruments.* Those deferred outflows of resources and deferred inflows of resources should be adjusted to reflect the difference between the acquisition value and the carrying value of acquired hedged items. Any remaining deferred outflows of resources or deferred inflows of resources associated with derivatives should be accounted for by the acquiring government in conformity with the provisions of paragraph 23 of GASBS 53.

Consideration

A distinguishing feature of a government acquisition (compared with a government merger) is the existence of consideration as part of the transaction. GASBS 69 provides that the consideration provided by the acquiring government should be measured as of the acquisition date as the sum of the values of the assets remitted or liabilities incurred to the former owners of the acquired entity, as determined in conformity with the requirements above. Consideration may include financial and nonfinancial assets, for example, cash, investments, or capital assets. In addition, a liability incurred may represent an obligation to provide consideration to the former owners of the acquired entity. For example, a government may issue a note payable in addition to, or in lieu of, cash to the former owners of an organization in exchange for the net assets of that organization. However, for purposes of GASBS 69, negative net position of an entity recognized in a government merger or a transfer of operations (that is, a net liability assumed by the combined government) does not, by itself, constitute consideration given.

In addition, a government acquisition may include a potential transfer of cash or other assets that is contingent upon specified events in the future. Contingent consideration should be recognized in conformity with the accounting and financial reporting requirements for contingencies contained in GASBS 62.

For circumstances in which the consideration provided exceeds the net position acquired, GASBS 69 provides that the acquiring government should report the difference as a deferred outflow of resources. The deferred outflow of resources should be attributed to future periods in a systematic and rational manner, based on professional judgment, considering the relevant circumstances of the acquisition. The length of the attribution period may be determined by considering such factors as the following:

(a) The estimated service lives of capital assets acquired, when acquisitions are largely based on the expected use of those capital assets.
(b) The estimated remaining service life for acquisitions of landfills that are capacity-driven.
(c) The expected length of contracts acquired.
(d) The estimated remaining service life of technology acquired, if the acquisition is based on the expected efficiencies of a technology system.

A government should periodically review and revise its estimate of the attribution period in subsequent reporting periods.

NOTE: The deferred outflow of resources recognized where the consideration given exceeds the net position of the entity acquired would be termed goodwill in the private sector. An important difference (in addition to the name) is that the deferred outflow of resources is amortized over some period as determined above, whereas in the private sector goodwill is not amortized, and is only evaluated for impairment.

Where the consideration provided in a government acquisition is less than the net position acquired, the acquiring government should eliminate the excess net position acquired by reducing the acquisition values assigned to the noncurrent assets (other than financial assets) that are acquired, unless the conditions of the acquisition arrangement indicate that a contribution should be recognized by the acquiring government, as discussed below. If the allocation reduces the acquisition value of the acquired noncurrent assets (other than financial assets) to zero, the remainder of the excess should be recognized as a special item in the flows statements.

If the seller intends to accept a lower price in order to provide economic aid to the acquiring government without directly receiving equal value in exchange, GASBS 69 provides that the acquiring government should recognize a contribution. The provisions of an arrangement would generally indicate whether economic aid is intended.

Acquisition costs. Acquisition costs are the costs the acquiring government incurs to effect a government acquisition. GASBS 69 provides that acquisition costs include, but are not limited to, fees for legal, accounting, valuation, professional, or consulting services. The acquiring government should recognize an expense/expenditure for acquisition costs in the periods in which the costs are incurred and the services are received. In addition, the costs to issue debt should be recognized in conformity with applicable accounting and financial reporting requirements for state and local governments.

NOTE: In March 2017 the GASB issued Statement No. 85 (GASBS 85), Omnibus 2017, which includes guidance for acquisitions prior to the effective date of GASBS 69. For those acquisitions, GASBS 85 provides that where consideration provided exceeded the net position acquired, a deferred outflow of resources should be reported for the difference, consistent with the accounting guidance in this section. In addition, negative goodwill should not be reported.

GASBS 85 is effective for reporting periods beginning after June 15, 2017. Earlier application is permitted by topic to the extent that all of the requirements associated with a single topic are implemented simultaneously. The goodwill requirement discussed above is a single topic and can be implemented early by itself, if so desired by a reporting government.

Intra-Entity Government Acquisitions

When accounting for government acquisitions within the same financial reporting entity, GASBS 69 provides that the acquiring government should recognize the assets, deferred outflows of resources, liabilities, and deferred inflows of resources at the *carrying values* of the selling entity. The difference between the acquisition price and the carrying value of the net position acquired should be reported as a special item by the acquiring government in its separately issued statements and reclassified as transfers or subsidies, as appropriate, in the financial statements of the reporting entity. In addition, application of the provisions of GASBS 69 is the same for both discretely presented and blended component units. That is, the provisions should first be applied in the separate financial statements of the component unit.

Reporting Government Acquisitions on a Provisional Basis

In some cases, where the initial measurement of certain assets, deferred outflows of resources, liabilities, or deferred inflows of resources is not finalized by the end of the reporting period in which the government acquisition occurs, the acquiring government should recognize estimated amounts for the items for which the measurement is not finalized. GASBS 69 provides that the acquiring government should prospectively update the estimated amounts reported as of the acquisition date to reflect new information obtained about facts and circumstances that existed as of the acquisition date that, if known, would have affected the measurement of amounts recognized as of that date.

Reporting Government Acquisitions in Governmental Fund Financial Statements

GASBS 69 states that in a government acquisition, the assets, deferred outflows of resources, liabilities, and deferred inflows of resources that will be reported in governmental funds should be recognized pursuant to the financial reporting requirements for governmental funds. The net fund balance acquired should be recognized by the acquiring government as a special item in the statement of revenues, expenditures, and changes in fund balances in the period of acquisition.

Transfers of Operations

For transfers of operations, as described earlier in this discussion of GASBS 69, the effective transfer date is the date the transferee government obtains control of the assets and becomes obligated for the liabilities of the operation transferred. GASBS 69's rules for when a transfer of operations is reported by a transferee (receiving) government are as follows:

- A continuing government should report a transfer of operations as a transaction in its financial statements for the reporting period in which it occurs.
- If a transfer of operations results in the formation of a new government, the new government's initial reporting period begins at the effective transfer date. Transfers of operations should be recognized by the disposing government in conformity with the provisions for disposals of government operations discussed later in this section.

The basic guidance of GASBS 69 is that the transferee government should recognize the *carrying values* of assets, deferred outflows of resources, liabilities, and deferred inflows of resources of the operations of the transferor government or nongovernmental entity as of the effective transfer date.

Similar to merger accounting, there may be certain adjustments of carrying value needed to record the transferred operations. For example, if the assets, deferred outflows of resources, liabilities, or deferred inflows of resources of one or more of the transferor entities' operations are not recognized and measured in conformity with authoritative guidance for state and local governments, those elements should be adjusted to bring them into conformity with that guidance before the transferee government recognizes the assets, deferred outflows of resources, liabilities, and deferred inflows of resources related to a transferred operation.

As with mergers, GASBS 69 provides that the transferee government should not recognize additional assets, deferred outflows of resources, liabilities, or deferred inflows of resources that authoritative guidance for state and local governments does not require or permit the transferor to recognize (for example, intangible assets that were not required to be reported). The net position received or assumed by a continuing transferee government should be reported as a special item. The assets, deferred outflows of resources, liabilities, and deferred inflows of resources of an operation received when establishing a new government should be included in the statement of net position at the beginning of its initial reporting period.

Again, similar to mergers, the entities involved in a transfer of operations may have measured the assets, deferred outflows of resources, liabilities, or deferred inflows of resources by applying different, but acceptable, methods of accounting in their separate financial statements. GASBS 69 permits transferee governments to adjust the amounts of those assets, deferred outflows of resources, liabilities, or deferred inflows of resources to reflect a consistent method of accounting as long as those methods comply with the accounting and financial reporting requirements for state and local governments. If adjustments to reflect a consistent method of accounting are made, they should be applied to the balances carried forward into the transferee government's financial statements. An explanation of those adjustments should be disclosed in the notes to the financial statements.

Assets, deferred outflows of resources, liabilities, or deferred inflows of resources associated with the operations reported in the transferor government's separate financial statements that are based on accounting estimates should be carried forward into the balances of a transferee government's financial statements without modifications. If changes in accounting estimates are made, they should be recognized in the flows statements of the transferee government. This treatment is consistent with that of GASBS 69 for mergers.

GASBS 69 provides that if decisions are made before the effective transfer date to dispose of capital assets and the transferee government will use those capital assets until the disposal occurs, those capital assets should be measured and reported at the carrying values by the transferee government. However, if the transferee government will not use those capital assets identified for disposal, they should be evaluated for impairment, to determine whether their initial carrying values should be adjusted. The transferee government should provide an explanation of adjustments for impairment in the notes to the financial statements. Similarly, if decisions are made before the effective transfer date that the manner or duration of use of specific capital assets that will not be disposed of will change, the transferee government should evaluate those capital assets for impairment.

Reporting Transfers of Operations in Governmental Fund Financial Statements

For transfers of operations, the assets, deferred outflows of resources, liabilities, and deferred inflows of resources that will be reported in governmental funds should be recognized under GASBS 69 pursuant to the financial reporting requirements for governmental funds. Transferee governments should recognize the net fund balance of an operation it receives as a special item in the statement of revenues, expenditures, and changes in fund balances in the period in which the transfer occurs.

Disposals of Government Operations

GASBS 69 provides that a disposing government should recognize a gain or loss on the disposal of operations, if applicable. Of particular note, gains or losses on the disposal of operations should be reported as a special item in the period in which the disposal occurs, based on either the effective transfer date of a transfer of operations or the date of sale for operations that are sold.

GASBS 69 specifies that the amount of the gain or loss on the disposal of operations should not include adjustments and costs associated with the normal operating activities of the operation up to the measurement date. The disposing government should include only those costs that are directly associated with the disposal of operations when determining the amount of the gain or loss to report.

NOTE: For gain or loss calculations, GASBS 69's requirements discussed in the preceding paragraph are meant to ensure that the disposing government doesn't include normal operating activities. For example, a disposing government should not be able to avoid recorded operating losses from a disposed operation that it incurred before disposal by attempting to include those losses in the loss calculation from disposal.

GASBS 69 specifies that costs directly associated with the disposal of government operations include, but are not limited to, benefits provided to a government's employees for involuntary terminations, contract termination costs, or other associated costs, such as fees for professional services. Those costs should be recognized and measured in accordance with the following GASBS 69 specifications:

(a) The costs of benefits provided to a government's employees for involuntary terminations should be measured and recognized in accordance with GASB Statement No. 47, *Accounting for Termination Benefits* (GASBS 47). However, if the use of existing financial reporting requirements to recognize costs directly associated with a disposal of government operations results in initial recognition of those costs in a period earlier than the measurement dates in GASBS 69, those costs associated with a disposal of operations would not be included in the gain or loss on the disposal of government operations.
(b) Contract termination costs related to a disposal of operations should be recognized when it is probable that a liability has been incurred and the amount of the obligation can be reasonably estimated.
(c) Other costs incurred during the disposal period that are directly associated with the disposal of operations should be included in the gain or loss recognized. In addition, the disposing government should accrue any known costs of future goods and services related to the transfer or sale of an operation as of the effective date of the disposal, when it is probable that a liability has been incurred and the amounts of the obligation can be reasonably estimated.

Reporting Disposals of Government Operations in Governmental Fund Financial Statements

GASBS 69 provides that the disposal of operations should be reported as a special item in the statement of revenues, expenditures, and changes in fund balances in the period in which the disposal occurs. The disposing government should recognize an amount equal to the fund balance of an operation it disposes of, net of consideration, if any. The special item should include expenditures directly associated with the disposal of operations, as discussed above.

Notes to the Financial Statements

GASBS 69 includes a number of disclosure requirements, which are discussed below. Certain requirements apply to broad categories of transactions while others relate only to specific types of transactions. The disclosures for mergers and transfers are the same in many instances since they are both recorded at carrying value, with some adjustment.

All government combinations. For each government combination, the government should include the following information in the notes to financial statements for the period in which the combination occurs:

(a) A brief description of the government combination, including identification of the entities involved in the combination and whether the participating entities were included within the same financial reporting entity.

(b) The date of the combination.
(c) A brief description of the primary reasons for the combination.

Government mergers and transfers of operations. The new government or continuing government also should disclose the following information:

(a) The amounts recognized as of the merger date or the effective transfer date as follows:
    1. Total assets—distinguishing between current assets, capital assets, and other assets.
    2. Total deferred outflows of resources.
    3. Total liabilities—distinguishing between current and long-term amounts.
    4. Total deferred inflows of resources.
    5. Total net position by component.
(b) A brief description of the nature and amount of significant adjustments made to bring into conformity the individual accounting policies or to adjust for impairment of capital assets resulting from the merger or transfer.
(c) The initial amounts recognized by the new or continuing government, if different from the values in (a) and the differences that arise from modifying the carrying values in (a) by the adjustments in (b).

Government acquisitions. In the period in which an acquisition occurs, the acquiring government also should disclose the following information:

(a) A brief description of the consideration provided.
(b) The total amount of net position acquired as of the date of acquisition.
(c) A brief description of contingent consideration arrangements, including the basis for determining the amount of payments that are contingent.

Disposals of government operations. In the period in which operations are transferred or sold, the disposing government should identify the operations and provide a brief description of the facts and circumstances leading to the disposal of those operations. In addition, the disposing government should identify and disclose the following information about the disposed government operations if not separately presented in its financial statements:

(a) Total expenses, distinguishing between operating and nonoperating, if applicable.
(b) Total revenues, distinguishing between operating and nonoperating, if applicable.
(c) Total governmental fund revenues and expenditures, if applicable.

SUMMARY

Defining the reporting entity for a state or local government or other governmental unit can be a difficult task because of the variety of relationships in which governments typically are involved. Applying the concepts described above under GASBS 14 should enable governments to effectively define the reporting entity and accomplish financial reporting objectives.

Exhibit 4 provides a questionnaire that is useful to periodically review the status of all component units, and is particularly useful when new entities are created. These new entities should be asked to complete the questionnaire as a basis for their consideration as potential component units.

Exhibit 4: Potential component unit evaluation questionnaire

(*Name of primary government*) is in the process of determining which organizations should be included in its financial reporting entity under generally accepted accounting principles. To assist (*name of primary government*) in accomplishing this objective, please provide the following information about (*name of potential component unit*) for evaluation as a component unit of (*name of primary government*).

Your assistance is greatly appreciated. Please return the completed questionnaire by (*date*) to (*name and address of individual receiving completed questionnaires*). If you need assistance in completing this questionnaire, please call (*name and telephone number of individual who can provide assistance*).

General Inquiries

1. What is your organization's fiscal year-end?

   ____

2. Are the organization's financial statements audited by independent auditors?
   Yes ______ No ______

   If yes, please provide the name, address, telephone number, and a contact person for the organization's independent auditors.

   (a) ____

   ____

3. Does your organization have an audit committee? Yes ______ No ______

   Please indicate the basis of accounting used by your organization in preparing its financial statements:

   Cash ______ Modified Accrual ______ Accrual ______ Other (please describe)

4. ____

   ____

5. Is your organization included as a component unit in the financial statements of any reporting entity? Yes ______ No ______

   If yes, please provide the name of the reporting entity and the basis for inclusion in that reporting entity as a component unit.

   (a) ____

   ____

Primary Government Characteristics

6. Does your organization have a separately elected governing body?
   Yes ______ No ______

Separate Legal Standing

7. Was your organization created as either a body corporate or a body corporate and politic?
   Yes ______ No ______
   (a) If yes, please attach to the completed questionnaire a copy of the law, statute, legislative resolution, or executive order that created your organization.
8. Does your organization have the explicit capacity to have a name? Yes ______ No ______
9. Does your organization have the right to sue and to be sued in its own name without recourse to a state or local government unit? Yes ______ No ______
10. Does your organization have the right to buy, sell, lease, or mortgage property in its own name?
    Yes ______ No ______

Fiscal Independence

11. Can your organization determine its budget without the (*name of primary government*) having the authority to substantively approve and modify that budget? Yes ______ No ______
12. Can your organization levy taxes or set rates or charges without approval by (*name of primary government*)? Yes ______ No ______
13. Can your organization issue bonded debt without the substantive approval of (*name of primary government*)? Yes ______ No ______

Financial Accountability

Appointment of a Voting Majority of Governing Board

14. Does the (*name of primary government*) appoint a majority of your organization's governing board? Yes ______ No ______
15. Do the financial decisions of your organization's governing board require more than a simple majority? Yes ______ No ______
    If yes, please provide details of the voting requirements.
    (a) ______________________________
    ____
    (b) If yes, does the (*name of primary government*) appoint enough governing board members to have a voting majority on the financial decisions? Yes ______ No ______
16. If the (*name of primary government*) has appointment authority for governing board members, is its appointment limited by a nomination process for governing board members? Yes ______ No ______
    If yes, please explain the facts and circumstances of the nomination process.
    (a) ______________________________
    ____
    (b) ______________________________

Imposition of Will

17. Does the (*name of primary government*) have the ability to remove appointed members of your organization's governing board at will? Yes ______ No ______
18. Does the (*name of primary government*) have the ability to modify or approve the budget of your organization? Yes ______ No ______
19. Does the (*name of primary government*) have the ability to modify or approve rate or fee changes affecting revenues of your organization? Yes ______ No ______
20. Does the (*name of primary government*) have the ability to veto, overrule, or modify the decisions (other than those included in 18 and 19 above) of your organization's governing board? Yes ______ No ______
21. Does the (*name of primary government*) have the ability to appoint, hire, reassign, or dismiss those persons responsible for the day-to-day operations and management of your organization? Yes ______ No ______
22. Are there any other conditions that may indicate that the (*name of primary government*) has the ability to impose its will on your organization? Yes ______ No ______
    (a) If yes, please provide details.
    ____
    ____
    ____

Financial Benefit or Burden

23. Is the (*name of primary government*) legally entitled to or can it otherwise access your organization's resources? Yes ______ No ______
24. Is the (*name of primary government*) legally obligated to assume or has it otherwise assumed the obligation to finance the deficits of, or provide financial support to, your organization? Yes ______ No ______
25. Is the (*name of primary government*) obligated for the debt of your organization? (In responding to question 25, consider questions 26 through 32.) Yes ______ No ______
26. Is the (*name of primary government*) legally obligated to honor deficiencies to the extent that proceeds from other default remedies are insufficient? Yes ______ No ______
27. Is the (*name of primary government*) required to temporarily cover deficiencies with its own resources until funds from the primary repayment source or other default remedies are available? Yes ______ No ______
28. Is the (*name of primary government*) required to provide funding for reserves maintained by your organization, or to establish its own reserves or guarantee fund for the debt? Yes ______ No ______
29. Is the (*name of primary government*) authorized to provide funding reserves maintained by your organization or to establish its own reserve or guarantee fund? Yes ______ No ______

    (a) Has such a fund been established? Yes ______ No ______
30. Is the (*name of primary government*) authorized to provide financing for a fund maintained by your organization for the purpose of purchasing or redeeming your organization's debt, or to establish a similar fund on its own? Yes ______ No ______

    (a) Has such a fund been established? Yes ______ No ______
31. Does your organization explicitly indicate by contract, such as by bond agreement or offering statement, that in the event of default by your organization, (*name of primary government*) may cover deficiencies, although it has no legal obligation to do so? Yes ______ No ______ (Note that the bond offering statement may specifically refer to a law that authorizes the [*name of primary government*] to include an appropriation in its budget to provide funds, if necessary, to honor the debt of your organization.)
32. Have there been legal decisions with the state or other jurisdiction or previous actions of the (*name of primary government*) related to actual or potential defaults on your organization's debt that make it probable that the (*name of primary government*) will assume responsibility for the debt of your organization in the event of default? Yes ______ No ______

Financial Accountability as a Result of Fiscal Dependency—Governing Board Majority Not Appointed by (name of primary government)

33. Does your organization have a separately elected governing board? Yes ______ No ______ (If yes, proceed to question 36.)
34. Is your governing board appointed by another government other than the (*name of primary government*)? Yes ______ No ______
35. Is your organization's board jointly appointed? Yes ______ No ______
36. Is your organization fiscally dependent on (*name of primary government*)? (For example, does [*name of primary government*] approve your organization's budget or levy property taxes for your organization?) Yes ______ No ______

(Name of primary government) *Not Financially Accountable*

37. Was your organization created solely for the benefit of the (*name of primary government*), even though your governing board may not be appointed by the (*name of primary government*)? Yes ______ No ______

38. Is your organization closely related to or affiliated with the (*name of primary government*) in any other way? Yes ______ No ______

    ____

    ____

    ____

    (a) If yes, please provide details of the relationship or affiliation.

Blending or Discrete Presentation

39. Is your organization's governing body substantially the same as that of the (*name of primary government*)? Yes ______ No ______
40. Is there sufficient representation of the (*name of primary government*)'s entire governing body on your organization's governing body to allow complete control of your organization's activities? Yes ______ No ______
41. Does your organization provide services entirely, or almost entirely, to the (*name of primary government*) or otherwise exclusively, or almost exclusively, to benefit the (*name of primary government*), even though it may not provide the service directly to the (*name of primary government*) (for example, an internal service fund that provides goods or services to the [*name of primary government*] rather than the citizenry)? Yes ______ No ______

    (a) If yes, please provide a description of the services.

    ____

    ____

42. Are there any other factors that should be considered in evaluating your organization's potential for inclusion in the financial reporting entity of (*name of primary government*)? Yes ______ No ______

    (a) If yes, please describe these factors.

    ____

    ____

    ____

12 CASH AND INVESTMENTS—VALUATION AND DISCLOSURES

INTRODUCTION

This chapter describes the accounting and financial reporting guidance for cash and investments held by governmental entities. Several significant GASB statements affect the accounting and financial reporting requirements for cash and investments.

- GASB Statement No. 40 (GASBS 40), *Deposit and Investment Risk Disclosures—An Amendment of GASB Statement No. 3*, revised the required disclosures regarding risks associated with deposits and investments. GASBS 40 reduces some of the disclosures previously required by GASB Statement No. 3 (GASBS 3), *Deposits with Financial Institutions, Investments (Including Repurchase Agreements), and Reverse Repurchase Agreements* with regard to custodial credit risk. However, this statement adds additional required disclosures about credit risk, concentration of credit risk, interest rate risk, and foreign currency risk. Additional disclosures are also required for investments that have fair values that are highly sensitive to changes in interest rates as well as deposit and investment policies related to disclosed risks. The GASB staff issued an Implementation Guide to GASBS 40 (GASBS 40 Implementation Guide) that has been cleared for issuance by the GASB. The more significant, broad-based implementation issues covered in this question-and-answer format document are incorporated into the guidance included later in this chapter.
- GASB Statement No. 31 (GASBS 31), *Accounting and Financial Reporting for Certain Investments and for External Investment Pools*, was issued by the GASB to provide accounting guidance (really measurement guidance) for "certain" investments that are

likely to comprise the majority of a government's investment holdings. Essentially, GASBS 31 requires many of the investments included within its scope to be measured and reported in the financial statements at fair value.

- GASB Statement No. 72 (GASBS 72), *Fair Value Measurement and Application*, was issued by the GASB in February 2015. Upon its effective date, it will provide a new definition of *investments*. It also provides guidance in measuring fair value in financial statements and requires significant disclosures as to the fair value hierarchy it establishes. While GASBS 72 applies to all fair value measurements in the financial statements, as a practical matter, its greatest impact will be on disclosure requirements for investments.

Governments that have significant investment portfolios (often they will be pension plans) sometimes increase their investment returns by lending securities to another party and hold collateral in its place. GASB Statement No. 28 (GASBS 28), *Accounting and Financial Reporting for Securities Lending Transactions*, provides accounting guidance for these types of transactions and is discussed later in this chapter. If the government has investments in derivatives, the disclosure requirements of GASB Statement No. 53 (GASBS 53), *Accounting and Reporting for Derivative Instruments*, should be followed. GASBS 53 is discussed in Chapter 13.

This chapter describes the accounting and financial reporting requirements relating to:

- Measurement and valuation principles for investments under GASBS 31. It will also include the accounting and financial reporting requirements for external investment pools, included in GASBS 31.
- Disclosure requirements for cash deposits and investments required by GASBS 40.
- Provisions of GASBS 72, which are discussed separately until its requirements become effective, which is for financial statements for periods beginning after June 15, 2015.

The reader should note that the measurement and valuation of investments of defined benefit pension plans are included in GASB Statement No. 67 (GASBS 67), *Financial Reporting for Pension Plans—An Amendment of GASB Statement No. 25*. In addition, the measurement and valuation of investments for Section 457 deferred compensation plans are included in GASB Statement No. 2 (GASBS 2), *Financial Reporting of Deferred Compensation Plans Adopted under the Provisions of Internal Revenue Code Section 457*. GASBS 2 and GASBS 67 require that investments be reported at fair value, so there is consistency between the measurement requirements of GASBS 2, GASBS 25, and GASBS 31. However, GASBS 31 specifies that in valuing certain investments of defined benefit pension plans or Section 457 deferred compensation plans, the accounting and financial reporting guidance of GASBS 31 for determining fair value should be used. These specific investments, defined later in this chapter, are as follows:

- Securities subject to purchased put option contracts and written call option contracts.
- Open-end mutual funds.
- External investment pools.
- Interest-earning investment contracts.

The reader should refer to Chapter 8 for a complete discussion of Section 457 deferred compensation plans and Chapter 2 for a complete discussion of the requirements relating to defined benefit pension plans.

VALUATION OF INVESTMENTS

Prior to the issuance of GASBS 31, the authoritative literature related to the valuation of investments was found in the AICPA Audit and Accounting Guide (the AICPA Guide), *Audits of State and Local Governmental Units*. The AICPA Guide provided that governmental fund investments are generally reported at cost unless there are decreases in market value and the decline is not due to a temporary condition. This general requirement was sometimes difficult to apply in practice because many times it was difficult to determine whether the decline in the market value of the investment was temporary. In many cases, this decision was based on the government's intent and ability to hold securities until maturity. When securities were written down because of a decline in market value that was judged to be other than temporary, sometimes the market value of the security did recover. In this case, there was no basis in the professional accounting literature to write the investments back up to their previously recorded amounts.

The GASB issued GASBS 31 to address these concerns for most, but not all, of a government's investments. GASBS 31 also establishes accounting and financial reporting standards for all investments held by governmental external investment pools. These standards for external investment pools will be discussed later in this chapter. For governmental entities other than external investment pools, defined benefit pension plans, and Internal Revenue Code Section 457 deferred compensation plans, GASBS 31 establishes accounting and financial reporting standards for investments in:

- Interest-earning investment contracts (such as certificates of deposit with financial institutions, repurchase agreements, and guaranteed and bank investment contracts).
- External investment pools.
- Open-end mutual funds.
- Debt securities.
- Equity securities (including unit investment trusts and closed-end mutual funds), option contracts, stock warrants, and stock rights that have readily determinable market values.

For purposes of applying the above standards, several definitions must be considered. For example:

- An *external investment pool* is an arrangement that commingles (or pools) the moneys of more than one legally separate entity and invests, on the participants' behalf, in an investment portfolio. To meet this definition, one or more of the participants cannot be part of the sponsor's reporting entity. If a government-sponsored investment pool includes only the primary government and its component units, it is an internal, not an external, investment pool.
- An *interest-earning investment contract* is a direct contract, other than a mortgage or other loan, that a government enters into as a creditor of a financial institution, broker-dealer, investment company, insurance company, or other financial institution for which it directly or indirectly receives interest payments.

An *open-end mutual fund* is an investment company registered with the U.S. Securities and Exchange Commission (SEC) that issues shares of its stock to investors, invests in an investment portfolio on the shareholders' behalf, and stands ready to redeem its shares for an amount based on its current share price. An open-end mutual fund creates new shares to meet investor demand, and the value of an investment in the fund depends directly on the value of the underlying portfolio.

(Open-end mutual funds may include in their definition governmental external investment pools that are registered as investment companies with the SEC and that operate as open-end funds.)

A *debt security* is any security that represents a creditor relationship with an entity. Debt securities are also defined by GASBS 31 to include:

- Preferred stock that either is required to be redeemed by the issuing entity or is redeemable at the option of the investor.
- A collateralized mortgage obligation (CMO) or other instrument that is issued in equity form but is accounted for as a nonequity investment.

Option contracts, financial futures contracts, and forward contracts are not included in the GASBS 31 definition of debt security.

In applying the above definition, the following would be considered debt securities: U.S. Treasury securities, U.S. government agency securities, municipal securities, corporate bonds, convertible debt, commercial paper, negotiable certificates of deposit, securitized debt instruments (such as CMOs and real estate mortgage investment conduits—REMICs), and interest-only and principal-only STRIPS.

Not included in the definition of debt securities provided by GASBS 31 would be trade accounts receivable arising from sales on credit and loans receivable arising from real estate lending activities of proprietary activities. However, receivables that have been securitized would meet the definition of debt security.

The requirements of GASBS 31 for equity securities (which are described in bullet points later in this section) apply only to equity securities with readily determinable fair values. The reader should not confuse this requirement with that of GASBS 31 for debt securities, which requires that all debt securities be reported at fair value, without consideration for whether their fair value is readily determinable.

One practical implementation problem for a financial statement preparer is how to determine fair value, when fair value is not readily determinable. Fair value for a debt security would not be readily determinable when the debt security is thinly traded or quoted market prices are not available. The GASB Implementation Guide notes that in these situations, the security's value should be estimated, which will require a degree of professional judgment on the part of the financial statement preparer.

The first consideration for estimating fair value is to consider the market prices for similar securities. This would take into consideration a particular debt security's coupon interest rate and credit rating of the issuer. Another common valuation technique for debt securities is determining fair value by the present value of expected future cash flows using a discount rate commensurate with the level of risk inherent in the debt security.

As the complexity of the features embodied in debt securities increases, valuation techniques may need to be expanded to consider matrix pricing estimates and options pricing models to consider these added complexities.

A technique referred to by the Implementation Guide as "fundamental analysis" may also be considered. This technique takes into consideration the assets, liabilities, operating statement performance, management, and economic environment of the entity that issued the debt security. These factors are then considered to determine the fair value of the security.

The Implementation Guide also advises financial statement preparers and auditors to exercise caution in accepting an estimate of fair value of a security from the issuer or broker of that security. An attempt should be made to confirm these fair value estimates with independent sources.

- An *equity security* is any security that represents an ownership interest in an entity, including common, preferred, or other capital stock; unit investment trusts; and closed-end mutual funds. The term *equity security* does not include convertible debt or preferred stock that either are required to be redeemed by the issuing entity or are redeemable at the option of the investor.

The following special types of securities are included in the scope of GASBS 31:

- Option contracts, which are contracts giving the buyer (owner) the right, but not the obligation, to purchase from (call option) or sell to (put option) the seller (or writer) of the contract a fixed number of items (such as shares of equity securities) at a fixed or determinable price on a given date or at any time on or before a given date.
- Stock warrants, which are certificates entitling the holder to acquire shares of stock at a certain price within a stated period. Stock warrants are often made part of the issuance of bonds or preferred or common stock.
- Stock rights, which are rights given to existing stockholders to purchase newly issued shares in proportion to their holdings on a specific date.

One other important definition contained in GASBS 31 is *fair value*, which has replaced the term *market value* in recent accounting pronouncements concerning investments. The reason for the new term is to indicate that an investment's fair value may be determined even if there is no actual, well-defined market (such as a stock exchange) for the investment. Fair value then represents the "amount at which a financial instrument could be exchanged in a current transaction between willing parties, other than in a forced or liquidation sale."

In determining whether equity and certain other securities are valued in the financial statements at fair value, there is an additional criterion that must be met. The fair value must be readily determinable. The fair value of equity securities, option contracts, stock warrants, and stock rights is readily determinable if sales prices or bid-and-asked quotations are currently available on a securities exchange registered with the U.S. Securities and Exchange Commission (SEC) or in the over-the-counter market, provided that those prices and quotations for the over-the-counter market are publicly reported by the National Association of Securities Dealers Automated Quotations systems or by the National Quotation Bureau.

The fair value of equity securities, option contracts, stock warrants, and stock rights traded only in a foreign market is readily determinable if that foreign market is of a breadth and scope comparable to one of the U.S. markets referred to in the preceding paragraph.

GASBS 31 concludes that the fair value of restricted stock is not readily determinable. Restricted stock refers to equity securities whose sale is restricted at acquisition by legal or contractual provisions (other than in connection with being pledged as collateral) unless the restriction terminates within one year or the holder has the power by contract or otherwise to cause the requirement to be met within one year. Any portion of the security that can reasonably be expected to qualify for sale within one year, such as may be the case under SEC Rule 144 or similar rules of the SEC, is not considered restricted.

There are several additional investments that are not included within the scope of GASBS 31. An investment in equity securities that is accounted for under the equity method, as provided for in APB Opinion 18, *The Equity Method of Accounting for Investments in Common Stock*, is not included within the scope of GASBS 31, nor are investments in joint ventures or component units as provided in GASB Statement 14 (GASBS 14), *The Financial Reporting Entity*.

In addition, GASBS 31 does not apply to securities or other instruments if they are not held by the government for investment purposes, either for itself or for parties for which it serves as investment manager or other fiduciary. Exhibit 1 provides a listing of some of the transactions that were generally not intended to be covered by GASBS 31. GASBS 31 generally does apply to investments held in agency funds, because these investments are held in a fiduciary capacity and are invested on behalf of the beneficiary.

Exhibit 1: Transactions not covered by GASBS 31

The Implementation Guide for GASBS 31 provides a listing of some of the common transactions that were not intended to be covered by GASBS 31.

It is important to note that this list generally does not apply to governmental external investment pools, defined benefit plans, or Internal Revenue Code Section 457 deferred compensation plans, which generally report all of their investments at fair value (except for external investment pools that are 2a7-like [discussed later in this chapter], which report investments at amortized cost).

The listing (which is not meant to be a complete listing by Implementation Guide 31) is as follows:

- Seized debt securities that the government holds as evidence or as a potential fine.
- Contractors' deposits of debt securities.
- Real estate held for investment purposes.
- Investments in joint ventures.
- Equity securities accounted for under the equity method.
- Long-term securities placed in an irrevocable trust that meets the requirements of a legal or in-substance defeasance.
- Loans receivable arising from real estate lending activities.
- Securities and other instruments not held for investment purposes.
- Receivables that do not meet the definition of a security.
- Equity securities (including unit investment trusts and closed-end mutual funds), option contracts, stock warrants, and stock rights that do not have readily determinable fair values.
- Short sales of securities.
- Investments in component units.
- Restricted stock.
- Trade accounts receivable arising from sales on credit.

GASB STATEMENT NO. 52—*LAND AND OTHER REAL ESTATE HELD AS INVESTMENTS BY ENDOWMENTS*

The GASB issued Statement No. 52, *Land and Other Real Estate Held as Investments by Endowments* (GASBS 52), to address a very narrow question of reporting certain land real estate investments.

Endowments, which include permanent and term endowments and permanent funds, should report land and other real estate held as investments at fair value. Changes in fair value during the reporting period should be reported as investment income.

Endowments are also required to apply the applicable disclosure requirements of GASBS 31, *Accounting and Financial Reporting for Certain Investments and for External Investment Pools*, in its paragraph 15.

Specific Application of the Requirements of GASBS 31

Except as discussed in the following paragraphs, GASBS 31 requires that governmental entities, including governmental external investment pools, report investments at fair value in the balance sheet or statement of financial position. Fair value is the amount at which an investment could be exchanged in a current transaction between willing parties, other than in a forced liquidation or sale.

Generally, if a quoted market price is available for an investment, the fair value is calculated by multiplying the market price per share (or other trading unit) by the number of shares (or trading units) owned by the governmental entity. If an entity has purchased put option contracts or written call option contracts on securities, and it has those same securities among its investments, it should consider those contracts in determining the fair value of those securities to the extent that it does not report those contracts at fair value.

There are several exceptions to the general rule of reporting investments within the scope of GASBS 31 at fair value. These exceptions are described in the following paragraphs.

Interest-earning investment contracts. Valuation of investments in interest-earning investment contracts depends on whether the contracts held by the government are participating contracts or nonparticipating contracts.

- *Participating contracts* are investments whose value is affected by market changes that are tied to interest rate changes. If these contracts are negotiable or transferable, or if their redemption value considers market rates, they should be considered participating. Investments in participating contracts should generally be valued in the financial statements at fair value. However, participating interest-earning investment contracts that have a remaining maturity at the time of purchase of one year or less may be reported at amortized cost, provided that the fair value of the investment is not significantly affected by the impairment of the credit standing of the issuer or by other factors. (Note that the remaining maturity to be considered is that at the time the investment was purchased, not the remaining maturity at the balance sheet date.) Looking at the most extreme instance, if the counterparty to the contract declares bankruptcy and the fair value of the participating interest-bearing investment contract falls significantly, amortized cost would not be an appropriate measure for including this investment in the financial statements, even if the other conditions above are met. Also note that in determining the remaining maturity in applying the above test, it is the remaining maturity at the time of purchase, not the original maturity of the investment, which is considered. Accordingly, a five-year negotiable participating interest-bearing investment contract purchased six months before its maturity would meet the above test of having a remaining maturity of less than one year.
- *Nonparticipating contracts* are those such as nonnegotiable certificates of deposit, where the redemption terms do not consider market rates. Nonparticipating interest-earning investment contracts should be reported in the financial statements using a cost-based measure, provided that the fair value of those contracts is not significantly affected by the impairment of the credit standing of the issuer or other factors.

Money market investments. Money market investments are short-term, highly liquid debt instruments, including commercial paper, bankers' acceptances, and U.S. Treasuries and agency obligations. GASBS 31 does not include derivative securities within its definition of money market investments, nor does it include either of the following:

- Asset-backed securities, which are assets composed of, or collateralized by, loans or receivables. Collateralization can consist of liens on real property, leases, or credit-card debt.

- Structured notes, which are debt securities whose cash flow characteristics (such as coupon, redemption amount, or stated maturity) depend on one or more indexes, or that have embedded forwards or options.

Money market investments generally should be reported in the financial statements at fair value. Money market investments that have a remaining maturity at the time of purchase of one year or less may be reported at amortized cost, provided that the fair value of the investment is not significantly affected by the impairment of the credit standing of the issuer or by other factors. This exception is similar to that described above for participating interest-earning investment contracts.

External investment pools. For investments in external investment pools that are not registered with the SEC, regardless of sponsorship by a governmental entity (such as bank short-term investment funds, which are nongovernmental pools not required to be registered with the SEC), fair value should be determined by the fair value per share of the pool's underlying portfolio, unless it is a 2a7-like pool, discussed below. Legally binding guarantees provided or obtained by the pool sponsor to support share value should be considered in determining the fair value of the participants' investments and should be evaluated in light of the creditworthiness of the sponsor. If a governmental entity cannot obtain information from a pool sponsor to allow it to determine the fair value of its investment, it should estimate the fair value of that investment and make the disclosures discussed later in this chapter.

A *2a7-like pool* is an external investment pool that is not registered with the SEC as an investment company but has a policy that it operates in a manner consistent with the SEC's Rule 2a7 of the Investment Company Act of 1940. Rule 2a7 allows SEC-registered mutual funds to use amortized cost rather than market value to report net position to compute share prices, if certain conditions are met. Those conditions include restrictions on the types of investments held, restrictions on the term-to-maturity of individual investments and the dollar-weighted average of the portfolio, requirements for portfolio diversification, requirements for divestiture considerations in the event of security downgrades and defaults, and required actions if the market value of the portfolio deviates from amortized cost by a specified amount. Investment positions in 2a7-like pools should be determined by the pool's share price.

The GASB issued Statement No. 59 (GASBS 59), *Financial Instruments Omnibus*, to make slight changes to the language of GASBS 31 to make clear that the intent of the GASB is for 2a7-like pools to meet the requirements of SEC Rule 2a7 for mutual funds. Accordingly, the following paragraph replaces the similar requirements of that of GASBS 31 and addresses the SEC's Rule 2a7 references to boards of directors and their responsibilities:

> *Investments in 2a7-like pools should be measured at the net asset value per share provided by the pool. A 2a7-like pool is an external investment pool that operates in conformity with the Securities and Exchange Commission's (SEC) Rule 2a7 as promulgated under the Investment Company Act of 1940, as amended. The net asset value per share generally is calculated on a basis other than fair value, such as by the "amortized cost" method that provides a net asset value per share that approximates fair value. To qualify as a 2a7-like pool, the pool should satisfy all SEC requirements of Rule 2a7, including that a group of individuals fulfills the functions of a board of directors. The following conditions do not preclude a pool from being considered 2a7-like:*
>
> (a) *The principal executive officer of the pool, who can be an elected official, has the power to enter into contracts and make personnel decisions: however, investment policies should nevertheless be set by the group of individuals that fulfills functions of a board of directors.*
> (b) *The pool is not required to register with the SEC.*

In addition, the GASB issued Statement No. 79 (GASBS 79), *Certain External Investment Pools and Pool Participants*. Rule 2a7 was significantly amended in 2014 to essentially result in these external investment pools to report their net asset value at fair value. The GASB desired to allow pools that previously were reported at net asset value based upon amortized cost to continue to do so. As such, GASB established requirements, through GASBS 79, whereby pools meeting the requirement could continue to report their net asset value using amortized cost.

NOTE: What is currently a fairly straightforward determination will become a very detailed, very specific determination under GASBS 79, as the following discussion will demonstrate. Because the requirements for Rule 2a7 pools using amortized cost essentially no longer exist, the GASB adopted these very specific requirements as a replacement for those requirements.

Compliance with Amortized Cost Criteria

GASBS 79 provides that an external investment pool may elect to measure for financial reporting purposes all of its investments at amortized cost if it meets all of the following criteria, each of which are described in greater detail below:

(a) Transacts with its participants at a stable net asset value per share (for example, all contributions and redemptions are transacted at $1.00 net asset value per share).
(b) Meets the portfolio maturity requirements.
(c) Meets the portfolio quality requirements.
(d) Meets the portfolio diversification requirements.
(e) Meets the portfolio liquidity requirements.
(f) Meets the shadow pricing requirements.

GASBS 79 notes that an external investment pool that is significantly noncompliant with any of these criteria during the reporting period generally should not measure for financial reporting purposes all of its investments at amortized cost for that reporting period. Instead, that pool should apply the provisions of GASBS 31, as amended. Such a pool may still report short-term debt investments with remaining maturities of up to 90 days at the reporting date at amortized cost, provided that the fair value of those investments is not significantly affected by the impairment of the credit standing of the issuer or by other factors.

GASBS 79 provides that professional judgment should be used to determine if the noncompliance, individually or in the aggregate, is significant. Factors that may indicate the noncompliance is significant include, but are not limited to:

(a) The noncompliance was not promptly identified.
(b) The noncompliance was due, at least in part, to factors within the control of the external investment pool's management.
(c) The noncompliance was not an isolated incident.
(d) Necessary corrective or remedial action was not promptly taken.

Under GASBS 79, when an external investment pool did not measure all of its investments at amortized cost for financial reporting purposes in the previous reporting period, the pool may make an election to change from fair value measurement to amortized cost-based measurement in the subsequent reporting period, only if the pool meets all the criteria specified above and justifies a change in accounting principle as prescribed in paragraphs 73 and 74 of Statement No. 62,

Codification of Accounting and Financial Reporting Guidance Contained in Pre–November 30, 1989 FASB and AICPA Pronouncements.

Portfolio Maturity Requirements

In order to measure for financial reporting purposes all of its investments at amortized cost, a qualifying external investment pool should meet certain portfolio maturity requirements contained in GASBS 79. A qualifying external investment pool should maintain its portfolio maturity consistent with a stable net asset value per share, as provided in this section.

GASBS 79 provides the following:

- A qualifying external investment pool should acquire a security or other investment only if the investment has a remaining maturity of 397 calendar days or less.
- The portfolio of a qualifying external investment pool should maintain a weighted average maturity of 60 days or less. A weighted average maturity measure expresses investment time horizons—the time when investments become due and payable—in this case, days weighted to reflect the dollar size of individual investments. However, certain maturity shortening features, such as interest rate resets, should be taken into account. Those features are described below.
- The portfolio of a qualifying external investment pool should maintain a weighted average life of 120 days or less. A weighted average life measure expresses the average length of time that each dollar of principal remains unpaid without taking into account the maturity shortening features used in calculating the weighted average maturity.

For the purposes of applying the requirements above, GASBS 79 provides that the maturity of a security or other investment should be the period remaining until the date on which the total or remaining principal amount is required to be unconditionally repaid in accordance with the terms of the investment, unless the investment is one of the types described in the following paragraphs. If a security or other investment is subject to a demand feature and the qualifying external investment pool is not relying on that demand feature, that demand feature should be disregarded for the purposes of determining maturity.

GASBS 79 provides that if a security or other investment has a variable interest rate (one that changes on set dates) and its carrying value approximates fair value, the maturity of that security should be determined as follows:

(a) The maturity of a U.S. government security, including its agencies and instrumentalities, and any certificates of deposit insured by the U.S. government or its agencies and instrumentalities, should be the period remaining until the next readjustment of the interest rate.
(b) The maturity of an investment that is not a U.S. government security and for which the principal amount is due in 397 calendar days or less should be the shorter of the period remaining until the next readjustment of the interest rate or the period remaining until the principal amount can be recovered through demand.
(c) The maturity of an investment that is not a U.S. government security and for which the principal amount is due in more than 397 calendar days should be the longer of the period remaining until the next readjustment of the interest rate or the period remaining until the principal amount can be recovered through demand.

If a security or other investment has a floating interest rate (one that changes based on an index or other market conditions, which may reset daily or at another frequency) and its carrying value approximates fair value, GASBS 79 provides that the maturity of that security should be determined as follows:

(a) The maturity of a U.S. government security, including its agencies and instrumentalities, and any certificates of deposit insured by the U.S. government or its agencies and instrumentalities, should be one day.
(b) The maturity of an investment that is not a U.S. government security and for which the principal amount is due in 397 calendar days or less should be the shorter of the period remaining until the interest rate resets or the maturity date of the investment.
(c) The maturity of an investment that is not a U.S. government security and for which the principal amount is due in more than 397 calendar days should be the period remaining until the principal amount can be recovered through demand.

The maturity of a repurchase agreement or a portfolio lending agreement should be either (a) the period remaining until the date on which the repurchase (or return) of the underlying securities is scheduled to occur or (b) the duration of the notice period applicable to a demand for the repurchase (or return) of the securities, such as a put option.

In addition, the maturity of an investment in a money market fund or in another external investment pool should be the period within which the fund or the pool is required to make a payment upon redemption.

Portfolio Quality Requirements

GASBS 79 notes that an investment should be acquired by a qualifying external investment pool only if it presents minimal credit risk as provided in the following paragraphs.

A security that has been rated by a nationally recognized statistical rating organization (NRSRO) should be acquired only if the security is denominated in U.S. dollars and has a credit rating within the highest category of short-term credit ratings (or its long-term equivalent category). The highest category of short-term credit ratings (or its long-term equivalent category) as established by an NRSRO may have multiple subcategories or gradations indicating relative standing (that is, several different ratings may constitute the single highest category). If an external investment pool is aware that a security has multiple ratings and the rating categories conflict, the following provisions apply:

(a) If a security has two ratings, the security should be considered to be in the lower category.
(b) If a security has more than two ratings, the security should be considered to be in the highest category of ratings as determined by at least two ratings.

A security that has not been rated by any NRSRO may be acquired only if the security is denominated in U.S. dollars and is determined (based upon the qualifying external investment pool's analysis) to be of comparable credit quality to securities that have been rated within the highest category of short-term credit ratings (or its long-term equivalent category).

GASBS 79 provides that a qualifying external investment pool may continue to hold a security that meets the qualifications in the two paragraphs above at acquisition but subsequently experiences a decline in credit quality if, at the reporting date, the pool holds no more than 3% of its total assets in the following:

(a) Securities that have credit ratings within the second-highest category of short-term credit ratings (or its long-term equivalent category), and

(b) Securities that are not rated but are determined to be of comparable credit quality to securities that have been rated within the second-highest category of short-term credit ratings (or its long-term equivalent category).

At the reporting date, a qualifying external investment pool should not hold any security that has a credit rating below the second-highest category of short-term credit ratings (or its long-term equivalent category) or is determined to be of comparable credit quality to a security that has been rated below the second-highest category of short-term credit ratings (or its long-term equivalent category).

In addition, a security or other investment subject to a guarantee should be considered to have met the rating requirements described above if one of the following criteria is met:

(a) The guarantee has received a credit rating within the highest category of short-term credit ratings (or its long-term equivalent category) or, if no credit rating is available, is determined (based upon the qualifying external investment pool's analysis) to be of comparable quality.
(b) The guarantor has obtained a credit rating within the highest category of short-term credit ratings (or its long-term equivalent category) or, if no credit rating is available, is determined (based upon the qualifying external investment pool's analysis) to be of comparable quality. However, if a security or other investment is subject to a guarantee and the qualifying external investment pool is not relying on that guarantee, that guarantee should be disregarded for the purposes of determining quality.

GASBS 79 provides that a security or other investment subject to a conditional demand feature may be acquired if, in addition to meeting the credit rating requirements discussed above, the conditional demand feature has received a credit rating within the highest category of short-term credit ratings (or its long-term equivalent category) or, if no credit rating is available, is determined (based upon the qualifying external investment pool's analysis) to be of comparable quality. If a security or other investment is subject to a demand feature and the qualifying external investment pool is not relying on that demand feature, that demand feature should be disregarded for the purposes of determining quality.

In addition, securities held by a qualifying external investment pool should not be exposed to custodial credit risk as described by paragraph 9 of Statement 40.

GASBS 79 also provides that the credit quality of a deposit should be evaluated in terms of either the credit quality of the depository institution or the exposure of the deposit to custodial credit risk. A deposit should be one of the following:

(a) Held by a depository institution with a credit rating within the highest category of short-term credit ratings (or its long-term equivalent category) or determined (based upon the qualifying external investment pool's analysis) to be of comparable quality. If the depository institution has multiple ratings, the quality determination requirements described above should be applied.
(b) Insured or collateralized such that it is not exposed to custodial credit risk as described in paragraph 8 of Statement 40.

The credit quality of a repurchase agreement should be evaluated in terms of the credit quality of the counterparty or its parent and in terms of the credit quality of the underlying collateral. Any underlying collateral should meet the applicable credit quality requirements of described above. In addition, a counterparty or its parent should meet one of the following criteria:

(a) Be a primary dealer as defined by the Federal Reserve Bank of New York.
(b) Have a credit rating within the highest category of short-term credit ratings (or its long-term equivalent category), following the quality determination requirements provided earlier.
(c) Be determined (based upon the qualifying external investment pool's analysis) to be of comparable quality to (b).

A repurchase agreement should be collateralized fully by meeting both of the following criteria:

(a) The fair value of the securities collateralizing the repurchase agreement (including loss of interest that the qualifying external investment pool reasonably could expect to incur if the counterparty defaults) is at least equal to the resale price provided in the repurchase agreement.
(b) The securities collateralizing the repurchase agreement are not exposed to custodial credit risk.

Portfolio Diversification Requirements

In accordance with GASBS 79, a qualifying external investment pool should acquire a security or other investment only if, after acquisition, the external investment pool would hold no more than 5% of its total assets in investments of any one issuer of securities subject to the additional requirements set forth below.

GASBS 79 notes that some securities or other investments have credit support in the form of a guarantee or through a demand feature. A qualifying external investment pool should acquire a security or other investment with credit support only if, after acquisition, the qualifying external investment pool would hold no more than 10% of its total assets with any one issuer of credit support. An issuer of credit support also can be an issuer of securities or other investments. In that case, the securities or other investments to which the issuer has pledged credit support should be combined with the securities or other investments of the issuer itself so that the combined position related to that issuer is limited to no more than 10% of the pool's total assets. However, if a security or other investment is subject to a demand feature or guarantee and the external investment pool is not relying on that demand feature or guarantee, that demand feature or guarantee should be disregarded for the purposes of determining portfolio diversification.

GASBS 79 also provides that if a qualifying external investment pool holds securities at the reporting date with credit ratings within the second-highest category of short-term credit ratings (or its long-term equivalent category), such securities of any one issuer should be no more than one-half of 1% of the pool's total assets. If such securities are subject to demand features or guarantees, the qualifying external investment pool should hold at the reporting date no more than 2.5% of its total assets in such securities from any one provider of demand features or guarantees. If a security or other investment is subject to a demand feature or guarantee and the qualifying external investment pool is not relying on that demand feature or guarantee, that demand feature or guarantee should be disregarded for the purposes of determining portfolio diversification.

GASBS 79 notes that U.S. government securities, including its agencies and instrumentalities, and any certificates of deposit insured by the U.S. government or its agencies and instrumentalities are exempt from the diversity calculations described above.

For the purposes of calculating the diversification limits GASBS 79 provides, the following additional considerations should be made:

(a) Two or more issuers of securities should be considered to be a single issuer if one issuer controls the other or the two issuers are under common control. Control is assumed to be present if one entity owns more than 50% of the issuer's voting securities.
(b) The acquisition of a repurchase agreement should be considered to be the acquisition of the underlying securities if the repurchase obligation is collateralized fully without regard to maturity date.
(c) The acquisition of a refunded security should be considered to be the acquisition of the escrowed securities.
(d) A conduit debt obligation as described in paragraph 2 of Interpretation No. 2, *Disclosure of Conduit Debt Obligations*, should be considered to be issued by the entity responsible for the payments related to the obligation rather than the governmental issuer.
(e) An asset-backed security should be considered to be issued by the entity that issued the security except:

    1. If the obligations of a single entity constitute 10% or more of the assets that back the security, that entity itself should be considered to be the issuer of that portion of the asset-backed security. For example, an external investment pool holds asset-backed commercial paper that is 3% of the external investment pool's total assets. Fifteen percent of the assets that back the commercial paper are receivables from a single bank. For purposes of the diversification calculation, 0.45% of the pool's total assets are considered to be issued by that bank.
    2. If some or all of the assets that back the security are themselves asset-backed securities (secondary asset-backed securities), any entity that issues obligations constituting 10% or more of the assets that back the secondary securities should be considered to be the issuer of that portion of the asset-backed security. For example, an external investment pool holds asset-backed commercial paper that is 3% of the pool's total assets. Twenty percent of the assets that back the commercial paper are other asset-backed securities (secondary securities). Fifteen percent of the assets that back the secondary securities are receivables from a single bank. For purposes of the diversification calculation, 0.09% of the pool's total assets are considered to be issued by that bank.

Portfolio Liquidity Requirements

GASBS provides that qualifying external investment pool should hold liquid assets sufficient to meet reasonably foreseeable redemptions. This determination may be based on the pool's knowledge of the expected cash needs of its participants. A qualifying external investment pool should only acquire a security or investment if, after acquisition, the external investment pool meets the additional requirements set forth in GASBS 79 below.

A qualifying external investment pool should acquire an illiquid investment only if, after acquisition, the qualifying external investment pool would hold no more than 5% of its total assets in illiquid investments. GASBS 79 defines an illiquid investment is an investment that cannot be sold or disposed of in the ordinary course of operations at its amortized cost value within five business days. GASBS 79 uses the example of a nonparticipating interest earning investment contract as described in GASBS 31—such as a nonnegotiable certificate of deposit that does not mature within five business days—is an illiquid investment.

A qualifying external investment pool should acquire a security or other investment only if, after acquisition, the qualifying external investment pool would hold at least 10% of its total assets in daily liquid assets.

Under GASBS 79, only the following are daily liquid assets:

(a) Cash, including demand deposits and certificates of deposit that mature within one business day.
(b) U.S. government securities that are direct obligations.
(c) Securities that will mature within one business day, with maturity determined without taking into account the maturity shortening features described in the maturity requirements section above.
(d) Securities subject to a demand feature that is exercisable and payable within one business day.
(e) Amounts receivable and due unconditionally within one business day on pending sales of portfolio securities.

GASBS 79 also provides that a qualifying external investment pool should acquire a security or other investment only if, after acquisition, the qualifying external investment pool would hold at least 30% of its total assets in weekly liquid assets.

Under GASBS 79, only the following are weekly liquid assets:

(a) Cash, including demand deposits and certificates of deposit that mature within five business days and are expected to be held to maturity.
(b) U.S. government securities that are direct obligations.
(c) Securities that (1) are U.S. government securities that are not direct obligations, (2) are issued at a discount without provision for the payment of interest, and (3) have a remaining maturity of 60 days or less.
(d) Securities that will mature within five business days, with maturity determined without taking into account the maturity shortening features described in the maturity requirements section above.
(e) Securities subject to a demand feature that is exercisable and payable within five business days.
(f) Amounts receivable and due unconditionally within five business days on pending sales of portfolio securities.

The liquidity of an investment in a money market fund or another external investment pool should be evaluated consistent with any redemption gates or other limitations. GASBS 79 uses the example that an investment in another external investment pool that imposes a five-business-day redemption notice period is considered a weekly liquid asset.

If a security or other investment is subject to a demand feature or guarantee and the qualifying external investment pool is not relying on that demand feature or guarantee, that demand feature or guarantee should be disregarded for the purposes of determining portfolio liquidity.

Shadow Pricing Requirements

GASBS 79 defines *shadow price* as the net asset value per share of a qualifying external investment pool, calculated using total investments measured at fair value at the calculation date.

GASBS 79 provides that a qualifying external investment pool should calculate its shadow price at a minimum on a monthly basis. The monthly calculation of the shadow price should occur no earlier than five business days prior to and no later than the end of the month. At each calculation date, that shadow price should not deviate by more than one half of 1% from the net asset value per share calculated using total investments measured at amortized cost.

Accounting and Financial Reporting for Participants in External Investment Pools

While the above discussion focuses on the requirements for an external investment pool to use amortized cost to compute its net asset value, GASBS 79 also logically provides that if an external investment pool meets these criteria and measures all of its investments at amortized cost, the pool's participants also should measure their investments in that external investment pool at amortized cost for financial reporting purposes. If an external investment pool does not meet the criteria, the pool's participants should measure their investments in that pool at fair value.

Disclosures

Qualifying External Investment Pools

GASBS 79 provides that a qualifying external investment pool that measures for financial reporting purposes all of its investments at amortized cost should disclose the following in the notes to financial statements:

(a) The disclosures required for fair value measurements of GASBS 72 as they relate to the disclosures of the fair value of investments required by GASBS 31, particularly a summary of the fair value, the carrying amount (if different from fair value), the number of shares or the principal amount, ranges of interest rates, and maturity dates of each major investment classification.

(b) The presence of any limitations or restrictions on participant withdrawals (such as redemption notice periods, maximum transaction amounts, and the qualifying external investment pool's authority to impose liquidity fees or redemption gates).

Participants in External Investment Pools

GASBS 79 requires that participants in a qualifying external investment pool that measures for financial reporting purposes all of its investments at amortized cost disclose the presence of any limitations or restrictions on withdrawals (such as redemption notice periods, maximum transaction amounts, and the qualifying external investment pool's authority to impose liquidity fees or redemption gates) in notes to the financial statements.

FINANCIAL REPORTING REQUIREMENTS

All investment income, including changes in the fair value of investments, should be recognized as revenue in the operating statement (or other statement of activities). When identified separately as an element of investment income, the change in the fair value of investments should be captioned "net increase (decrease) in the fair value of investments." Consistent with reporting investments at fair value, interest income should be reported at the stated interest rate, and any premiums or discounts on debt securities should not be amortized.

GASBS 31 specifies that realized gains and losses on sales of investments should not be displayed separately from the net increase or decrease in the fair value of investments in the financial statements. However, realized gains and losses may be separately displayed in the separate reports of governmental external investment pools, discussed later in this chapter. Realized gains and losses may also be displayed in the financial statements of investment pools that are reported as investment trust funds of a reporting entity.

Internal Investment Pools

Internal investment pools are arrangements that commingle or pool the moneys of one or more fund or component unit of the reporting entity. Investment pools that include participation by legally separate entities that are not part of the same reporting entity as the pool sponsor are not internal investment pools, but rather are considered to be external investment pools.

The equity position of each fund or component unit in an internal investment pool should be reported as an asset in those funds and component units.

Assignments of Interest

The asset reported should be an investment or a cash equivalent, not a receivable from another fund. In some cases, the income from investments associated with one fund is assigned to another fund because of legal or contractual provisions. In that situation, GASBS 31 specifies that the accounting treatment should be based on the specific language of the legal or contractual provisions. That is, if the legal and contractual provisions require a transfer of the investment income to another fund, the income should be reported in the fund that is associated with the assets, with an operating transfer to the recipient fund. However, if the legal or contractual provisions require that the investment income be that of another fund, no transfer of resources should be reported. Instead, the amount should be recognized in the recipient fund.

If the investment income is assigned to another fund for other than legal or contractual reasons, the income should be recognized in the fund that reports the investments. The transfer of that income to the recipient fund should be reported as an operating transfer.

REQUIRED DISCLOSURES

The latter part of this chapter provides a comprehensive discussion of the disclosure requirements for investments as required by GASBS 40. In addition to these requirements, GASBS 31 imposed additional disclosure requirements on state and local governments relative to investments. These disclosures are as follows:

- The methods and significant assumptions used to estimate the fair value of investments, if that fair value is based on other than quoted market prices.
- The policy for determining which investments, if any, are reported at amortized cost.
- For any investments in external investment pools that are not SEC-registered, a brief description of any regulatory oversight for the pool and whether the fair value of the position in the pool is the same as the value of the pool shares.
- Any involuntary participation in an external investment pool.
- If an entity cannot obtain information from a pool sponsor to allow it to determine the fair value of its investment in the pool, the methods used and significant assumptions made in determining that fair value and the reasons for having had to make such an estimate.
- Any income from investments associated with one fund that is assigned to another fund.

An entity has the option to disclose realized gains and losses in the notes to the financial statements computed as the difference between the proceeds of the sale and the original cost of the investments sold.

External investment pools that elect to report (and other entities that disclose) realized gains and losses should also disclose that:

- The calculation of realized gains and losses is independent of a calculation of the net change in the fair value of investments.
- Realized gains and losses on investments that had been held in more than one fiscal year and sold in the current year were included as a change in the fair value of investments reported in the prior year(s) and the current year.

NOTE: What the GASB is addressing in these disclosure requirements is that the use of fair value for reporting investments affects the carrying amount of those investments, and correspondingly there is an impact on the net effect of the realized gain or loss in the year sold. Consider the following example: A government purchases an investment during year 1 at a cost of $100. At the end of year 1, the fair value of the investment increases to $110, resulting in the recognition of an unrealized gain in operations for year 1. In year 2, the government sells the investment for $125. The realized gain on this investment that would be disclosed is $25. However, the amount of the gain that actually flows through the operating statement in year 2 is only $15, since $10 of the gain was already recognized in year 1.

Accounting and Financial Reporting Standards for External Investment Pools and Individual Investment Accounts

In addition to providing accounting and financial reporting for investments held by governments, GASBS 31 also provides accounting and financial reporting guidelines for external investment pools and individual investment accounts.

Generally, the accounting and financial reporting guidelines presented in the preceding pages related to governments are applicable to all investments held by external investment pools, except that money market investments and participating insurance contracts must be reported by external investment pools at fair value and that 2a7-like pools may report their investments at amortized cost. One other clarification is that external investment pools may report short-term debt investments with remaining maturities of up to ninety days at the date of the financial statements at amortized cost, provided that the fair value of those investments is not significantly affected by the impairment of the credit standing of the issuer or by other factors. For an investment that was originally purchased with a longer maturity, the investment's fair value on the day it becomes a short-term investment should be the basis for purposes of applying amortized cost.

External investment pool financial reporting. Separate stand-alone annual financial reports for governmental external investment pools should include a statement of net position and a statement of changes in net position prepared on the economic resources measurement focus and the accrual basis of accounting. GASBS 31 does not require that a statement of cash flows be presented. All applicable GASB pronouncements should be used to prepare these stand-alone reports. In addition, the financial statements of governmental external investment pools should include the following disclosures:

- A brief description of any regulatory oversight, including whether the pool is registered with the SEC as an investment company.
- The frequency of determining the fair value of investments.

- The method used to determine participants' shares sold and redeemed and whether that method differs from that used to report investments.
- Whether the pool sponsor has provided or obtained any legally binding guarantees during the period to support the value of shares.
- The extent of involuntary participation in the pool, if any (involuntary participants are those required by legal provisions to invest in the external investment pool).
- A summary of the fair value, the carrying amount (if different from the fair value), the number of shares or the principal amount, ranges of interest rates, and maturity dates of each major investment classification.
- If the financial statements distinguish among different components of investment income (such as interest, dividend, and other income instead of the net increase or decrease in the fair value of investments), disclosure of the accounting policy for defining each of the components that it reports.

Financial reporting by sponsoring governments. GASBS 31 provides additional financial statement requirements for *sponsoring governments*, defined as governmental entities that provide investment services, whether an investment pool or individual investment accounts, to other entities, and therefore have a fiduciary responsibility for those investments.

A sponsoring government of an external investment pool should report the external portion of each pool as a separate investment trust fund (that is, a fiduciary fund) that reports transactions and balances using the economic resources measurement focus and the accrual basis of accounting.

- The external portion of an external investment pool is the portion of the pool that belongs to legally separate entities that are not part of the sponsoring government's financial reporting entity.
- The internal portion of each external investment pool is the portion of the pool that belongs to the primary government and its component units. The internal portion should be reported in the same manner as the equity in internal investment funds, described earlier in this chapter.

The sponsoring government should present in its financial statements for each investment trust fund a statement of net position and a statement of changes in net position. The accounting for investment trust funds is described in Chapter 11.

The following disclosures required by GASBS 31 depend on whether the external investment pool issues a separate report:

- If an external investment pool issues a separate report, the annual financial statements of the sponsoring government should describe how to obtain that report in the notes to the financial statements.
- If an external investment pool does not issue a separate report, the annual financial report of the sponsoring government should include the following in the notes to its financial statements for each pool:
    - The additional disclosures described above for that would have been included in the pool's separate report.
    - The disclosures required by GASBS 3 and GASB Statement No. 28 (GASBS 28), *Accounting and Financial Reporting for Securities Lending Transactions*, and other cash and investment standards.

- Condensed statements of net position and changes in net position (if a pool includes both internal and external investors, those condensed financial statements should include, in total, the net position held in trust for all pool participants, and the equity of participants should distinguish between internal and external portions).

Individual Investment Accounts

An individual investment account is an investment service provided by a governmental entity for other legally separate entities that are not part of the same reporting entity. With individual investment accounts, specific investments are required for individual entities, and the income from and changes in the value of those investments affect only the entity for which they were acquired. GASBS 31 requires that governmental entities that provide individual investment accounts to other, legally separate entities that are not part of the same reporting entity report those investments in one or more separate investment trust funds. The disclosure requirements relating to stand-alone reports for external investment pools would not apply to individual investment accounts.

DEPOSITS AND INVESTMENT RISK DISCLOSURES

As described in the first part of this chapter, some specific disclosure requirements for investments and external investment pools are a result of the issuance of GASBS 31. However, the main risk disclosure requirements for investments and deposits are provided in GASBS 40. The following section of the chapter describes the various types of risks to which governmental investors are subject, as well as providing the detailed disclosure requirements contained in GASBS 40.

Level of Detail

GASBS 40 states that its disclosure requirements generally should be made for the primary government including its blended component units. Accordingly, one would expect that the disclosure requirements relate to the cash and investment amounts for the primary government, both unrestricted and restricted, for both the governmental and business-type activities, in the government-wide statement of net position.

However, GASBS 40 provides guidance for when additional disclosures may be necessary at a greater level of detail. When risk exposures are significantly greater than the deposit and investment risks of the primary government, risk disclosures should also be made for:

- Governmental activities.
- Business-type activities.
- Major funds.
- Nonmajor funds in the aggregate.
- Fiduciary fund types.

As for discretely presented component units, the GASBS 40 Implementation Guide refers to the general guidance of GASB Statement No. 14, *The Financial Reporting Entity*, as amended by GASBS 34 as to reporting specific disclosures relative to component units. These guidelines are discussed in Chapter 6.

The Implementation Guide also clarifies that the previous disclosure requirements under GASBS 3 relating to risks that are higher during the fiscal year than at the end of the fiscal year no longer apply under GASBS 40, which looks at the risk exposure at the date of the financial statements as an indicator of potential loss of resources.

Deposit and Investment Policies

GASBS 40 requires that governments briefly describe their deposit or investment policies that are related to the risks that are required to be disclosed by the Statement. If a government has no deposit or investment policy that addresses a specific type of risk that the government is exposed to, the disclosure should indicate that there is no policy related to that risk.

The Implementation Guide clarifies that GASBS 40 does not require governments to adopt investment policies—it requires that the policies be disclosed related to the identified risks or a disclosure that a policy does not exist relative to a particular risk that is present, if that is the case. In addition, external investment policies, such as those contained in bond covenants, should be considered for disclosure when identified risks warrant such a disclosure. If a government is not exposed to a risk, no disclosure is required. For example, if a government is not exposed to credit risk because it invests only in obligations of the U.S. government or obligations explicitly guaranteed by the U.S. government, the government is not exposed to credit risk and a credit risk policy disclosure is not required.

Custodial Credit Risk

GASBS 40 provides that the disclosures about deposits and investments by the three risk custodial credit categories be changed. Basically, the disclosures are reduced to only requiring that amounts that fall within the former Category 3 (the riskiest as to custodial risk) be disclosed.

- For deposits, a government would need to disclose the amount of bank balances that are "exposed to custodial credit risk." For a deposit to be exposed to custodial risk means that it is uninsured, and:
  - Uncollateralized;
  - Collateralized with securities held by the pledging financial institution; or
  - Collateralized with securities held by the pledging financial institution's trust department or agent but not in the government's name.
- For investments, a government would need to disclose certain information about investments that are "exposed to custodial credit risk." For an investment to be exposed to custodial credit risk, it would be uninsured, not registered in the name of the government, and held by either:
  - The counterparty; or
  - The counterparty's trust department or agent but not in the government's name.

For investments that are exposed to custodial credit risk, the following disclosures would be required:

- The type of the investment.
- The reported amount.
- How the investments are held.

Investments in external investment pools, open-end mutual funds, and securities underlying reverse repurchase agreements would not be considered as exposed to custodial credit risk.

Securities Lending Transaction Disclosures

GASBS 40 modifies the disclosure requirements for securities lending transactions. The reported amounts for securities lending collateral and the underlying securities should be disclosed by type of investment and amount. Collateral that is reported in the statement of net position would follow the disclosure requirements for custodial credit risk described above unless it has been invested in a securities lending collateral pool or another type of investment that is not exposed to custodial credit risk. For the underlying securities, the custodial credit risk requirements would be as follows:

- If the collateral for the securities loan is reported on the statement of net position, the underlying securities would not be subject to the custodial credit risk disclosure requirements.
- If the collateral for the securities loan is not reported on the statement of net position, the custodial credit risk disclosures would apply. The disclosure would be based on the type of collateral and the custodial arrangements for the collateral securities.

Concentration of Credit Risk

Governments are required to disclose, by amount and issuer, investments (other than those issued or guaranteed by the U.S. government) in any one issuer that represents 5% or more of total investments. Note that the issuer is considered to be the entity invested in, and not the investment company manager or pool sponsor. These disclosure requirements also do not apply to investments in mutual funds, external investment pools, or other pooled investments.

While GASBS 40 disclosures focus on the primary government, including blended component units, it also requires that risk disclosures be made for governmental fund and business-type activities, individual major funds, nonmajor funds in the aggregate, or fiduciary fund types when the risk exposures are significantly greater than the deposit and investment risks of the primary government. GASBS 40 uses the example of a capital projects fund that is considered a major fund. If an investment in corporate bonds did not meet the 5% criterion for disclosure for total investments of the primary government, but the capital projects fund's only investment was that of the corporate bonds of one issuer, disclosure should be made for the concentration of credit risk for the capital projects fund.

Interest Rate Risk

The disclosures about interest rate risk contained in GASBS 40 are probably the most significant new area addressed. GASBS 40 requires that governments disclose information about the sensitivity to interest rates of their debt investments. This disclosure is accomplished by communicating either investment maturities or information developed about portfolio volatility under various scenarios.

The FASB issued Statement No. 59 (GASBS 59), *Financial Instruments Omnibus*, which clarified that the interest rate risk disclosures for a government's investments in mutual funds, external investment pools, or other pooled investments should be limited to investments in **debt** mutual funds, external **debt** investment pools, or other pooled **debt** investments.

Interest rate sensitivity information would be organized by investment type and amount using one of the prescribed methods described in GASBS 40 as follows:

- **Segmented time distributions.** This method groups investment cash flows into sequential periods in tabular form.

- **Specific identification.** This method presents a list of each investment, its amount, its maturity date, and any call options.
- **Weighted-average maturity.** This method expresses investment time horizons (the time when investments become due and payable) in years or months, weighted to reflect the dollar size of individual investments.
- **Duration.** This method uses the present value of cash flows, weighted for those cash flows as a percentage of the investment's full price to measure a debt investment's exposure to fair value changes arising from changing interest rates.
- **Simulation model.** This method estimates changes in an investment's fair value given hypothetical changes in interest rates.

Governments would be encouraged to select the disclosure method that is most consistent with the method actually used by them to identify and manage interest rate risk.

Specific disclosures are also required for investments whose contract terms cause the investments' fair value to be highly sensitive to interest rate changes. Both the interest rate sensitivity and contract terms of the investment would be disclosed. The contract terms would be considered to include such information as the amount of the investment, multipliers, benchmark indices, reset dates (i.e., the time that a bond's variable coupon is repriced to reflect changes in a benchmark index), and embedded options. GASBS 40 provides three examples of these types of investments.

- A variable-rate investment's coupon rate that amplifies the effect of interest rate changes by greater than a one-to-one ratio, such as 1.25 times the three-month London Interbank Offered Rate (LIBOR).
- A variable-rate investment's coupon amount varies inversely with a benchmark index, such as 4% minus the three-month LIBOR rate.
- An asset-backed investment that has repayments that are expected to vary significantly with interest rate changes.

Foreign Currency Risk

If a government's deposits or investments are exposed to foreign currency risk, the government should disclose the U.S. dollar balances of such deposits or investments, classified by currency denomination and investment type.

NEW FAIR VALUE MEASUREMENT AND APPLICATION STANDARD

GASBS 72 establishes general principles for measuring fair value and sets standards of accounting and financial reporting for assets and liabilities that are measured at fair value.

NOTE: It's important to note that while the discussion of GASBS 72 is included in this chapter, which discusses investment accounting and disclosures, which will be the most common area to which it applies, it applies to all assets and liabilities that are measured at fair value. An additional important area to which it will apply will be to interest rate swap agreements.

GASBS 72 defines *fair value* as the price that would be received to sell an asset or paid to transfer a liability in an orderly transaction between market participants at the measurement date. Fair value is thus market-based rather than being an entity-specific measurement. GASBS 72 views fair value as an exit price at the measurement date from the perspective of a market participant that controls the asset or is obligated for the liability.

NOTE: Much of the discussion that follows from GASBS 72 regarding measuring fair value is fairly theoretical in nature and is not likely to have a significant effect on the measurement of fair value for routine assets and liabilities, particularly investments. It's included here to give the reader a complete understanding of GASBS 72, including its underlying conceptual basis. GASBS 72 follows very closely the fair value measurement and disclosure standards promulgated several years ago by the FASB. It also reflects recent amendments to the FASB requirements regarding investments that are reported at net asset value, which is discussed later in this section.

Fair Value Measurement of Particular Assets and Liabilities

Because the focus of a fair value measurement is on a particular asset or liability, GASBS 72 provides that a government should take into account the characteristics of the asset or liability that market participants would consider when pricing the asset or liability at the measurement date. Such characteristics include the condition and location of the asset and restrictions, if any, on the sale or use of the asset that are characteristics of the asset and not characteristics of a specific government's ownership. The effect on the measurement arising from a particular characteristic will differ depending on how that characteristic would be taken into account by market participants.

Unit of Account

GASBS 72 provides guidance as to the unit of account that should be used in determining fair value measurements. The particular asset or liability measured at fair value might be either (a) a single asset or liability (for example, a financial instrument) or (b) a group, whether a group of assets, a group of liabilities, or a group of related assets and liabilities (a partnership is provided as an example).

Measurement, recognition, or disclosure of an asset or liability—whether a single asset or liability or a group—depends on the unit of account of the asset or liability. The unit of account refers to the level at which an asset or a liability is aggregated or disaggregated for measurement, recognition, or disclosure purposes. Once the unit of account is established, relevant measurement attributes and disclosures can be applied.

NOTE: The unit of accounts for investments will be the individual securities, such as a share of stock, a bond, or other security.

Markets

Under GASBS 72, a fair value measurement assumes that a transaction to sell an asset or transfer a liability takes place in either (a) a government's principal market or (b) a government's most advantageous market, in the absence of a principal market. The most advantageous market is determined after taking into account transaction costs and transportation costs.

However, GASBS 72 provides that a government need not undertake an exhaustive search of all possible markets to identify the principal market or, in the absence of a principal market, the most advantageous market. However, it should take into account all information that is reasonably available. In the absence of evidence to the contrary, the market in which the government normally would enter into a transaction to sell an asset or to transfer a liability is presumed to be the principal market or, in the absence of a principal market, the most advantageous market.

If there is a principal market for the asset or liability, the fair value measurement should represent the price in that market (whether that price is directly observable for an identical asset or whether it is determined using another valuation technique), even if the price in a different market is potentially more advantageous at the measurement date.

A government should have access to the principal (or most advantageous) market at the measurement date. The government's principal (or most advantageous) market (and, thus, market participants) should be considered from the perspective of the government, thereby allowing for differences between and among entities with different activities.

Although a government should be able to access the market, it does not need to be able to sell the particular asset or transfer the particular liability on the measurement date to be able to measure fair value on the basis of the price in that market.

Even if there are no observable market transactions to provide pricing information about the sale of an asset or the transfer of a liability at the measurement date, a fair value measurement should assume that a transaction takes place at that date, considered from the perspective of a market participant that controls the asset or is obligated for the liability. That assumed transaction establishes a basis for determining the price to sell the asset or to transfer the liability.

Market Participants

GASBS 72 provides that a government should measure the fair value of an asset or a liability using the assumptions that market participants would use in pricing the asset or liability, assuming that market participants act in their economic best interest. In developing those assumptions, a government need not identify specific market participants. Rather, the government should identify characteristics that distinguish market participants generally, considering factors specific to all of the following:

(a) The asset or liability.
(b) The principal or most advantageous market, as appropriate, for the asset or liability.
(c) Market participants with whom the government would enter into a transaction in that market.

NOTE: Again, for most of the investments held by governments, such as actively traded stocks and many fixed income securities, these specific considerations will not likely have an impact on the fair value measurements.

Price and Transaction Costs

The price in the principal (or most advantageous) market used to measure the fair value of an asset or a liability should not be adjusted for transaction costs even if those costs are separable. GASBS 72 concludes that transaction costs are not a characteristic of an asset or a liability. Rather, they are specific to a transaction and will differ depending on how a government enters into a transaction for the asset or liability.

Transaction costs do not include transportation costs. If location is a characteristic of the asset (as might be the case for a commodity), the price in the principal (or most advantageous) market should be adjusted for the costs, if any, that would be incurred to transport the asset from its current location to that market.

NOTE: As it relates to investments, this section would mean that, for example, in determining the fair value of an equity investment representing shares of stock in a publicly traded corporation on an active stock exchange, the government would use the share price as a basis for determining fair value and not adjust it for brokerage commissions that would be incurred if the stock were actually sold.

VALUATION TECHNIQUES AND APPROACHES

Valuation Techniques

The next section of GASBS 72 describes valuation techniques and approaches. As discussed below, three different valuation approaches are provided. Within a particular valuation approach, valuation techniques would be used to determine fair value.

GASBS 72 provides that a government should use valuation techniques that are appropriate under the circumstances and for which sufficient data are available to measure fair value, maximizing the use of relevant observable inputs and minimizing the use of unobservable inputs. A government should use valuation techniques consistent with one or more of three approaches to measuring fair value: the market approach, cost approach, and income approach. These approaches are described in the next section.

GASBS 72 provides that a single valuation technique is appropriate in some cases (for example, using quoted prices in an active market for identical assets or liabilities). In other cases, multiple valuation techniques are appropriate (such as using both a present value technique and a market multiples technique for a single asset or liability). In such cases, the results should be evaluated considering the reasonableness of the range of values indicated by those results. A fair value measurement is the point within that range that is most representative of fair value under the circumstances. If an asset or a liability is composed of multiple components, multiple valuation techniques also may be used.

Further, valuation techniques used to measure fair value should be applied consistently from period to period. However, a change in a valuation technique or its application (such as a change in the weighting of individual valuation techniques if multiple valuation techniques are used, or a change in an adjustment applied to a valuation technique) is appropriate if the change results in a measurement that is equally or more representative of fair value under the circumstances. GASBS 72 notes that might be the case if, for example, any of the following included events occur:

(a) New markets develop.
(b) New information becomes available.
(c) Information previously used is no longer available.
(d) Valuation techniques improve.
(e) Market conditions change.

If the transaction price is a fair value measurement at initial recognition and a valuation technique that uses unobservable inputs will be used to measure fair value in subsequent periods, the valuation technique should be calibrated so that, at initial recognition, the result of the valuation technique equals the transaction price. After initial recognition, when measuring fair value using a valuation technique or techniques that use unobservable inputs, a government should ensure that those valuation techniques reflect observable market data at the measurement date. For example, if the price of a building at acquisition differs from prices of similar buildings due to variances in building quality, the fair value of that building at subsequent measurement dates should be the observable market prices for similar buildings as of the subsequent measurement dates (observable market data), adjusted for building quality (unobservable inputs).

A revision resulting from a change in the valuation technique or its application should be accounted for as a change in accounting estimate in accordance with GASBS 72.

Valuation Approaches

As mentioned above, GASBS 72 provides for the use of three different valuation approaches. These are the market approach, cost approach, and income approach. The following provides the description of these approaches provided by GASBS 72.

Market Approach

The market approach to measuring fair value uses prices and other relevant information generated by market transactions involving identical or similar assets, liabilities, or groups of assets and liabilities. Using quoted market prices is a technique that is consistent with the market approach. Additional examples provided include the use of the market multiples technique and the matrix pricing technique.

The market multiples technique uses multiples or ratios (such as price-to-earnings or market-to-book-value ratios) derived from identical or similar assets, liabilities, or groups of assets and liabilities (often referred to as comparables) to determine the fair value of an asset or liability. Market multiples might be in ranges with a different multiple for similar assets, liabilities, or groups.

GASBS 72 provides the following example. The fair value of an investment in a company could be determined based on the price-to-earnings ratios of similar companies. However, similar companies may trade at different ratios; therefore, the selection of the appropriate ratio within the range of price-to-earnings ratios requires professional judgment, considering qualitative and quantitative factors specific to the measurement.

The matrix pricing technique is used principally to value some types of financial instruments, such as debt securities, without relying exclusively on quoted prices for the specific securities. Instead, matrix pricing relies on the securities' relationship to other benchmark quoted securities.

Cost Approach

The cost approach to measuring fair value reflects the amount that would be required currently to replace the present service capacity of an asset. From the perspective of a market participant seller, the price that would be received for the asset is based on the cost to a market participant buyer to acquire or construct a substitute asset of comparable utility, adjusted for obsolescence. Obsolescence can be physical, functional (technological), or economic (external).

Income Approach

The income approach to measuring fair value converts future amounts (for example, cash flows or revenues and expenses) to a single current amount (such as would be determined by using the discounted present value technique).

When the income approach is used, the fair value measurement reflects current market expectations about those future amounts. Valuation techniques consistent with the income approach include, for example, (a) the present value technique, (b) the option pricing model technique such as the Black-Scholes-Merton formula, and (c) the multiperiod excess earnings technique.

Inputs to Valuation Techniques

GASBS 72 next addresses the various inputs that are used in any of the three valuation approaches that it defined above. The focus is distinguishing on observable from unobservable inputs, which will be a key concept underlying the various levels in the fair value hierarchy.

Basic Principles

GASBS 72 provides that valuation techniques should maximize the use of relevant observable inputs and minimize the use of unobservable inputs. If there is a quoted price in an active market for an identical asset or an identical liability, a government should use that quoted price without adjustment if measuring fair value, except where specific adjustments are defined, which is discussed later in this section.

A government should select inputs that are consistent with the characteristics of the asset or liability that market participants would take into account in a transaction for the asset or liability. Under GASBS 72, in some cases, those characteristics result in the application of an adjustment, such as a control premium or noncontrolling interest discount. However, a fair value measurement should not incorporate a premium or discount that is inconsistent with the unit of account provision described above.

Premiums or discounts that reflect size as a characteristic of a government's holding are not permitted in the measurement of fair value under GASBS 72. The example that is provided is that of a blockage factor that when applied to a Level 1 input would adjust the quoted price of an asset or a liability because the market's normal daily trading volume is not sufficient to absorb the quantity held by a government. Conversely, if measuring the fair value of a controlling interest, a control premium is a characteristic of the asset or liability and, where applicable, could result in an adjustment of the fair value measurement.

Inputs Based on Bid and Ask Prices

If an asset or a liability measured at fair value has a bid price and an ask price, GASBS 72 provides that the price within the bid–ask spread that is most representative of fair value under the circumstances should be used to measure fair value regardless of where the input is categorized within the fair value hierarchy. If no price is more representative than another, the use of a bid price (for an asset position) and an ask price (for a liability position) is permitted. Mid-market pricing or other pricing conventions that are used by market participants for measuring fair value within a bid–ask spread also are permitted.

Fair Value Hierarchy

The most noticeable impact that GASBS 72 will have on government financial statements is the establishment of a fair value hierarchy and the categorization and disclosures related to assets and liabilities reported at fair value in the financial statements.

The fair value hierarchy categorizes the inputs to valuation techniques used to measure fair value into three levels. These levels are defined by GASBS 72 as follows:

Level 1 inputs are quoted prices (unadjusted) for identical assets or liabilities in active markets that a government can access at the measurement date.

Level 2 inputs are inputs (other than quoted prices included within Level 1) that are observable for an asset or liability, either directly or indirectly.

Level 3 inputs are unobservable inputs for an asset or liability.

The additional detail regarding these three levels that is provided by GASBS 72 is discussed below. The fair value hierarchy promulgated by GASBS 72 gives the highest priority to Level 1 inputs and the lowest priority to Level 3 inputs. In other words, fair value should be measured using the highest (or most objective) level possible. The highest level possible (Level 1) has the lowest numeric value of a level (1), so these shouldn't be confused. Further, GASBS 72 provides that if a price for an identical asset or liability is not observable, a government should measure fair value using another valuation technique that maximizes the use of relevant observable inputs and minimizes the use of unobservable inputs.

If the fair value of an asset or a liability is measured using inputs from more than one level of the fair value hierarchy, the measurement is considered to be based on the lowest priority level input that is significant to the entire measurement.

To illustrate this, GASBS 72 provides the following example. If there are three inputs significant to a certain fair value measurement, two of them are Level 2 inputs, and one is a Level 3 input, the fair value measurement would be categorized in Level 3 of the fair value hierarchy. Assessing the significance of a particular input to the entire measurement requires professional judgment, taking into account factors specific to the asset or liability.

GASBS 72 notes that the availability of relevant inputs and their relative subjectivity might affect the selection of appropriate valuation techniques. However, the fair value hierarchy prioritizes the inputs to valuation techniques, not the valuation techniques used to measure fair value. For example, a measurement of fair value that uses a present value technique might be categorized within either Level 2 or Level 3, depending on the inputs that are significant to the entire measurement and the level of the fair value hierarchy within which those inputs are categorized.

If an observable input requires an adjustment using an unobservable input and that adjustment results in a significantly higher or lower fair value measurement, the resultant measurement would be categorized within Level 3 of the fair value hierarchy. GASBS 72 uses the following example to illustrate this. If a market participant takes into account the effect of a restriction on the sale of an asset when determining the price for the asset, a government would adjust the quoted price to reflect the effect of that restriction. If that quoted price is a Level 2 input and the adjustment is an unobservable input that is significant to the entire measurement, the measurement would be categorized within Level 3 of the fair value hierarchy.

GASBS 72 provides much more detail about each of these levels, which is discussed below.

Level 1 Inputs

GASBS 72 provides that a quoted price for identical assets or liabilities in an active market provides the most reliable evidence of a Level 1 input of fair value and should be used to measure fair value without adjustment whenever available, except as specified below. Examples of markets in which inputs might be observable include exchange markets (such as the New York Stock Exchange), dealer markets (such as over-the-counter markets and the market for U.S. Treasury securities), brokered markets (brokers attempt to match buyers and sellers, but don't trade for their own account, such as electronic communications networks), and principal-to-principal markets (where transactions are negotiated independently with no intermediary).

GASBS 72 notes that a Level 1 input will be available for many financial assets and financial liabilities, some of which might be exchanged in multiple active markets (for example, on different exchanges). Therefore, the emphasis within Level 1 is on determining both of the following:

(a) The principal market for an asset or liability or, in the absence of a principal market, the most advantageous market for an asset or liability.
(b) Whether the government can enter into a transaction for an asset or liability at the price in that market at the measurement date.

GASBS 72 provides specific instances where a Level 1 input should be adjusted. Absent any of these specific conditions, the Level 1 input should not be adjusted:

(a) **Large number of similar assets or liabilities.** An adjustment to a Level 1 input should be made if (1) a government holds a large number of similar (but not identical) assets or liabilities (for example, debt securities) that are measured at fair value and (2) a quoted price in an active market is available but not readily accessible for each of those assets or liabilities individually, except as noted below. That is, given the large number of similar assets or liabilities held by the government, it would be difficult to obtain pricing information for each individual asset or liability at the measurement date. In this case, a government may measure fair value using an alternative pricing method that does not rely exclusively on quoted prices (for example, matrix pricing). However, the use of an alternative pricing method results in a fair value measurement categorized within either Level 2 or Level 3 of the fair value hierarchy.
(b) **Quoted price not representative of fair value.** An adjustment to a Level 1 input should be made if a quoted price in an active market does not represent fair value at the measurement date. That might be the case if, for example, significant events (such as transactions in a principal-to-principal market, trades in a brokered market, or announcements) take place after the close of a market but before the measurement date. A government should establish and consistently apply a policy for identifying those events that might affect fair value measurements. However, if the quoted price is adjusted for new information, the adjustment results in a fair value measurement categorized within either Level 2 or Level 3 of the fair value hierarchy.
(c) **Fair value of an asset not representative of fair value of a liability.** An adjustment to a Level 1 input should be made if (1) the fair value of a liability is measured using the quoted price for the identical item traded as an asset in an active market and (2) that price needs to be adjusted for factors specific to the asset that are not applicable to the liability. If no adjustment to the quoted price of the asset is required, the result is a fair value measurement categorized within Level 1 of the fair value hierarchy. However, any adjustment to the quoted price of the asset results in a fair value measurement categorized within either Level 2 or Level 3 of the fair value hierarchy.

GASBS 72 also provides that if a position in a single asset or liability (including a position comprising a large number of identical assets or liabilities, such as a holding of financial instruments) is held and the asset or liability is traded in an active market, the fair value of the asset or liability should be measured within Level 1 as the product of the quoted price for the individual asset or liability and the quantity held by a government. That is the case even if a market's normal daily trading volume is not sufficient to absorb the quantity held, and placing orders to sell the position in a single transaction might affect the quoted price.

NOTE: For investments, most actively traded equity securities will be categorized as Level 1, as will open-end mutual funds (where a daily quote to purchase additional shares at net asset value is available) and most Treasury securities (where market quotes can be obtained for the identical security).

Level 2 Inputs

GASBS 72 defines Level 2 inputs to include:

(a) Quoted prices for similar assets or liabilities in active markets.
(b) Quoted prices for identical or similar assets or liabilities in markets that are not active.
(c) Inputs other than quoted prices that are observable for the asset or liability, such as:

1. Interest rates and yield curves observable at commonly quoted intervals.
2. Implied volatilities.
3. Credit spreads.

(d) Market-corroborated inputs, in which inputs are derived principally from or corroborated by observable market data by correlation or other means.

For financial reporting purposes, if an asset or liability has a specified (contractual) term, a Level 2 input is required to be observable for substantially the full term of the asset or liability.

GASBS 72 notes that adjustments to Level 2 inputs will vary depending on factors specific to an asset or liability, including:

(a) The condition or location of the asset.
(b) The extent to which inputs relate to items that are comparable to the asset or liability (including those factors described in paragraph 61).
(c) The volume or level of activity in the markets within which the inputs are observed.

NOTE: For investments, many corporate and other fixed income securities are included in Level 2. Often individual bond issues are not actively traded, but fair value can be determined using bonds that are traded that have the same or similar maturity, interest rate, credit rating, and so on. Also, where pooled investment funds are provided by an investment firm, often a quote for these funds cannot be obtained from an active market because they are available only to the investment firm's clients, so these are often categorized as Level 1.

Level 3 Inputs

GASBS 72 provides that a government should develop Level 3 inputs using the best information available under the circumstances, which might include the government's own data. In developing unobservable inputs, a government may begin with its own data, but it should adjust those data if (a) reasonably available information indicates that other market participants would use different data or (b) there is something particular to the government that is not available to other market participants. GASBS 72 states that a government need not undertake exhaustive efforts to obtain information about market participant assumptions; however, a government should take into account all information about market participant assumptions that is reasonably available. Unobservable inputs developed in the manner described in this paragraph are considered market participant assumptions and meet the objective of a fair value measurement.

Assumptions about risk include the risk inherent in a particular valuation technique used to measure fair value (such as a pricing model) and the risk inherent in the inputs to the valuation technique. A measurement that does not include an adjustment for risk would not represent a fair value measurement if market participants would include one when pricing the asset or liability. For example, it might be necessary to include a risk adjustment if there is significant measurement uncertainty. That could be the case if (a) there has been a significant decrease in the volume or level of activity compared with normal market activity for the asset or liability, or similar assets or liabilities, and (b) a government has determined that the transaction price or quoted price does not represent fair value, as described in the following paragraphs.

NOTE: The more common Level 3 investments are investments in real estate, limited partnership interests, and certain hedge funds.

NOTE: As mentioned previously, these fair value hierarchy levels track closely those of the FASB requirements, as recently amended. One unintended outcome that sometimes arose upon implementation of the FASB standards was that financial statement users sometimes viewed the levels as a reflection on the quality of the investment, rather than as a reflection of the objectivity of the fair value measurement. Government financial statement preparers should be ready to explain this difference should the question arise upon implementation of these GASB requirements.

Measuring Fair Value If the Volume or Level of Market Activity for an Asset or a Liability Has Significantly Decreased

GASBS 72 notes that the fair value of an asset or a liability might be affected if there has been a significant decrease in the volume or level of activity in relation to normal market activity for the asset or liability (or similar assets or liabilities). Determining the price at which market participants would be willing to enter into a transaction at the measurement date under current market conditions if there has been a significant decrease in the volume or level of activity for the asset or liability depends on the facts and circumstances at the measurement date and requires professional judgment. To determine whether, on the basis of the available evidence, there has been a significant decrease in the volume or level of activity for an asset or liability, GASBS 72 provides that a government should evaluate the significance and relevance of factors such as the following:

(a) There are few recent transactions.
(b) Price quotations are not developed using current information.
(c) Price quotations vary substantially either over time or among market makers (for example, some brokered markets).
(d) Indices that previously were highly correlated with the fair values of an asset or liability are demonstrably uncorrelated with recent indications of fair value for that asset or liability.
(e) There is a significant increase in implied liquidity risk premiums, yields, or performance indicators (such as delinquency rates or loss severities) for observed transactions or quoted prices when compared with a government's estimate of expected cash flows, taking into account all available market data about credit and other nonperformance risk for the asset or liability.
(f) There is a wide bid–ask spread or a significant increase in the bid–ask spread.
(g) There is a significant decline in the activity of a market for new issues (that is, a primary market) for an asset or liability or similar assets or liabilities, or there is an absence of such a market.
(h) Little information is publicly available (for example, for transactions that take place in a principal-to-principal market).

If a government concludes that there has been a significant decrease in the volume or level of activity for an asset or liability in relation to normal market activity for the asset or liability (or similar assets or liabilities), further analysis of the transactions or quoted prices is needed. A decrease in the volume or level of activity on its own may not indicate that a transaction price or quoted price does not represent fair value or that a transaction in that market is not orderly, as described below. However, a government may determine that a transaction or quoted price does not represent fair value (for example, there may be transactions that are not orderly). If so, an adjustment to the transactions or quoted prices will be necessary if (a) the government uses those prices as a basis for measuring fair value, and (b) that adjustment is significant to the fair value measurement in its entirety. Adjustments also may be necessary in other circumstances (for example, if a price for a similar asset requires significant adjustment to make it comparable to the asset being measured, or if the price is stale).

Regardless of the valuation technique used, GASBS 72 provides that a government should include appropriate risk adjustments, including a risk premium reflecting the amount that market participants would demand as compensation for the uncertainty inherent in the cash flows of an asset or a liability. In some cases, determining the appropriate risk adjustment might be difficult. However, the degree of difficulty alone is not a sufficient basis on which to exclude a risk adjustment.

The risk adjustment should be reflective of an orderly transaction between market participants at the measurement date under current market conditions.

If there has been a significant decrease in the volume or level of activity for an asset or liability, a change in valuation technique or the use of multiple valuation techniques may be appropriate (for example, changing from a technique based on market-observed prices to an expected cash flow technique).

When weighing indications of fair value resulting from the use of multiple valuation techniques, GASBS 72 provides that a government should consider the reasonableness of the range of fair value measurements. The objective is to determine the point within the range that is most representative of fair value under current market conditions.

A wide range of fair value measurements may be an indication that further analysis is needed.

IDENTIFYING TRANSACTIONS THAT ARE NOT ORDERLY

The discussion in the previous section includes circumstances where a government may need to identify transactions that are not orderly. GASBS 72 notes that the determination of whether a transaction is orderly can be difficult if there has been a significant decrease in the volume or level of activity for an asset or liability in relation to normal market activity for the asset or liability (or similar assets or liabilities). In such circumstances, it is not appropriate to conclude that all transactions in that market are not orderly. A government should evaluate the circumstances of the transaction to determine whether, based on the available evidence, the transaction is orderly. GASBS 72 identifies the following as circumstances that may indicate that a transaction is not orderly:

(a) The period of exposure to the market before the measurement date was not adequate to allow for marketing activities that are usual and customary for transactions involving such assets or liabilities under current market conditions.
(b) There was a usual and customary marketing period, but the seller marketed the asset or liability to a single market participant.

(c) The seller is in or near bankruptcy (that is, the seller is distressed).
(d) The seller was required to sell to meet regulatory or legal requirements (that is, the seller was forced).
(e) The transaction price is an outlier when compared with other recent transactions for the same or a similar asset or liability.

GASBS 72 specifies that a government should consider all of the following when measuring fair value, including the determination of market risk premiums or discounts:

(a) If the evidence indicates that a transaction is orderly, a government should take into account that transaction price. The reliance on that transaction price compared with other indications of fair value will depend on the facts and circumstances, such as:
   1. The volume of the transaction.
   2. The comparability of the transaction to the asset or liability being measured.
   3. The proximity of the transaction to the measurement date.
(b) If the evidence indicates the transaction is not orderly, a government should place little, if any, weight (compared with other indications of fair value) on that transaction price.
(c) If a government does not have sufficient information to conclude that a transaction is orderly, it should take into account the transaction price.

However, that transaction price may not represent fair value (that is, the transaction price is not necessarily the sole or primary basis for measuring fair value or determining market risk premiums or discounts). If a government does not have sufficient information to conclude that particular transactions are orderly, the government should place less weight on those transactions when compared with other transactions that are known to be orderly.

GASBS 72 also notes that to determine whether a transaction is orderly, a government should consider information that is reasonably available. If a government is a party to a transaction, it is presumed to have sufficient information to determine whether the transaction is orderly.

USING QUOTED PRICES PROVIDED BY THIRD PARTIES

GASBS 72 provides that quoted prices provided by third parties, such as pricing services or brokers, may be used if a government has determined that the quoted prices provided by those parties are developed in accordance with the provisions of GASBS 72.

However, if there has been a significant decrease in the volume or level of activity for an asset or liability, a government should evaluate whether the quoted prices provided by third parties are developed using current information that reflects orderly transactions or a valuation technique that reflects market participant assumptions (including assumptions about risk). In weighting a quoted price as an input to a fair value measurement, a government should rely less on quoted prices that do not reflect the result of transactions (when compared with other indications of fair value that reflect the results of transactions).

GASBS 72 also provides that the nature of a quoted price (such as whether the quoted price is an indicative price or a binding offer) should be taken into account when considering the available evidence, with more consideration given to quoted prices provided by third parties that represent binding offers.

Measurement Principles

GASBS 72 next provides guidance in applying its fair value principles to nonfinancial assets and liabilities. Generally, measuring nonfinancial assets and liabilities requires additional considerations in addition to those discussed for financial assets.

Nonfinancial Assets

Highest and Best Use of Nonfinancial Assets

In measuring fair value for nonfinancial assets, the concept that nonfinancial assets have different uses, resulting in different fair value measurements, must be considered. GASBS 72 provides that if an accounting standard requires the application of fair value to a nonfinancial asset (for example, real property in certain circumstances), the fair value measurement takes into account a market participant's ability to generate resources by using the asset according to its highest and best use or by selling it to another market participant that would use the asset according to its highest and best use.

NOTE: In measuring fair value of nonfinancial assets, often the assistance of a professional appraiser is used. Certain of the concepts described in this section would likely be difficult, in many circumstances, without such professional help. It would be important to make sure the appraiser is familiar with these concepts from a financial reporting point of view, in contrast to appraisals done for tax purposes, such as the value of a donation of a nonfinancial asset.

GASBS 72 defines *highest and best use* as the use of a nonfinancial asset by market participants that would maximize the value of the asset or the group of assets and liabilities within which the asset would be used. Further, the highest and best use of a nonfinancial asset takes into account the use of the asset that is physically possible, legally permissible, and financially feasible, as described by GASBS 72 as follows:

(a) A use that is physically possible takes into account the physical characteristics of an asset that market participants would take into account when pricing the asset (for example, the location or size of a property).
(b) A use that is legally permissible takes into account any legal restrictions on the use of an asset that market participants would take into account when pricing an asset (for example, the current zoning regulations applicable to a property).
(c) A use that is financially feasible takes into account whether a use of an asset that is physically possible and legally permissible generates resources (taking into account the costs of converting the asset to that use) to produce an investment return that market participants would require from an investment in that asset put to that use.

GASBS 72 considers that highest and best use is determined from the perspective of market participants using relevant market data as of the measurement date, even if a government intends a different use for a nonfinancial asset. However, the government's current use of a nonfinancial asset that is measured at fair value is presumed to be its highest and best use unless market or other factors suggest that a different use by market participants would maximize the value of the asset.

The highest and best use of a nonfinancial asset is based on certain assumptions used to measure the fair value of an asset, which GASBS 72 describes as follows:

(a) The highest and best use of a nonfinancial asset may provide maximum value to market participants through its use in combination with other assets as a group (as installed or otherwise configured for use) or in combination with other assets and liabilities.

1. If the highest and best use of the nonfinancial asset is for use in combination with other assets or with other assets and liabilities, the fair value of the asset is the price that would be received in a current transaction to sell the asset assuming that the asset would be used with other assets or with other assets and liabilities and that those assets and liabilities (that is, its complementary assets and the associated liabilities) would be available to market participants.
2. Liabilities associated with the nonfinancial asset and with the complementary assets include liabilities that provide resources but do not include liabilities used to acquire assets other than those within the group of assets.
3. Assumptions about the highest and best use of a nonfinancial asset should be consistent for all of the assets (for which highest and best use is relevant) of the group of assets or the group of assets and liabilities within which the nonfinancial asset would be used.

(b) The highest and best use of a nonfinancial asset may provide maximum value to market participants on a stand-alone basis. In that case, the fair value of the nonfinancial asset is the price that would be received in a transaction as of the measurement date to sell the nonfinancial asset to market participants that would use the nonfinancial asset on a stand-alone basis.

GASBS 72 provides that the measurement of the fair value of a nonfinancial asset assumes that an asset is sold consistent with the unit of account provision discussed earlier. This is the case whether the fair value measurement assumes that the highest and best use of the nonfinancial asset is for use for an individual asset or for use for an asset in combination with other assets or with other assets and liabilities. If the highest and best use is for the asset in combination with other assets or with other assets and liabilities, a measurement of the fair value of a nonfinancial asset assumes that the market participant already holds the complementary assets and associated liabilities.

Liabilities

Next, GASBS 72 addresses fair value measurement considerations for liabilities. Surprisingly, measuring the fair value of liabilities is more common than the reader might at first think. Thus measurement considerations for liabilities would apply to an interest rate swap agreement that is in a liability position to a government, which is encountered often in practice.

Basic Principles

GASBS 72 provides that the measurement of the fair value of a liability assumes that the liability is transferred to a market participant at the measurement date. The transfer of a liability assumes the liability would remain outstanding and the market participant transferee would be required to fulfill the obligation. The liability would not be settled with the counterparty or otherwise extinguished on the measurement date. GASBS 72 notes that even if there is no observable market to provide pricing information about the transfer of a liability (for example, because contractual or other legal restrictions prevent the transfer of such items), there might be an observable market for such items if they are held by other parties as assets.

Liabilities Held by Other Parties as Assets

If a quoted price for the transfer of an identical or similar liability is not available and the identical item is held by another party as an asset, GASBS 72 provides that a government should measure the fair value of the liability from the perspective of a market participant that holds the identical item as an asset at the measurement date. In such cases, a government should measure the fair value of the liability as follows:

(a) Using the quoted price in an active market for the identical item held by another party as an asset, if that price is available.
(b) If the quoted price in (a) is not available, using other observable inputs, such as the quoted price in a market that is not active for the identical item held by another party as an asset.
(c) If the observable prices in (a) and (b) are not available, using another valuation technique, such as the following:

1. Quoted prices for similar liabilities held by other parties as assets (a market approach).
2. A present value technique that takes into account the future cash flows that a market participant would expect to receive from holding the liability as an asset (an income approach).

GASBS notes that a government should adjust the quoted price of a liability held by another party as an asset only if there are factors specific to the asset that are not applicable to the fair value measurement of the liability. A government should ensure that the price of the asset does not reflect the effect of a restriction preventing the sale of that asset. Some factors that may indicate that the quoted price of an asset should be adjusted to determine the fair value of a liability include the following:

(a) The quoted price for the asset relates to a similar (but not identical) liability held by another party as an asset. For example, the liability may have a particular characteristic (such as the credit quality of the issuer) that is different from that reflected in the fair value of the similar liability held as an asset.
(b) The unit of account for the asset is not the same as for the liability. For example, consider an insured interest rate swap that is in a liability position.

In some cases, the price for such an asset reflects a combined price for a financial instrument comprising both the amounts due from the issuer and a third-party credit enhancement (for example, debt that is used with a financial guarantee from a third party). If the unit of account for the swap liability is not the combined financial instrument, the objective would be to measure the fair value of the issuer's liability, not the fair value of the combined package.

Thus, in such cases, GASBS 72 notes that a government would adjust the observed price for the asset to exclude the effect of the third-party credit enhancement.

Nonperformance Risk

GASBS 72 provides that the fair value of a liability reflects the effect of nonperformance risk. Nonperformance risk includes, but may not be limited to, a government's own credit risk. Nonperformance risk is assumed to be the same before and after the transfer of the liability.

When measuring the fair value of a liability, GASBS 72 provides that a government should take into account the effect of its credit risk (credit standing) and any other factors that might influence the likelihood that the obligation will or will not be fulfilled. That effect may differ depending on the characteristics of the liability, such as (a) whether the liability is an obligation to deliver cash (a financial liability) or an obligation to deliver goods or services (a nonfinancial liability) and (b) the terms of credit enhancements related to the liability, if any.

Restrictions Preventing the Transfer of a Liability

GASBS 72 provides that a government should not include a separate input or an adjustment to other inputs relating to the existence of a restriction that prevents the transfer of the liability, when measuring the fair value of a liability. The effect of a restriction that prevents the transfer of a liability is either implicitly or explicitly included in the other inputs to the fair value measurement. GASBS 72 includes the following example. At the transaction date, both the creditor and the obligor accepted the transaction price for the liability with full knowledge that the obligation includes a restriction that prevents its transfer. As a result of the restriction being included in the transaction price, a separate input or an adjustment to an existing input is not required at the transaction date to reflect the effect of the restriction on transfer. Similarly, a separate input or an adjustment to an existing input is not required at subsequent measurement dates to reflect the effect of the restriction on transfer.

Application of Fair Value

One of the most important aspects of GASBS 72 outside of the fair value hierarchy is its impact on the accounting for investments. Not only does GASBS 72 broaden the requirement to measure and report investments at fair value; it also broadens and clarifies the definition of an investment. These requirements are described in the following section.

Application of Fair Value to Investments

Except for certain types of investments detailed below, GASBS 72 provides that investments should be measured at fair value. An investment is a security or other asset that (a) a government holds primarily for the purpose of income or profit and (b) has a present service capacity based solely on its ability to generate cash or to be sold to generate cash.

NOTE: The key words to note in the above definition of investments are that, in addition to securities, other assets that meet certain criteria under GASBS 72 are also included in the definition of investments. These concepts and requirements are discussed in the following paragraphs.

Present Service Capacity

GASBS 72 notes that investments indirectly enable a government to provide services. Assets are resources with present service capacity that a government controls at the time. Present service capacity refers to a government's mission to provide services.

GASBS 72 notes that while capital assets provide services directly, investments do not. Rather, investments are valuable to a government because investments can be used to pay for goods or services that in turn are used to provide services directly to its citizens. As an example, if converted to cash, an investment may allow a government to acquire or construct a capital asset, such as a bridge. The bridge is used to provide services to the government's constituency.

Held Primarily for Income or Profit

GASBS 72 notes that a government acquires an investment with the expectation of future income or profit. Evidence that a government holds an asset for income or profit also may be found in the fund that reports the asset. For example, income-producing real property in a pension plan suggests that the asset is held primarily for income or profit.

Present Service Capacity Based Solely on an Asset's Ability to Generate Cash or to Be Sold to Generate Cash

Certain financial instruments may generate cash to finance the provision of services. However, the fact that a financial instrument generates cash does not, in itself, mean that it is an investment. As an example, GASBS 72 notes that mortgage loans are not investments if the loans arise from a government's program that extends financing to first-time homebuyers. The present service capacity of the loans is not based solely on the loans' ability to generate cash.

GASBS 72 provides that the determination of whether an asset is held primarily for the purpose of income or profit or whether its present service capacity is based solely on its ability to generate cash or to be sold to generate cash is based on actions by a government's management at acquisition. Once the government determines whether the asset is an investment or another type of asset, the classification should be retained for financial reporting purposes, even if the government's usage of the asset changes over time. As an example, an asset that is initially reported as a capital asset and later is held for sale should not be reclassified as an investment.

NOTE: This is an important requirement of GASBS 72 that should not be overlooked, because intuitively one might think that a government would reclassify investments to and from other assets based upon their use over their lifetime. Rather, as described above, the determination is made at acquisition and retained for financial reporting purposes.

Investment Measurements and Other Statements

GASBS 72 provides that its provisions should be applied to the measurement of investments reported at fair value, related recognition of gains and losses, and disclosures. However, the following describes certain investments that are not measured at fair value. GASBS 72 provides that the following investments should be measured as it describes below:

(a) Investments in nonparticipating interest-earning investment contracts should be measured using a cost-based measure as provided in paragraph 8 of Statement 31.
(b) Investments in unallocated insurance contracts should be reported as interest-earning investment contracts according to the provisions of paragraph 8 of GASB Statement 31, and paragraph 4 of Statement No. 59, *Financial Instruments Omnibus*.
(c) Money market investments and participating interest-earning investment contracts that have a remaining maturity at the time of purchase of one year or less and are held by governments other than external investment pools should be measured at amortized cost as provided in paragraph 9 of GASBS 31.

NOTE: This provision applies to money market investments themselves (commercial paper, U.S. Treasury bills, etc., as defined in GASBS 31). It does not apply to a money market fund that invests in money market investments. Such a fund would be measured at fair value.

(d) Investments held by 2a7-like external investment pools may be measured at amortized cost as provided in paragraph 16 of Statement 31.
(e) Synthetic guaranteed investment contracts that are fully benefit-responsive should be measured at contract value as provided in paragraph 67 of Statement 53.
(f) Investments in 2a7-like external investment pools should be measured at the net asset value (NAV) per share (or its equivalent) determined by the pool as provided in paragraph 5 of GASBS 59.
(g) Investments in life insurance contracts should be measured at cash surrender value.

Investments in Life Settlement Contracts

GASBS 72 requires that investments in life settlement contracts should be measured at fair value. Life settlement contracts have the following characteristics, which are provided in GASBS:

(a) The government-investor does not have an insurable interest (an interest in the survival of the insured, which is required to support the issuance of an insurance policy).
(b) The government-investor provides consideration to the policy owner of an amount in excess of the current cash surrender value of the life insurance policy.
(c) The contract pays the face value of the life insurance policy to the government-investor when the insured dies.
(d) The government-investor is the policyholder.

Investments in Certain Entities That Calculate the Net Asset Value per Share (or Its Equivalent)

To fully understand this section, there are two definitions contained in GASBS 72 that must be understood: net asset value per share and readily determinable fair value.

Net Asset Value per Share

Net asset value per share is the amount of net assets attributable to each share of capital stock (other than senior equity securities; that is, preferred stock) outstanding at the close of the period. It excludes the effects of assuming conversion of outstanding convertible securities, whether or not their conversion would have a diluting effect.

Readily Determinable Fair Value

An equity security has a readily determinable fair value if it meets any of the following conditions:

- The fair value of an equity security is readily determinable if sales prices or bid-and-asked quotations are currently available on a securities exchange registered with the U.S. Securities and Exchange Commission or in the over-the-counter market, provided that those prices or quotations for the over-the-counter market are publicly reported by the National Association of Securities Dealers Automated Quotations systems or by OTC Markets Group, Inc. Restricted stock meets that definition if the restriction terminates within one year.

  (a) The fair value is readily determinable if that foreign market is of a breadth and scope comparable to one of the U.S. markets referred to in the paragraph above.
  (b) The fair value of an investment in a mutual fund is readily determinable if the fair value per share (unit) is determined and published and is the basis for current transactions.

GASBS 72 provides that a government is permitted to establish the fair value of an investment in a nongovernmental entity that does not have a readily determinable fair value by using the NAV per share (or its equivalent), such as member units or an ownership interest in partners' capital to which a proportionate share of net assets is attributed. This method of determining fair value is permitted if the NAV per share (or its equivalent) of the investment is calculated as of the government's measurement date generally in a manner consistent with the Financial Accounting Standards Board's measurement principles for investment companies. A government should determine that the NAV per share (or its equivalent) provided by the investee is determined in that manner.

If the NAV per share (or its equivalent) of an investment obtained from the investee is not determined as of a government's measurement date or is not calculated in a manner consistent with the measurement principles for investment companies, GASBS 72 provides that the government should consider whether an adjustment to the most recent NAV per share (or its equivalent) is necessary. The objective of any adjustment is to determine the NAV per share (or its equivalent) for the investment that is calculated as of the government's measurement date in a manner consistent with the measurement principles for investment companies.

A government should determine on an investment-by-investment basis whether the method of determining fair value above should be applied. The method of determining fair value should be applied consistently to the fair value measurement of the government's entire position in a particular investment, unless it is probable at the measurement date that the government will sell a portion of an investment at an amount different from the NAV per share (or its equivalent) as described in paragraph 74. In those situations, the government should account for the portion of the investment that is being sold in accordance with other guidance in this Statement (that is, the government should not apply the guidance for using net asset value to measure fair value).

GASBS 72 also provides that the method of determining fair value using net asset value should not be applied if, as of the government's measurement date, it is probable that the government will sell the investment for an amount different from the NAV per share (or its equivalent). A sale is considered probable only if all of the following criteria have been met as of the government's measurement date:

(a) The government, having the authority to approve the action, commits to a plan to sell the investment.
(b) An active program to locate a buyer and other actions required to complete the plan to sell the investment have been initiated.
(c) The investment is available for immediate sale subject only to terms that are usual and customary for sales of such investments (for example, a requirement to obtain approval of the sale from the investee, or a buyer's due diligence procedures).
(d) Actions required to complete the plan indicate that it is unlikely that significant changes to the plan will be made or that the plan will be withdrawn.

Recognizing Changes in Fair Value

GASBS 72 does not change the accounting for changes in the fair value of investments during the reporting period. Changes in the fair value of investments should be recognized as provided in GASBS 31, as amended, which is described earlier in this chapter. Changes in the fair value of derivative instruments during the reporting period should be recognized as provided in GASBS 53, as amended.

Application of Fair Value to Debt Securities

GASBS 72 provides that loans acquired or originated by a government—such as mortgage loans acquired by a housing finance agency—that have been securitized should be measured at fair value.

Equity Interests in Common Stock

Equity interests in common stock, as described in GASBS 62, should be accounted for using the equity method if they meet the criteria specified in GASBS 62 and are not specifically excluded below.

The following investments are excluded by GASBS using the equity method of accounting:

(a) Common stock held by:

1. External investment pools.
2. Pension or other postemployment benefit plans.
3. Internal Revenue Code Section 457 deferred compensation plans.
4. Endowments (including permanent and term endowments) or permanent funds.

(b) Investments in certain entities that calculate the NAV per share (or its equivalent) as provided by GASBS 72.

(c) Equity interest ownership in joint ventures or component units as provided in GASBS 14, as amended.

Equity interests in common stock that do not meet both the definition of an investment and the criteria in GASBS 62 for using the equity method should be accounted for using the cost method as provided in GASBS 62.

NOTE: In August 2018 the GASB issued Statement No. 90, Majority Equity Interests and amendment of GASB Statements No. 14 and 61 (GASBS 90), which provides guidance for governments in determining whether a majority interest in a corporation, partnership, etc., should be reported as an investment or as a component unit. GASBS 90 also describes the appropriate accounting treatment under each scenario, including when such interest that is accounted for as an investment should be measured using the equity method or at fair value. GASBS 90 is described in Chapter 11.

Acquisition Value

GASBS 72 notes that the price that would be paid to acquire an asset with equivalent service potential in an orderly market transaction at the acquisition date, or the amount at which a liability could be liquidated with the counterparty at the acquisition date, is referred to as acquisition value. GASBS 72 provides that the following assets should be measured at acquisition value:

(a) Donated capital assets, as provided in GASBS 34, as amended.

(b) Donated works of art, historical treasures, and similar assets as provided in GASBS 34, as amended.

(c) Capital assets that a government receives in a service concession arrangement as provided in GASBS 60.

Disclosures

GASBS 72 has significant disclosure requirements that will affect virtually all governments and governmental entities, as most entities have investments that are (or will be) measured at fair value. GASBS 72 provides that its required disclosures should be organized by type of asset or liability and the following should be taken into consideration when determining the level of detail and disaggregation and how much emphasis to place on each disclosure requirement:

(a) **The nature, characteristics, and risks of an asset or a liability.** Assets and liabilities that share the same nature, characteristics, or risks may be aggregated. The following example is included in GASBS 72: U.S. Treasury bills may be aggregated with short-term U.S. Treasury Separate Trading of Registered Interest and Principal Securities (STRIPS) because these investments have similar exposures to interest rate risk.
(b) **The level of the fair value hierarchy within which the fair value measurement is categorized.** A greater degree of uncertainty and subjectivity suggests that the number of types may need to be greater. For example, fair value measurements categorized within Level 3 of the fair value hierarchy may need greater disaggregation.
(c) **Whether GASBS 72 or another GASB Statement specifies a type for an asset or a liability.** Disclosures should be disaggregated by type as specified by relevant accounting standards. For example, GASBS 53 requires derivative instrument disclosures that distinguish between hedging derivative instruments and investment derivative instruments.
(d) **The objective or the mission of the government.** The level of aggregation or disaggregation may differ based upon the objective or mission of the government. The example provided in GASBS 72 concerns an external investment pool, the objective of which is to achieve income or profit, which suggests greater disaggregation compared to a general purpose government.
(e) **The characteristics of the government.** A government may be composed of governmental and business-type activities, individual major funds, nonmajor funds in the aggregate, or fiduciary fund types and component units. Additional disclosures may be appropriate if the risk exposure of a particular fund is significantly greater than the deposit and investment risks of the primary government. GASBS 72 provides the example of a primary government whose total investments may not be exposed to a concentration of credit risk. However, if the government's capital projects fund (a major fund) has all of its investments in one issuer of corporate bonds, disclosure should be made for the capital projects fund's exposure to a concentration of credit risk.
(f) **Relative significance of assets and liabilities.** The relative significance of assets and liabilities measured at fair value compared to total assets and liabilities should be evaluated in terms of the government structure as discussed in (e) above.
(g) **Whether separately issued financial statements are available.** A government may further aggregate disclosures if a component unit issues its own separate financial statements containing disaggregated information. In the example provided by GASBS 72, a state government may consider reduced disclosures of fair value measurements of investments in certain entities that calculate the NAV per share (or its equivalent) if the financial statements of the state's pension plan include that information.
(h) **Line items presented in the statement of net position.** A type of asset or liability will often require greater disaggregation than the line items presented in the statement of net position. GASBS 72 notes that the statement of net position reports "cash and investments" while GASBS 3 and GASBS 40, *Deposit and Investment Risk Disclosures*, require disclosures that focus on deposits and investments. These disclosure requirements are discussed earlier in this chapter.

GASBS 72 provides specific disclosure requirements regarding fair value. In doing so, it distinguishes between recurring and nonrecurring fair value measurements as follows:

- Recurring fair value measurements of assets or liabilities are those that other GASB Statements require or permit in the statement of net position at the end of each reporting period.
- Nonrecurring fair value measurements of assets or liabilities are those that other GASB Statements require or permit in the statement of net position in particular circumstances (for example, when a government measures a mortgage loan held for sale at the lower of carrying value or fair value in accordance with GASBS 62).

GASBS 72 provides that a government should disclose the following information for each type of asset or liability measured at fair value in the statement of net position (or governmental funds balance sheet) after initial recognition.

(a) For recurring and nonrecurring fair value measurements:

1. The fair value measurement at the end of the reporting period.
2. Except for investments discussed above that are measured at the NAV per share (or its equivalent) and meet the requirements discussed above, the level of the fair value hierarchy within which the fair value measurements are categorized in their entirety (Level 1, Level 2, or Level 3).
3. A description of the valuation techniques used in the fair value measurement.
4. If there has been a change in valuation technique that has a significant impact on the result (for example, changing from an expected cash flow technique to a relief from royalty technique or the use of an additional valuation technique), that change and the reason(s) for making it.

(b) For nonrecurring fair value measurements: the reason(s) for the measurement.

NOTE: It's important to understand that the investments reported at net asset value as discussed earlier are not categorized in the fair value hierarchy. This is consistent to recent changes that the FASB has adopted for reporting of these types of investments within its fair value hierarchy. However, there are additional disclosure requirements for these investments, as is discussed in the following section.

Additional Disclosures for Fair Value Measurements of Investments in Certain Entities That Calculate the Net Asset Value per Share (or Its Equivalent)

The disclosures in this section that are required under GASBS 72 apply to investments in entities that meet all of the following criteria: (a) calculate the NAV per share (or its equivalent), regardless of whether the method of determining fair value described above has been applied; (b) do not have a readily determinable fair value; and (c) are measured at fair value on a recurring or nonrecurring basis during the period. GASBS 72 notes that a government should disclose information that addresses the nature and risks of the investments and whether the investments are probable of being sold at amounts different from the NAV per share (or its equivalent).

To meet that objective, GASBS 72 provides that a government should disclose the following information for each type of investment:

(a) The fair value measurement of the investment type at the measurement date and a description of the significant investment strategies of the investee(s) in that type.

(b) For each type of investment that includes investments that can never be redeemed with the investees, but a government receives distributions through the liquidation of the underlying assets of the investees: the government's estimate of the period over which the underlying assets are expected to be liquidated by the investees.
(c) The amount of a government's unfunded commitments related to that investment type.
(d) A general description of the terms and conditions upon which a government may redeem investments in the type (for example, quarterly redemption with 60 days' notice).
(e) The circumstances in which an otherwise redeemable investment in the type (or a portion thereof) might not be redeemable (for example, investments subject to a redemption restriction, such as a lockup or gate).
(f) For those otherwise redeemable investments in (e) that are restricted from redemption as of the government's measurement date: the estimate of when the restriction from redemption might lapse; if an estimate cannot be made, disclose that fact and how long the restriction has been in effect.
(g) Any other significant restriction on the ability to sell investments in the type at the measurement date.
(h) If a government determines that it is probable that it will sell an investment(s) for an amount different from the NAV per share (or its equivalent) than the reported net asset value that is being used as fair value: the total fair value of all investments that meet the criteria described in the last paragraph of the section on entities that report at net asset value and any remaining actions required to complete the sale.
(i) If a group of investments would otherwise meet the criteria described in the last paragraph of the section on entities that report at net asset value but the individual investments to be sold have not been identified (for example, if a government decides to sell 20% of its investments in private equity funds but the individual investments to be sold have not been identified), such that the investments continue to qualify for the method of determining fair value based upon net asset value: the government's plans to sell and any remaining actions required to complete the sale(s).

NATURE OF SECURITIES LENDING TRANSACTIONS

Governmental entities, particularly large ones, sometimes enter into transactions in which they loan securities in their investment portfolios to broker-dealers and other entities in return for collateral that the governmental entity agrees to return to the broker-dealer or other borrower when that entity returns the borrowed security to the governmental entity. The GASB issued Statement No. 28 (GASBS 28), *Accounting and Financial Reporting for Securities Lending Transactions*, to provide accounting and financial reporting requirements for these types of transactions.

This section discusses the requirements of GASBS 28 and describes some of the implementation issues encountered by governments that have implemented the statement.

Securities lending transactions are defined by GASBS 28 as transactions in which governmental entities transfer their securities to broker-dealers and other entities for collateral—which may be cash, securities, or letters of credit—and simultaneously agree to return the collateral for the same securities in the future. The securities transferred to the broker-dealer or other borrower are referred to as the *underlying* securities.

The governmental lender in a securities lending transaction that accepts cash as collateral to the transactions has the risk of having the transaction bear a cost to it, or it may make a profit on the transaction. For example, assume that the governmental lender of the securities invests the cash received as collateral. If the returns on those investments exceed the agreed-upon rebate paid to the borrower, the securities lending transaction generates income for the government. However, if the investment of the cash collateral does not provide a return exceeding the rebate or if the investment incurs a loss in principal, part of the payment to the borrower would come from the government's resources.

Of course, the situation is different if the collateral for the transaction is not in the form of cash, but instead consists of securities or a letter of credit. In this case, the borrower of the security pays the lender a loan premium or fee in compensation for the securities loan. In some cases, the government may have the ability to pledge or sell the collateral securities before being required to return them to the borrower at the end of the loan.

Governmental entities that lend securities are usually long-term investors with large investment portfolios. Governmental entities that typically use these transactions include pension funds, state investment boards and treasurers, and college and university endowment funds. Governments that enter into securities lending transactions are usually long-term investors; a high rate of portfolio turnover would preclude the loaning of securities because the loan might extend for a period beyond the intended holding period. At the same time, securities lending transactions are generally used by governmental entities that are holders of large investment portfolios. There are several reasons for this, such as the degree of investment sophistication needed to authorize and monitor these types of transactions, as well as the existence of a "critical mass" of investments available to lend to allow the governmental entity lender to earn enough profit on these transactions to have an acceptable increase in the overall performance on the investment portfolio. In addition, many lending agents are not interested in being involved with securities lending transactions for smaller portfolios.

PREVIOUS ACCOUNTING TREATMENT

Prior to the issuance of GASBS 28, there were no governmental accounting standards that addressed the accounting and financial reporting for securities lending transactions. Usually, governments did not reflect the securities lending transaction in their financial statements. In other words, the underlying securities continued to be recorded on the balance sheets. There was no recognition of the fact that collateral had been received from the borrower and that there was a liability on the part of the government to return the collateral to the borrower.

One related type of transaction for which the GASB had already issued accounting guidance was reverse repurchase agreements, which are legally different but in economic substance the same as securities lending transactions. In reverse repurchase agreements, the underlying security is actually sold to the borrower/purchaser with the agreement that the security will be resold to the government at a later date. Governmental sellers of securities under reverse repurchase agreements account for these agreements in the balance sheet as transactions. The asset is recorded for the cash received (and subsequently invested) and the liability to return the cash is also recorded in the balance sheet. The original security (comparable in economic substance to the underlying security in a securities lending transaction) is removed from the balance sheet in reverse repurchase agreements because legally the security has been sold.

GASBS 28 applies to all state and local governmental entities that have had securities lending transactions during the period reported. Because securities lending transaction programs are often found in governmental entities with large investment portfolios, they are commonly found in the balance sheets (or statements of plan net position) for pension plans.

GASBS 28'S EFFECT ON THE BALANCE SHEET

GASBS 28 requires the following basic accounting treatment for securities lending transactions:

- The securities that have been lent (the underlying securities) should continue to be reported in the balance sheet.
- Collateral received by a government as a result of securities lending transactions should be reported as an asset in the balance sheet of the governmental entity if the following collateral is received:
  - Cash is received as collateral.
  - Securities are received as collateral, if the governmental entity has the ability to pledge or sell them without a borrower default.
  - Liabilities resulting from these securities lending transactions should also be reported in the balance sheet of the governmental entity. The governmental entity has a liability to return cash or securities that it received from the securities borrower when the borrower returns the underlying security to the government.

For purposes of determining whether a security received as collateral should be recorded as an asset, governmental lenders are considered to have the ability to pledge or sell collateral securities without a borrower default if the securities lending contract specifically allows it. If the contract does not address whether the lender can pledge or sell the collateral securities without a borrower default, it should be deemed not to have the ability to do so unless it has previously demonstrated that ability or there is some other indication of the ability to pledge or sell the collateral securities.

Securities lending transactions that are collateralized by letters of credit or by securities that the governmental entity does not have the ability to pledge or sell unless the borrower defaults should not be reported as assets and liabilities in the balance sheet. Thus, in these two cases only the underlying security remains recorded in the balance sheet of the lending governmental entity.

NOTE: The obvious result of applying the requirements of GASBS 28 is the "grossing up" of the governmental entity's balance sheet with an asset for the collateral received and a corresponding liability, which are both in addition to the underlying security, which remains recorded as an asset. This effect can be quite large when the governmental entity has a substantial investment portfolio and an active securities lending program. For example, a large governmental defined benefit pension plan with $50 billion in net position increased both assets and liabilities by $4.7 billion, representing almost 10% of the net asset amounts.

In determining the amount of collateral received by the governmental entity lender, generally the market value of securities received as collateral is slightly higher than the market value of the securities loaned, the difference being referred to as the margin. The margin required by the lending government may be different for different types of securities. For example, the governmental entity might require collateral of 102% of the market value of securities loaned for lending transactions involving domestic securities, and it might require collateral of 105% of the market value of securities loaned for lending transactions involving foreign securities.

GASBS 28'S EFFECT ON THE OPERATING STATEMENT

The above discussion focuses on the accounting and financial reporting requirements of GASBS 28 relative to grossing up a governmental entity's balance sheet. GASBS 28 has a similar effect on a governmental entity's operating statement—amounts will be grossed up, but there is no net effect of applying the requirements of the statement.

GASBS 28 requires that the costs of securities lending transactions be reported as expenditures or expenses in the governmental entity's operating statement. These costs should include:

- Borrower rebates. These payments from the lender to the borrower as compensation for the use of the cash collateral provided by the borrower should be reported as interest expenditures or interest expense.
- Agent fees. These are amounts paid by a lender to its securities lending agent as compensation for managing its securities lending transactions and should be reported along with similar investment management fees.

In either of the above two cases, these costs of securities lending transactions should not be netted with interest revenue or income from the investment of cash collateral, any other related investments, or loan premiums or fees.

When the above requirements are applied, investment income and expenses are effectively grossed up for the interest earned on the collateral securities received by the lending governmental entity (or on the invested cash received as collateral), and expenditures or expenses are increased for a similar amount representing the amounts that would be paid to the securities borrower in compensation for holding the collateral asset, as well as the investment management expenses relating to securities lending transactions. Prior to the issuance of GASBS 28, these amounts would typically be netted, with the net income from securities lending transactions reported as part of the investment income of the portfolio.

OBSERVATION: During the relatively recent turmoil in the financial markets, a number of governments and pension plans experienced losses related to their securities lending programs. It's useful to understand how these losses occurred. In most cases, the losses weren't a direct result of lending securities. Rather, losses occurred when the lending governments invested cash received as collateral for the loaned securities and the investments declined in value.

POOLED SECURITIES

If a government pools money from several funds for investment purposes and the pool, rather than the individual funds, has securities lending transactions, the governmental entity should report the assets and liabilities arising from the securities lending transactions in the balance sheets of the funds that have the risk of loss on the collateral assets. In many cases, this will involve a pro rata allocation to the various funds based on their equity in the pools.

In addition, the income and costs arising from pooled securities lending transactions should be reported in the operating statements of the funds. If the income from lending pool securities that represent equity owned by one fund becomes the asset of another fund because of legal or contractual provisions, the reporting treatment should be based on the specific language of those provisions. In other words, if the legal or contractual provision requires a transfer of the amounts to another fund, the income and costs should be reported in the fund that owns the equity, with an operating transfer to the recipient fund. However, if the legal or contractual provisions require that the securities lending income be that of another fund, no transfer of resources should be reported. Instead, the amounts should be reported as income and costs in the recipient fund.

If the amounts become the assets of another fund for reasons other than legal or contractual provisions (such as because of a management decision), the income and costs should be recognized in the fund that reports the equity. The transfer of those amounts to the recipient fund should be reported as an operating transfer.

The provisions of GASBS 28 for reporting assets, liabilities, income, and costs from securities lending transactions apply to the financial statements of a governmental reporting entity that sponsors an investment pool in which there are participating entities that are legally separate from the sponsoring government. The reporting requirements of GASBS 28 for assets, liabilities, income, and costs do not extend to the legally separate entities that participate in the pool. Thus, these legally separate entities do not need to obtain information from the sponsoring government about securities lending transactions to report in their own financial statements.

DISCLOSURE REQUIREMENTS

GASBS 28 contains a number of disclosure requirements relative to securities lending transactions.

- The governmental entity should disclose in the notes to the financial statements the source of the legal or contractual authorization for the use of securities lending transactions and any significant violations of those provisions that occurred during the period. This is consistent with the requirements to disclose the types of investments in which an entity is legally or contractually permitted to invest. Securities lending transactions can be viewed as a significant part of investing activities, and the governmental entity would typically be legally or contractually permitted to enter into these types of transactions.
- Governmental entities should also disclose in the notes to the financial statements a general description of the securities lending transactions that occurred during the period. This disclosure should include the types of securities lent, the types of collateral received, whether the government has the ability to pledge or sell collateral securities without a borrower default, the amount by which the value of the collateral provided is required to exceed the value of the underlying securities, any restrictions on the amount of the loans that can be made, and any loss indemnification provided to the governmental entity by its securities lending agents. The entity also should disclose the carrying amount and market or fair values of the underlying securities at the balance sheet date. (An indemnification is a securities lending agent's guarantee that it will protect the lender from certain losses. A securities lending agent is an entity that arranges the terms and conditions of loans, monitors the market values of the securities lent and the collateral received, and often directs the investment of cash collateral.)
- Governmental entities should also disclose whether the maturities of the investments made with cash collateral generally match the maturities of their securities loans, as well as the extent of such matching at the balance sheet date. This disclosure is intended to give the financial statement reader some information as to whether the governmental entity has subjected itself to risk from changes in interest rates by not matching the maturities of the securities held as collateral with the maturities of the securities lending transactions.
- GASBS 28 also requires disclosures relative to credit risk, if any, related to securities lending transactions. *Credit risk* is defined by GASBS 28 as the aggregate of the lender's exposure to the borrowers of its securities. In other words, if the borrower of the security does not return the security, what exposure does the lending government have? The effective use of collateral is clearly a good mechanism to reduce or eliminate credit risk. A lender has

exposure from credit risk if the amount a borrower owes the lender exceeds the amount the lender owes the borrower. The amount the borrower owes the lender includes the fair value of the underlying securities (including accrued interest), unpaid income distributions on the underlying securities, and accrued loan premiums or fees. The amount the lender owes the borrower includes the cash collateral received, the fair value of collateral securities (including accrued interest), the face value of letters of credit, unpaid income distributions on collateral securities, and accrued borrower rebates.

If the governmental entity lender has no credit risk, that fact should be stated in the notes to the financial statements. If there is some amount of credit risk, the net amount due to the borrower should be disclosed in the notes to the financial statements.

Credit risk must be evaluated on a borrower-by-borrower basis and may need to be evaluated by contract with individual borrowers. For example, amounts due to one borrower cannot be offset by amounts due from other borrowers, so in determining the amount of credit risk, the financial statement preparer must ensure that none of these amounts are offset. In addition, the governmental entity lender may not have the right to offset amounts due from one individual borrower from one loan with amounts due to the same borrower on another loan. In determining the amount of credit risk to disclose, the financial statement preparer must also make sure that these due-to and due-from amounts are not offset.

- GASBS 28 requires that governmental entities also disclose the amount of any losses on their securities lending transactions during the period resulting from the default of a borrower or lending agent. Amounts recovered from prior-period losses should also be disclosed if not separately displayed in the operating statement.
- As was more fully described earlier in this chapter, GASBS 40 requires that investments included on the balance sheet of a governmental entity as of the end of a reporting period be categorized in terms of custodial credit risk. Because the collateral for securities lending transactions is reported on the balance sheet of the lending governmental entity (when it meets the criteria described earlier in this chapter), the disclosures required by GASBS 40 for collateral included on the balance sheet are required to be made. GASBS 28, as amended by GASBS 40, provides the following specific guidance relative to securities lending transactions:
- Collateral that is reported in the balance sheet should meet the disclosure requirement for custodial credit risk as defined in GASBS 40, unless it has been invested in a securities lending collateral investment pool or another type of investment that is not exposed to custodial credit risk.
- Underlying securities are not subject to the disclosure requirements for custodial credit risk if the collateral for those loans is reported in the balance sheet. The reason for not classifying the underlying securities is that the custodial credit risk related to these securities is effectively reflected in the disclosures of the custodial credit risk of the collateral. The underlying securities are really not in the custody of the lending government, so custodial risk is transferred effectively to the securities held as collateral.

OBSERVATION: Recent turmoil in the financial markets highlights the importance of adequately disclosing the risks that a government may have related to a securities lending program. As described earlier, declines in the fair value of collateral may have an adverse impact on these transactions, and financial statement preparers should be diligent in ensuring that any real or potential losses are adequately accounted for and disclosed in the financial statements.

A sample of a note disclosure for securities lending transactions is provided in Exhibit 2.

Exhibit 2: Sample note disclosure for securities lending transactions

Securities Lending

State statutes and boards of trustees policies permit the City of Anywhere's Pension Systems (which are reported as Pension [and Other Employee Benefit] Trust Funds) to lend their securities (the underlying securities) to broker-dealers and other entities with a simultaneous agreement to return the collateral for the same securities in the future. The Systems' custodians lend the following types of securities: short-term securities, common stock, long-term corporate bonds, U.S. government and U.S. government agencies' bonds, asset-backed securities, and international equities and bonds held in collective investment funds. Securities on loan at year-end are classified as a Category 1 risk in the preceding schedule of custodial credit risk. (See Chapter 15 for disclosure requirements for investments, including risk categorization.) International securities are uncategorized. In return, the Systems receive collateral in the form of cash at 100% to 105% of the principal plus accrued interest for reinvestment. At year-end, the Systems had no credit risk exposure to borrowers because the amounts the Systems owe the borrowers exceed the amounts the borrowers owe the Systems. The contracts with the Systems' custodian require borrowers to indemnify the Systems if the borrowers fail to return the securities, if the collateral is inadequate, or if the borrowers fail to pay the Systems for income distributions by the securities' issuers while the securities are on loan.

All securities loans can be terminated on demand within a period specified in each agreement by either the Systems or the borrowers. Cash collateral is invested in the lending agents' short-term investment pools, which have a weighted-average maturity of 90 days. The underlying securities (fixed income) have an average maturity of ten years.

The Pension (and Other Employee Benefit) Trust Funds report securities loaned as assets on the statement of fiduciary net position. Cash received as collateral on securities lending transactions and investments made with that cash are also recorded as assets. Liabilities resulting from these transactions are reported on the statement of fiduciary net position. Accordingly, for the year ended June 30, 20XX, the Pension (and Other Employee Benefit) Trust Funds recorded the investments purchased with the cash collateral as Collateral from Securities Lending Transactions with a corresponding liability as Securities Lending Transactions.

As described earlier in this chapter, securities received as collateral for securities lending transactions are not always reported as assets on the balance sheet of the lending government. For purposes of complying with the GASBS 3 disclosure requirements, underlying securities should be classified by category of custodial risk if the collateral for those loans is not reported as an asset in the balance sheet of the lending government. The categories in which the underlying securities are classified should be based on the types of collateral and the custodial arrangements for the collateral securities.

Split-Interest Agreements

Indirectly related to a government's cash and investments are assets received from donors that include a corresponding liability to the donor over certain periods of time. These arrangements are referred to as split-interest agreements. To fill a void in accounting guidance for these types of agreements, the GASB issued Statement No. 81 (GASBS 81), *Irrevocable Split-Interest Agreements*. These requirements (for both the asset and liability accounting), are discussed below.

NOTE: Other than governmental colleges and universities and hospitals, the receipt of split-interest agreements by other governmental entities is likely to be rare.

GASBS 81 defines an *irrevocable split-interest agreement* as an agreement in which the donor enters into a trust or other legally enforceable agreement (with characteristics that are equivalent to a split-interest agreement) under which the donor transfers resources to an intermediary to administer for the benefit of at least two beneficiaries, one of which could be a government. Under an irrevocable split-interest agreement, the donor does not reserve, or confer to another person, the right to terminate the agreement at will and have the donated resources returned to the donor or a third party. Irrevocable split-interest agreements can be created through trusts or other legally enforceable agreements with characteristics that are equivalent to irrevocable split-interest agreements. Examples of irrevocable split-interest agreements provided by GASBS 81 include charitable lead trusts, charitable remainder trusts, and life interests in real estate.

GASBS 81 notes that the stipulations of individual agreements can vary with respect to the entity acting as the intermediary (which may or may not be required to be a third party), the assignment of benefits, the term of the agreement, and other general provisions. For example, some donors require that the government that has a beneficial interest also serve as the intermediary in the irrevocable split-interest agreement.

GASBS 81 also notes that a typical irrevocable split-interest agreement has two components: a lead interest and a remainder interest. Irrevocable split-interest agreements can provide resources to a government either throughout the term of the agreement in the form of periodic disbursements (lead interest) or as a final disbursement at the termination of the agreement (remainder interest). In some irrevocable split-interest agreements, the amount of the disbursements to the lead interest beneficiary is preestablished as a specific amount (annuity). However, other irrevocable split-interest agreements define the periodic disbursements to the lead interest beneficiary as a variable amount—for example, as a specific percentage of the fair value of the assets measured at each disbursement date (unitrust).

An irrevocable split-interest agreement terminates after a period-certain term (for example, a specified number of years); a life-contingent term (upon the occurrence of a specified event, commonly the death of either the donor or the lead interest beneficiary); or a combination of both terms. As an example, a life-contingent irrevocable split-interest agreement might stipulate that, at the death of the donor, the remainder interest be remitted to the government.

NOTE: For those familiar with not-for-profit organizations that have split-interest agreements, the conceptual accounting underlying GASBS 81 is not very different from the FASB requirements. Not-for-profit organizations do not have deferred inflows and outflows of resources that are displayed separately from assets and liabilities, however.

A Government Is the Intermediary

A Government Is the Remainder Interest Beneficiary

GASBS 81 provides that if a government is both the intermediary and the remainder interest beneficiary of an irrevocable split-interest agreement, the government should recognize the following:

(a) Assets for resources received or receivable.
(b) A liability for the lead interest that is assigned to other beneficiaries.
(c) A deferred inflow of resources for the government's unconditional remainder interest.

Under GASBS 81, assets recognized pursuant to irrevocable split-interest agreements should be measured in accordance with existing standards. For example, assets that meet the definition of an investment should be measured at fair value according to the provisions of GASBS 72, as appropriate. Assets that meet the definition of an investment also should be remeasured and reported at fair value at each reporting date.

Changes in assets recognized pursuant to irrevocable split-interest agreements—such as those resulting from interest, dividends, and changes in fair value—should be recognized as an increase or a decrease in the related deferred inflow of resources.

GASBS 81 also provides that the amount recognized as the liability representing the lead interest that has been assigned to other beneficiaries should be measured based on a settlement amount (the stream of payments that is expected to be provided to other beneficiaries). This measurement should be based on an established valuation technique that incorporates assumptions that reflect the specific provisions of the agreement. The assumptions that should be considered when measuring the amount recognized as the liability include (a) the payment provisions of the agreement, (b) the estimated rate of return of the assets, (c) the mortality rate (if the term is life-contingent), and (d) the discount rate if a present value technique is used.

Disbursements to other beneficiaries should reduce the liability. The amount reported as the liability should be remeasured at each financial reporting date, based on changes in the assumptions used to determine the settlement amount. The change resulting from the remeasurement of the amount recognized as the liability should be recognized as an increase or a decrease in the related deferred inflow of resources, as appropriate.

At the termination of the irrevocable split-interest agreement, the amount reported as a deferred inflow of resources that is associated with the agreement should be recognized as revenue. The elimination of any remaining liability should be recognized as a gain (or as revenue in governmental funds).

A Government Is the Lead Interest Beneficiary

If a government is both the intermediary and the lead interest beneficiary of an irrevocable split-interest agreement, GASBS 81 provides that the government should recognize the following:

(a) Assets for resources received or receivable.
(b) A deferred inflow of resources for the government's unconditional lead interest.
(c) A liability for the remainder interest that is assigned to other beneficiaries.

Under GASBS 81, assets recognized pursuant to irrevocable split-interest agreements should be measured in accordance with existing standards. For example, assets that meet the definition of an investment should be measured at fair value according to the provisions of GASBS 72, as appropriate. Assets that meet the definition of an investment also should be remeasured and reported at fair value at each reporting date.

Changes in assets recognized pursuant to irrevocable split-interest agreements—such as those resulting from interest, dividends, and changes in fair value—should be recognized as an increase or a decrease in the related liability.

Under GASBS 81, the amount recognized as the deferred inflow of resources representing the government's unconditional lead interest should be measured based on a settlement amount (the stream of payments that is expected to be provided to the government beneficiary). This measurement should be based on an established valuation technique that incorporates assumptions that reflect the specific provisions of the agreement.

The assumptions that should be considered when measuring the amount recognized as the deferred inflow of resources include (a) the payment provisions of the agreement, (b) the estimated rate of return of the assets, (c) the mortality rate (if the term is life-contingent), and (d) the discount rate if a present value technique is used.

The amount of the governmental benefit for the period should be recognized as revenue and a decrease in the deferred inflow of resources. The amount reported as a deferred inflow of resources should be remeasured at each financial reporting date, based on changes in the assumptions used to determine the settlement amount. In addition, the change resulting from the remeasurement of the amount recognized as the deferred inflow of resources should be recognized as an increase or a decrease in the related liability, as appropriate.

At the termination of the irrevocable split-interest agreement, when the assets are disbursed to other beneficiaries, the liability and any remaining deferred inflow of resources related to the agreement should be eliminated.

Life Interests in Real Estate

GASBS 81 notes that a life interest in real estate is a type of life-contingent irrevocable split-interest agreement in which the donor (or parties specified at inception by the donor) retains the right to use the asset, such as a residence.

When the real estate asset is recognized as an investment, the provisions of GASBS 81 described in the following paragraphs should be applied under both the current financial resources measurement focus and the economic resources measurement focus.

When the real estate asset is recognized as a capital asset, the provisions described below should be applied only under the economic resource measurement focus.

The asset should be recognized as either a capital asset or an investment, depending on the terms of the agreement and management's intent at the time of the donation. If the asset is recognized as a capital asset, the asset should be measured at acquisition value. If the asset meets the definition of an investment as defined in GASBS 72, it initially should be measured according to the provisions of that Statement.

A liability should be recognized if a government assumes a legal obligation to sacrifice financial resources pursuant to the provisions of the life interest in real estate agreement, such as, for insurance, maintenance or repairs of the asset. If a liability is recognized, it should be reduced as the government satisfies the obligations.

A related deferred inflow of resources should be recognized in the amount of the difference between the asset and the liability (if a liability is recognized).

GASBS 81 notes that if the asset is recognized as an investment, changes in the fair value of the investment should be recognized as an increase or a decrease in the related deferred inflow of resources. If the asset is recognized as a capital asset, a systematic and rational allocation of the asset's initial acquisition value should reduce the carrying value of the asset and the deferred inflow of resources throughout the life of the agreement.

At the termination of the agreement, revenue should be recognized for the deferred inflow of resources, and for any remaining portion of the liability.

A Third Party Is the Intermediary

Beneficial Interests

GASBS 81 notes that a beneficial interest is the right to a portion of the benefits from donated resources pursuant to an irrevocable split-interest agreement in which the donor enters into a trust—or other legally enforceable agreement with characteristics that are equivalent to irrevocable split-interest agreements—and transfers the resources to an intermediary. When a third party is the intermediary, a government shares beneficial interests with at least one other beneficiary.

Recognition

GASBS 81 provides that if a third party is the intermediary of an irrevocable split-interest agreement, a government should recognize an asset and a deferred inflow of resources when the government becomes aware of the agreement and has sufficient information to measure the beneficial interest, provided that the following criteria are met.

Asset Recognition Criteria

GASBS 81 provides that assets should be recognized for beneficial interests that meet *all* of the following criteria:

(a) The government is specified by name as beneficiary in the legal document underlying the donation.
(b) The donation agreement is irrevocable.
(c) The donor has not granted variance power to the intermediary with respect to the donated resources.
(d) The donor does not control the intermediary, such that the actions of the intermediary are not influenced by the donor beyond the specified stipulations of the agreement.
(e) The irrevocable split-interest agreement establishes a legally enforceable right for the government's benefit (an unconditional beneficial interest).

Measurement

GASBS 81 provides that the beneficial interest asset initially should be measured at fair value and remeasured at fair value at each financial reporting date. Changes in the fair value of the beneficial interest asset also should be recognized as an increase or a decrease in the related deferred inflow of resources.

If a government is the lead interest beneficiary, the government should recognize revenue for the beneficial interest applicable to the reporting period as stipulated in the irrevocable split-interest agreement. Also, the government should reduce the beneficial interest asset for the same amount for the reporting period.

GASBS 81 also provides that if a government is the remainder interest beneficiary, the government should recognize revenue for the beneficial interest at the termination of the agreement, as stipulated in the irrevocable split-interest agreement. Also, at the termination of the agreement, the beneficial interest asset and the related deferred inflow of resources should be eliminated.

SUMMARY

GASBS 31 provides governmental entities with accounting and financial reporting guidance for most of the investments that they hold; these investments generally are carried in the financial statements at fair value. In addition, GASBS 40 provides somewhat extensive disclosure requirements for investments and bank deposits held by governments. Coupled with the requirements of GASBS 28 for securities lending transactions, investments involve intricate accounting and financial reporting requirements that must be adhered to by governmental entities.

13 DERIVATIVE INSTRUMENTS

INTRODUCTION

The GASB issued Statement 53 (GASBS 53), *Accounting and Financial Reporting for Derivative Instruments*, to provide guidance on recognition, measurement, and disclosures, regarding derivative instruments. Common types of derivative instruments used by governments include interest rate and commodity swaps, interest rate locks, options, swaptions, forward contracts, and futures contracts. One significant matter to note is that the recognition and measurement provisions of GASBS 53 should not be applied to financial statements using the current financial resources measurement focus. This means that the financial statements of governmental funds would not recognize derivative financial instruments on the balance sheet in accordance with the requirements of GASBS 53. For purposes of applying GASBS 53, the statement of net position refers only to government-wide, proprietary fund, and fiduciary fund financial statements.

Scope

GASBS 53 defines a derivative instrument as a financial instrument or other contract that has all of the following characteristics:

1. *Settlement factors*. A derivative instrument has (1) one or more reference rates (including indexes or underlyings) and (2) one or more notional amounts (sometimes called the face amount) or payment provisions or both. Those terms determine the amount of the settlement or settlements and, in some cases, whether or not a settlement is required. GASBS 53 describes a reference rate as a specified interest rate, security price, commodity price, foreign exchange rate, index of prices or rates, or other variable (including the occurrence or nonoccurrence of a specified event such as a scheduled payment under a contract). A reference rate may be a price or rate of an asset or liability but is not the asset or liability itself and may be any variable that has changes that are observable or otherwise objectively verifiable. GASBS 53 provides the following examples of reference rates:

   (a) A security price or security price index.
   (b) A commodity price or commodity price index.
   (c) An interest rate or interest rate index.
   (d) A credit rating or credit index.
   (e) An exchange rate or exchange rate index.
   (f) An insurance index or catastrophe loss index.
   (g) A climatic or geological condition (such as temperature, earthquake severity, or rainfall), another physical variable, or a related index.

   Common reference rates are the London Interbank Offered Rate (LIBOR), the Securities Industry and Financial Markets Association (SIFMA) swap index, the AAA general obligations index published by Municipal Market Data, or a commodity pricing point.

   The notional amount is the number of currency units, shares, bushels, pounds, or other units specified in the derivative instrument. The notional amount and reference rate are key factors of a derivative instrument's settlement payment. Other factors, such as the change in a reference rate over time, also may enter the calculation of a settlement payment. Finally, a payment provision may specify a payment to be made if the reference rate behaves in a specified manner, such as the three-month average of fuel prices at a certain pricing point that exceeds a certain price.
2. *Leverage*. It requires no initial net investment or an initial net investment that is smaller than would be required for other types of contracts that would be expected to have a similar response to changes in market factors. GASBS 53 uses an interest rate swap as an example of leverage, in that an interest rate swap generally requires no initial net investment. The swap's fair value, however, will change as if the holder of the swap had made an initial net investment in a fixed-rate instrument with a principal amount equal to the swap's notional value.
3. *Net settlement*. Its terms require or permit net settlement, it can readily be settled net by a means outside the contract, or it provides for delivery of an asset that puts the recipient in a position not substantially different from net settlement.

GASBS 53 provides that a financial instrument or other contract meets the net settlement characteristic if its settlement provisions meet one of the following criteria:

1. Neither party is required to deliver an asset that is associated with the reference rate and that has a principal amount, stated amount, face value, number of shares, or other denomination that is equal to the notional amount (or the notional amount plus a premium or minus a discount) of the financial instrument. For example, most interest rate swaps do not require that either party deliver cash or interest-bearing assets with a principal amount equal to the notional amount of the contract.

2. One of the parties is required to deliver an asset, but there is a market mechanism that facilitates net settlement. An example of that type of market mechanism is a futures exchange that offers a ready opportunity to enter into an offsetting contract.
3. One of the parties is required to deliver an asset, but that asset is readily convertible to cash or is itself a derivative instrument.

GASBS 53 also identifies specific types of financial instruments that are not included in its scope:

1. Normal purchases and sales contracts.
2. Insurance contracts.
3. Certain financial guarantee contracts. (Financial guarantee contracts that provide for payments to be made in response to changes in a reference rate would be included in the scope of GASBS 53 if they meet the other definition criteria described above.)
4. Certain contracts which are not exchange traded. GASBS 53 provides that a contract is not included in its scope if the contract is not exchange-traded and its reference rate is based on one of the following:
   (a) A climatic, geological, or other physical variable.
   (b) A price or value of a nonfinancial asset. The nonfinancial asset should not be readily convertible to cash.
5. Loan commitments.

The GASB issued Statement No. 59 (GASBS 59), *Financial Instruments Omnibus*, which clarifies whether certain contracts (including financial guarantee contracts) are included in its scope. Specifically:

- Contracts with nonperformance penalties.

  Contract nonperformance penalties do not meet the net settlement characteristic included in the definition of a derivative instrument. GASBS 59 amends GASBS 53, paragraph 13, by adding the following sentences at the end of the paragraph:

> *Some construction or purchase contracts include nonperformance penalty provisions. A penalty payment for nonperformance, either fixed or variable, that is dependent on the failure of the counterparty to comply with a contract term does not meet the net settlement characteristic.*

- Certain financial guarantee contracts.

Financial guarantee contracts included in the scope of GASBS 53 are limited to financial guarantee contracts that are considered to be investment derivative instruments entered into primarily for the purpose of obtaining income or profit. GASBS 59 supersedes GASBS 53, paragraph 16, as follows:

> **Certain financial guarantee contracts.** *A financial guarantee contract that meets the definition of a derivative instrument and is not entered into as an investment derivative instrument primarily for the purpose of obtaining income or profit is outside the scope of this Statement. Examples are as follows:*
>
> (a) *A federal guarantee that protects a university from loss in its student accounts receivables.*
> (b) *A guarantee a state government provides for the nonpayment of the debt of an industrial development corporation.*

(c) *Bond insurance in which the government pays the premium, the bond insurance is associated with the government's debt, and the debt holder is the beneficiary.*

Financial guarantee contracts are included in the scope of GASBS 53 if they meet the definitions of a derivative instrument and an **investment** derivative instrument entered into primarily for the purpose of obtaining income or profit. An example is a credit default swap that a government enters into to take a position for gain or income in response to changes in a reference rate, such as a contract that provides for payments to be made if the credit rating of a debtor falls below a particular level.

Recognition and Measurement of Derivative Instruments

GASBS 53 provides that derivative instruments should be reported on the statement of net position and should be measured at their fair value. (An exception to fair value measurement relates to fully benefit-responsive synthetic guaranteed investment contracts, which are discussed later.) Fair value should be measured by the market price if there is an active market for the derivative instrument. If a market price is not available, a forecast of the expected cash flows may be used, provided that the expected cash flows are discounted. GASBS 53 also provides that formula-based methods and mathematical models are also acceptable means of determining fair value.

NOTE: Obtaining fair value information for derivative instruments is generally not difficult. One of the more commonly used types of derivative instrument for governments is the interest rate swap agreement. Fair value is generally reported to governments at least annually and generally more frequently. The government financial statement preparer should be comfortable that the party providing fair value information is using a reasonable fair value method which is consistently applied. In many cases, particularly for significant swap agreements, governments engage the services of a swap consultant to assist in valuation, as well as to assist in the calculation of hedging effectiveness, discussed later in this chapter.

NOTE: As derivative instruments are measured at fair value, readers should refer to Chapter 12 for recently issued requirements under GASB Statement No. 72, Fair Value Measurement and Application, regarding fair value measurement and significant new disclosure requirements.

The real complexities of GASBS 53 come into play in determining how changes in the fair value of derivative instruments from period to period are presented in the financial statements. The determination of how changes in the fair value of derivatives are reported in the financial statements is based upon whether or not the derivative instrument meets the criteria to be considered a hedging derivative instrument.

- Changes in the fair values of investment derivative instruments (i.e., a derivative that is entered into primarily for the purpose of obtaining income or profit, or a derivative that does not meet the criteria of a hedging derivative instrument) should be reported within the investment revenue classification in the "flow of financial resources" statement—the statement of activities, statement of revenues, expenses and changes in fund net position, or statement of changes in fiduciary net position.
- Changes in fair value of hedging derivative instruments are recognized through the application of hedge accounting. In hedge accounting, changes in the fair values of derivatives are reported as deferred inflows or deferred outflows on the statement of net position.

Clearly, determining whether a derivative instrument meets the criteria to be considered a hedging derivative instrument is critical to determining the proper accounting for changes in the fair value of these instruments. Changes in the fair values of hedging derivative instruments are only recorded on the "balance sheet" while changes in the fair values of investment derivative instruments flow through the "income statement." A significant part of GASBS 53 is devoted to setting the criteria that must be met to qualify a derivative for hedge accounting.

GASBS 53 also provides guidance for when hedge accounting should be terminated. Specifically, GASBS 53 provides that hedge accounting should cease to be applied upon the occurrence of one of the following termination events:

1. The hedging derivative instrument is no longer effective as determined by applying the criteria for hedge accounting.
2. The likelihood that a hedged expected transaction will occur is no longer probable.
3. The hedged asset or liability, such as a hedged bond, is sold or retired but not reported as a current refunding or advanced refunding resulting in a defeasance of debt.
4. The hedging derivative instrument is terminated.
5. A current refunding or advanced refunding resulting in the defeasance of the hedged debt is executed.
6. The hedged expected transaction occurs, such as the purchase of an energy commodity or the sale of bonds.

If a termination in hedge accounting is required by one of the above events, any balance in the deferred inflow or outflow accounts should be reported on the flow of resources statement within the investment revenue classification.

Hedging Derivative Instruments

GASBS 53 provides that a hedging derivative instrument is established if both of the following criteria are met:

1. The derivative instrument is associated with a hedgeable item (described below). Association is established by consideration of the facts and circumstances of the derivative instrument, including whether:
   (a) The notional amount of the derivative instrument is consistent with the principal amount or quantity of the hedgeable item.
   (b) The derivative instrument will be reported in the same fund, if applicable, as the hedgeable item.
   (c) The term or time period of the derivative instrument is consistent with the term or time period of the hedgeable item.

A derivative instrument that is associated with a hedgeable item, but has yet to be determined effective in significantly reducing the identified financial risk, is referred to in GASBS 53 as a potential hedging derivative instrument.

2. The potential hedging derivative instrument is effective in significantly reducing the identified financial risk. Effectiveness is established if the changes in cash flows or fair values of the potential hedging derivative instrument substantially offset the changes in cash flows or fair values of the hedgeable item.

GASBS 53 defines hedgeable items as those that expose a government to identified financial risks that can be expressed in terms of exposure to adverse changes in cash flows or fair values. Hedgeable items can be all or a specific portion of:

1. A single asset or liability, for example, an entire bond issue or a specific portion of a bond issue.
2. Groups of similar assets or liabilities. If similar assets or similar liabilities are aggregated and hedged as a group, all of the individual assets or individual liabilities in the group are required to be exposed to the same identified financial risk that is being hedged.
3. An expected transaction.

Assets and liabilities that are measured at fair value—such as investments in many debt securities—do not qualify as hedgeable items.

For an expected transaction to be a hedgeable item, GASBS 53 provides that the occurrence of the expected transaction should be probable, supported by observable facts such as:

1. The frequency, volume, and amount of past transactions.
2. The financial, operational, and legal ability of the government to carry out the transaction (for example, whether the voters have approved a bond issue or tax levy).
3. The extent of loss or disruption to a government's activities that could result if the transaction does not occur.
4. The government's budget or other planning documents.

If an expected transaction is a hedgeable item, the evaluation of effectiveness should consider the probable terms of the expected transaction compared to the terms of the potential hedging derivative instrument.

GASBS 53 also provides that a transaction or expected transaction between a primary government and a discretely presented component unit can be a hedgeable item. However, a transaction wholly within a primary government—for example, a commitment to sell electricity by a city's electric utility (an enterprise fund of the city) to the city's general fund governmental operations—cannot be a hedgeable item.

Evaluating the Effectiveness of a Hedge

Since the determination of whether or not a derivative instrument is considered an effective hedge has a significant impact on the treatment of changes in its fair value on a government's activities statement, determining whether a hedge is effective or not comprises a significant portion of GASBS 53's discussions and requirements.

Under GASBS 53, potential hedging derivative instruments should be evaluated for effectiveness as of the end of each reporting period using a method described in the following pages. GASBS 53 specifies the extent to which these methods are required to be applied in the evaluation of effectiveness as follows:

1. Evaluation of effectiveness in the first reporting period. If a potential hedging derivative instrument is first evaluated using the **consistent critical terms method** (described below) and does not meet the criteria for effectiveness of that method, at least one **quantitative method** (also described below) also should be applied before concluding that the potential hedging derivative instrument is ineffective.

   If a potential hedging derivative instrument is first evaluated using a quantitative method and does not meet the criteria for effectiveness of that method, a government may, but is not required to, apply another quantitative method before concluding that the potential hedging derivative instrument is ineffective. However, if it is determined that a potential hedging derivative instrument is ineffective in the first reporting period, evaluation of effectiveness in subsequent reporting periods should not be performed for financial reporting purposes.

2. Evaluation of effectiveness in subsequent reporting periods. All potential hedging derivative instruments that were determined to be hedging derivative instruments in the prior reporting period should be reevaluated at the end of the current reporting period using the method that was applied in the prior reporting period. If that method is applied and the hedging derivative instrument no longer meets the criteria for effectiveness of that method, a government may, but is not required to, apply another method before concluding that the hedging derivative instrument is no longer effective.

Some potential hedging derivative instruments are designed to offset changes in cash flows or fair values of the hedgeable item in one direction. They are referred to as "one-sided hedges." Examples are options (such as caps and floors) that provide increases in cash flows or fair values if a market price exceeds or declines below a certain price or rate. In such cases, effectiveness should be evaluated consistent with the objective of the potential hedging derivative instrument. In other words, does the derivative instrument provide the hedge that the government sought by entering into the derivative contract? Other considerations may still be necessary such as whether relevant dates of the potential hedging derivative instrument are consistent with those of the hedgeable item.

GASBS 53 provides that effectiveness generally should be evaluated by considering overall changes in fair values or cash flows of the potential hedging derivative instrument. In a hybrid instrument, the potential hedging derivative instrument should be separated from the companion instrument for purposes of this assessment. Some potential hedging derivative instruments, however, have characteristics that permit separate evaluation of time value or interest. That separation may be significant in the evaluation of effectiveness if the hedging portion of the potential hedging derivative instrument excludes either the time value or the interest portion. GASBS 53 provides that separation is permissible if either of the following criteria is met:

1. The potential hedging derivative instrument is an option and effectiveness is evaluated by consideration of only the change in either:
   (a) The option's **intrinsic value**, excluding the option's change in time value from the assessment of effectiveness.
   (b) The option's minimum value, excluding the option's change in volatility value from the assessment of effectiveness. The option's minimum value is its intrinsic value adjusted for the effect of discounting. The volatility value is a key input in an option's fair value.
2. The potential hedging derivative instrument is a forward contract and effectiveness is evaluated by consideration of only the change in spot prices, excluding either the change in time value or the interest portion.

Methods for Determining the Effectiveness of a Hedge

The two basic methods to determine whether or not a derivative instrument is an effective hedge are categorized as the consistent critical terms method and the quantitative method, which is really comprised of several different quantitative methods. GASBS 53 discusses the application of these two methods separately for hedgeable items that are existing or expected financial instruments and hedgeable items that are existing or expected commodity transactions.

The Hedgeable Item Is an Existing or Expected Financial Instrument

If the hedgeable item is an existing financial instrument or an expected transaction that is expected to result in a financial instrument, GASBS 53 provides that effectiveness should be evaluated using the criteria in this section.

Certain financial risks may cause variability in portions of the overall changes in cash flows or fair values of financial instruments. Those risks may be individually hedged, provided that effectiveness can be measured. Risks that may be hedged include interest rate, tax, credit, and foreign currency risks. If interest rate risk is the hedged risk, the evaluation of effectiveness should be based on an appropriate benchmark interest rate. For tax-exempt debt, GASBS 53 provides that the Securities Industry and Financial Markets Association (SIFMA) swap index and the AAA general obligations index are appropriate benchmark interest rates. For taxable debt, the appropriate benchmark interest rates are the interest rate on direct Treasury obligations of the U.S. government and the London Interbank Offered Rate (LIBOR). However, if LIBOR or a percentage of LIBOR is employed as a hedge of tax-exempt debt, hedge effectiveness should be evaluated using one of the quantitative methods.

Consistent Critical Terms Method

The consistent critical terms method, as defined by GASBS 53, evaluates effectiveness by qualitative consideration of the critical terms of the hedgeable item and the potential hedging derivative instrument. If the critical terms of the hedgeable item and the potential hedging derivative instrument are the same or similar in certain circumstances, then the changes in cash flows or fair values of the potential hedging derivative instrument will substantially offset the changes in cash flows or fair values of the hedgeable item.

GASBS 53 provides the following discussions as to how to apply the consistent critical terms method to various types of financial instruments:

Interest rate swaps—cash flow hedges. (As interest rate swaps are probably the most common derivative instrument used by state and local governments, the application of the consistent critical terms method to interest rate swaps is important for governments to understand. Fortunately, this represents one of the most straightforward applications of a method to determine the effectiveness of a hedge.) An interest rate swap is an effective cash flow hedge under the consistent critical terms method if all of the following criteria are met:

1. The notional amount of the interest rate swap is the same as the principal amount of the hedgeable item throughout the life of the hedging relationship. This criterion is met if the notional amount of the interest rate swap and principal amount of the hedgeable item are equal for each hedged interest payment, even if the hedged item amortizes or otherwise adjusts subsequent to the inception of the hedge.
2. Upon association with the hedgeable item, the interest rate swap has a zero fair value.
3. The formula for computing net settlements under the interest rate swap is the same for each net settlement. That is, the fixed rate is the same throughout the term of the interest rate swap. Likewise, each variable payment of the interest rate swap is based on the same variable, such as the same reference rate or index.
4. The reference rate of the interest rate swap's variable payment is consistent with one of the following:

    (a) The reference rate or payment of the hedgeable item. For example, an interest rate swap provides variable payments to the government equal to the total variable payments of variable-rate bonds. This is a cost-of-funds hedge.

(b) A benchmark interest rate if interest rate risk is the hedged risk. The reference rate cannot be multiplied by a coefficient, such as some specified percentage of LIBOR, but it may be adjusted by addition or subtraction of a constant, such as the SIFMA swap index plus 10 basis points, provided that the constant is specifically attributable to the effects of state-specific tax rates.

5. The interest receipts or payments of the interest rate swap occur during the term of the hedgeable item, and no interest receipts or payments of the interest rate swap occur after the term of the hedgeable item. For example, an interest rate swap that hedges the first 10 years of a 15-year variable-rate bond meets this criterion.
6. The reference rate of the interest rate swap does not have a floor or cap unless the hedgeable item has a floor or cap. If the hedgeable item has a floor or cap, the interest rate swap has a floor or cap on the variable interest rate that is comparable to the floor or cap on the hedgeable item.
7. The time interval of the reference rate, commonly referred to as the designated maturity, employed in the variable payment of the interest rate swap is the same as the time interval of the rate reset periods of the hedgeable item. Examples that meet this criterion include an interest rate swap with a variable payment referenced to:

   (a) The SIFMA swap index—a seven-day index—that hedges variable-rate bonds with a rate reset every seven days; and
   (b) An interest rate swap with a variable payment referenced to the one-month LIBOR index that hedges taxable variable-rate bonds with a monthly rate reset.

8. The frequency of the rate resets of the variable payment of the swap and the hedgeable item are the same.
9. The rate reset dates of the interest rate swap are within six days of the rate reset dates of the hedgeable item.
10. The periodic interest rate swap payments are within 15 days of the periodic payments of the hedgeable item.

Interest rate swaps—fair value hedges. GASBS 53 provides that an interest rate swap is an effective fair value hedge under the consistent critical terms method if all of the following criteria are met:

1. The notional amount of the interest rate swap is the same as the principal amount of the hedgeable item throughout the life of the hedging relationship. This criterion is met if the notional amount of the interest rate swap and principal amount of the hedgeable item are equal over the entire term of the hedgeable item, even if the hedgeable item amortizes or otherwise adjusts subsequent to the inception of the hedge.
2. Upon association with the hedgeable item, the interest rate swap has a zero fair value.
3. The formula for computing net settlements under the interest rate swap is the same for each net settlement. That is, the fixed rate is the same throughout the term of the interest rate swap. Likewise, each variable payment of the interest rate swap is based on the same variable, such as the same reference rate or index.
4. An interest rate swap that hedges interest rate risk has a variable payment based on a benchmark interest rate without multiplication by a coefficient, such as some specified percentage of LIBOR. The benchmark interest rate, however, may be adjusted by addition or subtraction of a constant, such as the SIFMA swap index plus 10 basis points, provided that the constant is specifically attributed to the effect of state-specific tax rates.

5. The hedgeable item is not prepayable (that is, the hedgeable item is not able to be settled by either party prior to its scheduled maturity). This criterion does not apply to a call option in an interest-bearing hedgeable item that is matched by a mirror-image call option in an interest rate swap if both of the following criteria are met:
   (a) A mirror-image call option matches the terms of the call option in the hedgeable item. The terms include maturities, strike price, related notional amounts, timing and frequency of payments, and dates on which the instruments may be called.
   (b) The government is the writer of one call option and the holder (or purchaser) of the other call option. For example, a government issues callable fixed-coupon bonds and enters into an interest rate swap as a fair value hedge. The government has "purchased" and holds a call option in its issued bonds because those bonds carry a higher interest rate due to the bond's call option. In regard to the interest rate swap, it has a similar call option held by the interest rate swap's counterparty. If the callable bonds and the interest rate swap contain these features, the changes in fair value generated by the similar call options offset. A similar exception applies if the put option in an interest-bearing asset or liability is matched by a mirror-image put option in the interest rate swap.
6. The expiration date of the interest rate swap is on or about the maturity date of the hedgeable item so that the government will not be exposed to interest rate risk or market risk.
7. The reference rate of the interest rate swap has neither a floor nor a cap.
8. The reference rate of the interest rate swap resets at least every 90 days so that the variable payment or receipt is considered to be at a market rate.

Forward contracts. GASBS 53 provides that a forward contract is effective under the consistent critical terms method if all of the following criteria are met:

1. The forward contract is for the purchase or sale of the same quantity or notional amount and at the same time as the hedgeable item.
2. Upon association with the hedgeable item, the forward contract has a zero fair value.
3. The reference rate of the forward contract is consistent with the reference rate of the hedgeable item.

The change in the discount or premium on the forward contract should be excluded from the assessment of effectiveness and included within the investment revenue classification, or the change in expected cash flows of the expected transaction should be based on the forward price of the hedgeable item.

Quantitative Methods

GASBS 53 specifies three quantitative methods that may be used to evaluate effectiveness: the synthetic instrument method, the dollar-offset method, and the regression analysis method. Quantitative methods other than those specifically described in this Statement also may be used to evaluate effectiveness, provided that they meet the criteria of paragraph 48.

The quantitative methods of evaluating effectiveness may use historical data—past rates, prices, or payments. If there are new market conditions, however, the evaluation of effectiveness should be limited to using fair values, such as in the application of the dollar-offset method, or in certain instances, regression analysis of fair values. New market conditions are caused by asymmetrical changes in market supply or demand. GASBS 53 identifies a change in income tax rates of individual taxpayers that affects the demand for tax-exempt debt as an example of an event that suggests new market conditions.

Synthetic Instrument Method

The synthetic instrument method evaluates effectiveness by combining the hedgeable item and the potential hedging derivative instrument to simulate a third synthetic instrument. A potential hedging derivative instrument is effective if its total variable cash flows substantially offset the variable cash flows of the hedgeable item. This method is limited to cash flow hedges in which the hedgeable items are interest bearing and carry a variable rate. An example is the combination of a pay-fixed, receive-variable interest rate swap with a variable-rate bond to create a synthetic fixed-rate bond. GASBS 53 specifies that the synthetic instrument method may be applied to evaluate a potential hedging derivative instrument's effectiveness if all of the following criteria are met:

1. The notional amount of the potential hedging derivative instrument is the same as the principal amount of the associated variable-rate asset or liability throughout the life of the hedging relationship. This criterion is met if the notional amount of the swap and principal amount of the hedgeable item match for each hedged interest payment, even if the hedged item amortizes or otherwise adjusts subsequent to the inception of the hedge.
2. Upon association with the variable-rate asset or liability, the potential hedging derivative instrument has a zero fair value or the forward price is at-the-market.
3. The formula for computing net settlements under the potential hedging derivative instrument is the same for each net settlement, that is, the same fixed rate, reference rate, and constant adjustment, if any, throughout the term of the potential hedging derivative instrument.
4. The interest receipts or payments of the potential hedging derivative instrument occur during the term of the variable-rate asset or liability, and no interest receipts or payments occur after the term of the variable-rate asset or liability. For example, a swap that hedges the first 10 years of a 15-year variable-rate bond meets this criterion.

Under the synthetic instrument method, GASBS 53 provides that a potential hedging derivative instrument is effective if the actual synthetic rate is substantially fixed. The actual synthetic rate represents the aggregate payment experience of the variable-rate asset or liability and the potential hedging derivative instrument. GASBS 53 specifies that the actual synthetic rate should be within a range of 90% to 111% of the fixed rate of the potential hedging derivative instrument to be substantially fixed. It uses the example of when a swap's fixed payment rate is 5%, an actual synthetic interest rate that falls within a range between 4.50% (90% of 5.00%) and 5.55% (111% of 5.00%) is substantially fixed. Further, the results of this analysis should be evaluated as follows:

1. If the actual synthetic rate is within the required range for the current reporting period, the actual synthetic rate is substantially fixed.
2. If the actual synthetic rate is outside the required range for the current reporting period, the actual synthetic rate should be calculated on a life-to-date basis. If the actual synthetic rate on a life-to-date basis is within the required range, the actual synthetic rate is substantially fixed.
3. If a short time period has elapsed since inception of the hedge and the actual synthetic rate is outside the required range, the evaluation may include hypothetical payments, as

if the hedge had been established at an earlier date. Effectiveness should then be reevaluated. For example, the first reporting period ends 90 days into a 10-year hedge, and when the government prepares its financial statements, it finds that the actual synthetic rate for the 90-day period is outside the 90% to 111% range. In that case, hypothetical payments from periods prior to the establishment of the hedge may be added to the evaluation. If that analysis shows a synthetic rate within the required range, the actual synthetic rate is substantially fixed.

Dollar-Offset Method

The second quantitative method that can be used under GASBS 53 to determine hedge effectiveness is the dollar-offset method. The dollar-offset method evaluates effectiveness by comparing the changes in expected cash flows or fair values of the potential hedging derivative instrument with the changes in expected cash flows or fair values of the hedgeable item. GASBS 53 provides that this evaluation may be made using changes in the current period or on a life-to-date basis. If the changes of either the hedgeable item or the potential hedging derivative instrument are divided by the other and the result is within a range of 80 to 125% in absolute terms, these changes substantially offset and the potential hedging derivative instrument is effective. For example, if actual results are such that the fair value decrease of the potential hedging derivative instrument is $120 and the fair value increase of the hedgeable item is $100, the dollar-offset percentage can be measured as 120/100, which is 120%, or as 100/120, which is 83%. In either case, the potential hedging derivative instrument is determined to be effective.

Regression Analysis Method

The third quantitative method that can be used under GASBS 53 to determine hedge effectiveness is the regression analysis method. The regression analysis method evaluates effectiveness by considering the statistical relationship between the cash flows or fair values of the potential hedging derivative instrument and the hedgeable item. GASBS 53 provides that the changes in cash flows or fair values of the potential hedging derivative instrument substantially offset the changes in cash flows or fair values of the hedgeable item if all of the following criteria are met:

1. The R-squared of the regression analysis is at least 0.80.
2. The F-statistic calculated for the regression model demonstrates that the model is significant using a 95% confidence interval.
3. The regression coefficient for the slope is between −1.25 and −0.80.

The regression analysis should be based on sufficient data to determine if the potential hedging derivative instrument is effective as of the end of the reporting period. In assessing the sufficiency of the data, the period of time that the potential hedging derivative instrument is expected to hedge an identified financial risk in the future should be considered. Other results of the regression analysis method may need to be considered when evaluating effectiveness. The use of the regression analysis method requires appropriate interpretation and understanding of the statistical inferences. These statistical techniques are beyond the scope of this book and if this method is utilized, an individual with sufficient knowledge of statistics may need to be consulted to ensure that calculations and interpretations of calculations are appropriate.

GASBS 53 provides separate guidance in using the regression analysis method for cash flow hedges and fair value hedges, as follows.

Cash flow hedges. If a potential hedging derivative instrument is employed as a cash flow hedge, the relationship analyzed should be relevant cash flows, rates, or fair values of the potential hedging derivative instrument and the hedgeable item. GASBS 53 provides that the regression analysis should be conducted as follows:

1. The dependent variable for a cash flow hedge evaluated using cash flows or rates should be relevant cash flows or rates of the hedgeable item. The independent variable should be the relevant cash flows or rates of the potential hedging derivative instrument. If the evaluation is based on rates, the rates used as data in the regression analysis should be representative of the hedging relationship.
2. The dependent variable for a cash flow hedge evaluated using fair values should be the changes in fair values of the hypothetical derivative instrument. The independent variable should be the changes in fair values of the potential hedging derivative instrument. The hypothetical derivative instrument generally should have terms that exactly match the critical terms of the variable-rate hedgeable item. That is, the hypothetical derivative instrument and the hedgeable item should have the same notional amount and repricing dates, and mirror-image caps and floors, if applicable. The maturity of the hypothetical derivative instrument, however, should be the same as the maturity of the potential hedging derivative instrument. The hypothetical derivative instrument's reference rate should be consistent with the reference rate of the hedgeable item. The hypothetical derivative instrument should have a zero fair value upon association of the hedging relationship.

Fair value hedges. If a potential hedging derivative instrument is employed as a fair value hedge, the relationship analyzed should be the changes in fair values of the potential hedging derivative instrument and the hedgeable item. The dependent variable in the regression analysis represents changes in fair values of the hedgeable item (for example, fixed-rate bonds), and the independent variable represents changes in fair values of the potential hedging derivative instrument (for example, a pay-variable, receive-fixed interest rate swap).

Other Quantitative Methods

In addition to the three quantitative methods discussed above, GASBS 53 permits the use of other quantitative methods to determine hedge effectiveness if the specific method meets all of the following criteria:

1. Through identification and analysis of critical terms, the method demonstrates that the changes in cash flows or fair values of the potential hedging derivative instrument substantially offset the changes in cash flows or fair values of the hedgeable item.
2. Replicable evaluations of effectiveness are generated that are sufficiently complete and documented such that different evaluators using the same method and assumptions would reach substantially similar results.
3. Substantive characteristics of the hedgeable item and the potential hedging derivative instrument that could affect their cash flows or fair values are considered.

The Hedgeable Item Is an Existing or Expected Commodity Transaction

As mentioned previously in this section, GASBS 53 has separate guidance for using the consistent critical terms method and quantitative methods for evaluating the effectiveness of hedges of existing or expected commodity transactions. This guidance is provided in the following sections.

Consistent Critical Terms Method

GASBS 53 provides that the consistent critical terms method evaluates effectiveness by qualitative consideration of the critical terms of the hedgeable item and the potential hedging derivative instrument. If the critical terms of the hedgeable item and the potential hedging derivative instrument are the same, or similar in certain circumstances as described in the following sections, the changes in cash flows or fair values of the potential hedging derivative instrument will substantially offset the changes in cash flows or fair values of the hedgeable item.

Commodity swaps—cash flow hedges. GASBS 53 provides that a commodity swap is an effective cash flow hedge under the consistent critical terms method if all of the following criteria are met:

1. The commodity swap is for the purchase or sale of the same quantity (notional amount) of the same hedgeable item at the same time and delivery location as the hedgeable item.
2. Upon association with the hedgeable item, the commodity swap has a zero fair value.
3. The reference rate of the commodity swap is consistent with the reference rate of the hedgeable item.
4. The reference rate of the commodity swap does not have a floor or cap unless the hedgeable item has a floor or cap. Floors and caps place limits on expected cash flows. If the hedgeable item has a floor or cap, the commodity swap has a comparable floor or cap on the variable commodity price.

Commodity swaps—fair value hedges. GASBS 53 provides that a commodity swap is an effective fair value hedge under the consistent critical terms method if all of the following criteria are met:

1. The commodity swap is for the purchase or sale of the same quantity (notional amount) of the same hedgeable item at the same time and delivery location as the hedgeable item.
2. Upon association with the hedgeable item, the commodity swap has a zero fair value.
3. The hedgeable item is not prepayable (that is, the hedgeable item is not able to be settled by either party prior to its scheduled maturity). GASBS 53 provides that this criterion does not apply to a call option in a hedgeable item that is matched by a mirror-image call option in a commodity swap if both of the following criteria are met:

   (a) A mirror-image call option matches the terms of the call option in the hedgeable item. The terms include maturities, strike price, related notional amounts, timing and frequency of payments, and dates on which the instruments may be called.
   (b) The government is the writer of one call option and the holder (or purchaser) of the other call option.

4. The expiration date of the commodity swap is on or about the maturity or termination date of the hedgeable item so that the government will not be exposed to market risk.
5. The reference rate of the commodity swap has neither a floor nor a cap.
6. The reference rate of the commodity swap resets at least every 90 days so that the variable payment or receipt is considered to be at a market rate.

Forward contracts. GASBS 53 provides that a forward contract is effective under the consistent critical terms method if all of the following criteria are met:

1. The forward contract is for the purchase or sale of the same quantity (notional amount) of the same hedgeable item at the same time and location as the hedgeable item.

2. Upon association with the hedgeable item, the fair value of the forward contract is zero.
3. The reference rate of the forward contract is consistent with the reference rate of the hedgeable item.

The change in either the discount or premium on the forward contract should be excluded from the assessment of effectiveness and included within the investment revenue classification, or the change in expected cash flows of the expected transaction should be based on the forward price of the hedgeable item.

Quantitative Methods

GASBS 53 provides the following guidance in applying the quantitative methods for determining hedge effectiveness of existing or expected commodity transactions. The quantitative methods of evaluating effectiveness may use historical data—past rates, prices, or payments. If there are new market conditions, however, the evaluation of effectiveness should be limited to using fair values, such as in the application of the dollar-offset method, or in certain instances, regression analysis of fair values. New market conditions are caused by asymmetrical changes in market supply or demand. The examples of events that suggest new market conditions exist provided by GASBS 53 are new sources of commodity supplies, such as a new natural gas pipeline, and supply disruptions arising from natural disasters, such as hurricanes and earthquakes.

Synthetic Instrument Method

GASBS 53 provides that the synthetic instrument method evaluates effectiveness by combining the hedgeable item and the potential hedging derivative instrument to simulate a third synthetic instrument. A potential hedging derivative instrument is effective if its variable cash flows will substantially offset the variable cash flows of the hedgeable item. This method is limited to cash flow hedges in which the hedgeable items have a variable price or rate; that is, the variable cash flows of the potential hedging derivative instrument offset the variable cash flows of the hedgeable item to create an essentially fixed price or rate. GASBS 53 provides that this method may be applied to evaluate a potential hedging derivative instrument's effectiveness if both of the following criteria are met:

1. The notional quantity of the potential hedging derivative instrument is the same as the quantity of the hedgeable item.
2. Upon association with the hedgeable item, the potential hedging derivative instrument has a zero fair value or the forward price is at-the-market.

Under the synthetic instrument method, GASBS 53 provides that a potential hedging derivative instrument is effective if the synthetic price is substantively fixed. The synthetic price as of the evaluation date—the end of the reporting period—is compared to the synthetic price expected at the establishment of the hedge by calculation of an effectiveness percentage. If the effectiveness percentage is within a range of 90% to 111%, the synthetic price is substantively fixed.

Dollar-Offset Method

GASBS 53 provides that the dollar-offset method evaluates effectiveness by comparing the changes in expected cash flows or fair values of the potential hedging derivative instrument with the changes in expected cash flows or fair values of the hedgeable item. This evaluation may be made under GASBS 53 using changes in the current period or on a life-to-date basis. If the changes of either the hedgeable item or the potential hedging derivative instrument are divided by the other and the result is within a range of 80 to 125% in absolute terms, these changes will substantially offset and the potential hedging derivative instrument is determined to be effective. The example provided by GASBS 53 is that if actual results are such that the fair value decrease on the potential hedging derivative instrument is $120 and the fair value increase on the hedgeable item is $100, the dollar-offset percentage can be measured as 120/100, which is 120%, or as 100/120, which is 83%. In either case, the potential hedging derivative instrument is effective.

Regression Analysis Method

The regression analysis method evaluates effectiveness under GASBS 53 by considering the statistical relationship between the cash flows or fair values of the potential hedging derivative instrument and the hedgeable item. GASBS 53 provides that the changes in cash flows or fair values of the potential hedging derivative instrument substantially offset the changes in cash flows or fair values of the hedgeable item if all of the following criteria are met:

1. The R-squared of the regression analysis is at least 0.80.
2. The F-statistic calculated for the regression model demonstrates that the model is significant using a 95% confidence interval.
3. The regression coefficient for the slope is between −1.25 and −0.80.

The regression analysis should be based on sufficient data to determine if the potential hedging derivative instrument is effective as of the end of the reporting period. In assessing the sufficiency of the data, the period of time that the potential hedging derivative instrument is expected to hedge an identified financial risk in the future should be considered. Other results of the regression analysis method may need to be considered when evaluating effectiveness. The use of the regression analysis method requires appropriate interpretation and understanding of the statistical inferences. As mentioned earlier in the previous discussion on regression analysis, it may be necessary to obtain the consultation of someone familiar with statistical techniques to ensure that the calculations and interpretations of calculations under this method are appropriate.

In addition, GASBS 53 provides specific guidance on the use of regression analysis for evaluating the effectiveness of cash flow hedges and fair value hedges. These are described as follows.

Cash flow hedges. If a potential hedging derivative instrument is employed as a cash flow hedge, GASBS 53 provides that the relationship analyzed should be relevant cash flows, prices, or fair values of the potential hedging derivative instrument and the hedgeable item. The regression analysis should be conducted as follows:

1. The dependent variable for a cash flow hedge evaluated using cash flows or prices should be relevant cash flows or prices of the hedgeable item. The independent variable should be the relevant cash flows or prices of the potential hedging derivative instrument. If the evaluation is based on prices, the prices used as data in the regression analysis should be representative of the hedging relationship.
2. The dependent variable for a cash flow hedge evaluated using fair values should be the changes in fair values of the hypothetical derivative instrument. The independent variable should be the changes in fair values of the potential hedging derivative instrument. The hypothetical derivative instrument generally should have terms that exactly match the critical terms of the variable-price hedgeable item. That is, the hypothetical derivative instrument and the hedgeable item should have the same notional amount and repricing

dates, and mirror-image caps and floors. The maturity of the hypothetical derivative instrument, however, should be the same as the maturity of the potential hedging derivative instrument. The hypothetical derivative instrument's reference rate should be consistent with the reference rate of the hedgeable item. The hypothetical derivative instrument should have a zero fair value upon association of the hedging relationship.

Fair value hedges. If a potential hedging derivative instrument is employed as a fair value hedge, the relationship analyzed should be the changes in fair values of the potential hedging derivative instrument and the hedgeable item. The dependent variable in the regression analysis represents changes in fair values of the hedgeable item (for example, a fixed-price commodity contract), and the independent variable represents changes in fair values of the potential hedging derivative instrument (for example, a pay-variable, receive-fixed commodity swap).

Other Quantitative Methods

In addition to the three quantitative methods discussed above, GASBS 53 permits the use of other quantitative methods to determine hedge effectiveness if the specific method meets all of the following criteria:

1. Through identification and analysis of critical terms, the method demonstrates that the changes in cash flows or fair values of the potential hedging derivative instrument substantially offset the changes in cash flows or fair values of the hedgeable item.
2. Replicable evaluations of effectiveness are generated that are sufficiently complete and documented such that different evaluators using the same method and assumptions would reach substantially similar results.
3. Substantive characteristics of the hedgeable item and the potential hedging derivative instrument that could affect their cash flows or fair values are considered.

Hybrid Instruments

GASBS 53 also provides guidance for evaluating the effectiveness of hedging derivatives that are part of hybrid instruments. While derivative instruments often are stand-alone instruments, such as futures contracts, a derivative instrument also may accompany a companion instrument such as a debt instrument, a lease, an insurance contract, or a sale or purchase contract. An embedded derivative instrument may be a call option in a bond, a cap or floor in a sale or purchase contract, or an interest rate swap in a debt instrument. Alternatively, some derivative instruments may include investing or borrowing transactions. These instruments may give rise to hybrid instruments, which consist of a derivative instrument and a companion instrument.

GASBS 53 defines a hybrid instrument to be an instrument that meets all of the following criteria:

1. The companion instrument is not measured on the statement of net position at fair value.
2. A separate instrument with the same terms as the derivative instrument would meet the definition of a derivative instrument.
3. The economic characteristics and risks of the derivative instrument are not closely related to the economic characteristics and risks of the companion instrument. GASBS 53 considers that this would be the case in any of the following circumstances:

    (a) *Up-front payment with off-market terms.* As a result of a derivative instrument that has off-market terms, an up-front payment is received. Off-market terms that generate an up-front payment—a borrowing—are not closely related to the characteristics and risks of the derivative instrument. For example, a government enters into a pay-fixed, receive-variable interest rate swap that has an above-market fixed payment, resulting in an up-front payment to the government.

(b) *Written option that is in-the-money.* A written option that is in-the-money has intrinsic value. A government that writes or sells such an option to a counterparty receives an up-front payment, resulting in a borrowing for financial reporting purposes. The initial intrinsic value of the written option is not closely related to the characteristics and risks of the derivative instrument.

(c) *Inconsistent reference rate.* The derivative instrument has a reference rate that is inconsistent with the market of the companion instrument. For example, a debt instrument that has a variable coupon rate based on an equity index would not be closely related to the embedded derivative instrument (the variable-rate coupon). The economic characteristics and risks of the derivative instrument—an equity-based reference rate—are not closely related to the economic characteristics and risks of the companion instrument—a debt instrument. Alternatively, a variable coupon based on LIBOR would be closely related to the companion instrument.

(d) *Potential negative yield.* A hybrid instrument could be settled in such a way that an investor would not recover substantially all of its investment. For example, a government issues a note at an above-market interest rate with terms that provide that if market rates exceed a certain level, the coupon rate resets to zero for the remaining term-to-maturity of the instrument. The embedded derivative—the terms of the note which provide for the possibility of a rate reset and a negative yield—would not be closely related to the economic characteristics and risks of the companion instrument.

(e) *Leveraged yield.* The yield of the companion instrument is leveraged. A leveraged yield occurs if the embedded derivative instrument meets both of the following criteria:

    (i) The holder's *initial* rate of return on the companion instrument is at least doubled.
    (ii) The rate of return is at least twice what the market return would be for an instrument with the same terms as the companion instrument.

An embedded derivative instrument that is a component of a hybrid instrument should be recognized and measured in accordance with the requirements of GASBS 53. Such a derivative instrument also may be a hedging derivative if it meets the requirements of GASBS 53, which provides that the companion instrument should be recognized and measured in accordance with the reporting requirements that are applicable to that companion instrument—such as the financial reporting requirements for a debt instrument, a lease, or an insurance contract.

On-behalf payments included in derivative instrument payments. A government may enter into a derivative instrument with off-market terms that are intended to recover costs assumed by the counterparty on behalf of the government. For example, a government enters into a pay-fixed, receive-variable interest rate swap with a fixed rate that has been increased to compensate the counterparty for legal and advisory fees. GASBS 53 provides that those costs should be reported as expenditures or expenses consistent with the manner in which those payments would have been reported if the government had made payment directly.

The GASB issued Statement No. 64 (GASBS 64), *Derivative Instruments: Application of Hedge Accounting to Termination Provisions*, to clarify whether certain events relating to replacing a counterparty to a derivative (or the counterparty's credit support providers) would be subject to the termination provision of GASBS 53 as described above. GASBS 64 amends paragraph 22d of GASBS 53 to clarify when the application of hedge accounting should continue upon the replacement of a swap counterparty or a swap counterparty's credit support provider. Under GASBS 64, under certain circumstances, the replacements would not trigger the termination provisions of GASBS 53, as described below.

Under GASBS 53, as revised by GASBS 64, the hedging derivative instrument is terminated unless an effective hedging relationship continues as provided in the following provisions. An effective hedging relationship continues when all of the following criteria are met:

1. Collectability of swap payments is considered to be probable. (When collectability of payments is not probable, such as when a swap counterparty, or a swap counterparty's credit support provider, has entered into bankruptcy and the swap is not collateralized or does not remain insured, an effective hedging relationship does not continue.)
2. The swap counterparty of the interest rate swap or commodity swap, or the swap counterparty's credit support provider, is replaced with an assignment or in-substance assignment. (Bold terms are defined below.)
3. The government enters into the assignment or in-substance assignment in response to the swap counterparty, or the swap counterparty's credit support provider, either committing or experiencing an act of default or a termination event as both are described in the swap agreement.

GASBS 64 provides the following definitions of assignment and in-substance assignment:

Assignment. An assignment occurs when a swap agreement is amended to replace an original swap counterparty, or the swap counterparty's credit support provider, but all of the other terms of the swap agreement remain unchanged.

A swap counterparty replaced in the current reporting period may have previously replaced another swap counterparty in the past. As used in GASBS 64, the term *original* as it applies to the swap counterparty or the swap counterparty's credit support provider may include a swap counterparty that has replaced the original swap counterparty, or a credit support provider that has replaced the swap counterparty's original credit support provider.

In-substance assignment. An in-substance assignment occurs when all of the following criteria are met:

- The original swap counterparty, or the swap counterparty's credit support provider, is replaced.
- The original swap agreement is ended, and the replacement swap agreement is entered into on the same date. GASBS 64 notes that a swap agreement replaced in the current reporting period may have previously replaced another swap agreement in the past. Accordingly, as used in GASBS 64, the term *original swap agreement* may include a replacement swap agreement.
- The terms that affect changes in fair values and cash flows in the original and replacement swap agreements are identical. These terms include, but are not limited to, notional amounts; terms to maturity; variable payment terms; reference rates; time intervals; fixed-rate payments; frequencies of rate resets; payment dates; and options, such as floors and caps.

- Any difference between the original swap agreement's exit price and the replacement swap's entry price is attributable to the original swap agreement's exit price being based on a computation specifically permitted under the original swap agreement. Exit price represents the payment made or received as a result of terminating the original swap. Entry price represents the payment made or received as a result of entering into a replacement swap.

Synthetic Guaranteed Investment Contracts

GASBS 53 provides that fully benefit-responsive Synthetic Guaranteed Investment Contracts (SGICs), which are the combination of the underlying investments and the wrap contract, should be reported at contract value. Under GASBS 53, an SGIC is fully benefit-responsive if all of the following criteria are met:

1. The SGIC prohibits the government from assigning or selling the contract or its proceeds to another party without the consent of the issuer.
2. Prospective interest crediting rate adjustments are provided to plan participants and the government on a designated pool of investments by a financially responsible third party. Those adjustments provide assurance that the probability of future rate adjustments that would result in an interest crediting rate of less than zero is remote. The pool of investments in total meets both of the following criteria:
   (a) Is of high credit quality such that the possibility of credit loss is remote.
   (b) May be prepaid or otherwise settled in such a way that the government and plan participants would recover contract value.
3. The terms of the SGIC require all permitted participant-initiated transactions with the government to occur at contract value with no conditions, limits, or restrictions. Permitted participant-initiated transactions are those transactions allowed by the government, such as withdrawals for benefits, loans, or transfers to other investment choices.
4. Some events may limit a government's ability to transact with participants at contract value. Examples are premature termination of contracts, layoffs, plan terminations, bankruptcies, and early retirement incentives. The probability of such an event occurring within one year of the date of the financial statements is remote.
5. The government allows participants reasonable access to their investments. GASBS 53 provides that the following conditions do not affect the benefit responsiveness of an SGIC:
   (a) In plans with a single investment choice, restrictions on access to assets by active participants are consistent with the objective of the plan (for example, retirement benefits).
   (b) Participants' access to their account balances is limited to certain specified times during the plan year (for example, semiannually or quarterly) to control the administrative costs of the plan.
   (c) Administrative provisions that place short-term restrictions (for example, three or six months) on transfers to competing fixed-income investment options to limit arbitrage among those investment options (that is, equity wash provisions). If plan participants are allowed access at contract value to all or a portion of their account balances only upon termination of their participation in the plan, participants would not have reasonable access to their investments.

Notes to the Financial Statements

GASBS 53 has many specific disclosure requirements for derivative instruments that are listed in this section. Disclosure information for similar derivative instrument types may be provided individually or aggregated. GASBS 53 directs that to determine whether derivative instruments are the same type, the commonly known term for the derivative instrument (for example, swaps, swaptions, rate caps, futures contracts, and options written or purchased), the nature of the derivative instrument (for example, receive-fixed or pay-fixed interest rate swaps), the hedged item, if any, and the reference rate should be considered.

Summary Information

GASBS 53 requires that governments provide a summary of their derivative instrument activity during the reporting period and balances at the end of the reporting period. The information disclosed should be organized by governmental activities, business-type activities, and fiduciary funds. The information should then be divided into the following categories—hedging derivative instruments (distinguishing between fair value hedges and cash flow hedges) and investment derivative instruments. Within each category, derivative instruments should be aggregated by type (for example, receive-fixed swaps, pay-fixed swaps, swaptions, rate caps, basis swaps, or futures contracts). Information presented in the summary should include:

1. Notional amount.
2. Changes in fair value during the reporting period and the classification in the financial statements where those changes in fair value are reported.
3. Fair values as of the end of the reporting period and the classification in the financial statements where those fair values are reported. If derivative instrument fair values are based on other than quoted market prices, the methods and significant assumptions used to estimate those fair values should be disclosed. However, if the fair value is developed by a pricing service, there is no requirement to disclose significant assumptions if the pricing service considers those assumptions to be proprietary and, after making every reasonable effort, the pricing service declines to make that information available. This fact, however, should be disclosed.
4. Fair values of derivative instruments reclassified from a hedging derivative instrument to an investment derivative instrument. There also should be disclosure of the deferral amount that was reported within investment revenue upon the reclassification.

GASBS 53 permits the disclosure of the information required above in a columnar display, narrative form, or a combination of both.

Hedging Derivative Instruments

GASBS 53 provides that the following note disclosures be provided for all hedging derivative instruments.

Objectives. For hedging derivative instruments, governments should disclose their objectives for entering into those instruments, the context needed to understand those objectives, the strategies for achieving those objectives, and the types of derivative instruments entered into.

Terms. For hedging derivative instruments, governments should disclose significant terms, including:

1. Notional amount.
2. Reference rates, such as indexes or interest rates.

3. Embedded options, such as caps, floors, or collars.
4. The date when the hedging derivative instrument was entered into and when it is scheduled to terminate or mature.
5. The amount of cash paid or received, if any, when a forward contract or swap (including swaptions) was entered into.

Risks. For hedging derivative instruments, governments should disclose, if applicable, their exposure to the following risks that could give rise to financial loss. Risk disclosures are limited to hedging derivative instruments that are reported as of the end of the reporting period. Disclosures required by this paragraph may contain information that also is required by other paragraphs. However, these disclosures should be presented in the context of a hedging derivative instrument's risk:

1. *Credit risk.* If a hedging derivative instrument reported by the government as an asset exposes a government to credit risk, the government should disclose that exposure as credit risk and disclose the following information. These credit risk disclosures do not extend to derivatives that are exchange-traded, such as futures contracts. For those derivatives, disclosures for amounts held by broker/dealers are evaluated by applying the custodial credit risk disclosures found in Statements 3, *Deposits with Financial Institutions, Investments (including Repurchase Agreements), and Reverse Repurchase Agreements*, and 40, *Deposit and Investment Risk Disclosures*.

    (a) The credit quality ratings of counterparties as described by nationally recognized statistical rating organizations—rating agencies—as of the end of the reporting period. If the counterparty is not rated, the disclosure should indicate that fact.
    (b) The maximum amount of loss due to credit risk, based on the fair value of the hedging derivative instrument as of the end of the reporting period, that the government would incur if the counterparties to the hedging derivative instrument failed to perform according to the terms of the contract, without respect to any collateral or other security, or netting arrangement.
    (c) The government's policy of requiring collateral or other security to support hedging derivative instruments subject to credit risk, a summary description and the aggregate amount of the collateral or other security that reduces credit risk exposure, and information about the government's access to that collateral or other security.
    (d) The government's policy of entering into master netting arrangements, including a summary description and the aggregate amount of liabilities included in those arrangements. Master netting arrangements are established when (1) each party owes the other determinable amounts, (2) the government has the right to set off the amount owed with the amount owed by the counterparty, and (3) the right of setoff is legally enforceable.
    (e) The aggregate fair value of hedging derivative instruments in asset (positive) positions net of collateral posted by the counterparty and the effect of master netting arrangements.
    (f) Significant concentrations of net exposure to credit risk (gross credit risk reduced by collateral, other security, and setoff) with individual counterparties and groups of counterparties. A concentration of credit risk exposure to an individual counterparty may not require disclosure if its existence is apparent from the disclosures required by other parts of this paragraph; for example, a government has entered into only one interest rate swap. Group concentrations of credit risk exist if a number of counterparties are engaged in similar activities and have similar economic characteristics

that would cause their ability to meet contractual obligations to be similarly affected by changes in economic or other conditions.

2. *Interest rate risk.* If a hedging derivative instrument increases a government's exposure to interest rate risk, the government should disclose that increased exposure as interest rate risk and also should disclose the hedging derivative instrument's terms that increase such a risk. The determination of whether a hedging derivative instrument increases interest rate risk should be made after considering, for example, the effects of the hedging derivative instrument and any hedged debt.
3. *Basis risk.* If a hedging derivative instrument exposes a government to basis risk, the government should disclose that exposure as basis risk and also should disclose the hedging derivative instrument's terms and payment terms of the hedged item that creates the basis risk.
4. *Termination risk.* If a hedging derivative instrument exposes a government to termination risk, the government should disclose that exposure as termination risk and also the following information, as applicable:
   (a) Any termination events that have occurred.
   (b) Dates that the hedging derivative instrument may be terminated.
   (c) Out-of-the-ordinary termination events contained in contractual documents, such as "additional termination events" contained in the schedule to the International Swap Dealers Association master agreement.
5. *Rollover risk.* If a hedging derivative instrument exposes a government to rollover risk, the government should disclose that exposure as rollover risk and also should disclose the maturity of the hedging derivative instrument and the maturity of the hedged item.
6. *Market-access risk.* If a hedging derivative instrument creates market-access risk, the government should disclose that exposure as market-access risk.
7. *Foreign currency risk.* If a hedging derivative instrument exposes a government to foreign currency risk, the government should disclose the U.S. dollar balance of the hedging derivative instrument, organized by currency denomination and by type of derivative instrument.

Hedged debt. If the hedged item is a debt obligation, governments should disclose the hedging derivative instrument's net cash flows based on the requirements established by Statement 38, *Certain Financial Statement Note Disclosures*, paragraphs 10 and 11.

Other quantitative methods of evaluating effectiveness. If effectiveness is evaluated by application of a quantitative method not specifically identified in GASBS 53, governments should disclose the following information. However, there is no requirement to disclose information that a pricing service considers to be proprietary and after making every reasonable effort the pricing service declines to make available. This fact, however, should be disclosed.

1. The identity and characteristics of the method used.
2. The range of critical terms the method tolerates.
3. The actual critical terms of the hedge.

Investment Derivative Instruments

For investment derivative instruments, GASBS 53 requires governments to disclose their exposure to the following risks that could give rise to financial loss. Risk disclosures are limited to investment derivative instruments that are reported as of the end of the reporting period.

Disclosures required by this section may contain information that also is required by other sections. However, these disclosures should be presented in the context of an investment derivative instrument's risk:

1. *Credit risk.* If an investment derivative instrument exposes a government to credit risk (that is, the government reports the investment derivative instrument as an asset), the government should disclose that exposure.
2. *Interest rate risk.* If an investment derivative instrument exposes a government to interest rate risk, the government should disclose that exposure consistent with the disclosures required by GASBS 40, paragraphs 14 and 15. Further, an investment derivative instrument that is an interest rate swap is an additional example of an investment that has a fair value that is highly sensitive to interest rate changes as discussed in GASBS 40, paragraph 16. The fair value, notional amount, reference rate, and embedded options should be disclosed.
3. *Foreign currency risk.* If an investment derivative instrument exposes a government to foreign currency risk, the government should disclose that exposure consistent with the disclosures required by GASBS 40, paragraph 17.

Contingent Features

GASBS 53 provides that governments should disclose contingent features that are included in derivative instruments held at the end of the reporting period, such as a government's obligation to post collateral if the credit quality of the government's hedgeable item declines. For derivative instruments with contingent features reported as of the end of the reporting period, disclosure should include:

1. The existence and nature of contingent features and the circumstances in which the features could be triggered.
2. The aggregate fair value of derivative instruments that contain those features.
3. The aggregate fair value of assets that would be required to be posted as collateral or transferred in accordance with the provisions related to the triggering of the contingent liabilities.
4. The amount, if any, that has been posted as collateral by the government as of the end of the reporting period.

Hybrid Instruments

If a government reports a hybrid instrument, GASBS 53 requires that disclosures of the companion instrument be consistent with disclosures required of similar transactions, for example, disclosures for debt instruments. In that case, the existence of an embedded derivative with the companion instrument should be indicated in the disclosures of the companion instrument. For example, if a government has entered into a hybrid instrument that consists of a borrowing for financial reporting purposes and an interest rate swap, the government's disclosure should indicate the existence of the interest rate swap within the debt disclosure.

Synthetic Guaranteed Investment Contracts

Governments that report an SGIC that is fully benefit-responsive, as described above, are required to disclose the following information in the notes to the financial statements as of the end of the reporting period:

1. A description of the nature of the SGIC.
2. The SGIC's fair value (including separate disclosure of the fair value of the wrap contract and the fair value of the corresponding underlying investments).

SUMMARY

The accounting and financial reporting requirements for derivative instruments can be quite complex. Most of the complexity involves determining whether or not a derivative instrument is an effective hedge. This is an important determination as it has a significant impact on the way changes in fair value from period to period are reported. Regardless of the complexities, it is important that governments now have long-awaited guidance on accounting and reporting for derivative instruments.

14 CAPITAL ASSETS

INTRODUCTION

Capital assets used in governmental activities are reported in the government-wide statement of net position, but are not reported in the fund financial statements. Capital assets used in proprietary funds are recorded by these funds. Information on recording capital assets in proprietary funds is included in Chapter 7.

This chapter describes the accounting and financial reporting basics. The following topics will be addressed:

- Basic accounting for capital assets.
- Valuation of assets recorded, including accumulated depreciation.
- Recording infrastructure assets.
- Intangible assets.
- Capital asset impairment.
- Service concession arrangements.
- Capitalization of interest.
- Asset retirement obligations.
- Other financial reporting and disclosure considerations.

Because of the nature of governmental financial reporting and operations, certain fixed assets are recorded in funds and others are recorded only in the government-wide financial statements. Generally, fixed assets for the proprietary funds (the enterprise funds and the internal service funds) are recorded in the funds themselves.

In addition, fixed assets associated with trust funds are accounted for through those trust funds. For example, the principal or *corpus* amount of private-purpose funds may include fixed assets. In such cases, the fixed assets should be accounted for in the appropriate private-purpose trust fund. This assists in compliance with terms of the trust instrument, provides a deterrent to mismanagement of trust assets, and facilitates accounting for depreciation where the trust principal must be maintained intact.

Capital assets other than those accounted for in the proprietary funds or trust funds are considered capital assets used in governmental activities, which are accounted for only in the government-wide financial statements rather than in the individual governmental funds.

The reason that capital assets used in governmental activities are not recorded in the governmental funds is that the measurement focus of the governmental funds is the current financial resources measurement focus. Capital assets do not represent current financial resources available for expenditure, but rather are considered items for which financial resources have been used and for which accountability should be maintained. Accordingly, they are considered not to be assets of the governmental funds, but are rather accounted for as assets of the government as a whole. NCGAS 1 determined that the primary purposes for governmental fund accounting are to reflect its revenues and expenditures (that is, the sources and uses of its financial resources) and its assets, related liabilities, and net financial resources available for appropriation and expenditure. To best meet these objectives, capital assets need to be excluded from the governmental fund accounts and instead recorded only in the government-wide financial statements. Note that conceptually GASBS 34 is similar, as will be described later in this chapter. Instead of recording these fixed assets in an account group, however, they are recorded in the government-wide statement of net position.

The types of assets that should be included as capital assets used in governmental activities are those typically termed *capital assets*, that is, those that meet the capitalization criteria of the government. The more common classes used to categorize capital assets by governments are as follows:

- Land.
- Buildings.
- Equipment.
- Improvements other than buildings.
- Construction in progress.
- Intangibles.
- Infrastructure.

In addition, capital assets include those acquired in substance through noncancelable leases. Lease capitalization and disclosure requirements are more fully described in Chapter 19. The cost of infrastructure assets is also included in capital assets used in governmental activities. This requirement is discussed more fully in a later section of this chapter.

Capitalization Policy

To determine what assets will be treated as capital assets (regardless of whether it is a capital asset used in governmental or business-type activities or a capital asset of a proprietary fund) in practice, governments typically set thresholds for when assets may be considered for capitalization. For example, a government may determine that in order to be treated as a capitalized asset, an asset should cost at least $5,000 and have a useful life of five years. Note that this threshold applies only to items that are appropriately capitalizable by their nature. For example, a repair or maintenance expenditure of $7,000 would not be capitalized even if the threshold were $5,000. The threshold would apply to items that would normally be capitalized and is used to prevent too many small assets from being capitalized, which becomes difficult for governments to manage. Continuing the $5,000 threshold example, a personal computer purchased for $4,000 would not be capitalized. However, ten personal computers purchased as part of the installation of an integrated computer network would be eligible for capitalization in this example.

NOTE: Governments often have capitalization thresholds that, in the author's opinion, are far too low. Perhaps in their zeal to provide accountability for assets purchased with public resources, large governments exist that have capitalization thresholds of $100 to $500. Often, these thresholds have been in place for many years (sometimes from when the government first recorded general capital assets) and have not been adjusted for inflation. This presents a waste of resources in accounting for the details of these numerous small assets. Governments should periodically review their capitalization thresholds to make sure that they make sense, given their significance to the government's financial statements. To address the accountability issue that is likely to arise in raising these thresholds, keep in mind that assets that do not have to be recorded still must be safeguarded. In considering these accountability issues, the government must also consider that accountability standards may be imposed on the government from outside sources. For example, some federal and state contracts or grants may specify a capitalization level for tracking assets that are acquired with funds provided under the contract or grant. Although this level must be adhered to for contract or grant management purposes, the level should not determine the capitalization threshold established for financial reporting purposes.

Governments sometimes set or keep abnormally low capitalization rates because of sensitivity to their stewardship responsibilities for public resources. Other reasons, however, are more practical. For example, many governments can only issue general long-term debt for the acquisition or construction of capital assets. Therefore, the lower the capitalization threshold, the more assets can be purchased (for example, by a capital projects fund, which obtains its funds from the issuance of general long-term debt). These somewhat low dollar-amount items can be purchased and paid for over the life of the general long-term debt, with no impact on general fund resources, which are generally more subject to budget sensitivities.

VALUATION OF ASSETS RECORDED

As a general rule, capital assets should be initially recorded at cost. *Cost* is defined as the consideration that is given or received, whichever is more objectively determinable. In most instances, cost will be based on the consideration that the government gave for the asset, because that will provide the most objective determination of the cost of the asset.

The cost of a capital asset includes not only its purchase price or construction cost, but also any ancillary costs incurred that are necessary to place the asset in its intended location and in condition where it is ready for use. Ancillary charges will depend on the nature of the asset acquired or constructed, but typically include costs such as freight and transportation charges, site preparation expenditures, professional fees, and legal claims directly attributable to the asset acquisition or construction. An example of legal claims directly attributable to an asset acquisition is liability claims resulting from workers or others being injured during the construction of an asset, or damage done to the property of others as a direct result of the construction activities.

It is relatively easy to ascertain the costs of capital assets that are purchased currently. Contracts, purchase orders, and payment information is available to determine the acquisition or construction costs. The cost of a capital asset includes not only its purchase price or construction cost, but also whatever ancillary charges are necessary to place the asset in its intended location and in condition for its intended use. Thus, among the costs that should be capitalized as part of the cost of a capital asset are the following:

- Professional fees, such as architectural, legal, and accounting fees.
- Transportation costs, such as freight charges.
- Legal claims directly attributable to the asset acquisition.
- Title fees.
- Closing costs.
- Appraisal and negotiation fees.
- Surveying fees.
- Damage payments.
- Land preparation costs.
- Demolition costs.
- Insurance premiums during the construction phase.
- Capitalized interest (discussed later in this chapter).

The reporting of capital assets by governments was not always common. As governments worked to adopt the requirements of NCGAS 1, they were faced with the task of establishing capital asset records and valuation after many years of financial reporting without them. In these situations, many of the supporting documents and records that might contain original cost information were no longer available to establish the initial cost of these previously unrecorded assets.

Governments often found it necessary to estimate the original costs of these assets on the basis of such documentary evidence as may be available, including price levels at the time of acquisition, and to record these estimated costs in the appropriate fixed asset records. While this problem will diminish in size as governments retire or dispose of these assets with estimated costs, the notes to the financial statements should disclose the extent to which fixed asset costs have been estimated and the method (or methods) of estimation. Similar consideration needs to be made for the retroactive recording of infrastructure assets under GASBS 34.

Governments sometimes acquire capital assets by gift. When these fixed assets are recorded, they should be recorded at their estimated fair value at the time of acquisition by the government.

Capital Asset Accounting

As described earlier in this chapter, in the government-wide financial statements, capital assets should be reported at historical cost. Cost includes capitalized interest and ancillary costs (freight, transportation charges, site preparation fees, professional fees, etc.) necessary to place an asset into its intended location and condition for use.

One of the most significant aspects of GASBS 34 is its definition of what is included in capital assets: land, improvements to land, easements, buildings, building improvements, vehicles, machinery, equipment, works of art and historical treasures, infrastructure, and all other tangible and intangible assets that are used in operations and that have initial useful lives extending beyond a single reporting period. The GASB 34 Implementation Guide defines land improvements to consist of betterments, other than building, that ready land for its intended use. Examples provided of land improvements include site improvements such as excavations, fill, grading, and utility installation; removal, relocation, or reconstruction of the property of others, such as railroads and telephone and power lines; retention walls; parking lots, fencing, and landscaping.

Included in this definition are infrastructure assets. Previously, governments (not including proprietary funds) had the option of capitalizing infrastructure assets, and many, if not most, did not. (Infrastructure assets are defined by GASBS 34 as "long-lived capital assets that normally are stationary in nature and normally can be preserved for a significantly greater number of years than most capital assets.") Examples of infrastructure assets are roads, bridges, tunnels, drainage systems, water and sewer systems, dams, and lighting systems.

All governments are required to report general infrastructure capital assets prospectively. Retroactive capitalization of infrastructure assets required by GASBS 34 becomes more complicated.

- Phase 3 governments (governments with total annual revenues of less than $10 million) did not have to retroactively record infrastructure assets, although they are encouraged to do so.
- Phase 1 governments (governments with total annual revenues of $100 million or more) and Phase 2 governments (governments with total annual revenues of $10 million, but less than $100 million) were required to retroactively report all major general infrastructure assets. Specifically, Phase 1 and Phase 2 governments were required to capitalize and report major general fixed assets that were acquired in fiscal years ending after June 30, 1980, or that received major renovations, restorations, or improvements during that period.

DEPRECIATION OF CAPITAL ASSETS

Depreciation expense and the related accumulated depreciation are recorded in the government-wide statement of activities and in proprietary funds in a manner similar to that used by commercial entities.

In calculating depreciation, governments should follow the same acceptable depreciation methods used by commercial enterprises. There is actually very little authoritative guidance issued by the FASB and its predecessor standard-setting bodies. In fact, the financial statement preparer would need to go back to AICPA Accounting Research Bulletins to find an original definition of *depreciation accounting*, which is a system of accounting that aims to distribute the cost or other basic value of tangible capital assets, less any salvage value, over the estimated useful life of the unit (which may be a group of assets) in a systematic and rational manner. Viewed differently, depreciation recognizes the cost of using up the future economic benefits or service potentials of long-lived assets.

In addition to obtaining the original cost information described in the preceding section to this chapter, a government must determine the salvage value (if any) of an asset, the estimated useful life of the asset, and the depreciation method that will be used.

In practice, many governments usually assume that there will be no salvage value to the asset that they are depreciating. Governments tend to use things for a long time, and many of the assets that they record are useful only to the government, so there is no ready after-market for these assets. For example, what is the salvage value of a fully depreciated sewage treatment plant? Similarly, there is probably no practical use for used personal computer equipment, because governments are inclined to use these types of assets until they are virtually obsolete, which makes salvage value generally low. However, these governmental operating characteristics aside, if the government determines that there is likely to be salvage value for an asset being depreciated, the estimated salvage value should be deducted from the cost of the capital asset to arrive at the amount that will be depreciated. (In certain accelerated depreciation methods, such as the double-declining balance method, salvage value is not considered.)

Next, the government should determine the estimated useful lives of the assets that will be depreciated. Usually assets are grouped into asset categories and a standard estimated life or a range of estimated lives is used for each class.

Following are some common depreciable asset categories:

- Buildings.
- Leasehold improvements.
- Machinery and equipment.
- Office equipment.
- Infrastructure, including roads, bridges, parks, etc.

Two areas to keep in mind are that land is not depreciated, because it is assumed to have an indefinite life. Costs accumulated as an asset representing construction work in progress are also not depreciated until the assets being constructed are placed in service. In addition, as will be discussed in Chapter 22, capital assets that are recorded as a result of capital lease transactions are also considered part of the depreciable assets of a governmental organization.

The final component of the depreciation equation that a government needs to determine is the method that it will use. The most common method used by governments is the straight-line method of depreciation in which the amount to be depreciated is divided by the asset's useful life, resulting in the same depreciation charge in each year.

Accelerated methods of depreciation, such as the sum-of-the-year's digits and the double-declining balance methods, may also be used. However, their use is far less popular than the straight-line method. Although proprietary funds do use a measurement focus and basis of accounting that result in a determination of net income similar to that of a commercial enterprise, there is less emphasis on the bottom line of proprietary activities than there would be for a publicly traded corporation, for instance. Reflecting this lower degree of emphasis, governments sometimes elect to follow the straight-line method of depreciation more for simplicity purposes, rather than for analyzing whether their assets actually do lose more of their value in the first few years of use.

Governments should also disclose their depreciation policies in the notes to the financial statements. For the major classes of capital assets, the range of estimated useful lives that are used in the depreciation calculations should be disclosed. The governmental organization should also disclose the depreciation method used in computing depreciation.

Since the government-wide financial statements are prepared using the economic resources measurement focus, depreciation on capital assets is recorded. This was another highly controversial issue of GASBS 34. In response to commentary that infrastructure assets do not depreciate in value in the traditional sense, GASBS 34 allows a "modified approach" as to depreciation on qualifying infrastructure assets, as discussed below.

The theory behind using the modified approach is that infrastructure assets are different than what would be considered a "typical" capital asset. For example, say a garbage truck is a typical capital asset that has an estimated life of 10 years. It would be expected that the government would sell or "junk" the truck after 10 years and buy a new one. The cost of the original truck is charged as depreciation expense over its 10-year life, which matches the period over which its benefits were received by the government.

Now try to apply this theory to an infrastructure asset, such as a bridge. Even a newly constructed bridge has an estimated life of 40 to 50 years; is it likely that the government will really stop using the bridge after 40 or 50 years and build a new one? Probably not. What is more likely to happen is that the government will perform not only standard repair work on the bridge almost immediately after it is placed in service, but will also perform significant capital improvements to the bridge over time to keep it in a good state of repair throughout its existence. These capital improvements will likely extend the useful life of the bridge far beyond the otherwise expected useful life of 40 or 50 years. The modified approach as applied to infrastructure assets is an attempt to recognize the existence of the fact pattern discussed in this paragraph. Depreciation on infrastructure assets under the optional modified approach is not recorded as long as the government keeps the asset (in this case the bridge) at a set level of condition or state of repair. All costs to keep the asset in the stated condition level are expensed as incurred, regardless of whether they are standard repairs or are part of a major capital improvement.

Basically, depreciation rules (aside from the modified approach) follow those currently used by proprietary funds, as well as by commercial enterprises, which are described earlier in this section. Capital assets are reported in the statement of net position net of accumulated depreciation. (Capital assets that are not depreciated, such as land, construction in progress, and infrastructure assets using the modified approach, should be reported separately from capital assets being depreciated in the statement of activities.) Depreciation expense is recorded in the statement of activities and is reported as an expense of the individual programs or functions that have identifiable depreciable assets. Capital assets are depreciated over their estimated useful lives, except for land and land improvements and infrastructure assets using the modified approach.

Depreciation expense may be calculated by individual assets or by classes of assets (such as infrastructure, buildings and improvements, vehicles, and machinery and equipment). In addition, depreciation may be calculated for networks of capital assets or for subsystems of a network of capital assets. A network of assets is composed of all assets that provide a particular type of service for a government. A network of infrastructure assets may be only one infrastructure asset that is composed of many components. A subsystem of a network of assets is composed of all assets that make up a similar portion or segment of a network of assets. The GASBS 34 Implementation Guide provides the example of a water distribution system of a government, which could be considered a network. The pumping stations, storage facilities, and distribution mains could be considered subsystems of that network.

Modified Approach

Infrastructure assets that are part of a network or subsystem of a network are not required to be depreciated if two requirements are met.

1. The government manages the eligible infrastructure assets using an asset management system that has the following characteristics:
    (a) An up-to-date inventory of eligible infrastructure assets is maintained.
    (b) Condition assessments of the eligible infrastructure assets are performed and summarized using a measurement scale.
    (c) An estimate is made each year of the annual amount to maintain and preserve the eligible infrastructure assets at the condition level established and disclosed by the government.
2. The government documents that the eligible infrastructure assets are being preserved approximately at or above a condition level established and disclosed by the government. The condition level should be established and documented by administrative or executive policy, or by legislative action.

GASBS 34 requires that governments using the modified approach should document that:

1. Complete condition assessments of eligible infrastructure assets are performed in a consistent manner at least every three years.
2. The results of the most recent complete condition assessments provide reasonable assurance that the eligible infrastructure assets are being preserved approximately at or above the condition level established and disclosed by the government.

When the modified approach is used, GASBS 34 requires governments to present the following schedules, derived from asset management systems, as RSI for all eligible infrastructure assets that are reported using the modified approach:

1. The assessed condition, performed at least every three years, for at least the three most recent complete condition assessments, indicating the dates of the assessments.
2. The estimated annual amount calculated at the beginning of the fiscal year to maintain and preserve at (or above) the condition level established and disclosed by the government compared with the amounts actually expensed for each of the past five reporting periods.

The following are the GASBS 34 specified disclosures that should accompany this schedule:

1. The basis for the condition measurement and the measurement scale used to assess and report condition. For example, a basis for *condition measurement* could be distresses found in pavement surfaces. A *scale* used to assess and report condition could range from zero for failed pavement to 100 for a pavement in perfect condition.

2. The condition level at which the government intends to preserve its eligible infrastructure assets reported using the modified approach.
3. Factors that significantly affect the trends in the information reported in the required schedules, including any changes in the measurement scale, the basis for the condition measurement, or the condition assessment methods used during the periods covered by the schedules. If there is a change in the condition level at which the government intends to preserve eligible infrastructure assets, an estimate of the effect of the change on the estimated annual amount to maintain and preserve those assets for the current period also should be disclosed.

Failure to meet these conditions would preclude a government from continuing to use the modified approach.

NOTE: When the modified approach is used, depreciation expense is not recorded for the qualified infrastructure assets. Rather, all maintenance and preservation costs for those assets should be expensed in the period that they are incurred. Maintenance costs are those costs that allow an asset to continue to be used during its originally established useful life. Preservation costs (which would be capitalized if the modified approach was not being used) are considered to be those costs that extend the useful life of an asset beyond its originally estimated useful life, but do not increase the capacity or efficiency of the assets. Additions and improvements to assets that increase their capacity (i.e., the level of service provided by the assets) or efficiency (i.e., the level of service is maintained, but at a lower cost) are capitalized under both the modified approach and the depreciation approach.

The GASB issued Statement 51, *Accounting and Financial Reporting for Intangible Assets* (GASBS 51), to address practice issues that had arisen as to the accounting and reporting for intangible assets and to provide guidance for how intangible assets, including internally developed intangible assets, should be accounted for and reported.

Definition

GASBS 51 defines an intangible asset as an asset that possesses all of the following characteristics:

1. *Lack of physical substance.* An asset may be contained in or on an item with physical substance, for example, a compact disc in the case of computer software. An asset also may be closely associated with another item that has physical substance, for example, the underlying land in the case of a right-of-way easement. These modes of containment and associated items should not be considered when determining whether or not an asset lacks physical substance.
2. *Nonfinancial nature.* In the context of this Statement, an asset with a nonfinancial nature is one that is not in a monetary form similar to cash and investment securities, and it represents neither a claim or right to assets in a monetary form similar to receivables, nor a prepayment for goods or services.
3. *Initial useful life extending beyond a single reporting period.*

GASBS 51 includes in its scope all intangible assets except for the following:

1. Assets that meet the description in the preceding paragraph if the assets are acquired or created primarily for the purpose of directly obtaining income or profit. These assets generally should follow authoritative guidance for investments.

2. Assets resulting from capital lease transactions reported by lessees.
3. Goodwill created through the combination of a government and another entity.

Accounting and Financial Reporting for Intangible Assets Using the Economic Resources Measurement Focus

GASBS 51 provides that all intangible assets included in its scope be classified as capital assets. Accordingly, existing authoritative guidance related to the accounting and financial reporting for capital assets, including the areas of recognition, measurement, depreciation (termed *amortization* for intangible assets), impairment, presentation, and disclosures, should be applied to intangible assets as applicable. The provisions of GASBS 51 described in the following paragraphs should be applied to intangible assets in addition to the existing authoritative guidance for capital assets.

An intangible asset should be recognized in the statement of net position only if it is identifiable. GASBS 51 considers an intangible asset to be identifiable when either of the following conditions is met:

1. The asset is separable, that is, the asset is *capable* of being separated or divided from the government and sold, transferred, licensed, rented, or exchanged, either individually or together with a related contract, asset, or liability.
2. The asset arises from contractual or other legal rights, regardless of whether those rights are transferable or separable from the entity or from other rights and obligations.

Internally Generated Intangible Assets

GASBS 51 considers intangible assets to be considered internally generated if they are created or produced by the government or an entity contracted by the government, or if they are acquired from a third party but require more than minimal incremental effort on the part of the government to begin to achieve their expected level of service capacity.

Outlays incurred related to the development of an internally generated intangible asset that is identifiable should be capitalized only upon the occurrence of all of the following:

1. Determination of the specific objective of the project and the nature of the service capacity that is expected to be provided by the intangible asset upon the completion of the project.
2. Demonstration of the technical or technological feasibility for completing the project so that the intangible asset will provide its expected service capacity.
3. Demonstration of the current intention, ability, and presence of effort to complete or, in the case of a multiyear project, continue development of the intangible asset.

Only outlays incurred subsequent to meeting the above criteria should be capitalized.

Outlays incurred prior to meeting those criteria should be expensed as incurred.

Internally generated computer software. Computer software is a common type of intangible asset that is often internally generated. Computer software should be considered internally generated if it is developed in-house by the government's personnel or by a third-party contractor on behalf of the government. Commercially available software that is purchased or licensed by the government and modified using more than minimal incremental effort before being put into operation also should be considered internally generated for purposes of this Statement. For example, licensed financial accounting software that the government modifies to add special reporting capabilities would be considered internally generated.

The activities involved in developing and installing internally generated computer software can be grouped into the following stages:

1. *Preliminary Project Stage*. Activities in this stage include the conceptual formulation and evaluation of alternatives, the determination of the existence of needed technology, and the final selection of alternatives for the development of the software.
2. *Application Development Stage*. Activities in this stage include the design of the chosen path, including software configuration and software interfaces, coding, installation to hardware, and testing, including the parallel processing phase.
3. *Postimplementation/Operation Stage*. Activities in this stage include application training and software maintenance.

Data conversion should be considered an activity of the application development stage only to the extent it is determined to be necessary to make the computer software operational, that is, in condition for use. Otherwise, data conversion should be considered an activity of the postimplementation/operation stage.

For internally generated computer software, the recognition criteria described above should be considered to be met only when both of the following occur:

1. The activities noted in the preliminary project stage are completed.
2. Management implicitly or explicitly authorizes and commits to funding, at least currently in the case of a multiyear project, the software project.

Accordingly, outlays associated with activities in the preliminary project stage should be expensed as incurred. For commercially available software that will be modified to the point that it is considered internally generated, 1 and 2 above generally could be considered to have occurred upon the government's commitment to purchase or license the computer software.

Once the recognition criteria have been met, as described above, outlays related to activities in the application development stage should be capitalized. Capitalization of such outlays should cease no later than the point at which the computer software is substantially complete and operational. Outlays associated with activities in the postimplementation/operation stage should be expensed as incurred.

GASBS 51 notes that the activities within the stages of development described above may occur in a sequence different from that shown. GASBS 51 provides that the recognition guidance for outlays associated with the development of internally generated computer software set forth above should be applied based on the nature of the activity, not the timing of its occurrence. For example, outlays associated with application training activities that occur during the application development stage should be expensed as incurred.

Outlays associated with an internally generated modification of computer software that is already in operation should be capitalized in accordance if the modification results in any of the following:

1. An increase in the functionality of the computer software, that is, the computer software is able to perform tasks that it was previously incapable of performing.
2. An increase in the efficiency of the computer software, that is, an increase in the level of service provided by the computer software without the ability to perform additional tasks.
3. An extension of the estimated useful life of the software.

If the modification does not result in any of the above outcomes, the modification should be considered maintenance, and the associated outlays should be expensed as incurred.

OBSERVATION: The specific recognition criteria described above are likely to result in governments capitalizing fewer costs related to implementation of new software systems. Under prior practices, governments may have considered all reasonable costs associated with converting to new software to be capital costs. The recognition criteria described above will cause governments to classify and evaluate the various costs for the various stages of these types of projects and determine which of the costs are appropriate to capitalize.

Specific Amortization Issues

GASBS 51 provides that the useful life of an intangible asset that arises from contractual or other legal rights should not exceed the period to which the service capacity of the asset is limited by contractual or legal provisions. Renewal periods related to such rights may be considered in determining the useful life of the intangible asset if there is evidence that the government will seek and be able to achieve renewal and that any anticipated outlays to be incurred as part of achieving the renewal are nominal in relation to the level of service capacity expected to be obtained through the renewal. Such evidence should consider the required consent of a third party and the satisfaction of conditions required to achieve renewal, as applicable.

Under GASBS 51, an intangible asset is considered to have an indefinite useful life if there are no legal, contractual, regulatory, technological, or other factors that limit the useful life of the asset. A permanent right-of-way easement is the example provided of an intangible asset that should be considered to have an indefinite useful life. GASBS 51 provides that intangible assets with indefinite useful lives should *not* be amortized. If changes in factors and conditions result in the useful life of an intangible asset no longer being indefinite, the asset should be tested for impairment because a change in the expected duration of use of the asset has occurred. The carrying value of the intangible asset, if any, following the recognition of any impairment loss should be amortized in subsequent reporting periods over the remaining estimated useful life of the asset.

Impairment Indicator

In addition to the indicators included in GASB Statement No. 42 (GASBS 42), *Accounting and Financial Reporting for Impairment of Capital Assets and for Insurance Recoveries* (which is discussed in the following section), a common indicator of impairment for internally generated intangible assets is development stoppage, such as stoppage of development of computer software due to a change in the priorities of management. Internally generated intangible assets impaired from development stoppage should be reported at the lower of carrying value or fair value.

Accounting and Financial Reporting for Intangible Assets Using the Current Financial Resources Measurement Focus

GASBS 51 provides that outlays associated with intangible assets subject to its provisions should be reported as expenditures when incurred in financial statements prepared using the current financial resources measurement focus.

Retroactive reporting of intangible assets considered to have indefinite useful lives as of the effective date of GASBS 51 is not required but is permitted. Retroactive reporting of internally generated intangible assets (including ones that are in development as of the effective date of GASBS 51) also is not required but is permitted to the extent that the approach in paragraph 8 can be effectively applied to determine the appropriate historical cost of an internally generated intangible asset as of the effective date of the Statement.

The provisions of GASBS 51 related to intangible assets with indefinite useful lives should be applied retroactively only for intangible assets previously subjected to amortization that have indefinite useful lives as of the effective date of the Statement. Accumulated amortization related to these assets reported prior to the implementation of the Statement should be restated to reflect the fact that these assets are not to be amortized.

Impairment of Capital Assets

The GASB issued Statement 42, *Accounting and Financial Reporting for Impairment of Capital Assets and for Insurance Recoveries* (GASBS 42), to provide guidance for accounting for the impairment of capital assets. GASBS 42 also addresses the accounting for insurance recoveries, but by far the most significant aspects of the new statement will concern impairment of capital assets. GASBS 42 applies to all of the capital assets of a government, including its infrastructure assets.

Many readers may be familiar with the Financial Accounting Standards Board's Statement 144, *Accounting for the Impairment or Disposal of Long-Lived Assets* (SFAS 144). While GASBS 42 addresses the same basic topic as SFAS 144, its approach is actually quite different from what is found in the FASB Statement. In SFAS 144, determination of impairment is based upon expected cash flows from the asset that is being evaluated for impairment. In the governmental environment, many or most capital assets don't provide cash flows, nor are they expected to provide cash flows. GASBS 42 presents the GASB's solutions as to how to identify and measure impairment in the governmental environment.

Definition of Impairment

GASBS 42 defines asset impairment as a significant, unexpected decline in the service utility of a capital asset. The events or circumstances that lead to impairments are not considered normal and ordinary, meaning that they wouldn't be expected to occur during the useful life of the capital asset at the time that it was acquired.

GASBS 42 provides guidance on what is meant by the term *service utility*. The service utility of a capital asset is the usable capacity that, at the time of acquisition, was expected to be used to provide service. The current usable capacity of a capital asset may be due to normal or expected decline in useful life or it may be due to impairing events, which are discussed in the following pages.

Determining Whether a Capital Asset Is Impaired

GASBS 42 provides a two-step process in determining whether a capital asset is impaired:

1. Identifying potential impairments.
2. Testing for impairment.

Each of these steps is described in greater detail below.

Identifying events or circumstances that may indicate impairment. The events contemplated by GASBS 42 that may indicate impairment are prominent events, meaning that they are conspicuous or known to the government, and would be expected to have been discussed by governing boards, management, and/or the media. The following are provided by GASBS 42 as indicators of impairment:

1. Evidence of physical damage, such as for a building damaged by fire or flood, when the level of damage is such that restoration efforts are needed to restore service utility.

2. Enactment or approval of laws or regulations, or other changes in environmental factors, such as new water quality standards that a water treatment plant does not meet and cannot be modified to meet.
3. Technological development or evidence of obsolescence, such as that related to a major piece of diagnostic or research equipment that is used, because newer equipment provides better service.
4. A change in the manner or expected duration of usage of a capital asset, such as the closure of a school prior to the end of its useful life. Note that if the government were no longer using the asset, the asset would be evaluated for impairment even if the government decided to sell the asset.
5. Construction stoppage, such as stoppage of construction of a building due to lack of funding.

NOTE: It is important to understand that GASBS 42 expects a government to address whether there has been an impairment of a capital asset based upon the impairment indicators listed above. For example, the government would likely be expected to be aware of a major fire in one of its buildings that would cause it to evaluate whether there is an impairment to be recorded for that building. On the other hand, a building (or part of a building) may become unusable because of the gradual damage caused by termites or mold, for example. The government would not be expected to be aware of this situation and is not obligated to inventory its capital assets to make sure that these conditions do not exist. An impairment loss, in this case, would only be evaluated when the government becomes aware of the actual situation.

Testing for impairment. If an asset has been identified as potentially impaired by the indicators described above, the second step is to determine if impairment has incurred. GASBS 42 provides that the asset should be tested for impairment if both of the following factors are present:

- The magnitude of the decline in service utility is significant. GASBS 42 does not provide any specific methods to evaluate "significant" but does provide the example of expenses associated with the continued operation and maintenance or costs associated with restoration being "significant" in relationship to the current service utility of the asset.
- The decline in service utility is unexpected. This means that the restoration cost or other impairment circumstance is not part of the normal life cycle of the capital asset.

If both of these tests are met and the capital asset is determined to be impaired, the government would use the guidance of GASBS 42 in the following section to measure that impairment. If an asset was indicated to be impaired, but does not meet both of these two tests, GASBS 42 provides that the estimates used in depreciation calculations, such as remaining useful life and salvage value, should be reevaluated and changed if considered necessary.

Measuring Impairment

To measure the impairment for capital assets meeting the above tests, the government should next determine whether the impaired capital assets will be used by the government. Impaired capital assets that will no longer be used by the government should be reported at the lower of carrying value or fair value. This also applies to capital assets impaired from construction work stoppage, which are also reported at the lower of carrying or fair value.

For impaired capital assets that will continue to be used by the government, determination of the amount of the impairment (the historical cost that should be written off) is more complicated. GASBS 42 provides three different methods that are described below.

- *Restoration cost method.* The amount of the impairment is derived from the estimated costs to restore the utility of the capital asset, not including any amounts attributable to improvements or additions. The estimated restoration cost is converted to historical cost either by restating the estimated restoration cost using an appropriate cost index or by applying a ratio of estimated restoration cost over estimated *replacement* cost to the carrying amount of the asset.
- *Service units method.* The amount of the impairment is derived from isolating the historical cost of the service utility that cannot be used due to the impairment event or change in circumstances. The amount of the service units impaired is determined by evaluating the service units provided by the capital asset both before and after the impairment.
- *Deflated depreciated replacement cost method.* The amount of the impairment is derived from obtaining a current cost for a capital asset to replace the current level of service estimated. The estimated current cost is then depreciated (since the capital asset being replaced is not new) and deflated to convert the cost to historical cost dollars.

GASBS 42 identifies generally which method should be used from the various causes of impairment as follows:

1. Impairments from physical damage—restoration cost method.
2. Impairments from enactment or approval of laws or regulations, or other changes in environmental factors or from technological development or obsolescence—service units method.
3. Impairments from a change in manner or duration of use—deflated depreciated replacement cost method or service units method.

Reporting Impairment Losses

GASBS 42 provides that most impairment losses should be considered permanent (requiring a write-down of the asset) unless evidence is available to demonstrate that the impairment will be temporary. Impairment losses (other than temporary impairments) should be reported in the statement of activities and statement of revenues, expenses, and changes in fund net position, if appropriate, as a program or operating expense, special item, or extraordinary item in accordance with the guidance of GASBS 34. If not apparent from the face of the financial statements, a general description, amount, and the financial statement classification of the impairment loss should be disclosed in the notes to the financial statements. The carrying amount of impaired capital assets that are idle at year-end should be disclosed, regardless of whether the impairment is considered permanent or temporary.

Once an impairment loss has been recorded for an asset, the value of that asset should not be written up in the future if events affecting the circumstances of the impairment change.

Insurance Recoveries

In the governmental fund financial statements, GASBS 42 provides that restoration or replacement of a capital asset should be reported as a separate transaction from the insurance recovery. The insurance recovery is reported as another financing source or an extraordinary item, as appropriate.

In the government-wide financial statements (and in proprietary fund financial statements) the restoration or replacement of an impaired capital asset is also reported as a separate transaction from the impairment loss and associated insurance recovery. The impairment loss should be reported net of the associated insurance recovery when the recovery and loss occur in the same year. Insurance recoveries in subsequent years should be reported as program revenue or as an extraordinary item, as appropriate. Insurance recoveries should only be recognized when realized or realizable. If an insurance company has admitted or acknowledged coverage, an insurance recovery would be considered by GASBS 42 to be realizable.

If not apparent from the financial statements, the amount and classification of insurance recoveries should be disclosed.

DISCLOSURES RELATING TO CAPITAL ASSETS

GASBS 34 requires that information about changes in capital assets used in governmental activities and business-type activities be disclosed about major classes of capital assets. Exhibit 1 is an illustrative note disclosure for capital assets.

Exhibit 1 Illustrative capital asset note disclosure

Capital asset activity for the year ended June 30, 20XX, was as follows (in thousands):

	Primary Government			
	Beginning Balance	***Increases***	***Decreases***	***Ending Balance***
Governmental activities:				
Capital assets not being depreciated:				
Land and improvements	$x,xxx	$x,xxx	$(x,xxx)	$x,xxx
Construction in progress	x,xxx	x,xxx	(x,xxx)	x,xxx
Total capital assets not being depreciated	x,xxx	x,xxx	(x,xxx)	x,xxx
Other capital assets:				
Buildings and improvements	$x,xxx	$x,xxx	$(x,xxx)	$x,xxx
Equipment	x,xxx	x,xxx	(x,xxx)	x,xxx
Roads and highways	x,xxx	x,xxx	(x,xxx)	x,xxx
Total other capital assets at historical cost	x,xxx	x,xxx	(x,xxx)	x,xxx
Less accumulated depreciation for:				
Buildings and improvements	$x,xxx	$x,xxx	$(x,xxx)	$x,xxx
Equipment	x,xxx	x,xxx	(x,xxx)	x,xxx
Roads and highways	x,xxx	x,xxx	(x,xxx)	x,xxx
Total accumulated depreciation	x,xxx	x,xxx	(x,xxx)	x,xxx
Other capital assets, net	x,xxx	x,xxx	(x,xxx)	x,xxx
Governmental activities capital assets, net	$x,xxx	$x,xxx	$(x,xxx)	$x,xxx

Depreciation expense was charged to functions as follows:	
Governmental activities:	
General government	$ xxx
Public safety	xxx
Health and sanitation	xxx
Culture and recreation	xx
Transportation	xx
Total governmental activities depreciation expense	$x,xxx

	Primary Government			
	Beginning Balance	***Increases***	***Decreases***	***Ending Balance***
Business-type activities:				
Capital assets not being depreciated:				
Land and improvements	$x,xxx	$x,xxx	$(x,xxx)	$x,xxx
Construction in progress	x,xxx	x,xxx	(x,xxx)	x,xxx
Total capital assets not being depreciated	x,xxx	x,xxx	(x,xxx)	x,xxx
Other capital assets:				
Distribution and collection systems	$x,xxx	$x,xxx	$(x,xxx)	$x,xxx
Buildings and equipment	x,xxx	x,xxx	(x,xxx)	x,xxx
Total other capital assets at historical cost	x,xxx	x,xxx	(x,xxx)	x,xxx

	Primary Government			
	Beginning Balance	***Increases***	***Decreases***	***Ending Balance***
Less accumulated depreciation for:				
Distribution and collection systems	$(x,xxx)	$(x,xxx)	$x,xxx	$(x,xxx)
Buildings and equipment	(x,xxx)	(x,xxx)	x,xxx	(x,xxx)
Total accumulated depreciation	(x,xxx)	(x,xxx)	x,xxx	(x,xxx)
Other capital assets, net	x,xxx	x,xxx	x,xxx	x,xxx
Business-type activities capital assets, net	$x,xxx	$x,xxx	$(x,xxx)	$x,xxx

Depreciation expense was charged to functions as follows:

Business-type activities:	
Water	$ xxx
Sewer	xxx
Total business-type activities depreciation expense	$x,xxx

SERVICE CONCESSION ARRANGEMENTS

The GASB issued Statement No. 60 (GASBS 60), *Accounting and Financial Reporting for Service Concession Arrangements*, to provide accounting guidance for certain transactions that are broadly referred to as public-private (or public-public) partnerships, but more specifically called service concession arrangements. A service concession arrangement is an arrangement between a transferor (a government) and an operator (governmental or nongovernmental entity) in which (1) the transferor conveys to an operator the right and related obligation to provide services through the use of infrastructure or another public asset (a "facility") in exchange for significant consideration and (2) the operator collects and is compensated by fees from third parties.

GASBS 60 applies only to those arrangements in which specific criteria determining whether a transferor has control over the facility are met. One of the key questions answered by GASBS 60 regarding these types of arrangements is what entity records the asset? Does the transferor government keep the asset on its books, or is the asset recorded by the operator? As will be discussed in greater detail below, GASBS 60 provides that a transferor reports the facility subject to a service concession arrangement as its capital asset, generally following existing measurement, recognition, and disclosure guidance for capital assets. New facilities constructed or acquired by the operator or improvements to existing facilities made by the operator are reported at fair value by the transferor. A liability is recognized, for the present value of significant contractual obligations to sacrifice financial resources imposed on the transferor, along with a corresponding deferred inflow of resources. Revenue is recognized by the transferor in a systematic and rational manner over the term of the arrangement.

In short, there are several key items to keep in mind when applying GASBS 60 to a service concession arrangement:

- The government transferring the operation of the asset (transferor) will keep the asset recorded on its books.
- A new or improved facility will be recorded by the government at present value.
- A liability may need to be recognized for obligations that the government undertakes as part of the arrangement.
- The offset to a new asset recorded or a liability incurred is defined as a deferred inflow or outflow of resources that will be recognized over the life of the arrangement.
- Any up-front payment received (net of any obligations occurred) is also defined as a deferred inflow of resources and recognized over the life of the arrangement.

Keeping these basic tenets in mind will make understanding the specific requirements of GASBS 60 easier to achieve.

In addition, it's important to note that the provisions of GASBS 60 are applied to the financial statements of governments that are prepared using the economic resources measurement focus, which would include proprietary funds as well as government-wide financial statements.

Service Concession Arrangements within the Scope of GASBS 60

GASBS 60 establishes guidance for accounting and financial reporting for service concession arrangements, which as used in GASBS 60 are defined as an arrangement between a government (the transferor) and an operator (which may be a governmental entity [governmental operator] or a nongovernmental entity) in which all of the following criteria are met:

1. The transferor conveys to the operator the right and related obligation to provide public services through the use and operation of a capital asset (referred to in this Statement as

a "facility") in exchange for significant consideration, such as an up-front payment, installment payments, a new facility, or improvements to an existing facility. These services relate to the primary function of the facility (GASBS 60's example is operating a city zoo) rather than ancillary services operated in conjunction with the facility (for example, operating the souvenir stand at a city zoo).
2. The operator collects and is compensated by fees from third parties. GASBS 60's scope excludes agency relationships (that is, an arrangement in which an operator accepts payments from third parties and remits those payments to the transferor for an established fee).
3. The transferor determines or has the ability to modify or approve what services the operator is required to provide, to whom the operator is required to provide the services, and the prices or rates that can be charged for the services.
4. The transferor is entitled to significant residual interest in the service utility of the facility at the end of the arrangement.

GASBS 60 notes that service concession arrangements within its scope include, but are not limited to:

1. Arrangements in which the operator will design and build a facility and will obtain the right to collect fees from third parties (for example, construction of a municipal complex for the right to lease a portion of the facility to third parties).
2. Arrangements in which the operator will provide significant consideration in exchange for the right to access an existing facility (for example, a parking garage) and collect fees from third parties for its usage.
3. Arrangements in which the operator will design and build a facility for the transferor (for example, a new toll road), finance the construction costs, provide the associated services, collect the associated fees, and convey the facility to the government at the end of the arrangement.

Transferor Accounting and Financial Reporting for Facilities and Related Payments Received from an Operator

GASBS 60 provides that if the facility associated with a service concession arrangement is an existing facility, the transferor should continue to report the facility as a capital asset.

Further, if the facility associated with a service concession arrangement is a new facility purchased or constructed by the operator, or an existing facility that has been improved (i.e., increases the capacity or efficiency of the facility rather than preserve its useful life) by the operator, the transferor should report (1) the new facility or the improvement as a capital asset at fair value when it is placed in operation, (2) any contractual obligations as liabilities, and (3) a corresponding deferred inflow of resources equal to the difference between (1) and (2).

GASBS 60 also provides that a transferor should recognize a liability for certain obligations to sacrifice financial resources under the terms of the arrangement. Liabilities associated with the service concession arrangement should be recorded at their present value if a contractual obligation is significant and meets either of the following criteria:

1. The contractual obligation directly relates to the facility (for example, obligations for capital improvements, insurance, or maintenance on the facility). This obligation could relate to ownership of the facility or could arise from the transferor's responsibility to ensure that the facility remains fit for the particular purpose of the arrangement.
2. The contractual obligation relates to a commitment made by the transferor to maintain a minimum or specific level of service in connection with the operation of the facility

(GASBS 60 uses the example of providing a specific level of police and emergency services for the facility or providing a minimum level of maintenance to areas surrounding the facility).

After initial measurement, the capital asset is subject to existing requirements for depreciation, impairment, and disclosures. However, GASBS 60 provides that the capital asset should not be depreciated if the arrangement requires the operator to return the facility to the transferor in its original or an enhanced condition. The corresponding deferred inflow of resources should be reduced and revenue should be recognized in a systematic and rational manner over the term of the arrangement, beginning when the facility is placed into operation.

If a liability is recorded to reflect a contractual obligation to sacrifice financial resources as described above, the liability should be reduced as the transferor's obligations are satisfied. As obligations are satisfied, a deferred inflow of resources should be reported and the related revenue should be recognized in a systematic and rational manner over the remaining term of the arrangement. Improvements made to the facility by the operator during the term of the service concession arrangement should be capitalized as they are made and also are subject to requirements for depreciation, impairment, and disclosures.

If a service concession arrangement requires up-front or installment payments from the operator, GASBS 60 provides that the transferor should report (1) the up-front payment or present value of installment payments as an asset, (2) any contractual obligations as liabilities, and (3) related deferred inflow of resources equal to the difference between (1) and (2). Revenue should be recognized as the deferred inflow of resources is reduced. This revenue should be recognized in a systematic and rational manner over the term of the arrangement. A liability should be recognized if the transferor has contractual obligations that meet the criteria described above.

Governmental Operator Accounting and Financial Reporting for the Right to Access Facilities and Related Payments to a Transferor

If the operator is a government operator, GASBS 60 provides that the governmental operator report an intangible asset for the right to access the facility and collect third-party fees from its operation at cost (such as the amount of an up-front payment or the cost of construction of or improvements to the facility). The cost of improvements to the facility made by the governmental operator during the term of the service concession arrangement should increase the governmental operator's intangible asset if the improvements increase the capacity or efficiency of the facility. The intangible asset should be amortized over the term of the arrangement in a systematic and rational manner.

GASBS 60 notes that some agreements require a facility to be returned in a specified condition. If information that is prominent (conspicuous or known to the governmental operator) indicates the facility is not in the specified condition and the cost to restore the facility to that condition is reasonably estimable, then a liability and, generally, an expense to restore the facility should be reported. Governmental operators are not required to perform additional procedures to identify potential condition deficiencies beyond those already performed as part of their normal operations or those that may be required by the agreement.

Accounting for Revenue Sharing Arrangements

GASBS 60 also addresses service concession arrangements that include provisions for revenue sharing. A governmental operator that shares revenues with a transferor should report all revenue earned and expenses incurred—including the amount of revenues shared with the transferor—that are associated with the operation of the facility. In this circumstance, the transferor should recognize only its portion of the shared revenue when earned in accordance with the terms of the arrangement.

If revenue sharing arrangements contain amounts to be paid to the transferor regardless of revenues earned (for example, annual installments in fixed amounts), then the present value of those amounts should be reported by the transferor and governmental operators as if they were installment payments at the inception of the arrangement.

Required Disclosures

GASBS 60 provides that the following should be disclosed in the notes to financial statements of transferors and governmental operators for service concession arrangements:

1. A general description of the arrangement in effect during the reporting period, including management's objectives for entering into it and, if applicable, the status of the project during the construction period.
2. The nature and amounts of assets, liabilities, and deferred inflows of resources related to the service concession arrangement that are recognized in the financial statements.
3. The nature and extent of rights retained by the transferor or granted to the governmental operator under the arrangement.

GASBS 60 notes that some arrangements may include provisions for guarantees and commitments. For example, a transferor may become responsible for paying the debt of the operator in the event of a default, or the arrangement may include a minimum revenue guarantee to the operator. For each period in which a guarantee or commitment exists, GASBS 60 requires disclosures about guarantees and commitments, including identification, duration, and significant contract terms of the guarantee or commitment.

GASBS 60 provides that disclosure information for multiple service concession arrangements may be provided individually or in the aggregate for those that involve similar facilities and risk.

CAPITALIZATION OF INTEREST

Some capital assets that are reported in proprietary funds are constructed. These funds would include in the cost of those constructed assets any interest cost that would ordinarily be capitalized under the accounting rules similar to those used for commercial enterprises. This accounting guidance is now promulgated for governments in GASBS 62, which adopted requirements essentially identical to those previously contained in FASB requirements.

NOTE: In June 2018 the GASB issued Statement No. 89 Accounting for Interest Cost Incurred before the End of a Construction Period (GASBS 89), which effectively eliminates the concept of capitalized interest in governmental accounting. GASBS 89 provides that interest cost incurred before the end of a construction period be recognized as an expense in the period in which the cost is incurred for financial statements prepared on the economic resources measurement focus. Accordingly, interest cost incurred before the end of a construction period will not be included in the historical cost of a capital asset reported in a business-type entity or enterprise fund. GASBS 89 also confirms that financial statements prepared using the current financial resources measurement focus should report interest incurred before the end of the construction period as an expenditure.

GASBS 89 is effective for reporting periods beginning after December 15, 2019, with earlier application encouraged. Fortunately, the requirements of GASBS 89 are to be applied prospectively, so interest costs capitalized under current standards does not have be derecognized upon implementation.

NOTE: This chapter provides information on interest capitalization on capital assets constructed by proprietary funds. Capitalization of interest on capital assets used in governmental activities is also not recorded under GASBS 34.

Interest cost is capitalized for assets that require an acquisition period to get them ready for use. The acquisition period is the period beginning with the first expenditure for a qualifying asset and ending when the asset is substantially complete and ready for its intended use. The interest cost capitalization period starts when three conditions are met:

- Expenditures have occurred.
- Activities necessary to prepare the asset (including administrative activities before construction) have begun.
- Interest cost has been incurred.

The amount of interest cost capitalized should not exceed the actual interest cost applicable to the proprietary fund that is incurred during the reporting period. To compute the amount of interest cost to be capitalized for a reporting period, the average cumulative expenditures for the qualifying asset during the reporting period must be determined. In order to determine the average accumulated expenditures, each expenditure must be weighted for the time it was outstanding during the reporting period.

To determine the interest rate to apply against the weighted-average of expenditures computed in the preceding paragraph, the government should determine if the construction is being financed with a specific borrowing. If it is, which in the governmental environment is fairly likely, then the interest rate of that specific borrowing should be used. In other words, this interest rate, multiplied by the weighted-average of expenditures on the qualifying assets, would be the amount of interest that is capitalized. If no specific borrowing is made to acquire the qualifying asset, the weighted-average interest rate incurred on other borrowings outstanding during the period is used to determine the amount of interest cost to be capitalized.

As stated above, the amount of interest capitalized should not exceed the interest cost of the reporting period. In addition, interest is not capitalized during delays or interruptions, other than brief interruptions, that occur during the acquisition or development phase of the qualifying asset.

Background

As described earlier in this chapter, the historical cost of acquiring an asset includes the costs incurred necessary to bring the asset to the condition and location necessary for its intended use. If an asset requires a period in which to carry out the activities necessary to bring it to that location and condition, the interest cost incurred during that period as a result of expenditures for the asset is part of the historical cost of the asset.

The objectives of capitalizing interest are the following:

- To obtain a measure of acquisition cost that more closely reflects the enterprise's total investment in the asset; and
- To charge a cost that relates to the acquisition of a resource that will benefit future periods against the revenues of the periods benefited.

Conceptually, interest cost is capitalizable for all assets that require time to get them ready for their intended use, called the *acquisition period*. However, in certain cases, because of cost/benefit considerations in obtaining information, among other reasons, interest cost should not be capitalized. Accordingly, SFAS 34 specifies that interest cost should not be capitalized for the following types of assets:

- Inventories that are routinely manufactured or otherwise produced in large quantities on a repetitive basis.
- Assets that are in use or ready for their intended use in the earnings activities of the entity.
- Assets that are not being used in the earnings activities of the enterprise and are not undergoing the activities necessary to get them ready for use.
- Assets that are not included in the balance sheet.
- Investments accounted for by the equity method after the planned principal operations of the investee begin.
- Investments in regulated investees that are capitalizing both the cost of debt and equity capital.
- Assets acquired with gifts or grants that are restricted by the donor or the grantor to acquisition of those assets to the extent that funds are available from such gifts and grants. (Interest earned from temporary investment of those funds that is similarly restricted should be considered an addition to the gift or grant for this purpose.)
- Land that is not undergoing activities necessary to get it ready for its intended use.
- Certain oil- and gas-producing operations accounted for by the full cost method.

After consideration of the above exceptions, interest should be capitalized for the following types of assets, referred to as *qualifying assets*:

- Assets that are constructed or otherwise produced for an entity's own use, including assets constructed or produced for the enterprise by others for which deposits or progress payments have been made.
- Assets that are for sale or lease and are constructed or otherwise produced as discrete projects, such as real estate developments.
- Investments (equity, loans, and advances) accounted for by the equity method while the investee has activities in progress necessary to commence its planned principal operations, provided that the investee's activities include the use of funds to acquire qualifying assets for its operations.

Amount of Interest to Be Capitalized

The amount of interest cost to be capitalized for qualifying assets is intended to be that portion of the interest cost incurred during the assets' acquisition periods that could theoretically be avoided if expenditures for the assets had not been made, such as avoiding interest by not making additional borrowings or by using the funds expended for the qualifying assets to repay borrowings that already exist.

The amount of interest that is capitalized in an accounting period is determined by applying an interest rate (known as the capitalization rate) to the average amount of the accumulated expenditures for the asset during the period. (Special rules may apply when qualifying assets are financed with tax-exempt debt. These rules are discussed later in this chapter.) The capitalization rates used in an accounting period are based on the rates applicable to borrowings outstanding during the accounting period. However, if an entity's financing plans associate a specific new borrowing with a qualifying asset, the enterprise may use the rate on that specific borrowing as the capitalization rate to be applied to that portion of the average accumulated expenditures for the asset not in excess of the amount of the borrowing. If the average accumulated expenditures for the asset exceed the amounts of the specific new borrowing associated with the asset, the capitalization rate applicable to this excess should be a weighted-average of the rates applicable to the other borrowings of the entity.

GASBS 62 provides specific guidance on determining which borrowings should be considered in the weighted-average rate mentioned in the previous paragraph. The objective is to obtain a reasonable measure of the cost of financing the acquisition of the asset in terms of the interest cost incurred that otherwise could have been avoided. Judgment will likely be required to make a selection of borrowings that best accomplishes this objective in the particular circumstances of the governmental entity. For example, capitalized interest for capital assets constructed and financed by revenue bonds issued by a water and sewer authority should consider the interest rate of the water and sewer authority's debt, rather than general obligation bonds of the government. The revenue bonds are likely to show a different, probably lower, rate than that of the general obligation bonds.

In addition to the above guidance on the calculation of the amount of capitalized interest, the amount of interest that is capitalized in an accounting period cannot exceed the total amount of interest cost incurred by the entity in that period.

Capitalization Period

Generally, the capitalization period begins when the following three conditions are met:

1. Expenditures for assets have been made.
2. Activities that are necessary to get the asset ready for its intended use are in progress.
3. Interest cost is being incurred.

(The beginning of the capitalization period for assets financed with tax-exempt debt is described later in this chapter.)

Interest capitalization continues as long as the above three conditions continue to be met. The term *activities* is meant to be construed broadly. It should be considered to encompass more than physical construction. Activities are all the steps required to prepare the asset for its intended use, and might include:

- Administrative and technical activities during the preconstruction phase.
- Development of plans or the process of obtaining permits from various governmental authorities.
- Activities undertaken after construction has begun in order to overcome unforeseen obstacles, such as technical problems, labor disputes, or litigation.

If the governmental entity suspends substantially all activities related to the acquisition of the asset, interest capitalization should cease until activities are resumed. However, brief interruptions, interruptions that are externally imposed, and delays inherent in the asset acquisition process do not require interest capitalization to be interrupted.

When the asset is substantially completed and ready for its intended use, the capitalization period ends. The term *substantially complete* is used to prohibit the continuing of interest capitalization in situations in which completion of the asset is intentionally delayed. Interest cost should not be capitalized during periods when the entity intentionally defers or suspends activities related to the asset, because interest incurred during such periods is a holding cost and not an acquisition cost.

Capitalization of Interest Involving Tax-Exempt Borrowings and Certain Gifts and Grants

SFAS 62 addresses tax-exempt borrowings used to finance qualifying assets. Generally, interest earned by an entity is not offset against the interest cost in determining either interest capitalization rates or limitations on the amount of interest cost that can be capitalized. However, in situations where the acquisition of qualifying assets is financed with the proceeds of tax-exempt borrowings and those funds are externally restricted to finance the acquisition of specified qualifying assets or to service the related debt, this general principal is changed. The amount of interest cost capitalized on qualifying assets acquired with the proceeds of tax-exempt borrowings that are externally restricted as specified above is the interest cost on the borrowing less any interest earned on related interest-bearing investments acquired with proceeds of the related tax-exempt borrowings from the date of the borrowing until the assets are ready for their intended use.

In other words, when a specific tax-exempt borrowing finances a project, a governmental entity will earn interest income on bond proceeds that are invested until they are expended or required to be held in debt service reserve accounts. These interest earnings should be offset against the interest cost in determining the amounts of interest to be capitalized. Conceptually, the true interest cost to the government is the net of this interest income and interest cost. However, this exception to the general rule of not netting interest income against interest expense relates only to this specific exception relating to tax-exempt borrowings and where amounts received under gifts and grants are restricted to use in the acquisition of the qualifying asset.

Disclosures

In addition to the accounting requirements specified above, there are two disclosure requirements relating to capitalized interest:

1. For an accounting period in which no interest cost is capitalized, the amount of interest cost incurred and charged to expense during the period should be disclosed.
2. For an accounting period in which some interest cost is capitalized, the total amount of interest cost incurred during the period and the amount thereof that has been capitalized should be disclosed.

Example

The following example demonstrates some of the basic requirements and considerations in calculating and accounting for capitalized interest.

Assume that an airport authority is building a new runway at a cost of $1,000,000. Construction will start on January 1, 20XX and will be completed and placed in service by June 30, 20XX, which is also the authority's year-end. A bond issue of $800,000, whose proceeds must be used to build the runway, bears interest at a rate of 5%. Bond proceeds are invested in an account earning 4% interest until the proceeds are expended. The remaining amount needed for the construction, $200,000, will be funded internally by the airport authority after the $800,000 of bond proceeds are used up. The airport authority's total interest cost for this period is $200,000, and its similar borrowings bear a weighted-average interest rate of 6%.

The monthly expenditures and interest costs and income on the bond proceeds are calculated as listed below, and the following schedule would be the first step in calculating the amount of capitalized interest:

Month	*Expenditures*	*Cumulative Exp.*	*Mth. Int. Cost*	*Mth. Int. Income*
Jan	$100,000	100,000	417	2,333
Feb	100,000	200,000	833	2,000
Mar	200,000	400,000	1,667	1,333
Apr	200,000	600,000	2,500	667
May	200,000	800,000	3,333	
Jun	200,000	1,000,000	4,333[1]	–
	13,083	6,333		

This amount is calculated at $800,000 @ 5% for one month ($3,333) and $200,000 @ 6% for one month ($1,000).

If the airport authority issued taxable debt to build the runway, the amount of capitalized interest to be recorded is $13,083. If the airport authority issued tax-exempt debt that was specifically restricted to finance the acquisition of the specific qualified asset, the interest cost capitalized would be $6,750 ($13,083 less $6,333). Also note that in the case of the tax-exempt debt example, if the airport authority issued monthly financial statements, the "negative" amount of capitalized interest in January, for example, of $1,916 ($2,333 less $417) would actually be reduced from the cost of the construction-in-progress that would have been recorded as an asset in the monthly financial statements.

Also note that if the amounts expended were reasonably equal over the monthly periods, calculation of the capitalized interest would closely approximate the monthly amounts. For example, $800,000 expended over six months results in an average outstanding expenditure of $400,000, which at 5% annual rate equals $10,000 plus $200,000 outstanding for one month at 6% equals $1,000, for a total of $11,000.

Asset Retirement Obligations

In November 2016 the GASB issued Statement No. 82 (GASBS 83), *Certain Asset Retirement Obligations*, to address accounting and financial reporting for certain asset retirement obligations. As its name states, the GASB only addresses asset retirement obligations that meet certain criteria.

GASBS 83 defines asset retirement obligations (ARO) as a legally enforceable liability associated with the retirement of a tangible capital asset (that is, the tangible capital asset is permanently removed from service). The retirement of a tangible capital asset encompasses its sale, abandonment, recycling, or disposal in some other manner; however, it does not encompass the temporary idling of a tangible capital asset.

Under GASBS 83 AROs result from the normal operations of tangible capital assets, whether acquired or constructed, and include legally enforceable liabilities associated with all of the following activities:

(a) Retirement of a tangible capital asset.
(b) Disposal of a replaced part that is a component of a tangible capital asset.
(c) Environmental remediation associated with the retirement of a tangible capital asset that results from the normal operation of that capital asset.

GASBS 83 also applies to legally enforceable liabilities of a lessor in connection with the retirement of its leased property if those liabilities meet the definition of an ARO.

GASBS 83 does not apply to the following:

(a) Obligations that arise solely from a plan to sell or otherwise dispose of a tangible capital asset.
(b) Obligations associated with the preparation of a tangible capital asset for an alternative use.

(c) Obligations for pollution remediation, such as asbestos removal, that result from the other-than-normal operation of a tangible capital asset.
(d) Obligations associated with maintenance, rather than retirement, of a tangible capital asset.
(e) The cost of a replacement part that is a component of a tangible capital asset.
(f) Landfill closure and postclosure care obligations, including those not covered by GASB Statement No. 18, *Accounting for Municipal Solid Waste Landfill Closure and Postclosure Care Costs*.
(g) Conditional obligations to perform asset retirement activities.

NOTE: In analyzing whether a potential asset retirement obligation is within the scope of GASBS 83, consider that a common example used is the decommissioning of a nuclear power plant, where there are certain significant legally required obligations that must be undertaken to retire the plant. Conversely, obligations to move or dispose of desks and chairs when a government moves out of a leased space would likely not meet the criteria of GASBS 83 as listed above.

RECOGNITION

Recognition of an ARO

GASBS 83 provides that a government should recognize an ARO when the liability is incurred and reasonably estimable. Incurrence of a liability is manifested by the occurrence of both an external obligating event and an internal obligating event resulting from normal operations. An obligating event refers to an event whose occurrence determines the timing for recognition of an ARO.

GASBS 83 considers an external obligating event to be one of the following:

(a) Approval of federal, state, or local laws or regulations.
(b) Creation of a legally binding contract.
(c) Issuance of a court judgment.

GASBS 83 considers an internal obligating event to be one of the following:

(a) For contamination-related AROs, the event is the occurrence of contamination. Contamination refers only to contamination that (1) is a result of the normal operation of a tangible capital asset (such as nuclear contamination of a nuclear reactor vessel as a result of the normal operation of a nuclear power plant) and (2) is not in the scope of GASB Statement 49, *Accounting and Financial Reporting for Pollution Remediation Obligations,* as amended.
(b) For non-contamination-related AROs:
   1. If the pattern of incurrence of the liability is based on the use of the tangible capital asset, the event is placing that capital asset into operation and consuming a portion of the usable capacity by the normal operations of that capital asset. GASBS 83 uses the example of an internal obligating event to recognize a liability for the retirement of a coal strip mine is the excavation of the coal strip mine and using a portion of the capacity of the coal strip mine.

2. If the pattern of incurrence of the liability is not based on the use of the tangible capital asset, the event is placing that capital asset into operation. For example, the internal obligating event to recognize a liability for the retirement of a wind turbine is placing the wind turbine into operation.
3. If the tangible capital asset is permanently abandoned before it is placed into operation, the event is the permanent abandonment itself. For example, the internal obligating event to recognize a liability for the retirement of a tangible capital asset that is permanently abandoned during construction is the abandonment of the construction.

(c) For AROs related to acquired tangible capital assets, the event is the acquisition of the tangible capital asset. For example, the internal obligating event to recognize a liability for an acquired power plant with an existing ARO is the acquisition of the power plant.

GASBS 83 notes that the action of completing a plan to retire a tangible capital asset is not, by itself, an internal obligating event.

Recognition of a Deferred Outflow of Resources

When an ARO is recognized, GASBS 83 provides that a government also should recognize a corresponding deferred outflow of resources.

However, if a tangible capital asset is permanently abandoned before it is placed into operation, a government should immediately report an outflow of resources (for example, an expense) rather than a deferred outflow of resources when an ARO is recognized.

INITIAL MEASUREMENT

Initial Measurement of an ARO

GASBS 83 provides that a government should determine the types of activities to be included in the measurement of an ARO based on relevant legal requirements, that is, the relevant laws, regulations, contracts, or court judgments. The legal requirements resulting from laws and regulations should be based on applicable federal, state, or local laws or regulations that have been approved as of the financial reporting date, regardless of their effective dates.

GASBS 83 also provides that the measurement of an ARO should be based on the best estimate of the current value of outlays expected to be incurred. Current value is the amount that would be paid if all equipment, facilities, and services included in the estimate were acquired at the end of the current reporting period.

Under GASBS 83 the best estimate should be determined using all available evidence. This approach requires probability weighting of potential outcomes when sufficient evidence is available or can be obtained at reasonable cost. When probability weighting cannot be accomplished at reasonable cost, the most likely amount in the range of potential outcomes should be used. The determination of that amount should take into consideration all other available evidence that can be obtained at reasonable cost, including the potential for higher or lower outcomes.

Initial ARO Measurement Exception for a Minority Owner

GASBS 83 notes that a government may have a minority share (less than 50%) of ownership interest in an undivided interest arrangement in which (a) the government and one or more other entities jointly own a tangible capital asset to the extent of each entity's ownership interest and (b) each joint owner is liable for its share of the ARO.

When a nongovernmental entity is the majority owner of the jointly owned tangible capital asset, the nongovernmental majority owner normally would report its ARO in accordance with the guidance of another recognized accounting standards setter. For example, a governmental utility district may have a 10% ownership interest in a power plant with a related ARO, for which 75% of the ownership interest belongs to a publicly traded energy company that reports using Financial Accounting Standards Board guidance.

In addition, a government may have a minority share of ownership interest in a jointly owned tangible capital asset in an undivided interest arrangement in which (1) none of the joint owners has a majority ownership (more than 50%) and (2) a nongovernmental joint owner has the operational responsibility for the jointly owned tangible capital asset and reports the associated ARO in accordance with the guidance of another recognized accounting standards setter.

In those situations, the provisions for initial measurement of an ARO as described in GASBS 83 do not apply to a government's minority share of an ARO associated with a jointly owned tangible capital asset. Instead, the government's minority share of an ARO should be reported using the measurement produced by the nongovernmental majority owner, or the nongovernmental minority owner that has operational responsibility, following the guidance of another recognized accounting standards setter. The ARO should not be adjusted to conform to the liability measurement and recognition requirements in this Statement. The measurement date of such an ARO should be no more than one year and one day prior to the government's financial reporting date.

NOTE: This can be a significant benefit to a government in measuring an asset retirement obligation. If the nongovernmental majority owner is calculating and reporting its ARO based upon the accounting principles promulgated by the Financial Accounting Standards Board, there would be no need for the government to try to remeasure its share of the liability using GASBS 83's guidance.

Initial Measurement of a Deferred Outflow of Resources

GASBS 83 provides that a government should initially measure a deferred outflow of resources associated with an ARO at the amount of the corresponding liability upon initial measurement.

SUBSEQUENT MEASUREMENT AND RECOGNITION

Subsequent Measurement and Recognition of an ARO

GASBS 83 provides that subsequent to initial measurement, a government should at least annually adjust the current value of its ARO for the effects of general inflation or deflation. A government also should at least annually evaluate all relevant factors to determine whether the effect of one or more of those factors is expected to significantly increase or decrease the estimated outlays associated with the ARO. GASBS 83 provides that a government should remeasure the ARO only when the results of the evaluation indicate there is a significant change in the estimated outlays. Factors that may lead to a significant change in the estimated outlays include, but are not limited to the following:

(a) Price increases or decreases due to factors other than general inflation or deflation for specific components of the estimated outlays.
(b) Changes in technology.
(c) Changes in legal or regulatory requirements resulting from changes in laws, regulations, contracts, or court judgments.
(d) Changes in the type of equipment, facilities, or services that will be used to meet the obligations to retire the tangible capital asset.

GASBS 83 provides that changes in the estimated outlays should be recognized as an increase or decrease in the carrying amount of the ARO in one of the following ways:

(a) For a liability that increases or decreases before the time of retirement of the tangible capital asset, a government should adjust the corresponding deferred outflow of resources.
(b) For a liability that increases or decreases at or after retirement of the tangible capital asset, at which time the corresponding deferred outflow of resources has been fully recognized as outflows of resources, a government should recognize an outflow of resources or an inflow of resources in the reporting period in which the increase or decrease occurs.

Subsequent ARO Measurement Exception for a Minority Owner

For a government that has a minority share of an ARO as described above, GASBS 83 provides that the provisions for subsequent liability measurement and recognition described above do not apply. Instead, subsequent to initial measurement, such a government should continue to report its minority share of an ARO using the measurement produced by the nongovernmental majority owner or the nongovernmental minority owner that has operational responsibility as described earlier.

The measurement date of such an ARO should be no more than one year and one day prior to the government's financial reporting date.

Subsequent Measurement and Recognition of a Deferred Outflow of Resources

Upon initial measurement of a deferred outflow of resources for an ARO, GASBS 83 requires a government to recognize a reduction of the deferred outflow of resources as an outflow of resources (for example, expense) in a systematic and rational manner over a period of time, in one of the following ways:

(a) For a deferred outflow of resources initially reported at the beginning of a tangible capital asset's estimated useful life, the reduction of the deferred outflow of resources should be recognized as an outflow of resources (for example, expense) over the *entire* estimated useful life of the tangible capital asset.
(b) For a deferred outflow of resources initially reported after a tangible capital asset has been placed into operation, but before the end of its estimated useful life, the reduction of the deferred outflow of resources should be recognized as an outflow of resources (for example, expense) over the *remaining* estimated useful life of the tangible capital asset, starting from the point at which the deferred outflow of resources is initially recognized.

RECOGNITION AND MEASUREMENT IN FINANCIAL STATEMENTS PREPARED USING THE CURRENT FINANCIAL RESOURCES

Measurement Focus

In financial statements prepared using the current financial resources measurement focus, GASBS 83 provides that liabilities and expenditures should be recognized for goods and services used for asset retirement activities upon receipt of those goods and services, to the extent that the amounts are normally expected to be liquidated with expendable available financial resources. Those amounts are normally expected to be liquidated with expendable available financial resources to the extent that they are due and payable. The accumulation of resources in a governmental fund for eventual payment of unmatured general long-term indebtedness, including AROs, does not constitute an outflow of current financial resources and should not result in the recognition of an additional governmental fund liability or expenditure. In the statement of revenues, expenditures, and changes in fund balances, any facilities and equipment acquisitions associated with asset retirement activities should be reported as expenditures.

Effects of Funding and Assurance Provisions

If a government is subject to legal, regulatory, or contractual requirements to provide funding and assurance for its AROs by setting aside assets restricted for payment of the AROs, the government should disclose that fact in accordance with the disclosure requirements discussed below.

Providing funding and assurance that a government will be able to satisfy its AROs does not satisfy or extinguish the related liabilities, nor should the assets restricted for payment of AROs be used to offset the related liabilities. Any costs associated with complying with funding and assurance provisions should be accounted for separately from the AROs.

Notes to Financial Statements

GASBS 83 provides that a government should disclose the following information about its AROs, except for its minority share of an ARO:

(a) A general description of the AROs and associated tangible capital assets, as well as the source of the obligations (whether they are a result of federal, state, or local laws or regulations, contracts, or court judgments).
(b) The methods and assumptions used to measure the liabilities.
(c) The estimated remaining useful life of the associated tangible capital assets.
(d) How any legally required funding and assurance provisions associated with AROs are being met; for example, surety bonds, insurance policies, letters of credit, guarantees by other entities, or trusts used for funding and assurance.
(e) The amount of assets restricted for payment of the liabilities, if not separately displayed in the financial statements.

If an ARO or portions thereof has been incurred by a government but is not yet recognized because it is not reasonably estimable, the government should disclose that fact and the reasons therefor.

If a government has a minority share of an ARO, GASBS 83 provides that the government should disclose the following information about its minority share:

(a) A general description of the ARO and associated tangible capital asset, including:
   1. The total amount of the ARO shared by the nongovernmental majority owner or the nongovernmental minority owner that has operational responsibility, other minority owners, if any, and the reporting government.
   2. The reporting government's minority share of the total amount of the ARO, stated as a percentage.
   3. The dollar amount of the reporting government's minority share of the ARO.

(b) The date of the measurement of the ARO produced by the nongovernmental majority owner or the nongovernmental minority owner that has operational responsibility, if that date differs from the government's reporting date.

(c) How any legally required funding and assurance provisions associated with the government's minority share of an ARO are being met, for example, surety bonds, insurance policies, letters of credit, guarantees by other entities, or trusts used for funding and assurance.

(d) The amount of assets restricted for payment of the government's minority share of the ARO, if not separately displayed in the financial statements.

Effective Date and Transition

The requirements of GASBS 83 are effective for reporting periods beginning after June 15, 2018. Earlier application is encouraged. Changes adopted to conform to the provisions of GASBS 83 should be applied retroactively by restating financial statements, if practicable, for all prior periods presented. If restatement for prior periods is not practicable, the cumulative effect, if any, of applying GASBS 83 should be reported as a restatement of beginning net position (or fund balance or fund net position, as applicable) for the earliest period restated. In the first period that this Statement is applied, the notes to the financial statements should disclose the nature of the restatement and its effect. Also, the reason for not restating prior periods presented should be disclosed.

SUMMARY

GASBS 34 significantly changes the way in which capital assets used in governmental activities of a government are reported. Implementation of the retroactive infrastructure reporting requirements is an important consideration for most governments, as are recent requirements for recording intangible assets and the impairment of assets.

15 DEBT AND OTHER OBLIGATIONS

OVERVIEW OF THE ACCOUNTING FOR DEBT AND OTHER OBLIGATIONS

Prior to the implementation of the financial reporting model for governments as promulgated by GASBS 34, long-term debt and certain other obligations related to governmental activities were accounted for in the general long-term debt account group. Under GASBS 34, long-term debt and certain other obligations are also generally not reported in the governmental funds. They are usually reported as liabilities on the government-wide statement of net position or as liabilities of proprietary funds. This chapter describes the accounting for long-term debt and certain other obligations and describes several issues as to when certain obligations might be reported in governmental funds.

Other long-term liabilities typically found in the government-wide statement of net assets are specifically covered in other chapters of this guide. These liabilities (and the references to the related chapters) are as follows:

- Capital leases and operating leases with scheduled rent increases (Chapter 19).
- Compensated absences (Chapter 18).
- Judgments and claims (Chapter 21).
- Landfill closure and postclosure costs (Chapter 16).
- Postemployment-related liabilities (Chapter 17).

Readers should review these chapters to determine the appropriate recognition of these liabilities in the government-wide financial statements.

In addition, when governments "sell" or pledge future revenues or receivables, recent accounting rules provide guidance for when these types of transactions should be accounted for as sales, or whether they should be accounted for as borrowings. This chapter also discusses the requirements of GASB Statement No. 48 (GASBS 48), *Sales and Pledges of Receivables and Future Revenues and Intra-Entity Transfers of Assets and Future Revenues*, which provides guidance to accounting for these types of transactions.

This chapter also describes the accounting and reporting requirements of GASB Statement No. 49 (GASBS 49), *Accounting and Financial Reporting for Pollution Remediation Obligations*, which provides guidance for when and at what amount a liability should be recorded for pollution remediation obligations.

In addition, this chapter also describes the accounting and financial reporting requirements of GASB Statement No. 70 (GASBS 70), *Accounting and Financial Reporting for Nonexchange Financial Guarantees*.

Funds using proprietary fund accounting record all liabilities (both long-and short-term) in the funds themselves as well as in the government-wide financial statements. Since the governmental funds only record liabilities expected to be satisfied with expendable and available financial resources, governmental long-term liabilities are generally not recorded in the governmental funds as these liabilities are reported on the government-wide statement of net position. For several different types of these liabilities, there may be instances where the liability or a portion of the liability may also be reported in a governmental fund, if the obligation will be satisfied with current financial resources. The reader should keep this in mind in considering the various types of liabilities discussed in this and related chapters to ensure that the obligations are recorded in the correct place. The reader should also read the discussion later in this section for more information about when liabilities are recorded in governmental funds.

The following sections discuss the accounting for general long-term bonds and other debt that might be recorded in the government-wide financial statements. A separate chapter (Chapter 19) discusses the accounting and reporting for capital leases and operating leases with scheduled rent increases. The balance of the amounts recorded in the government-wide financial statements represents specific accrued liability-type items. While specific requirements and calculation of these items are discussed in the chapters referred to above, a review of the overall accounting for accrued liabilities as it relates to long-term obligation warrants special attention.

First, as a general rule, accrued liabilities should be automatically recorded in the governmental funds themselves when due, regardless of whether they will be liquidated with current resources. Usually, accrued liabilities for salaries and accounts payable for goods and services received prior to the end of the fiscal year, but paid in the following fiscal year, fall into this category. These typical, standard accruals, as mentioned, should be recorded in the governmental fund and the government-wide financial statements.

The most common liabilities other than debt items that are generally only recorded in the government-wide financial statements are as follows:

- Judgments and claims.
- Compensated absences.
- Unfunded pension liabilities.
- Special termination benefits.
- Landfill closure and postclosure costs.
- Capital lease obligation and operating leases with scheduled rent increases.

In these cases, a liability should not be recognized in the governmental fund only to the extent that the liability would not "normally be liquidated with expendable available resources." The method of determining how a liability would normally be liquidated with expendable available resources is not provided in any GASB or NCGA pronouncement, although the GAAFR does provide some general practice guidance.

Some governments previously had policies whereby they set aside money in their current budget to fund liabilities incurred during the period, even though those liabilities were not paid until some future budget period. A result of funding liabilities on an ongoing basis is the accumulation of resources in the fund. These resources, currently available in the fund at the end of each fiscal year, will eventually be used to liquidate the liability. Therefore, by their nature, these funded liabilities were considered to be liquidated with expendable available resources, even though the liquidation may not take place until some time far into the future. Accordingly, funded liabilities were reported as fund liabilities regardless of when the liabilities will be liquidated. However, the GAAFR specifies that this practice should not affect the recognition of expenditures and fund liabilities, which would only be recognized as the related liability becomes due, regardless of the liability being advance funded. This change is a result of GASB Interpretation 6, which is discussed more fully in Chapter 3.

Contrast the funded liability situation to the unfunded liability situation, where the government is not setting aside current resources to pay these unfunded liabilities. The government is relying on the resources of future periods to liquidate these liabilities when they become due. Accordingly, it can be concluded that these liabilities will not be liquidated with expendable available resources, even though the liabilities may be liquidated in the very near future. Unfunded liabilities will be paid with amounts that have not yet been provided as of the end of the fiscal year. Accordingly, unfunded liabilities for the special cases listed above should be reported only in the government-wide financial statements.

The example of compensated absences can be used to further demonstrate the unfunded example. Most governments report their entire liability for compensated absences only in the government-wide financial statements. These same governments use the pay-as-you-go method for actually making the payments. For example, when sick day or vacation time is paid, it is paid from the normal recurring payroll while conceptually reducing the liability in the government-wide financial statements. Lump-sum payments are treated in a similar manner. However, compensated absences should be accrued in the fund for employees who have terminated service as of year-end but have not yet been paid for the vested compensated absences that are payable to them. This is specifically because these amounts are now "due" to the employees, even though they have not been paid.

The approach described above applies only to the specific liability items listed above. All other liabilities related to governmental funds must be reported in the funds themselves, regardless of (1) when they are expected to be paid and (2) funding. In other words, a government could not report the accounts payable of its governmental fund in the government-wide financial statements and not the general fund simply because it was behind on payments or because the amounts weren't actually due until a significant time after the fiscal year-end.

When determining whether a government funds one of the above special liabilities, it is important to consider that the criterion is based on whether a government normally liquidates the liability with expendable available financial resources. If a government ordinarily funds a certain type of liability, but fails to do so in a given year, the liability should continue to be reported in the governmental fund because it would normally be liquidated from expendable available financial resources based on the government's existing funding policies.

In addition, liabilities that are payable on demand as of the balance sheet date, other than those related to compensated absences, must be reported as fund liabilities, regardless of whether they are funded. For example, if a government settles a claim or receives a final judgment on a claim prior to the fiscal year-end, but does not actually pay the settlement or judgment until the next fiscal year, the fund from where judgments and claims are normally paid should record a liability for the settlement or judgment amount, regardless of whether it is funded.

GASBS 34 requires certain disclosures about long-term liabilities. These disclosures should include both long-term debt (such as bonds, notes, loans, and leases payable) and other long-term liabilities (such as compensated absences, judgments and claims, landfill liabilities, net pension obligations, etc.). These disclosures are normally presented in the form of a table in the notes to the financial statements and should include:

- Beginning- and end-of-year balances, regardless of whether prior year data are presented on the government-wide financial statements.
- Increases and decreases, presented separately.
- The portions of each item that are due within one year of the date of the financial statement.
- Which governmental funds typically have been used to liquidate other long-term liabilities (such as compensated absences and pension liabilities) in prior years.

DEBT DISCLOSURES UNDER GASB 88

In March 2019 the GASB issued Statement No. 88, *Certain Disclosures Related to Debt, including Direct Borrowings and Direct Placements* (GASBS 88). For purposes of its disclosure requirements, GASBS 88 defines debt as a liability that arises from a contractual obligation to pay cash (or other assets that may be used in lieu of payment of cash) in one or more payments to settle an amount that is fixed at the date the contractual obligation is established. This definition is meant to clarify that the debt disclosures apply to private placements of debt, for which there had been some diversity in practice. In addition, existing disclosures and proposed additional information are to be provided for direct borrowings and direct placements of debt separately from other debt. For disclosure purposes, debt does not include leases, except for contracts reported as a financed purchase of an underlying asset, or accounts payable.

In addition to the current disclosure requirements related to debt, GASBS 88 requires a government to disclose the following summarized information about the following:

- Amount of unused lines of credit.
- Assets pledged as collateral for debt.
- Terms specified in debt agreements related to significant (1) events of default with finance-related consequences, (2) termination events with finance-related consequences, and (3) subjective acceleration clauses.

NOTE: In applying the third bulleted item, the words "significant" and "finance-related consequences" are important, and although not defined in GASBS 88, should be read as they are generally understood in identifying which events of default to disclose. A typical bond indenture has a long list of events of default. The financial statements are not required to disclose every listed event of default to comply with GASBS 88.

GASBS 88 also provides that in the notes to the financial statements, a government should provide separate information in debt disclosures regarding (a) direct borrowings and direct placements of debt from (b) other debt. This applies to both existing and new debt disclosure requirements.

Effective Date

The requirements of GASBS 88 are effective for reporting periods beginning after June 15, 2018, with earlier application encouraged. It applies to the notes to the financial statements for all periods presented.

DEMAND BONDS

Demand bonds are debt instruments that create a potential call on a state or local government's current financial resources. The accounting question that arises is whether the liability for demand bonds should be recorded as a liability of the fund that receives the proceeds, or whether the debt should be included only in the government-wide statement of net position. The GASB issued guidance through GASB Interpretation 1 (GASBI 1), *Demand Bonds Issued by State and Local Governmental Entities*, which is reflected in the discussion of the following accounting question.

Demand bonds are debt issuances that have demand provisions (termed "put" provisions) as one of their features that gives the bondholder the right to require that the issuer redeem the bonds within a certain period, after giving some agreed-upon period of notice, usually 30 days or less. In some cases, the demand provisions are exercisable immediately after the bonds have been issued. In other cases, there is a waiting period of, for example, five years until the put provisions of the bonds may be exercised by the bondholder. These provisions mean that the bondholder is less subject to risks caused by rising interest rates. Because the bondholder is assured that he or she can receive the par value of the bond at some future date, a demand bond has some features and advantages of a short-term investment for the bondholder, in addition to being a potential long-term investment. Accordingly, depending on the current market conditions, governments can issue these types of bonds at a lower interest rate than would be possible with bonds that did not have the demand bonds' put provision.

Because the issuance of demand bonds represents significant potential cash outlays by governments, steps are usually taken to protect the government from having to fund from its own cash reserves demand bonds redeemed by bondholders. First, governments usually appoint remarketing agents whose function is to resell bonds that have been redeemed by bondholders. In addition, governments usually obtain letters of credit or other arrangements that would make funds available sufficient to cover redeemed bonds.

To provide for long-term financing in the event that the remarketing agents are unable to sell the redeemed bonds within a specified period (such as three to six months), the government issuing demand bonds generally enters into an agreement with a financial institution to convert the bonds to an installment loan repayable over a specified period. This type of arrangement is known as a "take-out" agreement and may be part of the letter of credit agreement or a separate agreement.

From the perspective of the government issuing debt in the form of demand bonds, the most important elements of the transaction are the standby liquidity agreement and the take-out agreement. The standby liquidity agreement assures the availability of short-term funds to redeem the bonds that are put by the bondholder pending resale by the remarketing agent. In addition, the take-out agreement is of equal or more importance because it provides assurance that the issuer will be able to repay any borrowings under the standby liquidity agreement and preserves the long-term nature of the basic debt.

As addressed by GASBI 1, demand bonds are those that by their terms have demand provisions that are exercisable at the balance sheet date or within one year from the date of the balance sheet. These bonds should be reported by governments in the general long-term debt account group, provided all of the following conditions delineated in GASBI 1 are met:

- Before the financial statements are issued, the issuer has entered into an arm's-length financing (take-out) agreement (an arm's-length agreement is an agreement with an unrelated third party, with each party acting in his or her own behalf) to convert bonds put (but not resold) into some other form of long-term obligation.
- The take-out agreement does not expire within one year from the date of the issuer's balance sheet.
- The take-out agreement is not cancelable by the lender or the prospective lender during that year, and obligations incurred under the take-out agreement are not callable during that year.
- The lender, prospective lender, or investor is expected to be financially capable of honoring the take-out agreement.

Regarding the conditions above, if the take-out agreement is cancelable or callable because of violations that can be objectively verified by both parties and no violations have occurred prior to issuance of the financial statements, the demand bonds should be classified and recorded as long-term debt. If violations have occurred and a waiver has been obtained before issuance of the financial statements, the bonds should also be classified and recorded as long-term debt. Otherwise, the demand bonds should be classified and recorded as liabilities of the governmental fund.

If the take-out agreement is cancelable or callable because of violations that cannot be objectively verified by both parties, the take-out agreement does not provide sufficient assurance of long-term financing capabilities, and the bonds should be classified as liabilities of the fund.

If a government exercises a take-out agreement to convert demand bonds that have been redeemed into an installment loan, the installment loan should be reported in the general long-term debt account group.

If the above conditions are not met, the demand bonds should be recorded as a liability of a governmental fund, such as the capital projects fund. The selection of the fund to record the liability is determined by which fund receives the bond proceeds from the issuance of the demand bonds. Most often, this is the capital projects fund.

In addition, if a take-out agreement expires while its related demand bonds are still outstanding, the government should report a fund liability in the fund for the demand bonds that were previously reported in the general fixed asset account group. The liability is reported as a liability of the fund that originally reported the proceeds of the bond. A corresponding debit to "Other financing uses" would need to be made at this time to record the fund liability.

In addition to the accounting requirements relative to demand bonds, GASBI 1 requires that a number of disclosures be made about this type of bond and the related agreements. These disclosures are in addition to the normal disclosures required about debt and include the following:

- General description of the demand bond program.
- Terms of any letters of credit or other standby liquidity agreements outstanding.
- Commitment fees to obtain the letters of credit and any amounts drawn on them outstanding as of the balance sheet date.
- A description of the take-out agreement, including its expiration date, commitment fees to obtain that agreement, and the terms of any new obligation under the take-out agreement.
- The debt service requirements that would result if the take-out agreement were to be exercised.

If a take-out agreement has been exercised converting the bonds to an installment loan, the installment loan should be reported as general long-term debt, and the payment schedule under the installment loan should be included as part of the schedule of debt service requirements to maturity.

Using the criteria and requirements of GASBI 1, Exhibit 1 is an illustrative footnote disclosure for demand bonds included in the general long-term debt account group.

Exhibit 1: Illustrative footnote disclosure for demand bonds in the general long-term debt account group

The noncurrent liabilities reported in the government-wide statement of net position include $XXX,XXX of general obligation demand bonds maturing serially through June 30, 20XY, backed by the full faith, credit, and taxing power of the City. The bonds were issued pursuant to an ordinance adopted by the City Council on July 1, 20XX. The proceeds of the bonds were used to provide funds for certain capital improvements. The redemption schedule for these bonds is included in the bond redemption schedule in Note XX. The bonds are subject to purchase on the demand of the holder at a price equal to principal plus accrued interest on three days' notice and delivery to the City's remarketing agent, XYZ Remarketing Company. The remarketing agent is authorized to use its best efforts to sell the repurchased bonds at a price equal to 100% of the principal amount by adjusting the interest rate.

Under an irrevocable letter of credit issued by Friendly Bank, the trustee or the remarketing agent is entitled to draw an amount sufficient to pay the purchase price of bonds delivered to it. The letter of credit is valid through September 30, 20XX, and carries a variable interest rate equal to the difference between the institution's prime lending rate (currently 8%) and the rate payable on the bonds.

If the remarketing agent is unable to resell any bonds that are "put" within six months of the "put" date, the City has a take-out agreement with Friendly Bank to convert the bonds to an installment loan payable over a five-year period bearing an adjustable interest rate equal to the bank's prime lending rate. The take-out agreement expires on September 30, 20XX. If the take-out agreement were to be exercised because the entire issue of $XXX,XXX of demand bonds was "put" and not resold, the City would be required to pay $XX,XXX a year for five years under the installment loan agreement, assuming an 8% interest rate.

The City is required to pay Friendly Bank an annual commitment fee for the letter of credit of 1% per year of the outstanding principal amount of the bonds, plus XXX days of interest at a rate of 8% unless subsequently changed. The City has paid a take-out agreement fee of $XX,XXX (1/10 of 1% of $XXX,XXX) to Friendly Bank. In addition, the remarketing agent receives an annual fee of 1/10 of 1% of the outstanding principal amount of the bonds.

ADVANCE REFUNDINGS

Accounting for transactions relating to the advance refunding of long-term debt was described in Chapter 6. While that discussion focused on the flow of funds through a debt service fund when an advance refunding occurs, the critical accounting decision to be made for advance refundings of general long-term debt is whether the liability of the refunded debt is removed from the government-wide statement of net position. That accounting decision and the related disclosure requirements for advance refundings are the focus of the following discussion.

NOTE: The Tax Cuts and Jobs Act of 2017 provided that interest on bonds issued as part of an advance refunding of debt would essentially no longer be tax exempt for federal tax purposes. This will likely significantly reduce the number of advance refunding transactions. Note that refunding bonds (used to pay off bonds that have reached a callable date and are actually paid off) are not impacted.

NOTE: The reader should refer to Chapter 9, which describes changes to the reporting of amounts related to debt refunding upon the effectiveness of GASB Statement No. 65 (GASBS 65), Items Previously Reported as Assets and Liabilities.

For current refundings and advance refundings resulting in a defeasance of debt reported by governmental activities, business-type activities, and proprietary funds, the difference between the reacquisition price and the net carrying amount of old debt should be reported as a deferred outflow of resources or a deferred inflow of resources and recognized as a component of interest expense in a systematic and rational manner over the remaining life of the old debt or the life of the new debt, whichever is shorter.

Prior to the expiration of the lease term, if a change in the provisions of a lease results from a refunding by the lessor of tax-exempt debt, including an advance refunding, in which (1) the perceived economic advantages of the refunding are passed through to the lessee and (2) the revised agreement is classified as a capital lease by the lessee, then the lessee should adjust the lease obligation to the present value of the future minimum lease payments under the revised lease. The adjustment of the lease obligation to present value should be made using the effective interest rate applicable to the revised agreement. The resulting difference should be reported as a deferred outflow of resources or a deferred inflow of resources. The deferred outflow of resources or the deferred inflow of resources should be recognized as a component of interest expense in a systematic and rational manner over the remaining life of the old debt or the life of the new debt, whichever is shorter.

In addition, under GASBS 65 issuance costs for debt are no longer reported as assets in the government-wide or proprietary fund financial statements.

GASB Statement No. 7 (GASBS 7), *Advance Refundings Resulting in Defeasance of Debt*, provides significant background and accounting guidance for determining the appropriate accounting for these activities.

There are several reasons why a government might desire to refund its debt in advance of the debt's maturity date. The following are some of these reasons a government may advance refund its debt:

1. Most frequently, governments refinance debt to take advantage of more favorable interest rates. If interest rates have declined for similar securities, it is likely that the government can realize savings by advance refunding its older debt.
2. Governments may also refinance debt to change the structure of debt service payments, such as by shortening or lengthening the period.
3. Governments might also refinance debt to escape from unfavorable bond covenants, such as restrictions on issuing additional debt.

Because the benefits that a government may realize from the above reasons are likely to be available before the debt is actually due or redeemable, it is necessary for a government to advance refund the debt. A government accomplishes an advance refunding by taking the proceeds of the new debt issued to refinance the old debt and placing the proceeds in an escrow account that is subsequently used to provide funds to do the following, at minimum:

- Meet periodic principal and interest payments of the old debt until the call or maturity date.
- Pay the call premium, if redemption is at the call date.
- Redeem the debt at the call date or the maturity date.

Most advance refunding transactions result in a defeasance of the debt, enabling the government to remove the amount of the old debt from the government-wide statement of net position. A defeasance can be either legal or in substance:

- A legal defeasance occurs when debt is legally satisfied based on certain provisions in the instrument, even though the debt is not actually repaid.
- An in-substance defeasance is the far more common type of defeasance. An in-substance defeasance occurs when debt is considered defeased for accounting purposes even though a legal defeasance has not occurred.

GASBS 7 prescribes the criteria that must be met before debt is considered defeased for accounting and reporting purposes. The government must irrevocably place cash or assets with an escrow agent in a trust to be used solely for satisfying scheduled payments of both interest and principal of the defeased debt, and the possibility that the debtor will be required to make future payments on that debt is remote. The trust is restricted to owning only monetary assets that are essentially risk-free as to the amount, timing, and collection of interest and principal. The monetary assets should be denominated in the currency in which the debt is payable. GASBS 7 also prescribes that for debt denominated in U.S. dollars, risk-free monetary assets are essentially limited to:

- Direct obligations of the U.S. government (including state and local government securities that the U.S. Treasury issues specifically to provide state and local governments with required cash flows at yields that do not exceed the Internal Revenue Service's arbitrage limits).
- Obligations guaranteed by the U.S. government.
- Securities backed by U.S. government obligations as collateral and for which interest and principal payments generally flow immediately through to the security holder.

Determining the benefit of an advance refunding of long-term debt is not simply a matter of comparing the values of the old debt being refunded and the new debt that is being issued to provide the proceeds to accomplish the advance refunding. In fact, it may be necessary in a refunding to issue new debt in an amount greater than the old debt. In these cases, savings may result if the total new debt service requirements (principal and interest) are less than the old debt service requirements.

Although the difference in total cash flows between the old and the new debt service payments provides some indication of the effect of an advance refunding transaction, that transaction should also be examined from a time-value-of-money perspective. The value on a given date of a series of future payments is less than the sum of those payments because of the time value of money, commonly referred to as the present value of a future payment stream. The present value of the future payment stream provides a more meaningful measure of the savings or costs resulting from a refunding.

GASBS 7 defines the economic gain or loss on a refunding transaction as the difference between the present value of the new debt service requirements and the present value of the old debt service requirements. The interest rate used to determine the present value of these two payment streams should be an interest rate that reflects the estimate of the amount of earnings required on the assets placed in the escrow account, adjusted for any issuance costs that will result in a lower amount of funds actually being invested in the escrow account.

Determining the effective interest rate that is used to discount the cash flow streams on both the old and new debt service payments is an important component in determining the economic gain or loss on an advance refunding. As stated above, this rate is affected by costs that are allowable, which will be paid out of the escrow account. The U.S. Treasury Department regulations limit the amount that a government may earn on funds from tax-exempt debt issuances that are invested by the government, including investments in escrow accounts that are used to pay debt service on the old debt in an advance refunding transaction.

NOTE: The purpose of the limitations is to prevent governments from issuing tax-exempt debt to obtain funds to invest in otherwise taxable securities. Because governments are not subject to income taxes, there would otherwise be a great opportunity to take advantage of these "arbitrage" earnings. For example, a government may be able to issue tax-exempt debt with an interest rate of 4% and at the same time purchase U.S. Treasury securities with a taxable interest rate of 6%. Since the government is not subject to income taxes, in this example it would have 2% more in earnings for every dollar it borrows, ignoring debt issuance costs. The U.S. Treasury requires that, after a complex set of calculations over a five-year period of time, arbitrage earnings be rebated to the U.S. Treasury.

Because of the arbitrage rebate requirements, a government would generally be able to earn on its escrow funds an interest rate equal to the amount that it was paying in interest on the debt that it issued to obtain the funds to put in the escrow account. An adjustment to the interest rate allowed on the escrow funds can be made for certain advance refunding costs which the U.S.

Treasury Department deems "allowable," which means that they can be recouped in part through the escrow earnings. The term *allowable* used above relates to the fact that the U.S. Treasury Department allows certain issuance costs to be deducted from bond proceeds before determining the maximum allowable yield of the escrow fund. Because the escrow fund is invested for a period shorter than the life of the bond, or at the time of the refunding Treasury securities are yielding less than the escrow's legal maximum rate, not all allowable costs can be recovered. To the extent that these costs are recovered by escrow earnings, they effectively cost the issuing entity nothing, and are therefore ignored in computing the effective interest rate. If the costs cannot be recovered, they should be considered in the determination of the effective interest rate, as described above.

Having at least some of these costs allowable and eligible for recoupment from the escrow earnings means that a slightly higher rate would be allowed on the escrow earnings, which is clearly a benefit to a government in evaluating whether a particular advance refunding transaction would be favorable to it. The more that the escrow fund can earn, the smaller the escrow requirement. The smaller the escrow requirement, the less new debt a government must issue to accomplish the refunding transaction. One caveat to this benefit, however, is that the maximum allowable rate that can be earned on the escrow funds is simply that—a maximum rate. Market conditions may be such that a government may only be able to earn an interest rate on the escrow funds that is actually less than the maximum allowable rate.

NOTE: GASBS 7 provides three examples of the calculation of economic gains and losses in a nonauthoritative appendix that are helpful in understanding the components of the calculation. In practice, many governments will rely on underwriters or independent financial advisors to assist them in calculating these amounts. This is particularly true when there are numerous factors that are present in the refunding transaction, such as call dates for the old bonds, variability in coupon rates, and so on.

GASBS 7 requires that governments that defease debt through an advance refunding provide a general description of the transaction in the notes to the financial statements in the year of the refunding. At a minimum, the disclosures should include (1) the difference between the cash flows required to service the old debt and the cash flows required to service the new debt and complete the refunding, and (2) the economic gain or loss resulting from the transaction.

- When measuring the difference between the two cash flows, additional cash used to complete the refunding paid from resources other than the proceeds of the new debt (for example, for issuance costs or payments to the escrow agent) should be added to the new debt flows. Accrued interest received at the bond issuance date should be excluded from the new debt cash flows. If the new debt is issued in an amount greater than that required for the refunding, only that portion of debt service applicable to the refunding should be considered when determining these cash flows.
- As stated above, economic gain or loss is the difference between the present value of the old debt service requirements and the present value of the new debt service requirements, discounted at the effective interest rate and adjusted for additional cash paid, as described in the preceding paragraph.

The effective interest rate is the rate that, when used to discount the debt service requirements on the new debt, produces a present value equal to the proceeds of the new debt (including accrued interest), net of any premiums or discounts and any underwriting spread and issuance costs that are not recoverable through escrow earnings. Issuance costs include all costs incurred to issue the bonds, including, but not limited to, insurance costs (net of rebates from the old debt, if any), financing costs (such as rating agency fees), and other related costs (such as printing, legal, administrative, and trustee expenses).

In addition to these primary disclosures, GASBS 7 also provides additional disclosure guidance as follows:

- In all periods following an advance refunding for which debt that is defeased in substance remains outstanding, the amount, if any, of outstanding debt at the end of the reporting period should be disclosed. These disclosures should distinguish between the primary government and its discretely presented component units.
- The disclosures discussed in the preceding paragraphs should distinguish between the primary government's funds and account groups and its discretely presented component units. The reporting entity's financial statements should present the funds and account groups of the primary government (including its blended component units) and provide an overview of the discretely presented component units.

The reporting entity's financial statements should make those discretely presented component unit disclosures essential to the fair presentation of its general-purpose financial statements, fair presentation being a matter of professional judgment. Financial statement preparers should keep in mind that there are circumstances when aggregating disclosure information can be misleading. Reporting entities are not precluded from providing additional or separate disclosures for both the primary government and its discretely presented component units. For example, a significant loss in one fund may be offset by a significant gain in another fund. In this circumstance, additional or separate disclosure by each fund should be made. (See Exhibit 2.)

Exhibit 2: Illustrative note disclosures for year of advance refund and subsequent periods

The following illustrative note disclosures for the year of the advance refund and subsequent periods in which the old debt is outstanding are based on the guidance of GASBS 7.

Sample Note Disclosure—in the Year of the Advanced Refunding

On April 1, 20XX, the City issued $XXX,XXX in general obligation bonds with an average interest rate of X.XX% to advance refund $XXX,XXX of outstanding 20XX-series bonds with an average interest rate of X.XX%. The net proceeds of $XXX,XXX (after payment of $XX,XXX in underwriting fees, insurance, and other issuance costs) plus an additional $XX,XXX of 20XX-series sinking-fund monies were used to purchase U.S. government securities. Those securities were deposited in an irrevocable trust with an escrow agent to provide for all future debt service payments on the 20XX-series bonds. As a result, the 20XX-series bonds are considered to be defeased and the liability for these bonds has been removed from the government-wide statement of net position.

The City advance refunded the 20XX-series bonds to reduce its total debt service payments over the next XX years by almost $XX,XXX and to obtain an economic gain (difference between the present values of the debt service payments on the old and new debt) of $X,XXX.

Sample Note Disclosure—Periods Following an Advance Refunding

In prior years, the City defeased certain general obligation bonds by placing the proceeds of new bonds in an irrevocable trust to provide for all future debt service payments on the old bonds. Accordingly, the trust account assets and the liability for the defeased bonds are not included in the City's financial statements. On June 30, 20XX, $XXX,XXX of bonds outstanding were considered defeased.

After implementation of GASBS 34, the accounting for the gain or loss from an advance refunding of debt needs to be considered in the government-wide financial statements. The gain or loss for accounting purposes is basically calculated as the difference between the carrying amount of the old and new debt. Any gain or loss is deferred in the government-wide statements and amortized over the life of the new debt, preferably by the effective interest method of amortization.

Note that GASB Statement No. 62 (GASBS 62), *Codification of Accounting and Reporting Guidance Contained in Pre-November 30, 1989 FASB and AICPA Pronouncements*, provides that if debt is extinguished other than by a current or advance refunding, such as extinguished through a troubled debt restructuring or by using financial resources that did not arise from debt proceeds, the gain or loss described above is recognized immediately in the flows statement in the period of extinguishment.

GASB Statement No. 86—*Certain Debt Extinguishment Issues (GASBS 86)*

In May 2017, the GASB issued GASB Statement No. 86, *Certain Debt Extinguishment Issues* (GASBS 86), which addresses a fairly narrow set of issues regarding debt extinguishment. These issues are discussed next.

Accounting and Financial Reporting for In-Substance Defeasance of Debt Using Only Existing Resources

Statement No. 7, *Advance Refundings Resulting in Defeasance of Debt*, requires that debt be considered defeased in substance if the debtor irrevocably places refunding debt proceeds with an escrow agent in a trust to be used solely for satisfying scheduled payments of both principal and interest of the defeased debt. The trust also is required to meet certain conditions for the transaction to qualify as an in-substance defeasance, as described above. GASBS 86 establishes essentially the same requirements if a government places only existing resources in a trust to extinguish the debt. Any difference between the reacquisition price (the amount required to be placed in the trust) and the net carrying amount of the debt defeased in substance using only existing resources would be recognized as a separately identified gain or loss in the period of the defeasance in financial statements using the economic resources measurement focus.

Governments that defease debt using only existing resources are required to provide a general description of the transaction in the notes to the financial statements in the period of the defeasance. In all periods following an in-substance defeasance of debt using only existing resources, the amount of that debt that remains outstanding at period-end would be disclosed.

Prepaid Insurance Related to Extinguished Debt

For governments that extinguish debt, whether through a legal extinguishment or through an in-substance defeasance, GASBS 86 requires that any remaining prepaid insurance related to the extinguished debt be included in the net carrying amount of that debt for the purpose of calculating the difference between the reacquisition price and the net carrying amount of the debt.

Notes to Financial Statements for In-Substance Defeasance Transactions

GASBS 86 notes that one of the criteria for determining an in-substance defeasance is that the trust be limited to holding only monetary assets that are classified as being essentially risk free. If the substitution of essentially risk-free monetary assets by monetary assets that are not essentially risk free is not prohibited, governments would disclose that fact in the period in which the debt is defeased in substance. In subsequent periods, governments would disclose the amount of debt defeased in substance that remains outstanding for which that risk of substitution exists.

NOTE: One implementation question not addressed by GASBS 86 is: How could an in-substance defeasance be accomplished if monetary assets that are not essentially risk free are used to defease the debt? Having disclosure requirements related to monetary assets that are not essentially risk free results in this question.

Effective Date and Transition

The requirements of GASBS 86 are effective for reporting periods beginning after June 15, 2017. Earlier application is encouraged.

BOND, REVENUE, AND TAX ANTICIPATION NOTES

Bond, revenue, and tax anticipation notes are a mechanism for state and local governments to obtain financing in the form of a short-term note that the government intends to pay off with the proceeds of a long-term bond. Bond anticipation notes were discussed in Chapter 5 and are further discussed in the following paragraphs. Revenue and tax anticipation notes are also sources of short-term financing for governments. However, these short-term notes are not anticipated to be repaid from bond proceeds. They are expected to be paid from future collections of tax revenues, often real estate taxes, or other sources of revenue, often federal or state categorical aid. Therefore, these notes should be reported as a fund liability in the fund that receives the proceeds from the notes.

The accounting question for bond anticipation notes is whether the notes should be recorded as a short-term liability in the fund that received the proceeds of the notes (usually the capital projects fund), or whether certain prescribed conditions are met to enable the notes to be treated as a noncurrent liability and recorded only in the government-wide financial statements. What distinguishes bond anticipation notes from revenue and tax anticipation notes is that the bond anticipation notes are expected to be paid with the proceeds of a long-term financing. If certain circumstances are met, the bond anticipation notes may be recorded only in the government-wide financial statements, instead of reporting them as a liability in the governmental fund that received their proceeds, most often the capital projects fund.

NOTE: Under GASBS 34, the same considerations are made as to whether the bond anticipation notes are recorded as a fund liability. In the government-wide statements, the liability will always be recorded; however, it must be determined whether the liability is reported as a current or noncurrent liability.

NCGA Interpretation 9 (NCGAI 9), *Certain Fund Classifications and Balance Sheet Accounts*, addresses the question of how bond, revenue, and tax anticipation notes should be reflected in the financial statements of a government, particularly how they should be accounted for by governmental funds. This guidance is particularly relevant for the capital projects fund, because this is the fund that usually receives the proceeds of bonds issued to finance major asset acquisitions or construction.

NCGAI 9 prescribes that if all legal steps have been taken to refinance the bond anticipation notes and the interest is supported by an ability to consummate refinancing the short-term notes on a long-term basis in accordance with the criteria set forth in FASB Statement No. 6 (SFAS 6), *Classification of Short-Term Obligations Expected to Be Refinanced* (see below), they should be shown as a fund liability, although they would be recorded as a liability on the government-wide statement of net position. However, if the necessary legal steps and the ability to consummate refinancing criteria have not been met, then the bond anticipation notes should be reported as a fund liability in the fund receiving the proceeds.

The requirements of SFAS 6 referred to above are as follows:

> *The enterprise's intent to refinance the short-term obligation on a long-term basis is supported by an ability to consummate the refinancing demonstrated in either of the following ways:*
>
> (a) Post-balance-sheet date issuance of long-term obligation or equity securities. After the date of an enterprise's balance sheet, but before that balance sheet is issued, a long-term obligation … has been issued for the purpose of refinancing the short-term obligation on a long-term basis; or
>
> (b) Financing agreement. Before the balance sheet is issued, the enterprise entered into a financing agreement that clearly permits the enterprise to refinance the short-term obligation on a long-term basis on terms that are readily determinable, and all of the following conditions are met:
>
> (i) The agreement does not expire within one year (or operating cycle) from the date of the enterprise's balance sheet and during that period the agreement is not cancelable by the lender or the prospective lender or investor (and obligations incurred under the agreement are not callable during that period) except for the violation of a provision with which compliance is objectively determinable or measurable.
>
> (ii) No violation of any provision of the financing agreement exists at the balance sheet date and no available information indicates that a violation has occurred thereafter but prior to the issuance of the balance sheet, or, if one exists at the balance sheet date or has occurred thereafter, a waiver has been obtained.
>
> (iii) The lender or the prospective lender or investor with which the enterprise has entered into the financing agreement is expected to be financially capable of honoring the agreement.

For purposes of applying the above provisions of SFAS 6, a "violation of a provision" is a failure to meet a condition set forth in the agreement or breach or violation of a provision such as a restrictive covenant, representation, or warranty, whether or not a grace period is allowed or the lender is required to give notice. In addition, when a financing agreement is cancelable for violation of a provision that can be evaluated differently by the parties to the agreement (for instance, when compliance with the provision is not objectively determinable or measurable), it does not comply with the condition of b(ii) above.

NOTE: To meet the above-described conditions to record short-term bond anticipation notes as long-term debt, a government either has to have completed the financing after the balance sheet date but before the financial statements are issued, or must have a solid agreement in place to obtain the long-term financing after the financial statements are issued. This appears to be a fairly narrow opening to avoid recording the financing as a long-term liability in the general long-term debt account group. However, the chance of complying with these conditions may be better than it appears, because the requirements of the bond anticipation notes themselves will likely require that concrete agreements to issue the long-term bonds are in place before the lenders provide the short-term financing through the bond anticipation notes.

SPECIAL ASSESSMENT DEBT

As described in Chapter 5, the capital projects fund typically accounts for capital projects financed with the proceeds of special assessment debt. More often than not, special assessment projects are capital in nature and are designed to enhance the utility, accessibility, or aesthetic value of the affected properties. The projects may also provide improvements or additions to a government's capital assets, including infrastructure. Some of the more common types of capital special assessments include streets, sidewalks, parking facilities, and curbs and gutters.

The cost of a capital improvement special assessment project is usually greater than the amount the affected property owners can or are willing to pay in one year. To finance the project, the affected property owners effectively mortgage their property by allowing the government to attach a lien on it so that they can pay their *pro rata* share of the improvement costs in installments. To actually obtain funds for the project, the government usually issues long-term debt to finance the project. Ordinarily, the assessed property owners pay the assessments in installments, which are timed to be due based on the debt service requirements of the debt that was issued to fund the projects. The assessed property owners may also elect to pay for the assessment immediately or at any time thereafter, but prior to the installment due dates. When the assessed property owners satisfy their obligations, the government removes the liens from the respective properties.

GASB Statement No. 6 (GASBS 6), *Accounting and Reporting for Special Assessments*, defines *special assessment debt* as those long-term obligations secured by a lien on the assessed properties, for which the primary source of repayment is the assessments levied against the benefiting properties. Often, however, the government will be obligated in some manner to provide resources for repayment of special assessment debt in the event of default by the assessed property owners. It is also not uncommon for a local government to finance an improvement entirely with the proceeds of a general obligation debt and to levy special assessments against the benefiting property owners to provide some of the resources needed to repay the debt.

The primary source of funds for the repayment of special assessment debt is the assessments against the benefiting property owners. The government's role and responsibilities in the debt may vary widely. The government may be directly responsible for paying a portion of the project cost, either as a public benefit or as a property owner benefiting from the improvement. General government resources repay the portion of the debt related to the government's share of the project cost. These costs of capital projects would be expenditures of the capital projects fund. On the other hand, the government may have no liability for special assessment debt issues. Between these two extremes, the government may pledge its full faith and credit as security for the entire special assessment bond issue, including the portion of the bond issue to be paid by assessments against the benefiting property owners. (Further information on determining the extent of a government's responsibility for special assessment debt is provided below.)

If the government is obligated in some manner to assume the payment of related debt service in the event of default by the property owners, all transactions related to capital improvements financed by special assessments should be reported in the same manner, and on the same basis of accounting, as any other capital improvement and financing; that is, transactions of the construction phase of the project should be reported in a capital projects fund (or other appropriate fund), and transactions of the debt service phase should be reported in a debt service fund, if a separate fund is used.

At the time of the levy of a special assessment, special assessments receivable should be recorded in the capital projects fund, offset by the same amount recorded as deferred revenues.

The government should consider the collectibility of the special assessment receivables and determine whether the receivables should be offset with a valuation allowance. The deferred revenue amount should then be decreased because revenues are recognized when they become measurable and available.

The extent of a government's liability for debt related to a special assessment capital improvement can vary significantly. The government may be primarily liable for the debt, as in the case of a general obligation bond, or it may have no liability whatsoever for the special assessment debt. Often, however, the government will be obligated in some manner for the special assessment debt because it provides a secondary source of funds for repayment of the special assessment debt in the event of default by the assessed property owners. The determination of whether the government is obligated in some manner for the debt is important because if so, the special assessment debt will be reported as a liability in the government-wide financial statements.

GASBS 6 provides guidance as to when a government is obligated in some manner for special assessment debt. A government is obligated in some manner for special assessment debt if (1) the government is legally obligated to assume all or part of the debt in the event of default or (2) the government may take certain actions to assume secondary liability for all or part of the debt, and the government takes, or has given indication that it will take, those actions. Conditions that indicate that a government is obligated in some manner include:

1. The government is obligated to honor deficiencies to the extent that lien foreclosure proceeds are insufficient.
2. The government is required to establish a reserve, guarantee, or sinking fund with other resources.
3. The government is required to cover delinquencies with other resources until foreclosure proceeds are received.
4. The government must purchase all properties "sold" for delinquent assessments that were not sold at public auction.
5. The government is authorized to establish a reserve, guarantee, or sinking fund, and it establishes such a fund. If a fund is not established, the considerations in items 7 and 8 below may provide evidence that the government is obligated in some manner.
6. The government may establish a separate fund with other resources for the purpose of purchasing or redeeming special assessment debt, and it establishes such a fund. If a fund is not established, the considerations in items 7 and 8 below may provide evidence that the government is obligated in some manner.
7. The government explicitly indicates by contract, such as bond agreement or offering statement, that in the event of default it may cover deficiencies, although it has no legal obligation to do so.
8. Legal decisions within the state or previous actions by the government related to defaults on other special assessment projects make it probable that the government will assume responsibility for the debt in the event of default.

Given the broad nature of the situations when a government is obligated in some manner for the debt, GASBS 6 concludes that being "obligated in some manner" is intended to include all situations other than those in which (1) the government is prohibited (by constitution, charter, statute, ordinance, or contract) from assuming the debt in the event of default by the property owner or the government is not legally liable for assuming the debt and makes no statement, or gives no indication, that it will or may honor the debt in the event of default.

Following are the accounting requirements for debt issued to finance capital projects that will be paid wholly or partly from special assessments against benefited property owners:

- General obligation debt that will be repaid in part from special assessments should be reported like any other general obligation debt.
- Special assessment debt for which the government is obligated in some manner should be reported in the government-wide statement of net position, except for the portion, if any, that is a direct obligation of an enterprise fund or is expected to be repaid from operating revenues of an enterprise fund. (Note that the enterprise fund portion would also be included in the debt reported on the government-wide statement of net position.)
    - The portion of the special assessment debt that will be repaid from property owner assessments should be reported as "special assessment debt with government commitment."
    - The portion of special assessment debt that will be repaid from general resources of the government (the public benefit portion, or the amount assessed against government-owned property) should be reported in the government-wide statement of net position like other general obligation debt.
- Special assessment debt for which the government is not obligated in any manner should not be displayed in the government's financial statements. However, if the government is liable for a portion of that debt (the public benefit portion, or as a property owner), that portion should be reported in the government-wide statement of net position.

GASBS 6 requires that when the government is obligated in some manner for special assessment debt, the notes to the financial statements should include the normal long-term disclosures about the debt. In addition, the government should describe the nature of the government's obligation, including the identification and description of any guarantee, reserve, or sinking fund established to cover defaults by property owners. The notes should also disclose that the amounts of delinquent special assessment receivables are not separately displayed on the face of the financial statements.

In addition, the statistical section of the CAFR, if one is prepared, should present a schedule of special assessment billings and collections of those billings for the last ten years if the government is obligated in some manner for the related special assessment debt.

If the government is not obligated in any manner for special assessment debt, the notes to the financial statements should disclose the amount of the debt and the fact that the government is in no way liable for repayment but is only acting as agent for the property owners in collecting assessments, forwarding the collections to bondholders, and initiating foreclosure procedures, where appropriate.

POLLUTION REMEDIATION OBLIGATIONS

The GASB issued Statement No. 49 (GASBS 49), *Accounting and Financial Reporting for Pollution Remediation Obligations*, on issues related to accounting and financial reporting requirements for pollution remediation obligations. GASBS 49 specifies five obligating events, which, if any one were to occur, governments would be required to estimate the components of expected pollution remediation outlays and determine whether outlays for those components should be accrued as a liability or, if appropriate, capitalized when goods or services are acquired. These obligating events are identified later in this section.

GASBS 49 does not apply to:

- Landfill closure and postclosure care obligations that are within the scope of GASBS 18, *Accounting for Municipal Solid Waste Landfill Closure and Postclosure Care Costs*.
- Other future pollution remediation activities that are required upon retirement of an asset (known as asset retirement obligations) during periods preceding the retirement. However, GASBS 49 would apply to those activities at the time of the retirement if obligating events are met and a liability has not been recorded previously.
- Recognition of asset impairments or liability recognition for unpaid claims by insurance activities. For asset impairments, the guidance of GASBS 42, *Accounting and Financial Reporting for Impairment of Capital Assets and Insurance Recoveries*, should be used, and for insurance activities, the guidance of GASBS 10, *Accounting and Financial Reporting for Risk Financing and Related Insurance Issues*, should be used.
- Pollution prevention or control obligations with respect to current operations, such as obligations to install smokestack scrubbers, treat effluent, or use environment-friendly products. GASBS 49 also does not apply to fines, penalties, and other nonremediation outlays, such as liability for civil wrongs arising from exposure to toxic substances, product and workplace safety outlays, litigation support involved with potential recoveries, and outlays borne by society at large rather than by a specific government.

GASBS 49 defines a pollution remediation obligation as an obligation to address the current or potential detrimental effects of existing pollution by participating in pollution remediation activities. Pollution remediation activities include the following:

- Precleanup activities, such as the performance of a site assessment, site investigation, and corrective measures feasibility study and the design of a remediation plan.
- Cleanup activities, such as neutralization, containment, or removal and disposal of pollutants and site restoration.
- Government oversight and enforcement-related activities, such as work performed by an environmental regulatory authority dealing with the site and chargeable to the government.
- Operation and maintenance of the remedy, including required monitoring of the remediation effort.

Pollution remediation obligations do not include pollution prevention or control obligations with respect to current operations. Pollution remediation outlays are considered by GASBS 49 to include all direct outlays attributable to pollution remediation activities (including payroll, benefits, equipment, facilities, materials, and legal and other professional services) and may include estimated indirect outlays, such as general overhead. Outlays related to nature resource damage, such as revegetation outlays, are included only if incurred as part of a pollution remediation effort.

GASBS 49 provides a framework for the recognition and measurement of pollution remediation liabilities that incorporates the following components:

- **Obligation events.** Once an obligation event occurs, a government should determine whether one or more components of a pollution remediation obligation are recognizable as a liability.
- **Components and benchmarks.** Components of a liability, such as legal services, site investigation, or postremediation monitoring, should be recognized as they become reasonably estimable. GASBS 49 provides benchmarks for determining when various components become reasonably estimable.

- **Measurement, including the expected cash flow technique.** Measurement of pollution remediation obligations is based on the current value of outlays expected to be incurred. The components of the liability are measured using the expected cash flow technique (explained later), which measures that liability as the sum of probability-weighted amounts in a range of possible estimated amounts, which is the estimated mean or average.

When a government knows or reasonably believes that a site is polluted, the government should determine whether one or more components of a pollution remediation obligation are recognizable when any of the following events specified in the Statement occurs:

- The government is compelled to take remediation action because pollution creates an imminent endangerment to public health or welfare or the environment, leaving it little or no discretion to avoid remediation action.
- The government is in violation of a pollution prevention-related permit or license (such as a Resource Conservation and Recovery Act permit) or similar permits under state law.
- The government is named, or evidence indicates that it will be named, by a regulator as a responsible party or potentially responsible party for remediation, or as a government responsible for sharing costs.
- The government is named, or evidence indicates that it will be named, in a lawsuit to compel the government to participate in remediation.
- The government commences, or legally obligates itself to commence, cleanup activities, or monitoring or operation and maintenance of the remediation effort. If these activities are voluntarily commenced and none of the other obligation events have occurred relative to the entire site, the amount recognized as an obligation should be based on the portion of the remediation project that the government has initiated and is legally required to complete.

Recognition Benchmarks

GASBS 49 requires that pollution remediation liabilities be recognized as the ranges of their components become reasonably estimable (special rules apply to government funds, as discussed later). If all components of the liability cannot be estimated, the government must recognize a liability as the range of each component of the liability (such as legal services, site investigation, or required remediation monitoring) becomes known.

The range of an estimated remediation liability is expected to be defined and periodically refined, as necessary, as different stages in the remediation process occur. Certain stages of a remediation effort or process and of a responsible (or potentially responsible) party involvement provide benchmarks that should be considered when evaluating the extent to which a range of potential outlays for a remediation effort or process is reasonably estimable. GASBS 49 provides, however, that these benchmarks should not be applied in a manner that would delay recognition beyond the point at which a reasonable estimate of the range of the component of the liability can be made. GASBS 49 requires, at a minimum, the estimate of a pollution remediation liability be evaluated as each of the following benchmarks occur:

- Receipt of an administrative order compelling a government to take a response action or risk penalties.
- Participation, as a responsible party or potentially responsible party, in the site assessment or investigation.

- Completion of a corrective measures feasibility study.
- Issuance of an authorization to proceed.
- Remediation design and implementation, through and including operation and maintenance, and postremediation monitoring.

Measurement of Liabilities

Pollution remediation liabilities should be measured at their current value, which is the amount that would be paid if all equipment, facilities, and services included in the estimate were acquired during the current period. The current value of a pollution remediation liability should be based on reasonable and supportable assumptions about future events that may affect the eventual settlement of the liability. GASBS 49 provides that the current value should be based on applicable federal, state, or local laws and regulations that have been approved, regardless of their effective date, and the existing technology expected to be used for the cleanup. The probabilities of these various expectations affect the probability-weighted measurement of the liability discussed in the following section. GASBS 49 requires that the liabilities be measured using the expected cash flow technique, which measures the liability as the sum of probability-weighted amounts in a range of possible estimated amounts—the estimated mean or average. This technique uses all expectations about possible cash flows.

To use GASBS 49's example, an estimated cash flow might be \$100, \$200, or \$300 with probabilities of 10%, 60%, and 30%, respectively. The expected cash flow is calculated as the sum of \$100 times 10%, \$200 times 60%, and \$300 times 30%, or \$220.

GASBS 49 provides that estimates of a pollution remediation liability should be adjusted when benchmarks are met or when new information indicates changes in estimated outlays due to, for example, changes in the remediation plan or operating conditions. These changes may include the type of equipment, facilities, and services that will be used; price increases or reductions for specific outlay components, such as ongoing monitoring requirements; changes in technology; or changes in legal or regulatory requirements.

Accounting for Recoveries

Recoveries expected from other parties, and expected insurance recoveries, would affect the measurement of the liability and the related expense as follows:

- Expected recoveries reduce the measurement of the government's pollution remediation expenditure or expense, and, if they are not yet realized or realizable, also reduce the measurement of the government's pollution remediation liability.
- If the expected recoveries are realized or realizable, they should be recognized separately from the liability as recovery assets, such as cash or receivables.

Capitalization of Pollution Remediation Outlays

GASBS 49 provides that generally pollution remediation outlays should be recognized as an expense when a liability is recognized. However, pollution remediation liabilities should be capitalized in the government-wide and proprietary fund statements when goods and services are acquired if acquired for any of the following circumstances:

- To prepare property in anticipation of a sale.
- To prepare property for use when the property was acquired with known or suspected pollution that was expected to be remediated.

- To perform pollution remediation that restores a pollution-caused decline in service utility that was recognized as an asset impairment.
- To acquire property, plant, and equipment that have a future alternative use.

NOTE: In practice, most pollution remediation outlays will not meet the criteria of GASBS 49 for capitalization. Conceptually this makes sense, as there is no real asset created by the remediation of pollution, except in the limited instances provided by GASBS 49 where the remediation activities produce some identifiable and realizable benefits to the government. Concepts aside, many governments were likely to have been previously capitalizing these types of costs as they were actually incurred. For governments that can only issue debt to fund capital assets, the implementation of GASBS 49 may well affect their funding of these types of costs.

Display in Governmental Fund Financial Statements

Liabilities for pollution remediation activities that normally are liquidated with expendable available resources should be recognized upon receipt of goods and services used in the remediation process. The accumulation of resources in a governmental fund for eventual payment of unmatured general long-term indebtedness, including pollution remediation liabilities, does not constitute an outflow of current financial resources and should not result in the recognition of an additional governmental fund liability or expenditure. Estimated recoveries of pollution remediation outlays from insurers and other responsible (or potentially responsible) parties for which the government is performing remediation activities should reduce any associated pollution remediation expenditures when the recoveries are measurable and available.

Disclosures

GASBS 49 requires the following disclosures for recognized pollution remediation liabilities and recoveries of pollution remediation outlays:

1. The nature and source of pollution remediation obligations (for example, federal, state, or local laws and regulations).
2. The amount of the estimated liability (if not apparent from the financial statements), the methods and assumptions used for the estimate, and the potential for changes due to, for example, price increases or reductions, technology, or applicable laws or regulation.
3. Estimated recoveries reducing the liability.

For pollution remediation liabilities, or portions thereof that are not yet recognized because they are not reasonably estimable, the government should disclose a general description of the nature of the pollution remediation activities.

ACCOUNTING FOR CONTINGENCIES

GASBS 62 incorporates the concepts of accounting for contingencies currently found in FASB literature into the governmental GAAP hierarchy. GASBS 62 defines a contingency as an existing condition, situation, or set of circumstances involving uncertainty as to possible gain (referred to as a gain contingency) or loss (referred to as a loss contingency) to a government that will ultimately be resolved when one or more future events occur or fail to occur. Resolution of the uncertainty may confirm the acquisition of an asset, or the reduction of a liability, or the loss or impairment of an asset, or the incurrence of a liability.

GASBS 62 also distinguishes between a contingency and a loss. The fact that an estimate is involved does not, in and of itself, constitute the type of uncertainty referred to in the definition of a contingency. GASBS 62 uses depreciation as an example. The fact that estimates are used to allocate the known cost of a depreciable asset over the period of use by a government does not make depreciation a contingency; the eventual expiration of the utility of the asset is not uncertain. Thus, depreciation of assets is not a contingency as defined, nor are such matters as recurring repairs, maintenance, and overhauls, which interrelate with depreciation. Also, amounts owed for services received, such as advertising and utilities, are not contingencies even though the accrued amounts may have been estimated; there is nothing uncertain about the fact that those obligations have been incurred.

GASBS 62 includes the following risks of loss from the following kinds of events that are included within its scope:

(a) Collectibility of receivables.
(b) Guarantees of indebtedness of others.
(c) Agreements to repurchase receivables (or to repurchase the related property) that have been sold.
(d) Claims for delays or inadequate specifications on contracts.

GASBS 62 identifies the following risks of loss from the following kinds of events that are *not* included within its scope:

(a) Torts.
(b) Theft of, damage to, or destruction of assets.
(c) Business interruption.
(d) Errors or omissions.
(e) Job-related illnesses or injuries to employees.
(f) Acts of God.
(g) Pollution remediation obligations.

The accounting and financial reporting standards for the risks of loss associated with items (a) through (f) are provided in GASBS 10, as amended. The accounting and financial reporting standards for the risks of loss associated with item (g) are provided in GASBS 49.

Probability Classifications for Loss Contingencies

When a loss contingency exists, the likelihood that the future event or events will confirm the loss or impairment of an asset or the incurrence of a liability can range from probable to remote. GASBS 62 uses the terms *probable*, *reasonably possible*, and *remote* to identify three areas within that range, as follows:

(a) **Probable.** The future event or events are likely to occur.
(b) **Reasonably possible.** The chance of the future event or events occurring is more than remote but less than likely.
(c) **Remote.** The chance of the future event or events occurring is slight.

Accrual of Loss Contingencies

GASBS 62 provides that an estimated loss from a loss contingency should be accrued if both of the following conditions are met:

(a) Information available prior to issuance of the financial statements indicates that it is probable that an asset had been impaired or a liability had been incurred at the date of the financial statements. It is implicit in this condition that it should be probable that one or more future events will occur confirming the fact of the loss.
(b) The amount of loss can be reasonably estimated.

The purpose of these two conditions is to require accrual of losses when they are reasonably estimable and relate to the current or a prior period. When condition (a) above is met, that is, it is probable that an asset had been impaired or a liability had been incurred, and information available indicates that the estimated amount of loss is within a range of amounts, it follows that some amount of loss has occurred and can be reasonably estimated. When some amount within the range appears at the time to be a better estimate than any other amount within the range, that amount should be accrued. When no amount within the range is a better estimate than any other amount, however, the minimum amount in the range should be accrued.

Disclosure of Loss Contingencies

GASBS 62 includes disclosure requirements related to loss contingencies. Disclosure of the nature of an accrual made, and in some circumstances the amount accrued, may be necessary for the financial statements not to be misleading.

If no accrual is made for a loss contingency because one or both of the conditions above are not met, or if an exposure to loss exists in excess of the amount accrued, disclosure of the contingency should be made when there is at least a reasonable possibility that a loss or an additional loss may have been incurred. The disclosure should indicate the nature of the contingency and should give an estimate of the possible loss or range of loss or state that such an estimate cannot be made. Disclosure is not required of a loss contingency involving an unasserted claim or assessment when there has been no manifestation by a potential claimant of an awareness of a possible claim or assessment unless it is considered probable that a claim will be asserted and there is a reasonable possibility that the outcome will be unfavorable.

After the date of a government's financial statements but before those financial statements are issued, information may become available indicating that an asset was impaired or a liability was incurred after the date of the financial statements or that there is at least a reasonable possibility that an asset was impaired or a liability was incurred after that date. The information may relate to a loss contingency that existed at the date of the financial statements. On the other hand, the information may relate to a loss contingency that did not exist at the date of the financial statements. GASBS 62 provides that disclosure of those kinds of losses or loss contingencies may be necessary, however, to keep the financial statements from being misleading. If disclosure is deemed necessary, the financial statements should indicate the nature of the loss or loss contingency and give an estimate of the amount or range of loss or possible loss or state that such an estimate cannot be made.

GASBS 62 provides that certain loss contingencies should be disclosed in financial statements even though the possibility of loss may be remote. The common characteristic of those contingencies is a guarantee, normally with a right to proceed against an outside party in the event that the guarantor is called upon to the satisfy the guarantee. Examples include guarantees of indebtedness of others and guarantees to repurchase receivables (or, in some cases, to repurchase the related property) that have been sold or otherwise assigned. Those loss contingencies, and others that in substance have the same characteristic, should be disclosed. The disclosure should include the nature and amount of the guarantee. Consideration should be given to disclosing, if estimable, the value of any recovery that could be expected to result, such as from the guarantor's right to proceed against an outside party.

In applying the requirements of GASBS 62, the term *guarantees of indebtedness of others* includes indirect guarantees of indebtedness of others. An indirect guarantee of the indebtedness of another arises under an agreement that obligates a government to transfer resources to another entity upon the occurrence of specified events, under conditions whereby (1) the resources are legally available to creditors of the second entity and (2) those creditors may enforce the second entity's claims against the government under the agreement.

General or Unspecified Operations Risks

General or unspecified operations risks do not meet the conditions for accrual provided above, and no accrual for loss should be made. No disclosure about these risks is required by GASBS 62.

Gain Contingencies

Contingencies that might result in gains usually are not reflected in the accounts since to do so might be to recognize revenue prior to its realization. GASBS 62 provides that adequate disclosure should be made of contingencies that might result in gains, but care should be exercised to avoid misleading implications as to the likelihood of realization.

GASB STATEMENT NO. 70—*ACCOUNTING AND FINANCIAL REPORTING FOR NONEXCHANGE FINANCIAL GUARANTEE TRANSACTIONS (GASBS 70)*

In April 2013, the GASB issued GASBS 70 to address certain reporting issues with certain guarantee transactions. Some governments guarantee financial obligations of other governments or nongovernmental entities in which equal value is not received in return for the guarantee—a nonexchange transaction. When a government extends a financial guarantee that is a nonexchange transaction, the government has agreed to indemnify a third party if the entity that issued the guaranteed obligation does not fulfill its requirements under the obligation. Generally, these types of guarantees are extended by governments as part of their mission to assist other governments, nongovernmental entities, or individuals within the government's jurisdiction. Similarly, a government may receive a financial guarantee for an obligation it has issued in which equal value is not provided by the government in return. The Exposure Draft uses the example of a school district that receives a financial guarantee from the state for the district's debt service payments on construction bonds the school district has issued.

GASBS 70 establishes accounting and financial reporting standards for financial guarantees that are nonexchange transactions (nonexchange financial guarantees) extended or received by a government. GASBS 70 defines a *nonexchange financial guarantee* as a guarantee of an obligation of a legally separate entity or individual, including a blended or discretely presented component unit, which requires the guarantor to indemnify a third-party obligation holder under specified conditions. GASBS 70 does not apply to guarantees related to special assessment debt within the scope of GASB Statement No. 6, *Accounting and Financial Reporting for Special Assessments*.

Accounting and Financial Reporting for Nonexchange Financial Guarantee Transactions

GASBS 70 requires that a government that has extended a nonexchange financial guarantee consider qualitative factors in assessing the likelihood that the government will make a payment in relation to the guarantee. Examples provided by GASBS 70 of such qualitative factors relevant to the entity that has issued the guaranteed obligation include, but are not limited to, the following:

1. Initiation of the process of entering into bankruptcy or a financial reorganization.
2. Breach of a debt contract in relation to the guaranteed obligation, such as a failure to meet rate covenants, failure to meet coverage ratios, or default or delinquency in interest or principal payments.
3. Indicators of significant financial difficulty, such as failure to make payments to paying agents or trustees on a timely basis, drawing on a reserve fund to make debt service payments, initiation of a process to intercept receipts to make debt service payments, debt holder concessions, significant investment losses, loss of a major revenue source, significant increase in noncapital disbursements in relation to operating or current revenues, or commencement of financial supervision by another government.

GASBS 70 notes that some governments extend similar nonexchange guarantees to more than one individual or entity. GASBS 70 provides the example of a state government that guarantees debt issued for construction of capital assets for qualifying school districts within the state. When a government extends similar guarantees to a group, the government should consider applicable qualitative factors in relation to the issuers in the group or should consider relevant historical data to assess the likelihood that the government will make a payment in relation to those guarantees. For example, a government that has historical data on the default frequency of a group of guarantees should consider that data in relation to its outstanding guarantees to assess the likelihood that it will make a payment on one or more of the guarantees within the group.

Recognition and Measurement in Economic Resources Financial Statements

When qualitative factors or historical data as discussed above indicate that it is more likely than not that a government will make a payment on nonexchange financial guarantees it extended, the government would recognize a liability and an expense in financial statements prepared using the economic resources measurement focus. The amount recognized should be the discounted present value of the best estimate of the future outflows expected to be incurred as a result of the guarantee. As used in GASBS 70, the term *more likely than not* means a likelihood of more than 50%. If there is no best estimate of the future outflows expected to be incurred, but a range of estimated future outflows can be established in which no amount within that range appears to be a better estimate than any other amount, the minimum amount in that range would be recognized.

Recognition and Measurement in Current Financial Resources Financial Statements

When qualitative factors or historical data as discussed above indicate that it is more likely than not that a government will make a payment on nonexchange financial guarantees it extended, the government would recognize a fund liability and an expenditure in financial statements prepared using the current financial resources measurement focus to the extent the liability is normally expected to be liquidated with expendable available financial resources. Liabilities for nonexchange financial guarantees extended are normally expected to be liquidated with expendable available financial resources when payments are due and payable on the guaranteed obligation.

Governments Receiving a Financial Guarantee

When a government is required to repay a guarantor for payments made on the government's obligations, the government would reclassify that portion of its liability for the guaranteed obligation as a liability to the guarantor. The government that issued the guaranteed obligation should continue to report the obligation as a liability until all or a portion of the liability is legally released, such as when a Plan of Adjustment is confirmed by the court in the case of bankruptcy. Interest expense/expenditures reported should be reduced by the interest-related payments made by the guarantor that are not required to be repaid.

When a government is legally released as an obligor from its own obligations and from any liability to the guarantor, the government would recognize revenue to the extent of the reduction of guaranteed liabilities.

Intra-Entity Nonexchange Financial Guarantees Involving Blended Component Units

GASBS 70 provides that when a government that extends a nonexchange financial guarantee recognizes a liability for the guarantee, the government that issued the guaranteed obligation should recognize a receivable equal to the amount of the liability recognized by the government that extended the guarantee, only if the government that issued the guaranteed obligation is one of the following:

(a) A blended component unit of that government.
(b) A primary government that includes the government that extended the guarantee as a blended component unit within its reporting entity.
(c) Within the same reporting entity and both parties are blended component units of the same primary government.

Disclosures

GASBS 70 includes a number of disclosure requirements.

A government that extends nonexchange financial guarantees should disclose the following information about the guarantees by type of guarantee:

1. A description of the obligations that are guaranteed identifying:
   (a) The legal authority and limits for providing financial guarantees.
   (b) The relationship to the entity or entities issuing the obligations that are guaranteed.
   (c) The length of time of the guarantees.
   (d) Arrangements for recovering payments from the issuers of the obligations that are guaranteed.
2. The total amount of all guarantees extended that are outstanding at the reporting date.

A government that recognizes a nonexchange financial guarantee liability or has made payments during the reporting period on nonexchange financial guarantees extended should disclose the following information:

(a) A brief description of the timing of recognition and measurement of the liabilities and information about the changes in recognized guarantee liabilities, including the following:
   1. Beginning-of-period balances.
   2. Increases, including initial recognition and adjustments increasing estimates.

    3. Guarantee payments made and adjustments decreasing estimates.
    4. End-of-period balances.
- (b) Cumulative amounts of indemnification payments that have been made on guarantees extended that are outstanding at the reporting date.
- (c) Amounts expected to be recovered from indemnification payments that have been made through the reporting date.

Governments That Issue Guaranteed Obligations

A government that has one or more outstanding obligations at the reporting date that have been guaranteed by another entity as part of a nonexchange transaction should disclose the following information about the guarantee(s) by type of guarantee:

- (a) The name of the entity providing the guarantee.
- (b) The amount of the guarantee.
- (c) The length of time of the guarantee.
- (d) The amount paid, if any, by the entity extending the guarantee on obligations of the government during the current reporting period.
- (e) The cumulative amount paid by the entity extending the guarantee on outstanding obligations of the government.
- (f) A description of requirements to repay the entity extending the guarantee.
- (g) The outstanding amounts, if any, required to be repaid to the entity providing the guarantee.

If a government has issued a guaranteed obligation for which payments have been made during the reporting period by the entity that extended the guarantee and that guaranteed obligation is no longer outstanding at the end of the reporting period, regardless of whether the government has any other outstanding guaranteed obligations at the end of the reporting period, it should disclose:

- (a) The amount paid by the entity that extended the guarantee on obligations of the government during the current reporting period.
- (b) The cumulative amount paid by the entity that extended the guarantee on outstanding obligations of the government.
- (c) A description of requirements to repay the entity that extended the guarantee.
- (d) The outstanding amounts, if any, required to be repaid to the entity that provided the guarantee.

GASB STATEMENT NO. 58—*ACCOUNTING AND FINANCIAL REPORTING FOR CHAPTER 9 BANKRUPTCIES (GASBS 58)*

The GASB issued GASBS 58 to provide guidance to municipalities that enter Chapter 9 bankruptcies. Chapter 9 of the U.S. Bankruptcy Code is intended to protect a financially distressed government from its creditors while it develops and negotiates a plan for adjusting its debts. Chapter 9 of the U.S. Bankruptcy Code allows *municipalities* to file for bankruptcy if specifically authorized to do so by state law. The bankruptcy code defines a municipality as a "political subdivision or public agency or instrumentality of a State" (Section 101). This can include cities, counties, special taxing districts, school districts, certain hospital authorities, airport authorities, or other revenue producing enterprises.

GASBS 58 establishes accounting and financial reporting standards for all governments that have petitioned for relief under Chapter 9 of the U.S. Bankruptcy Code or have been granted relief under the provisions of Chapter 9, including governments that enter into bankruptcy and are not expected to emerge as a going concern. GASBS 58 does not apply to troubled debt restructurings that occur outside of bankruptcy. GASBS 58 provides that its disclosure requirements cease to apply for periods following the fiscal year in which the bankruptcy case is closed or the government has its petition dismissed.

Accounting Recognition

GASBS 58 provides that when the Plan of Adjustment is confirmed by the court, the pre-petition liabilities that are subject to the plan are discharged, and the government is bound to the new debt and payment terms in the plan, governments should recognize gains (or losses) from adjustments to those liabilities (and assets, as discussed below) as of the confirmation date or a later date when all significant conditions existing prior to the plan's becoming binding are resolved.

In addition, a confirmed Plan of Adjustment may call for payments that are contingent upon future events. In GASBS 58's provided example, a government may be required to make certain payments if tax collections exceed a specified amount or if the government is able to issue new debt. GASBS provides that the government should recognize a liability for a contingent future payment if it meets the recognition requirements in paragraph 14 of NCGA Statement 4, *Accounting and Financial Reporting Principles for Claims and Judgments and Compensated Absences*. Additional recognition guidance for employer obligations relating to employee benefit plans is provided below.

NOTE: The NCGA Statement and paragraph above references FASB Statement No. 5 (now at FASB Accounting Standards Codification Section 450) for guidance. Basically, a liability for the future payment would be recorded when it is probable that a liability has occurred at the date of the financial statements and the amount of the loss can be reasonably estimated.

GASBS 58 provides specific guidance on the various types of liabilities that might typically be recorded on the municipality's financial statements, as discussed below.

Accounts Payable, Notes, and Debt Obligations

Subject to the requirements for certain specific liabilities discussed below, a contractual obligation to pay on demand or on fixed or determinable dates (for example, accounts payable, notes, debentures and bonds, and related accrued interest) that is included in a confirmed Plan of Adjustment should be remeasured.

GASBS 58 provides that measurement should be based on the payment terms specified in the confirmed Plan of Adjustment. Reductions in future interest payments that have not been accrued, if any, should result in lower interest costs reported in future periods. Reductions to the pre-petition principal and accrued interest payable amounts, if any, should be reported as gains to the extent that the adjusted principal and accrued interest payable amounts in the confirmed Plan of Adjustment are less than the carrying amounts of the debt, including unamortized premium or discount and accrued interest payable. Any remaining unamortized issuance costs associated with a liability that has been adjusted should be expensed. If the adjusted principal and accrued interest payable amounts in the confirmed Plan of Adjustment are greater than the carrying amounts (which may be encountered with deep discount debt), the difference should be reported as an adjustment to interest costs in future periods.

If the Plan of Adjustment does not indicate whether it reduces the principal amount or interest payments, then the debt should be adjusted, and a gain reported, by an amount equal to the difference between the present value of the future payments under the confirmed Plan of Adjustment and the carrying amount of the pre-petition debt. The present value of the future payments should be computed using the effective rate of interest for the original debt.

Capital Leases

GASBS 58 provides that if the provisions of a capital lease are modified in a way that changes the amount of the remaining minimum lease payments and the modification either (1) does not give rise to a new agreement or (2) does give rise to a new agreement but such agreement is also classified as a capital lease, then the present balances of the asset and the obligation should be adjusted by an amount equal to the difference between the present value of the future minimum lease payments under the revised or new agreement and the carrying amount of the pre-petition obligation. The present value of the future minimum lease payments under the revised or new agreement should be computed using the rate of interest used to record the lease initially. A termination of a capital lease should be accounted for by removing the asset and obligation, with a gain or loss recognized for the difference.

Pensions and Other Postemployment Benefits

The method of measuring changes to an employer's pension or other postemployment benefit (OPEB) obligations depends on whether the confirmed Plan of Adjustment results in (1) rejection or (2) amendment of the pension or OPEB plan.

1. If an employer's obligation for unsecured plan benefits is rejected and becomes general unsecured debt, then the change should be accounted for as a termination of the pension or OPEB plan and a new liability recognized in its place. Any assets or liabilities that the employer has recognized related to the terminated plan should be eliminated. Any new liability established in the confirmed Plan of Adjustment should be recognized consistent with standards of accounting for liabilities arising from judgments. The gain (or loss) upon termination of the pension or OPEB plan and the outflow of economic resources related to the establishment of the new liability should be reported as provided in paragraph 12.
2. If an employer's liability for benefits is not rejected, the financial effects of benefit changes should be accounted for by applying the standards of accounting and financial reporting for amendments of a pension or OPEB plan.

Other Liabilities

GASBS 58 notes that payment provisions in a confirmed Plan of Adjustment also should be incorporated into the remeasurement of other liabilities that are measured and reported based on payment expectations (for example, pollution remediation liabilities).

Other Matters

GASBS 58 provides additional requirements relative to certain specific areas as follows:

- If a government is not expected to emerge from bankruptcy as a going concern, then the government's assets should be remeasured and reported at a value that represents the amount expected to be received as of the date of the confirmation of the Plan of Adjustment.
- Gains (or losses) resulting from remeasurement of liabilities or assets in bankruptcy should be reported as an extraordinary item. Additional guidance for governmental funds is provided below.
- Professional fees and similar types of costs directly related to the bankruptcy proceedings should be reported as an expense or expenditure as incurred.
- If the new payment terms affect liabilities (and assets) reported in the governmental funds, those amounts should be adjusted. Adjustments to the reported amount of governmental fund liabilities (and assets), if any, should be reported as an extraordinary item.

Disclosure Requirements

GASBS 58 provides that governments that have filed for bankruptcy should disclose the following:

1. Pertinent conditions and events giving rise to the petition for bankruptcy.
2. The expected or known effects of such conditions and events, including:
   (a) The principal categories of the claims subject to compromise or that already have been adjusted.
   (b) The principal changes in terms and the major features of settlement.
   (c) The aggregate gain expected to occur by remeasuring liabilities subject to a proposed Plan of Adjustment, or realized, as appropriate; or a statement that any gain is not yet reasonably estimable and the reasons therefore.
   (d) Contingent claims not subject to reasonable estimation.
3. Significance of those conditions and events on the levels of service and operations of the government, and any mitigating factors, such as assumption of services by other governments.
4. Possibility of termination of the government, or any plans to terminate the government, as appropriate.
5. How to obtain a copy of the government's Plan of Adjustment or a statement that a plan is not yet available and an estimate of when it will be completed.

SALES AND PLEDGES OF RECEIVABLES AND FUTURE REVENUES

The GASB issued GASB Statement No. 48, *Sales and Pledges of Receivables and Future Revenues and Intra-Entity Transfers of Assets and Future Revenues* (GASBS 48), to address accounting and financial reporting issues relating to sales and pledges of receivables and future revenues. GASBS 48 provides guidance for transactions in which future cash flows from collecting specific receivables or from specific future revenues are exchanged for immediate cash payments, usually as a single lump sum. These types of transactions are often referred to as securitizations, although the new statement does not use this specific term. GASBS 48 also supersedes the specific accounting guidance for tobacco settlement authorities previously contained in GASBTB 2004-1.

The primary accounting question that is addressed by GASBS 48 is whether a transaction should be accounted for as a sale or as a collateralized borrowing. GASBS 48 has an inherent assumption that these types of transactions are collateralized borrowings. For these transactions to be accounted for as a sale, GASBS 48 defines a series of criteria which must be met to qualify as a sale. In addition, GASBS 48 provides accounting guidance for those instances where these types of transactions are accounted for as a sale.

The GASB has based the determination of whether a transaction is a sale or collateralized borrowing on whether a government's continuing involvement with the receivables or future revenue rights has transferred. A significant aspect of this determination is the degree to which the selling or pledging government (the transferor) retains or relinquishes (to the transferee) control over the receivables or future revenues that are transferred.

OBSERVATION: GASBS 48 generally results in fewer of these types of transactions being recorded as sales than under prior standards. In addition, even when sales accounting is appropriate for transactions involving future revenue streams, in many instances the revenue will be deferred and recognized over the life of the agreement. This will always be the case when the transaction is between entities within the same financial reporting entity.

Assessing a government's continuing involvement. GASBS 48 has separate criteria for assessing a government's continuing involvement for receivables and for future revenues. The following are the criteria provided:

Receivables. A transaction in which a government receives proceeds (or is entitled to receive proceeds) in exchange for the rights to future cash flows from receivables should be reported as a sale if the government's continuing involvement with those receivables is effectively terminated. A government's continuing involvement is considered effectively terminated if *all* of the following criteria are met:

1. The transferee's ability to subsequently sell or pledge the receivables is not limited by constraints imposed by the transferor government or through other means, such as organizational or structured restrictions.
2. The transferor does not have the option or ability to unilaterally substitute for or reacquire specific accounts from among the receivables transferred. However, the ability to substitute for defective accounts, at the option of the transferee, would not violate this criterion.
3. The sale agreement is not cancelable by either party, including cancellation through payment of a lump sum or transfer of rights or other assets.
4. The receivables and the cash resulting from their collection have been isolated from the transferor government (as discussed below).

In determining whether receivables have been isolated from the transferor government (item 4 above) GASBS 48 provides the following criteria:

1. The transferee should have legal standing from the transferor (using the criteria for determining whether an organization is a legally separate entity in GASB Statement No. 14, *The Financial Reporting Entity*, as amended).
2. Generally, banking arrangements should be designed to eliminate access by the transferor and its component units (other than the transferee) to cash generated by collecting the

receivables. Access is eliminated when payments on individual accounts are made directly to a custodial account maintained for the benefit of the transferee. However, if the transferor continues to service the accounts or if obligors misdirect their payments on transferred accounts to the transferor, the following requirements apply:

(a) The payments to the transferee should be made only from the resources generated by the specific receivables rather than from the transferor's own resources. The transferor should have no obligation to advance amounts to the transferee before it collects equivalent amounts from the underlying accounts.

(b) Cash collected by the transferor on behalf of the transferee should be remitted to the transferee without significant delay. In addition, any earnings on the invested collections should be passed on to the transferee.

(c) The transferor should consider proceeds received from the transferee as satisfaction of individual accounts. The transferor should indicate in its records which accounts have been transferred and which collections pertain to those accounts.

3. Provisions in the transfer agreement (or provided by statutes, charters, or other governing documents or agreements) should protect the transferee from the claims of the transferor's creditors.

Future revenues. GASBS 48 provides that a transaction in which a government receives proceeds in exchange for cash flows from specific future revenues should be reported as a sale if the government's continuing involvement with those revenues meets *all* of the following criteria:

1. The transferor government will not maintain an active involvement in the future generation of those revenues. (Active involvement is determined based on the criteria in the next section.)
2. The transferee's ability (or the ability of its ultimate holder/owner of the future cash flows) to subsequently sell or pledge the future cash flows is not limited by constraints imposed by the transferor either in the transfer agreement or by other means.
3. The cash resulting from collection of the future revenues has been isolated from the transferor government. (See items 2 and 2a and 2b above.)
4. The contract or agreement between the original resource provider and the transferor government does not prohibit a transfer or assignment of those resources.
5. The sale agreement is not cancelable by either party, including cancellation through payment of a lump sum or transfer of other rights or assets.

For purposes of determining a government's active involvement for item 1 above, GASBS 48 provides that active involvement generally requires a substantive action or performance by the government. Governments need to distinguish the primary or fundamental activity or process that generates a specific revenue from those that, although associated with the revenue, are tangential, or incidental, or are undertaken to protect the revenue. The following are examples that would be considered active involvement:

1. The government produces or provides the goods or services that are exchanged for the revenues.
2. The government levies or assesses taxes, fees, or charges that can directly influence the revenue base or the rates applied to that base to generate revenues. For example, the revenue bases for property, sales, and income taxes are taxable real estate parcels, taxable retail sales, or taxable income, respectively. Under GASBS 48, the taxing government can directly influence any of those bases by establishing minimum taxable levels, granting

exemptions, providing credits, or excluding certain transactions. The taxing government may initiate, activate, or determine tax rates pertaining to each revenue base.
3. The government is required to submit applications for grants or contributions from other governments, organizations, or individuals to obtain the revenues.
4. The government is required to meet grant or contribution performance contingencies to qualify for those resources.

GASBS 48 also provides examples when governments may remain associated with specific revenues in ways that do not constitute the primary or fundamental activity that generates the revenue and thus would not be considered to be actively involved in the generation of revenues as follows:

1. Holding title to revenue-producing assets, such as leases, rents, or royalty income.
2. Owning a contractual right to a stream of future revenues, such as rights to tobacco settlement revenues.
3. Satisfying the "required characteristics" eligibility requirements contained in GASB Statement No. 33, *Accounting and Financial Reporting for Nonexchange Transactions*.
4. Agreeing to refrain from specified acts or transactions, such as agreeing to noncompetition restrictions.

NOTE: The GASB was very specific in citing collecting the stream of future tobacco settlement revenues as an example that does not constitute active involvement. This will cause sales of future revenue streams of tobacco settlement revenues to be accounted for as sales, rather than borrowings. While this may seem to be the same as the accounting treatment prior to the issuance of GASBS 48, it is the deferral provisions of GASBS 48 discussed later in this section that will create the biggest change in accounting for these types of transactions.

Accounting for transactions that do not qualify as sales. A transaction not meeting the sale reporting criteria described above should be reported as a collateralized borrowing. The receivables or future revenues should be considered for financial statement purposes as pledged rather than sold. Proceeds received by the pledging government should be reported as a liability in its statement of net position and as another financing source in its governmental funds, if the governmental funds receive the proceeds. A transferee government should recognize a receivable for the amounts paid to the pledging government.

Accounting for transactions that do qualify as sales. If the sales reporting criteria are met, the transaction should be reported as a sale, using the following guidance:

- In a sale of receivables, the selling government should no longer recognize as an asset the receivables sold. Except for reporting in governmental funds, the difference between the proceeds and the carrying amount of the receivables should be recognized as a gain or loss in the period of sale. In governmental funds, the difference between the proceeds received and the receivables sold (net of allowances and deferred revenues) should be recognized as revenue.
- In a sale of future revenues, the selling government should report the proceeds as revenue or deferred revenue in both the government-wide and fund financial statements. GASBS 48 provides that generally revenue should be deferred and recognized over the duration of the sales agreement; however, there may be instances wherein recognition in the period of sale is appropriate. For transactions with parties outside the financial reporting entity, deferral is required if the future revenue sold was not recognized previously because the

event that would have resulted in revenue recognition had not yet occurred. Consummation of the future revenue sale transaction is not a substitute for a revenue recognition event and consequently the revenue from the sale should be deferred. However, revenue should be recognized at the time of the sale only if the revenue sold was not recognized previously because of uncertainty of realization or the inability to reliably measure the revenue.

Intra-Entity Transfers of Assets and Future Revenues

When accounting for the transfer of capital and financial assets within the same financial reporting entity, GASBS 48 provides that the transferee (recipient) should recognize the assets or future revenues received at the carrying amount of the transferor. The difference between the amount paid (exclusive of amounts that may be refundable) and the carrying value of the receivables transferred should be reported as a gain or loss by the transferor and as a revenue or expenditure/expense by the transferee in their separately issued financial statements, but should be reclassified as transfers or subsidies, as appropriate, in the financial statements of the reporting entity.

For an intra-entity sale of future revenues, the transferor government has reported no carrying value for the rights sold because the asset recognition criteria have not been met. Accordingly, the transferee government should not recognize an asset and related revenue until recognition criteria appropriate to that type of revenue are met. Instead, the transferee government should report the amount paid as a deferred charge to be amortized over the duration of the transfer agreement. The transferor government should defer the recognition of revenue from the sale in its government-wide and fund financial statements and recognize it over the duration of the sale agreement.

Amortization of Deferred Revenues and Charges

GASBS 48 provides that deferred revenues and charges arising from a sale of future revenues should be amortized over the life of the sale agreement using a systematic and rational measure. For example, periodic amortization could be determined by the ratio of resources received from the sale by the transferor to the estimated total future revenues sold by the transferee.

Residual Interest

As part of the proceeds received, a transferor government may acquire a subordinate or junior note or a residual interest representing the right to collections that exceed a stipulated level (such as the debt service requirements of the transferee). GASBS 48 provides that a transferor government should recognize a note or residual interest as an asset, representing a residual interest in:

- Excess receivable collections, giving consideration to the likelihood of realization.
- Excess future revenues, when the asset recognition criteria appropriate to the specific type of revenue that underlies the note or certificate have been met.

A transferee government should recognize a liability to remit residuals to the transferor government, based on the recognition criteria contained in the following section relating to recourse and other obligations.

- **Recourse and other obligations.** A transferor government should recognize estimated liabilities arising from the purchase and sale agreement when information available prior to the issuance of the financial statements indicates that it is probable that a liability has been incurred at the date of the financial statements and the amount of the obligation can be reasonably estimated.
- **Pledges of future revenues when resources are not received by the pledging government.** A government may pledge future cash flows of specific revenues without receiving resources in exchange for that pledge. For example, a government may pledge resources to a component unit that issues debt. The debt-issuing component unit then pledges those future payments from the pledging government as security for its own debt.

The pledging government should not recognize a liability and, in the above example, the component unit should not recognize a receivable for the pledged revenues at the time of the pledge.

The pledging government should continue to recognize revenue from the pledged amounts and should recognize a liability to the component unit and an expenditure/expense simultaneously with the recognition of the revenues pledged. The component unit should recognize revenue when the pledged government is obligated to make the payments.

Disclosures related to future revenues that are pledged or sold. For purposes of these disclosure requirements, GASBS 48 defines pledged revenues as those specific revenues that have been formally committed to directly collateralize or secure debt of the pledging government, or directly or indirectly collateralize or secure debt of a component unit. For each period in which the secured debt remains outstanding, pledging governments should disclose the following:

- Identification of the specific revenue pledged and the approximate amount of the pledge. Generally, the approximate amount would equal the remaining principal and interest requirements of the secured debt.
- Identification of, and general purpose for, the debt secured by the pledged revenue.
- The term of the commitment—that is, the period of time during which the revenue will not be available for other purposes.
- The relationship of the pledged amount to the total for the specific revenue, if estimable.
- A comparison of the pledged revenues recognized during the period to the principal and interest requirements for the debt directly or indirectly collateralized by those revenues.

In the year of the sale, governments that sell future revenue streams should disclose information about the specific revenues sold, including:

- Identification of the specific revenue sold, including the approximate amount, and the significant assumptions used in determining the approximate amount.
- The period to which the sale applies.
- The relationship of the sold amount to the total for that specific revenue, if estimable.
- A comparison of the proceeds of the sale and the present value of the future revenues sold, including the significant assumptions used in determining present value.

NOTE: The reader should refer to Chapter 9, which describes changes to the reporting of amounts related to sales and pledges of revenues upon the effectiveness of GASB Statement No. 65, Items Previously Reported as Assets and Liabilities.

GASB STATEMENT NO. 47—*ACCOUNTING FOR TERMINATION BENEFITS (GASBS 47)*

The GASB issued GASBS 47 to provide accounting and financial reporting guidance for termination benefits. Termination benefits are benefits provided by employers to employees as an inducement to hasten the termination of the employees' services. Termination benefits may be voluntary (generally when the employee has a choice as to whether or not he or she wants to take advantage of the termination benefits) or involuntary (generally when the employee has no choice but to accept termination of his or her services and the resulting termination benefit). Termination benefits include early retirement incentives, severance benefits, and other termination-related benefits. GASBS 47 does not include in its scope the accounting for unemployment compensation.

GASBS 47 notes that judgment will be required in determining whether the nature of a benefit arrangement is to provide benefits in exchange for the early termination of services (in which case it would be considered a termination benefit) or to provide benefits in exchange for employee services, including pension benefits or other postemployment benefits (OPEBs). (Accounting for postemployment benefits is discussed in Chapter 17.) GASBS 47 provides examples of the relevant factors to be considered, including the employer's intent, the way in which the employees generally view the benefits, whether the benefit is conditioned on termination of employment prior to the normal retirement age, and the length of time for which the benefits have been made available.

GASBS 47 prescribes measurement criteria for calculating the cost of termination benefits. Separate rules are provided for health-care-related termination benefits and non-health-care-related termination benefits. Each of these measurement criteria is described below.

Health-care-related termination benefits. Health-care-related termination benefits, including health care continuation under the Consolidated Omnibus Budget Reconciliation Act (COBRA), should be measured by an employer by calculating the discounted present value of the expected future benefit payments. The following additional guidelines are provided:

1. *Projection of benefits.* If the event giving rise to the health-care-related termination benefits is a large-scale, age-oriented program, the employer should segregate benefits provided to terminated employees and their beneficiaries from those provided to active employees for measurement purposes. The employer should project its expected future benefit payments based on the projected total claims costs, or age-adjusted premiums approximating claims costs, for terminated employees. The expected termination benefit payment for each future period is the difference between (a) the projected claims costs, or age-adjusted premiums approximating claims costs, for terminated employees and (b) the payments, if any, to be made by the terminated employees.

   If the event is not a large-scale, age-related program, the employer should segregate the benefits provided to terminated employees and their beneficiaries from those provided to active employees for measurement purposes and should project the employer's expected future benefit payments for terminated employees. The use of projected claims costs, or age-adjusted premiums approximating claims costs, is not required. In other words, unadjusted premiums may be used as the basis for the projection of future benefits.

OBSERVATION: The requirements of GASBS 47 for health-care-related termination benefits have a similar conceptual background as GASBS 45 for OPEB plan benefits as they relate to the explicit rate subsidy concept for health care premiums. In other words, if health care termination benefits are specifically provided to an age group that is comprised of older employees, the measurement of cost should not be based on a blended health care premium rate, because the older recipients of the benefit are assumed to use a greater amount of health care benefits. The cost of providing these benefits cannot, in effect, be subsidized by using a blended rate that includes the younger employees remaining in the workforce. In the first example above, since the termination benefit is based on age, a rate calculation for the effective age group should be calculated and used to project the future benefit costs.

---

2. *Health care cost trend rate.* The projection of expected future benefit payments should include an assumption regarding the health care cost trend rate for the periods covered by the employer's commitment to provide the benefits.
3. *Discount rate.* GASBS 47 provides that the discount rate used to calculate present value should be determined by giving consideration to the estimated yield, over the period of time the benefits are to be provided, on the investments that are expected to be used to finance the payment of benefits, with consideration given to the nature and mix of current and expected benefits. (For pay-as-you-go benefits, this will be strongly influenced by the interest earned on current available cash balances rather than a longer-term rate such as that used by funded defined benefit pension plans.)

Non-health-care-related termination benefits. GASBS 47 provides that if the benefit terms establish an obligation to pay specific amounts on fixed or determinable dates, the cost of the benefits is to be calculated as the discounted present value of expected future benefit payments, including an assumption regarding changes in future cost levels during periods covered by the employer's commitment to provide the benefits.

If the benefit terms do not establish an obligation to pay specific amounts on fixed or determinable dates, the cost of the benefits should be calculated as either (1) the discounted present value of expected future benefit payments, including an assumption regarding changes in the future benefit levels, or (2) the undiscounted total of estimated future benefit payments at current cost levels.

When the costs are discounted, GASBS 47 provides the same guidance for selecting a discount rate as discussed above.

Recognition of Termination Liabilities and Expense in Accrual Basis Financial Statements

Voluntary termination benefits. For voluntary termination benefits, an employer should recognize a liability and expense in accrual basis financial statements when the employees accept the offer and the amounts can be estimated. GASBS 47 provides that the measurement of the liability should be updated, and any incremental liability or expense (both positive and negative) should be recognized as of the end of each subsequent reporting period.

Involuntary termination benefits. For purposes of applying the provisions of GASBS 47, an involuntary termination is a plan that:

- Identifies, at a minimum, the number of employees to be terminated, the job classifications or functions that will be affected and their locations, and when the terminations are expected to occur.
- Establishes the terms of the termination benefits in sufficient detail to enable employees to determine the type and amount of benefits they will receive if they are involuntarily terminated.

For involuntary termination benefits, a liability and expense should be recognized in accrual basis financial statements when a plan of termination has been approved by those with the authority to commit the employer to the plan, the plan has been communicated to employees, and the amounts can be estimated. GASBS 47 provides that the measurement of the liability should be updated, and any incremental liability or expense (both positive and negative) should be recognized as of the end of each subsequent reporting period.

If the involuntary termination requires the employee to render future service in order to receive termination benefits, a liability and expense for the portion of the involuntary termination benefits that will be provided only after completion of future service should be recognized ratably over the future service period. GASBS 47 provides that the measurement of the liability should be updated, and any incremental liability or expense (both positive and negative) should be recognized as of the end of each subsequent reporting period.

Recognition of Termination Benefit Liabilities and Expenditures in Modified Accrual Basis Financial Statements

In governmental fund financial statements prepared on a modified accrual basis of accounting, liabilities and expenditures for termination benefits are recognized to the extent the liabilities are normally expected to be liquidated with expendable available financial resources.

Effect of Termination Benefit on an Employer's Defined Benefit Pension or OPEB Obligations

The effects of a termination benefit on an employer's defined benefit pension or OPEB obligations should be accounted for and reported in accordance with GASBS 27 or GASBS 45, respectively.

Disclosures

GASBS 47 has several specific disclosure requirements relating to termination benefits. These are as follows:

1. In the period in which an employer becomes obligated for termination benefits and in any additional period in which employees are required to render future service in order to receive involuntary termination benefits, the employer should disclose a description of the termination arrangement, such as information about the types of benefits provided, the number of employees affected, and the period of time over which benefits are expected to be provided.
2. In the period in which an employer becomes obligated for termination benefits, the cost of the termination benefits should be disclosed, if not otherwise identifiable from the financial statements. An employer that provides termination benefits that affect defined benefit pension or OPEB obligations should disclose in the notes the change in the actuarial accrued liability for the pension or OPEB plan attributable to the termination benefits.
3. In all periods in which termination benefit liabilities are reported, disclosure should be made of the significant methods (such as whether benefits are measured at the discounted present value of expected future benefit payments) and assumptions (such as the discount rate and health care cost trend rate, if applicable) used to determine liabilities.
4. If a termination benefit that otherwise meets the recognition criteria of GASBS 47 but is not recognized because the expected benefits are not estimable, that fact should be disclosed.

SUMMARY

This chapter summarized the accounting and reporting for long-term debt and various other obligations. The financial statement preparer needs to consider not only the long-term debt that should be reported, but also the long-term portions of other liabilities that are not required to be reported in governmental funds. In addition, the relationship of certain debt-related issues, such as reporting special assessment debt and demand bonds, should be coordinated with the accounting for other governmental funds, particularly the capital projects fund and the debt service fund.

16 LANDFILL CLOSURE AND POSTCLOSURE CARE COSTS

INTRODUCTION

The GASB issued Statement 18 (GASBS 18), *Accounting for Municipal Solid Waste Landfill Closure and Postclosure Care Costs,* to address a very specific issue, the accounting and financial reporting for landfill closure and postclosure care costs. However, since many governmental entities operate these types of facilities, GASBS 18 affected many governmental entities.

GASBS 18 was issued in response to requirements promulgated by the U.S. Environmental Protection Agency (EPA). Landfill operators became obligated to meet certain requirements of the EPA as to closure and postclosure requirements. The postclosure requirements extend for a period of thirty years. Landfill operators are also subject to closure and postclosure care costs resulting from state and local laws and regulations. The GASB issued GASBS 18 to require governments to recognize the liability for these closure and postclosure conditions as the landfill is being used, so that by the time the landfill becomes full and no longer accepts waste, the liability is recorded in the financial statements of the governmental entity that operates the landfill and is responsible for these requirements.

This chapter describes the applicability and requirements of GASBS 18. It also provides examples of detailed calculations of the liabilities for these types of costs that must be recorded in the governmental entity's financial statements.

APPLICABILITY

The provisions of GASBS 18 apply to all state and local governmental entities, including public benefit corporations and authorities, governmental utilities, governmental hospitals and other health care facilities, and governmental colleges and universities. GASBS 18 establishes accounting and financial reporting standards for municipal solid waste landfill (hereafter MSWLF, or simply landfill) closure and postclosure care costs that are required by federal, state, and local laws and regulations. In order to meet these requirements, financial statement preparers need to understand (1) what a MSWLF is and how it operates and (2) closure and postclosure care costs that will be incurred and are covered by this Statement. These two items are addressed in the following paragraphs.

MUNICIPAL SOLID WASTE LANDFILLS

A municipal solid waste landfill is an area of land or an excavation that receives household waste. What makes a landfill "municipal" is not the ownership of the landfill, but the type of waste that is received by the landfill—municipal waste means household waste. Thus, a private, nongovernmental enterprise could own and operate a MSWLF (although it wouldn't be subject to the requirements of GASBS 18).

Landfills (which, for purposes of this chapter, is used interchangeably with MSWLF) operate in many different ways. Their operating methods, along with their closure and postclosure care plans, are filed with regulatory bodies. Many landfills operate on a "cell" basis, where the total landfill is divided into sections that are used one at time. Each cell can then be closed when it reaches capacity and the waste is then received by the next cell that will be used.

Certain of the closure materials and equipment used to contain wastes and to monitor the environmental impact of landfill operations (such as liners and leachate collection systems) must be installed before the cells are ready to receive waste. These prereception activities are sometimes needed in order to comply with federal, state, or local regulations or requirements. After each cell (or the entire landfill, if it is operated as one large cell) is filled to capacity and no longer accepts waste, a final cover is applied to the cell. Sometimes even when the landfill is operated as a number of cells, the final cover is not applied until the entire landfill is filled to capacity and no longer accepts solid waste.

Estimated Total Current Cost of Closure and Postclosure Care

There are a variety of costs that the operator of a landfill will incur for protection of the environment. These costs will be incurred during the period that the landfill is in operation and after the landfill is closed and no longer accepting waste. GASBS 18 addresses the recording of costs relating both to the closure of the landfill and to costs incurred after the landfill is closed (postclosure costs). These costs include the cost of equipment and facilities (such as leachate collection facilities and final cover) as well as the cost of services (such as postclosure maintenance and monitoring costs). Certain of these costs, which result in the disbursement of funds near or after the date that the landfill stops accepting solid waste and during the postclosure period, are included in the "estimated total current cost" of landfill closure and postclosure care, regardless of whether they are capital or operating in nature. (Current cost is the amount that would be paid if all equipment, facilities, and services included in the estimate were acquired during the current period.)

NOTE: Conceptually, GASBS 18 is similar, although not the same, as the recording of an asset retirement obligation discussed in Chapter 14. The idea is that as waste is being added to the landfill and the landfill is being filled up, the expense of taking care of the landfill after it is closed should be matched to the period of time during which the government receives the benefit of the landfill—which is during the period it accepts the waste. At the same time, recording a liability for closure and postclosure care costs recognizes the obligation of the government to comply with federal and other laws after the landfill's closure.

GASBS 18 requires that the estimated total current cost of landfill closure and postclosure care, based on the applicable federal, state, and local laws and regulations, include the following:

- The cost of equipment expected to be installed and facilities expected to be constructed (based upon the landfill's operating plan) near or after the date that the landfill stops accepting solid waste and during the postclosure period. Equipment and facilities that are considered as part of these costs should only be those that will be used exclusively for the landfill. This may include gas monitoring and collection systems, storm water management systems, groundwater monitoring wells, and leachate treatment facilities. The costs for equipment and facilities that are shared by more than one landfill should be allocated to each user landfill based on the percentage of use by each landfill.
- The cost of final cover (sometimes called capping) expected to be applied near or after the date that the landfill stops accepting waste.
- The cost of monitoring and maintaining the expected usable landfill area during the postclosure period. Postclosure care may include maintaining the final cover; monitoring groundwater; monitoring and collecting methane and other gases; collecting, treating, and transporting leachate; repairing or replacing equipment; and remedying or containing environmental hazards.

In determining the estimated total current costs, the governmental financial statement preparer should consider whether all of the requirements of the EPA, as well as state or local requirements, apply as to what facilities need to be installed and what activities need to take place for the closure and postclosure periods. In other words, what is the government operating the landfill required to do and what does it plan to do to close and thereafter care for the landfill? The current costs of these facilities and activities need to be considered as part of the total estimated current cost.

NOTE: The calculation of the estimated current cost of closure and postclosure care for a landfill realistically requires the assistance of either in-house or consulting engineers. Some consulting engineers have teamed with accounting or financial consulting firms to prepare these estimates and calculations for governmental entities, including the preparation of the required disclosures in a draft footnote. While using these services may be effective or convenient, the financial statement preparer ultimately takes responsibility for the amounts recorded and disclosed, and should therefore seek to understand and concur with the calculations, even if outside specialists are used.

After the governmental entity makes an initial calculation of the estimated current cost of landfill closure and postclosure costs, the estimate should be adjusted each year to reflect any changes that should be made to the estimate. For example, the current cost or the estimated costs may increase or decrease simply due to inflation or deflation. On the other hand, there may be changes in the operating conditions of the landfill that may affect the closure and postclosure costs. These changes might include the type of equipment that will need to be acquired, as well as facilities or services that will be used to perform closure and postclosure care. In addition, there may be changes in cost estimates due to changes in the technologies that will be used for closure and postclosure care activities, changes in the expected usable landfill area, and changes in closure and postclosure legal and regulatory requirements that must be considered.

Recording Closure and Postclosure Care Costs—Proprietary Funds and Government-Wide Financial Statements

The true impact of applying GASBS 18's requirements of recognizing a liability is seen in the government-wide financial statements and in proprietary funds. This is because as a liability is recorded proportionally each year for total estimated current costs, a corresponding expense is recorded in the operating statements. This results in a matching of the period in which the cost of the closure and postclosure care activities occur with the period that is benefited by the landfill activities—that is, when the solid wastes are actually put into the landfill. As described later in this chapter, governmental funds do not recognize the estimated closure and postclosure care costs. These funds record an expenditure when the actual closure and postclosure care costs are expended.

For landfill activities reported using proprietary fund accounting and reporting, and for reporting in the government-wide financial statements, a portion of the estimated total current cost of landfill closure and postclosure costs is recognized as an expense and as a liability in each period that the landfill accepts solid waste. Recognition should begin on the date that the landfill begins accepting solid waste, continue in each period that it accepts waste, and be completed by the time that it stops accepting waste. Estimated total current cost is assigned to periods based on the landfill use rather than on the passage of time. Accordingly, some measure of landfill capacity used each period is used to compare with the total landfill capacity, such as cubic yards of solid waste, airspace, or any other reasonable measure.

Using this approach, the current period amount to be expensed is calculated as follows:

$$\frac{\text{Estimated total current cost} \times \text{Cumulative capacity used}}{\text{Total estimated capacity}} - \text{Amount previously recognized}$$

Example

For example, assume that a landfill begins operating on the first day of a governmental entity's fiscal year and is being accounted for by a proprietary fund. The postclosure monitoring period required by law is thirty years. The total estimated current costs are $500,000, determined as follows:

1. Equipment and facilities costs	
Near date landfill stops accepting waste	$ 10,000
During closure/postclosure period:	
• Maintenance and upgrading of leachate treatment system	5,000
• Expected renewals and replacements of storm water and erosion control facilities ($5,000 per year)	150,000
• Monitoring and well replacements (10 wells at $3,000 each)	30,000
2. Final cover costs, including vegetative cover	10,000
3. Postclosure care cost	
• Inspection and maintenance of final cover ($2,000 per year)	60,000
• Groundwater monitoring ($5,000 per year)	150,000
• On-site leachate pretreatment and off-site treatment (1,000,000 gallons @ $.05)	50,000
• Projected remediation costs based on similarly situated landfills	35,000
	$ 500,000

The landfill capacity is 1,000,000 cubic yards of solid waste, and 20,000 cubic yards of solid waste are deposited in the landfill during the first fiscal year. The calculation of the expense and liability to be recorded in this fiscal year for closure and postclosure costs is calculated as follows:

Year 1

$$\frac{\$500,000 \times 20,000 - 0}{1,000,000} = \$10,000$$

The following journal entry would be recorded:

Expenses—landfill closure and postclosure care costs	10,000	
Liability—landfill closure and postclosure		10,000

To record expenses for landfill closure and postclosure costs

Year 2

Continuing the above example, assume that both an increase in the general price level and changes in the specific costs of certain equipment and services have been determined. In addition, it is determined that the actual remaining capacity of the landfill is only 950,000 cubic yards because during the year a certain area of the landfill could not be used. During Year 2, 25,000 cubic yards of solid waste were deposited in the landfill. The total estimated current cost for closure and postclosure care is calculated as follows:

1. Equipment and facilities costs	
Near date landfill stops accepting waste	$ 10,500
During closure/postclosure period:	
• Maintenance and upgrading of leachate treatment system	5,000
• Expected renewals and replacements of storm water and erosion control facilities ($4,000 per year)	120,000
• Monitoring and well replacements (10 wells at $3,250 each)	32,500
2. Final cover costs, including vegetative cover	12,000
3. Postclosure care cost	
• Inspection and maintenance of final cover ($2,000 per year)	60,000
• Groundwater monitoring ($5,500 per year)	165,000
• On-site leachate pretreatment and off-site treatment (1,000,000 gallons @ $.06)	60,000
• Projected remediation costs based on similarly situated landfills	45,000
	$510,000

The calculation of the expense/liability provision for Year 2 is computed as follows:

Year 2

$$\frac{\$510,000 \times 45,000}{950,000}$$

–$10,000 = $24,158 less $10,000 amount recognized in Year 1 = $14,158

The following journal entry would be recorded:

Expenses—landfill closure and postclosure care costs	14,158	
Liability—landfill closure and postclosure care costs		14,158

To record expenses for landfill closure and postclosure costs for Year 2 of landfill operations

Equipment, facilities, services, and final cover that are included in the estimated total current cost should be reported as a reduction of the accrued liability for the landfill closure and postclosure care when they are acquired.

Capital assets that will be used exclusively for a landfill that are not included as part of the calculation of closure and postclosure care should be fully depreciated by the date that the landfill stops accepting solid waste. If capitalized, facilities and equipment installed or constructed for a single cell should be depreciated over the estimated useful life of that cell. If these capital assets are shared among landfills, the portion assigned to each landfill should be fully depreciated by the date that each stops accepting solid waste.

NOTE: The above accounting used by a proprietary fund would be similar to that used in the government-wide financial statements prepared under the new financial reporting model. The liability recorded would be segregated into its current and noncurrent portions.

Recording Closure and Postclosure Care Costs—Governmental Funds

For landfills reported using governmental fund accounting and financial reporting, the measurement and recognition of the accrued liability for landfill closure and postclosure care should be consistent with the calculations described above for proprietary funds. However, the governmental funds should recognize expenditures and fund liabilities using the modified accrual basis of accounting. The remainder of the liability that is not recorded in the fund would only be reflected in the government-wide financial statements.

NOTE: The total estimated current costs for landfill closure and postclosure costs include only those costs that will be incurred near or after the date that the landfill no longer accepts solid waste. Accordingly, in practice, during the years of operation of the landfill, none of the liability for landfill closure and postclosure care costs will be recorded in the governmental fund. The full amount of the calculated liability is recorded in the general long-term debt account group.

Eventually, the equipment and facilities needed for closure and postclosure care of the landfill will be purchased by the governmental fund. When that occurs, the governmental fund will recognize an expenditure for the costs that will use the current expendable financial resources of the governmental fund.

In recording capital assets related to closure and postclosure care, GASBS 18 provides that equipment and facilities included in the estimated total current cost of closure and postclosure care should not be reported as capital assets. Governments that are only able to use bond proceeds for capital expenditures may find themselves unable to finance their equipment and facilities related to landfill closure and postclosure with bond proceeds. Specific requirements for individual government will need to be checked.

Equipment, facilities, services, and final cover included in the estimated total current cost should be reported as a reduction of the recorded liability for the landfill closure and postclosure care when they are acquired. In the operating statement, facilities and equipment acquisitions included in estimated total current cost should be reported as closure and postclosure care expenditures.

Reporting Changes in Estimates

When the formula for determining the periodic liability accrual for landfill closure and postclosure care costs is used, any changes in the estimated total current costs that occur before the landfill stops accepting solid waste are reported in the period of the changes and an adjustment is made to the calculation using the formula. (The example provided in this chapter demonstrates how a change in the estimated total current costs from $500,000 to $510,000 is generally treated as a change in an accounting estimate and recognized prospectively in the calculation, since it is allocated over the remaining estimated life of the landfill.)

On the other hand, accounting for a horizontal expansion of the landfill is handled differently. This type of change is viewed by GASBS 18 as an expansion of the landfill capacity and should not affect the factors used to calculate the accrued liability for the closure and postclosure costs of the original landfill. In this case, a separate calculation of the closure and postclosure care costs for the expanded portion of the landfill would need to be made for each financial reporting period.

Changes in the estimated total current cost for landfill closure and postclosure care may also occur after the date that the landfill stops accepting solid waste. These changes may include changes due to inflation (or deflation), changes in technology, changes in closure and postclosure care requirements, corrections of errors in estimation, and changes in the extent of environmental remediation that is required. Changes in these estimates should be reported in the period in which the change is probable and reasonably estimable. Recording these changes by governmental funds within the governmental fund itself must also take into account the modified accrual basis of accounting and consideration for whether the costs will be paid from the fund's current expendable financial resources.

Accounting for Assets Placed in Trust

Landfill owners or operators may be required by EPA (or state or local laws or regulations) rules to provide financial assurances for closure, postclosure care, and remediation of each landfill. This financial assurance may require the owners or operators to place assets with third-party trustees. For example, owners and operators that use surety bonds to provide financial assurance for closure and postclosure care are required by the EPA to establish a surety standby trust fund and make deposits directly into this standby trust fund.

These amounts should be reported in the fund (e.g., the general fund, special revenue fund, or enterprise fund) used to report the landfill's operations. These assets should be identified by an appropriate description, such as "amounts held by trustee." Any investment earnings on amounts set aside to finance closure and postclosure care costs should be reported as revenue and not as reductions of the estimated total current cost of landfill closure and postclosure care costs and the related accrued liability.

RESPONSIBILITY FOR LANDFILL CLOSURE AND POSTCLOSURE CARE ASSUMED BY ANOTHER ENTITY

The owner or operator of a landfill may transfer all or part of its responsibilities for closure and postclosure care to another entity. A typical example is where a private company agrees to provide closure and postclosure care as part of its contract to operate a government-owned landfill.

Owners and operators of landfills should report a liability for closure and postclosure care costs whenever an obligation to bear these costs has been retained. However, GASBS 18 provides that even when the liability has been transferred, a governmental entity may be contingently liable under applicable federal, state, or local laws and regulations. Accordingly, the governmental entity should also consider the financial capability or stability of any other entity that assumes the responsibility to meet the closure and postclosure care obligations when these obligations become due.

If it appears that the entity assuming the responsibility will not be able to meet its obligations and it is probable that the landfill owner will be required to pay closure and postclosure care costs, then the amount of the obligation should be reported in accordance with the guidance provided for proprietary and governmental funds earlier in this chapter for measuring and recording the accrued liability for closure and postclosure care costs.

DISCLOSURES

GASBS 18 contains several disclosure requirements that relate to landfill closure and postclosure costs, as follows (see Exhibit 1):

- The nature and source of landfill closure and postclosure care requirements—federal, state, or local laws and regulations.
- The fact that the recognition of a liability for closure and postclosure costs is based on landfill capacity used to date.
- The reported liability for closure and postclosure care at the balance sheet date (if not apparent from the financial statements) and the estimated total current cost of closure and postclosure care remaining to be recognized.
- The percentage of landfill capacity used to date and estimated remaining landfill life in years.
- The way in which financial assurance requirements relating to closure and postclosure requirements are being met; in addition, any assets restricted for payment of closure and postclosure care costs should be disclosed if this amount is not apparent from the financial statements.
- The nature of the estimates and the potential for changes due to inflation or deflation, technology, or applicable laws and regulations.

Exhibit 1: Illustrative note disclosure for landfill closure and postclosure care costs

Note X: Closure and Postclosure Care Costs

The City has one active landfill available for solid waste disposal, which is located in the city at 123 Waste Way. A portion of the total estimated current cost of the closure and postclosure care is to be recognized in each period the landfill accepts solid waste. The operations of the landfill are accounted for in the general fund. For governmental funds, the measurement and recognition of the liability for closure and postclosure care are based on total estimated current cost and landfill usage to date. Expenditures and fund liabilities are recognized using the modified accrual basis of accounting. The remainder of the liability is reported only in the government-wide financial statements.

When the landfill stops accepting solid waste, the City is required by federal and state law to close the landfill, including final cover, storm water management, landfill gas control, and to provide postclosure care for a period of thirty years following closure. The City is also obligated under a consent order with the State Department of Environmental Protection to conduct certain corrective measures associated with the landfill. The corrective measures include construction and operation of a leachate mitigation system and closure, postclosure, and groundwater monitoring activities for the sections of the landfill no longer accepting solid waste.

The liability for these activities as of June 30, 20XX, is $XXX,XXX based on the cumulative landfill capacity used to date. The total estimated current cost is $X,XXX,XXX; therefore, the costs remaining to be recognized are $XXX,XXX. The liability for closure and postclosure care costs is based on the cumulative capacity used to date of the landfill of XX%. Cost estimates are based on current data, including contracts awarded by the City, contract bids, and engineering studies. These estimates are subject to adjustment to account for inflation and for any changes in landfill conditions, regulatory requirements, technologies, or cost estimates.

The City is required by state and federal laws and regulations to make annual contributions to a trust fund to finance closure and postclosure care. The City is in compliance with these requirements, and at June 30, 20XX, investments of $XXX,XXX at fair value are held for these purposes. The City expects that future inflation costs will be paid from the interest earnings on these annual contributions. However, if interest earnings are inadequate or additional postclosure care requirements are determined (due to changes in technology or applicable laws and regulations, for example), these costs may need to be covered from future tax revenues.

SUMMARY

The accounting and financial reporting for landfills is an important consideration for the financial statement preparer of a governmental entity that operates or owns a landfill. While the accounting itself for landfill closure and postclosure costs is not complicated, the determination and estimation of these future costs often requires the work of a specialist to assist the financial statement preparer in complying with the accounting and disclosure requirements of GASBS 18.

17 POSTEMPLOYMENT BENEFITS—PENSION AND OTHER

INTRODUCTION

This chapter describes the accounting and financial reporting for postemployment benefits, including pensions and benefits other than pensions provided to retirees (i.e., other postemployment benefits [OPEBs]) by state and local governmental entities. Accounting and financial reporting for pensions have been an area for which guidance from the GASB was developed over a very long period. Governmental employers are well known as significant users of pensions and OPEBs as important benefits for their employees. Defined benefit pension plans remain an important governmental employee benefit, despite their declining popularity in the private sector. Governments generally pay their employees less than what their counterparts in private industry make. However, one factor offsetting these somewhat lower salaries is fairly generous pension benefits that retiring employees enjoy at a relatively young age, along with one or more OPEB plan benefits, such as retiree health care insurance. Accordingly, the accounting and financial reporting for pension and OPEB costs and financial reporting by governmental pension and OPEB plans is an important area.

This chapter has been significantly revised to reflect the substantial changes in the accounting for pensions and OPEB benefits that have recently been adopted. The changes to accounting for pension benefits occurred several years ago. The changes in accounting for OPEB benefits are being adopted by governments at the present time, although some may have adopted the OPEB standards earlier than required. Fortunately, the concepts in the new OPEB standards closely track those of the pension standards, so adoption of the OPEB standards and understanding their conceptual basis should be somewhat easier to adopt. Since these two sets of standards are so closely aligned, both the pension and the OPEB standards will be addressed together, with differences pointed out where appropriate. Specifically, this chapter addresses these new (or recent) GASB statements:

- GASB Statement No. 68 (GASBS 68), *Accounting and Financial Reporting for Pensions—An Amendment of GASB Statement No. 27*
- GASB Statement No. 71 (GASBS 71), *Pension Transition for Contributions Made Subsequent to the Measurement Date—An Amendment of GASB Statement No. 68*
- GASB Statement No. 73 (GASBS 73), *Accounting and Financial Reporting for Pensions and Related Assets That Are Not within the Scope of GASB Statement No. 68, and Amendments to Certain Provisions of GASB Statements No. 67 and No. 68*
- GASB Statement No. 75 (GASBS 75), *Accounting and Financial Reporting for Postemployment Benefits Other Than Pensions*
- GASB Statement No. 82 (GASBS 82), *Pension Issues—An Amendment of GASB Statements No. 67, No. 68, and No. 73*
- GASB Statement No. 85 (GASBS 85), *Omnibus 2017*

SCOPE AND APPLICABILITY

GASBS 68 applies to the financial statements of all state and local governmental employers whose employees (or volunteers who provide services to state and local governments) are provided with pensions though pension plans that are administered through trusts (meeting certain criteria, as discussed below) and to the financial statements of state and local government nonemployer contributing entities that have a legal obligation to make contributions directly to such pension plans.

The requirements of GASBS 68 apply to these entities regardless of whether the employer's financial statements are presented in separately issued, stand-alone statements or are included in the financial reports of another government.

GASBS 68 establishes the following criteria for determining whether pension plans should be considered as being administered through trusts or equivalent arrangements (jointly referred to as trusts):

(a) Contributions from employers and nonemployer contributing entities to the pension plan and earnings on those contributions are irrevocable.
(b) Pension plan assets are dedicated to providing pensions to plan members in accordance with the benefit terms.
(c) Pension plan assets are legally protected from the creditors of employers, nonemployer contributing entities, and the pension plan administrator. If the plan is a defined benefit pension plan, plan assets also are legally protected from creditors of the plan members.

GASBS 75 extends the approach to accounting and financial reporting established in GASBS 68 to all postemployment benefits other than pensions, with modifications as necessary to reflect that for accounting and financial reporting purposes, any assets accumulated for pensions that are not provided through plans that are not administered though trusts (as determined in accordance with GASBS 68's criteria) should not be considered pension plan assets. GASBS 75 includes requirements for employers that have OPEB plans that are not administered through trusts, which is far more prevalent in practice than those that are administered by trusts. Thus, many of the accounting and disclosure requirements of GASBS 75 related to plans administered by trusts are similar to those for plans without trusts, with the exception of there being no trust assets to reduce the amount of the OPEB liability that is recorded.

GASBS 68 only applies to pension plans that meet the criteria for being administered by a trust as described above. However, in order to keep GASBS 68 and GASBS 75 conceptually similar, the GASB issued GASBS 73 to provide accounting and financial reporting requirements for pension plans that are not administered by trusts. Thus, the accounting and financial reporting requirements for pension and OPEB benefits include those plans administered by trusts and those plans not administered by trusts.

The majority of the requirements of GASBS 68 and 75 relate to governmental employers that have defined benefit pension plans; however, there is some guidance in the Statement for employers with defined contribution pension plans.

A **defined contribution plan** is defined by GASBS 68 as "Pensions having terms that (a) provide an individual account for each employee; (b) define the contributions that an employer is required to make (or the credits that it is required to provide) to an active employee's account for periods in which that employee renders service; and (c) provide that the pensions an employee will receive will depend only on the contributions (or credits) to the employee's account, actual earnings on investments of those contributions (or credits), and the effects of forfeitures of contributions (or credits) made for other employees, as well as pension plan administrative costs, that are allocated to the employee's account." In a defined contribution plan, the amounts that are ultimately received by the plan member as pension benefits depend only on the amount that was contributed to the member's account and the earnings on the investment of those contributions. In addition, in some cases, forfeitures of benefits by other plan members may also be allocated to a member's account. Accordingly, in this type of pension plan there is no guaranteed pension benefit based on an employee's salary, length of service, and so forth.

A **defined benefit pension plan** is defined by GASBS 68 as "Pensions for which the income or other benefits that the employee will receive at or after separation from employment are defined by the benefit terms. The pensions may be stated as a specified dollar amount or as an amount that is calculated based on one or more factors such as age, years of service, and compensation." (A pension that does not meet the criteria of a defined contribution pension is classified as a defined benefit pension for purposes of this Statement.) GASBS 68 provides that the term *pensions* includes the following:

(a) Retirement income.
(b) Postemployment benefits other than retirement income (such as death benefits, life insurance, and disability benefits) that are provided through a pension plan.

Pension benefits do not include postemployment healthcare benefits and termination payments. Postemployment benefits other than retirement income that are provided separately from a pension plan and postemployment healthcare benefits should be accounted for as other postemployment benefits in accordance with GASBS 75.

Other postemployment benefits are all postemployment benefits other than retirement income (such as death benefits, life insurance, disability, and long-term care) that are provided separately from a pension plan, as well as postemployment healthcare benefits, regardless of the manner in which they are provided. Other postemployment benefits do not include termination benefits. If the postemployment benefits are paid from employee benefit plans that do not pay pension benefits in addition to the postemployment benefits, then these plans are not subject to the accounting requirements of GASBS 68. They are considered other postemployment benefits (OPEB) plans and would use the accounting guidance of GASBS 75. GASBS 75 further clarifies the term *OPEB* to include the following examples:

(a) Postemployment healthcare benefits—including medical, dental, vision, hearing, and other health-related benefits—whether provided separately from or provided through a pension plan.
(b) Other forms of postemployment benefits—for example, death benefits, life insurance, disability, and long-term care—when provided separately from a pension plan.

Example

Assume that the Municipal Employees Retirement System (MERS) is a defined benefit pension plan that provides retirement benefits as well as postemployment disability and health care benefits to its members. GASBS 68's requirements for defined benefit pension plans apply to the retirement benefits and the disability benefits. In accounting for the costs of the postemployment health care benefits, the employer would follow the accounting guidance of GASBS 75.

Further, assume that the same employer that contributes to MERS has a separate employee benefit plan that provides group life insurance benefits to its employees. Because these benefits are not provided by a plan that also provides retirement income to its members, the group life insurance postemployment benefits would be considered OPEBs and would adopt the accounting guidance of GASBS 75, rather than GASBS 68.

Financial Reporting for Benefits by Employers

As previously mentioned, the accounting for OPEB plans by employers is provided by GASBS 75. GASBS 75 addresses accounting and financial reporting requirements for both defined benefit OPEB and defined contribution OPEB.

Defined benefit plan is a pension or OPEB plan for which the benefits that the employee will receive at or after separation from employment are defined by the benefit terms. The OPEB may be stated as (a) a specified dollar amount; (b) an amount that is calculated based on one or more factors such as age, years of service, and compensation; or (c) a type or level of coverage such as prescription drug coverage or a percentage of health insurance premiums.

Defined contribution plan is a pension or OPEB plan having terms that:

(a) Provide an individual account for each employee.
(b) Define the contributions that an employer or nonemployer contributing entity is required to make (or credits that it is required to provide) to an active employee's account for periods in which that employee renders service.
(c) Provide that the pension or OPEB an employee will receive will depend only on the contributions (or credits) to the employee's account, actual earnings on investments of those contributions (or credits), and the effects of forfeitures of contributions (or credits) made for other employees, as well as pension or OPEB plan administrative costs, that are allocated to the employee's account.

If the pension or OPEB to be provided has all of the terms identified in (a)–(c) above, the requirements of GASBS 68 or 75 for defined contribution plans apply. If the benefits to be provided does not have all of the above terms—for example, if the benefit is a function of factors other than those identified in (c) above—the requirements of GASBS 68 or 75 for defined benefit plans apply.

Types of Defined Benefit Pension and OPEB Plans and Employers

Defined benefit pension and OPEB plans (other than insured plans that are discussed later) are classified first according to the number of employers whose employees are provided with pension or OPEB benefits through the plan. A plan can be either a single-employer or multi-employer plan based upon the number of employers with employees in the plan; however, there are a few special rules.

For purposes of this classification, a primary government and its component units are considered to be one employer. If a defined benefit pension or OPEB plan is used to provide pension or OPEB benefits to the employees of only one employer, the OPEB plan should be classified for financial reporting purposes as a **single-employer defined benefit plan**. If a defined benefit pension or OPEB plan is used to provide benefits to the employees of more than one employer, the plan should be classified for financial reporting purposes as a **multiple-employer defined benefit plan**.

A multiple-employer defined benefit pension or OPEB plan is then classified according to whether obligations and plan assets are shared by employers.

In a multiple-employer defined benefit plan that is administered through a trust, if the assets of the plan are pooled for investment purposes but separate accounts are maintained for each individual employer so that each employer's share of the pooled assets is legally available to pay the benefits of only its employees, the pension or OPEB plan should be classified as an **agent multiple-employer defined benefit plan**. As will be discussed later in this chapter, the accounting and financial reporting requirements for agent multi-employer plans are similar to single-employer plans.

In a multiple-employer defined benefit plan that is administered through a trust, if the OPEB obligations to the employees of more than one employer are pooled and the plan assets can be used to pay the benefits of the employees of any employer that provides pension or OPEB through the plan, the plan should be classified as a **cost-sharing multiple-employer defined benefit plan**.

Special Funding Situations

Both GASBS 68 and GASBS 75 provide a considerable amount of guidance regarding the accounting and financial reporting for pension and OPEB benefits when special funding situations exist. These requirements are consistent with the requirements for single employer, agent multi-employer, and cost-sharing multi-employer plans discussed herein and are not repeated in this chapter, although both GASBS 68 and 75 address them separately. Readers interested in the specific reporting requirements of GASBS 68 and 75 for special funding situations may find referring to these GASB statements helpful.

Special funding situations are circumstances in which a nonemployer entity is legally responsible for providing financial support for pension or OPEB benefits of the employees of another entity by making contributions *directly to* a pension or OPEB plan that is administered through a trust (including making benefit payments as the OPEB comes due for benefits provided through such a plan), or by making benefit payments directly as the benefit comes due in circumstances in which the pension or OPEB benefit is provided through a plan that is not administered through a trust (including amounts paid using nonemployer contributing entity assets held by others), *and* either of the following criteria is met:

(a) The amount of contributions or benefit payments for which the nonemployer entity legally is responsible is *not* dependent upon one or more events or circumstances unrelated to the pension or OPEB.

GASBS 68 and 75 provide examples of conditions in which such an amount is not dependent, including (1) a circumstance in which the nonemployer entity is required by statute to contribute a defined percentage of an employer's payroll directly to an OPEB plan that is administered through a trust, (2) a circumstance in which the nonemployer entity is required to pay retiree health insurance premiums as the premiums come due (OPEB plans only), and (3) a circumstance in which the nonemployer entity is required by the terms of a pension or OPEB plan to contribute directly to the plan a statutorily defined proportion of the employer's required contributions to the plan.

In contrast, examples of situations in which the amount of contributions is dependent upon an event or circumstance that is unrelated to pension or OPEB benefits include (i) a circumstance in which the nonemployer entity is required to make contributions to a pension or OPEB plan that is administered through a trust based on a specified percentage of a given revenue source or equal to the amount by which the nonemployer entity's ending fund balance exceeds a defined threshold amount and (ii) a circumstance in which the amount of benefit payments required to be made by the nonemployer entity as pension or OPEB benefits come due is limited by a given revenue source or by the amount by which the nonemployer entity's fund balance exceeds a defined threshold.

(b) The nonemployer entity is the only entity with a legal obligation to provide financial support directly to a pension or OPEB plan that is used to provide pension or OPEB benefits to employees of another entity.

Special funding situations do not include circumstances in which resources are provided *to the employer,* regardless of the purpose for which those resources are provided.

1. For defined benefit pension and OPEB plans, requirements for accounting and financial reporting by employers and by governmental nonemployer contributing entities with special funding situations are generally consistent with the accounting and financial reporting requirements for employers. Requirements for governmental nonemployer entities

that have a legal obligation to provide financial support directly to a defined benefit pension or OPEB plan that is used to provide pension or OPEB benefits to employees of another entity but do not meet the criterion above are discussed later in this chapter.

2. For defined contribution pension and OPEB plans, requirements for accounting and financial reporting by employers and by governmental nonemployer contributing entities with special funding situations are generally consistent with those of defined contribution plan requirements contained in GASBS 68 and 75.

Defined Benefit Pensions and OPEB Benefits Other Than Insured Benefits

GASBS 68 and 75 provide that liabilities, expense/expenditures, deferred outflows of resources, and deferred inflows of resources should be reported for the following, as applicable:

(a) Liabilities to employees for pensions and OPEB benefits.
(b) Payables to defined benefit pension and OPEB plans that are administered through a trust.

Liabilities to employees for defined benefit pension and OPEB should be reported separately. However, pension or OPEB benefits provided through different pension or OPEB plans may be displayed in the aggregate, and net pension or OPEB assets for defined benefit OPEB provided through different pension or OPEB plans that are administered through trusts may be displayed in the aggregate. Aggregated defined benefit pension liabilities should be displayed separately from aggregated net defined benefit pension assets. Aggregated OPEB liabilities should be displayed separately from aggregated net OPEB assets.

Single and Agent Employers

Recognition and measurement in financial statements prepared using the economic resources measurement focus and accrual basis of accounting—single and agent employers that do not have a special funding situation.

Net Pension and OPEB Liability

GASBS 68 and 75 provide that a liability should be recognized for the net pension or OPEB liability. The net pension or OPEB liability should be measured as the portion of the actuarial present value of projected benefit payments that is attributed to past periods of employee service in conformity with the requirements described below (total pension or OPEB liability), net of the pension or OPEB plan's fiduciary net position. The pension or OPEB plan's fiduciary net position should be determined using the same valuation methods that are used by the pension or OPEB plan for purposes of preparing its statement of fiduciary net position. The net pension or OPEB liability should be measured as of a date (measurement date) no earlier than the end of the employer's prior fiscal year and no later than the end of the employer's current fiscal year, consistently applied from period to period.

Timing and Frequency of Actuarial Valuations

Under GASBS 68 and 75, the total pension or OPEB liability should be determined by (a) an actuarial valuation as of the measurement date or (b) the use of update procedures to roll forward to the measurement date amounts from an actuarial valuation as of a date no more than 30 months and 1 day earlier than the employer's most recent fiscal year-end.

If update procedures are used and significant changes occur between the actuarial valuation date and the measurement date, professional judgment should be used to determine the extent of procedures needed to roll forward the measurement from the actuarial valuation to the measurement date, and consideration should be given to whether a new actuarial valuation is needed. For purposes of this determination, the effects of changes in the discount rate resulting from changes in the pension or OPEB plan's fiduciary net position or from changes in the municipal bond rate, if applicable, should be among the factors evaluated. For accounting and financial reporting purposes, an actuarial valuation of the total pension or OPEB liability should be performed at least biennially. More frequent actuarial valuations are encouraged.

Selection of Assumptions

Unless otherwise specified in GASBS 68 or 75, the selection of all assumptions used in determining the total pension or OPEB liability and related measures should be made in conformity with Actuarial Standards of Practice issued by the Actuarial Standards Board. For this purpose, a *deviation,* as the term is used in Actuarial Standards of Practice, from the guidance in an Actuarial Standard of Practice should not be considered to be in conformity with the requirement in this paragraph. The pension or OPEB plan, employer, and, if any, governmental nonemployer contributing entities that make contributions to the pension or OPEB plan, should use the same assumptions when measuring similar or related pension or OPEB information.

Projection of Benefit Payments

Projected benefit payments should include all benefits (including refunds of employee contributions) to be provided to current active and inactive employees through the pension or OPEB plan (including amounts for OPEB to be paid by employers or nonemployer contributing entities as the benefits come due) in accordance with the benefit terms and any additional legal agreements to provide benefits that are in force at the measurement date. Usually, a written document is the best evidence of the benefit terms. However, in some cases, the substantive plan may differ from the written document. Accordingly, other information also should be taken into consideration in determining the benefits to be provided, including other communications between the employer and employees (active and inactive) and an established pattern of practice with regard to the sharing of benefit-related costs with inactive employees.

Projected benefit payments should include the effects of automatic postemployment benefit changes, including automatic cost-of-living adjustments (automatic COLAs). In addition, projected benefit payments should include the effects of (a) projected ad hoc postemployment benefit changes, including ad hoc cost-of-living adjustments (ad hoc COLAs), to the extent that they are considered to be substantively automatic; (b) projected salary changes (in circumstances in which the OPEB formula incorporates future compensation levels); and (c) projected service credits (both in determining an employee's probable eligibility for benefits and in the projection of benefit payments in circumstances in which the OPEB formula incorporates years of service). Administrative costs associated with providing OPEB should be excluded from projected benefit payments.

Under GASBS 75, projected OPEB benefit payments also should include taxes or other assessments expected to be imposed on benefit payments using the rates in effect at the measurement date or, if different rates have been approved by the assessing government to be applied in future periods, the rates approved by the assessing government associated with the periods in which the assessments on the benefit payments will be imposed.

Projected OPEB benefit payments should be based on claims costs, or age-adjusted premiums approximating claims costs, in conformity with Actuarial Standards of Practice issued by the Actuarial Standards Board. For this purpose, a *deviation,* as the term is used in Actuarial Standards of Practice, from the guidance in an Actuarial Standard of Practice should not be considered to be in conformity with the requirement in this paragraph.

A legal or contractual cap on benefit payments for OPEB each period should be considered in projecting benefit payments, if the cap is assumed to be effective taking into consideration whether the cap has been enforced in the past and other relevant factors and circumstances.

Under both GASBS 68 and 75, benefit payments to be provided by means of an allocated insurance contract should be excluded from projected benefit payments if (a) the contract irrevocably transfers to the insurer the responsibility for providing the benefits, (b) all required payments to acquire the contract have been made, and (c) the likelihood is remote that the employer, nonemployer contributing entities, if any, or the pension or OPEB plan will be required to make additional payments to satisfy the benefit payments covered by the contract.

Discount Rate

GASBS 68 and 75 provided that the discount rate should be the single rate that reflects the following:

(a) The long-term expected rate of return on pension or OPEB plan investments that are expected to be used to finance the payment of benefits, to the extent that the pension or OPEB plan's fiduciary net position is projected to be sufficient to make projected benefit payments and the pension or OPEB plan assets are expected to be invested using a strategy to achieve that return.

(b) A yield or index rate for 20-year, tax-exempt general obligation municipal bonds with an average rating of AA/Aa or higher (or equivalent quality on another rating scale), to the extent that the conditions in (a) are not met.

NOTE: Many OPEB plans are on a "pay as you go" basis and do not accumulate assets in a trust to pay future benefits. In those plans, the bond yield will have a far more significant impact on the discount rate than pension plans, which tend to be at least partially funded to provide future benefits.

Comparing Projections of Fiduciary Net Position to Projected Benefit Payments

GASBS 68 and 75 provide that the amount of the pension or OPEB plan's projected fiduciary net position and the amount of projected benefit payments should be compared in each period of projected benefit payments. Projections of the pension or OPEB plan's fiduciary net position should incorporate all cash flows for contributions from the employer and nonemployer contributing entities, if any, intended to finance benefits of current active and inactive employees (status at the measurement date) and all cash flows for contributions from current active employees. It should not include (a) cash flows for contributions from the employer or nonemployer contributing entities intended to finance the service costs of future employees or (b) cash flows for contributions from future employees, unless those contributions are projected to exceed service costs for those employees. In each period, contributions from the employer and nonemployer contributing entities should be considered to apply, first, to service costs of employees in the period and, second, to past service costs, unless the effective pension or OPEB plan terms related to contributions indicate that a different relationship between contributions to the pension or OPEB plan from nonemployer contributing entities and service costs should be applied. Contributions from active employees should be considered to be applied to service costs before contributions from the employer and nonemployer contributing entities.

In applying these concepts, GASBS 68 and 75 provide that professional judgment be applied to project cash flows for contributions from the employer and nonemployer contributing entities in circumstances in which (a) those contribution amounts are established by statute or contract or (b) a formal, written policy related to those contributions exists. Application of professional judgment should consider the most recent five-year contribution history of the employer and nonemployer contributing entities as a key indicator of future contributions from those sources and should reflect all other known events and conditions. In circumstances other than those described in (a) and (b), the amount of projected cash flows for contributions from the employer and nonemployer contributing entities should be limited to an average of contributions from those sources over the most recent five-year period and may be modified based on consideration of subsequent events. For this purpose, the basis for the average (for example, percentage of the payroll contributed or percentage of the actuarially determined contribution made) should be a matter of professional judgment.

If the evaluations discussed above can be made with sufficient reliability without a separate projection of cash flows into and out of the pension or OPEB plan, alternative methods may be applied in making the evaluations.

Calculating the Discount Rate

For each future period, if the amount of the pension or OPEB plan's fiduciary net position is projected to be greater than or equal to the benefit payments that are projected to be made in that period and the pension or OPEB plan assets up to that point are expected to be invested using a strategy to achieve the long-term expected rate of return, GASBS 68 and 75 provide that the actuarial present value of benefit payments projected to be made in the period should be determined using the long-term expected rate of return on those investments. The long-term expected rate of return should be based on the nature and mix of current and expected pension or OPEB plan investments over a period representative of the expected length of time between (a) the point at which an employee begins to provide service to the employer and (b) the point at which all benefits to the employee have been paid. For this purpose, the long-term expected rate of return should be determined net of pension or OPEB plan investment expense but without reduction for pension or OPEB plan administrative expense. The municipal bond rate discussed above should be used to calculate the actuarial present value of all other benefit payments.

Under both GASBS 68 and 75, the discount rate is the single rate of return that, when applied to all projected benefit payments, results in an actuarial present value of projected benefit payments equal to the total of the actuarial present values determined in conformity with both statements.

Attribution of the Actuarial Present Value of Projected Benefit Payments to Periods

GASBS 68 and 75 provide that the entry age actuarial cost method be used to attribute the actuarial present value of projected benefit payments of each employee to periods in conformity with the following:

(a) Attribution should be made on an individual employee-by-employee basis.
(b) Each employee's service costs should be level as a percentage of that employee's projected pay. For purposes of this calculation, if an employee does not have projected pay, the projected inflation rate should be used in place of the projected rate of change in salary.

(c) The beginning of the attribution period should be the first period in which the employee provides service under the benefit terms, notwithstanding vesting or other similar terms.
(d) The service costs of all pension and OPEB benefits should be attributed through all assumed ages of exit from active service.
(e) Each employee's service costs should be determined based on the same benefit terms reflected in that employee's actuarial present value of projected benefit payments.

NOTE: This is a significant departure from previous standards, which permitted various actuarial attribution methods to be used.

Pension and OPEB Expense, Deferred Outflows of Resources and Deferred Inflows of Resources Related to Pensions and OPEB, and Support of Nonemployer Contributing Entities

GASBS 68 and 75 provide that changes in the net pension or OPEB liability should be recognized in pension or OPEB expense in the current reporting period except as indicated below. If the alternative measurement method is not used to measure the total pension or OPEB liability, each of the following should be recognized in pension or OPEB expense, beginning in the current reporting period, using a systematic and rational method over a closed period equal to the average of the expected remaining service lives of all employees that are provided with pension or OPEB benefits through the plan (active and inactive employees) determined as of the beginning of the measurement period:

1. Differences between expected and actual experience with regard to economic or demographic factors (differences between expected and actual experience) in the measurement of the total pension or OPEB liability.
2. Changes of assumptions about future economic or demographic factors or of other inputs (changes of assumptions or other inputs).

The portion of (1) and (2) not recognized in pension or OPEB expense should be reported as deferred outflows of resources or deferred inflows of resources related to pension or OPEB.

The difference between projected and actual earnings on pension or OPEB plan investments should be recognized in OPEB expense using a systematic and rational method over a closed five-year period, beginning in the current reporting period. The amount not recognized in pension or OPEB expense should be reported as deferred outflows of resources or deferred inflows of resources related to pension or OPEB. Deferred outflows of resources and deferred inflows of resources arising from differences between projected and actual pension or OPEB plan investment earnings in different measurement periods should be aggregated and reported as a net deferred outflow of resources related to pension or OPEB or a net deferred inflow of resources related to pension or OPEB.

Contributions to the pension or OPEB plan from the employer should not be recognized in OPEB expense. Contributions to the pension or OPEB plan from nonemployer contributing entities that are not in a special funding situation should be recognized as revenue.

Contributions to the pension or OPEB plan from the employer subsequent to the measurement date of the net pension or OPEB liability and before the end of the reporting period (excluding amounts associated with the employer from nonemployer contributing entities that are not in a special funding situation) should be reported as a deferred outflow of resources related to pension or OPEB.

Recognition in Financial Statements Prepared Using the Current Financial Resources Measurement Focus and Modified Accrual Basis of Accounting—All Single and Agent Employers

In financial statements prepared using the current financial resources measurement focus and modified accrual basis of accounting, GASBS 68 and 75 provide that a net pension or OPEB liability should be recognized to the extent the liability is normally expected to be liquidated with expendable available financial resources. Pension or OPEB expenditures should be recognized equal to the total of (a) amounts paid by the employer to the pension or OPEB plan, including amounts paid for pension or OPEB as the benefits come due, and (b) the change between the beginning and ending balances of amounts normally expected to be liquidated with expendable available financial resources. A net pension or OPEB liability is normally expected to be liquidated with expendable available financial resources to the extent that benefit payments have matured—that is, benefit payments are due and payable and the pension or OPEB plan's fiduciary net position is not sufficient for payment of those benefits.

Notes to Financial Statements—All Single and Agent Employers

NOTE: These disclosure requirements combine the general requirements of both GASBS 68, as amended, and GASBS 75. Disclosures for pension and OPEB plans would be reported separately. The term "aggregate" as used below refers to the "aggregate pension" amounts and "aggregate OPEB" amounts, both reported separately.

The total (aggregate for all pension or OPEB amounts, regardless of the type of pension or OPEB plans through which the benefit is provided and whether the pension or OPEB plans are administered through a trust) of the employer's pension or OPEB liabilities, net pension or OPEB assets, deferred outflows of resources and deferred inflows of resources related to pension or OPEB, and pension or OPEB expense/expenditures for the period associated with defined benefit pension or OPEB liabilities to employees, as applicable, should be disclosed if the total amounts are not otherwise identifiable from information presented in the financial statements.

The information specified below should be disclosed for benefits provided through each single-employer or agent pension or OPEB plans in which the employer participates. Disclosures related to more than one pension or OPEB plan should be combined in a manner that avoids unnecessary duplication.

In circumstances in which the employees of a primary government and its component units are provided with pension or OPEB benefits through the same single-employer or agent pension or OPEB plan, the note disclosures in the reporting entity's financial statements should separately identify amounts associated with the primary government (including its blended component units) and those associated with its discretely presented component units.

Plan Description

GASBS 68 and 75 provide that the following information should be disclosed about the pension or OPEB plans through which benefits are provided:

(a) The name of the plan, identification of the entity that administers the plan, and identification of the plan as a single-employer or agent pension or OPEB plan.
(b) A brief description of the benefit terms, including (1) the classes of employees covered; (2) the types of benefits; (3) the key elements of the benefit formulas; (4) the terms or

policies, if any, with respect to automatic postemployment benefit changes, including automatic COLAs, ad hoc postemployment benefit changes, including ad hoc COLAs, and the sharing of benefit-related costs with inactive employees; and (5) the authority under which benefit terms are established or may be amended. If the plan is closed to new entrants, that fact should be disclosed.

(c) The number of employees covered by the benefit terms, separately identifying numbers of the following:
   1. Inactive employees currently receiving benefit payments.
   2. Inactive employees entitled to but not yet receiving benefit payments.
   3. Active employees.

(d) A brief description of contribution requirements, including (1) the basis for determining the employer's contributions to the plan (for example, statute, contract, an actuarial basis, or some other manner); (2) identification of the authority under which contribution requirements of the employer, nonemployer contributing entities, if any, and employees are established or may be amended; (3) legal or contractual maximum contribution rates, if applicable; and (4) the contribution rates (in dollars or as a percentage of covered payroll) of the employer, nonemployer contributing entities, if any, and employees for the reporting period. Also, the amount of contributions recognized by the plan from the employer during the reporting period, excluding amounts resulting from contributions recognized by the plan as noncurrent receivables, if not otherwise disclosed.

(e) Whether the plan issues a stand-alone financial report (or the plan is included in the report of another government) that is available to the public and, if so, how to obtain the report (for example, a link to the plan report on the employer's website).

Information about the Net OPEB Liability

Assumptions and Other Inputs

Significant assumptions and other inputs used to measure the total pension or OPEB liability, including assumptions about inflation, healthcare cost trend rates (OPEB plans only), salary changes, ad hoc postemployment benefit changes (including ad hoc COLAs), and the sharing of benefit-related costs with inactive employees, should be disclosed, as applicable. For all significant assumptions, if different rates are assumed for different periods, information should be disclosed about what rates are applied to the different periods of the measurement.

1. In addition, GASBS 68 and 75 provide that the following information related to assumptions and other inputs should be disclosed, as applicable:
   (a) The fact that projections of the sharing of benefit-related costs are based on an established pattern of practice.
   (b) The source of the mortality assumptions (for example, the published tables on which the assumptions are based or that the assumptions are based on a study of the experience of the covered group).
   (c) The dates of experience studies on which significant assumptions are based.
   (d) If the alternative measurement method is used to measure the total pension or OPEB liability, the source of or basis for all significant assumptions selected. Measures of the net OPEB liability calculated using (1) a healthcare cost trend rate that is 1-percentage-point higher than the assumed healthcare cost trend rate and (2) a healthcare

cost trend rate that is 1-percentage-point lower than the assumed healthcare cost trend rate.

2. The following information should be disclosed about the discount rate:
   (a) The discount rate applied in the measurement of the total pension or OPEB liability and the change in the discount rate since the prior measurement date, if any.
   (b) Assumptions made about projected cash flows into and out of the plan, such as contributions from the employer, nonemployer contributing entities, and employees.
   (c) The long-term expected rate of return on plan investments and a brief description of how it was determined, including significant methods and assumptions used for that purpose.
   (d) If the discount rate incorporates a municipal bond rate, the municipal bond rate used and the source of that rate.
   (e) The periods of projected benefit payments to which the long-term expected rate of return and, if used, the municipal bond rate are applied in determining the discount rate.
   (f) The assumed asset allocation of the plan's portfolio, the long-term expected real rate of return for each major asset class, and whether the expected rates of return are presented as arithmetic or geometric means, if not otherwise disclosed.
   (g) Measures of the net pension or OPEB liability calculated using (1) a discount rate that is 1-percentage-point higher and (2) a discount rate that is 1-percentage-point lower than the discount rate selected using the requirements discussed above.

The Plan's Fiduciary Net Position

All information required by GASBS 68 and 75 and other financial reporting standards about the elements of the plan's basic financial statements (that is, all information about the plan's assets, deferred outflows of resources, liabilities, deferred inflows of resources, and fiduciary net position) should be disclosed. However, if (a) a financial report that includes disclosure about the elements of the plan's basic financial statements is available on the Internet, either as a standalone financial report or included as a fiduciary fund in the financial report of another government, and (b) information is provided about how to obtain the report, reference may instead be made to the other report for these disclosures. In this circumstance, it also should be disclosed that the plan's fiduciary net position has been determined on the same basis used by the plan, and a brief description of the plan's basis of accounting, including the policies with respect to benefit payments (including refunds of employee contributions) and the valuation of plan investments, should be included. If significant changes have occurred that indicate that the disclosures included in the plan's financial report generally do not reflect the facts and circumstances at the measurement date, information about the substance and the magnitude of the changes should be disclosed.

Changes in the Net Pension or OPEB Liability

For the current reporting period, a schedule of changes in the net pension or OPEB liability is required by GASBS 68 and 75. The schedule should separately include the information indicated below. If the employer has a special funding situation, the information in subparagraphs (a)–(c) should be presented for the collective net pension or OPEB liability.

(a) The beginning balances of the total pension or OPEB liability, the plan's fiduciary net position, and the net pension or OPEB liability.
(b) The effects during the period of the following items, if applicable, on the balances in subparagraph (a):
   1. Service cost
   2. Interest on the total pension or OPEB liability
   3. Changes of benefit terms
   4. Differences between expected and actual experience in the measurement of the total pension or OPEB liability
   5. Changes of assumptions or other inputs
   6. Contributions from the employer
   7. Contributions from nonemployer contributing entities
   8. Contributions from active employees and inactive employees not yet receiving benefit payments OPEB plan net investment income
   9. Benefit payments (including refunds of employee contributions and amounts from employers or nonemployer contributing entities for pension or OPEB as the benefits came due) OPEB plan administrative expense
   10. Other changes, separately identified if individually significant
(c) The ending balances of the total pension or OPEB liability, the plan's fiduciary net position, and the net pension or OPEB liability.
(d) If the employer has a special funding situation:
   1. The nonemployer contributing entities' total proportionate share of the collective net pension or OPEB liability
   2. The employer's proportionate share of the collective net pension or OPEB liability

In addition, the following information should be disclosed, if applicable:

(a) The measurement date of the net pension or OPEB liability; the date of the actuarial valuation or alternative measurement method calculation on which the total pension or pension or OPEB liability is based; and, if applicable, the fact that update procedures were used to roll forward the total pension or OPEB liability to the measurement date. If the alternative measurement method is used to measure the total pension or OPEB liability, the fact that this alternative method was used in place of an actuarial valuation also should be disclosed.
(b) If the employer has a special funding situation, the employer's proportion (percentage) of the collective net pension or OPEB liability, the basis on which its proportion was determined, and the change in its proportion since the prior measurement date.
(c) A brief description of changes of assumptions or other inputs that affected measurement of the total pension or OPEB liability since the prior measurement date.
(d) A brief description of changes of benefit terms that affected measurement of the total pension or OPEB liability since the prior measurement date.
(e) The amount of benefit payments in the measurement period attributable to the purchase of allocated insurance contracts, a brief description of the benefits for which allocated insurance contracts were purchased in the measurement period, and the fact that the obligation for the payment of benefits covered by allocated insurance contracts has been transferred from the employer to one or more insurance companies.
(f) A brief description of the nature of changes between the measurement date of the net pension or OPEB liability and the employer's reporting date that are expected to have a

significant effect on the net pension or OPEB liability, and the amount of the expected resultant change in the net pension or OPEB liability, if known.

(g) The amount of pension or OPEB expense recognized by the employer in the reporting period.

(h) The employer's balances of deferred outflows of resources and deferred inflows of resources related to pension or OPEB, classified as follows, if applicable:

1. Differences between expected and actual experience in the measurement of the total pension or OPEB liability
2. Changes of assumptions or other inputs
3. Net difference between projected and actual earnings on plan investments
4. If the employer has a special funding situation, changes in the employer's proportion and differences between (a) the employer's contributions (other than those associated with the individual employer's separately financed specific liabilities to the plan) and (b) the employer's proportionate share of certain contributions
5. The employer's contributions to the plan subsequent to the measurement date of the net OPEB liability

(i) A schedule presenting the following:

1. For each of the subsequent five years, and in the aggregate thereafter, the net amount of the employer's balances of deferred outflows of resources and deferred inflows of resources in subparagraph (h) that will be recognized in the employer's OPEB expense
2. If the employer does not have a special funding situation, the amount of the employer's balance of deferred outflows of resources in subparagraph (h) that will be recognized as a reduction of the net OPEB liability
3. If the employer has a special funding situation, the amount of the employer's balance of deferred outflows of resources in subparagraph (h) that will be included as a reduction of the collective net OPEB liability.

(j) The amount of revenue recognized for the support provided by nonemployer contributing entities (see paragraph 43d or paragraphs 106 and 107), if any.

Required Supplementary Information—All Single and Agent Employers

GASBS 68 and 75 provide that the required supplementary information identified in subparagraphs (a)–(d), as applicable, should be presented separately for each single-employer and agent OPEB plan through which pension or OPEB is provided. The information indicated in subparagraphs (a) and (b) should be determined as of the measurement date of the net pension or OPEB liability and may be presented in a single schedule. The information in subparagraphs (c) and (d) should be determined as of the employer's most recent fiscal year-end. If a primary government and one or more of its component units provide pension or OPEB through the same single-employer or agent plan, required supplementary information in the reporting entity's financial statements should present information for all benefits provided by the reporting entity through the single-employer or agent plan.

(a) A 10-year schedule of changes in the net pension or OPEB liability that separately presents the information required about the pension or OPEB liability in the notes for each year.

(b) A 10-year schedule presenting the following for each year:

1. If the employer does not have a special funding situation:
   (a) The total pension or OPEB liability
   (b) The pension or OPEB plan's fiduciary net position

(c) The net pension or OPEB liability
(d) The pension or OPEB plan's fiduciary net position as a percentage of the total pension or OPEB liability
(e) The covered-employee payroll
(f) The net pension or OPEB liability as a percentage of covered-employee payroll

2. If the employer has a special funding situation, information about the collective net pension or OPEB liability:
   (a) The total pension or OPEB liability
   (b) The pension or OPEB plan's fiduciary net position
   (c) The collective net pension or OPEB liability
   (d) The nonemployer contributing entities' total proportionate share (amount) of the collective net pension or OPEB liability
   (e) The employer's proportionate share (amount) of the collective net pension or OPEB liability
   (f) The covered-employee payroll
   (g) The employer's proportionate share (amount) of the collective net pension or OPEB liability as a percentage of covered-employee payroll
   (h) The pension or OPEB plan's fiduciary net position as a percentage of the total pension or OPEB liability

(c) If an actuarially determined contribution is calculated, a 10-year schedule presenting the following for each year:
1. The actuarially determined contribution of the employer. For purposes of this schedule, actuarially determined contributions should exclude amounts, if any, associated with payables to the pension or OPEB plan that arose in a prior fiscal year and those associated with separately financed specific liabilities of the individual employer to the pension or OPEB plan.
2. The amount of contributions recognized by the pension or OPEB plan in relation to the actuarially determined contribution of the employer. For purposes of this schedule, contributions should exclude amounts resulting from contributions recognized by the pension or OPEB plan as noncurrent receivables.
3. The difference between the actuarially determined contribution of the employer and the amount of contributions recognized by the pension or OPEB plan in relation to the actuarially determined contribution of the employer.
4. The covered-employee payroll.
5. The amount of contributions recognized by the pension or OPEB plan in relation to the actuarially determined contribution of the employer as a percentage of covered-employee payroll.

(d) If an actuarially determined contribution is not calculated and the contribution requirements of the employer are statutorily or contractually established, a 10-year schedule presenting the following for each year:
1. The statutorily or contractually required employer contribution. For purposes of this schedule, statutorily or contractually required contributions should exclude amounts, if any, associated with payables to the plan that arose in a prior fiscal year and those associated with separately financed specific liabilities of the individual employer to the plan.
2. The amount of contributions recognized by the plan in relation to the statutorily or contractually required employer contribution. For purposes of this schedule, contributions

should exclude amounts resulting from contributions recognized by the plan as non-current receivables.

3. The difference between the statutorily or contractually required employer contribution and the amount of contributions recognized by the plan in relation to the statutorily or contractually required employer contribution.
4. The covered-employee payroll.
5. The amount of contributions recognized by the plan in relation to the statutorily or contractually required employer contribution as a percentage of covered-employee payroll.

Notes to Required Schedules

GASBS 68 and 75 require significant methods and assumptions used in calculating the actuarially determined contributions, if any, be presented as notes to the schedule described above. In addition, for each of the schedules required, information should be presented about factors that significantly affect trends in the amounts reported (for example, changes of benefit terms, changes in the size or composition of the population covered by the benefit terms, or the use of different assumptions). Information about investment-related factors that significantly affect trends in the amounts reported should be limited to those factors over which the pension or OPEB plan or the participating governments have influence (for example, changes in investment policies). Information about external, economic factors (for example, changes in market prices) should not be presented. (The amounts presented for prior years should not be restated for the effects of changes—for example, changes of benefit terms or changes of assumptions—that occurred subsequent to the measurement date of that information.)

COST-SHARING EMPLOYERS

Recognition and measurement in financial statements prepared using the economic resources measurement focus and accrual basis of accounting—cost-sharing employers that do not have a special funding situation.

Proportionate Share of the Collective Net Pension or OPEB Liability

GASBS 68 and 75 require that a liability be recognized for the employer's proportionate share of the collective net pension or OPEB liability, measured as of a date (measurement date) no earlier than the end of the employer's prior fiscal year and no later than the end of the employer's current fiscal year, consistently applied from period to period. The employer's proportionate share of the collective net pension or OPEB liability should be measured by:

(a) Determining the employer's proportion—a measure of the proportionate relationship of (1) the employer (and, to the extent associated with the employer, nonemployer contributing entities, if any, that provide support for the employer but that are not in a special funding situation) to (2) all employers and all nonemployer contributing entities. The basis for the employer's proportion should be consistent with the manner in which contributions to the pension or OPEB plan, excluding those associated with separately financed specific liabilities of an individual employer to the pension or OPEB plan, are determined. The use of the employer's projected long-term contribution effort to the pension or OPEB plan (including that of nonemployer contributing entities that provide support for the employer but that are not in a special funding situation) as compared to the total projected long-term contribution effort of all employers and all nonemployer contributing entities to determine the employer's proportion is encouraged.

(b) Multiplying the collective net pension or OPEB liability determined in accordance with the requirements of GASBS 68 and 75, as applicable, by the employer's proportion calculated in (a).

To the extent that different contribution rates are assessed based on separate relationships that constitute the collective net pension or OPEB liability (for example, separate rates are calculated based on an internal allocation of liabilities and assets for different classes or groups of employees), the determination of the employer's proportionate share of the collective net pension or OPEB liability should be made in a manner that reflects those separate relationships.

The employer's proportion should be established as of the measurement date, unless the employer's proportion is actuarially determined, in which case a proportion established at the date of the actuarial valuation used to determine the collective net pension or OPEB liability may be used.

OPEB Expense and Deferred Outflows of Resources and Deferred Inflows of Resources Related to OPEB

GASBS 68 and 75 provide that pension or OPEB expense and deferred outflows of resources and deferred inflows of resources related to OPEB should be recognized for the items discussed below, as applicable.

Proportionate Share

Pension and OPEB expense, as well as deferred outflows of resources and deferred inflows of resources related to pension or OPEB, should be recognized for the employer's proportionate shares of collective pension or OPEB expense and collective deferred outflows of resources and deferred inflows of resources related to pension or OPEB. The employer's proportionate shares should be determined using the employer's proportion of the collective net pension or OPEB liability.

Change in Proportion

Under GASBS 68 and 75, if there is a change in the employer's proportion of the collective net pension or OPEB liability since the prior measurement date, the net effect of that change on the employer's proportionate shares of the collective net pension or OPEB liability and collective deferred outflows of resources and deferred inflows of resources related to pension or OPEB, determined as of the beginning of the measurement period, should be recognized in the employer's pension or OPEB expense, beginning in the current reporting period, using a systematic and rational method over a closed period. For this purpose, the length of the expense recognition period should be equal to the average of the expected remaining service lives of all employees that are provided with pension or OPEB through the pension or OPEB plan (active employees and inactive employees) determined as of the beginning of the measurement period. The amount not recognized in the employer's pension or OPEB expense should be reported as a deferred outflow of resources or deferred inflow of resources related to pension or OPEB.

Contributions during the Measurement Period

For contributions to the pension or OPEB plan, other than those to separately finance specific liabilities of an individual employer or nonemployer contributing entity to the plan, the difference during the measurement period between (a) the total amount of such contributions from the employer (and amounts associated with the employer from nonemployer contributing entities that are not in a special funding situation) and (b) the amount of the employer's proportionate share of the total of such contributions from all employers and all nonemployer contributing entities should be recognized in the employer's pension or OPEB expense, beginning in the current reporting period, using a systematic and rational method over a closed period. For this purpose, the length of the expense recognition period should be equal to the average of the expected remaining service lives of all employees that are provided with pension or OPEB through the plan (active employees and inactive employees) determined as of the beginning of the measurement period. The amount not recognized in the employer's pension or OPEB expense should be reported as a deferred outflow of resources or deferred inflow of resources related to pension or OPEB.

For contributions to the pension or OPEB plan to separately finance specific liabilities of the individual employer to the pension OPEB plan, the difference during the measurement period between (a) the amount of such contributions from the employer (and amounts associated with the employer from nonemployer contributing entities that are not in a special funding situation) and (b) the amount of the employer's proportionate share of the total of the contributions in (a), determined using the employer's proportion of the collective net pension or OPEB liability, should be recognized in the employer's pension or OPEB expense.

For contributions made by others to the pension or OPEB plan during the measurement period to separately finance specific liabilities to the plan (excluding amounts associated with the employer from nonemployer contributing entities that are not in a special funding situation), the amount of the employer's proportionate share of the total of such contributions determined using the employer's proportion of the collective net pension or OPEB liability should be recognized as a reduction of the employer's pension or OPEB expense.

Employer Contributions Subsequent to the Measurement Date

Contributions to the pension or OPEB plan from the employer subsequent to the measurement date of the collective net pension or OPEB liability and before the end of the employer's reporting period (excluding amounts associated with the employer from nonemployer contributing entities that are not in a special funding situation) should be reported as a deferred outflow of resources related to pension or OPEB.

Support of Nonemployer Contributing Entities Not in a Special Funding Situation

GASBS 68 and 75 provide that revenue should be recognized in an amount equal to (a) the change in the collective net pension or OPEB liability arising from contributions to the pension or OPEB plan during the measurement period from nonemployer contributing entities that are not in a special funding situation to separately finance specific liabilities of the individual employer to the plan and (b) the employer's proportionate share of the change in the collective net pension or OPEB liability arising from contributions to the plan during the measurement period from nonemployer contributing entities for purposes other than the separate financing of specific liabilities to the plan.

Measurement of the Collective Net Pension or OPEB Liability, Collective Pension or OPEB Expense, and Collective Deferred Outflows of Resources and Deferred Inflows of Resources Related to Pension or OPEB

Collective Net Pension or OPEB Liability

GASBS 68 and 75 provide that the collective net pension or OPEB liability should be measured as the total pension or OPEB liability (determined in conformity with the requirements described below), net of the pension or OPEB plan's fiduciary net position. However, if certain criteria are met, the total pension or OPEB liability may be measured in conformity with the alternative measurement method described later in this chapter. The pension or OPEB plan's fiduciary net position should be determined using the same valuation methods that are used by the pension or OPEB plan for purposes of preparing its statement of fiduciary net position.

Timing and Frequency of Actuarial Valuations

GASBS 68 and 75 provide that the total pension or OPEB liability be determined by (a) an actuarial valuation as of the measurement date or (b) the use of update procedures to roll forward to the measurement date amounts from an actuarial valuation as of a date no more than 30 months and 1 day earlier than the employer's most recent fiscal year-end. If update procedures are used and significant changes occur between the actuarial valuation date and the measurement date, professional judgment should be used to determine the extent of procedures needed to roll forward the measurement from the actuarial valuation to the measurement date, and consideration should be given to whether a new actuarial valuation is needed. For purposes of this determination, the effects of changes in the discount rate resulting from changes in the pension or OPEB plan's fiduciary net position or from changes in the municipal bond rate, if applicable, should be among the factors evaluated. For accounting and financial reporting purposes, an actuarial valuation of the total pension or OPEB liability should be performed at least biennially. More frequent actuarial valuations are encouraged by GASBS 68 and 75.

Selection of Assumptions

The selection of all assumptions used in determining the total pension or OPEB liability and related measures is required by GASBS 68 and 75 to be made in conformity with Actuarial Standards of Practice issued by the Actuarial Standards Board. For this purpose, a *deviation,* as the term is used in Actuarial Standards of Practice, from the guidance in an Actuarial Standard of Practice should not be considered to be in conformity with the requirement in this paragraph. The pension or OPEB plan, employers, and, if any, governmental nonemployer contributing entities that make contributions to the pension or OPEB plan should use the same assumptions when measuring similar or related pension or OPEB information.

Projection of Benefit Payments

GASBS 68 and 75 provide that projected benefit payments include all benefits (including refunds of employee contributions) to be provided to current active and inactive employees through the pension or OPEB plan (including amounts for pension or OPEB to be paid by employers or nonemployer contributing entities as the benefits come due) in accordance with the benefit terms and any additional legal agreements to provide benefits that are in force at the measurement date. Usually, a written document is the best evidence of the benefit terms. However, in some cases, the substantive plan may differ from the written document. Accordingly, other information also should be taken into consideration in determining the benefits to be provided, including other communications between the employer and employees (active and inactive) and an established pattern of practice with regard to the sharing of benefit-related costs with inactive employees.

Projected benefit payments should include the effects of automatic post-employment benefit changes, including automatic COLAs. In addition, projected benefit payments should include the effects of (a) projected ad hoc postemployment benefit changes, including ad hoc COLAs, to the extent that they are considered to be substantively automatic; (b) projected salary changes (in circumstances in which the benefit formula incorporates future compensation levels); and (c) projected service credits (both in determining an employee's probable eligibility for benefits and in the projection of benefit payments in circumstances in which the benefit formula incorporates years of service). Administrative costs associated with providing pension or OPEB should be excluded from projected benefit payments.

Projected OPEB benefit payments also should include taxes or other assessments expected to be imposed on benefit payments using the rates in effect at the measurement date or, if different rates have been approved by the assessing government to be applied in future periods, the rates approved by the assessing government associated with the periods in which the assessments on the benefit payments will be imposed.

Projected OPEB benefit payments should be based on claims costs, or age-adjusted premiums approximating claims costs, in conformity with Actuarial Standards of Practice issued by the Actuarial Standards Board. For this purpose, a *deviation,* as the term is used in Actuarial Standards of Practice, from the guidance in an Actuarial Standard of Practice should not be considered to be in conformity with the requirement in this paragraph.

A legal or contractual cap on benefit payments for OPEB each period should be considered in projecting benefit payments, if the cap is assumed to be effective taking into consideration whether the cap has been enforced in the past and other relevant factors and circumstances.

Both pension and OPEB benefit payments to be provided by means of an allocated insurance contract should be excluded from projected benefit payments if (a) the contract irrevocably transfers to the insurer the responsibility for providing the benefits, (b) all required payments to acquire the contract have been made, and (c) the likelihood is remote that the employers, nonemployer contributing entities, if any, or pension or OPEB plan will be required to make additional payments to satisfy the benefit payments covered by the contract.

Discount Rate

GASBS 68 and 75 provide that the discount rate should be the single rate that reflects the following:

(a) The long-term expected rate of return on pension or OPEB plan investments that are expected to be used to finance the payment of benefits, to the extent that (1) the plan's fiduciary net position is projected to be sufficient to make projected benefit payments and (2) plan assets are expected to be invested using a strategy to achieve that return.

(b) A yield or index rate for 20-year, tax-exempt general obligation municipal bonds with an average rating of AA/Aa or higher (or equivalent quality on another rating scale), to the extent that the conditions in (a) are not met.

Comparing Projections of the OPEB Plan's Fiduciary Net Position to Projected Benefit Payments

For purposes of applying the requirements above, the amount of the plan's projected fiduciary net position and the amount of projected benefit payments should be compared in each period of projected benefit payments. Projections of the plan's fiduciary net position should incorporate all cash flows for contributions from employers and nonemployer contributing entities, if any, intended to finance benefits of current active and inactive employees (status at the measurement date) and all cash flows for contributions from current active employees. It should not include (a) cash flows for contributions from employers or nonemployer contributing entities intended to finance the service costs of future employees or (b) cash flows for contributions from future employees, unless those contributions are projected to exceed service costs for those employees. In each period, contributions from employers and nonemployer contributing entities should be considered to apply, first, to service costs of employees in the period and, second, to past service costs, unless the effective plan terms related to contributions indicate that a different relationship between contributions to the plan from nonemployer contributing entities and service costs should be applied. Contributions from active employees should be considered to be applied to service costs before contributions from employers and nonemployer contributing entities.

GASBS 68 and 75 provide that professional judgment be applied to project cash flows for contributions from employers and nonemployer contributing entities in circumstances in which (a) those contribution amounts are established by statute or contract or (b) a formal, written policy related to those contributions exists. Application of professional judgment should consider the most recent five-year contribution history of the employers and nonemployer contributing entities as a key indicator of future contributions from those sources and should reflect all other known events and conditions.

In circumstances other than those described in (a) and (b), the amount of projected cash flows for contributions from employers and nonemployer contributing entities should be limited to an average of contributions from those sources over the most recent five-year period and may be modified based on consideration of subsequent events. For this purpose, the basis for the average (for example, percentage of the payroll contributed or percentage of the actuarially determined contribution made) should be a matter of professional judgment.

If these evaluations can be made with sufficient reliability without a separate projection of cash flows into and out of the plan, alternative methods may be applied in making the evaluations.

Calculating the Discount Rate

For each future period, if the amount of the plan's fiduciary net position is projected to be greater than or equal to the benefit payments that are projected to be made in that period and plan assets up to that point are expected to be invested using a strategy to achieve the long-term expected rate of return, the actuarial present value of benefit payments projected to be made in the period should be determined using the long-term expected rate of return on those investments. The long-term expected rate of return should be based on the nature and mix of current and expected plan investments over a period representative of the expected length of time between (a) the point at which an employee begins to provide service to the employer and (b) the point at which all benefits to the employee have been paid. For this purpose, the long-term expected rate of return should be determined net of plan investment expense but without reduction for plan administrative expense. The municipal bond rate discussed above should be used to calculate the actuarial present value of all other benefit payments.

For purposes of GASBS 68 and 75, the discount rate is the single rate of return that, when applied to all projected benefit payments, results in an actuarial present value of projected benefit payments equal to the total of the actuarial present values.

Attribution of the Actuarial Present Value of Projected Benefit Payments to Periods

GASBS 68 and 75 required the entry age actuarial cost method to be used to attribute the actuarial present value of projected benefit payments of each employee to periods in conformity with the following:

(a) Attribution should be made on an individual employee-by-employee basis.
(b) Each employee's service costs should be level as a percentage of that employee's projected pay. For purposes of this calculation, if an employee does not have projected pay, the projected inflation rate should be used in place of the projected rate of change in salary.
(c) The beginning of the attribution period should be the first period in which the employee provides service under the benefit terms, notwithstanding vesting or other similar terms.
(d) The service costs of all benefits should be attributed through all assumed ages of exit from active service.
(e) Each employee's service costs should be determined based on the same benefit terms reflected in that employee's actuarial present value of projected benefit payments.

Collective Pension and OPEB Expense and Collective Deferred Outflows of Resources and Deferred Inflows of Resources Related to Pension and OPEB

GASBS 68 and 75 provide that changes in the collective net pension or OPEB liability be included in collective pension or OPEB expense in the current measurement period except as indicated below:

(a) If the alternative measurement method is not used to measure the total pension or OPEB liability, each of the following should be included in collective pension or OPEB expense, beginning in the current measurement period, using a systematic and rational method over a closed period equal to the average of the expected remaining service lives of all employees that are provided with pension or OPEB through the pension or OPEB plan (active employees and inactive employees) determined as of the beginning of the measurement period:
    1. Differences between expected and actual experience with regard to economic or demographic factors (differences between expected and actual experience) in the measurement of the total pension or OPEB liability
    2. Changes of assumptions about future economic or demographic factors or of other inputs (changes of assumptions or other inputs)

    The portion of (1) and (2) not included in collective pension or OPEB expense should be included in collective deferred outflows of resources or deferred inflows of resources related to pension or OPEB.
(b) The difference between projected and actual earnings on pension or OPEB plan investments should be included in collective pension or OPEB expense using a systematic and rational method over a closed five-year period, beginning in the current measurement period. The amount not included in collective pension or OPEB expense should be included in collective deferred outflows of resources or deferred inflows of resources related to pension or OPEB. Collective deferred outflows of resources and deferred inflows of resources arising from differences between projected and actual plan investment earnings in different measurement periods should be aggregated and included as a

net collective deferred outflow of resources related to pension or OPEB or a net collective deferred inflow of resources related to pension or OPEB.

(c) Contributions to the pension or OPEB plan from employers or nonemployer contributing entities should not be included in collective pension or OPEB expense.

Recognition in Financial Statements Prepared Using the Current Financial Resources Measurement Focus and Modified Accrual Basis of Accounting—All Cost-Sharing Employers

In financial statements prepared using the current financial resources measurement focus and modified accrual basis of accounting, an employer's proportionate share of the collective net pension or OPEB liability should be recognized to the extent the liability is normally expected to be liquidated with expendable available financial resources. GASBS 68 and 75 provide that pension and OPEB expenditures be recognized equal to the total of (a) amounts paid by the employer to the pension or OPEB plan, including amounts paid for pension or OPEB as the benefits come due, and (b) the change between the beginning and ending balances of amounts normally expected to be liquidated with expendable available financial resources. A net pension or OPEB liability is normally expected to be liquidated with expendable available financial resources to the extent that benefit payments have matured—that is, benefit payments are due and payable and the pension or OPEB plan's fiduciary net position is not sufficient for payment of those benefits.

Notes to Financial Statements—All Cost-sharing Employers

The following summarized the disclosure requirements of GASBS 68 and 75. The term "aggregate" refers to aggregate pension or OPEB amounts. Accordingly, pension and OPEB disclosures should be provided separately in the financial statements and required supplementary information.

The total (aggregate for all pension or OPEB, regardless of the type of plans through which the benefit is provided and whether the plans are administered through a trust of the employer's pension or OPEB liabilities, net pension or OPEB assets, deferred outflows of resources and deferred inflows of resources related to pension or OPEB, and pension or OPEB expense/expenditures for the period associated with pension or OPEB liabilities to employees, as applicable, should be disclosed if the total amounts are not otherwise identifiable from information presented in the financial statements.

The information described below should be disclosed for benefits provided through each cost-sharing pension or OPEB plan in which the employer participates. Disclosures related to more than one pension or OPEB plan should be combined in a manner that avoids unnecessary duplication.

Plan Description

The following information should be disclosed about the pension or OPEB plan through which benefits are provided:

(a) The name of the plan, identification of the entity that administers the plan, and identification of the plan as a cost-sharing plan.

(b) A brief description of the benefit terms, including (1) the classes of employees covered; (2) the types of benefits; (3) the key elements of the benefit formulas; (4) the terms or policies, if any, with respect to automatic postemployment benefit changes, including automatic COLAs, ad hoc postemployment benefit changes, including ad hoc COLAs, and the sharing of benefit-related costs with inactive employees; and (5) the authority under which benefit terms are established or may be amended. If the plan is closed to new entrants, that fact should be disclosed.

(c) A brief description of contribution requirements, including (1) the basis for determining the employer's contributions to the plan (for example, statute, contract, an actuarial basis, or some other manner); (2) identification of the authority under which contribution requirements of employers, nonemployer contributing entities, if any, and employees are established or may be amended; (3) legal or contractual maximum contribution rates, if applicable; and (4) the contribution rates (in dollars or as a percentage of covered payroll) of employers, nonemployer contributing entities, if any, and employees for the reporting period. Also, the amount of contributions recognized by the plan from the employer during the reporting period, excluding amounts resulting from contributions recognized by the plan as noncurrent receivables, if not otherwise disclosed.

(d) Whether the plan issues a stand-alone financial report (or the plan is included in the report of another government) that is available to the public and, if so, how to obtain the report (for example, a link to the plan report on the employer's website).

Information about the Employer's Proportionate Share of the Collective Net Pension or OPEB Liability

Assumptions and Other Inputs

Significant assumptions and other inputs used to measure the total pension or OPEB liability, including assumptions about inflation, healthcare cost trend rates (for OPEB plans), salary changes, ad hoc postemployment benefit changes (including ad hoc COLAs), and the sharing of benefit-related costs with inactive employees, should be disclosed, as applicable. For all significant assumptions, if different rates are assumed for different periods, information should be disclosed about what rates are applied to the different periods of the measurement.

In addition, the following information related to assumptions and other inputs should be disclosed, as applicable:

(a) The fact that projections of the sharing of benefit-related costs are based on an established pattern of practice

(b) The source of the mortality assumptions (for example, the published tables on which the assumptions are based or that the assumptions are based on a study of the experience of the covered group)

(c) The dates of experience studies on which significant assumptions are based

(d) If the alternative measurement method is used to measure the total pension or OPEB liability, the source of or basis for all significant assumptions selected

(e) Measures of the employer's proportionate share of the collective net OPEB liability calculated using (1) a healthcare cost trend rate that is 1-percentage-point higher than the assumed healthcare cost trend rate and (2) a healthcare cost trend rate that is 1-percentage-point lower than the assumed healthcare cost trend rate

The following information should be disclosed about the discount rate:

(a) The discount rate applied in the measurement of the total pension or OPEB liability and the change in the discount rate since the prior measurement date, if any

(b) Assumptions made about projected cash flows into and out of the plan, such as contributions from employers, nonemployer contributing entities, and employees

(c) The long-term expected rate of return on plan investments and a brief description of how it was determined, including significant methods and assumptions used for that purpose
(d) If the discount rate incorporates a municipal bond rate, the municipal bond rate used and the source of that rate
(e) The periods of projected benefit payments to which the long-term expected rate of return and, if used, the municipal bond rate are applied in determining the discount rate
(f) The assumed asset allocation of the plan's portfolio, the long-term expected real rate of return for each major asset class, and whether the expected rates of return are presented as arithmetic or geometric means, if not otherwise disclosed
(g) Measures of the employer's proportionate share of the collective net pension or OPEB liability calculated using (1) a discount rate that is 1-percentage-point higher than that used under the requirements of GASBS 68 and 75 and (2) a discount rate that is 1-percentage-point lower than that required by paragraph 79

The Pension or OPEB Plan's Fiduciary Net Position

All information required by GASBS 68 and 75 and other financial reporting standards about the elements of the pension or OPEB plan's basic financial statements (that is, all information about the plan's assets, deferred outflows of resources, liabilities, deferred inflows of resources, and fiduciary net position) should be disclosed. However, if (a) a financial report that includes disclosure about the elements of the plan's basic financial statements is available on the Internet, either as a stand-alone financial report or included as a fiduciary fund in the financial report of another government and (b) information is provided about how to obtain the report, reference may instead be made to the other report for these disclosures. In this circumstance, it also should be disclosed that the plan's fiduciary net position has been determined on the same basis used by the plan, and a brief description of the plan's basis of accounting, including the policies with respect to benefit payments (including refunds of employee contributions) and the valuation of plan investments should be included. If significant changes have occurred that indicate that the disclosures included in the plan's financial report generally do not reflect the facts and circumstances at the measurement date, information about the substance and the magnitude of the changes should be disclosed.

Additional Information

GASBS 68 and 75 require the following additional information should be disclosed, if applicable:

(a) The employer's proportionate share (amount) of the collective net pension or OPEB liability and, if an employer has a special funding situation, (1) the portion of the nonemployer contributing entities' total proportionate share (amount) of the collective net pension or OPEB liability that is associated with the employer and (2) the total of the employer's proportionate share (amount) of the collective net pension or OPEB liability and the portion of the nonemployer contributing entities' total proportionate share of the collective net pension or OPEB liability that is associated with the employer.
(b) The employer's proportion (percentage) of the collective net pension or OPEB liability, the basis on which its proportion was determined, and the change in its proportion since the prior measurement date.
(c) The measurement date of the collective net pension or OPEB liability; the date of the actuarial valuation or alternative measurement method calculation on which the total pension

or OPEB liability is based; and, if applicable, the fact that update procedures were used to roll forward the total pension or OPEB liability to the measurement date. If the alternative measurement method is used to measure the total OPEB liability, the fact that this alternative method was used in place of an actuarial valuation also should be disclosed.

(d) A brief description of changes of assumptions or other inputs that affected measurement of the total pension or OPEB liability since the prior measurement date.

(e) A brief description of changes of benefit terms that affected measurement of the total pension or OPEB liability since the prior measurement date.

(f) A brief description of the nature of changes between the measurement date of the collective net pension or OPEB liability and the employer's reporting date that are expected to have a significant effect on the employer's proportionate share of the collective net pension or OPEB liability, and the amount of the expected resultant change in the employer's proportionate share of the collective net pension or OPEB liability, if known.

(g) The amount of pension or OPEB expense recognized by the employer in the reporting period.

(h) The employer's balances of deferred outflows of resources and deferred inflows of resources related to pension or OPEB, classified as follows, if applicable:
1. Differences between expected and actual experience in the measurement of the total pension or OPEB liability
2. Changes of assumptions or other inputs
3. Net difference between projected and actual earnings on pension or OPEB plan investments
4. Changes in the employer's proportion and differences between (a) the employer's contributions (other than those associated with the individual employer's separately financed specific liabilities to the plan) and (b) the employer's proportionate share of certain contributions
5. The employer's contributions to the plan subsequent to the measurement date of the collective net pension or OPEB liability

(i) A schedule presenting the following:
1. For each of the subsequent five years, and in the aggregate thereafter, the net amount of the employer's balances of deferred outflows of resources and deferred inflows of resources in subparagraph (h) that will be recognized in the employer's pension or OPEB expense
2. The amount of the employer's balance of deferred outflows of resources in subparagraph (h) that will be included as a reduction of the collective net pension or OPEB liability.

(j) The amount of revenue recognized for the support provided by nonemployer contributing entities, if any.

Required Supplementary Information—All Cost-Sharing Employers

GASBS 68 and 75 require certain information to be reported as required supplementary information, as identified in this section.

(a) and (b), as applicable, should be presented separately for each cost-sharing pension or OPEB plan through which pension or OPEB is provided. The information indicated in subparagraph (a) should be determined as of the measurement date of the collective net pension or OPEB liability. The information in subparagraph (b) should be determined as of the employer's most recent fiscal year-end.

(a) A 10-year schedule presenting the following for each year:
 1. If the employer does not have a special funding situation:
 (a) The employer's proportion (percentage) of the collective net pension or OPEB liability
 (b) The employer's proportionate share (amount) of the collective net pension or OPEB liability
 (c) The employer's covered-employee payroll
 (d) The employer's proportionate share (amount) of the collective net pension or OPEB liability as a percentage of the employer's covered-employee payroll
 (e) The pension or OPEB plan's fiduciary net position as a percentage of the total pension OPEB liability
 2. If the employer has a special funding situation:
 (a) The employer's proportion (percentage) of the collective net pension or OPEB liability
 (b) The employer's proportionate share (amount) of the collective net pension or OPEB liability
 (c) The portion of the nonemployer contributing entities' total proportionate share (amount) of the collective net pension or OPEB liability that is associated with the employer
 (d) The total of (b) and (c)
 (e) The employer's covered-employee payroll
 (f) The employer's proportionate share (amount) of the collective net pension or OPEB liability as a percentage of the employer's covered-employee payroll
 (g) The pension or OPEB plan's fiduciary net position as a percentage of the total pension or OPEB liability

(b) If the contribution requirements of the employer are statutorily or contractually established, a 10-year schedule presenting the following for each year:
 1. The statutorily or contractually required employer contribution. For purposes of this schedule, statutorily or contractually required contributions should exclude amounts, if any, associated with payables to the plan that arose in a prior fiscal year and those associated with separately financed specific liabilities of the individual employer to the plan.
 2. The amount of contributions recognized by the plan in relation to the statutorily or contractually required employer contribution. For purposes of this schedule, contributions should exclude amounts resulting from contributions recognized by the OPEB as noncurrent receivables.
 3. The difference between the statutorily or contractually required employer contribution and the amount of contributions recognized by the plan in relation to the statutorily or contractually required employer contribution.
 4. The employer's covered-employee payroll.
 5. The amount of contributions recognized by the plan in relation to the statutorily or contractually required employer contribution as a percentage of the employer's covered-employee payroll.

Notes to Required Schedules

GASBS 68 and 75 provide that information about factors that significantly affect trends in the amounts reported in the above schedules (for example, changes of benefit terms, changes in the size or composition of the population covered by the benefit terms, or the use of different assumptions) should be presented as notes to the schedules. Information about investment-related factors that significantly affect trends in the amounts reported should be limited to those factors over which the plan or the participating governments have influence (for example, changes in investment policies). Information about external, economic factors (for example, changes in market prices) should not be presented. (The amounts presented for prior years should not be restated for the effects of changes—for example, changes of benefit terms or changes of assumptions—that occurred subsequent to the measurement date of that information.)

ALTERNATIVE MEASUREMENT METHOD FOR OPEB LIABILITIES

In place of an actuarial valuation, GASBS 75 provides that the total OPEB liability may be measured using the alternative measurement method if fewer than 100 employees (active and inactive) are provided with benefits through the OPEB plan as of the beginning of the measurement period. The specific requirements for the calculation are contained in GASBS 75.

DEFINED CONTRIBUTION PENSION AND OPEB PLANS

In financial statements prepared using the economic resources measurement focus and accrual basis of accounting, GASBS 68 and 75 provide that the following should be recognized by employers that do not have a special funding situation for defined contribution pension or OPEB:

(a) Pension or OPEB expense equal to the amount of contributions or credits to employees' accounts that are defined by the benefit terms as attributable to employees' services in the period, net of forfeited amounts that are removed from employees' accounts. Amounts that are reallocated to the accounts of other employees should not be considered forfeited amounts for this purpose.

(b) A change in the pension or OPEB liability equal to the following:

1. If the pension or OPEB is provided through a defined contribution plan that is administered through a trust, the difference between amounts recognized as pension or OPEB expense and amounts paid by the employer to the pension or OPEB plan
2. If the pension or OPEB is provided through a defined contribution plan that is not administered through a trust, the difference between amounts recognized as pension or OPEB expense and amounts paid by the employer as the benefits come due during the fiscal year

In financial statements prepared using the current financial resources measurement focus and modified accrual basis of accounting, pension or OPEB expenditures should be recognized equal to the total of (a) amounts paid by the employer for pension or OPEB as the benefits come due and (b) the change between the beginning and ending balances of amounts normally expected to be liquidated with expendable available financial resources. A liability for defined contribution pension or OPEB should be recognized to the extent the liability is normally expected to be liquidated with expendable available financial resources. A liability for defined contribution pension or OPEB is normally expected to be liquidated with expendable available financial resources to the extent that contributions are due and payable pursuant to legal requirements, including contractual arrangements.

Notes to Financial Statements

GASBS 68 and 75 provide that the following information should be disclosed in notes to financial statements about each defined contribution plan to which an employer is required to contribute:

(a) The name of the plan, identification of the entity that administers the plan, and identification of the plan as a defined contribution plan.
(b) A brief description of the benefit terms (including terms, if any, related to vesting and forfeitures and the policy related to the use of forfeited amounts) and the authority under which benefit terms are established or may be amended.
(c) If the pension or OPEB is provided through a defined contribution OPEB plan that is administered through a trust, the contribution (or crediting) rates (in dollars or as a percentage of salary) for employees, the employer, and nonemployer contributing entities, if any, and the authority under which those rates are established or may be amended.
(d) If the pension or OPEB is provided through a defined contribution plan that is not administered through a trust:
   1. The fact that there are no assets accumulated in a trust. If provided through a plan that is administered through a trust and that trust does not meet the criteria in paragraph of GASBS 68 and 75, each criterion that the trust does not meet should be disclosed.
   2. Identification of the authority under which requirements for the employer and nonemployer contributing entities, if any, to pay pension or OPEB as the benefits come due are established or may be amended. Also, the amount paid by the employer for pension or OPEB as the benefits came due during the reporting period, if not otherwise disclosed.
(e) The amount of pension or OPEB expense recognized by the employer in the reporting period.
(f) The amount of forfeitures reflected in pension or OPEB expense recognized by the employer in the reporting period.
(g) The amount of the employer's liability outstanding at the end of the period, if any.

Effective Date and Transition

GASBS 68 was effective for financial statements for fiscal years beginning after June 15, 2014, with earlier application encouraged.

In addition, the information for all periods for the ten-year schedules that are required to be presented as required supplementary information may not be available initially. In these cases, during the transition period, GASBS 68 provides that information should be presented for as many years as are available. However, the schedules should not include information that is not measured in accordance with the requirements of GASBS 68.

GASB STATEMENT NO. 71, *PENSION TRANSITION FOR CONTRIBUTIONS MADE SUBSEQUENT TO THE MEASUREMENT DATE—AN AMENDMENT OF GASB STATEMENT NO. 68* (GASBS 71)

In November 2015 the GASB issued GASBS 71 to correct an anomaly when GASBS 68 would be implemented regarding employer contributions.

GASBS 68 requires a state or local government employer (or nonemployer contributing entity in a special funding situation) to recognize a net pension liability measured as of a date (the measurement date) no earlier than the end of its prior fiscal year. If a state or local government employer or nonemployer contributing entity makes a contribution to a defined benefit pension plan between the measurement date of the reported net pension liability and the end of the government's reporting period, GASBS 68 requires that the government recognize its contribution as a deferred outflow of resources. In addition, GASBS 68 requires recognition of deferred outflows of resources and deferred inflows of resources for changes in the net pension liability of a state or local government employer or nonemployer contributing entity that arise from other types of events. At transition to GASBS 68, if it is not practical for an employer or nonemployer contributing entity to determine the amounts of all deferred outflows of resources and deferred inflows of resources related to pensions, GASBS 68 required that beginning balances for deferred outflows of resources and deferred inflows of resources not be reported.

As a result, if it is not practical to determine the amounts of all deferred outflows of resources and deferred inflows of resources related to pensions, contributions made after the measurement date of the beginning net pension liability could not have been reported as deferred outflows of resources at transition. This could have resulted in a significant understatement of an employer or nonemployer contributing entity's beginning net position and expense in the initial period of implementation.

GASBS 71 amends GASBS 68 to require that, at transition, a government recognize a beginning deferred outflow of resources for its pension contributions, if any, made subsequent to the measurement date of the beginning net pension liability. GASBS 68 will continue to require that beginning balances for other deferred outflows of resources and deferred inflows of resources related to pensions be reported at transition only if it is practical to determine all such amounts.

In other words, governments are required to record (not just not precluded from recording) contributions made after the measurement date as a deferred outflow of resources for its pension contributions, if any, are made subsequent to the measurement date of the beginning net pension liability.

GASBS 71 should be implemented simultaneously with GASBS 68.

GASB STATEMENT NO. 73, *ACCOUNTING AND FINANCIAL REPORTING FOR PENSIONS AND RELATED ASSETS THAT ARE NOT WITHIN THE SCOPE OF GASB STATEMENT 68, AND AMENDMENTS TO CERTAIN PROVISIONS OF GASB STATEMENTS NO. 67 AND NO. 68* (GASBS 73)

The GASB issued GASBS 73 in June 2015 to establish requirements for defined benefit pensions that are not within the scope of GASBS 68. It also provides requirements for assets that are accumulated for purposes of providing those pensions.

GASBS 73 establishes standards of accounting and financial reporting for defined benefit pensions and defined contribution pensions that are provided to the employees of state and local governmental employers and are not within the scope of Statement 68. Statement 68 establishes requirements for pensions that are provided through pension plans that are administered through trusts or equivalent arrangements (hereafter jointly referred to as trusts) in which the following criteria are met:

(a) Contributions from employers and nonemployer contributing entities to the pension plan and earnings on those contributions are irrevocable.

(b) Pension plan assets are dedicated to providing pensions to plan members in accordance with the benefit terms.

(c) Pension plan assets are legally protected from the creditors of employers, nonemployer contributing entities, and the pension plan administrator. If the plan is a defined benefit pension plan, plan assets also are legally protected from creditors of the plan members.

NOTE: From a practical perspective, GASBS 73 extends all of the accounting and disclosure guidance from GASBS 68 to employers that provide defined benefit pensions and defined contribution pensions but do not meet the criteria listed above. In other words, if these criteria are met, follow GASBS 68. If they are not met, follow GASBS 73, whose requirements are essentially the same as those of GASBS 68.

As the assets of pension plans covered under GASBS 68 are maintained in irrevocable trusts, GASBS 73 addresses the question of reporting assets that are being accumulated to pay pension benefits, but are not contained in an irrevocable trust.

GASBS 73 provides that if a pension plan is not administered through a trust that meets the criteria noted above, any assets accumulated for pension purposes should continue to be reported as assets of the employer or nonemployer contributing entity.

Further, if a pension plan is not administered through a trust that meets the criteria above, GASBS 73 provides that a government that holds assets accumulated for pension purposes in a fiduciary capacity should report the assets in an agency fund. The amount of assets accumulated in excess of liabilities for benefits due to plan members and accrued investment and administrative expenses should be reported as a liability to participating employers or nonemployer contributing entities. If the agency fund is included in the financial report of an employer whose employees are provided with benefits through the pension plan or a nonemployer contributing entity that pays benefits as the pensions come due, balances reported in the agency fund should exclude amounts that pertain to the employer or nonemployer contributing entity that reports the agency fund. Instead, those amounts should continue to be reported as required, as described in the previous paragraph.

Amendments to GASBS 67 and 68

GASBS 73 also amends GASBS 67 and 68 with regard to the following issues:

1. Information that is required to be presented as notes to the ten-year schedules of required supplementary information about investment-related factors that significantly affect trends in the amounts reported.
2. Accounting and financial reporting for separately financed specific liabilities of individual employers and nonemployer contributing entities for defined benefit pensions.
3. Timing of employer recognition of revenue for the support of nonemployer contributing entities not in a special funding situation.

The following are the specific amendments and clarifications of GASBS 67 and 68 that are included in GASBS 73:

Notes to Schedules of Required Supplementary Information

For purposes of applying paragraph 34 of Statement 67 or paragraph 47, paragraph 82, or paragraph 115 of Statement 68, information about investment-related factors that significantly affect trends in the amounts reported should be limited to those factors over which the pension plan or participating governments have influence (for example, changes in investment policies). Information about external, economic factors (for example, changes in market prices) should not be presented.

Payables to Defined Benefit Pension Plans

For purposes of applying Statement 67 or Statement 68, a separately financed specific liability is a specific contractual liability to a defined benefit pension plan for a one-time assessment to an individual employer or nonemployer contributing entity of an amount resulting from, for example, (a) an increase in the total pension liability due to an individual employer joining a pension plan or a change of benefit terms specific to an individual employer or (b) a contractual commitment for a nonemployer contributing entity to make a one-time contribution for purposes of reducing the net pension liability. The term *separately financed* is used to differentiate those payables to the pension plan from payables to the pension plan that originate from the portion(s) of the total pension liability that is pooled by two or more employers (or by a single, agent, or cost-sharing employer and a nonemployer contributing entity in a special funding situation) for financing purposes. Payables to the pension plan for unpaid (legal, contractual, or statutory) financing obligations associated with the pooled portion of the total pension liability are not considered to be separately financed specific liabilities, even if separate payment terms have been established for those payables. In the reporting period in which any payable to the pension plan arises, the full amount of the payable should be recognized as a contribution to the pension plan.

For purposes of applying the requirements in paragraph 32c(1) or paragraph 32c(2) of Statement 67 or paragraph 46c(1), paragraph 46d(1), paragraph 81b(1), or paragraph 114b(1) of Statement 68 for information to be presented in contribution-related schedules of required supplementary information, actuarially determined contributions, contractually required contributions, and statutorily required contributions should exclude amounts, if any, associated with payables to the pension plan that arose in a prior fiscal year and those associated with separately financed specific liabilities of the individual employer or nonemployer contributing entity, as applicable, to the pension plan.

A single employer that has a special funding situation should recognize additional revenue for the portion of expense recognized by the governmental nonemployer contributing entity in conformity with paragraph 105 of Statement 68. A cost-sharing employer that has a special funding situation should recognize additional revenue and pension expense for the portion of expense recognized by the governmental nonemployer contributing entity in conformity with paragraph 105 of Statement 68 for the change in the total pension liability associated with a separately financed specific liability of the individual governmental nonemployer contributing entity that is associated with the employer.

Contributions made by others to a pension plan during the measurement period to separately finance specific liabilities to the pension plan should be recognized as follows:

(a) For a cost-sharing employer, the amount of the employer's proportionate share of the total of such contributions (excluding amounts associated with the employer from nonemployer contributing entities not in a special funding situation) determined using the employer's proportion of the collective net pension liability should be recognized as a reduction of the employer's pension expense.
(b) For a governmental nonemployer contributing entity in a special funding situation, the amount of the governmental nonemployer contributing entity's proportionate share of the total of such contributions determined using the governmental nonemployer contributing entity's proportion of the collective pension liability should be recognized as a reduction of the governmental nonemployer contributing entity's expense.
(c) For an employer that has a special funding situation, the amounts required to be recognized in conformity with paragraph 90 or paragraphs 94 and 95 of Statement 68, as applicable, should be reduced by the employer's proportionate share of the total of the amounts recognized by nonemployer contributing entities in conformity with paragraph 121b of this Statement that are associated with the employer.

Revenue Recognition for Support of Nonemployer Contributing Entities Not in a Special Funding Situation

In financial statements prepared using the economic resources measurement focus and accrual basis of accounting, employers should recognize revenue for the support of a nonemployer contributing entity that is not in a special funding situation in the reporting period in which the contribution of the nonemployer contributing entity is reported as a change in the net pension liability or collective net pension liability, as applicable.

Effective Date and Transition

The requirements of GASBS 73 that address accounting and financial reporting by employers and governmental nonemployer contributing entities for pensions that are not within the scope of GASBS 68 are effective for financial statements for fiscal years beginning after June 15, 2016.

The requirements of GASBS 73 that address financial reporting for assets accumulated for purposes of providing those pensions are effective for fiscal years beginning after June 15, 2015.

GASB STATEMENT NO. 82, *PENSION ISSUES—AN AMENDMENT OF GASB STATEMENTS NO. 67, NO. 68, AND NO. 73* (GASBS 82)

In March 2016 the GASB issued GASBS 82 to clarify a few issues that had arisen during the implementation of GASBS 68. The following are the three issues addressed.

Presentation of Payroll-Related Measures in Required Supplementary Information

Statements 67 and 68 required presentation of covered-employee payroll, which is the payroll of employees that are provided with pensions through the pension plan, and ratios that use that measure, in schedules of required supplementary information. GASBS 82 amends requirements to instead require the presentation of covered payroll, defined as the payroll on which contributions to a pension plan are based, and ratios that use that measure.

Selection of Assumptions

GASBS 82 clarifies that a *deviation*, as the term is used in Actuarial Standards of Practice issued by the Actuarial Standards Board, from the guidance in an Actuarial Standard of Practice, is not considered to be in conformity with the requirements of Statement 67, Statement 68, or Statement 73 for the selection of assumptions used in determining the total pension liability and related measures.

Classification of Employer-Paid Member Contributions

GASBS 82 also clarifies that payments that are made by an employer to satisfy contribution requirements that are identified by the pension plan terms as plan member contribution requirements should be classified as plan member contributions for purposes of Statement 67 and as employee contributions for purposes of Statement 68. It also requires that an employer's expense and expenditures for those amounts be recognized in the period for which the contribution is assessed and classified in the same manner as the employer classifies similar compensation other than pensions (for example, as salaries and wages or as fringe benefits).

Effective Date

The requirements of GASBS 82 are effective for reporting periods beginning after June 15, 2016, except for the requirements for the selection of assumptions in a circumstance in which an employer's pension liability is measured as of a date other than the employer's most recent fiscal year-end. In that circumstance, the requirements for the selection of assumptions are effective for that employer in the first reporting period in which the measurement date of the pension liability is on or after June 15, 2017. Earlier application is encouraged.

GASB STATEMENT NO. 75, *ACCOUNTING AND FINANCIAL REPORTING FOR POSTEMPLOYMENT BENEFITS OTHER THAN PENSIONS* (GASBS 75)

In June 2015 the GASB issued GASBS 75 to change the way governments measure and report OPEB plan benefits. The concepts and essential requirements of GASBS 75 for OPEB plan benefits are based on those of GASBS 68 for pension benefits. The requirements of GASBS 75 are incorporated into this chapter.

Effective Date

GASBS 75 is effective for fiscal years beginning after June 15, 2017. Earlier application is encouraged.

GASB STATEMENT NO. 85, *OMNIBUS 2017* (GASBS 85)

In March 2017 the GASB issued GASB Statement No. 85 (GASBS 85), *Omnibus 2017*, which includes a number of provisions related to accounting and financial reporting for OPEB plan benefits upon adopting the requirements of GASBS 75. These provisions are discussed next.

Timing of the Measurement of Pension or OPEB Liabilities and Expenditures Recognized in Financial Statements Prepared Using the Current Financial Resources Measurement Focus

In financial statements prepared using the current financial resources measurement focus, GASBS 85 provides that liabilities to employees for defined benefit pensions or defined benefit OPEB plans should be measured as of the end of the reporting period. All expenditures for defined benefit pensions or defined benefit OPEB plans, including (a) amounts for payables to a pension or OPEB plan and (b) amounts for costs incurred by the employer related to the administration of defined benefit pensions or defined benefit OPEBs provided through a pension or OPEB plan that is not administered through a trust, should be measured for the reporting period.

Recognition and Measurement of On-Behalf Payments for Pensions or OPEBs in Employer Financial Statements

In financial statements prepared using the current financial resources measurement focus, an employer should recognize expenditures for on-behalf payments for pensions or OPEBs equal to the total of (a) amounts paid during the reporting period by nonemployer contributing entities to the pension or OPEB plan (or for benefits as they come due) and (b) the change between the nonemployer contributing entities' beginning and ending balances of amounts normally expected to be liquidated with expendable available financial resources. Both (a) and (b) include amounts for payables to a pension or OPEB plan.

Except for the circumstances as identified in the following paragraph, in financial statements prepared using the current financial resources measurement focus, an employer should recognize revenue equal to the amount of expenditures determined in accordance with the requirements above.

For on-behalf payments that are not legally required to be made by a nonemployer contributing entity for defined contribution pensions or defined contribution OPEBs, an employer should apply the revenue recognition requirements of GASBS 24. For on-behalf payments for pensions or OPEBs, the provisions of GASBS 24 related to on-behalf payments for fringe benefits should not be applied.

Presentation of Payroll-Related Measures in Required Supplementary Information by OPEB Plans and Employers That Provide OPEBs

GASBS 85 provides that for single-employer defined benefit OPEB plans (single-employer OPEB plans) and cost-sharing multiple-employer defined benefit OPEB plans (cost-sharing OPEB plans), the measure of payroll that is required by GASBS 75 to be presented in schedules of required supplementary information (and used in ratios that are presented in required supplementary information) should be covered payroll. Covered payroll is the payroll on which contributions to the OPEB plan are based. If contributions to the OPEB plan are not based on a measure of pay, no measure of payroll should be presented.

For employers that provide OPEBs through OPEB plans that are administered through trusts that meet the criteria established in GASBS 75, the measure of payroll that is required to be presented in schedules of required supplementary information (and used in ratios that are presented in required supplementary information) should be one of the following, as applicable:

(a) Covered payroll (as defined above), if contributions to the OPEB plan are based on a measure of pay.
(b) Covered-employee payroll (as defined in paragraph 246 of GASBS 75), if contributions to the OPEB plan are not based on a measure of pay.

Classification of Employer-Paid Member Contributions for OPEB Plans

GASBS 85 notes that in some circumstances, payments are made by the employer to satisfy contribution requirements that are identified by the OPEB plan terms as plan member contribution requirements. For purposes of applying GASBS 74, those amounts should be classified as plan member contributions. For purposes of applying GASBS 75, including for purposes of determining a cost-sharing employer's proportion, those amounts should be classified as employee contributions. An employer's expense and expenditures for those amounts should be recognized in the period for which the contribution is assessed and classified in the same manner as the employer classifies similar compensation other than OPEBs (for example, as salaries and wages or as fringe benefits).

Alternative Measurement Method for OPEB Plans

The following specific modifications may be incorporated into application of the alternative measurement:

(a) *Expected point in time at which plan members (employees) will exit from active service.* The assumption should reflect past experience and future expectations for the covered group. For active plan members (employees) covered under the terms of the OPEB plan, the assumption may incorporate (1) a single assumed age at which plan members (employees) will exit from active service or (2) an assumption that plan members (employees) will exit from active service upon attaining a certain number of years of service.

(b) *Turnover.* The requirements of paragraph 56e and paragraph 57a or 57b, as applicable, of GASBS 74 or paragraph 225e and paragraph 226a or 226b, as applicable, of GASBS 75 may be applied to determine the assumed probability that an active plan member (employee) will remain employed until the assumed age at which the plan member (employee) will meet employment-related eligibility requirements to receive benefits.

OPEBs Provided through Certain Multiple-Employer Defined Benefit OPEB Plans

The paragraphs below address defined benefit OPEB plan benefits provided through a cost-sharing OPEB plan that (a) is not a state or local governmental OPEB plan, (b) is used to provide defined benefit OPEBs both to employees of state or local governmental employers and to employees of employers that are not state or local governmental employers, and (c) has no predominant state or local governmental employer (either individually or collectively with other state or local governmental employers that provide OPEBs through the OPEB plan). The paragraphs below apply to the financial statements of state and local governmental employers whose employees are provided with defined benefit OPEBs through cost-sharing OPEB plans that have the characteristics in the previous paragraph. Those requirements apply whether the government's financial statements are presented in stand-alone financial reports or are included in the financial reports of another government.

Recognition and Measurement

OPEB expense should be recognized in an amount equal to the employer's required contributions to the OPEB plan for the reporting period, and a payable should be reported for unpaid required contributions at the end of the reporting period. OPEB expense also should be recognized for separate liabilities to the OPEB plan that arise in the reporting period (for example, for amounts assessed to an individual employer upon joining a cost-sharing OPEB plan), and a payable should be reported for unpaid amounts at the end of the reporting period.

OPEB expenditures should be recognized in an amount equal to the employer's required contributions to the OPEB plan that are associated with pay periods within the reporting period. In addition, for separate liabilities to the OPEB plan, OPEB expenditures should be recognized equal to the total of (a) amounts paid by the employer in relation to the payable and (b) the change between the beginning and ending balances of amounts normally expected to be liquidated with expendable available financial resources.

A payable should be recognized to the extent it is normally expected to be liquidated with expendable available financial resources—that is, for (a) the unpaid required contributions that are associated with pay periods within the reporting period and (b) the portion of any separate liabilities to the OPEB plan that is due and payable pursuant to contractual arrangements or legal requirements.

Notes to Financial Statements

For each cost-sharing OPEB plan that has the characteristics described above through which the employer provides OPEB plan benefits, the following should be disclosed:

(a) Name of the OPEB plan, identification of the entity that administers the OPEB plan, and identification of the OPEB plan as a cost-sharing OPEB plan.
(b) Whether the OPEB plan issues a publicly available financial report and, if so, how to obtain the report.
(c) A brief description of the benefit terms, including:
   1. The number of the government's employees covered.
   2. The types of benefits provided.
   3. The authority under which benefit terms are established or may be amended.
(d) A brief description of the contribution requirements, including:
   1. The basis for determining the employer's contributions to the OPEB plan (for example, pursuant to a collective-bargaining agreement).
   2. Identification of the authority under which contribution requirements of the employer and its employees are established or may be amended.
   3. The required contribution rates of the employer and its employees for the reporting period.
   4. The amount, in dollars, of the employer's required contributions for the reporting period.
   5. The expiration date(s) of the collective-bargaining agreement(s) requiring contributions to the OPEB plan, if any.
   6. A description of any minimum contributions required for future periods by the collective-bargaining agreement(s), statutory obligations, or other contractual obligations, if applicable.
   7. Whether the employer is subject to any provisions regarding withdrawal from the OPEB plan.
(e) The following information about the employer's payables, if any:
   1. If not otherwise identifiable, the balance of payables.
   2. Significant terms related to the payables.
   3. A description of what gave rise to the payables (for example, required contributions to the OPEB plan or a contractual arrangement for contributions to the OPEB plan related to past service upon entrance into the arrangement).

Required Supplementary Information

A schedule of the employer's required contributions for each of the 10 most recent fiscal years should be presented as required supplementary information.

The schedule should separately identify amounts associated with each OPEB plan.

Notes to the Required Schedule

Information about factors that significantly affect trends in the amounts reported (for example, changes in the size of the population covered by the benefit terms or changes in required contribution rates) should be presented in notes to the required schedule.

Effective Date

GASBS 85 is effective for reporting periods beginning after June 15, 2017. Earlier application is permitted by topic to the extent that all of the requirements associated with a single topic are implemented simultaneously. The pension requirements discussed above are a single topic and can be implemented early by themselves, if so desired by a reporting government. The pension requirements and the OPEB requirements are considered a single topic for purposes of implementing the OPEB requirements.

SUMMARY

The overall requirements of GASBS 68 and 75 for accounting for pensions and OPEBs by governmental entities include a number of very specific and detailed requirements that the financial statement preparer must be familiar with to ensure compliance.

18 COMPENSATED ABSENCES

INTRODUCTION

Governmental entities almost always provide benefits to their employees in the form of *compensated absences*—which is a catchall phrase for instances where an employee is not at work, but is still paid. Vacation pay and sick leave represent the most common and frequently used forms of compensated absences.

One of the objectives in accounting for compensated absences is the matching of compensation expense with the benefits received from an employee's work. In other words, as an employee works and earns vacation and sick leave that will be paid or used in the future, there should be some recognition that a liability and an expense have occurred during the time that the employee is providing the services. Of course, using the basis of accounting and measurement focus of governmental funds, the liability for compensated absences is generally not recorded by the fund, but is instead only recorded in the government-wide statement of net position. There is no corresponding expenditure in the governmental fund until these amounts are actually paid or when they are due to be paid.

The GASB made some slight modifications to the then existing requirements of FASB Statement 43 (SFAS 43), *Accounting for Compensated Absences* (now FASB ASC 710-10), and issued a GASB Statement that addressed the accounting and financial reporting for compensated absences for all governmental entities, regardless of the basis of accounting and measurement focus used. The resulting statement was GASB Statement 16 (GASBS 16), *Accounting for Compensated Absences*. This chapter describes the accounting and financial reporting requirements for compensated absences, which are based on the requirements of GASBS 16.

SCOPE OF GASBS 16

GASBS 16 establishes accounting and financial reporting requirements for compensated absences for state and local governmental entities. Compensated absences are absences from work for which employees are still paid, such as vacation, sick leave, and sabbatical leave. GASBS 16's requirements apply regardless of which reporting model or fund type is used by the governmental entity to report its transactions and prepare its financial statements. Therefore, GASBS 16 applies to all state and local governmental entities, including public benefit corporations and authorities, public employee retirement systems, governmental utilities, governmental hospitals and other health care providers, and governmental colleges and universities. It also applies to governmental colleges and universities. The accounting and financial reporting requirements for governmental colleges and universities are more fully discussed in Chapter 23.

Simply because GASBS 16's requirements generally apply to all governmental entities does not mean that the presentation of the amounts in the various different types of entities' financial statements calculated using its guidance will be the same. The amounts calculated as a liability under GASBS 16 will be the same regardless of the basis of accounting or measurement focus used by the entity or fund to which the liability applies. However, the recording of the liability and recognition of compensation expense or expenditure in preparing fund financial statements will be different based on whether the liability relates to a governmental fund (which uses the modified accrual basis of accounting and the current financial resources measurement focus) or a fund or entity that uses proprietary fund accounting (which uses the accrual basis of accounting and the economic resources measurement focus). Under the new financial reporting model, the government-wide financial statements will report the liability and compensation expense using the accrual basis of accounting and the economic resources measurement focus. Additional discussions of these differences will be described later in this chapter.

BASIC PRINCIPLE

The underlying principle for accounting for compensated absences is that a liability for compensated absences that are attributable to services already rendered and are not contingent on a specific event outside the control of the employer and the employee should be accrued as employees earn the rights to the benefits. On the other hand, compensated absences that relate to future services or are contingent on a specific event outside the control of the employer and employee should be accounted for in the period those services are rendered or those events take place. A later section of this chapter discusses differences in accounting between governmental funds and proprietary funds/government-wide financial statements for the liability for compensated absences.

While this conceptual principle sounds good, to put it into practice the three main types of compensated absences—vacation, sick leave, and sabbatical leave—need to be examined individually to determine when to actually calculate the liability. Guidance is provided later in this chapter as to how to compute the liability, once it is determined that a liability should be recorded.

Vacation Leave (and Other Compensated Absences with Similar Characteristics)

GASBS 16 requires that a liability be accrued for vacation leave and other compensated absences with similar characteristics and should be recorded as the benefits are earned by the employees if both of these conditions are met:

1. The employees' rights to receive compensation are attributable to services already rendered.
2. It is probable that the employer will compensate the employees for the benefits through paid time off or some other means, such as cash payments at termination or retirement.

For purposes of applying these requirements, other compensated absences have characteristics similar to vacation leave if paid time off is not contingent on a specific event outside the control of the employer and the employee. These types of leave include leave whose use is conditional only on length of service, an event that is essentially controllable by the employer or employee, rather than arising from an unforeseen and uncontrollable event such as an illness.

In applying this criterion, three different scenarios will arise:

1. The employee is entitled to the vacation pay, and no other criteria need be met. A liability for this amount should be recorded.

   An employer governmental entity would accrue a liability for vacation leave and other compensated leave with similar characteristics that were earned but not used during the current or prior periods and for which the employees can receive compensation in a future period.

   Some governmental entities provide their employees with military leave. Recording a liability in advance of such leave is not appropriate under GASBS 16 because an employee's right to compensation for military leave is not earned based on past service. Instead, compensation is based on the future military service. In other words, if the employee resigned prior to the start of his or her military leave, he or she would not be entitled to any compensation relating to the future military leave. No military leave was specifically "earned" during the time that the employee was working.
2. The employee has earned time, but the time is not yet available for use or payment because the employee has not yet met certain conditions.

   Benefits that have been earned but that are not yet available for use as paid time off or as some other form of compensation because employees have not met certain conditions (such as a minimum service period for new employees) should be recorded as a liability to the extent that it is probable that the employees will meet the conditions for compensation in the future.
3. The employee has earned vacation benefits, but the benefits are expected to lapse and not result in compensation to the employee.

   Benefits that have been earned but that are expected to lapse and thus not result in compensation to employees should not be accrued as a liability.

Exhibit 1 provides an example of a simple liability calculation for vacation leave.

Exhibit 1: Example of liability calculation for vacation leave

An employee has 20 vacation days as of the end of a fiscal year and currently earns $100 per day. No minimum length of service is required to be eligible for paid vacation leave on termination. In addition, salary-related taxes and salary-based, incremental other costs (discussed later in this chapter) equal 8% of the salary earned. The vacation liability is calculated as

$$20 \text{ days} \times \$100 = \$2{,}000 + 8\%\text{salary} - \text{related costs}\left(\$160\right) = \text{a total liability to record of } \$2{,}160$$

Assume that a government requires a minimum employment period of 1 year before an employee can take vacation leave or be compensated for unused leave at termination. If the employee in the above example was a new employee and the government estimated that 50% of its new employees leave before being eligible for vacation leave or termination payments, the government would estimate its liability as follows:

$$\$2{,}160\left(\text{as above}\right) \times 50\% = \$1{,}080$$

Sick Leave (and Other Compensated Absences with Similar Characteristics)

GASBS 16 requires that a liability for sick leave and other compensated absences with similar characteristics should be accrued using one of the following termination approaches:

- The termination payment method.
- The vesting method.

(For the purpose of determining which compensated absences would have similar characteristics to sick leave, financial statement preparers should consider whether the paid time off is contingent on a specific event outside the control of both the employer and the employee. An example of this situation would be jury duty.)

The following are descriptions of the two methods of recording a liability for sick leave.

Termination payment method. A liability should be accrued for sick leave as the benefits are earned by the employees if it is probable that the employer will compensate the employees for the benefits through cash payments conditioned on the employees' termination or retirement (referred to as the *termination payments*).

An additional explanation of termination payments may be necessary to implement this requirement. Termination payments usually are made directly to employees. In some cases, however, a government's sick leave policy may provide for the value of sick leave at termination to be satisfied by payments to a third party on behalf of the employee. For example, some governments allow the value of a sick leave termination payment to be used to pay a retiring employee's share of postemployment health care insurance premiums. These amounts, just as cash payments made directly to employees, are termination payments for purposes of applying GASBS 16. However, termination payments do not include sick leave balances for which employees only receive additional service time credited for pension benefit calculation purposes.

In applying the termination payment method, a liability is recorded only to the extent that it is probable that the benefits will result in termination payments, rather than be taken as absences due to illness or other contingencies, such as medical appointments or funerals. The liability that is recorded would be based on an estimate using the governmental entity's historical experience of making termination payments for sick leave, adjusted for the effect of any changes that have taken place in the governmental entity's termination payment policy and other current factors that might be relevant to the calculation.

NOTE: Some governments compensate employees for sick leave at termination based on some reduced payment scheme. For example, the government may have a policy that an employee must have a minimum of ten years of service to be entitled to any termination payment for sick leave, and the termination payment may be calculated based on some fraction of the total unused sick days that the terminating employee has at the date of termination. For example, a government might have a policy that only employees with a minimum of ten years of service will be compensated for sick leave and that compensation will be equal to the compensation for one-third of the total of the unused sick days that the employee has left on termination.

Exhibit 2 provides an example of the sick leave liability using the termination payment method.

Exhibit 2: Using termination payment method to calculate sick leave liability

This exhibit demonstrates how a government might calculate its sick leave liability using the termination payments method. Two different applications of the method are used. One application uses the number of sick days paid upon an employee's termination in the calculation. The second application of the method uses the actual sick leave payment made to terminating employees.

Step 1 Obtain historical information about sick leave payments made to terminating employees over some reasonable period, such as the last 5 years.

For this example, both the number of sick days paid and the amount of the payments is obtained. In practice only one of these types of information is needed.

Fiscal Year	*# of Employees Terminated*	*# Sick Days Paid*	*$ of Sick Leave Paid*	*Avg. Years Work*
20X1	5	50	$5,000	20
20X2	1	8	1,000	10
20X3	2	15	2,000	15
20X4	3	20	3,000	12
20X5	4	25	4,000	10
		118	$15,000	67

Step 2 Calculate the adjusted sick leave termination cost for each year worked.

Method 1—Using the number of sick days paid

	Total sick days paid	118
×	Current average daily pay rate	$100
=		$11,800
×	Percentage of sick leave paid	50%
=	Adjusted sick leave payments	$5,900

Divide the adjusted sick leave payments ($5,900) by the average years worked (67 × 15 employees, or 1,005) to arrive at the sick leave payments per year worked ($6).

Method 2—Using the actual sick leave payments

First, adjust the amounts paid in the five-year period to what the payments would have been at the current salary rates:

Fiscal Year	*$ of Sick Leave Paid*	*Adjusted to Current Salaries*
20X1	$5,000	7,000
20X2	1,000	1,100
20X3	2,000	2,200
20X4	3,000	3,100
20X5	4,000	4,000
	$15,000	$17,400
Retiree rate factor ×		71%*
Adjusted sick leave payments		$12,354
Divide by years worked		1,005
Sick leave per year worked		$12

**This factor represents the difference between the average daily pay rate for active employees ($100, as calculated in method 1) and the retiree pay rate (assume $140 in this example) or 100/140 = 71%.*

Note that there is no requirement to multiply this amount by the percentage of sick pay that is actually paid (50% in this example) because this is already reflected in the amounts of sick leave actually paid.

Step 3 Calculate the year-end liability for sick leave.

Two additional pieces of information are needed for this step. First, assume the total person years worked by all active employees (assume that there are 100 employees who have worked a total often years, or 1,000 years). Second, the additional salary-related costs that are required for these payments (assume 8%).

	Method 1	*Method 2*
Total person years worked	1,000	1,000
Sick leave rate per year	$6	$12
Sick leave liability	$6,000	$12,000
Additional salary-related payments (@8%)	480	960
Total liability	$6,480	$12,960

Note that the calculated liability under each method is quite different. This was done for illustrative purposes to show that the amounts calculated can be different. In actual practice with a larger employee population, the two methods are more likely to result in similar, but not necessarily the same, liability amounts.

Vesting method. As an alternative to the termination payment method described above, an employer governmental entity may use the method described as the "vesting" method under GASBS 16 (see Exhibit 3). Under the vesting method, a governmental entity should estimate its accrued sick leave liability based on the sick leave accumulated at the balance sheet date by those employees who currently are eligible to receive termination payments, as well as other employees who are expected to become eligible in the future to receive such payments. To calculate the liability, these accumulations should be reduced to the maximum amount allowed as a termination payment. Accruals for those employees who are expected to become eligible in the future should be based on assumptions concerning the probability that individual employees or classes or groups of employees will become eligible to receive termination payments.

Both of these methods should usually produce a similar amount for the liability that a government should record for sick leave and other compensated absences with similar characteristics.

Exhibit 3: Using vesting method to calculate sick leave liability

This exhibit provides an example of calculating sick leave liability using the vesting method.

Assume in this example that an employee must have ten years of service before they can vest in payments for sick leave upon termination and that a maximum of 60 days of sick leave can be paid. Sick leave is paid at a reduced rate of 50%.

There are only five employees who work for this government. Their relative payroll information is provided below.

Employee	*Length of Service*	*Sick Leave Balance*	*Daily Pay Rate*
1	14	32 days	$100
2	8	20 days	80
3	20	65 days	110
4	1	2 days	60
5	5	10 days	75

Step 1 Determine which employees will vest in their sick leave payments. Based upon this government's experience, employees who attain seven years of service are likely to remain the additional three years and vest in their sick leave balances. Employees with less than seven years of service are accordingly removed from the calculation, because it is assumed that they will not reach the ten-year requirement. (In practice, governments may fine-tune this assumption. For example, probabilities can

be assigned to each year, such as 10% of employees with one year of service reach the ten-year requirement, 20% of employees with two years of service, etc.) In addition, governments may also fine-tune the assumption based on actual experience with different groups of employees, such as civilian employees or uniformed service employees.

NOTE: A governmental entity using one of these methods to calculate the liability may consider viewing the liability calculation from the alternative method to determine if a similar liability results. If the amounts of the liability vary widely between the two methods and the government cannot explain the differences, the government can then go back and review the assumptions used in the two methods to see if any of these assumptions can be improved to make the resulting liability more understandable under both methods.

In this example, employees 1, 2, and 3 will assume to vest in sick leave.

Step 2 Calculate the amount of vested sick leave pay

Employee	*Sick leave balance*	*Sick leave up to max.*	*Daily pay rate*	*Reduced pay %*	*Sick leave liability*
1	32 days	32 days	$100	50%	$1,600
2	20 days	20 days	80	50%	800
3	65 days	60 days	110	50%	3,300
Total sick leave liability					$5,700
Additional salary related payments (at 8%)					456
Total liability					$6,156

Sabbatical Leave

Determining how or if a liability for sabbatical leave should be calculated and reported is based on the nature and terms of the sabbatical leave available to employees. The accounting for sabbatical leave depends on whether the compensation during the sabbatical is for service during the period of the leave itself, or instead for past service.

Some governmental entities permit sabbatical leave from normal duties so that employees can perform research or public service or can obtain additional training to enhance the reputation of or otherwise benefit the employer. In this case, the sabbatical constitutes a change in assigned duties and the salary paid during the leave is considered compensation for service during the period of the leave. The nature of the sabbatical leave is considered to be restricted. In this situation, the sabbatical leave should be accounted for in the period the service is rendered. A liability should not be reported in advance of the sabbatical.

On the other hand, sometimes sabbatical leave is permitted to provide compensated unrestricted time off. In this situation, the salary paid during the leave is compensation for past service. Accordingly, in this situation, a liability should be recorded during the periods the employees earn the right to the leave if it is probable that the employer will compensate the employees for the benefits through paid time off or some other means.

NOTE: In the two extreme cases of sabbatical leave described above, restricted and unrestricted, the determination of whether a liability is recorded seems clear. However, in actual practice, the nature of sabbatical leave may not be as clear as in these two examples. For example, an employee may be given compensated time off to pursue research or other learning experience that is completely at the discretion of the employer.

Determination of whether this compensation is related to past service may require the use of considerable judgment on the part of the financial statement preparer. Governmental employers should develop a reasonable policy for whether a liability is recorded and apply this policy consistently among similarly situated employees who are provided with compensated sabbatical leave.

Other Factors Affecting the Liability Calculation

Two other factors need to be considered by the governmental financial statement preparer in calculating liability amounts for compensated absences—the rate of pay that is used to calculate the liability and the additional salary-related costs that should be considered for accrual. These two factors are discussed in the following paragraphs.

GASBS 16 specifies that the liability for compensated absences should be based on the salary rates in effect at the balance sheet date. There is no need to project future salary increases into a calculation that considers that when the vacation or sick leave is actually paid, it is likely to be at a higher rate of pay than that in place at the balance sheet date. On the other hand, if a governmental employer pays employees for compensated absences at other than their pay rates or salary rates (sometimes at a lower amount that is established by contract, regulation, or policy), then the other rate that is in effect at the balance sheet date should be used to calculate the liability.

As for salary-related payments, GASBS 16 specifies that an additional amount should be accrued as a liability for those payments associated with compensated absences. These amounts should be recorded at the rates in effect at the balance sheet date. Salary-related payments subject to accrual are those items for which an employer is liable to make a payment directly and incrementally associated with payments made for compensated absences on termination. These salary-related payments would include the employer's share of Social Security and Medicare taxes and might also include an employer's contribution to a pension plan. For example, an accrual for the required contribution to a defined contribution or a cost-sharing multiple-employer defined benefit pension plan should be made if the employer is liable for a contribution to the plan based on termination payments made to employees for vacation leave, sick leave, or other compensated absences. An additional accrual should not be made relating to single-employer or agent multiemployer defined benefit plans.

In applying the requirements of the preceding paragraph, the accrual should be made based on the entire liability for each type of compensated absence to which the salary-related payments apply. In other words, payments directly and incrementally associated with the payment of sick leave termination payments should be accrued for the entire sick leave liability. Salary-related payments associated with termination payments of vacation leave should be accrued for the entire vacation leave liability, including leave that might be taken as paid time off, rather than paid as termination payments.

NOTE: The calculation of the liability for compensated absences can be very complicated for governmental entities. Often there are various groups of employees that are working under various union contracts and have a wide range of benefits, in addition to the benefits earned by nonunion employees. A further complication is that as compensated absence benefits are changed, long-term employees are sometimes "grandfathered" to remain eligible for compensated absences under older rules that are more favorable to the employee. All of these differences [compounded by governmental entities usually having (1) a large number of employees and (2) payroll or human resource computer systems that may not lend themselves to readily capturing leave balances] make the compensated absence liability calculation subject to the use of estimates and historical payment patterns to determine reasonable liability amounts. Sometimes, a sample of employees is taken, liabilities calculated in detail, and the results extrapolated to the workforce as a whole. Governments should carefully weigh the costs and benefits of spending an inordinate amount of time in calculating a precise amount for this estimate, as a reasonable estimate of the liability would serve the financial statement user equally well.

FINANCIAL REPORTING CONSIDERATIONS

The accounting and financial reporting for compensated absences for state and local governments must take into consideration the differences between the governmental fund and the proprietary fund accounting basis and measurement focus with respect to:

- Fund long-term liabilities and general long-term liabilities.
- Current liabilities and noncurrent liabilities.

The accounting and financial reporting differ on whether the liability is recorded in a proprietary fund or a governmental fund. The differences are not in how the amount of the liability is calculated. Both types of funds calculate the liability in the manner described in the preceding sections in this chapter. The difference in the accounting and financial reporting relates to where and how the liability is recorded.

For governmental funds, the long-term portion of the liability for compensated absences is one that is recorded in the government-wide statement of net position. Consistent with the modified accrual basis of accounting and the current financial resources measurement focus, the long-term portion of the compensated absence liability will not be liquidated with the expendable available financial resources of the governmental funds to which it relates. The amount of the compensated absences accrued as a liability (with a corresponding expenditure accrual) within a governmental fund at the end of the fiscal year is the amount of the total compensated absence liability that will be paid with expendable available resources. The amounts recorded in the governmental fund should only be recorded when the amounts become due. For example, an employee leaves the government and is due a payment for compensated absences but has not yet received payment. The balance of the liability for compensated absences is recorded only in the government-wide statement of net position.

NOTE: As a practical matter, many governments report the entire liability for compensated absences that relate to governmental funds only in the government-wide statement of net position and report expenditures for compensated absences generally on a pay-as-you-go basis. While technically a small portion of the governmental fund liability may be paid from expendable available resources, recognizing the expenditure only when the amounts for compensated absences are actually paid does not usually result in a large distortion in the expenditures reported in the governmental funds. However, in the year of a significant government downsizing, where large numbers of employees are receiving termination payments for vacation time, sick leave, and other leave, the amount of the expenditures in one year could differ significantly from prior years and may require closer examination to determine if at least some portion of the liability should be recorded in the governmental funds because these amounts may be due to employees and not paid.

For proprietary funds, the accounting and financial reporting for recording the liability for compensated absences resembles more closely that used by commercial enterprises. The total applicable compensated absence liability is recorded in the proprietary funds, and the corresponding amount of the liability that must be accrued is recorded as an expense in the proprietary fund.

NOTE: When a government reports under the GASBS 34 financial reporting model, the government-wide financial statements record compensated absences in a manner similar to that used by proprietary funds. However, the liability that is recorded needs to be reported in two components—the amount estimated to be due in one year and the amount estimated to be due in more than one year. Furthermore, changes in the liability reported on the government-wide statement of net position (and not the governmental fund) will result in an increase or decrease of expense reported on the government-wide statement of activities. This increase or decrease in expense will need to be allocated by program/function on the government-wide statement of activities.

SUMMARY

This chapter has presented the basic accounting requirements and guidelines for governments to use in calculating the liability for compensated absences. These general rules should ideally be used to develop a working model for estimating this liability, allowing the governmental entity to meet the requirements of GASBS 16 in a useful and cost-effective manner.

19 ACCOUNTING FOR LEASES

INTRODUCTION

Accounting for leases is one of the more technically challenging areas in accounting, including governmental accounting. This chapter describes the accounting and financial reporting requirements for both lessees and lessors. Essentially, these accounting requirements depend on whether the lease is classified as an operating lease or a capital lease. This classification is made in the same manner by governmental entities as by commercial enterprises. Two important differences must be considered, however. The first is whether the lease is accounted for by a governmental fund or a proprietary fund. The accounting and financial reporting requirements differ significantly. The second is whether an operating lease has scheduled rent increases inherent in its terms and conditions. The accounting for such scheduled rent increases differs for governmental entities from the accounting used by commercial enterprises for scheduled rent increases.

In future years, lease accounting will be substantially changed by the provisions of GASB Statement No. 87, *Leases*, which is described at the end of this chapter.

This chapter provides guidance for all of these situations, first from the point of view of the lessee and second from the point of view of the lessor.

ACCOUNTING BASIS

The accounting and financial reporting requirements discussed in this chapter originate with NCGA Statement 5 (NCGAS 5), *Accounting and Financial Reporting Principles for Lease Agreements of State and Local Governments*. NCGAS 5 directed state and local governments to use the accounting and financial reporting standards of FASB Statement 13 (SFAS 13), *Accounting for Leases*, including subsequent amendments, which is now FASB ASC Section 840. GASB Statement No. 62 (GASBS 62), *Codification of Accounting and Financial Reporting Guidance Contained in Pre–November 30, 1989 FASB and AICPA Pronouncements*, incorporated the substance of existing lease accounting standards into requirements.

NOTE: One important consideration in lease accounting for capital leases for governments concerns leases between a primary government and its component units. The accounting differs for blended component units and discretely presented component units:

- ***Blended component units.*** *Capital leases between the primary government and a blended component unit (or between two component units) should not be reported as capital leases in the financial reporting entity's financial statements. The component unit's debt and assets under the lease are reported as a form of the primary government's debts and assets.*
- ***Discretely presented component units.*** *Capital leases between the primary government and a discretely presented component unit should be accounted for as usual capital leases under GASBS 62 as described in this chapter. However, related receivables and payables should not be combined with other amounts due to or from component units or with capital lease receivables and payables with organizations outside of the reporting entity. In these cases, governments may want to consider elimination of entries for the lease assets and liabilities, since a double counting of these assets and liabilities results from this accounting treatment.*

The accounting for leases is derived from the view that a lease that transfers substantially all of the benefits and risks of ownership should be accounted for as the acquisition of an asset and the incurrence of a liability by the lessee (that is, a capital lease), and as a sale or financing by the lessor (that is, a sales-type, direct-financing, or leveraged lease). Other leases should be accounted for as operating leases—in other words, the rental of property.

NOTE: The reader should refer to Chapter 9, which describes changes to the reporting of amounts related to leases upon the effectiveness of GASB Statement No. 65, Items Previously Reported as Assets and Liabilities. Specifically:

- ***Initial direct costs of operating leases.*** *The lessor should recognize initial direct costs of an operating lease as expense/expenditure in the period incurred.*
- ***Sale-leaseback transactions.*** *The gain or loss on the sale of property that is accompanied by a leaseback of all or any part of the property for all or part of its remaining economic life should be recorded as a deferred inflow of resources or a deferred outflow of resources, respectively, and recognized in a systematic and rational manner over the arrangement in proportion to the recognition of the lease asset if a capital lease, or in proportion to the related gross rental charged to expense/expenditure over the lease term of an operating lease, subject to certain exceptions.*

NOTE: In March 2017, the GASB issued Statement No. 87, Leases (GASBS 87), which will result in significant changes in the accounting for leases. GASBS 87 is similar in concept to a project completed by the FASB, although the accounting requirements are not at all identical. The requirements of GASBS 87 are described later in this chapter. The existing guidance is maintained in the chapter and should be used until implementation of GASBS 87.

GASBS 62 defines a lease as an agreement conveying the right to use capital assets (land and/or depreciable assets) usually for a stated period of time. It includes agreements that, although not nominally identified as leases, meet the above definition. This definition does not include agreements that are contracts for services that do not transfer the right to use capital assets from one contracting party to the other. On the other hand, agreements that do transfer the right to use capital assets meet the definition of a lease for purposes of applying the following provisions even though substantial services by the contractor (lessor) may be called for in connection with the operation or maintenance of such assets. GASBS 62 lease requirements do not apply to lease agreements concerning the rights to explore for or to exploit natural resources such as oil, gas, minerals, and timber. Nor do they apply to licensing agreements for items such as motion picture films, plays, manuscripts, patents, and copyrights.

Lessee Accounting

A lessee accounts for a lease as one of the following:

- Capital lease.
- Operating lease.

If a lease meets any one of the following four classification criteria, it is a capital lease:

1. The lease transfers ownership of the property to the lessee by the end of the lease term. (To be a capital lease, a land lease must meet either this criterion or criterion 2 below.)
2. The lease contains a bargain purchase option. A *bargain purchase option* is a provision allowing the lessee, at its option, to purchase the lease property for a price sufficiently lower than the expected fair value of the property at the date the option becomes exercisable, and that exercise of the option appears, at the inception of the lease, to be reasonably assured.
3. The lease term is equal to 75% or more of the estimated economic life of the leased property. However, if the beginning of the lease term falls within the last 25% of the total estimated economic life of the lease property, including earlier years of use, this criterion should not be used for purposes of classifying the lease. The *estimated economic life* of leased property is defined as the estimated remaining period during which the property is expected to be economically usable by one or more users, with normal repairs and maintenance, for the purpose for which it was intended at the inception of the lease without limitation of the lease term.

NOTE: A good example of the "economic" life of an asset that is being leased would be the life of a personal computer. While the actual hardware may be expected to function perfectly well for ten years, it would be hard to justify an economic life of more than three to five years, given the rapid changes in technology.

---

4. The present value at the beginning of the lease term of the minimum lease payments, excluding executory costs, equals or exceeds 90% of the excess of the fair value of the leased property. If the beginning of the lease term falls within the last 25% of the total estimated economic life of the lease property, including earlier years of use, this criterion should not be used for purposes of classifying the lease.

Minimum lease payments include only those payments that the lessee is obligated to make or can be required to make in connection with the leased property. Contingent rentals should not be considered part of the minimum lease payments. Exhibit 1 defines minimum lease payments in accordance with GASBS 62.

Exhibit 1: Definition of minimum lease payments

In classifying leases as capital and operating and in recording leases, the determination of what are the minimum lease payments under the lease is likely to be an important consideration. Accordingly, GASBS 62 provides some specific guidance in determining what should be considered as part of the minimum payments under a lease.

Recording operating and capital leases by the lessee. The following pages provide an illustration of how a lessee would record both an operating lease and a capital lease. The recording is also affected by whether the fund that is recording the lease is a governmental or a proprietary fund. These differences are also illustrated.

Operating lease. The recording of an operating lease is basically the same for both governmental funds and proprietary funds. The lease is accounted for as any other recurring payment. Remember that an operating lease is treated simply as a rental of property with no assets or liabilities recorded, assuming that the governmental entity makes the lease payments on time and there are no overlapping prepaid periods.

Assume that a government leases a van for a monthly lease payment of $400 for a two-year period. Payments are due on the first day of each month. The lease is determined to be an operating lease, since none of the criteria for capitalizing a lease are met. The following journal entries are recorded by both governmental and proprietary funds:

Rental expenditures/expense—transportation equipment	400	
Cash		400

To record monthly lease payment for van

This is a simplistic example of an operating lease. Later in this chapter situations involving more complex transactions, such as leases with scheduled rent increases, will be discussed.

Capital lease. In recording a capital lease, the governmental entity records an amount equal to the present value of the minimum lease payments. (However, the amount recorded should not exceed the fair value of the property being leased.) Both an asset and a liability are recorded because a capital lease is accounted for as if the lessee had actually purchased the leased property. In other words, it records the leased property on its books as an asset and records the same amount as a liability, reflecting that the substance of the lease transaction is that the lessee is purchasing the asset from and financing the purchase with the lessor.

Modifying the illustration presented above, assume that the government leases the same van for $400 per month, but the life of the lease is five years and after the five-year period the governmental entity can purchase the van from the lessor for $1. In this case, the capital lease criterion that a bargain purchase option exists is met. In addition, the lease is arguably for 75% of the economic life of the van, meeting a second lease capitalization criterion. (Although in this case at least two criteria are met, only one of the four criteria actually needs to be met to require the lease to be accounted for as a capital lease.) Assume that the lessee is unable to determine the implicit interest rate that the lessor used in the lease, and will use its incremental borrowing rate of 6% to perform the present value calculations. The lease term begins June 1 with the first payment due on June 1, with interest paid in advance. The government has a June 30 fiscal year-end.

The $400 monthly payments for five years represent total payments of $24,000 over the life of the lease. The present value of these minimum lease payments using the 6% interest rate is $20,690.

In recording capital leases by a lessee, there are significant differences in the accounts used by governmental funds and proprietary funds. The following illustrates those differences, incorporating the above example.

Governmental fund. In governmental funds, the primary emphasis is on the flow of financial resources, and expenditures are recognized on the modified accrual basis of accounting. Accordingly, if a lease agreement is to be financed from general governmental resources, it must be accounted for and reported on a basis consistent with governmental fund accounting principles.

Capital assets used in governmental activities acquired through lease agreements should be reported only in the government-wide statement of net position at the inception of the agreement in an amount determined by the criteria of SFAS 13 (FASB ASC 840), as amended. A liability in the same amount should be recorded simultaneously in the government-wide statement of net position. When a capital lease represents the acquisition or construction of a general capital asset, it should be reflected as an expenditure and another financing source, consistent with the accounting and financial reporting for general obligation bonded debt. (See Chapter 5 for further information on accounting for general capital asset acquisition by a capital projects fund.) Subsequent governmental fund lease payments are accounted for consistently with the principles for recording debt service on general obligation debt. (See Chapter 6 for accounting for debt service payments by a debt service fund.)

NOTE: While governments may choose to account for general government capital lease transactions in capital projects funds and debt service funds, they are not required to do so unless otherwise required by law, regulation, or contract. For simplicity, the following example assumes that the general government capital lease transactions are accounted for by the general fund. For entries that would be recorded in the government-wide financial statements, see the later description of accounting for proprietary funds.

General Fund

Expenditures—capital leases	20,690	
Other financing sources—capital leases		20,690

To record capital lease transaction

The above entries record the execution of the capital lease itself. The following entries would be recorded subsequent to the signing of the lease. Assume that the only payment made during the fiscal year is one $400 payment, which consists of $100 of interest and $300 of principal (amounts have been rounded for simplicity).

General Fund

Expenditures—capital lease—principal	300	
Expenditures—capital lease—interest	100	
Cash		400

To record payment made on capital lease

NOTE: If the government does not record debt service expenditure by object, the entire $400 could be debited to "Expenditures—capital lease" instead of breaking out the interest and principal portions of the lease payment.

Government-wide financial statements and proprietary funds. All assets and liabilities of proprietary funds are accounted for and reported in the respective proprietary fund. Therefore, transactions for proprietary fund capital leases are accounted for and reported entirely within the individual proprietary fund. Assets and liabilities for capital lease transactions of governmental funds are reported only in the government-wide financial statements.

Using the same illustration as above, the following journal entries would be recorded by the proprietary fund or in the government-wide financial statements for capital leases:

Fixed assets—van	20,690	
Amounts due under capital leases		20,690

To record execution of capital lease agreement

Interest expense	100	
Amounts due under capital leases	300	
Cash		400

To record first month's lease payment

Depreciation expense	345	
Accumulated depreciation—fixed assets—van		345

To record depreciation expense for leased van

NOTE: The depreciation period in the above example was assumed to be the same as the term of the lease. If a lease is capitalized because of the existence of a bargain purchase option or because the title to the asset transfers to the lessee at the end of the lease (criteria 1 and 2 above), the lessee is free to use a depreciation period that is consistent with its normal depreciation policy. Accordingly, if the lessee normally depreciates vans over ten years, it should depreciate the van over a ten-year period. However, if criteria 1 and 2 are not met, and the lease is capitalized because either criterion 3 or 4 is met, then the period for depreciation should be the lease term, rather than the lessee's normal depreciation policy.

Disclosure requirements. Both governmental funds and proprietary funds and the government-wide financial statements are required to provide disclosures about leases. These disclosure requirements are as follows:

(A) For capital leases:

1. The gross amount of assets recorded under capital leases as of the date of each balance sheet presented by major classes according to nature or function. (This information may be combined with comparable information for owned assets.)
2. Future minimum lease payments as of the date of the latest balance sheet presented, in the aggregate and for each of the five succeeding fiscal years, with separate deductions from the total for the amount representing executory costs, and any profit thereon, included in the minimum lease payments and for the amount of the imputed interest necessary to reduce the net minimum lease payments to present value.
3. The total of minimum sublease rentals to be received in the future under noncancelable subleases as of the date of the latest balance sheet presented.
4. Total contingent rentals actually incurred for each period for which an income statement is presented.

5. Assets recorded under capital leases and the accumulated amortization thereon should be separately identified in the lessee's balance sheet or in the footnotes. Similarly, the related obligations should be separately identified in the balance sheet as obligations under capital leases. (For governmental funds, this should be applied as separately identified in the general fixed asset account group and general long-term debt account group.)

(B) For operating leases having initial or remaining noncancelable lease terms in excess of one year:
1. Future minimum rental payments required as of the date of the latest balance sheet presented, in the aggregate and for each of the five succeeding fiscal years.
2. The total of minimum rentals to be received in the future under noncancelable subleases as of the date of the latest balance sheet presented.

(C) For all operating leases: rental expense for each period for which an income statement is presented, with separate amounts for minimum rentals, contingent rentals, and sublease rentals. Rental payments under the leases with terms of a month or less that were not renewed need not be included.

(D) A general description of the lessee's leasing arrangements including, but not limited to, the following:
1. The basis on which contingent rental payments are determined.
2. The existence of terms of renewal or purchase options and escalation clauses.
3. Restrictions imposed by lease agreements, such as those concerning dividends (governmental entities might interpret these as transfers), additional debt, and further leasing.

Example 2 illustrates disclosures that might be used as the basis of a lessee's lease disclosures for both operating and capital leases.

Example 1: Sample disclosure—capital and operating leases

The City leases a significant amount of property and equipment from others. Leased property having elements of ownership is recorded as capital leases in the general fixed asset account group. The related obligations, in amounts equal to the present value of the minimum lease payments payable during the remaining term of the leases, are recorded in the government-wide statement of net position. Leased property not having elements of ownership is classified as operating leases. Both capital and operating lease payments are recorded as expenditures when payable. Total expenditures on such leases for the fiscal year ended June 30, 20X1, were $XXX,XXX.

As of June 30, 20X1, the City (excluding discretely presented component units) had future minimum payments under capital and operating leases with a remaining term in excess of one year as follows:

	Capital	**Operating**	**Total**
Fiscal year ending June 30:			
20X2	$xxx	$xx	$x,xxx
20X3	$xxx	$xx	$x,xxx
20X4	$xxx	$xx	$x,xxx
20X5	$xxx	$xx	$x,xxx
20X6	$xxx	$xx	$x,xxx

	Capital	Operating	Total
20X7–20X11	$xxx	$xx	$x,xxx
20X12–20X16	$xxx	$xx	$x,xxx
Future minimum payments	$xxx	$xx	$x,xxx
Less interest	$xxx		
Present value of future minimum payments	$xxx		

Lessor Accounting

Lessors also classify leases according to whether they are in-substance sales of property or equipment or true rentals of property or equipment. A lessor classifies leases into one of the following categories:

- Operating leases.
- Direct-financing leases.
- Sales-type leases.
- Leveraged leases.

For governmental entities, the two predominant leases are operating leases and direct-financing leases. Sales-type leases arise when there is a manufacturer's profit built into the lease payment. Leveraged leases involve the financing of the lease through a third-party creditor. Both of these types of leases are not common in the leasing activities of governmental entities, but are included in GASBS 62.

The direct-financing lease for a lessor is the equivalent of the capital lease for a lessee. A direct-financing lease transfers substantially all of the risk and rewards of ownership from the lessor to the lessee. In a direct-financing lease, the owner of the property is in substance financing the purchase of the property by the lessee, which is evident from the title of this type of lease.

GASBS 62 requires that a lease be classified as a direct-financing lease when any of the four capitalization criteria (described earlier in the chapter) are met and when both of the following additional criteria are satisfied:

- Collectibility of the minimum future lease payments is reasonably predictable. However, a lessor is not precluded from classifying a lease as a direct-financing lease simply because the receivable is subject to an estimate of uncollectibility based on the experience with groups of similar receivables.
- No important uncertainties surround the amount of nonreimbursable costs yet to be incurred by the lessor under the lease. Important uncertainties might include commitments by the lessor to guarantee performance of the leased property in a manner more extensive than the typical product warranty or to effectively protect the lessee from obsolescence of the leased property. However, the necessity of estimated executory costs to be paid by the lessor does not by itself constitute an important uncertainty for purposes of this criterion.

The lessor's investment in the lease consists of the present value of the minimum lease payments, including any residual values that accrue to the benefit of the lessor and any rental payments guaranteed by a third party not related to the lessor or lessee (similar to a leveraged lease). In determining the present value of the minimum lease payments, the interest rate implicit in the lease is used. This rate is the discount rate that, when applied to the minimum lease payments and the residual value accruing to the benefit of the lessor, causes the aggregate present value at the beginning of the lease term to be equal to the fair value of the leased property to the lessor at the inception of the lease.

NOTE: This sounds more complicated than it is. Simply, it means that a lessor that enters into a direct-financing lease agreement does so at the fair value of the property being leased. Included in the monthly lease payments is an interest factor that reflects the fact that the lessor is receiving the money over time, rather than at once. The interest rate needed to discount the monthly lease payments to arrive at the fair value of the property at the beginning of the lease is the implicit interest rate.

Once the present value of the minimum lease payments is determined, this amount is compared with the carrying amount of the asset that is recorded on the books of the lessor at the time the lease is signed. The difference between the present value of the minimum lease payments and the carrying amount is recorded as deferred income at the time the lease is signed. The amount of deferred income is amortized into income over the lease term, using the effective interest method.

As was seen with accounting for capital leases by lessees, whether the fund recording the lease is a governmental fund or a proprietary fund has a significant effect on how leases, particularly capital leases, are accounted for and reported. The following illustrations of journal entries use the same facts as the examples of accounting by the lessee, but instead are provided by the lessor. One additional assumption is that the asset being leased has a carrying amount on the books of the lessor of $20,000, which is the original cost of $22,000 and accumulated depreciation of $2,000. These amounts are recorded in the general fixed asset account group for governmental funds and on the balance sheet of proprietary funds. In addition, assume that $20,690 is the fair value of the van being leased on the beginning date of the lease.

Operating lease—governmental and proprietary funds. Both governmental and proprietary funds would record the operating lease similarly. The journal entry that would be recorded is as follows:

Cash	400	
Rental income		400

To record rental income from the rental of a van

NOTE: The van still remains recorded in the government-wide statement of net position and the balance sheet of the proprietary fund. Depreciation would continue to be recorded on the asset.

Direct financing lease—governmental funds. In governmental funds, lease receivables and deferred revenues should be used to account for leases receivable when a state or local government is the lessor in a lease situation. Only the portion of lease receivables that represents revenue/other financing sources that are measurable and available should be recognized as revenue/other financing sources in governmental funds. The remainder of the receivable remains deferred. In the government-wide financial statements, the accounting for a direct financing lease would be the same as that described in the next section for proprietary funds.

The following journal entry is recorded at the inception of the lease:

General Fund

Lease payments receivable ($400 monthly for 60 months)	24,000

Deferred revenue—lease principal payments		20,690
Deferred revenue—lease interest payments		3,310

To record execution of direct-financing lease

When the general fund receives the first lease payment of $400, the following journal entry is recorded:

General Fund

Cash	400	
Deferred revenue—lease principal payments	300	
Deferred revenue—lease interest payments	100	
Lease receivable		400
Revenue—lease principal payments		300
Revenue—interest		100

To record receipt of first payment on direct financing lease

Note that the 1994 GAAFR recommends that lease principal payments be reported as revenue, although reporting these payments as other financing sources is acceptable.

There are two factors that need to be considered by governmental funds in recording direct financing leases: initial direct costs and allowance for uncollectible accounts.

Initial direct costs. The governmental entity may incur costs related to the negotiation and execution of the lease, such as legal and accounting costs, credit investigations, and so on. The governmental fund would recognize these costs as expenditures when incurred, with an equal amount of unearned revenue recognized in the same period. Assuming initial direct costs of $250 in this example, the following journal entries would be recorded:

General Fund

Expenditures—lease direct costs	250	
Cash		250

To record initial direct expenditures for lease

Deferred revenue—lease interest payments	250	
Revenue—lease principal payments		250

To record initial direct expenditures for lease

The effect of these entries is to reduce the amount of interest income that will be recognized over the life of the lease, which is appropriate, considering that the net income on the lease is lower because of the $250 of initial direct cost payments. In this example, the implicit interest rate in the lease is thus less than the 6% rate that has been assumed before these direct costs.

Allowance for uncollectible accounts. If the government has experience with similar types of leases or enters into a large number of leases, the government may determine that an allowance for uncollectible lease payments is appropriate. For this lease, assume that an allowance of $200 is deemed appropriate. The following journal entry is recorded:

General Fund

Deferred revenue—lease principal payments	200	
Allowance for uncollectible lease receivables		200

To record an allowance for uncollectible lease receivables

Government-wide financial statements and proprietary funds. Direct-financing leases in the government-wide financial statements and in proprietary funds are recorded in the same way that commercial enterprises would record these leases. One significant difference is that since the asset being leased is already on the balance sheet of the proprietary fund, the amount of deferred revenue to be amortized is much smaller, consisting of the deferred interest income on the lease and the difference between the fair value of the asset leased and the carrying amount of the asset.

The following are sample journal entries considering the above facts:

Proprietary Fund

Lease receivable	24,000	
Accumulated depreciation—van	1,000	
Fixed asset—van		22,000
Deferred revenue—direct financing lease		3,000

To record execution of a direct financing lease for a van

Assuming that the implicit interest rate approximates 6%, the following journal entry is recorded when the first lease payment is received:

Cash	400	
Deferred revenue—direct financing lease	100	
Lease receivable		400
Interest income		100

To record receipt of first month's lease payment on a direct financing lease

For initial direct costs, the amount of the costs paid is recorded as a reduction of the deferred revenue on the lease.

Deferred revenue—direct financing lease	250	
Cash		250

To reduce deferred revenue on lease for initial direct costs

To set up an allowance for uncollectible accounts, the following journal entry would be recorded:

Deferred revenue—direct financing lease	200	
Allowance for uncollectible lease receivable		200

To set up an allowance for uncollectible lease receivable

As can be seen from the above examples, lessors that use proprietary fund accounting use the guidance of GASBS 62 as amended and interpreted in virtually the same manner as commercial enterprises.

As mentioned above, GASBS 62 also includes the distinctions for leveraged and sales-type leases. The following requirements deal with leveraged leases from the standpoint of the lessor.

Leveraged leases. For purposes of applying the requirements of GASBS 62, a leveraged lease is defined as one having all of the following characteristics:

(a) Except for the exclusion of leveraged leases from the definition of a direct financing lease, it otherwise meets that definition. Leases that meet the definition of sales-type leases set forth in paragraph 212b(1) should not be accounted for as leveraged leases but should be accounted for as sales-type leases.

(b) It involves at least three parties: a lessee, a long-term creditor, and a lessor (commonly called the equity participant).

(c) The financing provided by the long-term creditor is nonrecourse as to the general credit of the lessor (although the creditor may have recourse to the specific property leased and the unremitted rentals relating to it). The amount of the financing is sufficient to provide the lessor with substantial leverage in the transaction.

(d) The lessor's net investment, as described below, declines during the early years once the investment has been completed, and rises during the later years of the lease before its final elimination. Such decreases and increases in the net investment balance may occur more than once.

A lease meeting the preceding definition should be accounted for by the lessor using the method described below. A lease not meeting the definition of a leveraged lease should be accounted for by a lessor as another type of lease, as defined earlier in this chapter.

The lessor should record an investment in a leveraged lease net of the nonrecourse debt. The net of the balances of the following accounts should represent the initial and continuing investment in leveraged leases:

(a) Rentals receivable, net of that portion of the rental applicable to principal and interest on the nonrecourse debt.

(b) The estimated residual value of the leased asset. The estimated residual value generally should not exceed the amount estimated at the inception of the lease.

Given the original investment and using the projected cash receipts and disbursements over the term of the lease, the rate of return on the net investment in the years in which it is positive should be computed. The rate is that rate which, when applied to the net investment in the years in which the net investment is positive, will distribute the revenue to those years, and is distinct from the interest rate implicit in the lease. In each year, whether positive or not, the difference between the net cash flow and the amount of revenue recognized, if any, should serve to increase or reduce the net investment balance.

If the projected net cash receipts over the term of the lease are less than the lessor's initial investment, the deficiency should be recognized as a loss at the inception of the lease. Likewise, if at any time during the lease term the application of the method described above would result in a loss being allocated to future years, that loss should be recognized immediately. This situation might arise in cases in which one of the important assumptions affecting revenue is revised, as described in the following paragraph.

Any estimated residual value and all other important assumptions affecting estimated total revenue from the lease should be reviewed at least annually. If during the lease term the estimate of the residual value is determined to be excessive and the decline in the residual value is judged to be other than temporary, or if the revision of another important assumption changes the estimated total revenue from the lease, the rate of return and the allocation of revenue to positive investment years should be recalculated from the inception of the lease using the revised assumption. The accounts constituting the net investment balance should be adjusted to conform to the recalculated balances, and the change in the net investment should be recognized as a gain or loss in the year in which the assumption is changed. An upward adjustment of the estimated residual value should not be made.

When leveraged leasing is a significant part of the lessor's operations, the components of the net investment balance in leveraged leases should be disclosed in the notes to the financial statements.

Sales-type leases. Sales-type leases are leases that give rise to gain or loss. GASBS 62 provides the following accounting guidance to be followed by lessors:

(a) The minimum lease payments (net of amounts, if any, included therein with respect to executor costs such as insurance and maintenance to be paid by the lessor, together with any gain thereon) plus the unguaranteed residual value accruing to the benefit of the lessor should be recorded as the gross investment in the lease.

(b) The difference between the gross investment in the lease in (a) above and the sum of the present values of the two components of the gross investment should be recorded as a liability. The discount rate to be used in determining the present values should be the interest rate implicit in the lease. The net investment in the lease should consist of the gross investment less the related liability. The liability should be recognized as revenue over the lease term so as to produce a constant periodic rate of return on the net investment in the lease. The net investment in the lease should be subject to the same considerations as other assets in classification as current or noncurrent assets in a classified statement of net position. Contingent rentals should be included in the flows statement when accruable.

(c) The present value of the minimum lease payments (net of executor costs, including any gain thereon), computed at the interest rate implicit in the lease, should be recorded as the sales price. The cost or carrying amount, if different, of the leased property, plus any initial direct costs, less the present value of the unguaranteed residual value accruing to the benefit of the lessor, computed at the interest rate implicit in the lease, should be recognized in the same period.

(d) The estimated residual value should be reviewed at least annually. If the review results in a lower estimate than had been previously established, a determination should be made as to whether the decline in estimated residual value is other than temporary. If the decline in estimated residual value is judged to be other than temporary, the accounting for the transaction should be revised using the changed estimate. The resulting reduction in the net investment should be recognized as a loss in the period in which the estimate is changed. An upward adjustment of the estimated residual value should not be made.

(e) In leases containing a residual guarantee or a penalty for failure to renew the lease at the end of the lease term, following the method of amortization described in (b) above will result in a balance of minimum lease payments receivable at the end of the lease term that will equal the amount of the guarantee or penalty at that date. In the event that a renewal or other extension of the lease term renders the guarantee or penalty inoperative, the existing balances of the minimum lease payments receivable and the estimated residual value should be adjusted for the changes resulting from the revised agreement, subject to the limitation on the residual value imposed by (d) above, and the net adjustment should be charged or credited to a liability.

(f) Except for a change in the provisions of a lease that results from a refunding by the lessor of tax-exempt debt, including an advance refunding, in which the perceived economic advantages of the refunding are passed through to the lessee by a change in the provisions of the lease agreement and the revised agreement is classified as a direct financing lease, a change in the provisions of a lease, a renewal or extension of an existing lease, and a termination of a lease prior to the expiration of the lease term should be accounted for as follows:

1. If the provisions of a lease are changed in a way that changes the amount of the remaining minimum lease payments and the change either does not give rise to a new agreement or does give rise to a new agreement but such agreement is classified as a direct financing lease, the balance of the minimum lease payments receivable and the estimated residual value, if affected, should be adjusted to reflect the change, subject to the limitation on the residual value imposed by subparagraph (d) above, and the net adjustment should be charged or credited to a liability. If the change in the lease provisions gives rise to a new agreement classified as an operating lease, the remaining net investment should be removed from the accounts, the leased asset should be recorded as an asset at the lower of its original cost, present fair value, or present carrying amount, and the net adjustment should be charged to revenue in the period. The new lease should thereafter be accounted for as any other operating lease.
2. Except when a guarantee or penalty is rendered inoperative as described in (e) above, a renewal or an extension of an existing lease should be accounted for as follows:
   (a) If the renewal or extension is classified as a direct financing lease, it should be accounted for as described in subparagraph f(1) above.
   (b) If the renewal or extension is classified as an operating lease, the existing lease should continue to be accounted for as a sales-type lease to the end of its original term, and the renewal or extension should be accounted for as any other operating lease.
   (c) If a renewal or extension that occurs at or near the end of the term of the existing lease is classified as a sales-type lease, the renewal or extension should be accounted for as a sales-type lease.
3. A termination of the lease should be accounted for by removing the net investment from the accounts, recording the leased asset at the lower of its original cost, present fair value, or present carrying amount, and the net adjustment should be charged to revenue in the period.

If prior to the expiration of the lease term a change in the provisions of a lease results from the refunding by the lessor of tax-exempt debt, including an advance refunding, in which the perceived economic advantages of the refunding are passed through to the lessee and the revised agreement is classified as a direct financing lease by the lessor, the change should be accounted for as follows:

(a) If a change in the provisions of a lease results from a refunding of tax-exempt debt, including an advance refunding that results in a defeasance of debt, the lessor should adjust the balance of the minimum lease payments receivable and the estimated residual value. The adjustment of the liability should be the amount required to adjust the net investment in the lease to the sum of the present values of the two components of the gross investment based on the interest rate applicable to the revised lease agreement. The combined adjustment resulting from applying the two preceding sentences should be recognized as a gain or loss over the remaining life of the old debt or the life of the new debt, whichever is shorter.

(b) If a change in the provisions of a lease results from an advance refunding that results in a defeasance of debt, the lessor should systematically recognize, as revenue, any reimbursements to be received from the lessee for costs related to the debt to be refunded, such as unamortized discount or issue costs or a call premium, over the remaining life of the old debt or the life of the new debt, whichever is shorter.

Disclosure requirements. There are a number of disclosure requirements contained in GASBS 62 that must be made, where applicable, by governmental entities that are lessors. When leasing is a significant part of a lessor's activities, the following information with respect to leases should be disclosed in the financial statements or the footnotes to the financial statements:

(A) For direct financing leases:

1. The components of the net investment in the leases as of the date of each balance sheet presented:
   (a) Future minimum lease payments to be received, with separate deductions for (1) amounts representing executory costs, included in the minimum leases payments and (2) the accumulated allowance for uncollectible minimum lease payments receivable.
   (b) The unguaranteed residual values accruing to the benefit of the lessor.
   (c) The amount of initial direct costs.
   (d) The amount of unearned income.
2. Future minimum lease payments to be received for each of the five succeeding fiscal years as of the date of the latest balance sheet presented.
3. Total contingent rentals included in revenue for each period for which an operating statement is presented.

(B) For operating leases:

1. The cost and carrying amount, if different, of property on lease or held for leasing by major classes of property according to nature or function, and the amount of accumulated depreciation (where applicable) in total as of the date of the latest balance sheet presented.
2. Minimum rentals on noncancelable leases as of the date of the latest balance sheet presented, in the aggregate and for each of the five succeeding fiscal years.
3. Total contingent rentals included in income for each period for which an operating statement is presented.

(C) A general description of the lessor's leasing arrangements.

Exhibit 2 provides a sample footnote disclosure that might be used by a governmental entity that is a lessor with both direct financing and operating leases.

Exhibit 2: Sample footnote disclosure by lessor with both direct financing and operating leases

The City leases certain City-owned property to others for use as ports and terminals. These leases are classified as direct-financing leases and expire at various intervals over the next 20 years.

The following are the components of the City's net investment in direct financing leases as of June 30, 20X1 (when a balance sheet for the prior year is presented, this information would be presented for both years):

Total minimum lease payments to be received	$xxx,xxx
Less amounts representing executory costs	x,xxx
Minimum lease payments receivable	$xxx,xxx
Less allowance for uncollectible lease payments	x,xxx
Net minimum lease payments receivable	$xxx,xxx

Estimated residual values of lease property	x,xxx
	xxx,xxx
Less unearned income	xx,xxx
Net investment in direct financing leases	$ xx,xxx

Minimum lease payments do not include contingent rentals that may be received under the lease contracts only if certain operating conditions are achieved. Contingent rentals in fiscal year ended June 30, 20X1, amounted to $X,XXX.

At June 30, 20X1, minimum lease payments for each of the five succeeding fiscal years are asfollows:

Fiscal Year	*Amount*
20X2	$x,xxx
20X3	x,xxx
20X4	x,xxx
20X5	x,xxx
20X6	x,xxx
20X7-20X11	x,xxx
20X12-20X16	x,xxx
Total minimum lease payments	$x,xxx

The City also leases City-owned property to others for use as marketplaces. Total rental revenue on these operating leases for the fiscal year ended June 30, 20X1, was $X,XXX. The City's investment in property on operating leases consisted of buildings of $XX,XXX, less accumulated depreciation of $X,XXX, which amounts are recorded in the City's general fixed asset account group.

The City may receive contingent rentals on these operating leases only if certain operating conditions are achieved. Contingent rentals in fiscal year ended June 30, 20X1, amounted to $X,XXX.

At June 30, 20X1, minimum lease payments for each of the five succeeding fiscal years are asfollows:

Fiscal Year	*Amount*
20X2	$x,xxx
20X3	x,xxx
20X4	x,xxx
20X5	x,xxx
20X6	x,xxx
20X7-20X11	x,xxx
20X12-20X16	x,xxx
Total future rental payments	$x,xxx

OTHER LEASING ISSUES FOR GOVERNMENTAL ENTITIES

In addition to the specific considerations for accounting and financial reporting for leases that pertain to governmental entities that are lessees and lessors, there are two additional cross-cutting matters related to leasing activities that need to be considered:

- Operating leases with scheduled rent increases.
- Fiscal funding and cancellation clauses.

These topics, followed by the topic of GASB Statement No. 87, *Leases*, are addressed in the remaining sections of this chapter.

Operating Leases with Scheduled Rent Increases

GASB Statement No. 13 (GASBS 13), *Accounting for Operating Leases with Scheduled Rent Increases*, establishes accounting requirements for those types of leases that differ from the accounting and financial reporting for those by commercial organizations. GASBS 13's requirements for operating leases with scheduled rent increases apply regardless of whether a governmental or proprietary fund is used to account for the lease. The requirements apply to all state and local governmental entities, including public benefit corporations and authorities, public employee retirement systems, governmental utilities, hospitals, other health care providers, colleges, and universities.

Scheduled rent increases are fixed by contract. The increases take place with the passage of time and are not contingent on future events. The increases in rent may be based, for example, on such factors as anticipated increases in costs or anticipated appreciation of property values, although the amount of the increase is specified in the lease agreement. Scheduled rent increases are not contingent rentals, in which the changes in rent payments are based on changes in future specific economic factors, such as future sales volume or future inflation.

Measurement criteria. Transactions that arise from operating leases with scheduled rent increases should be measured based on the terms and conditions of the lease contract when the pattern of payment requirements, including the increases, is systematic and rational.

NOTE: For example, a governmental entity leases office space for a three-year period in which the rents are as follows: year 1, $1,000; year 2, $1,100; year 3, $1,200. The governmental entity would recognize an expenditure/expense of $1,000 in year 1, $1,100 in year 2, and $1,200 in year 3. This is different from the requirements of commercial accounting, where the total payments under the lease ($3,300) would be recognized on a straight-line basis over the life of the lease, or in this case $1,100 in each year.

In applying this requirement, GASBS 13 provides the following examples of payment schedules that are considered systematic and rational:

- Lease agreements specify scheduled rent increases over the lease term that are intended to cover (and are reasonably associated with) economic factors relating to the property, such as the anticipated effects of property value appreciation or increases in costs due to factors such as inflation. Rent increases because of property value appreciation may result from the maturation of individual properties as well as from general appreciation of the market. Lower lease property values (and rents) may exist, for example, when a new office building has only a few tenants, but more are expected in the future.
- Lease payments are required to be made on a basis that represents the time pattern in which the lease property is available for use by the lessee.

In some cases, an operating lease with scheduled rent increases contains payment requirements in a particular year or years that are artificially low when viewed in the context of earlier or later payment requirements. This situation may take place, for example, when a lessor provides a rent reduction or rent holiday that is in substance a financing arrangement between the lessor and the lessee. Another example provided by GASBS 13 is where a lessor provides a lessee with reduced rents as an inducement to enter into the lease. In this case, GASBS 13 stipulates that the operating lease transactions be measured using either of the following methods:

1. **The straight-line method.** This is the method described above that is normally used by commercial enterprises in accounting for all operating leases with scheduled rent increases. The periodic rental expenditure/expense and rental revenue are equal to the total amount of the lease payments divided by the total number of periodic payments to be made under the lease. Continuing with the example provided above, the lessor would record the following entries in each of the three years of the lease by the lessor:

Year 1		
Cash	1,000	
Lease receivable	100	
Lease revenue		1,100
Year 2		
Cash	1,100	
Lease revenue		1,100
Year 3		
Cash	1,200	
Lease revenue		1,100
Lease receivable		100

2. **The fair value method.** The operating lease transactions may be measured based on the estimated fair value of the rental. The difference between the actual lease payments and the fair value of the lease property should be accounted for using the interest method, whereby an interest amount (whether expenditure/expense or revenue) is recorded at a constant rate based on the amount of the outstanding accrued lease receivable or payable. However, if the fair value of the rental is not reasonably estimable, the straight-line method should be used.

In applying these requirements for using the straight-line and estimated fair value methods, there is a distinction in the accounting between governmental funds and proprietary funds:

- Entities that report operating leases with scheduled rent increases in proprietary and similar trust funds should recognize rental revenue or expense each period as it accrues over the lease term, as described above for the straight-line and estimated fair value methods. This would apply to the government-wide financial statements as well.
- Entities that report operating leases with scheduled rent increases in governmental funds should recognize rental revenue or expenditures each period using the modified accrual basis of accounting. That is, the amount recognized as rental revenue (either on a straight-line basis or on an estimated fair value basis) should be recognized as revenue to the extent that it is available to finance expenditures of the fiscal period. Accrued receivables should be reported in the fund and offset by deferred revenue for the portion not yet recognized as revenue. The lessee should recognize expenditures and fund liabilities to the extent that the amounts are payable with expendable, available financial resources. Any remaining accrued liabilities calculated in accordance with either the straight-line basis or the estimated fair value basis should be reported in the government-wide financial statements.

Fiscal Funding and Cancellation Clauses

In applying the criteria of GASBS 62 to lease agreements of state and local governments, legal restrictions of governments must be considered. One type of legal restriction relates to debt limitation and debt incurrence that prohibits governments from entering into obligations extending beyond the current budget year. Because of this type of restriction, a governmental lease agreement usually contains a clause (called either a *fiscal funding clause* or a *cancellation clause*) that permits the governmental lessee to terminate the agreement on an annual basis if funds are not appropriated to make required payments.

> *A cancelable lease, such as a lease containing a fiscal funding clause [a clause that generally provides that the lease is cancelable if the legislature or other funding authority does not appropriate the funds necessary for the governmental unit to fulfill its obligations under the lease agreement] be evaluated to determine whether the uncertainty of possible lease cancellation is a remote contingency ... a lease which is cancelable (1) only upon occurrence of some remote contingency ... shall be considered noncancelable for purposes of this definition.*

The economic substance of most lease agreements with fiscal funding clauses is that they are essentially long-term contracts, with only a remote possibility that the lease will be canceled because of the fiscal funding clause. Accordingly, fiscal funding clauses should not prohibit lease agreements from being capitalized. If a lease agreement meets all other capitalization criteria except for the noncancelable criterion, the likelihood of the lease being canceled must be evaluated, and if the possibility of cancellation is remote, the lease should be capitalized.

GASB Statement No. 87—*Leases*

In March 2017, the GASB issued Statement No. 87, *Leases* (GASBS 87), which will result in significant changes in the accounting for leases. GASBS 87 is similar in concept to a project completed by the FASB, although the accounting requirements are not at all identical.

The following is a summary of the provisions of GASBS 87:

Definition of a Lease

A lease is defined as a contract that conveys control of the right to use another entity's nonfinancial asset (the underlying asset) as specified in the contract for a period of time in an exchange or exchange-like transaction. Examples of nonfinancial assets include buildings, land, vehicles, and equipment. Any contract that meets this definition would be accounted for under the proposed leases guidance, unless specifically excluded.

Lease Term

The lease term is defined as the period during which a lessee has a noncancelable right to use an underlying asset, plus the following periods, if applicable, covered by a lessee's or lessor's option to:

(a) Extend the lease if it is reasonably certain, based on all relevant factors, that the lessee will exercise that option.
(b) Terminate the lease if it is reasonably certain, based on all relevant factors, that the lessee will not exercise that option.

A fiscal funding or cancellation clause would be considered in determining the lease term only when it is reasonably certain that the clause will be exercised.

Lessees and lessors would reassess the lease term only if one or more of the following occur:

(a) The lessee or lessor elects to exercise an option even though it was previously determined that it was reasonably certain that the lessee or lessor would not exercise that option.
(b) The lessee or lessor elects to not exercise an option even though it was previously determined that it was reasonably certain that the lessee or lessor would exercise that option.
(c) An event specified in the lease contract that requires an extension or termination of the lease takes place.

Lessee Accounting

A lessee would recognize a lease liability and a lease asset at the beginning of a lease, unless the lease is a short-term lease or transfers ownership of the underlying asset. The lease liability would be measured at the present value of payments expected to be made for the lease term. The lease asset would be measured at the amount of the initial measurement of the lease liability, plus any payments made to the lessor at or before the beginning of the lease and certain indirect costs.

A lessee would reduce the lease liability as payments are made and recognize an outflow of resources for interest on the liability. The lessee would amortize the lease asset in a systematic and rational manner over the shorter of the lease term or the useful life of the underlying asset. The notes to the financial statements would include a description of leasing arrangements, the amount of lease assets recognized, and a schedule of future lease payments to be made.

Lessor Accounting

A lessor would recognize a lease receivable and a deferred inflow of resources at the beginning of a lease, with certain exceptions (including a short-term lease or a lease that transfers ownership of the underlying asset). A lessor would not derecognize the asset underlying the lease. The lease receivable would be measured at the present value of lease payments expected to be received for the lease term. The deferred inflow of resources would be measured at the value of the lease receivable plus any payments received at or prior to the beginning of the lease that relate to future periods.

A lessor would recognize interest revenue on the lease receivable and an inflow of resources (for example, revenue) from the deferred inflow of resources in a systematic and rational manner over the term of the lease. The notes to the financial statements would include a description of leasing arrangements and the total amount of revenue recognized from leases.

NOTE: This is a significant departure from the FASB standard, which does not significantly change lessor accounting for what are currently referred to as operating leases.

Contracts with Multiple Components and Contract Combinations

Generally, a government would account for the lease and nonlease components of a lease as separate contracts. If a lease involves multiple underlying assets, lessees and lessors generally would account for each underlying asset as a separate lease contract. To allocate consideration required under the contract to different components, lessees and lessors would use contract prices for individual components if reasonable based on observable stand-alone prices. Under certain circumstances, multiple components in a lease contract would be accounted for as a single lease unit. Contracts that are entered into at or near the same time with the same counterparty and meet certain criteria would be considered part of the same lease contract and would be evaluated in accordance with the guidance on contracts with multiple components.

NOTE: Nonlease components might involve maintenance contracts that are part of a rental payment.

Short-Term Leases

A short-term lease would be defined as a lease that, at the beginning of the lease, has a maximum possible term under the contract of 12 months or less, including any options to extend, regardless of its probability of being exercised. Lessees and lessors would recognize short-term lease payments as outflows of resources or inflows of resources, respectively, based on the payment provisions of the contract.

Lease Terminations and Modifications

An amendment to a lease contract would be considered a lease modification, unless the lessee's right to use the underlying asset decreases, in which case it would be a partial termination. A lease termination would be accounted for by reducing the carrying values of the lease liability and lease asset by a lessee, or the lease receivable and deferred inflow of resources by the lessor, with any difference being recognized as a gain or loss. A lease modification generally would be accounted for by remeasuring the lease liability and adjusting the related lease asset by a lessee, or remeasuring the lease receivable and adjusting the related deferred inflow of resources by a lessor.

Subleases and Leaseback Transactions

Subleases would be treated as transactions separate from the original lease. The original lessee that becomes the lessor in a sublease would account for the original lease and the sublease as separate transactions as a lessee and lessor, respectively.

A transaction would qualify for sale-leaseback accounting only if it includes a qualifying sale. Otherwise, it is a borrowing. The sale and leaseback portions of a transaction would be accounted for as separate sale and lease transactions, except that any difference between the carrying value of the capital asset that was sold and the net proceeds from the sale would be reported as a deferred inflow of resources or a deferred outflow of resources and recognized over the term of the leaseback.

A lease-leaseback transaction would be accounted for as a net transaction. The gross amounts of each portion of the transaction would be disclosed.

Effective Date and Transition

The requirements of GASBS 87 are effective for reporting periods beginning after December 15, 2019. Earlier application is permitted. Leases would be recognized and measured using the facts and circumstances that exist at the beginning of the period of implementation (or, if applied to earlier periods, the beginning of the earliest period restated). However, lessors would not restate the assets underlying their existing sales-type or direct financing leases. Any residual assets for those leases would become the carrying values of the underlying assets.

SUMMARY

The accounting and financial reporting for lease agreements is an area that usually presents an interesting challenge to financial statement preparers. This challenge is due to the diversity in the types and nature of lease agreements that must be accounted for, as well as the complexity of the accounting rules that must be applied. The financial statement preparer for a governmental entity must be familiar with the requirements of commercial accounting for leases in order to effectively and correctly apply this guidance to lease agreements that are entered into by a governmental entity.

20 NONEXCHANGE TRANSACTIONS

The term *nonexchange transaction* may sound to some as being some esoteric type of transaction that might not be frequently encountered, so governmental financial statement preparers may at first think that this chapter will not have broad applicability.

However, once it is understood that taxes are nonexchange transactions, it becomes clear that nonexchange transactions include accounting and financial reporting requirements for a significant part of a governmental entity's typical transactions.

GASB Statement 33 (GASBS 33), *Accounting and Financial Reporting for Nonexchange Transactions*, divides all transactions into two categories:

1. Exchange transactions, in which each party to a transaction receives and gives up something of essentially the same value.
2. Nonexchange transactions, in which a government gives or receives value without directly receiving or giving something equal in value in the exchange.

As will be more fully described below, nonexchange transactions therefore include very significant items of revenues and expenditures for governmental activities, such as taxes (including property, sales, and income taxes) as well as revenues provided by federal and state aid programs.

NOTE: The GASB issued this Statement because there was very little professional guidance in existence for recognizing nonexchange transactions on an accrual basis, which the GASB correctly anticipated was needed when the accrual basis of accounting is used on a government-wide perspective under the GASBS 34 financial reporting model. In addition, the GASB believed that the existing guidance for nonexchange transactions that are recorded on a modified accrual basis (which will continue at the fund level under the new financial reporting model) could also use some clarification and standardization.

Classes of Nonexchange Transactions

GASBS 33 identifies four classes of nonexchange transactions:

1. *Derived tax revenues*. These are transactions that result from assessments imposed by governments on exchange transactions. Included in this class are personal and corporate income taxes and sales taxes.

2. *Imposed nonexchange revenues.* These are transactions that result from assessments by governments on nongovernmental entities (including individuals) other than assessments on exchange transactions. Included in this class are property taxes, fines and penalties, and property forfeitures.
3. *Government-mandated nonexchange transactions.* These are transactions that occur when one government (including the federal government) at one level provides resources to a government at another level and requires that government use them for a specific purpose (referred to as purpose restriction). The provider may also require that the resources be used within a specific time (referred to as a time restriction). Included in this class are federal aid programs that state and local governments are mandated to perform and state programs that local governments are mandated to perform. GASBS 33 identifies two significant characteristics of transactions in this class of nonexchange transactions:
   (a) A government mandates that a government at another level (the recipient government) must perform or facilitate a particular program in accordance with the providing government's enabling legislation, and provides resources for that purpose.
   (b) There is a fulfillment of eligibility requirements (including time requirements) in order for a transaction to occur.
4. *Voluntary nonexchange transactions.* These are transactions that result from legislative or contractual agreements, other than exchanges, entered into willingly by two or more parties. Included in this class are certain grants and entitlements and donations by nongovernmental entities. While these transactions are not imposed on the provider or the recipient, the fulfillment of purpose restrictions, eligibility requirements, and time requirements may be necessary for a transaction to occur.

Accounting and Financial Reporting Requirements

GASBS 33 has different accounting standards for revenue recognition under the accrual basis of accounting and the modified accrual basis of accounting. Under either basis of accounting, recognition of nonexchange transactions in the financial statements is required unless the transactions are not measurable (reasonably estimable) or are not probable (likely to occur). Transactions that are not recognized because they are not measurable should be disclosed.

Accrual-basis requirements. In using the guidance of GASBS 33 for nonexchange transactions that are accounted for under the accrual basis of accounting, it is important to note that there are different standards for time requirements and purpose restrictions in determining whether a transaction has occurred:

- Time requirements—When a nonexchange transaction is government mandated or voluntary, compliance with time requirements is necessary for the transaction to occur. Time requirements must be met for a provider to record a liability or expense and for a recipient to record a revenue and a receivable. For imposed nonexchange transactions, a government should recognize a receivable when it has an enforceable legal claim to the resources, but should not recognize revenue until the period when the use of the resources is required or first permitted.

- Purpose restrictions govern what a recipient is allowed to do with the resources once it receives them. Recognition of assets, liabilities, revenues, and expenses should not be delayed because of purpose restrictions. An exception arises in a grant or agreement in which the resource provider will not provide resources unless the recipient has incurred allowable expenditures under the grant or agreement. This is an eligibility requirement. In that case, there is no reward (i.e., no asset, liability, revenue, or expense) recognition until the recipient expends the resources. (This exception relates to what was once referred to as *expenditure-driven revenue*.) Cash or other assets provided in advance should be reported as advances by providers and as deferred revenues by recipients.

NOTE: Particular attention should be paid to government-mandated nonexchange transactions as to time requirements, particularly when a purpose restriction would not delay the recognition of revenue. This type of nonexchange transaction includes grants from one level of government to another. Many times, grant programs are awarded based upon the fiscal year of the grantor government. For example, let us say that a state government is going to make a grant to a city within the state. The state's fiscal year-end is March 31 and the city's is June 30. If there are no purpose restrictions (such as eligibility requirements) that would cause the government to not be able to be entitled to the resources, a grant made for the state fiscal year beginning April 1 would be recognized in full by the government in the fiscal year that ends the immediately following June 30.

In addition to these general requirements for the accrual basis of accounting, GASBS 33 provides specific guidance for each class of nonexchange transaction:

- *Derived tax revenues*. Assets from derived tax revenues are recognized as revenue in the period when the exchange transaction on which the tax is imposed occurs or when the resources are received, whichever occurs first. Resources received by a government in anticipation of an assessable exchange transaction should be reported as deferred revenue until the period of the exchange.
- *Imposed nonexchange revenues*. Assets from imposed nonexchange revenue transactions are to be recognized in the period when an enforceable legal claim to the assets arises or when the resources are received, whichever occurs first. For property taxes, this is generally (but not always) the date when the government has a right to place a lien on the property (the lien date).

  Revenues from imposed nonexchange revenue transactions should be recognized in the same period that the assets are recognized, unless the enabling legislation includes time requirements. If so, the government should report the resources as deferred revenues until the time requirements are met. This means that revenues from property taxes would be recognized in the period for which the taxes are levied, even if the lien date or the due date for payment occurs in a different period.

NOTE: The GASB issued an amendment to GASBS 33 to address a potential problem in applying this Statement in situations where a government shares its own derived tax revenues or imposed nonexchange transactions with other governments. This amendment, issued in the form of GASB Statement 36, Recipient Reporting for Certain Shared Nonexchange Revenues—An Amendment of GASBS 33, is discussed later in this chapter.

- *Government-mandated nonexchange transactions and voluntary nonexchange transactions.* GASBS 33 provides that a transaction for these two classes of transactions does not occur (other than the provision of cash in advance) and should not be recognized until all eligibility requirements are met. In other words, the provider has not incurred a liability and the recipient does not have a receivable, and recognition of revenues and expenses for resources received or provided in advance should be deferred.

NOTE: The reader should refer to Chapter 9, which describes the reporting of amounts related to government-mandated and voluntary nonexchange transactions on the effectiveness of GASB Statement No. 65, Items Previously Reported as Assets and Liabilities.

For government-mandated nonexchange transactions and voluntary nonexchange transactions, resources transmitted before the eligibility requirements are met (excluding time requirements) should be reported as assets by the provider and as liabilities by the recipient. Resources received or recognized as receivable before time requirements are met, but after all other eligibility requirements have been met, should be reported as a deferred outflow of resources by the provider and a deferred inflow of resources by the recipient. GASBS 65 points out that recognition of assets and revenues should not be delayed pending completion of purely routine requirements, such as the filing of clients for allowable costs under a reimbursement program.

The GASB issued GASB Statement 36 (GASBS 36), *Recipient Reporting for Certain Shared Nonexchange Revenues—An Amendment of GASB Statement 33*, to provide a technical correction of a requirement contained in GASBS 33. There are a number of circumstances in which a government may share its revenues with another government. Under GASBS 33 as originally issued, a resource-providing government and a recipient government may have recognized these revenues at different times. GASBS 36 supersedes paragraph 28 of GASBS 33 to eliminate this potential discrepancy. Both the resource-providing government and the recipient government should comply with the requirements of GASBS 33, as amended, for voluntary or government-mandated nonexchange transactions, as appropriate. Because some recipient governments receive these shared revenues through a continuing appropriation, they may rely on periodic notification by the provider government of the accrual-basis information necessary for compliance. If the resource-providing government does not notify the recipient government in a timely manner, the recipient government should use a reasonable estimate of the amount to be accrued. In this instance before amendment, GASBS 33 would have called upon the recipient government to record these revenues on a basis of cash collections instead of using an estimate.

The eligibility requirements are specified by GASBS 33 to comprise one or more of the following:

1. The recipient (and secondary recipients, if applicable) has the characteristics specified by the provider.
2. If specified, the time requirements specified by the provider have been met (that is, the period when resources are required to be used or when use is first permitted has begun). If the provider is a nongovernmental entity and does not specify a period, the applicable period is the first in which use is permitted. If the provider is a government and does not specify a period, the following requirements apply:
   (a) The applicable period for both the provider and recipients is the provider's fiscal year and begins on the first day of that year. The entire amount of the provider's award should be recognized at that time by the recipient as well as the provider.
   (b) If the provider has a biennial budgetary process, each year of the biennium should be considered a separate period, with proportional allocation of the total resources

provided or to be provided for the biennium, unless the provider specifies a different allocation.

3. The provider offers resources on a reimbursement basis, the related legislative or contractual requirements stipulate that the provider will reimburse the recipient for allowable expenditures, and the recipient has made allowable expenditures under the applicable program.
4. The provider's offer of resources is contingent on a specified action of the recipient and that action has occurred (applies only to voluntary nonexchange transactions).

Recipients should recognize assets and revenues from government-mandated or voluntary nonexchange transactions when all applicable eligibility requirements are met. If private donations to a government meet the above criteria, including promises to give, they should be recognized in the financial statements of the government.

Modified accrual basis. The preceding discussion describes the proposed transaction recognition criteria using the accrual basis of accounting. GASBS 33 also addresses revenue recognition using the modified accrual basis of accounting. Revenues from nonexchange transactions should be recognized in the accounting period when they become measurable and available. While this is consistent with current practice (except for the elimination of the "due date" criteria under GASBI 5, *Property Tax Revenue Recognition in Governmental Funds*), GASBS 33 provides the following guidance for each of the four classes of nonexchange transactions:

1. *Derived tax revenues.* Recipients should recognize revenues in the period when the underlying exchange transaction has occurred and the resources are available.
2. *Imposed nonexchange revenues—property taxes.* The guidance of GASBI 5 should be applied, which is current GAAP.
3. *Imposed nonexchange revenues—other than property taxes.* Revenues should be recognized in the period when an enforceable legal claim has arisen and the resources are available.
4. *Government-mandated nonexchange transactions and voluntary nonexchange transactions.* Revenues should be recognized in the period when all applicable eligibility requirements have been met and the resources are available.

NOTE: The reader should refer to Chapter 9, which describes changes to the reporting of amounts related to imposed nonexchange transactions upon the effectiveness of GASB Statement No. 65, Items Previously Reported as Assets and Liabilities.

For imposed nonexchange transactions deferred inflows of resources should be recognized when resources are received or recognized as a receivable before (1) the period for which property taxes are levied or (2) the period when resources are required to be used or when use is first permitted for all other imposed nonexchange revenues in which the enabling legislation includes time requirements. This will change the terminology and financial statement display of the journal entries presented below, as "deferred revenues" will be replaced with deferred inflows of resources.

Some examples of how some of the more common resources of governments would be recorded follow.

Property Taxes

Property taxes represent a significant source of revenue for many governments, particularly local governments. These governments, therefore, must make sure that they apply governmental accounting principles appropriately in reporting property tax revenues.

Property taxes recorded in a governmental fund should be accounted for as an imposed nonexchange revenue using the modified accrual basis. When a property tax assessment is made, it is to finance the budget of a particular period, meaning that the property taxes are intended to provide funds for the expenditures of that particular budget period. The revenue produced from any property tax assessment should be recognized in the fiscal period for which it is levied, provided that the "available" criterion of the modified accrual basis of accounting is met. (*Available* means that the property taxes are due to the government or past due and receivable within the current period, and are collected within the current period or expected to be collected soon enough thereafter to be used to pay current liabilities.) Property taxes that are due or past due must be collected within 60 days after the period for which they were levied. For example, if property taxes are levied for a fiscal year that ends on June 30, 20X1, property taxes that were assessed and due for this period (and prior periods) can be recognized as revenue as long as they are collected by August 29, 20X1.

NOTE: As a practical matter, some governments find that it is easier to use the two months following year-end for accruing this revenue, rather than a strict interpretation of 60 days. These governments find that their monthly closing process facilitates the recording of these revenue accruals, rather than attempting to cut off one or two days before the actual month end.

If unusual circumstances justify a period of greater than 60 days, the government should disclose the length of the period and the circumstances that justify its use. For example, in unusual circumstances, a government may be able to demonstrate that property taxes received after 60 days would be available to pay current liabilities if the current liabilities will be paid sometime after 60 days after year-end. Thus, there are two criteria that must be met before property tax revenue is to be recognized:

1. The property taxes are levied to finance the expenditures of the budget period reported.
2. The collections of these property taxes must take place no later than 60 days after the end of the reported period.

The GASB issued Interpretation 5 (GASBI 5), *Property Tax Revenue Recognition in Governmental Funds*, which eliminated the former criteria that the property taxes must be due or past due within the reported period in order to be recognized.

In recording property taxes, there is a difference as to when a receivable is recorded for property tax revenue and when the related revenue is recognized. A receivable should be recorded on the balance sheet for property tax receivables (net of estimated uncollectible property taxes receivable) on the date that the property taxes are levied. To the extent that property taxes receivable exceed the amount of revenue that may be recognized under the "available" criterion, the difference should be recorded as deferred revenue. Accordingly, revenue should only be recognized for the amount of the property taxes receivable amount on the balance sheet at the end of the fiscal year for the amounts of the property tax receivable that were collected 60 days after the balance sheet date. The difference between the property tax receivable at the fiscal year-end and the amount recognized as property tax revenue should be recorded as deferred property tax revenue.

In addition, when property taxes are collected in advance of the year for which they are levied, the advance collections should be recorded as deferred revenue. These advance collections should not be recognized as revenue until the period for which they were levied is reached.

Some representative journal entries should clarify the accounting for property tax revenues.

Assumptions

Property taxes in the amount of $100,000 are levied during the current fiscal year to provide resources for budgetary expenditures of the current fiscal year. The taxes are due to be paid within the fiscal year reported. Historical experience indicates that 1% of the property taxes will be uncollectible. The government has decided to record all property tax collections during the year as revenues and to then adjust the accounts at the end of the year to record property taxes receivable and deferred property tax revenues.

Following are the sample journal entries for recording these taxes on a modified accrual basis:

1. The government levies the $100,000 of property taxes.

Property taxes receivable	100,000	
Allowance for uncollectible property taxes		1,000
Property tax revenue		99,000

To record property tax levy

2. The government collects $80,000 of property taxes prior to its fiscal year-end.

Cash	80,000	
Property taxes receivable		80,000

To record collections of the property tax levy

3. The government collects $10,000 of the fiscal year's property taxes within 60 days of the end of the fiscal year. The actual amount of property tax revenue to be recognized for the year is $80,000 collected during the year, plus $10,000 collected after the end of the fiscal year, or $90,000. Since $99,000 was recorded as property tax revenue on the date of the property tax levy, an adjustment must be recorded to reduce the amount recognized as property tax revenue.

Property tax revenue	9,000	
Deferred inflow of resources—uncollected property tax revenue		9,000

To record deferred revenue for property tax receivables that do not meet the criteria to be recognized as property tax revenue

Two other journal entries are also possible related to property taxes:

4. The government determines that $500 of the property taxes receivable are specifically identified as not being collected, even after consideration of tax liens on the property. The following entry is recorded:

Allowance for uncollectible property taxes	500	
Property taxes receivable		500

To write off uncollectible property taxes

5. The government is having cash flow difficulties and offers a discount to property tax payers who prepay the subsequent fiscal year's property taxes, and as a result, $5,000 of the subsequent year's tax levy is collected in the current fiscal year. Since these collections are for the subsequent fiscal year's tax levy, they are recorded as deferred revenue in the current fiscal year as follows:

Cash	5,000	
Deferred inflow of resources—prepaid property tax revenues		5,000

To record early collections of the subsequent fiscal year's property tax levy

The sequence of these journal entries may change, based on the operating procedures of the government. For example, the government may record all collections of property tax revenue as a deferred inflow of resources and then recognize the proper amount of property tax revenue at year-end, and then again when the 60-day subsequent period collections are determined. The sequence of the journal entries is not as important as the government recognizing only the appropriate amount of property tax revenue and recording the proper amount of property taxes receivable and deferred property tax revenues.

In addition to recording the transactions described above properly, the government should also periodically review the propriety of the allowance for uncollectible real estate taxes and consider writing off against the allowance for those taxes from specific taxpayers that are not likely to be collected. The government should also determine whether the allowance for uncollectible taxes is understated.

NOTE: Since property taxes are almost always accounted for by a governmental fund, the accounting for the allowance for uncollectible property taxes is somewhat unique. Because property tax revenues are recognized only when collected within the fiscal year or within 60 days after the fiscal year, the property tax levy receivable at year-end is offset by (1) those property taxes collected within 60 days after the fiscal year-end, (2) the allowance for uncollectible property taxes, and (3) deferred real estate taxes. By definition, any additional property taxes deemed uncollectible must have their related "credit" in the deferred property revenue account. Therefore, if a government determines that its allowance for uncollectible property taxes should be increased, the following entry would be recorded:

Deferred inflow of resources—uncollected property tax revenue	xx,xxx	
Allowance for uncollectible property taxes		xx,xxx

This is unique to the modified accrual basis of accounting for property taxes, because increasing an allowance for an uncollectible receivable has no impact on the operating statement of the entity. It is strictly a journal entry affecting two balance sheet accounts.

Unless they must be used to support a specific program, property taxes are reported as general revenues on the government-wide statement of activities. Converting the property tax revenue recorded in the governmental funds on a modified accrual basis to the accrual basis for purposes of accounting for the government-wide statements is fairly easy. Conceptually, the difference in the revenue between the two bases of accounting is the amount that was deferred as not collected within 60 days under the modified accrual method. Basically, the government would reverse entry 3 listed above as follows for the government-wide statements:

Deferred inflow of resources—uncollected property tax revenue	9,000	
Property tax revenue		9,000

To recognize as revenue property taxes collected after 60 days on the government-wide financial statements

The difference in the actual amount of revenue recognized under the two different accounting bases, however, will not actually be $9,000 in this example, because similar entries would have been recorded in the prior year to set up deferred revenue on the modified accrual basis and then reverse it for the government-wide statements. The actual effect on the revenue recognized between the two methods would be the difference in the amounts deferred under the modified accrual basis from one year to the next, since the prior year entry would have been reversed.

NOTE: There is a danger in referring to the above adjustment as a journal entry, because it implies that it would be recorded in a general ledger. This entry would not be recorded on the governmental fund's general ledger since it pertains only to the government-wide financial statements and not the fund financial statements. In fact, many governments seem to be recording the adjustments needed to prepare the government-wide statements on spreadsheets. Because accountants think in terms of double-sided journal entries, these will continue to be used in this book to describe the adjustments for the government-wide statements—just be careful as to where they are "recorded."

Income and Sales Taxes, and Other Derived Tax Revenues

Income taxes usually represent a significant source of revenue to governments. Sales taxes are another common form of significant revenue provider that is used by governments to fund operations. In addition, other forms of derived taxes, such as cigarette taxes, provide revenues to many state and local governments. What these taxes have in common is that they are derived from taxes imposed on exchange transactions.

On a modified accrual basis, the revenue from these taxes is fairly easy to determine because the availability criteria focus governments' attention on the collections from these taxes shortly after year-end. In practice, many governments have been using a one-month or two-month collection period after year-end (depending on the nature of the tax and how and when tax returns are filed) to determine the amounts that are recorded on the modified accrual basis. On the accrual basis, revenue recognition becomes more complicated in that estimates of what will be ultimately received for taxes imposed on exchange transactions occurring during the governments' fiscal year are required. Since many governments do not have fiscal years that match the calendar year and since many of these taxes are based on calendar-year tax returns, the calculations are further complicated.

Taxpayer-assessed revenues are difficult to measure for a number of reasons. First, the reporting period for these revenues is often a calendar year, and the majority of governments have a fiscal year that is other than the calendar year, and accordingly there are overlapping reporting periods. Second, the tax returns or remittance forms taxpayers use to remit these taxes are usually not due until several months after the calendar year-end and are subject to extension requests. Third, these types of taxes, particularly income taxes, are subject to estimated payment requirements throughout the year, and the final amount of the tax is determined when the tax return form is actually completed. Finally, since the revenues are taxpayer-assessed, it is sometimes difficult for the government to satisfactorily estimate the amount of tax it will ultimately receive based on historical information, because the taxes are generally based on the relative strength of the economy during the calendar year reported by the taxpayer. Historical information does not always have a direct correlation with the current status of the economy.

In some cases taxpayer-assessed revenues are collected by a level of government different from the government that is the actual beneficiary of the tax. For example, a state may be responsible for collecting sales taxes, although portions of the sales taxes collected are actually revenues of counties or cities located within the state. In these cases, the state will remit sales tax collections to the local governments (counties, cities, etc.) periodically. Similar situations exist where states collect personal income taxes imposed by major cities within the state.

The local governments receiving taxes collected by another level of government should apply the same criteria of recognizing these revenues (i.e., when they are measurable and available). If the collecting government remits the local government's portion of the taxes promptly, the local government is likely to recognize revenue in similar amounts to that which they would recognize if they collected the revenues themselves. On the other hand, if the collecting government imposes a significant delay until the time that it remits the portion of the collections due the local government to that local government, consideration must be given to when these revenues actually become available to the local government, given their delay in receiving the revenues from the collecting government.

NOTE: While the measurable criterion can usually be met by effective use of accounting estimates, the available criterion is more direct. For reporting on the modified accrual basis of accounting, some governments choose to use the same 60-day criterion used for property taxes collected after year-end for determining the amount of these revenues that should be considered available. Before adopting this general rule, the government should ensure that the tax relates back to the fiscal year for which the estimate is being made. For example, sales tax returns are often due monthly following the month of the sale. Assume that a government with a June 30 year-end requires sales tax returns to be filed and taxes remitted by the 20th day of the month following the date of the sales. In this case, sales taxes remitted with the July 20 sales tax returns would relate to sales in June and would appropriately be accrued back to the fiscal year that ended June 30. However, the sales taxes remitted with the August 20 sales tax returns would relate to sales in July of the new fiscal year and should not be accrued back to the fiscal year that ended on June 30, despite being collected within 60 days of the June 30 year-end.

In addition to accruing revenues for taxpayer-assessed taxes, governments must make the appropriate liability accruals for refunds that they are required to make based on tax returns that are filed. Governments should use actual refunds made after the fiscal year-end, combined with estimates for refunds made using a combination of historical experience and information about the economy of the fiscal year reported. When a government records this liability accrual, it should record the accrual as a reduction of the related tax revenue presented in the general or special revenue fund and as a liability of the fund. The liability should be recorded in the fund through a reduction of the related revenue rather than simply recording a refund liability in the general long-term debt account group. Tax refunds are likely to be a liability to be liquidated with current financial resources, and accordingly, a fund liability rather than a general long-term debt account group liability, is recorded. Netting the tax refunds with the related tax revenues also provides a more accurate picture of the amount of tax revenues that should actually have been recorded by the government.

Adjustments for the Accrual Basis of Accounting

In order to report the derived revenues from the taxes described in the previous paragraphs on the accrual basis of accounting and economic resources measurement focus, the government needs to consider the taxes that will be collected after the availability period that is used for reporting these revenues on a modified accrual basis. The government needs to calculate how much revenue it "earns" during its fiscal year from exchange transactions that occurred during that fiscal year.

Consider the following example: A taxpayer prepares an income tax return for the calendar year ended December 31, 20X1. The taxpayer had withholdings taken from her salary during the year. In addition, the taxpayer made estimated tax payments throughout the year, with the final estimated payment made on January 15, 20X2. The taxpayer filed an extension request on April 15, 20X2, and paid an amount she estimated would be due with the final return. The return was filed on August 15, 20X2, which resulted in a refund that the taxpayer applied to her estimated payments for the calendar year ending December 31, 20X2. When completing her 20X2 tax return, the taxpayer discovers an error in the 20X1 return and files an amended return on May 15, 20X3, requesting an additional refund. How much would the government ultimately be entitled to receive in taxes from the earnings of the taxpayer during the government's fiscal year ended June 30, 20X1?

To approximate the answer to this question, a government would need to look at each component of the various tax events that are described above and determine how best to record the revenues (or refund) that occur from those events. The government has to assume that it is virtually impossible for it to have actual information in time for it to prepare its own financial statements on a timely basis. Furthermore, the fact that the tax year and the government's fiscal year are different essentially assures that some estimation process is required.

Each government's tax procedures and requirements are different, and different taxes work in different ways, so there is no set of prescribed procedures that can be suggested that will result in the best method in every case. Nevertheless, there are some general processes and procedures that might prove helpful. In the example described above, the government would probably be best off breaking the various tax events into groups and handling each in the most practical way. For example, withholding taxes are based on salary earnings and usually must be remitted to governments in a very short period of time. Perhaps withholding taxes received during the year should be recognized by the government in the year received. Similarly, estimated tax payments are often received quarterly and should correspond with estimates of earnings for each particular quarter. The estimated tax receipts related to the four quarters that comprise the government's fiscal year might be assumed to be recorded within that fiscal year. Tax payments received with returns and refunds made with returns filed on a timely basis (or received with extension request) might be aggregated and assumed to occur ratably over the calendar year. Accordingly, of the amounts received (or refunded) for calendar year 20X0, the government might assume that half were received in its 20X0 fiscal year and half in its 20X1 fiscal year. Projection of the first half of 20X2 would be needed and could be based on past history and adjusted for known factors, such as changes in tax rates or rising or declining incomes. Further, the government might determine that the amounts received or paid with amended returns are very small and may choose to simply account for these in the same period received or paid.

Note that not all derived tax revenues will be this difficult to calculate. For example, many governments require that sales taxes be remitted on a monthly basis. It should be fairly easy to match the receipts of sales tax revenues to the months of the fiscal year to which those taxes relate. For example, for a June 30 year-end, if sales taxes relating to the month of June are due to be remitted by July 20, the government would accrue the July receipts back to June, since that is when the sales on which the sales tax revenues were derived occurred.

NOTE: Historically, when governments accounted for taxpayer-assessed revenues, many set up a receivable and recognized revenue for the amounts that were measurable and available and recorded in a governmental fund using the modified accrual basis of accounting. An alternative approach would have been to estimate the ultimate amounts that were receivable (similar to the above calculation) and then record the total receivable, with revenue recognized for the amount of the receivable that was available and deferred revenue recorded for the difference between the total receivable and the amount recognized as revenue because it was available.

In adopting GASBS 34, governments that only recorded the amount of the receivable as equal to the amount of revenue recognized should consider changing to the alternative of recording the total receivable. In addition to being a more correct way of recording these amounts, recording the total receivable along with deferred revenue at the fund level makes conversion and reconciliation of the fund amounts with the government-wide amounts much easier. All the governments would need to do each year for the government-wide statements is reverse the amount of deferred revenue and recognize revenue for this amount in the government-wide statements. Note that since a deferred revenue amount is also recorded in the prior year (and is the deferred revenue opening balance), the actual effect on revenue of adjusting to the accrual basis of accounting in the government-wide statements will be the change in the deferred revenue amounts from one year to the next. What makes this approach attractive is that the amount of the receivable for these derived revenues will be the same on the fund and government-wide financial statements. In addition, the reconciliation of the fund financial statements amounts to the government-wide amounts can be attributed to either the existence of the deferred revenue amount (on the statement of net position) or the changes in the deferred revenue amount (on the statement of activities). In other words, these revenues would work essentially the same way that the property tax revenues described in the previous section are recorded.

Grants and Other Financial Assistance

State and local governments typically receive a variety of grants and other financial assistance. At the state level, this financial assistance may be primarily federal financial assistance. At the local government level, the financial assistance may be federal, state, or other intermediate level of local government. Financial assistance generally is legally structured as a grant, contract, or cooperative agreement. The financial assistance might take the form of entitlements, shared revenues, pass-through grants, food stamps, and on-behalf payments for fringe benefits and salary.

What financial assistance should be recorded? Governments often receive grants and other financial assistance that they are to transfer to or spend on behalf of a secondary recipient of the financial assistance. These agreements are known as *pass-through grants*. All cash pass-through grants should be reported in the financial statements of the primary recipient government and should be recorded as revenues and expenditures of that government.

There may be some infrequent cases when a recipient government acts only as a cash conduit for financial assistance. Guidance on identifying these cases is provided by GASB Statement 24 (GASBS 24), *Accounting and Financial Reporting for Certain Grants and Other Financial Assistance*. In these cases, the receipt and disbursement of the financial assistance should be reported as transactions of an agency fund. A recipient government serves as a cash conduit if it merely transmits grantor-supplied money without having administrative or direct financial involvement in the program. Some examples of a recipient government that would be considered to have administrative involvement in a program are provided by GASBS 24, as follows:

- The government monitors secondary recipients for compliance with program-specific requirements.
- The government determines eligibility of secondary recipients or projects, even if grantor-supplied criteria are used.
- The government has the ability to exercise discretion in how the funds are allocated.

A recipient government has direct financial involvement if, as an example, it finances some direct program costs because of grantor-imposed matching requirements or is liable for disallowed costs.

Revenue recognition of grants and other financial assistance. Grants, entitlements, or shared revenues recorded in the general and special revenue funds should be recognized as revenue in the accounting period in which they become susceptible to accrual (they are measurable and available). In applying these criteria, the financial statement preparer must consider the legal and contractual requirements of the particular financial assistance being considered.

Financial assistance in the form of shared revenues and entitlements is often restricted by law or contract more in form than in substance. Only a failure on the part of the recipient to comply with prescribed regulations would cause a forfeiture of the resources. Such resources should be recorded as revenue at the time of receipt, or earlier if the susceptibility to accrual criteria are satisfied. If entitlements and shared revenues are collected in advance of the period that they are intended to finance, they should be recorded as deferred revenue.

Grants are nonexchange transactions that would be classified as either government-mandated or voluntary nonexchange transactions. The accounting for both of these transactions is similar and is described earlier in this chapter. Many of the government-mandated grants that are received by governments are expenditure driven. These are covered later in this section. In many of the remaining grants, the key accounting component is when eligibility requirements are met, which determine when it is appropriate for the recipient government to recognize the grant as revenue. If the actual cash is received before the eligibility requirements have been met, the cash should be recorded as a deferred revenue until the eligibility requirements are met. On the other hand, if the eligibility requirements have been met and the cash has not yet been received by the recipient government, the recipient government would record a receivable and revenue for the grant revenue that it is owed. For recording this amount in a governmental fund on the modified accrual basis of accounting, the availability criteria should be examined to see if the revenue should be recognized or recorded as deferred revenue. In practice, grant revenue is usually received within a timeframe where the availability criteria are met (this is also discussed later, in the expenditure-driven revenue section).

One of the more important eligibility requirements is the time requirement, where the time period in which a grant is to be spent is specified. For example, if a state government provides formula-based education aid to a local government or a school district and specifies that the aid is for the school year that begins in September and ends in June, that is the period of time for which the grant revenue would be recognized. Few, if any, differences between the modified accrual basis of accounting on the fund level and the accrual basis of accounting at the government-wide level should arise. However, if no time period is specified (and all other eligibility requirements are met), the total amount of the grant would be recognized as revenue immediately. For example, assume that a state government with a December 31 year-end provides a grant to a local government in its budget for its fiscal year, which begins on January 1, 20X1. The local government has a fiscal year of June 30. If there are no time requirements and all other eligibility criteria are met, the grant appropriation at the state level is available on January 1, 20X1, the first day of the state's fiscal year. In this case, the local government would recognize the revenue from the whole grant on January 1, 20X1.

NOTE: In the above example, governments prior to adoption of GASBS 33 probably would have recognized half of the grant revenue in this example in the fiscal year ended June 30, 20X1, and half in the fiscal year ended June 30, 20X2. Under GASBS 33, the entire grant would be recognized in the fiscal year ended June 30, 20X1.

Expenditure-driven grants and other financial assistance revenue. Many grants and other financial aid programs are on a cost-reimbursement basis, whereby the recipient government "earns" the grant revenue when it actually makes the expenditures called for under the grant. This type of arrangement is described as "expenditure-driven" revenue, since the amount of revenue that should be recognized is directly related to the amount of expenditures incurred for allowable purposes under the grant or other contractual agreement. (Of course, the amount of revenue recognized under a grant or contract should not exceed the total allowable revenue for the period being reported, regardless of the amount of expenditures.) Updating the terminology for GASBS 33, making the expenditure is simply an eligibility requirement. To be eligible for the grant revenue, you must make the expenditure. The accounting for most expenditure-driven grants is likely to remain the same under GASBS 33 as it was prior to adoption of GASBS 33.

In accounting for expenditure-driven revenue, governments typically make the expenditures first and then claim reimbursement from the grantor or other aid provider. In this case, a receivable should be established, provided that the criteria for recording revenue under the modified accrual basis of accounting are satisfied. For expenditure-driven revenues, determining whether the "available" criterion is met is difficult for some grants and other sources of aid. First, there will be a time lag from when the government actually makes the expenditures under the grant, accumulates the expenditure information to conform with some predetermined billing period, and submits the claim for reimbursement to the grantor or other aid provider. Sometimes the grantors and other aid providers delay disbursing payments to the recipient organizations while they review the reimbursement claims submitted by the recipient organization. In some cases, the aid providers even perform some limited types of audit procedures on claims for reimbursement. Often, the actual receipt of cash for expenditure-driven revenues exceeds the period normally considered "available" to pay current obligations. Governments, however, do record the receivable from the grantor or other aid provider and the related grant revenue, despite it being unclear as to whether the "available" criterion will be met. The reason for not requiring that the available criteria be met is that the government has already recognized the expenditures for these grants and other aid programs. Without recognizing the related grant revenue, the governmental fund's operating statements will indicate that there was a use of resources for these grants and other programs when, in fact, these programs are designed to break even and result in no drain of financial resources on the government. As additional guidance, the GAAFR indicates that in practice, it is uncommon for the recognition of revenue related to reimbursement grants to be deferred based on the availability criterion of modified accrual accounting. Nevertheless, deferral ought to be considered in situations where reimbursement is not expected within a reasonable period. Financial statement preparers and auditors should consider this guidance on current practice in accounting for expenditure-driven revenue.

NCGA Statement 2 provides that when expenditure is the prime factor for determining eligibility for reimbursement, revenue should be recognized when the expenditure is made.

Practice Issues

The first practice issue that a governmental financial statement preparer accounting for nonexchange revenues in governmental fund types will encounter (as with the financial reporting model discussed next) is that information will need to be developed on two bases of accounting—accrual and modified accrual for the government-wide and fund financial statements, respectively. This will clearly result in the modification or enhancement of financial systems to be able to capture revenue information on an accrual basis.

The second practice issue relates to ensuring that, when applicable, the eligibility requirements are met before revenue is recognized in the financial statements. In addition, the timing requirements may also need careful consideration, including where a resource provider does not specify a time requirement, and one needs to be implied using the guidance of the Statement.

Governments that have evaluated the impact of GASBS 33 are finding that its greatest impact is in the area of governmental grants. Applying GASBS 33 tends to result in recording receipts from certain grants as revenue rather than as deferred revenue under prior accounting practice.

21 RISK FINANCING AND INSURANCE-RELATED ACTIVITIES/PUBLIC ENTITY RISK POOLS

INTRODUCTION

Governmental organizations are subject to many of the same risks of "doing business" as commercial enterprises, including risks related to various torts, property damage awards, personal injury cases, and so forth.

Governments are most often self-insured for these types of risks. Sometimes the government establishes or participates in a *public entity risk pool* that acts somewhat like an insurer against various types of risks.

This chapter is divided into two main sections. The first addresses the accounting and financial reporting guidance for the risk financing and insurance-related activities of state and local governments (other than public entity risk pools). The second section of this chapter addresses the accounting and financial reporting requirements for public entity risk pools.

The primary accounting and financial reporting guidance for both of the sections listed above is found in GASB Statement 10 (GASBS 10), *Accounting and Financial Reporting for Risk Financing and Related Insurance Issues*. This guidance was enhanced by the GASB's *Guide to Implementation of GASB Statement 10*, which provides GASB staff guidance on the application of GASBS 10. The GASB issued Statement 30 (GASBS 30), *Risk Financing Omnibus*, which was a way of fine-tuning the previously issued guidance to address some of the problems that state and local governmental entities were having in operating under the provisions of GASBS 10. The guidance from all three of these sources is included in this chapter.

RISK FINANCING AND INSURANCE ACTIVITIES OF STATE AND LOCAL GOVERNMENTS (OTHER THAN PUBLIC ENTITY RISK POOLS)

As will be seen in the following discussion, the accounting and financial reporting for risk financing contained in GASBS 10 are quite similar to the accounting requirements originally contained in the FASB's Statement of Financial Accounting Standards 5 (SFAS 5), *Accounting for Contingencies*, now included in GASB Statement No. 62 (GASBS 62), *Codification of Accounting and Financial Reporting Guidance Contained in Pre–November 30, 1989, FASB and AICPA Pronouncements*. These requirements are also discussed in Chapter 15. GASBS 10 includes in its scope the risks of loss from the following kinds of events:

- Torts (wrongful acts, injuries, or damages not involving a breach of contract for which a civil action can be brought).
- Theft or destruction of, or damage to, assets.
- Business interruption.
- Errors or omissions.
- Job-related illnesses or injuries to employees.
- Acts of God (events beyond human origin or control, such as natural disasters, lightning, windstorms, and earthquakes).

The accounting and financial reporting requirements discussed in this section also apply to losses resulting when a governmental entity agrees to provide accident and health, dental, and other medical benefits to its employees and retirees and their dependents and beneficiaries, based on covered events that have already occurred. For example, a retiree incurs a doctor bill that will be reimbursed by the government for a doctor's visit occurring prior to the end of the government's fiscal year. However, these requirements do not apply to postemployment benefits that governmental employers expect to provide to current and future retirees, their beneficiaries, and their dependents in accordance with the employer's agreement to provide those future benefits. Also excluded from these requirements are Medicaid insurance plans provided to low-income state residents under Title XIX of the Federal Social Security Act.

GASBS 10 provides that when a risk of loss or a portion of the risk of loss from the types of events listed above has not been transferred to an unrelated third party, state and local governmental entities should report an estimated loss from a claim as an expenditure/expense and a liability if both of the following conditions are met:

1. Information available before the financial statements are issued indicates that it is probable that an asset had been impaired or a liability had been incurred at the date of the financial statements. (The date of the financial statements means the end of the most recent accounting period for which financial statements are being presented.) It is implicit in this condition that it must be probable that one or more future events will also occur, confirming the fact of the loss.
2. The amount of the loss can be reasonably estimated.

In determining whether the amount of a loss can be reasonably estimated, it is quite possible that the amount of the loss can reasonably be estimated as a range of amounts, rather than as one specific amount. If this is the case, the amount of the loss is still considered to be reasonably estimable. First, determine if some amount within the range appears to be a better estimate than any other amount within the range, and use this amount for the estimate. Second, if no amount within the range is a better estimate than any other amount, the minimum amount of the range should be used as an estimate to be accrued.

When a loss contingency exists, the likelihood that the future event or events will confirm the loss or impairment of an asset or the incurrence of a liability can range from probable to remote. GASBS 10 uses the terms *probable*, *reasonably possible*, and *remote* to identify three areas within that range. The terms are defined as follows:

1. *Probable* —The future event or events are likely to occur.
2. *Reasonably possible* —The chance of the future event or events is more than remote, but less than likely.
3. *Remote* —The chance of the future event or events occurring is slight.

Disclosure of Loss Contingencies

If no accrual is made for a loss contingency because it has not met the conditions of being probable or reasonably estimable, disclosure of the loss contingency should be met if it is at least reasonably possible that a loss may have been incurred. The disclosure should indicate the nature of the contingency and should give either an estimate of the possible loss or range of loss or state that such an estimate cannot be made. Disclosure is not required of a loss contingency involving an unreported claim or assessment if there has been no manifestation of a potential claimant or an awareness of a possible claim or assessment, unless it is considered probable that a claim will be asserted and there is a reasonable possibility that the outcome will be unfavorable.

A disclosure of loss contingency should also be made when an exposure to loss exists in excess of the amount accrued in the financial statements and it is reasonably possible that a loss or additional loss may have been incurred. For example, if a loss is probable and is estimated with a range of amounts and the lower amount of the range is accrued in the financial statements, the reasonably possible amount of the loss in excess of the amount accrued should be disclosed.

A remote loss contingency is not required to be accrued or disclosed in the financial statements.

The following summarizes the expenditure/expense and liability recognition and disclosure requirements under GASBS 10:

Likelihood of Loss Contingency	*Accounting/Disclosure*
Probable and can be reasonably estimated	Recognize expenditure/expense and liability
Probable and cannot be reasonably estimated	Disclosure required/no expenditure/expense and liability recognition
Reasonably possible	Disclosure required/no expenditure/expense and liability recognition
Remote	No disclosure required/no expenditure/expense and liability recognition

Incurred but not reported claims. GASBS 10 requires that incurred but not reported claims (IBNR) be evaluated. When a loss can be reasonably estimated and it is possible that a claim will be asserted, the expenditure/expense and liability should be recognized.

IBNR claims are claims for uninsured events that have occurred but have not yet been reported to the governmental entity. IBNR claims include (1) known losses expected to be presented later as claims, (2) unknown loss events expected to become claims, and (3) expected future developments on claims already reported.

NOTE: IBNR claims that are probable and reasonably estimable are typically the recurring types of claims that occur in a fairly predictable pattern. For example, a government might know that each year approximately 25% of the "trip-and-fall" claims that actually occur prior to the end of the government's fiscal year (that is, someone falls on a government's sidewalk and sues for actual damages or pain and suffering) are not asserted until after the government's financial statements are issued for that year-end. The number and average settlement of these claims usually can be reasonably estimated, and it is probable that they will be asserted. In this case, recognition of an expenditure/expense and liability is recorded in the financial statements for the government's fiscal year in which the actual loss occurred—that is, the fiscal year in which people actually fell and were injured on the government's sidewalk.

Amount of loss accrual. Estimates for claims liabilities, including IBNR, should be based on the estimated ultimate cost of settling the claims, including the effects of inflation and other societal and economic factors, using experience adjusted for current trends and any other factors that would modify experience.

NOTE: In the trip-and-fall claims mentioned above, the government may know the number of these claims filed in its past. However, perhaps an ice and snow storm occurs during the last month of the government's fiscal year. The number of claims filed is likely to increase and this should be considered in estimating IBNR claims. On the other hand, maybe the government has replaced a significant part of its crumbling sidewalks during the fiscal year and would expect the number of trip-and-fall claims to decrease in the fiscal year reported. This adjustment to prior experience should also be considered in estimating the potential liability.

GASBS 10 specifies that claims liabilities should include specific, incremental claim adjustment expenditures/expenses. In other words, incremental costs should include only those costs incurred because of a claim. For example, the cost of outside legal counsel on a particular claim is likely to be treated as an incremental cost. However, assistance from internal legal staff on a claim may be incremental because the salary costs for internal staff normally will be incurred regardless of the claim.

Discounting. The practice of presenting claims liabilities at the discounted present value of estimated future cash payments is neither mandated nor prohibited by GASBS 10. However, claims liabilities associated with structured settlements should be discounted if they represent contractual obligations to pay money on fixed or determinable dates. A structured settlement is a means of satisfying a claim liability and consists of an initial cash payment to meet specific present financial needs combined with a stream of future payments designed to meet future financial needs. For example, a government may enter into a settlement with someone injured by a government vehicle, whereby the government agrees to pay the injured party's hospital claims up front, and then a monthly fixed amount for the remaining life of the injured party. The monthly payment cash flow streams should be discounted when a government recognizes this loss in its financial statements.

Annuity contracts. A governmental entity may purchase an annuity contract in a claimant's name to satisfy a claim liability. If the likelihood that the entity will be required to make future payments on the claim is remote, the governmental entity is considered to have satisfied its primary liability to the claimant. Accordingly, the annuity contract should not be reported as an asset by the governmental entity, and the liability for the claim should be removed from the governmental entity's balance sheet. However, GASBS 10 requires that the aggregate outstanding amount of liabilities that are removed from the governmental entity's balance sheet be disclosed as long as those contingent liabilities are outstanding. On the other hand, if annuity contracts used to settle claims for which the claimant has signed an agreement releasing the governmental entity from further obligation and for which the likelihood that the governmental entity will be required to make future payments on those claims is remote, then the amount of the liability related to these annuity contracts should not be included in this aggregate disclosure. If it is later determined that the primary liability will revert back to the governmental entity, the liability should be reinstated on the balance sheet.

Use of a single fund. GASBS 10 requires that if a single fund is used to account for a governmental entity's risk financing activities, that fund should be either the general fund or an internal service fund. Entities reported as proprietary funds or trust funds and that are component units of a primary government may participate in a risk financing internal service fund of that primary government. However, other stand-alone entities that are reported as proprietary or trust funds and are not considered to be a part of another financial reporting entity should not use an internal service fund to report their own risk financing activities.

NOTE: GASB Statement No. 66 (GASBS 66), Technical Corrections—2012, an Amendment of GASB Statements No. 10 and No. 62, removes the provision cited above that limits fund-based reporting of an entity's risk financing activities to the general fund and the internal service fund type. GASBS 66 is effective for financial statements for periods beginning after December 15, 2012, with earlier application encouraged.

Risk Retention by Entities Other than Pools

The following summarizes the accounting and financial reporting considerations that must be made when either the general fund or an internal service fund is used to account for risk retained by entities other than pools.

General fund. An entity that uses the general fund to account for its risk financing activities should recognize claims liabilities and expenditures in accordance with the criteria described earlier in this chapter.

Claims liabilities should be reduced by amounts expected to be recovered through excess insurance. Excess insurance is a way to transfer the risk of loss from one party to another when the risk transferred is for amounts that exceed a certain sum. For example, a government may retain the risk of loss for amounts below a relatively high dollar amount, such as $5 million. However, the governmental entity may transfer the risk (that is, buy insurance) for losses in excess of this $5 million amount. Any amounts that are expected to be recovered from this excess amount should be deducted from claim liability recorded in the general fund.

NOTE: Readers should refer to Chapter 15, which discusses recording liabilities in governmental funds and on the government-wide statement of net position. There are certain liabilities of governmental funds (which obviously include the general fund) that, when not liquidated with expendable financial resources, are not recorded as liabilities of the fund, but are instead recorded as liabilities only in the government-wide statement of net position. Liabilities for claims and judgments discussed in this chapter are one of these liabilities recorded in the government-wide statement of net position when they are not expected to be liquidated with expendable financial resources. Thus, when the general fund is used to account for risk financing activities, the liability recognized in the financial statements may well be reported in the government-wide statement of net position, since most, if not all, of the liability will not be liquidated with expendable financial resources. Note that for the claims and judgments liability recorded on the government-wide statement of net position, changes in the liability from the beginning of the year to the end of the year will result in an addition or reduction to the claims and judgments expense reported on the government-wide statement of net position.

One useful way in which governments can determine how much, if any, of the judgments and claims liability should be reported in the general fund itself is to look at those liabilities that have been settled in principle, but not payment, prior to the end of the fiscal year, and accrue these settlements as expenditures and liabilities in the general fund as of the end of the fiscal year, with the remainder of the judgments and claims liability recorded in the general long-term debt account group.

For example, the governmental entity with a June 30 fiscal year-end may agree with a claimant to settle a personal injury case for $10,000. The claimant and the governmental entity reach this agreement on June 25, but because various releases and other legal formalities need to be executed, a check is not presented to the claimant until September 15, which is in the next fiscal year. Using this method, an expenditure and a liability for $10,000 would be recorded in the general fund as of June 30, since it is reasonable to believe that this amount will be paid from expendable available resources. On the other hand, if no settlement had been reached, the governmental entity would use the probable and reasonably estimable criteria to determine whether it would recognize a liability for this claim. If these criteria were met, a liability would be recorded in the government-wide statement of net position for the governmental entity's estimate of the settlement amount, which may or may not be discounted, at the option of the government.

While the "single" fund for accounting for risk financing activities may be met by accounting for these activities in the general fund, that does not mean that the general fund cannot allocate the costs of claims that are recognized to other funds. GASBS 10 provides that the governmental entity may use any method it chooses to allocate loss expenditures/expenses to other funds of the entity. Consistent with the discussion of interfund transactions for reimbursements, as described in Chapter 20, the allocated amounts should be treated as expenditures in the funds to which they are allocated and as a reduction of the expenditures of the general fund, from which the costs are allocated. (However, if the total amount so allocated exceeds the total expenditures and liabilities, the excess should be treated as operating transfers.)

NOTE: In preparing the government-wide statement of activities, the total claims and judgments expense (which includes amounts recognized as expenditures in the general fund as well as changes in the long-term liability recorded only on the government-wide statement of net position) needs to be allocated by the functions-program reported on the statement of activities.

Keep in mind that proprietary funds use the accrual basis of accounting and the economic resources measurement focus. Accordingly, the recording of liabilities related to these funds should follow that for proprietary funds; that is, the expense and the liability should be recorded in the proprietary fund itself, and not in the general long-term debt account group.

Internal service fund. A governmental entity may elect to use an internal service fund to account for its risk financing activities. Claims expenses and liabilities should be recognized using the criteria described in the earlier part of this chapter. As is the case when the general fund is used to account for risk financing activities, claims expenses should be reduced by amounts expected to be recovered through excess insurance. In addition, claim amounts that are probable but not reasonably estimable should be disclosed, in addition to the disclosures of losses that are reasonably possible.

The internal service fund may use any basis considered appropriate to charge other funds of the governmental entity. However, GASBS 10 includes three conditions that must be met in charging these amounts to other funds:

1. The total charge by the internal service fund to the other funds for the period reported is calculated in accordance with the earlier section of this chapter; *or*
2. The total charge by the internal service fund to the other funds is based on an actuarial method or historical cost information adjusted over a reasonable period of time so that internal service fund revenues and expenses are approximately equal. (The actuarial method can be any one of several techniques that actuaries use to determine the amounts and timing of contributions needed to finance claims liabilities so that the total contributions plus compounded earnings on them will equal the amounts needed to satisfy claims liabilities. It may or may not include a provision for anticipated catastrophic losses.)
3. In addition to item 2 above, the total charge by the internal service fund may include a reasonable provision for expected future catastrophic losses.

Charges made by internal service funds in accordance with these provisions should be recognized as revenue by the internal service fund and as expenditures/expenses by the other funds of the governmental entity. Deficits, if any, in the internal service fund resulting from application of items 2 and 3 above do not need to be charged back to the other funds in any one year, as long as adjustments are made over a reasonable period of time. A deficit fund balance in an internal service fund, however, should be disclosed in the notes to the financial statements. Retained earnings in an internal service fund resulting from application of item 3 above should be reported as equity designated for future catastrophic losses in the notes to the financial statements.

On the other hand, if the charge by an internal service fund to the other funds of the governmental entity is greater than the amount resulting from application of the preceding three conditions, the excess should be reported in both the internal service fund and the other funds as an operating transfer. However, if the charge by the internal service fund to the other funds fails to recover the full cost of claims over a reasonable period of time, any deficit fund balance in the internal service fund should be charged back to the other funds and reported as an expenditure/expense of those funds.

NOTE: These principles for the charging of costs by the internal service fund for risk financing are similar to those normally used by internal service funds for charging of other costs. Refer to Chapter 10 and Chapter 20 for additional information.

Governmental Entities That Participate in Risk Pools

As will be more fully described in the second part of this chapter, a governmental entity may participate in a public entity risk pool when there is a transfer or a pooling of risk. On the other hand, a governmental entity may participate in a public entity risk pool when there is no transfer of risk to the public entity risk pool, but rather the governmental entity contracts with the pool to service the governmental entity's uninsured claims. The following two sections describe the governmental entity's accounting and financial reporting considerations in each of these two instances.

Entities Participating in Public Entity Risk Pools with Transfer or Pooling of Risk

If a governmental entity participates in a pool in which there is a transfer or pooling (or sharing) of risks among the participants, the governmental entity should report its premium or required contribution as an insurance expenditure or expense. If the pooling agreement permits the pool to make additional assessments to its members, the governmental entity should consider the likelihood of additional assessments and report an additional expenditure or expense and liability if an assessment is probable and can be reasonably estimated. Assessment amounts that are probable but not reasonably estimable should be disclosed, along with disclosure of assessments that are reasonably possible.

NOTE: In other words, instead of the governmental entity evaluating the likelihood of losses due to claims that it directly pays, the governmental entity is making the same considerations as to the likelihood that it will need to pay more money to the public entity risk pool because of the claims experience of the pool requiring additional resources.

If the pool agreement does not provide for additional member assessments and the pool reports a deficit for its operations, the pool member should consider the financial capacity or stability of the pool to meet its obligations when they become due. If it is probable that the governmental entity will be required to pay its own obligations if the pool fails, the amount of those obligations should be reported as an expenditure/expense and as a liability if they can be reasonably estimated. Additionally, the same disclosure requirements for losses that are probable but not estimable and for losses that are reasonably possible apply.

Capitalization contributions. When state or local governmental entities join to form a public entity risk pool or when a governmental entity joins an established pool, the pooling agreement may require that a capitalization contribution be made to the pool to meet the initial or ongoing capital minimums established by the pooling agreement itself or by statute or regulation.

A capitalization contribution to a public entity risk pool with a transfer or pooling of risk should be reported as a deposit if it is probable that the contribution will be returned to the governmental entity either upon the dissolution of or the approved withdrawal from the pool. This determination should be based on the governmental entity's review of the provisions of the pooling agreement and an evaluation of the pool's financial capacity to return the contribution. (Governmental funds that record the capitalization contribution as a deposit should reserve a fund balance to indicate that the deposit is not appropriable for expenditure.)

If it is not probable that the contribution will be returned to the governmental entity, the following guidance should be used, depending on the fund type or type of entity involved:

- *Proprietary funds*. The contribution should be reported initially as an asset (prepaid insurance), and an expense should be recognized over the period for which the pool is expected to provide coverage. The periods expected to be covered should be consistent with the periods for which the contribution is factored into the pool's determination of premiums, but should not exceed ten years if this period is not readily determinable.
- *Governmental funds*. The entire amount of the capitalization contribution may be recognized as an expenditure in the period of the contribution. Reporting the capitalization contribution as prepaid insurance is not required. However, if the governmental entity elects, the governmental fund can initially report the capitalization contribution as an asset (prepaid insurance), and expenditures should be allocated and recognized over the

periods for which the pool is expected to provide coverage. Similar to the method used by proprietary funds, the periods expected to be covered should be consistent with the periods for which the contribution is factored into the pool's determination of premiums paid, but should not exceed ten years if the period is not determinable.

NOTE: Government-wide financial statements report capitalization contributions in a manner similar to proprietary funds. Judgment will be required to determine whether the asset recorded is a current or noncurrent asset based upon the facts of the particular situation.

Entities Participating in Public Entity Risk Pools without Transfer or Pooling of Risk

Governmental entities sometimes contract with other entities to service their uninsured claims. In this situation, there is no transfer of risk to the pool or pooling of risk with other pool participants. The governmental entity should recognize and measure its claims liabilities and related expenditures/expenses in accordance with the requirements described earlier in this chapter (essentially as if the governmental entity were servicing its own claims). Payments to the pool, including capitalization contributions, should be reported either as deposits or as reductions of the claim liability, as appropriate. A deposit should be recorded when the payment is not expected to be used to pay claims. A reduction of the claims liability should be made when payments to the pool are used to pay claims as they are incurred.

Other Matters for Entities Other than Public Entity Risk Pools

In addition to some disclosure requirements (which follow the next section), GASBS 10 provides some other specific guidance for accounting and financial reporting for risk financing activities for governmental entities that are not public entity risk pools. These additional topics are as follows, and are discussed in the following paragraphs:

1. Insurance-related transactions:
   (a) Claims-made policies.
   (b) Retrospectively rated policies.
   (c) Policyholder or pool dividends.
2. Entities providing claims servicing or insurance coverage to others.

Insurance-related transactions

Claims-made policies. A *claims-made* policy or contract is a type of policy that covers losses from claims asserted against the policyholder during the policy period, regardless of whether the liability-imposing events occurred during the current period or any previous period in which the policyholder was insured under the claims-made contract or other specified period before the policy period (the policy retroactive date). For example, a governmental entity may purchase a claims-made policy to cover claims made during its fiscal year, July 1, 2000, through June 30, 2001. A claim resulting from an accident that occurred on May 1, 2000, that was filed on July 31, 2000, would be covered by this claims-made policy. However, an accident that occurred on August 1, 2000, for which a claim was not filed until August 31, 2001, would not be covered by the policy, unless of course the policy was renewed for the next fiscal year.

While this type of policy represents a transfer of risk within the policy limits to the insurer or public entity risk pool for claims and incidents reported to the insurer or the pool, there is no transfer of risk for claims and incidents not reported to the insurer or pool. As a result, a governmental entity that is insured under a claims-made policy should account for the estimated cost of those claims and incidents not reported to the insurer as it would for other IBNR claims as described in the earlier part of this chapter.

If, on the other hand, the governmental entity purchases "tail coverage," the premium or contribution for this additional insurance would be accounted for as an expenditure or expense in the financial statements of the period presented. *Tail coverage* is a type of insurance policy that is designed to cover claims incurred before but reported after the cancellation or expiration of a claims-made policy. It is also referred to as *extended discovery coverage*. In this case, the risk for the IBNR claims up to the limit of the policy is transferred to the insurance company or pool that is providing the tail insurance coverage.

Retrospectively rated policies. A *retrospectively rated* policy is one that uses a method of determining the final amount of an insurance premium by which the initial premium is adjusted based on actual experience during the period of coverage, sometimes subject to minimum and maximum adjustment limits. It is designed to encourage safety by the insured (since increased claims will result in higher premiums) and to compensate the insurer if larger than expected losses are incurred.

A governmental entity with a retrospectively rated policy or contract where the minimum or required contribution is based primarily on the entity's loss experience should account for the minimum premium as an expenditure or expense over the period of the coverage under the policy and should also accrue estimated losses from reported and unreported claims in excess of the minimum premium. This accrual should be determined as would other claims accrual as was described earlier in this chapter. However, any estimated losses should not be accrued in excess of a stipulated maximum premium or contribution requirement.

If the governmental entity is insured under a retrospective policy that is based on the experience of a group of entities, it would account for the claims costs as in the preceding paragraph, although it would use the group's experience in determining any additional amounts that would need to be accrued to reflect anticipated premium adjustments. In addition, GASBS 10 specifies that the governmental entity should disclose:

- That it is insured under a retrospectively rated policy.
- That premiums are accrued based on the ultimate cost of the experience to date of a group of entities.

In addition, if the governmental entity cannot estimate losses on its retrospective policies, it should disclose the existing contingency in the notes to the financial statements, provided that the additional liability for premiums is probable or reasonably possible.

Policyholder or pool dividends. If a governmental entity receives or is entitled to receive a policyholder dividend or return of contribution related to its insurance or pool participation contract, that dividend should be recognized as a reduction of original insurance expenditures or expenses at the time that the dividend is declared.

This treatment is appropriate since policyholder dividends are payments made or credits extended to the insured by the insurer, usually at the end of the policy year, that result in a reduction in the net insurance cost to the policyholder. The accounting treatment in the preceding paragraph is appropriate regardless of whether the dividends are paid in cash to the policyholder or are applied to the insured to reduce premiums due for the next policy year.

Entities providing claims servicing or insurance coverage to others. Sometimes a governmental entity may provide insurance-like services to other entities. The circumstances of the nature and extent of the services provided need to be considered to determine the most appropriate accounting treatment. The following general principles apply:

- If a governmental entity provides insurance or risk management coverage to other entities outside the government's reporting entity that is separate from its own risk management activities and involves a material transfer or pooling of risk among the participants, then these activities should be accounted for as a public entity risk pool. (See the second part of this chapter for further details.)
- If a governmental entity provides risk transfer or pooling coverage combined with its own risk management activities to individuals or organizations outside of its reporting entity, those activities should continue to be reported in the general fund or internal service fund only as long as the governmental entity is the predominant participant in the fund. If the governmental entity is not the predominant participant in the fund, then the combined activities should be accounted for as a public entity risk pool, using an enterprise fund and the accounting and financial reporting requirements described in the second part of this chapter.
- If a governmental entity provides claims servicing functions which are not insurance functions for individuals and organizations that are not a part of its financial reporting entity, amounts collected or due from those individuals or organizations and paid (or to be paid) to settle claims should be reported as a net asset or liability on an accrual basis, as appropriate. In other words, as a claims service, the governmental entity may collect more from the other entity than it has paid out to settle claims on behalf of the other entity, in which case it owes the excess amount back to the other entity. On the other hand, the governmental entity may have paid out more to settle claims for the other entity than it has received from the other entity, in which case it has a receivable for the difference from the other entity. In addition, the operating statement of the governmental entity should report claims servicing revenue and administrative costs as described in the second section of this chapter.

Disclosure Requirements

In addition to the accounting requirements relating to risk financing activities described in the preceding section of this chapter, GASBS 10 also contains a number of disclosure requirements relating to these activities. GASBS 10 specifies that the following information should be disclosed in the notes to the financial statements, when applicable:

1. A description of the risks of loss to which the entity is exposed and the ways in which those risks of loss are handled (such as purchase of commercial insurance, participation in a public entity risk pool, or risk retention).
2. A description of significant reductions in insurance coverage in the prior year by major categories of risk. (Whether the amount of settlements exceeded insurance coverage for each of the past three years should also be indicated.)
3. If an entity participates in a risk pool, a description of the nature of the participation, including the rights and the responsibilities of both the entity and the pool.
4. If an entity retains the risk of loss (even when it accounts for these activities in a separate internal service fund), the following should be disclosed:
   (a) The basis for estimating the liabilities for unpaid claims, including the effects of specific, incremental claim adjustment expenditures or expenses, salvage, and subrogation,

and whether other allocated or unallocated claim adjustment expenditures or expenses are included.

(b) The carrying amount of liabilities for unpaid claims that are recorded at present value in the financial statements and the range of rates used to discount those liabilities.

(c) The aggregate outstanding amount of claims liabilities for which annuity contracts have been purchased in the claimant's names and for which the related liabilities have been removed from the balance sheet. Annuity contracts used to settle claims where the claimant has signed an agreement releasing the entity from further obligation and for which the likelihood that the pool will be required to make future payments on those claims is remote should not be included in this disclosure.

5. A reconciliation of changes in the aggregate liabilities for claims for the current fiscal year and the prior fiscal year, using the following tabular format:
   (a) Amount of claims liabilities at the beginning of each fiscal year.
   (b) Incurred claims, representing the total of a provision for events of the current fiscal year and any change (increase or decrease) in the provision for events of prior fiscal years.
   (c) Payments on claims attributable to events of both the current fiscal year and prior fiscal years.
   (d) Any other material items, with an appropriate explanation.
   (e) Amount of claims liability at the end of each fiscal year.

Chapter 11 discusses the determination of a government's reporting entity, including a discussion of disclosure requirements for a primary government and its discretely presented component units. The guidance in that chapter should be considered in determining what disclosures should be included in the financial statements of a reporting entity that includes blended and discretely presented component units.

ACCOUNTING AND FINANCIAL REPORTING FOR PUBLIC ENTITY RISK POOLS

This section of the chapter describes the accounting and financial reporting requirements for risk financing and insurance-related activities of public entity risk pools. These standards are primarily derived from those of GASBS 10, as subsequently amended by GASBS 30.

What Is a Public Entity Risk Pool?

A *public entity risk pool* is a cooperative group of governmental entities joining together to finance an exposure, liability, or risk. The risks may include property and liability risks, workers, or employee health care. The pool may be a stand-alone entity or be included as part of a larger governmental entity that acts as the pool's sponsor.

The agreements between the governmental entities that participate in the public entity risk pools and the pool itself are known as *participation contracts*. These are formal written contracts that describe, among other things, the period, amount of the risk coverage that the pool will provide for the participating governmental entity, and the contribution the participant must pay for that coverage. The participation contract is synonymous with a *policy*, a term used in the commercial insurance field to refer to the contract between an insurer and an insured that describes the period and amount of risk coverage to be provided to the insured.

A governmental entity that is a pool's sponsor may or may not participate in the pool for its own risk management function. For example, a state may host, but not participate in, a risk management pool that provides workers' compensation protection for all of the local school districts in the state. Conversely, a state may already pool its general liability risk internally and decide to extend that pooling to local governments unable to obtain private insurance coverage within the state. Entities that participate in the state pool may share risks with other participants, including the state.

The rules as to when risk financing activities should be accounted for as part of the operations of a sponsoring government or when they should be accounted for as a public entity risk pool were discussed earlier in this chapter.

Stand-alone public entity risk pools are established under authorizing statute by agreement of any number of state and local governmental entities. Stand-alone pools are sometimes organized or sponsored by municipal leagues, school associations, or other types of associations of governmental entities. A stand-alone pool is frequently operated by a board including one member from each participating government. Generally, a public entity risk pool has no publicly elected officials and no power to tax.

There are four basic types of public entity risk pools. They are:

1. **Risk-sharing pool**—An arrangement by which governments pool risks and funds and share in the cost of losses.
2. **Insurance-purchasing pool**—An arrangement by which governments pool funds or resources to purchase commercial insurance products. (This arrangement is also referred to as a *risk-purchasing group.*)
3. **Banking pool**—An arrangement by which monies are made available on a loan basis for pool members in the event of loss.
4. **Claims-servicing or account pool**—An arrangement in which a pool manages separate accounts for each pool member from which the losses of that member are paid.

NOTE: Only the risk-sharing and insurance-purchasing pools are considered to represent a transfer of risk. The banking pool and claims-servicing pool do not represent a transfer of risk and are not covered by the guidance presented in this section for public entity risk pools. These entities simply report amounts collected or due from pool participants, including capitalization contributions, and paid or to be paid to settle claims as a net asset or liability on an accrual basis to or from the pool participants.

Determining whether a transfer of some or all of a risk has occurred is likely to require the exercise of professional judgment by the financial statement preparer. Risk retention and risk transfer are not mutually exclusive or absolute. Premiums paid or required contributions to a public entity risk pool may be made under a number of conditions and circumstances. For example, the contribution may not be adjustable, regardless of the loss experience. On the other hand, the contribution may be adjustable dollar-for-dollar for amounts that losses paid exceed or are less than the original contribution. Variations of adjustment schemes between these two extremes are also common, such as adjusting contributions only when loss experience falls outside of some agreed-upon range of amounts. In addition, if the public entity risk pool does not have sufficient assets to pay the claims against its participating governments, it is not possible for the governments to have transferred their risks to the risk pool, since they will be ultimately liable if the risk pool fails to pay the claims.

Risks of loss from the following kinds of events are included within the scope of this discussion of public entity risk pools that represent a transfer of risk:

- Torts (wrongful acts, injuries, or damages not involving a breach of contract for which a civil action can be brought).

- Theft or destruction of, or damage to, assets.
- Business interruption.
- Errors or omissions.
- Job-related illnesses or injuries to employees.
- Acts of God (events beyond human origin or control, such as natural disasters, lightning, windstorms, and earthquakes).
- Other risks of loss of participating entities assumed under a policy or a participation contract issued by a public entity risk pool.

The rules discussed in this section also apply to losses assumed under contract by a public entity risk pool when a participating employer agrees to provide accident and health, dental, and other medical benefits to its employees and retirees and their dependents and beneficiaries based on covered events that have already occurred. The scope of this section excludes all post-employment benefits that governmental employers expect to provide to current and future retirees. In addition, the scope of GASBS 10's guidance for public entity risk pools excludes Medicaid insurance plans provided to low-income state residents under Title XIX of the Federal Social Security Act, although it is unlikely that a state would use a public entity risk pool for Medicaid insurance plans anyway.

Specific Accounting and Financial Reporting Requirements

In addition to the background information provided by GASBS 10 described above, the accounting and financial reporting requirements discussed in the following sections should enable the financial statement preparer to effectively account for and report the activities of a public entity risk pool.

Fund type to use. All public entity risk pools should account for their activities in an enterprise fund, regardless of whether there is a transfer or pooling of risk. Accordingly, public entity risk pools should use proprietary fund accounting and apply all applicable GASB pronouncements and certain FASB pronouncements as well. Accounting and financial reporting considerations for proprietary funds are more fully described in Chapter 10. This is one of the few instances where the use of a specific fund is required by GAAP for governments.

Premium revenue recognition. Premiums and required contribution revenues should be matched to the risk protection provided, and accordingly should be recognized as revenue over the contract period in proportion to the amount of risk protection provided. For example, if a public entity risk pool receives $8,000 in premiums to provide liability insurance up to $5 million for a two-year period, $4,000 of premium revenue is recognized in each year. In a few cases, the period of risk differs significantly from the contract period, and premiums should be recognized as revenue over the period of risk in proportion to the amount of risk protection provided. Usually this results in premiums being recognized as revenue evenly over the contract period (or period of risk, if different). In some cases, the amount of risk protection changes according to a predetermined schedule, and the recognition of premium revenue should be adjusted accordingly. For example, using the same facts as in the previous example, but assuming that the amount of the insurance increases to $7 million in the second year of the contract, premium revenue is recognized as follows:

Year 1	$8,000 × $5 million/($5 million + $7 million) = $3,333
Year 2	$8,000 × $7 million/($5 million + $7 million) = $4,667

The allocation of a higher premium to year 2 of the contract correctly reflects the fact that a greater amount of insurance is being provided in the second year of the contract.

Revenue recognition for retrospectively rated policy premiums and for reporting-form contracts is slightly more difficult. Recall from the first section of the chapter that a retrospectively rated policy is a type of policy that uses a method of determining the final amount of an insurance premium by which the initial premium is adjusted based on actual experience during the period of coverage, sometimes subject to minimum and maximum adjustment limits. It is designed to encourage safety by the insured (since increased claims will result in higher premiums) and to compensate the insurer if larger than expected losses are incurred. *Reporting-form* contracts are policies in which the policyholder is required to report the value of property insured to the insurer at certain intervals. The final premium on the contract is determined by applying the contract rate to the average of the values reported.

For both retrospectively rated policies and reporting-form policies, the following premium revenue recognition requirements should be used:

1. If the ultimate premium is reasonably estimable, the estimated ultimate premium should be recognized as revenue over the contract period. The estimated ultimate premium should be revised to reflect current experience. (This is assumed to be the most likely case.)
2. If the ultimate premium cannot be reasonably estimated, the cost recovery method or the deposit method should be used until the ultimate premium becomes reasonably estimable:
   (a) Under the cost recovery method, premiums are recognized as revenue in an amount equal to estimated claims costs as insured events occur until the ultimate premium is reasonably estimable, and recognition of income should be postponed until that time. For example, assume that $50,000 in premium revenue has been received for the fiscal year on a retrospective policy, but is still subject to adjustment. In addition, estimated claims costs for insured events for the same period are $35,000. The following journal entry would be recorded for premium revenue:

Cash	50,000	
Premium revenue		35,000
Unearned premium revenue		15,000

To record premium revenue earned and deferred

   (b) Under the deposit method, premiums are not recognized as revenues and claims costs are not charged to expense until the ultimate premium is reasonably estimable. Revenue recognition is postponed until this time. Assuming the same facts as in the preceding example, the following journal entries would be recorded:

Cash	50,000	
Unearned premium revenue		50,000

To record receipt of deferred premium revenue

At the same time, as claims costs are paid, they are not charged to expenses, but are set up as a deferred charge. The cumulative effect of this recording is reflected in the following journal entry:

Unrecognized claims costs	35,000	
Cash		35,000

To record payment of claims costs that are deferred pending recognition of related premium revenue

One other revenue recognition issue highlighted by GASBS 10 involves a situation where a portion of a premium is specifically identified as being collected for future catastrophic losses. (A *catastrophic loss* is considered a conflagration, earthquake, windstorm, explosion, or similar event resulting in substantial losses or an unusually large number of unrelated and unexpected losses occurring in a single period.) In this case, the amount specifically identified should be recognized as revenue over the contract period. In addition, that amount should be separately identified as a reservation of pool equity if it is contractually restricted for that specific future use or if it is legally restricted for that specific use by an organization or individual outside the reporting entity.

Claim cost recognition. The basic principle for claim cost recognition by public entity risk pools is that a liability for unpaid claims (including IBNR) should be accrued when insured events occur. For claims-made policies, a liability should be accrued in the period in which the event that triggers coverage under the policy or participation contract occurs.

The recorded liability should be based on the estimated ultimate cost of settling the claims (including the effects of inflation and other societal and economic factors), using experience adjusted for current trends and any other factors that would modify experience.

NOTE: These societal factors are difficult to predict and fall into the category of "you'll know them when you see them." For example, a city was found to have used lead-based paint in some of its subsidized housing. Peeling paint eaten by children living in these apartments became a reason for various medical problems encountered by these children. Assume that these claims followed the normal claims experience of the city for these types of liabilities. However, at some point, a high level of publicity and large advertising campaigns in targeted neighborhoods by attorneys greatly changed the city's claims patterns with respect to lead-based paint claims, resulting in a change in the model used to estimate the ultimate liability for these cases.

Claims accruals for IBNR claims should be made if it is probable that a loss has been incurred and the amount can be reasonably estimated. Changes in estimates of claims costs resulting from the continuous review process and differences between estimates and payments for claims should be recognized in results of operations of the period in which the estimates are changed or payments are made.

Estimated recoveries on unsettled claims should be evaluated in terms of their estimated and realizable value and deducted from the liability for unpaid claims. Estimated recoveries on settled claims also should be deducted from the liability for unpaid claims. Two examples of these recoveries are salvage and subrogation:

- *Salvage* represents the amount received by a public entity risk pool from the sale of property (usually damaged property) on which the pool has paid a total claim to the insured and has obtained title to the property.
- *Subrogation* is the right of the insurer to pursue any course of recovery of damages in its name or the name of the policyholder against a third party who is liable for costs of an insured event that have been paid by the insurer.

Claims adjustment expenses. Liabilities for claims adjustment expenses should be accrued when the related liability for unpaid claims is accrued. Claims adjustment expenses include all costs that are expected to be incurred in connection with the settlement of unpaid claims. These costs can be either allocated or unallocated.

- *Allocated claims adjustment expenses* are those that can be associated directly with specific claims paid or in the process of the settlement, such as legal and adjuster's fees.

- *Unallocated claims adjustment expenses* are other costs that cannot be associated with specific claims but are related to claims paid or in the process of settlement, such as salaries and other internal costs of the pool's claims department.

Discounting. The practice of presenting claims liabilities at the discounted present value of estimated future cash payments is neither mandated nor prohibited by GASBS 10. However, claims liabilities associated with structured settlements should be discounted if they represent contractual obligations to pay money on fixed or determinable dates. A structured settlement is a means of satisfying a claim liability and consists of an initial cash payment to meet specific present financial needs combined with a stream of future payments designed to meet future financial needs. For example, a public entity risk pool may enter into a settlement with someone injured by a participant government's vehicle, whereby the participant government agrees to pay the injured party's hospital claims up front, and then a monthly fixed amount for the remaining life of the injured party. The monthly payment cash flow streams should be discounted when the public entity risk pool recognizes this loss in its financial statements.

Annuity contracts. A public entity risk pool may purchase an annuity contract in a claimant's name to satisfy a claim liability. If the likelihood that the pool will be required to make future payments on the claim is remote, the public entity risk pool is considered to have satisfied its primary liability to the claimant. Accordingly, the annuity contract should not be reported as an asset by the public entity risk pool, and the liability for the claim should be removed from the public entity risk pool's balance sheet. However, GASBS 10 requires that the aggregate outstanding amount of liabilities that are removed from the public entity risk pool's balance sheet should be disclosed as long as those contingent liabilities are outstanding. On the other hand, if annuity contracts used to settle claims for which the claimant has signed an agreement releasing the public entity risk pool from further obligation and for which the likelihood that the public entity risk pool will be required to make future payments on those claims is remote, then the amount of the liability related to these annuity contracts should not be included in this aggregate disclosure.

Disclosure of loss contingencies. If no accrual is made for a loss contingency because it has not met the conditions of being probable or reasonably estimable, disclosure of the loss contingency should be made by the public entity risk pool if it is at least reasonably possible that a loss may have been incurred. The disclosure should indicate the nature of the contingency and should give an estimate of the possible loss or range of loss or state that such an estimate cannot be made. Disclosure is not required of a loss contingency involving an unreported claim or assessment if there has been no manifestation of a potential claimant or an awareness of a possible claim or assessment unless it is considered probable that a claim will be asserted and there is a reasonable possibility that the outcome will be unfavorable.

A disclosure of loss contingency should also be made when an exposure to loss exists in excess of the amount accrued in the financial statements by the public entity risk pool and it is reasonably possible that a loss or additional loss may have been incurred. For example, if a loss is probable and is estimated with a range of amounts and the lower amount of the range is accrued in the public entity risk pool's financial statements, the reasonably possible amount of the loss in excess of the amount accrued should be disclosed.

Policy/participation contract acquisition costs. Public entity risk pools sometimes incur acquisition costs when acquiring new or renewal participation contracts. These costs might include certain underwriting and policy issue costs as well as inspection fees that are primarily related to contracts issued or renewed during the period in which the costs are incurred. Underwriting costs are those costs related to the process of selecting, classifying, evaluating, rating, and assuming risks.

GASBS 10 provides that acquisition costs should be capitalized and charged to expense in proportion to premium revenue recognized. Rather than determining acquisition costs on an individual contract basis, these costs may be allocated by groups based on the types of contracts that are consistent with the pool's manner of acquiring, servicing, and measuring the revenue and expense elements of its contracts. Unamortized acquisition costs should be classified on the balance sheet as an asset.

A public entity risk pool may determine acquisition costs based on a percentage relationship of costs incurred to premiums from contracts issued or renewed for a specified period. In this case, the specified relationship and the period used, once determined, should be applied to applicable unearned premiums throughout the contract periods.

Other costs. Costs incurred during the period other than those related to claims, such as those relating to investment management, general administration, and policy maintenance, that do not vary with and are not primarily related to the acquisition of new and renewal contracts should be charged to expense as incurred.

Policyholder dividends. Policyholder dividends are payments made or credits extended to the insured by the public entity risk pool, usually at the end of the policy year, which result in reducing the net insurance cost to the policyholder. They are not determined based on the actual experience of an individual policyholder or a pool participant, but are instead based on the experience of the pool or a class of policies.

Policyholder dividends should be accrued as dividends expense using an estimate of the amount to be paid. Dividends used by policyholders to reduce premiums should also be reported as premium income. Policyholder dividends include amounts returned to pool participants from excess premiums for future catastrophic losses.

Experience refunds. Experience refunds are based on the experience of individual policyholders or pool participants (in contrast to policyholder dividends, which are based on the experience of the pool or a class of policies). If the pool has experience refund arrangements that exist under experience-rated contracts, a separate liability should be accrued for these amounts. The liability is based on the experience of the policyholder and the provisions of the contract. Revenue from the policyholder is reduced by amounts that are expected to be paid in the form of refunds. In other words, when a liability for a refund is established, it is done so by decreasing revenue instead of increasing an expense account.

Premium deficiency. A premium deficiency is the amount by which expected claims costs (including IBNR) and all expected claim adjustment expenses, expected dividends to policyholders or pool participants, unamortized acquisition costs, and incurred policy maintenance costs exceed related unearned premium revenue. In other words, when all aspects of a particular insurance policy or contract are considered, the public entity risk pool will incur a loss on the policy or contract.

If a premium deficiency exists, unamortized acquisition costs should be expensed to the extent of the premium deficiency. Deficiencies in excess of unamortized acquisition costs should be recognized as a premium deficiency liability as of the balance sheet date and as a premium deficiency expense.

NOTE: The substance of this requirement of GASBS 10 is that known losses on insurance contracts or policies are recognized as liabilities and expensed immediately.

The premium deficiency liability should be adjusted in future reporting periods as expected costs are incurred so that no premium deficiency liability remains at the end of the period covered by the policies or contracts.

Premium deficiencies that result from risk-sharing pool participation contracts also should be reported as revenue (and a corresponding assessment receivable) at the time the pool determines that a deficiency is reasonably estimable, provided that the pool has an enforceable legal claim to the amounts and their collectability is probable.

Reinsurance. Reinsurance is a transaction in which an assuming enterprise (reinsurer) for a consideration (i.e., a premium) assumes all or part of a risk that was originally undertaken by another enterprise (known as the ceding enterprise). The legal rights of the insured are not affected by the reinsurance transaction. The ceding enterprise that issued the original insurance contract remains liable to the insured for the payment of policy benefits. This is similar to, but not exactly the same as, excess insurance. Excess insurance is the transfer of risk of loss from one party (the insured) to another (the excess insurer) in which the excess insurer provides insurance in excess of a certain, usually large, amount. For example, a public entity risk pool may purchase insurance to transfer the risk of aggregate losses above $5 million by its pool participants.

Amounts that are recoverable from reinsurers or excess insurers and that relate to paid claims and claim adjustment expenses should be classified as assets (with an appropriate allowance for uncollectible amounts) and as reductions of expenses. Estimated amounts recoverable from reinsurers that relate to the liabilities for unpaid claims and claim adjustment expenses should be deducted from those liabilities rather than reported as assets. Unearned premiums on contracts that are ceded to a reinsurer by a pool should be netted with related premiums paid to but not yet earned by the reinsurer. Receivables and payables from the same reinsurer, including amounts withheld, also should be netted. Reinsurance premiums paid and reinsurance recoveries on claims may be netted against earned premiums and incurred claims costs, respectively, in the operating statement.

Proceeds from reinsurance transactions that represent recovery of acquisition costs should reduce applicable unamortized acquisition costs in such a manner that net acquisition costs are capitalized and charged to expense in proportion to net revenue recognized (similar to the examples that were provided in the previous section relating to acquisition costs). If the pool has agreed to service all of the related ceded insurance contracts without reasonable compensation, a liability should be accrued for estimated excess future service costs (that is, maintenance costs) under the reinsurance contracts.

To the extent that a reinsurance or excess insurance contract does not, despite its form, provide for indemnification of the pool by the reinsurer against loss or liability, the premium paid less the premium to be retained by the reinsurer should be accounted for as a deposit by the pool. Those contracts may be structured in various ways but, regardless of form, if their substance is that all or part of the premium paid by the pool is a deposit, amounts paid should be accounted for as deposits. A net credit resulting from the contract should be reported as a liability of the pool.

Capitalization contributions made to other public entity risk pools. In some cases, public entity risk pools participate in other public entity risk pools, such as excess pooling arrangements. A participant pool that makes a capitalization contribution should apply the guidance contained in the first part of this chapter. The participant pool also should apply pertinent reinsurance accounting guidance. The participant pool may be required to net certain amounts related to the excess pool, or it may be required to treat certain amounts paid to the excess pool as a deposit.

Capitalization contracts received. The accounting for capitalization contributions by a public entity risk pool depends on whether it is probable that the contribution will be returned.

If it is probable that capitalization contributions will be returned, a pool should report contributions received as a liability.

If it is not probable that capitalization contributions will be returned, a pool should report the contributions as unearned premiums. Premium revenue should be allocated and recognized over the periods for which coverage is expected to be provided by the pool. The periods expected to be covered should be consistent with the periods for which the contribution is factored into the determination of premiums but should not exceed ten years if not readily determinable.

Investments. The accounting and financial reporting for investments held by public entity risk pools is governed by GASB Statement 31 (GASBS 31), *Accounting and Financial Reporting for Certain Investments and for External Investment Pools*. GASBS 31 includes in its scope all debt securities and equity securities with readily determinable market values and certain other, similar investments, which are recorded in the financial statements at their fair values. These guidelines are covered in depth in Chapter 12.

Since public entity risk pools operate similarly to insurance companies, their range of investments tends to be greater than those that are covered by GASBS 31. Accordingly, much of the accounting and financial reporting guidance for investments that was originally included by the GASB in GASBS 10 relating to investments is still applicable. These specialized investment areas are discussed in the following paragraphs:

1. *Mortgage loans*. Mortgage loans should be reported at their outstanding principal balances if they were acquired at par value. They should be stated at amortized cost if they were purchased at a discount or a premium. In either case, an allowance for estimated uncollectible amounts, if any, should be recorded. Amortization and other related charges or credits should be charged or credited to investment income. Any changes in the allowance for estimated uncollectible amounts relating to mortgage loans should be included in realized gains and losses.
2. *Real estate investments*. Real estate investments should be reported at cost less accumulated depreciation and less an allowance for any impairment in the value of the real estate investment. Depreciation and other related charges and credits should be charged or credited to investment income. Any changes in the allowance for impairment in value related to real estate investments should be included in realized gains and losses.
3. *Other investments*. All other investments should be reported at cost plus or minus any unamortized premium or discount. If the fair value of an investment declines below its carrying amount and it is probable that a loss will be realized in the future, an estimated loss should be reported as a realized loss in the pool's operating statement and as a reduction of the carrying amount of the investment.
4. *Loan origination fees*. In addition to the above guidance, GASBS 10 specifies that loan origination fees should be accounted for as originally prescribed in FASB Statement 91 (SFAS 91), *Accounting for Nonrefundable Fees and Costs Associated with Originating Loans and Initial Direct Costs of Leases* (now included in GASBS 62), which established the accounting for nonrefundable fees and costs associated with lending, committing to lend, and purchasing a loan or group of loans. GASBS 62 specifies the following accounting for fees and initial direct costs associated with leasing:
   (a) Loan origination fees should be recognized over the life of the related loan as an adjustment of yield.
   (b) Certain direct loan origination costs should be recognized over the life of the related loan as a reduction of the loan's yield.
   (c) All loan commitment fees should be deferred except for certain retrospectively determined fees. Commitment fees meeting specified criteria should be recognized over the loan commitment period. All other commitment fees should be recognized as an adjustment of yield over the related loan's life or, if the commitment expires unexercised, recognized in income on expiration of the commitment.

(d) Loan fees, certain direct loan origination costs, and purchase premiums and discounts on loans should be recognized as an adjustment of yield generally using the interest method based on the contractual terms of the loan. Prepayments may be anticipated in certain circumstances.

(e) Real estate used in operations. Real estate used predominantly in the public entity risk pool's operations (as opposed to an investment in real estate) should be classified as such. Depreciation and other real estate operating costs on real estate used in operations should be classified as operation expenses, consistent with this real estate's classification on the balance sheet. Imputed investment income and rental expense should not be recognized for real estate used in a public entity risk pool's operations.

Disclosure Requirements and Required Supplementary Information

In addition to the accounting guidance described above, public entity risk pools must meet a number of disclosure requirements relative to their activities and must also prepare and disclose certain required supplementary information in accordance with GASBS 10, as amended by GASBS 30. The following are the disclosure and supplementary information requirements:

Disclosure requirements. Public entity risk pools should make the following disclosures:

1. A description of the risk transfer or pool agreement, including the rights and responsibilities of the pool and the pool participants. (Also provide a brief description of the number and types of entities participating in the pool.)
2. The basis for estimating the liabilities for unpaid claims and claim adjustment expenses. (Pools should state that the liabilities are based on an estimated ultimate cost of settling the claims, including the effects of inflation and other societal and economic factors.)
3. The nature of acquisition costs capitalized, the method of amortizing those costs, and the amount of those costs amortized for the period.
4. The face amount and carrying amount of liabilities for unpaid claims and claim adjustment expenses that are recorded at present value in the financial statements and the range of annual interest rates used to discount those liabilities.
5. Whether the pool considers anticipated investment income in determining whether a premium deficiency exists.
6. The nature and significance of excess insurance or reinsurance transaction to the pool's operations, including the type of coverage, reinsurance premiums ceded, and the estimated amounts that are recoverable from excess insurers and reinsurers and that reduce the liabilities as of the balance sheet date for unpaid claims and claim adjustment expenses.
7. A reconciliation of total claims liabilities, including an analysis of changes in aggregate liabilities for claims and claim adjustment expenses for the current fiscal year and the prior fiscal year, in the following tabular format:
   (a) Amount of liabilities for unpaid claims and claim adjustment expenses at the beginning of each fiscal year.
   (b) Incurred claims and claim adjustment expenses:
      (i) Provision for insured events of the current fiscal year.
      (ii) Increase (decrease) in the provision for insured events of prior fiscal years.

(c) Payments:

(i) Claims and claim adjustment expenses attributable to insured events of the current fiscal year.

(ii) Claims and claim adjustment expenses attributable to insured events of prior fiscal years.

(d) Other, including an explanation of each material item.

(e) Amount of liabilities for unpaid claims and claim adjustment expenses at the end of each fiscal year.

8. The aggregate outstanding amount of liabilities for which annuity contracts have been purchased from third parties in the claimant's name and for which the related liabilities have been removed from the balance sheet. (However, annuity contracts used to settle claims for which the claimant has signed an agreement releasing the entity from further obligation and for which the likelihood that the pool will be required to make future payments on those claims is remote should not be included in this disclosure.)

Required supplementary information. Required supplementary information consists of statements, schedules, statistical data, or other information that the GASB has determined necessary to supplement, although not required to be a part of, the general-purpose financial statements.

The following revenue and claims development information should be included as required supplementary information immediately after the notes to the financial statements in separate public entity risk pool financial reports. Pools that are included as part of a combined general government reporting entity and that do not issue separate financial statements should present the required supplementary information after the notes to the reporting entity's financial statements. If the reporting entity issues a comprehensive annual financial report, pools may present the required supplementary information as statistical information in a table that presents the following information:

1. Amount of gross premium (or required contribution) revenue, amount of premium (or required contribution) revenue ceded, and the amount of net reported premium (or required contribution) revenue (net of excess insurance or reinsurance), and reported investment revenue for each of the past ten fiscal years, including the latest fiscal year.
2. Amount of reported unallocated claim adjustment expenses and reported other costs for each of the past ten fiscal years, including the latest fiscal year.
3. The total gross amount of incurred claims and allocated claim adjustment expenses (both paid and accrued before the effect of loss assumed by excess insurers or reinsurers), loss assumed by excess insurers and reinsurers (both paid and accrued), and the total net amount of incurred claims and allocated claims adjustment expenses (both paid and accrued). The amounts should be presented as originally reported at the end of each of the past ten accident years (for occurrence-based policies or contracts), report years (for claims-made policies or contracts), or policy years, including the latest year. The amounts should be limited to provision for claims resulting from events that triggered coverage under the policy or participation contract in that year. If amounts are not present on an accident-year basis or a report-year basis, they should be reported on a policy-year basis. For purposes of this disclosure, a policy-year basis is a method that assigns incurred losses and claim adjustment expenses to the year in which the event that triggered coverage under the pool insurance policy or participation contract occurred. For occurrence-based coverage for which all members have a common contract renewal date, the policy-year basis is the same as the accident-year basis. For claims-made coverage, policy-year basis is the same as the report-year basis. The basis of reporting should be used consistently for all years presented.

4. The cumulative net amount paid as of the end of the accident year, report year, or policy year (as appropriate) and each succeeding year for each of the incurred claims and allocated expense amounts presented in item 3 above.
5. The reestimated amount for loss assumed by excess insurers or reinsurers as of the end of the current year for each of the accident years, report years, or policy years (as appropriate) presented in item 3 above.
6. The reestimated amount for net incurred claims and claim adjustment expenses as of the end of each succeeding year for each of the accident years, report years, or policy years (as appropriate) presented in item 3 above.
7. The change in net incurred claims and claim adjustment expenses from the original estimate, based on the difference between the latest reestimated amount present in item 6 above for each of the accident years, report years, or policy years (as appropriate) presented in item 3 above.

In addition, percentage information (such as the percentage of gross incurred claims and claim adjustment expenses assumed by excess insurers or reinsurers) may be presented but is not required. If presented, the information should not obscure or distort the required elements of the table.

In addition to the reconciliation of total claims liabilities (included in the list of disclosures above), a reconciliation of claims liabilities by type of contract, including an analysis of changes in liabilities for claims and claim adjustment expenses for the current fiscal year and the prior year, should be presented in the same table format as the disclosure required described above.

Because of the requirement in items 4 and 5 above for payments and reestimates in each of the succeeding ten years in the ten-year required supplementary information table, the format of the table is awkward and can be confusing. Exhibit 1 presents one format that might be used, based upon an example provided in GASBS 30.

Exhibit 1: Sample format for ten-year loss development information for public entity risk pool

The following table illustrates how the city of Anywhere's Public Entity Risk Pool (the Pool) earned revenue (net of reinsurance) and investment income compare to related costs of loss (net of loss assumed by reinsurers) and other expenses assumed by the Pool as of the end of each of the previous ten years. The rows of the table are defined as follows: (1) This line shows the total of each fiscal year's gross earned premiums and reported investment revenue, amounts of premiums ceded, and reported premiums (net of reinsurance) and reported investment revenue. (2) This line shows each fiscal year's other operating costs of the Pool including overhead and loss adjustment expenses not allocatable to individual claims. (3) This line shows the Pool's gross incurred losses and allocated loss adjustment expense, losses assumed by reinsurers, and net incurred losses and loss adjustment expense (both paid and accrued) as originally reported at the end of the year in which the event that triggered coverage occurred (called *accident year*). (4) This section of ten rows shows the cumulative net amounts paid as of the end of successive years for each accident year. (5) This line shows the latest reestimated amount of losses assumed by reinsurers for each accident year. (6) This section of ten rows shows how each accident year's net incurred losses increased or decreased as of the end of successive years. (This annual reestimation results from new information received on known losses, reevaluation of existing information on known losses, and emergence of new losses not previously known.) (7) This line compares the latest reestimated net incurred losses amount to the amount originally established (line 3) and shows whether this latest estimate of losses is greater or less than originally thought. As data for individual accident years mature, the correlation between the original estimates and reestimated amounts is commonly used to evaluate the accuracy of net incurred losses currently recognized in less mature accident years. The columns of the table show data for successive accident years.

	Fiscal and Accident Year Ended (in thousands of dollars)									
	20X0	***20X1***	***20X2***	***20X3***	***20X4***	***20X5***	***20X6***	***20X7***	***20X8***	***20X9***
1. Premiums and investment revenue:										
Earned	$x,xxx	$x,xxx	$x,xxx	$x,xxx	$x,xxx	$x,xxx	$x,xxx	$x,xxx	$x,xxx	$x,xxx
Ceded	x,xxx	x,xxx	x,xxx	x,xxx	x,xxx	x,xxx	x,xxx	x,xxx	x,xxx	x,xxx
Net earned	x,xxx	x,xxx	x,xxx	x,xxx	x,xxx	x,xxx	x,xxx	x,xxx	x,xxx	x,xxx
2. Unallocated expenses	x,xxx	x,xxx	x,xxx	x,xxx	x,xxx	x,xxx	x,xxx	x,xxx	x,xxx	x,xxx
3. Estimated losses and expenses, end of accident year:										
Incurred	x,xxx	x,xxx	x,xxx	x,xxx	x,xxx	x,xxx	x,xxx	x,xxx	x,xxx	x,xxx
Ceded	x,xxx	x,xxx	x,xxx	x,xxx	x,xxx	x,xxx	x,xxx	x,xxx	x,xxx	x,xxx
Net incurred(1)	x,xxx	x,xxx	x,xxx	x,xxx	x,xxx	x,xxx	x,xxx	x,xxx	x,xxx	x,xxx
4. Net paid (cumulative) as of:										
End of accident year	x,xxx	x,xxx	x,xxx	x,xxx	x,xxx	x,xxx	x,xxx	x,xxx	x,xxx	x,xxx
1 year later	x,xxx	x,xxx	x,xxx	x,xxx	x,xxx	x,xxx	x,xxx	x,xxx	x,xxx	
2 years later	x,xxx	x,xxx	x,xxx	x,xxx	x,xxx	x,xxx	x,xxx	x,xxx		
3 years later	x,xxx	x,xxx	x,xxx	x,xxx	x,xxx	x,xxx	x,xxx			
4 years later	x,xxx	x,xxx	x,xxx	x,xxx	x,xxx	x,xxx				
5 years later	x,xxx	x,xxx	x,xxx	x,xxx	x,xxx					
6 years later	x,xxx	x,xxx	x,xxx	x,xxx						
7 years later	x,xxx	x,xxx	x,xxx							
8 years later	x,xxx	x,xxx								
9 years later	x,xxx									
5. Reestimated ceded losses and expenses:	x,xxx	x,xxx	x,xxx	x,xxx	x,xxx	x,xxx	x,xxx	x,xxx	x,xxx	x,xxx
6. Reestimated net incurred losses and expenses:										
End of accident year(1)	x,xxx	x,xxx	x,xxx	x,xxx	x,xxx	x,xxx	x,xxx	x,xxx	x,xxx	x,xxx
1 year later	x,xxx	x,xxx	x,xxx	x,xxx	x,xxx	x,xxx	x,xxx	x,xxx	x,xxx	
2 years later	x,xxx	x,xxx	x,xxx	x,xxx	x,xxx	x,xxx	x,xxx	x,xxx		
3 years later	x,xxx	x,xxx	x,xxx	x,xxx	x,xxx	x,xxx	x,xxx			
4 years later	x,xxx	x,xxx	x,xxx	x,xxx	x,xxx	x,xxx				
5 years later	x,xxx	x,xxx	x,xxx	x,xxx	x,xxx					
6 years later	x,xxx	x,xxx	x,xxx	x,xxx						
7 years later	x,xxx	x,xxx	x,xxx							
8 years later	x,xxx	x,xxx								
9 years later	x,xxx									
7. Increase (decrease) in estimated net incurred losses and expenses from end of accident year(2)	x,xxx	x,xxx	x,xxx	x,xxx	x,xxx	x,xxx	x,xxx	x,xxx	x,xxx	x,xxx

[1] *Amounts on these lines should equal.*

[2] *This amount is the difference between the total of line 3 and the most recent year presented in line 6.*

During the transition period following implementation of GASBS 10, ten years of information about claims liabilities and claim adjustment expenses may not be available. Information required above should be presented for as many years as that information is available. In addition, if changes in a pool's loss, expense, reinsurance, excess insurance, or other transactions materially affect pool revenue, expenses, or liabilities in a manner not fairly disclosed or presented in the tables below, the pool should expand those disclosures to show additional detail to keep the schedules from being misleading or to keep trends from becoming obscure.

SUMMARY

Risk financing activities are typically very significant for state and local governmental entities, regardless of whether risks are transferred to public entity risk pools. This chapter addressed the accounting and financial reporting requirements for both the state and local governmental entities themselves, as well as those for public entity risk pools.

22 PENSION AND OPEB PLAN FINANCIAL STATEMENTS

INTRODUCTION

This chapter describes the accounting and financial reporting requirements for state and local government pension and OPEB plans. The GASB has issued GASB Statement No. 67 (GASBS 67), *Financial Reporting for Pension Plans—An Amendment of GASB Statement No. 25*, which significantly changes the financial reporting for pension plans. The requirements of GASBS 67, which are effective for financial statements for fiscal years beginning after June 15, 2013, are incorporated into this chapter.

The GASB has also issued GASB Statement No. 74 (GASBS 74), *Financial Reporting for Post-employment Benefit Plans Other than Pensions*, which applies similar concepts from GASBS 67 to OPEB plans. GASBS 74 is effective for financial statements for fiscal years beginning after June 15, 2016, with earlier application encouraged. GASBS 74 is also integrated into this chapter.

Although the accounting and financial reporting for OPEB plans is similar to that of defined benefit pension plans, this chapter will describe each separately as there are certain important differences in the nature of each type of plan, although the accounting principles employed are consistent.

GASB 67 REQUIREMENTS FOR PENSION PLAN ACCOUNTING AND FINANCIAL REPORTING

GASB Statement No. 67 (GASBS 67), *Accounting and Financial Reporting for Pensions—An Amendment of GASB Statement No. 25*

After issuing an Invitation to Comment, a Preliminary Views Document, and an Exposure Draft regarding pension accounting and financial reporting, the GASB has issued two final statements in this area. GASBS 67 addresses pension plan accounting and financial reporting. GASB Statement No. 68 (GASBS 68), *Accounting and Financial Reporting for Pensions—An Amendment of GASB Statement No. 27*, addresses employers' accounting for pensions. GASBS 68 is discussed in Chapter 17. GASBS 67 is discussed below.

Both GASBS 67 and GASBS 68 will have significant impacts on accounting and reporting by pension plans and employers that participate in these plans, particularly for defined benefit pension plans.

GASBS 67 amends the requirements of GASBS 25 and GASB Statement No. 50 (GASBS 50), *Pension Disclosures*, as they relate to pension plans that are administered through trusts, or equivalent arrangements, that meet certain criteria. The requirements of GASBS 25 and 50 would remain applicable to pension plans that are not covered by the scope of GASBS 67, and requirements applicable to defined contribution plans that provide postemployment benefits other than pensions would remain effective for those plans.

GASBS 67 establishes financial reporting standards for state and local governmental pension plans—defined benefit pension plans and defined contribution pension plans—that are administered through trusts or equivalent arrangements (hereafter jointly referred to as trusts) in which:

1. Contributions from employers and nonemployer contributing entities to the pension plan and earnings on those contributions are irrevocable. In some circumstances, contributions are made by the employer to satisfy plan member contribution requirements. If the contribution

amounts are recognized by the employer as salary expense, those contributions should be classified as plan member contributions under GASBS 67. Otherwise, those contributions should be classified as employer contributions.

2. Pension plan assets are dedicated to providing pensions to plan members in accordance with the benefit terms. GASBS 67 notes that the use of pension plan assets to pay pension plan administrative costs or to refund plan member contributions in accordance with benefit terms is consistent with this criterion.
3. Pension plan assets are legally protected from the creditors of employers, nonemployer contributing entities, and the pension plan administrator. If the plan is a defined benefit pension plan, plan assets also are legally protected from creditors of the plan members.

GASBS 67 notes that it focuses on provisions specific to pension plans. In addition, pension plans should continue to follow all other accounting and financial reporting requirements applicable to the transactions and other events reported in their basic financial statements, including notes to those statements, and required supplementary information. (In other words, requirements such as Management's Discussion and Analysis and otherwise required note disclosures, such as those related to investment risks, are still applicable to pension plans, even if not specifically mentioned in GASBS 67.)

GASBS 67 applies to state and local governmental pension plans, irrespective of whether (1) the pension plan's financial statements are included in a separate financial report issued by the pension plan or by the public employee retirement system that administers the pension plan (stand-alone pension plan financial report) or (2) the pension plan is included as a pension trust fund of another government.

GASBS 67 defines the term *pensions,* which includes the following:

1. Retirement income.
2. Postemployment benefits other than retirement income (such as death benefits, life insurance, and disability benefits) that are provided through a pension plan. Accordingly, under this definition, pensions do not include postemployment health care benefits and termination benefits. When postemployment benefits other than retirement income are provided separately from a pension plan, they are classified as other postemployment benefits (OPEB), and the plans through which those benefits are provided should be accounted for and reported as OPEB plans in accordance with Statement No. 43, *Financial Reporting for Postemployment Benefit Plans Other than Pension Plans,* as amended, and not in accordance with GASBS 67.

NOTE: The GASB has a separate project that will address accounting and financial reporting for OPEB plans and employers providing OPEB benefits. Accordingly, the requirements of GASBS 67 and GASBS 68 do not apply to OPEB benefits or OPEB plans.

GASBS 67 notes that termination benefits are primarily addressed in Statement No. 47, *Accounting for Termination Benefits*. The effects of a termination benefit on the defined benefit pension liabilities of an employer or governmental nonemployer contributing entity should be included in measures of those pension liabilities that are required by GASBS 67.

Defined benefit pensions are defined by GASBS 67 as pensions for which the income or other benefits that the plan member will receive at or after separation from employment are defined by the benefit terms. The pensions may be stated as a specified dollar amount or as an amount that is calculated based on one or more factors such as age, years of service, and compensation. In essence, the pension benefit is determined by plan terms rather than governed by the amount of assets contributed to the plan.

In contrast, defined contribution pensions are defined by GASBS 67 as pensions having terms that:

(a) Provide an individual account for each plan member.
(b) Define the contributions that an employer is required to make (or credits that it is required to provide) to an active plan member's account for periods in which that member renders service.
(c) Provide that the pensions a plan member will receive will depend only on the contributions (or credits) to the plan member's account, actual earnings on investments of those contributions (or credits), and the effects of forfeitures of contributions (or credits) made for other plan members, as well as pension plan administrative costs, that are allocated to the plan member's account.

If the pensions to be provided are a function of factors other than those identified in (c), above, the pension plan through which the pensions are provided should be classified as a defined benefit pension plan. Otherwise, the pension plan should be classified as a defined contribution pension plan.

Types of Defined Benefit Pension Plans

As in existing standards, GASBS 67 classifies defined benefit pension according to:

1. The number of employers whose employees are provided with pensions through the pension plan; and
2. Whether pension obligations and pension plan assets are shared.

For purposes of this classification, a primary government and its component units are considered to be one employer.

If a defined benefit pension plan is used to provide pensions to the employees of only one employer, the pension plan is classified for financial reporting purposes as a single-employer defined benefit pension plan (single-employer pension plan).

If a defined benefit pension plan is used to provide pensions to the employees of more than one employer, the pension plan is classified for financial reporting purposes as a multiple-employer defined benefit pension plan. Two additional subclassifications are needed for multi-employer plans:

1. If the assets of a multiple-employer defined benefit pension plan are pooled for investment purposes but separate accounts are maintained for each individual employer so that each employer's share of the pooled assets is legally available to pay the benefits of only its employees, the pension plan should be classified as an agent multiple-employer defined benefit pension plan (agent pension plan). For agent pension plans, the provisions of GASBS 67 apply at the aggregate plan level for each agent pension plan administered.
2. If the pension obligations to the employees of more than one employer are pooled and pension plan assets can be used to pay the benefits of the employees of any employer that provides pensions through the pension plan, the pension plan is considered to be a cost-sharing multiple-employer defined benefit pension plan (cost-sharing pension plan).

As will be described in much more detail below, the accounting and financial reporting requirements for single-employer and agent multiemployer plans are similar and are quite different from those used by cost-sharing pension plans.

GASBS 67 notes that state and local governments often act as fiduciaries for one or more pension plans, as well as other types of plans (such as OPEB plans or deferred compensation plans). If the financial report of a public employee retirement system or other government includes more than one pension plan that is within the scope of GASBS 67, the provisions of the statement should be applied separately to each such pension plan administered.

Number of Pension Plans

When all assets accumulated in a defined benefit pension plan for the payment of benefits may legally be used to pay benefits (including refunds of plan member contributions) to *any* of the plan members, GASBS 67 provides that the total assets should be reported as assets of one defined benefit pension plan even if administrative policy requires that separate reserves, funds, or accounts for specific groups of plan members, employers, or types of benefits be maintained. This is also the case if separate actuarial valuations are performed for different classes of plan or different groups of plan members because different contributions rates may apply for each class or group depending on the applicable benefit structures, benefit formulas, or other factors.

OBSERVATION: This last point is particularly important in the current economic times as a number of state and local governments have looked to amend the benefits or contribution rates for new employees to minimize their pension expenses. These changes may create new "tiers" within a plan, but for financial reporting purposes, they do not create a new plan.

However, under GASBS 67, a separate defined benefit pension plan should be reported for a portion of the total assets, even if the assets are pooled with other assets for investment purposes, if that portion of assets meets both of the following criteria:

1. The portion of assets is accumulated solely for the payment of benefits to certain classes or groups of plan members or to plan members who are the active or inactive employees of certain entities (for example, state government employees).
2. The portion of assets may not legally be used to pay benefits to other classes or groups of plan members or other entities' plan members (for example, local government employees).

Financial Statements

The basic financial statements of a defined benefit pension plan are not changed by GASBS 67. A defined benefit pension plan should present the following financial statements, prepared on the accrual basis of accounting:

1. *A statement of fiduciary net position,* which includes information about assets, deferred outflows of resources, liabilities, deferred inflows of resources, and fiduciary net position, as applicable, as of the end of the pension plan's reporting period.
2. *A statement of changes in fiduciary net position,* which includes information about the additions to, deductions from, and net increase (or decrease) in fiduciary net position for the pension plan's reporting period.

Statement of fiduciary net position. The following guidance is provided by GASBS 67 as to the types of accounts typically found in a statement of net position of a defined benefit pension plan.

Assets. Assets should be subdivided into (1) the major categories of assets held (for example, cash and cash equivalents, receivables, investments, and assets used in pension plan operations) and (2) the principal components of the receivables and investments categories.

Receivables. Receivables generally are short term and consist of contributions due as of the end of the reporting period from employers, nonemployer contributing entities, and plan members, and interest and dividends on investments. Amounts recognized as receivables for contributions should include only those due pursuant to legal requirements.

GASBS 67 provides that receivables for contributions that are payable to the pension plan more than one year after the end of the reporting period (for example, pursuant to installment contracts) should be recognized in full in the period the receivable arises. If a receivable is recognized at its discounted present value, interest should be accrued using the effective interest method, unless use of the straight-line method would not produce significantly different results.

Investments. Purchases and sales of investments should be recorded on a trade-date basis. Unless otherwise provided for in this section, pension plan investments—whether equity or debt securities, real estate, investment derivative instruments, or other investments—should be reported at their fair value at the end of the pension plan's reporting period. GASBS 67 reiterates that the fair value of an investment is the amount that the pension plan could reasonably expect to receive in a current sale between a willing buyer and a willing seller—that is, other than in a forced or liquidation sale. Fair value should be measured by the market price if there is an active market for the investment. If such prices are not available, fair value should be estimated. The fair value of open-end mutual funds, external investment pools, and interest-earning investment contracts should be determined as provided in GASB Statement 31, *Accounting and Financial Reporting for Certain Investments and for External Investment Pools,* and in Statement No. 59, *Financial Instruments Omnibus.*

Investments in life insurance should be reported at cash surrender value. Unallocated insurance contracts are reported as interest-earning investment contracts according to the provision of GASBS 31. Synthetic guaranteed investment contracts that are fully benefit responsive (as defined in Statement No. 53, *Accounting and Financial Reporting for Derivative Instruments*) are reported at contract value. The fair value of an investment should reflect brokerage commissions and other costs normally incurred in a sale, if determinable.

An allocated insurance contract is a contract with an insurance company under which a related payment to the insurance company is currently used to purchase immediate or deferred annuities for individual plan members. These contracts are also referred to as annuity contracts. GASBS 67 provides that allocated insurance contracts should be excluded from pension plan assets if (1) the contract irrevocably transfers to the insurer the responsibility for providing the benefits, (2) all required payments to acquire the contracts have been made, and (3) the likelihood is remote that the employer or the pension plan will be required to make additional payments to satisfy the benefit payments covered by the contract.

Liabilities. Pension plan liabilities generally consist of benefits (including refunds of plan member contributions) due to plan members and accrued investment and administrative expenses. Pension plan liabilities for benefits should be recognized when the benefits are currently due and payable in accordance with the benefit terms. Benefits payable from allocated insurance contracts excluded from pension plan assets as discussed above should be excluded from pension plan liabilities. As in prior guidance, the present values of future benefits that are expected to be paid to plan members are not included on the statement of net position as liabilities of the plan.

Fiduciary net position. GASBS 67 provides that assets, plus deferred outflows of resources, less liabilities, less deferred inflows of resources at the end of the pension plan's reporting period should be reported as *net position restricted for pensions.*

Statement of Changes in Fiduciary Net Position

Additions. The additions section of the statement of changes in fiduciary net position should include separate display of the following, where applicable:

1. Contributions from employers.
2. Contributions from nonemployer contributing entities (for example, state government contributions to a local government pension plan).
3. Contributions from plan members, including those transmitted by the employers.
4. Net investment income, including separate display of (1) investment income and (2) investment expense, including investment management and custodial fees and all other significant investment-related costs. The following section provides additional guidance on reporting net investment income.

Investment income. Under GASBS 67, investment income includes (1) the net increase (decrease) in the fair value of pension plan investments and (2) interest income, dividend income, and other income not included in (1). The components (1) and (2) of investment income may be separately displayed or combined and reported as one amount.

The net increase (decrease) in the fair value of investments should include realized gains and losses on investments that were both bought and sold during the period. GASBS 67 provides that realized and unrealized gains and losses should not be separately displayed in the financial statements. Realized gains and losses, computed as the difference between the proceeds of sale and the original cost of the investments sold, may be disclosed in notes to financial statements. GASBS 67 requires that such disclosure state:

1. The calculation of realized gains and losses is independent of the calculation of the net change in the fair value of pension plan investments.
2. Realized gains and losses on investments that had been held in more than one reporting period and sold in the current period were included as a change in the fair value reported in the prior period(s) and the current period.

Consistent with reporting investments at fair value, interest income should be reported at the stated interest rate. Any premiums or discounts on debt securities should not be amortized.

GASBS 67 also notes that the disclosure of default losses and recoveries on reverse repurchase agreements and securities lending transactions, as provided by GASB Statement No. 3, *Deposits with Financial Institutions, Investments (including Repurchase Agreements), and Reverse Repurchase Agreements,* and of GASB Statement 28, *Accounting and Financial Reporting for Securities Lending Transactions,* respectively, does not constitute a reporting of realized losses in accordance with GASBS 67 and would require reporting of all realized gains and losses for the year.

Investment expense. Investment-related costs are reported as investment expense if they are separable from (1) Investment income and (2) the administrative expense of the pension plan.

Deductions. GASBS 67 provides that the deductions section of the statement of changes in fiduciary net position should separately display, at a minimum, (1) benefit payments to plan members (including refunds of plan member contributions) and (2) total administrative expense.

Amounts paid by the pension plan to an insurance company pursuant to an allocated insurance contract that is excluded from pension plan assets, including purchases of annuities with amounts allocated from existing investments with the insurance company, should be included in amounts recognized as benefits paid. Dividends from an allocated insurance contract should be recognized as a reduction of benefit payments recognized in the period. Benefit payments should not include benefits paid by an insurance company in accordance with such a contract.

Net increase (decrease) in fiduciary net position. GASBS 67 provides that the difference between total additions and total deductions presented in the statement of changes in fiduciary net position should be reported as *the net increase (or decrease) in net position.*

Notes to Financial Statements

GASBS 67 requires a significant amount of note disclosures, as discussed in this section. The notes should include all disclosures required when the financial statements are presented (1) in a stand-alone pension plan financial report or (2) solely in the financial report of another government (as a pension trust fund). If (1) a defined benefit pension plan is included in the financial report of a government that applies the requirements of Statement 68 for benefits provided through the pension plan and (2) similar information is required by GASBS 67 and GASBS 68, the government should present the disclosures in a manner that avoids unnecessary duplication.

GASBS 67 provides that the following should be disclosed in notes to financial statements, as applicable:

1. Plan description:
   (a) The name of the pension plan, identification of the public employee retirement system or other entity that administers the pension plan, and identification of the pension plan as a single-employer, agent, or cost-sharing pension plan.
   (b) The number of participating employers (if the pension plan is a multiple-employer pension plan) and the number of nonemployer contributing entities, if any.
   (c) Information regarding the pension plan's board and its composition (for example, the number of trustees by source of selection or the types of constituency or credentials applicable to selection).
   (d) Classes of plan members covered and the number of plan members, separately identifying numbers of the following:
      (1) Inactive plan members (or their beneficiaries) currently receiving benefits.
      (2) Inactive plan members entitled to but not yet receiving benefits.
      (3) Active plan members.

   If the pension plan is closed to new entrants, that fact should be disclosed:
   (e) The authority under which benefit terms are established or may be amended and the types of benefits provided through the pension plan. If the pension plan or the entity that administers the pension plan has the authority to establish or amend benefit terms, a brief description should be provided of the benefit terms, including the key elements of the pension formulas and the terms or policies, if any, with respect to

automatic post-employment benefit changes, including automatic cost-of-living adjustments (automatic COLAs), and ad hoc postemployment benefit changes, including ad hoc cost-of-living adjustments (ad hoc COLAs).

(f) A brief description of contribution requirements, including (1) identification of the authority under which contribution requirements of employers, nonemployer contributing entities, if any, and plan members are established or may be amended and (2) the contribution rates (in dollars or as a percentage of covered payroll) of those entities for the reporting period. If the pension plan or the entity that administers the pension plan has the authority to establish or amend contribution requirements, disclose the basis for determining contributions (for example, statute, contract, an actuarial basis, or some other manner).

2. Pension plan investments:
   (a) Investment policies, including:
      (i) Procedures and authority for establishing and amending investment policy decisions.
      (ii) Policies pertaining to asset allocation.
      (iii) Description of significant investment policy changes during the reporting period.
   (b) A brief description of how the fair value of investments is determined, including the methods and significant assumptions used to estimate the fair value of investments if that fair value is based on other than quoted market prices.
   (c) Identification of investments (other than those issued or explicitly guaranteed by the U.S. government) in any one organization that represent 5% or more of the pension plan's fiduciary net position.
   (d) The annual money-weighted rate of return on pension plan investments calculated as the internal rate of return on pension plan investments, net of pension plan investment expense, and an explanation that a money-weighted rate of return expresses investment performance, net of pension plan investment expense, adjusted for the changing amounts actually invested. Pension plan investment expense should be measured on the accrual basis of accounting. Inputs to the internal rate of return calculation should be determined at least monthly. The use of more frequently determined inputs is encouraged.
3. Receivables—The terms of any long-term contracts for contributions to the pension plan between (1) an employer or nonemployer contributing entity and (2) the pension plan, and the balances outstanding on any such long-term contracts at the end of the pension plan's reporting period.
4. Allocated insurance contracts excluded from pension plan assets:
   (a) The amount reported in benefit payments in the current period that is attributable to the purchase of allocated insurance contracts.
   (b) A brief description of the pensions for which allocated insurance contracts were purchased in the current period.
   (c) The fact that the obligation for the payment of benefits covered by allocated insurance contracts has been transferred to one or more insurance companies.
5. Reserves—In circumstances in which there is a policy of setting aside, for purposes such as benefit increases or reduced employer contributions, a portion of the pensions plan's fiduciary net position that otherwise would be available for existing pensions or for pension plan administration:

(a) A description of the policy related to such reserves.
(b) The authority under which the policy was established and may be amended.
(c) The purposes for and conditions under which the reserves are required or permitted to be used.
(d) The balances of the reserves.

6. Deferred retirement option program (DROP) balances—If a pension plan includes terms that permit a plan member to be credited for benefit payments into an individual member account within the pension plan while continuing to provide services to the employer and to be paid a salary:
(a) A description of the DROP terms.
(b) The balance of the amounts held by the pension plan pursuant to the DROP.

Disclosures Specific to Single-Employer and Cost-Sharing Pension Plans

In addition to the information required by the preceding section, GASBS 67 also requires that the information identified below be disclosed in notes to financial statements. All information should be measured as of the pension plan's most recent fiscal year-end. Information about cost-sharing pension plans should be presented for the pension plan as a whole.

1. The components of the liability of the employers and nonemployer contributing entities to plan members for benefits provided through the pension plan (net pension liability), calculated in conformity with the requirements discussed below. (Unless otherwise indicated, references to a net pension liability also apply to the situation in which the pension plan's fiduciary net position exceeds the total pension liability, resulting in a net pension asset.)
(a) The total pension liability.
(b) The pension plan's fiduciary net position.
(c) The net pension liability.
(d) The pension plan's fiduciary net position as a percentage of the total pension liability.
2. Significant assumptions, and other inputs used to measure the total pension liability, including assumptions about inflation, salary changes, and ad hoc postemployment benefit changes (including ad hoc COLAs). With regard to mortality assumptions, the source of the assumptions (for example, the published tables on which the assumption is based or that the assumptions are based on a study of the experience of the covered group) should be disclosed. The dates of experience studies on which significant assumptions are based also should be disclosed. If different rates are assumed for different periods, information should be disclosed about what rates are applied to the different periods of the measurement.
(a) The following information should be disclosed about the discount rate:
(i) The discount rate applied in the measurement of the total pension liability and the change in the discount rate since the pension plan's prior fiscal year-end, if any.
(ii) Assumptions made about projected cash flows into and out of the pension plan, such as contributions from employers, nonemployer contributing entities, and plan members.
(iii) The long-term expected rate of return on pension plan investments and a description of how it was determined, including significant methods and assumptions used for that purpose.

(iv) If the discount rate incorporates a municipal bond rate, the municipal bond rate used and the source of that rate.
(v) The periods of projected benefit payments to which the long-term expected rate of return and, if used, the municipal bond rate applied to determine the discount rate.
(vi) The assumed asset allocation of the pension plan's portfolio, the long-term expected real rate of return for each major asset class, and whether the expected rates of return are presented as arithmetic or geometric means, if not otherwise disclosed.
(vii) Measures of the net pension liability calculated using (a) a discount rate that is 1 percentage point higher than that required by paragraph 40 and (b) a discount rate that is 1 percentage point lower than that required by paragraph 40.

3. The date of the actuarial valuation on which the total pension liability is based and, if applicable, the fact that update procedures were used to roll forward the total pension liability to the pension plan's fiscal year-end.

Required Supplementary Information

GASBS 67 provides that the required supplementary information presented by a defined benefit pension plan include all information described below when the financial statements are presented (1) in a stand-alone pension plan financial report or (2) solely in the financial report of another government (as a pension trust fund).

However, if (1) a defined benefit pension plan is included in the financial report of a government that applies the requirements of GASBS 68 for benefits provided through the pension plan and (2) similar information is required by GASBS 67 and GASBS 68, the government should present the information in a manner that avoids unnecessary duplication. This is a similar requirement to avoid duplication of information as was described in the note disclosures above.

Single-employer and cost-sharing pension plans. GASBS 67 provides that schedules of required supplementary information that include the information indicated in subparagraphs 1 through 4, below, be presented. The information in subparagraphs (a) and (b) may be presented in a single schedule. Information for each year should be measured as of the pension plan's most recent fiscal year-end. Information about cost-sharing pension plans should be presented for the pension plan as a whole.

1. A ten-year schedule of changes in the net pension liability, presenting for each year (1) the beginning and ending balances of the total pension liability, the pension plan's fiduciary net position, and the net pension liability, calculated in accordance with the requirements below, and (2) the effects on those items during the year of the following, as applicable:
   (a) Service cost.
   (b) Interest on the total pension liability.
   (c) Changes of benefit terms.
   (d) Differences between expected and actual experience with regard to economic or demographic factors in the measurement of the total pension liability.
   (e) Changes of assumptions about future economic or demographic factors or of other inputs.
   (f) Contributions from employers.
   (g) Contributions from nonemployer contributing entities.
   (h) Contributions from plan members.

- (i) Pension plan net investment income.
- (j) Benefit payments, including refunds of plan member contributions.
- (k) Pension plan administration expense.
- (l) Other changes, separately identified if individually significant.

2. A ten-year schedule presenting the following for each year:
   - (a) The total pension liability.
   - (b) The pension plan's fiduciary net position.
   - (c) The net pension liability.
   - (d) The pension plan's fiduciary net position as a percentage of the total pension liability.
   - (e) The covered-employee payroll.
   - (f) The net pension liability as a percentage of covered-employee payroll.
3. A ten-year schedule presenting for each year the information indicated in items (a) through (f), below, if an actuarially determined contribution is calculated for employers or nonemployer contributing entities. The schedule should identify whether the information relates to the employers, nonemployer contributing entities, or both.
   - (a) The actuarially determined contributions of employers or nonemployer contributing entities. For purposes of this schedule, actuarially determined contributions should exclude amounts, if any, to separately finance specific liabilities of an individual employer or nonemployer contributing entity to the pension plan.
   - (b) For cost-sharing pension plans, the contractually required contribution of employers or nonemployer contributing entities, if different from (a).
   - (c) The amount of contributions recognized during the fiscal year by the pension plan in relation to the actuarially determined contribution in (a). For purposes of this schedule, contributions should include only amounts recognized as additions to the pension plan's fiduciary net position resulting from cash contributions and from contributions recognized by the pension plan as current receivables.
   - (d) The difference between the actuarially determined contribution in item (a) and the amount of contributions recognized by the pension plan in relation to the actuarially determined contribution in (c).
   - (e) The covered-employee payroll.
   - (f) The amounts of contributions recognized by the pension plan in relation to the actuarially determined contributions in (c) as a percentage of covered-employee payroll in (e).
4. A ten-year schedule presenting for each fiscal year the annual money-weighted rate of return on pension plan investments.

Agent pension plans. GASBS 67 provides that agent plans should include a ten-year schedule presenting for each fiscal year the annual money-weighted rate of return on pension plan investments in required supplementary information.

Notes to the Required Schedules

GASBS 67 requires that significant methods and assumptions used in calculating the actuarially determined contributions, if any, should be presented as notes to the schedule required for actuarially determined contributions listed above. In addition, for each of the schedules presented as required supplemental information, information should be presented about factors that significantly affect trends in the amounts reported (for example, changes of benefit terms, changes in the size or composition of the population covered by the benefit terms, or the use of different assumptions). (The amounts presented for prior years should not be restated for the effects of changes—for example, changes of benefit terms or changes of assumptions—that occurred subsequent to the end of the fiscal year for which the information is reported.)

Measurement of the Net Pension Liability

The most significant changes in pension accounting and financial reporting promulgated by GASBS 67 and GASBS 68 are not in the financial statement formats and disclosure noted above. Rather, the most significant changes involve the measurement of the net pension liability and, in the case of GASBS 68, how employers account for the net pension liability. These measurements are discussed in the following sections.

It's important to note that the measurement requirements discussed in this section are also included in GASBS 68, so there is consistency between the two standards.

The net pension liability is measured as the total pension liability (determined in conformity with the requirements discussed below), net of the pension plan's fiduciary net position. The net pension liability is measured as of the pension plan's most recent fiscal year-end.

Total Pension Liability

Under GASBS 67, the total pension liability is the portion of the actuarial present value of projected benefit payments that is attributed to past periods of plan member service and measured in conformity with the following requirements.

Timing and frequency of actuarial valuations. GASBS 67 provides that the total pension liability should be determined by (1) an actuarial valuation as of the pension plan's most recent fiscal year-end or (2) the use of update procedures to roll forward to the pension plan's most recent fiscal year-end amounts from an actuarial valuation as of a date no more than 24 months earlier than the pension plan's most recent fiscal year-end. If update procedures are used and significant changes occur between the actuarial valuation date and the pension plan's fiscal year-end, GASBS 67 requires that professional judgment be used to determine the extent of procedures needed to roll forward the measurement from the actuarial valuation to the pension plan's fiscal year-end, and consideration should be given to whether a new actuarial valuation is needed. For purposes of this determination, the effects of changes in the discount rate resulting from changes in the pension plan's fiduciary net position or from changes in the municipal bond rate, if applicable, should be among the factors evaluated. For financial reporting purposes, an actuarial valuation of the total pension liability should be performed at least biennially. More frequent actuarial valuations are encouraged by GASBS 67.

Selection of assumptions. Unless otherwise specified in GASBS 67, the selection of all assumptions used in determining the total pension liability should be made in conformity with Actuarial Standards of Practice issued by the Actuarial Standards Board. The pension plan, employers, and, if any, governmental nonemployer contributing entities that make contributions to the pension plan should use the same assumptions when measuring similar or related pension information.

Projection of benefit payments. GASBS 67 provides that projected benefit payments should include all benefits to be provided to current active and inactive plan members as through the pension plan in accordance with the benefit terms and any additional legal agreements to provide benefits that are in force at the pension plan's fiscal year-end. Projected benefit payments should include the effects of automatic postemployment benefit changes, including automatic

COLAs. In addition, projected benefit payments should include the effects of (1) projected ad hoc postemployment benefit changes, including ad hoc COLAs, to the extent that they are considered to be substantively automatic; (2) projected salary changes (in circumstances in which the pension formula incorporates future compensation levels); and (3) projected service credits (both in determining a plan member's probable eligibility for benefits and in the projection of benefit payments in circumstances in which the pension formula incorporates years of service). Benefit payments to be provided by means of an allocated insurance contract excluded from pension plan should be excluded from projected benefit payments.

Considerations identified by GASBS 67 that might be relevant to determining whether ad hoc COLAs are substantively automatic include the historical pattern of granting the changes, the consistency in the amounts of the changes or in the amounts of the changes relative to a defined cost-of-living or inflation index, and whether there is evidence to conclude that changes might not continue to be granted in the future despite what might otherwise be a pattern that would indicate such changes are substantively automatic.

OBSERVATION: The requirement to include ad hoc COLAs that are substantively automatic in the calculation of projected benefit payments is a significant change being brought about by GASBS 67 and GASBS 68. Prior to these statements, ad hoc COLAs, even if substantively automatic, would not have been included in the projected benefit payment calculation.

Discount rate. GASBS 67 provides that the discount rate should be the single rate that reflects the following:

1. The long-term expected rate of return on pension plan investments that are expected to be used to finance the payment of benefits, to the extent that (1) the pension plan's fiduciary net position is projected to be sufficient to make projected benefit payments and (2) pension plan assets are expected to be invested using a strategy to achieve that return.
2. A yield or index rate for 20-year, tax-exempt general obligation municipal bonds with an average rating of AA/Aa or higher (or equivalent quality on another rating scale), to the extent that the conditions in (1) are not met.

OBSERVATION: This is a significant change in discount rate determination under GASBS 67 and GASBS 68. The new standards essentially let a government use its expected return on pension plan assets to the extent that the assets (and earnings) will be sufficient to pay plan benefits. To the extent it is not sufficient, a tax-exempt borrowing rate is used. In cases where the tax-exempt borrowing rate will be a factor in determining the discount rate (which is likely to be often) that rate is very likely to be less than the assumed rate of return on plan assets. A lower discount rate means a higher calculated amount of projected benefit payments.

Comparing projections of the pension plan's fiduciary net position to projected benefit payments. For purposes of determining the discount rate, GASBS 67 provides that the amount of the pension plan's projected fiduciary net position and the amount of projected benefit payments should be compared in each period of projected benefit payments. Projections of the pension plan's fiduciary net position should incorporate all cash flows for contributions from employers and nonemployer contributing entities, if any, intended to finance benefits of current active and inactive plan members (status at the pension plan's fiscal year-end) and all cash flows for contributions from current active plan members. It should not include (1) cash flows for contributions from employers or nonemployer contributing entities intended to finance the service costs of future plan members or (2) cash flows for contributions from future plan members, unless those contributions are projected to exceed service costs for those plan members.

In each period, contributions from employers and nonemployer contributing entities should be considered to apply, first, to service costs of plan members in the period and, second, to past service costs, unless the effective pension plan terms related to contributions indicate that a different relationship between contributions to the pension plan from nonemployer contributing entities and service costs should be applied. Member contributions should be considered to be applied to service costs before contributions from employers and nonemployer contributing entities.

GASBS 67 provides that professional judgment should be applied to project cash flows for contributions from employers and nonemployer contributing entities in circumstances in which (1) those contribution amounts are established by statute or contract or (2) a formal, written policy related to those contributions exists. Application of professional judgment should consider the most recent five-year contribution history of the employers and nonemployer contributing entities as a key indicator of future contributions from those sources and should reflect all other known events and conditions. In circumstances other that those described in (1) and (2), the amount of projected cash flows for contributions from employers and nonemployer contributing entities should be limited to an average of contributions from those sources over the most recent five-year period and may be modified based on consideration of subsequent events. For this purpose, the basis for the average (for example, percentage of covered payroll contributed or percentage of actuarially determined contributions made) should be a matter of professional judgment.

If the evaluations required above can be made with sufficient reliability without a separate projection of cash flows into and out of the pension plan, GASBS 67 permits alternative methods to be applied in making the evaluations.

Calculating the discount rate. For each future period, if the amount of the pension plan's fiduciary net position is projected to be greater than or equal to the benefit payments that are projected to be made in that period and pension plan assets up to that point are expected to be invested using a strategy to achieve the long-term expected rate of return, GASBS 67 provides that the actuarial present value of benefit payments projected to be made in the period should be determined using the long-term expected rate of return on those investments. The long-term expected rate of return should be based on the nature and mix of current and expected pension plan investments over a period representative of the expected length of time between (1) the point at which a plan member begins to provide service to the employer and (2) the point at which all benefits to the plan member have been paid. For this purpose, the long-term expected rate of return should be determined net of pension plan investment expense but without reduction for pension plan administrative expense. The municipal bond rate should be used to calculate the actuarial present value of all other benefit payments.

GASBS 67 states that the discount rate is the single rate of return that, when applied to all projected benefit payments, results in an actuarial present value of projected benefit payments equal to the total of the actuarial present values determined in conformity with the above discussion.

Attribution of the actuarial present value of projected benefit payments to periods. GASBS 67 requires that the entry age actuarial cost method should be used to attribute the actuarial present value of projected benefit payments of each plan member to periods in conformity with the following:

1. Attribution should be made on an individual plan-member-by-plan-member basis.
2. Each plan member's service costs should be level as a percentage of that member's projected pay. For purposes of this calculation, if a member does not have projected pay, the projected inflation rate should be used in place of the projected rate of change in salary.

3. The beginning of the attribution period should be the first period in which the member's service accrues pensions under the benefit terms, notwithstanding vesting or other similar terms.
4. The service costs of all pensions should be attributed through all assumed exit ages, through retirement. In pension plans in which the benefit terms include a DROP (as described in an earlier section), for purpose of GASBS 67, the date of entry into the DROP should be considered to be the plan member's retirement date.
5. Each plan member's service costs should be determined based on the same benefit terms reflected in that member's actuarial present value of projected benefit payments.

OBSERVATION: In addition to the requirements relating to substantively automatic COLAs and in the calculation of the discount rate, the requirement to use the entry age actuarial cost method is one of the more significant changes in pension accounting and financial reporting under GASBS 67 and GASBS 68. Under existing standards, governments and pension plans were permitted to select from a number of different actuarial cost methods that were tied to their required funding calculations. Instead of having the actuarial method for determining the projected pension liability based on the same method used by the government for funding calculations, all governments and pension plans must now use the same actuarial method for purposes of the pension liability calculation. This is a significant change.

Defined Contribution Pension Plans

GASBS 67 provides that the following information be disclosed in notes to financial statements of defined contributions pension plans:

1. Identification of the pension plan as a defined contribution pension plan.
2. Classes of plan members covered (for example, general employees or public safety employees), the number of plan members, participating employers (if the pension plan is a multiple-employer pension plan), and, if any, nonemployer contributing entities.
3. The authority under which the pension plan is established or may be amended.

Effective Date and Transition

GASBS 67 is effective for financial statements for fiscal years beginning after June 15, 2013. Earlier application is encouraged.

In the first period that GASBS 67 is applied, changes made to comply with the statement should be treated as an adjustment of prior periods, and financial statements presented for the periods affected should be restated. If restatement is not practical, the cumulative effect of applying the statement, if any, should be reported as a restatement of beginning net position for the earliest period restated. In the period GASBS 67 is first applied, the financial statements should disclose the nature of any restatement and its effect. Also, the reason for not restating prior periods presented should be explained.

In the fiscal year in which GASBS 67 is first implemented (transition year), the ten-year schedule of information about contributions required should be presented, if applicable. Pension plans are encouraged, but not required, by GASBS 67 to present all years of other required supplementary information retroactively. If retroactive information is not presented for the full ten years, required supplementary information should be presented for as many years for which information measured in conformity with the requirements of this Statement is available in the transition year and until ten years of such information is available. The schedules should not include information that is not measured in conformity with the requirements of this Statement.

GASBS 74 Requirements for OPEB Plans

In June 2015 the GASB issued GASB Statement No. 74 (GASBS 74), *Financial Reporting for Postemployment Benefit Plans Other Than Pensions*. GASBS 74 adopts virtually the same concepts from GASBS 67 for pension plans and applies them to OPEB plans.

GASBS 74 establishes financial reporting standards for state and local governmental OPEB plans—defined benefit OPEB plans and defined contribution OPEB plans—that are administered through trusts or equivalent arrangements (jointly referred to as trusts) in which:

(a) Contributions from employers and nonemployer contributing entities to the OPEB plan and earnings on those contributions are irrevocable.
(b) OPEB plan assets are dedicated to providing OPEB to plan members in accordance with the benefit terms.
(c) OPEB plan assets are legally protected from the creditors of employers, nonemployer contributing entities, and the OPEB plan administrator. If the plan is a defined benefit OPEB plan, plan assets also are legally protected from creditors of the plan members.

GASBS 74 also establishes financial reporting standards for governments that hold assets accumulated for purposes of providing OPEB through defined benefit OPEB plans that are *not* administered through trusts or equivalent arrangements that meet the above criteria.

GASBS 74 is not applicable to defined benefit OPEB plans in which benefits are financed through an arrangement whereby premiums are paid to an insurance company while employees are in active service, in return for which the insurance company unconditionally undertakes an obligation to pay the OPEB of those employees as defined in the OPEB plan terms. Such plans are referred to as insured plans.

Types of OPEB and OPEB Plans

GASBS 74 describes the term *OPEB* to include the following:

(a) Postemployment health care benefits—including medical, dental, vision, hearing, and other health-related benefits—whether provided separately from or provided through a pension plan.
(b) Other forms of postemployment benefits—for example, death benefits, life insurance, disability, and long-term care—when provided separately from a pension plan.

NOTE: It's important to note the other types of benefits that are considered OPEB benefits and make sure that they are included in applying the requirements of GASBS 74. Some financial statement preparers focus on retiree medical benefits, but the term is broader in scope.

GASBS 74 provides that OPEB does not include termination benefits or termination payments for sick leave. When postemployment benefits other than postemployment health care benefits are provided through a pension plan, they are classified as pensions, and the plans through which those benefits are provided should be accounted for and reported as pension plans, separate from the OPEB plan.

GASBS 74 includes the following definitions:

Defined benefit OPEB is OPEB for which the benefits that the plan member will receive at or after separation from employment are defined by the benefit terms. The OPEB may be stated as (a) a specified dollar amount; (b) an amount that is calculated based on one or more factors such as age, years of service, and compensation; or (c) a type or level of coverage such as prescription drug coverage or a percentage of health insurance premiums.

Defined contribution OPEB is OPEB having terms that:

(a) Provide an individual account for each plan member.
(b) Define the contributions that an employer or nonemployer contributing entity is required to make (or credits that it is required to provide) to an active plan member's account for periods in which that member renders service.
(c) Provide that the OPEB a plan member will receive will depend only on the contributions (or credits) to the plan member's account, actual earnings on investments of those contributions (or credits), and the effects of forfeitures of contributions (or credits) made for other plan members, as well as OPEB plan administrative costs, that are allocated to the plan member's account.

GASBS 74 provides that if the OPEB to be provided has all of the terms identified above, the OPEB plan through which the OPEB is provided should be classified as a defined contribution OPEB plan. Defined contribution OPEB plans that are administered through trusts that meet the criteria above should apply the requirements for note disclosures for plans administered through trusts, discussed later. If the OPEB to be provided does not have all of the above terms—for example, if the OPEB is a function of factors other than those identified in (c) above—the OPEB is classified as defined benefit OPEB, and the plan through which the OPEB is provided should be classified as a defined benefit OPEB plan.

Types of Defined Benefit OPEB Plans

Defined benefit OPEB plans other than insured plans are classified under GASBS 74 first according to the number of employers whose employees are provided with OPEB through the OPEB plan. (For purposes of this classification, a primary government and its component units are considered to be one employer.)

If a defined benefit OPEB plan is used to provide OPEB to the employees of only one employer, the OPEB plan should be classified for financial reporting purposes as a single-employer defined benefit OPEB plan.

If a defined benefit OPEB plan is used to provide OPEB to the employees of more than one employer, the OPEB plan should be classified for financial reporting purposes as a multiple-employer defined benefit OPEB plan.

Multiemployer plans are further classified by GASBS 74 as agent or cost-sharing plans. If a multiple-employer defined benefit OPEB plan is administered through a trust, the OPEB plan is then classified according to whether OPEB obligations and OPEB plan assets are shared by employers.

Agent Multiemployer Defined Benefit OPEB Plan

If the assets of the OPEB plan are pooled for investment purposes but separate accounts are maintained for each individual employer so that each employer's share of the pooled assets is legally available to pay the benefits of only its employees, the OPEB plan should be classified as an agent multiple-employer defined benefit OPEB plan (agent OPEB plan).

Cost-Sharing Multiemployer Defined Benefit OPEB Plan

If the OPEB obligations to the employees of more than one employer are pooled and OPEB plan assets can be used to pay the benefits of the employees of any employer that provides OPEB through the OPEB plan, the OPEB plan should be classified as a cost-sharing multiple-employer defined benefit OPEB plan (cost-sharing OPEB plan).

GASBS 74 distinguishes in its accounting and disclosure requirements among these types of plans, as described in the various requirements that follow.

GASBS 74 notes that a state or local government may act as the fiduciary entrusted with administering one or more OPEB plans. If the financial report of a government includes more than one OPEB plan, the provisions of GASBS 74 should be applied separately to each such OPEB plan administered. The following paragraph provides considerations under GASBS 74 that are relevant to the determination of the number of defined benefit OPEB plans administered through trusts.

Defined Benefit OPEB Plans That Are Administered through Trusts

Number of OPEB Plans

GASBS 74 provides that if, on an ongoing basis, all assets accumulated in a defined benefit OPEB plan for the payment of benefits may legally be used to pay benefits (including refunds of plan member contributions) to *any* of the plan members, the total assets should be reported as assets of one defined benefit OPEB plan even if:

(a) Administrative policy requires that separate reserves, funds, or accounts for specific groups of plan members, employers, or types of benefits be maintained (such as a reserve for plan member contributions, a reserve for disability benefits, or separate accounts for the contributions of state government versus local government employers); or
(b) Separate actuarial valuations are performed for different classes of plan members (for example, general employees and public safety employees) or different groups of plan members because different contribution rates may apply for each class or group depending on the applicable benefit structures, benefit formulas, or other factors.

A separate defined benefit OPEB plan should be reported for a portion of the total assets, even if the assets are pooled with other assets for investment purposes, if that portion of assets meets both of the following criteria:

(a) The portion of assets is accumulated solely for the payment of benefits to certain classes or groups of plan members or to plan members who are the active or inactive employees of certain entities (for example, state government employees).
(b) The portion of assets may not legally be used to pay benefits to other classes or groups of plan members or other entities' plan members (for example, local government employees).

Financial Statements

GASBS 74 provides that a defined benefit OPEB plan that is administered through a trust should present the following financial statements, prepared using the economic resources measurement focus and accrual basis of accounting:

(a) A *statement of fiduciary net position,* which includes information about assets, deferred outflows of resources, liabilities, deferred inflows of resources, and fiduciary net position, as applicable, as of the end of the OPEB plan's reporting period.
(b) A *statement of changes in fiduciary net position,* which includes information about the additions to, deductions from, and net increase (or decrease) in fiduciary net position for the OPEB plan's reporting period.

GASBS 74 provides specific guidance as to the presentation of these two financial statements. As to the presentation of the basic financial statements, GASBS 74's requirements do not differ significantly from the current requirements.

Statement of Fiduciary Net Position

Assets

GASBS 74 provides that OPEB plan assets should be subdivided into (a) the major categories of assets held (for example, cash and cash equivalents, receivables, investments, and capital assets) and (b) the principal components of the receivables and investments categories.

Receivables

GASB 74 notes that OPEB plan receivables generally are short-term and may arise from contributions from employers, nonemployer contributing entities, or plan members, or interest or dividends on investments. Contribution receivables should include amounts of benefit payments that are owed by employers or nonemployer contributing entities for OPEB as the benefits come due and that will not be reimbursed to the employers or nonemployer contributing entities using OPEB plan assets. Amounts recognized as receivables for contributions should include only those due pursuant to legal requirements.

GASBS 78 also provides that receivables for contributions that are payable to the OPEB plan more than one year after the end of the reporting period (for example, pursuant to installment contracts) should be recognized in full in the period the receivable arises. If a receivable is recognized at its discounted present value, interest should be accrued using the effective interest method, unless use of the straight-line method would not produce significantly different results.

Investments

Purchases and sales of investments should be recorded on a trade-date basis. GASBS 74 provides that allocated insurance contracts should be excluded from OPEB plan assets if (a) the contract irrevocably transfers to the insurer the responsibility for providing the benefits, (b) all required payments to acquire the contracts have been made, and (c) the likelihood is remote that the employer, nonemployer contributing entities, or OPEB plan will be required to make additional payments to satisfy the benefit payments covered by the contract.

Liabilities

Under GASBS 74, OPEB plan liabilities generally consist of benefit payments (including refunds of plan member contributions) due to plan members and accrued investment and administrative expenses. OPEB plan liabilities for benefits should be recognized when the benefits are currently due and payable in accordance with the benefit terms. OPEB plan liabilities should include amounts of benefit payments that are owed by employers or nonemployer contributing entities for OPEB as the benefits come due. Benefits payable from allocated insurance contracts excluded from OPEB plan assets should be excluded from OPEB plan liabilities.

Fiduciary Net Position

Assets, plus deferred outflows of resources, less liabilities, less deferred inflows of resources at the end of the OPEB plan's reporting period are to be reported as *net position restricted for OPEB*. This is consistent with the current presentation.

Statement of Changes in Fiduciary Net Position

Additions

Per GASBS 74, the additions section of the statement of changes in fiduciary net position should include separate display of the following, if applicable:

(a) Contributions from employers, including amounts for OPEB as the benefits come due that will not be reimbursed to the employers using OPEB plan assets.
(b) Contributions from nonemployer contributing entities (for example, state government contributions to a local government OPEB plan), including amounts for OPEB as the benefits come due that will not be reimbursed to the nonemployer contributing entities using OPEB plan assets.
(c) The total of contributions from active plan members and inactive plan members not yet receiving benefit payments, including those transmitted by employers.
(d) Net investment income, including separate display of (1) investment income and (2) investment expense, including investment management and custodial fees and all other significant investment-related costs (discussed below).

Investment Income

Under GASBS 74, investment income includes (a) the net increase (decrease) in the fair value of OPEB plan investments and (b) interest income, dividend income, and other income not included in (a). Components (a) and (b) of investment income may be separately displayed or combined and reported as one amount.

Investment Expense

GASBS 74 provided that investment-related costs should be reported as investment expense if they are separable from (a) investment income and (b) the administrative expenses of the OPEB plan.

Deductions

GASBS 74 provides that the deductions section of the statement of changes in fiduciary net position should separately display, at a minimum, (a) benefit payments to plan members (including refunds of plan member contributions and amounts from employers or nonemployer contributing entities for OPEB as the benefits come due) and (b) total administrative expense. Benefit payments should exclude amounts paid by inactive plan members.

Under GASBS 74, amounts paid by the OPEB plan, an employer, or a nonemployer contributing entity to an insurance company pursuant to an allocated insurance contract that is excluded from OPEB plan assets, including purchases of annuities with amounts allocated from existing investments with the insurance company, should be included in amounts recognized as benefit payments. Dividends from an allocated insurance contract should be recognized as a reduction of benefit payments recognized in the period. Benefit payments should not include benefits paid by an insurance company in accordance with such a contract.

Net Increase (Decrease) in Fiduciary Net Position

Finally, the difference between total additions and total deductions presented in the statement of changes in fiduciary net position should be reported as the *net increase* (or *decrease*) *in net position.*

Notes to Financial Statements

GASBS 74 has voluminous note disclosures and requirements for required supplementary information.

GASBS 74 also provides that the notes to financial statements of a defined benefit OPEB plan that is administered through a trust include all disclosures below, as applicable, if the financial statements are presented in a stand-alone OPEB plan financial report or solely in the financial report of another government. If (a) a defined benefit OPEB plan is included in the financial report of a government that applies the requirements of GASBS 74 for benefits provided through the OPEB plan and (b) similar information is required by both GASBS 74 and 75, the government should present the disclosures in a manner that avoids unnecessary duplication.

The following are the disclosures required by GASBS 74, along with the explanatory comments that provide information as to how certain disclosures and required supplementary information are presented, as applicable:

(a) Plan description:
   1. The name of the OPEB plan, identification of the entity that administers the OPEB plan, and identification of the OPEB plan as a single employer, agent, or cost-sharing OPEB plan.
   2. The number of participating employers (if the OPEB plan is an agent or cost-sharing OPEB plan) and the number of nonemployer contributing entities, if any.
   3. Information regarding the OPEB plan's board and its composition (for example, the number of trustees by source of selection or the types of constituency or credentials applicable to selection).
   4. The number of plan members, separately identifying numbers of the following:
      (a) Inactive plan members currently receiving benefit payments.
      (b) Inactive plan members entitled to but not yet receiving benefit payments.
      (c) Active plan members.

   If the OPEB plan is closed to new entrants, that fact should be disclosed.

   5. The authority under which benefit terms are established or may be amended, the types of benefits provided through the OPEB plan, and the classes of plan members covered. If the OPEB plan or the entity that administers the OPEB plan has the authority to establish or amend benefit terms, a brief description should be provided of the benefit terms, including the key elements of the OPEB formulas and the terms or policies, if any, with respect to automatic postemployment benefit changes, including automatic cost-of-living adjustments (automatic COLAs); ad hoc postemployment benefit changes, including ad hoc cost-of-living adjustments (ad hoc COLAs); and the sharing of benefit-related costs with inactive plan members.
   6. A brief description of contribution requirements, including (a) identification of the authority under which contribution requirements of employers, nonemployer contributing entities, if any, and plan members are established or may be amended; (b) the contribution rates (in dollars or as a percentage of covered payroll) of the employer, nonemployer contributing entities, if any, and plan members for the reporting period; and (c) legal or contractual maximum contribution rates, if applicable. If the OPEB plan or the entity that administers the OPEB plan has the authority to establish or amend contribution requirements, disclose the basis for determining contributions (for example, statute, contract, an actuarial basis, or some other manner).

(b) OPEB plan investments
   1. Investment policies, including:
      (a) Procedures and authority for establishing and amending investment policy decisions.
      (b) Policies pertaining to asset allocation.
      (c) Description of significant investment policy changes during the reporting period.
   2. Identification of investments (other than those issued or explicitly guaranteed by the U.S. government) in any one organization that represent 5% or more of the OPEB plan's fiduciary net position.
   3. The annual money-weighted rate of return on OPEB plan investments calculated as the internal rate of return on OPEB plan investments, net of OPEB plan investment expense, and an explanation that a money-weighted rate of return expresses investment performance, net of OPEB plan investment expense, adjusted for the changing amounts actually invested. OPEB plan investment expense should be measured on the accrual basis of accounting. Inputs to the internal rate of return calculation should be determined at least monthly. The use of more frequently determined inputs is encouraged.

(c) Receivables. The terms of any long-term contracts for contributions to the OPEB plan between (1) an employer or nonemployer contributing entity and (2) the OPEB plan, and the balances outstanding on any such long-term contracts at the end of the OPEB plan's reporting period.

(d) Allocated insurance contracts excluded from OPEB plan assets:
   1. The amount reported in benefit payments in the current period that is attributable to the purchase of allocated insurance contracts.
   2. A brief description of the OPEB for which allocated insurance contracts were purchased in the current period.
   3. The fact that the obligation for the payment of benefits covered by allocated insurance contracts has been transferred to one or more insurance companies.

(e) Reserves. In circumstances in which there is a policy of setting aside, for purposes such as benefit increases or reduced employer contributions, a portion of the OPEB plan's fiduciary net position that otherwise would be available for existing OPEB or for OPEB plan administration:
   1. A description of the policy related to such reserves.
   2. The authority under which the policy was established and may be amended.
   3. The purposes for and conditions under which the reserves are required or permitted to be used.
   4. The balances of the reserves.

Required Supplementary Information

Similar to the discussion preceding the note disclosure requirements above, GASBS 74 provides that required supplementary information presented by a defined benefit OPEB plan that is administered through a trust should include all information required below, as applicable, if the financial statements are included in a stand-alone OPEB plan financial report or solely in the financial report of another government. If (a) a defined benefit OPEB plan is included in the financial report of a government that applies the requirements of GASBS 75 for benefits provided through the OPEB plan and (b) similar information is required by both GASBS 74 and 75, the government should present the information in a manner that avoids unnecessary duplication.

The following is the Required Supplementary Information required by GASBS 74, as applicable.

Single-Employer and Cost-Sharing OPEB Plans

GASBS provides that schedules of required supplementary information that include the information indicated in (a) through (d) below should be presented. The information in (a) and (b) may be presented in a single schedule. Information for each year should be measured as of the OPEB plan's most recent fiscal year-end. Information about cost-sharing OPEB plans should be presented for the OPEB plan as a whole:

(a) A ten-year schedule of changes in the net OPEB liability, presenting for each year (1) the beginning and ending balances of the total OPEB liability, the OPEB plan's fiduciary net position, and the net OPEB liability, calculated in conformity with the applicable requirements of GASBS 74, and (2) the effects on those items during the year of the following, as applicable. If the alternative measurement method is used to measure the total OPEB liability, the information indicated in subparagraphs (4) and (5) may be presented as a single amount:

1. Service cost.
2. Interest on the total OPEB liability.
3. Changes of benefit terms.
4. Differences between expected and actual experience with regard to economic or demographic factors in the measurement of the total OPEB liability.
5. Changes of assumptions about future economic or demographic factors or of other inputs.
6. Contributions from employers, including amounts for OPEB as the benefits come due that will not be reimbursed to the employers using OPEB plan assets.
7. Contributions from nonemployer contributing entities, including amounts for OPEB as the benefits come due that will not be reimbursed to the nonemployer contributing entities using OPEB plan assets.
8. The total of contributions from active plan members and inactive plan members not yet receiving benefit payments.
9. OPEB plan net investment income.
10. Benefit payments (including refunds of plan member contributions and amounts from employers or nonemployer contributing entities for OPEB as the benefits come due).
11. OPEB plan administrative expense.
12. Other changes, separately identified if individually significant.

(b) A ten-year schedule presenting the following for each year:

1. The total OPEB liability.
2. The OPEB plan's fiduciary net position.
3. The net OPEB liability.
4. The OPEB plan's fiduciary net position as a percentage of the total OPEB liability.
5. The covered-employee payroll.
6. The net OPEB liability as a percentage of covered-employee payroll.

(c) A ten-year schedule presenting for each year the information indicated in items (1) through (6) below, if an actuarially determined contribution is calculated for employers or nonemployer contributing entities. The schedule should identify whether the information relates to the employers, nonemployer contributing entities, or both:
   1. The actuarially determined contributions of employers or nonemployer contributing entities. For purposes of this schedule, actuarially determined contributions should exclude amounts, if any, associated with payables to the OPEB plan that arose in a prior fiscal year and those associated with separately financed specific liabilities to the OPEB plan.
   2. For cost-sharing OPEB plans, the statutorily or contractually required contribution of employers or nonemployer contributing entities, if different from (1). For purposes of this schedule, statutorily or contractually required contributions should include amounts from employers or nonemployer contributing entities for OPEB as the benefits come due that will not be reimbursed to the employers or nonemployer contributing entities using OPEB plan assets and should exclude amounts, if any, associated with payables to the OPEB plan that arose in a prior fiscal year and those associated with separately financed specific liabilities to the OPEB plan.
   3. The amount of contributions, including amounts from employers or nonemployer contributing entities for OPEB as the benefits come due that will not be reimbursed to the employers or nonemployer contributing entities using OPEB plan assets, recognized during the fiscal year by the OPEB plan in relation to the actuarially determined contribution in (1). For purposes of this schedule, contributions should exclude amounts resulting from contributions recognized by the OPEB plan as noncurrent receivables.
   4. The difference between the actuarially determined contribution in (1) and the amount of contributions recognized by the OPEB plan in relation to the actuarially determined contribution in (3).
   5. The covered-employee payroll.
   6. The amount of contributions recognized by the OPEB plan in relation to the actuarially determined contribution in (3) as a percentage of covered-employee payroll in (5).

(d) A ten-year schedule presenting for each fiscal year the annual money-weighted rate of return on OPEB plan investments calculated as described above.

Agent OPEB Plans

A ten-year schedule presenting for each fiscal year the annual money-weighted rate of return on OPEB plan investments calculated as described above should be presented in required supplementary information.

Notes to the Required Schedules

In addition to the specific components of Required Supplementary Information listed above, GASBS 74 provides specifics about notes to be provided for the required schedules. Significant methods and assumptions used in calculating the actuarially determined contributions, if any, should be presented as notes to the schedule. In addition, for each required schedule, information should be presented about factors that significantly affect trends in the amounts reported (for example, changes of benefit terms, changes in the size or composition of the population covered by the benefit terms, or the use of different assumptions). Information about investment-related factors that significantly affect trends in the amounts reported should be limited to those factors over which the OPEB plan or the participating governments have influence (for example, changes in investment policies). Information about external, economic factors (for example, changes in market prices) should not be presented. (The amounts presented for prior years should not be restated for the effects of changes—for example, changes of benefit terms or changes of assumptions—that occurred subsequent to the end of the fiscal year for which the information is reported.)

Measurement of the Net OPEB Liability

NOTE: Having addressed the basic financial statements, required disclosures, and RSI, GASBS 74 next turns to the requirements for how the net OPEB liability is measured. This is the area with the substance of the changes promulgated by GASBS 74. The requirements are consistent with that of GASBS 75 as to employer calculations, where applicable.

GASBS 74 provides that the net OPEB liability should be measured as the total OPEB liability (determined in accordance with the requirements discussed below), net of the OPEB plan's fiduciary net position. The net OPEB liability should be measured as of the OPEB plan's most recent fiscal year-end.

Total OPEB Liability

The total OPEB liability is the portion of the actuarial present value of projected benefit payments that is attributed to past periods of plan member service in conformity with the requirements discussed in the following paragraphs. For smaller plans meeting certain conditions, an alternative measurement method is also provided.

Timing and Frequency of Actuarial Valuations

GASBS 74 provides that the total OPEB liability should be determined by (a) an actuarial valuation as of the OPEB plan's most recent fiscal year-end or (b) the use of update procedures to roll forward to the OPEB plan's most recent fiscal year-end amounts from an actuarial valuation as of a date no more than 24 months earlier than the OPEB plan's most recent fiscal year-end.

If update procedures are used and significant changes occur between the actuarial valuation date and the OPEB plan's fiscal year-end, GASBS 74 provides that professional judgment should be used to determine the extent of procedures needed to roll forward the measurement from the actuarial valuation to the OPEB plan's fiscal year-end, and consideration should be given to whether a new actuarial valuation is needed. For purposes of this determination, the effects of changes in the discount rate resulting from changes in the OPEB plan's fiduciary net position or from changes in the municipal bond rate, if applicable, should be among the factors evaluated. For financial reporting purposes, an actuarial valuation of the total OPEB liability should be performed at least biennially. GASBS 74 encourages more frequent actuarial valuations.

Selection of Assumptions

Unless otherwise specified, GASBS 74 provides that the selection of all assumptions used in determining the total OPEB liability should be made in conformity with Actuarial Standards of Practice issued by the Actuarial Standards Board. For this purpose, a *deviation*, as the term is used in Actuarial Standards of Practice, from the guidance in an Actuarial Standard of Practice should not be considered to be in conformity with this requirement. The OPEB plan, employers, and, if any, governmental nonemployer contributing entities that make contributions to the OPEB plan, including payments that are made for OPEB as the benefits come due and that will not be reimbursed to the employer or nonemployer contributing entity using OPEB plan assets, should use the same assumptions when measuring similar or related OPEB information.

Projection of Benefit Payments

GASBS 74 provides that projected benefit payments should include all benefits (including refunds of plan member contributions) to be provided to current active and inactive plan members through the OPEB plan (including amounts for OPEB to be paid by employers or nonemployer contributing entities as the benefits come due) in accordance with the benefit terms and any additional legal agreements to provide benefits that are in force at the OPEB plan's fiscal year-end. GASBS 74 notes that usually, a written document is the best evidence of the benefit terms. However, in some cases, the substantive plan may differ from the written document. Accordingly, GASBS 74 provides that other information also should be taken into consideration in determining the benefits to be provided, including other communications between the employer and plan members (active and inactive) and an established pattern of practice with regard to the sharing of benefit-related costs with inactive plan members.

Projected benefit payments should include the effects of automatic postemployment benefit changes, including automatic COLAs. In addition, projected benefit payments should include the effects of (a) projected ad hoc postemployment benefit changes, including ad hoc COLAs, to the extent that they are considered to be substantively automatic; (b) projected salary changes (in circumstances in which the OPEB formula incorporates future compensation levels); and (c) projected service credits (both in determining a plan member's probable eligibility for benefits and in the projection of benefit payments in circumstances in which the OPEB formula incorporates years of service). Administrative costs associated with providing OPEB should be excluded from projected benefit payments. Benefit payments to be provided by means of an allocated insurance contract excluded from OPEB plan assets in conformity should be excluded from projected benefit payments.

NOTE: While automatic COLA increases may have been a more significant factor in calculating the projected benefits for pensions, it is included here for consistency and may apply in some circumstances. Nevertheless, the concept of making sure that the projected benefit reflects the "substantive plan" is an important one for OPEBs as well as pensions.

GASBS 74 also provides that projected benefit payments also should include taxes or other assessments expected to be imposed on benefit payments using the rates in effect at the OPEB plan's fiscal year-end or, if different rates have been approved by the assessing government to be applied in future periods, the rates approved by the assessing government associated with the periods in which the assessments on the benefit payments will be imposed.

Projected benefit payments should be based on claims costs, or age-adjusted premiums approximating claims costs, in accordance with Actuarial Standards of Practice issued by the Actuarial Standards Board. For this purpose, a *deviation*, as the term is used in Actuarial Standards of Practice, from the guidance in an Actuarial Standard of Practice should not be considered to be in conformity with this requirement.

In addition, GASBS 74 notes that a legal or contractual cap on benefit payments for OPEB each period should be considered in projecting benefit payments, if the cap is assumed to be effective taking into consideration whether the cap has been enforced in the past and other relevant factors and circumstances.

Discount Rate

NOTE: While the requirement relating to the discount rate determination is very similar to GASBS 67 and 68, most OPEB plans are either unfunded or have little funding, so the rate will be more heavily influenced by the municipal bond rate.

GASBS 74 provides that the discount rate should be the single rate that reflects the following:

(a) The long-term expected rate of return on OPEB plan investments that are expected to be used to finance the payment of benefits, to the extent that (1) the OPEB plan's fiduciary net position is projected to be sufficient to make projected benefit payments and (2) OPEB plan assets are expected to be invested using a strategy to achieve that return.
(b) A yield or index rate for 20-year, tax-exempt general obligation municipal bonds with an average rating of AA/Aa or higher (or equivalent quality on another rating scale), to the extent that the conditions in (a) are not met.

Comparing Projections of the OPEB Plan's Fiduciary Net Position to Projected Benefit Payments

---

NOTE: The requirements discussed below are important for plans with assets because in determining the extent to which benefit payments can be paid out the plan assets, a projection of the amount and timing of the benefits needs to be considered, along with the nature and timing of expected contributions.

For purposes of applying the discount rate requirements above, GASBS 74 provides that the amount of the OPEB plan's projected fiduciary net position and the amount of projected benefit payments should be compared in each period of projected benefit payments. Projections of the OPEB plan's fiduciary net position should incorporate all cash flows for contributions from employers and nonemployer contributing entities, if any, intended to finance benefits of current active and inactive plan members (status at the OPEB plan's fiscal year-end) and all cash flows for contributions from current active plan members. Conversely, GASBS 74 provides that the projection should not include (a) cash flows for contributions from employers or nonemployer contributing entities intended to finance the service costs of future plan members or (b) cash flows for contributions from future plan members, unless those contributions are projected to exceed service costs for those plan members. In each period, contributions from employers and nonemployer contributing entities should be considered to apply, first, to service costs of plan members in the period and, second, to past service costs, unless the effective OPEB plan terms related to contributions indicate that a different relationship between contributions to the OPEB plan from nonemployer contributing entities and service costs should be applied. Contributions from active plan members should be considered to be applied to service costs before contributions from employers and nonemployer contributing entities.

GASBS 74 notes that professional judgment should be applied to project cash flows for contributions from employers and nonemployer contributing entities in circumstances in which (a) those contribution amounts are established by statute or contract or (b) a formal, written policy related to those contributions exists. Application of professional judgment should consider the most recent five-year contribution history of the employers and nonemployer contributing entities as a key indicator of future contributions from those sources and should reflect all other known events and conditions. In circumstances other than those described in (a) and (b), the amount of projected cash flows for contributions from employers and nonemployer contributing entities should be limited to an average of contributions from those sources over the most recent five-year period and maybe modified based on consideration of subsequent events. For this purpose, the basis for the average (for example, percentage of payroll contributed or percentage of actuarially determined contributions made) should be a matter of professional judgment.

GASBS 74 does allow that if the evaluations required by the above can be made with sufficient reliability without a separate projection of cash flows into and out of the OPEB plan, alternative methods may be applied in making the evaluations.

Calculating the Discount Rate

For each future period, GASBS 74 provides that if the amount of the OPEB plan's fiduciary net position is projected to be greater than or equal to the benefit payments that are projected to be made in that period and OPEB plan assets up to that point are expected to be invested using a strategy to achieve the long-term expected rate of return, the actuarial present value of benefit payments projected to be made in the period should be determined using the long-term expected rate of return on those investments. GASBS provides that the long-term expected rate of return should be based on the nature and mix of current and expected OPEB plan investments over a period representative of the expected length of time between (a) the point at which a plan member begins to provide service to the employer and (b) the point at which all benefits to the plan member have been paid. For this purpose, the long-term expected rate of return should be determined net of OPEB plan investment expense but without reduction for OPEB plan administrative expense.

The municipal bond rate discussed above is used to calculate the actuarial present value of all other benefit payments.

GASBS 74 considers the discount rate as the single rate of return that, when applied to all projected benefit payments, results in an actuarial present value of projected benefit payments equal to the total of the actuarial present values.

Attribution of the Actuarial Present Value of Projected Benefit Payments to Periods

GASBS 74 provides that the entry age actuarial cost method should be used to attribute the actuarial present value of projected benefit payments of each plan member to periods in conformity with the following:

(a) Attribution should be made on an individual plan-member-by-plan-member basis.
(b) Each plan member's service costs should be level as a percentage of that member's projected pay. For purposes of this calculation, if a member does not have projected pay, the projected inflation rate should be used in place of the projected rate of change in salary.
(c) The beginning of the attribution period should be the first period in which the member provides service under the benefit terms, notwithstanding vesting or other similar terms.
(d) The service costs of all OPEB should be attributed through all assumed ages of exit from active service.

(e) Each plan member's service costs should be determined based on the same benefit terms reflected in that member's actuarial present value of projected benefit payments.

NOTE: As with pensions, the GASB has selected one actuarial attribution method that must be used, which will result in better comparability among different governments.

Alternative Measurement Method

NOTE: As with the prior standard, the GASB has provided an alternative measurement method for smaller OPEB plans. The specifics of the requirements from GASBS 74 are detailed below. This is an alternative, but not necessarily easy, method. For practice experience with the prior standard, governments seemed more inclined to have an actuarial valuation, rather than to attempt this calculation on their own.

In place of an actuarial valuation, GASBS 74 provides that the total OPEB liability may be measured using the alternative measurement method discussed in this section if there are fewer than 100 plan members (active and inactive) as of the beginning of the OPEB plan's fiscal year.

If the alternative measurement method is used, GASBS 74 provides that one or more of the specific modifications discussed below may be incorporated into application of the requirements of the alternative method:

(a) *General considerations*. Assumptions other than those specifically identified in the alternative method might be needed depending on the benefits provided. Assumptions generally should be based on the actual experience of the covered group, to the extent that credible experience data are available, but should emphasize expected long-term future trends rather than give undue weight to recent past experience. However, GASBS 74 provides that grouping techniques that base the selection of assumptions on combined experience data for similar plans may be used, as discussed later in this section. The reasonableness of each assumption should be considered independently based on its own merits and its consistency with each other assumption. As an example, GASBS 74 notes that each assumption of which general inflation is a component should include the same assumption with regard to that component. In addition, consideration should be given to the reasonableness of the combined impact of all assumptions.

(b) *Expected point in time at which benefit payments will begin to be made*. The assumption should reflect past experience and future expectations for the covered group. For active plan members, the assumption may incorporate (1) a single assumed age at which benefit payments will begin to be made or (2) an assumption that benefit payments will begin to be made upon attaining a certain number of years of service.

(c) *Marital and dependency status*. These assumptions may be based on the current status of active and inactive plan members or on historical demographic data for inactive plan members.

(d) *Mortality*. The assumption should be based on current published mortality tables.

(e) *Turnover*. For purposes of allocating the present value of projected benefit payments to periods, the assumed probability that an active plan member will remain employed until the assumed age at which benefit payments will begin to be made generally should be based on the historical age-based turnover experience of the covered group, adjusted for any expected long-term future trends using the calculation method identified in the alternative method.

However, if experience data are not available, the probability of remaining employed until the assumed age at which benefit payments will begin to be made should be assigned using the method identified in the alternative method.

(f) *Health care cost trend rate*. Assumptions about changes in health care cost in future periods for which benefit payments are projected should be derived from an objective source.

(g) *Use of health insurance premiums*. If experience-rated health care benefits are provided through premium payments to an insurer or other service provider, the OPEB plan's current premium structure may be used as the initial per capita health care rates for the purpose of projecting health care benefit payments. However, if the same premium rates are given for both active employees and inactive plan members, age-adjusted premium rates for inactive plan members should be obtained from the insurer or, if that information cannot be obtained from the insurer, age-adjusted premiums for inactive plan members should be estimated using the method identified in the alternative method.

(h) *Coverage options*. If the terms of an OPEB plan provide inactive plan members with coverage options, assumptions regarding coverage choices should be based on the experience of the covered group, considering differences, if any, in choices of pre- and post-Medicare-eligible plan members.

(i) *Use of grouping*. Grouping techniques may be used. One such technique is to group plan members based on common demographic characteristics (for example, plan members within a range of ages or years of service), when the obligation for each plan member in the group is expected to be similar for commonly grouped individuals. Another technique is to group OPEB plans with similar expected costs and benefits.

NOTE: The above are areas where GASBS 74 permits, or does not permit, changes to be made to the alternative method. There is actually a good deal of judgment inherent in making actuarial calculations. The items listed above provide guidance as to when judgment and actual plan experience can be used to modify the alternative method.

The following is the alternative measurement methodology contained in GASBS 74. The calculation methods and default values should be used, if applicable, to meet the requirements to determine the probability that active plan members will remain employed until the expected point in time that benefit payments will begin to be made and to determine age-adjusted premiums for inactive plan members:

(a) For purposes of applying these requirements, if historical age-based turnover experience of the covered group is used, the following methodology should be used to calculate the probability of remaining employed until the assumed age at which benefit payments will begin to be made:

Age	Probability of Termination in Next Year (a)	Probability of Remaining Employed for Next Year (b)	Probability of Remaining Employed from Earliest Entry Age to Beginning of Year (c)	Probability of Remaining Employed from Age Shown to Assumed Age at Which Benefit Payments Will Begin to Be Made (d)

Column a: For each age (n) from the earliest entry age to assumed age at which benefit payments will begin to be made, list the age-based *probability of termination in the next year* for the covered group.

Column b: Compute the probability at each age of remaining employed for the next year. This value should be calculated as 1 – a.

Column c: Set the initial value in column c to equal 1.000. For each subsequent age (n), column c values should be calculated as: $c(n - 1) \times b(n - 1)$.

Column d: For each age (n), these values should be calculated as the product of the values in column b from age n to the year prior to the assumed age at which benefit payments will begin to be made.

(b) For purposes of applying the requirements of regarding turnover, if historical age-based turnover experience of the covered group is not used, historical age-based turnover should be derived from either:

1. Data maintained by the U.S. Office of Personnel Management regarding the most recent experience of the employee group covered by the Federal Employees Retirement System.
2. Data maintained by another entity, such as a public employee retirement system, which includes the covered group.

(c) For purposes of applying the requirements for health insurance premiums, when the same premiums are charged to active employees and inactive plan members and age-adjusted premium information for inactive plan members is not able to be obtained from the insurer or service provider, the following approach should be used to age-adjust premiums for purposes of projecting benefit payments:

1. To adjust premiums for ages under 65:
   (a) Identify the premium charged for active and inactive employees under age 65.
   (b) Calculate the average age of the employees to which the premium identified in step a applies.
   (c) For each employee under age 65, identify the greater of expected age at which benefit payments will begin to be made or current age.
   (d) Calculate the average of the ages identified in step c.
   (e) Calculate the midpoint age between the result of step d and age 65: result of step d + [0.5 × (65 – result of step d)].
   (f) Using the results of steps b and e, calculate a factor with the following formula: 1.04 (result of step e – result of step b).
   (g) Multiply the factor identified in step f by the premium identified in step a. The result is the current-year age-adjusted premium that should be used as the basis for projecting benefit payments for ages under age 65.
2. To adjust premiums for ages 65 or older:
   (a) Identify the premium charged for active and inactive employees age 65 or older.
   (b) Calculate the average age of the employees to which the premium identified in step a applies.
   (c) For each employee (whether age pre-65 or age 65 or older), identify the greater of current age or age 65.
   (d) Calculate the average of the ages identified in step c.
   (e) Calculate the average life expectancy of all employees.
   (f) Calculate the midpoint age between the result of step d and the result of step e: result of step d + [0.5 × (result of step e – result of step d)].

(g) Using the results of steps b and f, calculate a factor with the following formula: 1.04(64 – result of step b) × 1.03(result of step f – 64) (for plans with no Medicare coordination) or 0.5 × 1.04(64 – result of step b) × 1.03(result of step f – 64) (for plans with Medicare coordination).

(h) Multiply the factor identified in step g by the premium identified in step a. The result is the current-year age-adjusted premium that should be used as the basis for projecting benefit payments for age 65 or older.

GASBS 74 notes that the procedures described in item c(2) above would be applied only in cases in which inactive employees age 65 or older are included in a single, blended premium assessed by the insurer or service provider for active and inactive employees. If separate rates are assessed for inactive employees age 65 or older, preparers would follow the steps in paragraph c(1) for age-adjusting blended premiums for under age 65 and would use the separately assessed premium rates (without additional age adjustment) for age 65 or older.

NOTE: The following paragraphs are very important as to accounting for assets accumulated for OPEB benefits, both when they are held in a trust that meets the GASBS 74 criteria, or not held in a trust. These paragraphs are NOT specifically related to the alternative measurement method. They apply in all cases.

Assets Accumulated for Purposes of Providing OPEB through Defined Benefit OPEB Plans That Are Not Administered through Trusts

GASBS 74 provides that if an OPEB plan is not administered through a trust that meets the criteria listed at the very start of this GASBS 74 discussion, any assets accumulated for OPEB purposes should continue to be reported as assets of the employer or nonemployer contributing entity.

GASBS 74 further provides that if an OPEB plan is not administered through a trust that meets the criteria, a government that holds assets accumulated for OPEB purposes in a fiduciary capacity should report the assets in an agency fund. The amount of assets accumulated in excess of liabilities for benefits due to plan members and accrued investment and administrative expenses should be reported as a liability to participating employers or nonemployer contributing entities. If the agency fund is included in the financial report of an employer whose employees are provided with benefits through the OPEB plan or a nonemployer contributing entity that makes benefit payments as OPEB comes due, balances reported by the agency fund should exclude amounts that pertain to the employer or nonemployer contributing entity that reports the agency fund. Instead, those amounts should continue to be reported as stated in the preceding paragraph.

Defined Contribution OPEB Plans That Are Administered through Trusts

GASBS 74 requires that the following information be disclosed in notes to financial statements of a defined contribution OPEB plan that is administered through a trust that meets the criteria mentioned earlier:

(a) Identification of the OPEB plan as a defined contribution OPEB plan.

(b) The authority under which the OPEB plan is established or may be amended.

(c) Classes of plan members covered (for example, general employees or public safety employees).
(d) The number of plan members, participating employers (if the OPEB plan is used to provide OPEB to the employees of more than one employer), and, if any, nonemployer contributing entities.

EFFECTIVE DATE AND TRANSITION

The requirements of GASBS 74 are effective for fiscal years beginning after June 15, 2016. Earlier application is encouraged. Changes adopted to conform to the provisions of GASBS 74 should be applied retroactively by restating financial statements, if practical, for all prior periods presented. If restatement for prior periods is not practical, the cumulative effect, if any, of applying GASBS 74 should be reported as a restatement of beginning net position (or fund balance or fund net position, as applicable) for the earliest period restated. In the first period that GASB 74 is applied, the notes to the financial statements should disclose the nature of the restatement and its effect. Also, the reason for not restating prior periods presented should be disclosed.

SUMMARY

The accounting and financial reporting for defined benefit pension and OPEB plans is a specialized area that requires close coordination with the plan's actuary to develop and report all of the required disclosures. Pension and OPEB plan financial statement preparers, however, should understand the actuarial methods and assumptions to a sufficient extent that they are able to take responsibility for the plan's financial statements, including the required supplementary information.

23 EDUCATIONAL AND OTHER GOVERNMENTAL ENTITIES

INTRODUCTION

This chapter discusses the broad accounting and financial reporting requirements and practices for several groups of governmental organizations:

- School districts.
- Governmental colleges and universities.
- Governmental hospitals and other health care providers.
- Governmental not-for-profit organizations.
- Other public benefit corporations.

SCHOOL DISTRICTS

In examining the accounting and financial reporting for school districts, the main area to examine is how the accounting and financial reporting for school districts would differ from that for general-purpose governments, which has been described throughout this guide.

First, school districts are governmental entities subject to the jurisdiction of the Governmental Accounting Standards Board (GASB). Second, school districts would prepare a Comprehensive Annual Financial Report (CAFR) in conformity with GAAP, as would any general-purpose government.

Beyond these commonalties, however, there are some practical differences likely to be encountered in accounting and financial reporting by school districts when compared to general-purpose governments. The following paragraphs highlight some of these differences.

Legal Compliance

One difference from general-purpose governments that the preparer of a school district's financial statements is likely to encounter is the requirement to use a standardized chart of accounts. State governments generally require school districts to prepare special-purpose reports used for a number of purposes by states, including the monitoring of state aid programs to the school districts. In order to provide consistency among school districts in these special reports, state governments generally require school districts to follow a uniform chart of accounts. In many cases, this uniform chart of accounts is based on the U.S. Department of Education's publication Financial Accounting for Local and State School Systems. The use of a standardized chart of accounts by a school district should not in any way prevent the school district from preparing GAAP-based financial statements.

Fund Accounting

School districts should use fund accounting in conjunction with their various activities, using the guidance provided throughout this book. They are also subject to the requirements of GASBS 34 to present government-wide financial statements. Two activities that school districts are likely to encounter are as follows:

1. School districts generally report food service funds as either special revenue funds or enterprise funds. Federal commodities used in conjunction with these programs should be reported as inventory. Many school districts report the use of those commodities as revenues (with a corresponding expenditure) when the commodities are used. If a special revenue fund is used, the value of donated commodities should be reported as revenue when received.
2. Funds are often set up by school districts for student activities paid for from sources other than the school district's budget, such as special fundraising activities. For example, students may sell candy or other small items to support an after-school sports program. In these cases, the principal of the school is often responsible for administering these funds. Student activity funds should be included within the school's financial statements, if they are material. Student activity funds should be reported as a single special revenue fund or agency fund with subaccounts, if appropriate. An agency fund is appropriate if the assets of the student activity fund legally belong to the students. If not, a special revenue fund would be the more appropriate financial reporting classification for these funds. (A discussion of accounting for the cost of activities that include fundraising is provided later in this chapter.)

Reporting Entity

A school district may be included in the reporting entity of another government, depending on the individual circumstances and the application of GASB Statement 14 (GASBS 14), *The Financial Reporting Entity,* which is described in Chapter 6. Many school districts are independent and are not included as part of any other entity's financial reporting entity. There are, however, school districts that are dependent on other governmental entities and meet the criteria of GASBS 14 requiring inclusion in the financial reporting entity of another government.

In some cases, a school district may qualify for inclusion in the reporting entity of more than one entity. For example, a school district may qualify to be part of the financial reporting entity of a city, the county in which the city is located, and the state in which the county is located. The school district should be reported in the financial reporting entity of only one of these entities.

According to the 1994 GAAFR, as a general rule, the school district is reported in the financial reporting entity of the lowest level of government of which it qualifies as a component unit.

GASBS 14 provides specific guidance for elementary and secondary schools, noting the combination of funding sources from local taxation and state aid formulas. GASBS 14 notes that in most cases, the entity status of a school district will be readily apparent as either part of a primary government or a component unit of a local government because either its governing board is separately elected or a voting majority is appointed by the local government. In other cases, however, school districts' governing boards are appointed by state officials, and the state may appear to be financially accountable for the school district because of the state aid distribution. The financial statement preparer will need to exercise judgment as to whether the school district should be considered a component unit of the state or of the local government. Usually, the fiscal dependency is on the local government, not the financial burden on the state created by legislatively established education aid distribution formulas. This fiscal dependency on the local government generally should govern the determination of the appropriate reporting entity for school districts with these governance and funding characteristics.

GOVERNMENTAL COLLEGES AND UNIVERSITIES

The GASB issued Statement 35 (GASBS 35), *Basic Financial Statements—and Management's Discussion and Analysis—for Public Colleges and Universities*. GASBS 35 amended GASBS 34 to include public colleges and universities within its scope. Instead of requiring a specific new reporting model for public colleges and universities, GASBS 35 simply makes the provisions of GASBS 34 applicable to public colleges and universities.

Exhibits 1, 2, and 3 present sample statements based upon the example in GASBS 35.

Exhibit 1: Sample statement of net position of a public university

Somewhere State University
Statement of Net Position
June 20, 20XX

Assets	
Current assets:	
Cash and cash equivalents	$ xx,xxx
Short-term investments	xx,xxx
Accounts receivable, net	xx,xxx
Inventories	xx,xxx
Deposit with bond trustee	xx,xxx
Notes and mortgages receivable, net	xx,xxx
Other assets	xx,xxx
Total current assets	xxx,xxx
Noncurrent assets:	
Restricted cash and cash equivalents	xx,xxx
Endowment investments	xx,xxx
Notes and mortgages receivable, net	xx,xxx
Other long-term investments	xx,xxx
Investments in real estate	xx,xxx

(Continued)

Capital assets, net	xx,xxx
Total noncurrent assets	xxx,xxx
Total assets	xxx,xxx
Liabilities	
Current liabilities:	
Accounts payable and accrued liabilities	xx,xxx
Unearned revenue	xx,xxx
Long-term liabilities—current portion	xx,xxx
Total current liabilities	xx,xxx
Noncurrent liabilities:	
Deposits	xx,xxx
Unearned revenue	xx,xxx
Long-term liabilities	xx,xxx
Total noncurrent liabilities	xxx,xxx
Total liabilities	xxx,xxx
Net position	
Invested in capital assets, net of related debt	
Restricted for:	
Nonexpendable:	
Scholarships and fellowships	xx,xxx
Research	xx,xxx
Expendable:	
Scholarships and fellowships	xx,xxx
Research	xx,xxx
Instructional department uses	xx,xxx
Loans	xx,xxx
Capital projects	xx,xxx
Debt service	xx,xxx
Other	xx,xxx
Unrestricted	xx,xxx
Total net position	$xxx,xxx

Exhibit 2: Sample statement of revenues, expenses, and changes in net position of a public university

Somewhere State University
Statement of Revenues, Expenses, and Changes in Net Position
June 20, 20XX

Revenues	
Operating revenues:	
Student tuition and fees (net of scholarship allowances of $x,xxx)	$ xx,xxx
Patient services (net of charity care of $xx,xxx)	xx,xxx
Federal grants and contracts	xx,xxx
State and local grants and contracts	xx,xxx
Nongovernmental grants and contracts	xx,xxx
Sales and services of educational departments	xx,xxx
Auxiliary expenses:	
Residential life (net of scholarship allowances of $x,xxx)	xxx,xxx
Bookstore (net of scholarship allowances of $x,xxx)	xx,xxx

Other operating revenues	xx,xxx
Total operating revenues	xxx,xxx
Expenses	
Operating expenses:	
Salaries	
Faculty (physicians for the hospital)	xx,xxx
Exempt staff	xx,xxx
Nonexempt wages	xx,xxx
Benefits	xx,xxx
Scholarships and fellowships	xx,xxx
Utilities	xx,xxx
Supplies and other services	xx,xxx
Depreciation	xx,xxx
Total operating expenses	xxx,xxx
Operating income	xx,xxx
Nonoperating revenues (expenses)	
State appropriations	xx,xxx
Gifts	xx,xxx
Investment income (net of investment expense of $x,xxx for the primary institution and $x,xxx for the hospital)	xx,xxx
Interest on capital assets—related debt	(xx,xxx)
Other nonoperating revenues	xx,xxx
Net nonoperating revenues	xxx,xxx
Income before other revenues, expenses, gains, or losses	xxx,xxx
Capital appropriations	xx,xxx
Capital grants and gifts	xx,xxx
Additions to permanent endowments	xx,xxx
Increase in net position	xxx,xxx
Net position	
Net position—beginning of year	xxx,xxx
Net position—end of year	$xxx,xxx

Exhibit 3: Sample statement of cash flows of a public university

Somewhere State University
Statement of Cash Flows
June 20, 20XX

Cash flows from operating activities	
Tuition and fees	$ xx,xxx
Research grants and contracts	xx,xxx
Payments to suppliers	(xx,xxx)
Payments to employees	(xx,xxx)
Loans issued to students and employees	(xx,xxx)
Collection of loans to students and employees	xx,xxx
Auxiliary enterprise charges:	
Residence halls	xx,xxx
Bookstore	xx,xxx

(Continued)

Other receipts	xx,xxx
Net cash used by operating activities	(xx,xxx)
Cash flows from noncapital financing activities	
State appropriations	xx,xxx
Gifts and grants received for other than capital purposes:	
Private gifts for endowment purposes	xx,xxx
Net cash flows provided by noncapital financing activities	xx,xxx
Cash flows from capital and related financing activities	
Proceeds from capital debt	xx,xxx
Capital appropriations	xx,xxx
Capital grants and gifts received	xx,xxx
Proceeds from sale of capital assets	xx,xxx
Purchases of capital assets	(xx,xxx)
Principal paid on capital debt and lease	(xx,xxx)
Interest paid on capital debt and lease	(xx,xxx)
Net cash used by capital and related financing activities	(xx,xxx)
Cash flows from investing activities	
Proceeds from sales and maturities of investments	xx,xxx
Interest on investments	xx,xxx
Purchase of investments	(xx,xxx)
Net cash provided by investing activities	xx,xxx
Net increase in cash	xx,xxx
Cash—beginning of year	xx,xxx
Cash—end of year	$ xx,xxx
Reconciliation of net operating revenues (expenses) to net cash provided (used) by operating activities:	
Operating income (loss)	(xx,xxx)
Adjustments to reconcile net income (loss) to net cash provided (used) by operating activities:	
Depreciation expense	xx,xxx
Change in assets and liabilities:	
Receivables, net	xx,xxx
Inventories	xx,xxx
Deposit with bond trustee	xx,xxx
Other assets	(xx,xxx)
Accounts payable	(xx,xxx)
Unearned revenue	xx,xxx
Deposits held for others	(xx,xxx)
Compensated absences	xx,xxx
Net cash used by operating activities	$ (xx,xxx)

Reporting Entity Considerations

The provisions of GASBS 14 are applicable to determine the inclusion of a governmental college or university in the financial reporting entity of another governmental entity.

Costs of Activities That Include Fundraising

The AICPA has issued Statement of Position 98-2 (SOP 98-2, now at FASB ASC 958-720), Accounting for Costs of Activities of Not-for-Profit Organizations and State and Local

Governmental Entities That Include Fundraising, which has been cleared by the GASB. It therefore should be considered as category B in the hierarchy of generally accepted accounting principles for governments (see Chapter 2 for additional details of this hierarchy).

While not many governments participate in fundraising activities, many governmental colleges and universities do actively raise funds, and it is these organizations that the impact of the SOP will affect the most. That is not to say that other organizations, such as governmental health care providers, etc., will not also be required to comply with its requirements.

SOP 98-2 (FASB ASC 958-720) specifies criteria that it describes as purpose, audience, and content that, at a minimum, must be met before joint costs of joint activities can be allocated.

- If these three criteria are met, the costs of joint activities that are identifiable with a particular function should be charged to that function and joint costs should be allocated between fundraising and the appropriate program or management and general function.
- If these three criteria are not met, all costs of the joint activity should be reported as fundraising costs, regardless of whether these costs might otherwise be considered program or management and general costs if they had been incurred in a different activity. An exception to this rule is that costs of goods or services provided in exchange transactions that are part of joint activities (such costs of direct donor benefits of a special event, such as the cost of a meal provided at a fundraising dinner) should not be reported as fundraising.

The three criteria are as follows:

1. *Purpose*. The purpose criterion is met if the purpose of the joint activity includes accomplishing program or management and general functions:
   (a) *Program activities*. To accomplish program functions, the activity should call for specific action by the audience that will help accomplish the entity's mission. (For example, if the purpose of the not-for-profit organization is to encourage good health, then in mailing a brochure to an audience encouraging them to stop smoking, lose weight, etc., with suggestions as to how to go about these changes, the call to specific action requirement is met and the considerations in the following paragraphs should be examined.)
   (b) *Program and management and general activities*. For program activities that meet the call to action requirement (and for any management and general activity), determining whether the purpose criterion is met should be based upon the following considerations (SOP 98-2 lists these factors in their order of importance, and that is the same order in which they are presented herein):
      1. Whether compensation or fees for performing the activity are based on contributions received. The purpose criterion is not met if a majority of compensation or fees for any party's performance of any component of the discrete joint activity is based on contributions raised for that discrete activity.
      2. Whether a similar program or management and general activity is conducted separately and on a similar or greater scale. The purpose criterion is met if either of the two conditions are met:
         (a) *Condition 1*. The program component of the joint activity calls for a specific action by the recipient that will help accomplish the entity's mission and a similar program component is conducted without the fundraising component, using the same medium and on a scale that is similar to or greater than the scale on which it is conducted with fundraising.

   (b) *Condition 2.* A management and general activity that is similar to the management and general component of the joint activity being accounted for is conducted without the fundraising component, using the same medium and on a scale that is similar to or greater than the scale on which it is conducted with the fundraising.
 3. Other evidence, if the factors discussed above do not determine whether the purpose criterion is met. All available evidence, both positive and negative, should be considered.

2. *Audience.* SOP 98-2 (FASB ASC 958-720) presumes that the audience criterion is not met if the audience includes prior donors or is otherwise selected based on the ability or likelihood to contribute to the not-for-profit organization. This presumption can be overcome if the audience is also selected for one or more of the reasons listed below.

   The following reasons may be used to satisfy the audience criterion where the audience includes no prior donors and is not based on its ability or likelihood to contribute to the not-for-profit organizations (these factors may also be used to rebut the audience presumption described in the preceding paragraph):
   (a) The audience's need to use or reasonable potential for use of the specific action called for by the program component of the joint activity.
   (b) The audience's ability to take specific action to assist the not-for-profit organization in meeting the goals of the program component of the joint activity.
   (c) The not-for-profit organization is required to direct the management and general component of the joint activity to the particular audience or the audience has reasonable potential for use of the management and general component.
3. *Content.* The content criterion is met if the joint activity supports program or management or general functions, as follows:
   (a) *Program.* The joint activity calls for specific action by the recipient that will help accomplish the not-for-profit organization's mission. If the need for the benefits of the action is not clearly evident, information describing the action and explaining the need for and benefits of the action.
   (b) *Management and general.* The joint activity fulfills one or more of the not-for-profit organization's management responsibilities through a component of the joint activity.

SOP 98-2 (FASB ASC 958-720) clearly is very specific as to when joint costs can be allocated for joint activities and provides seventeen specific examples that should be used in applying the purpose, audience, and content criteria to individual circumstances.

Allocation Methods

While SOP 98-2's (FASB ASC 958-720) discussion of *when* joint costs may be allocated is very specific and detailed, its discussion of *how* to allocate joint costs is more flexible. The allocation methodology that is used must be rational and systematic, resulting in a reasonable allocation that is applied consistently given similar facts and circumstances. Appendix F of the SOP describes some commonly used allocation methods but does not require that one of the methods presented be used.

Incidental Activities

Provided its criteria are met, SOP 98-2 (FASB ASC 958-720) makes optional allocating joint costs in circumstances in which a fundraising, program, or management and general activity is conducted in conjunction with another activity and is incidental to the other activity. However, SOP 98-2 warns that in circumstances in which the program or management and general activity is incidental to the fundraising activities, it is unlikely that the conditions for allocating joint costs would be met.

NOTE: Generally, the requirements make it more difficult to allocate joint costs to program activities. The requirements that must be met are restrictive and meant to curb abuses of overallocation of joint costs to program activities. A high percentage of expenses being program expenses is a positive performance indicator for not-for-profit organizations. It is an indication that funds raised are not being spent for fundraising or for management and administrative activities, but rather for the program activities for which the organization exists.

The remainder of this chapter addresses some of these issues for the following special types of governmental entities:

- Governmental hospitals and other health care providers.
- Governmental not-for-profit organizations.
- Other public benefit corporations.

The entities described in this chapter are types of governmental entities that are likely to fall within the category of "special-purpose governments" under GASBS 34.

Special-Purpose Governments

GASBS 34 contains the concept of special-purpose governments and has reduced or modified financial statement requirements for these governments. GASBS 34 is written from the perspective of general-purpose governments, such as states, cities, towns, etc. Special-purpose governments are legally separate entities and may be component units or other stand-alone governments. GASBS 34's modified financial reporting requirements are only allowable, however, in certain circumstances.

For special-purpose governments engaged in a single governmental program, GASBS 34 allows that government-wide and fund financial statements be combined using a columnar format that reconciles individual line items of fund financial data to government-wide data in a separate column on the face of the financial statements. A governmental special-purpose government cannot be considered a special-purpose government if it budgets, manages, or accounts for its activities as multiple programs.

For special-purpose governments engaged only in business-type activities, only the financial statements for enterprise funds should be presented. These financial statements include:

- Management's discussion and analysis.
- Statement of net position or balance sheet.
- Statement of revenues, expenses, and changes in fund net position.
- Statement of cash flows.
- Notes to the financial statements.
- Required supplementary information, if applicable.

For special-purpose governments engaged only in fiduciary activities, only the financial statements for fiduciary funds should be presented. These financial statements include:

- Management's discussion and analysis.
- Statement of fiduciary net position.
- Statement of changes in fiduciary net position.
- Notes to the financial statements.

GOVERNMENTAL HOSPITALS AND OTHER HEALTH CARE PROVIDERS

There is no set of governmental accounting and financial reporting standards that specifically apply to governmental hospitals and other health care providers. (For simplicity, wherever this chapter refers to "hospitals," it is referring to both hospitals and other health care providers.) Originally, hospitals that were operated by governmental units were required to follow the requirements of the American Institute of Certified Public Accountants (AICPA) *Hospital Audit Guide,* as amended and interpreted. The *Hospital Audit Guide* was superseded in June 1996 by the AICPA Audit and Accounting Guide (1996 Guide), *Health-Care Organizations.*

The 1996 Guide was cleared for final issuance by the GASB. Accordingly, based on the GAAP hierarchy effective at that time, the 1996 Guide constitutes category (c) accounting and reporting guidance for governmental hospitals. (See Chapter 2 for a more complete discussion of the governmental accounting hierarchy.) GAAP hierarchy categories (c) and (d) are both sources of established accounting principles. If an accounting treatment is not specified by the GASB or FASB pronouncements made applicable by GASB Statements or Interpretations, an independent auditor, under AICPA rules, would need to be prepared to justify a conclusion that a treatment other than category (c) or (d) is generally accepted.

Because the accounting treatment recommended by the 1996 Guide can best be accomplished in an enterprise fund, governmental hospitals should be accounted for as an enterprise fund. This means that governmental hospitals that are using proprietary (enterprise) fund accounting and financial reporting should apply all applicable GASB pronouncements (including all NCGA Statements and Interpretations currently in effect), as well as certain FASB and Accounting Principles Board pronouncements. The applicability of GASB and FASB pronouncements to activities reported as proprietary funds is discussed in detail in Chapter 10. Readers should also be aware of the guidance of AICPA Statement of Position 98-2 (FASB ASC 958-720), *Accounting for Costs of Activities of Not-for-Profit Organizations and State and Local Governmental Entities That Include Fundraising,* discussed earlier in this chapter.

Reporting Entity Considerations

Although the nucleus of a financial reporting entity is usually a primary government, an organization other than a primary government (including hospitals and other health care providers) may serve as a nucleus for a reporting entity when it issues separate financial statements. The reporting entity considerations addressed in Chapter 6 should be considered when a governmental hospital or other health care provider issues separate financial statements.

In addition to the reporting entity considerations, the governmental hospital that is a component unit of another governmental unit should acknowledge that fact. This is accomplished by using a reference to the primary government in the title of a component unit's separately issued financial statements, such as "City Hospital Corporation—a component unit of the city of Example."

In addition, the notes to the financial statements should identify the primary government in whose financial reporting entity it is included and describe its relationship with the primary government.

GOVERNMENTAL NOT-FOR-PROFIT ORGANIZATIONS

In a number of instances, state and local government entities have used accounting and financial reporting principles that are applicable not to governments, but to not-for-profit organizations. In a typical situation, a government sets up a separate entity, often tax-exempt under Section 501(c)3 of the Internal Revenue Code, to accomplish some governmental function and purpose. For example, a city may establish such a not-for-profit organization to promote economic development within the city, such as by attracting new business to the city or by discouraging businesses from leaving the city. Although the state or local governmental entity retains control and accountability for the not-for-profit organization, resulting in its being reported as a component unit of the state or local government, the not-for-profit organization has all of the characteristics of a separate organization.

Governmental not-for-profit organizations should follow the accounting and financial reporting guidelines of GASBS 34.

OTHER PUBLIC BENEFIT CORPORATIONS

Governments often establish and incorporate *public benefit corporations* to assist the governmental entity in providing services to the citizenry. Some of these public benefit corporations are entities that actually operate facilities or a plant to provide services to citizens. For example, a water and sewer authority may operate and maintain a reservoir system, a water filtration plant, and a sewage treatment facility. A port authority may operate shipping terminal facilities. Other public benefit corporations may be more of a financing nature. For example, a housing finance authority may be established to provide financing for the development of affordable housing within the jurisdiction of the government. A dormitory authority may be established to provide financing for the construction of dormitory facilities for a governmental college or university.

The use of public benefit corporations seems to be increasing as governments recognize some of the benefits that these entities offer to the government. For example, in the case of a water and sewer authority, the authority may be able to sell revenue bonds based on a pledge of the fees that it charges to its users. These revenue bonds are likely to be able to be sold with a lower interest rate than would general obligation bonds of the government, since there is a revenue stream dedicated to their repayment, which, all things being equal, makes them a better credit risk than the general obligation bonds.

Governments also are recognizing the benefits of the flexibility that public benefit corporations offer. Usually these corporations operate without many of the restrictions that general governments operate under. For example, their employees may not be subject to civil service rules, or taxpayer approval may not be needed for a financing authority to issue bonds. Transactions can be structured between the public benefit corporation and the governmental entity to almost make it seem transparent to the governmental entity that a public benefit corporation is involved in the transactions. For example, a state that desired to build prison facilities used a public benefit corporation to issue bonds and to build the facility. The state then leased the facility from the public benefit corporation. The lease payments made by the state were exactly tied to the debt service payments that were being made on the bonds by the public benefit corporation.

In determining the accounting and financial reporting requirements for these types of public benefit corporations, the guidance in Chapter 7 for proprietary funds should be used. These entities almost always use the accounting and financial reporting principles of proprietary funds in a government's financial statements. Thus, these entities need to decide whether they will implement FASB statements issued after November 30, 1989, in accordance with GASBS 20. Additional information on this decision and the related requirements is provided in Chapter 7. Public benefit corporations are most often presented as discretely presented component units of a government, but they may also be blended, if they meet the reporting entity requirements to be reported as a blended component unit.

Where public benefit corporations issue debt, they almost always issue their own stand-alone financial statements, since these financial statements are needed to actually sell their debt. When these financial statements are issued, the public benefit corporation should consider whether there are any entities that should be included as a component unit of the public benefit corporation. The same criteria described in Chapter 11 should be considered in making this determination. In addition, when stand-alone financial statements of a public benefit corporation that is a component unit of a governmental entity are issued, those financial statements should indicate that the public benefit corporation is a component unit of the primary government.

Utilities

The above discussion indicates that public benefit corporations sometimes provide services similar to those provided by utilities. In the above discussion, the example of a water and sewer authority was provided, which would be considered the same as the activities of a utility.

Since utilities are a rate-regulated industry, there are certain standards in private-sector accounting that relate specifically to regulated industries. FASB Statement 71 (SFAS 71), *Accounting for the Effects of Certain Regulation* (now at FASB ASC Section 980), promulgates the standards for nongovernmental entities. GASB Statement No. 62 (GASBS 62), *Codification of Accounting and Financial Reporting Guidance Contained in the Pre–November 30, 1989 FASB and AICPA Pronouncements,* has incorporated this guidance into its requirements.

If a governmental public utility applies the provisions of GASBS 62 and its related pronouncements, the application needs to take into consideration that in the case of a governmental utility, the "regulator" (that is, the authority that governs the rates the utility charges) and the governmental entity that controls the governmental utility may be one and the same.

The requirements generally relate to the type of regulation where rates (that is, the price charged for the utility's service) are set at levels intended to recover the estimated costs of providing the regulated services or products, including the cost of capital, which includes interest and a provision for earnings on investments. (For governments, the cost of capital is likely to be only on the interest cost without a built-in "profit" on the government's investment in the utility.)

GASBS 62 requires that revenues and costs be matched. For a number of reasons, revenues intended to cover some costs are provided either before or after the costs are incurred. If regulation provides assurance that incurred costs will be recovered in the future, GASBS 62 requires enterprises to capitalize those costs. If current recovery is provided for costs that are expected to be incurred in the future, those receipts should be recorded as liabilities until the related costs have been incurred.

An important aspect of regulatory accounting is that when an asset can be recognized for costs that will be recovered in the future, GASBS 62 provides that:

Rate actions of a regulator can provide reasonable assurance of the existence of an asset. An enterprise shall capitalize all or part of an incurred cost that would otherwise by charged to expense if both of the following criteria are met:

1. It is probable that future revenue in an amount at least equal to the capitalized cost will result from inclusion of that cost in allowable costs for rate-making purposes.
2. Based on available evidence, the future revenue will be provided to permit recovery of the previously incurred cost rather than to provide for expected levels of similar future costs. If the revenue will be provided through an automatic rate-adjustment clause, this criterion requires that the regulator's intent clearly be to permit recovery of the previously incurred cost.

In the case of the governmental utility that has authority to set its own rates (or when the rates are set by the primary governments that control the public utility), application of these conditions as to the intent of the regulator are clearly more easily applied than when the regulator is an independent third party.

Rate actions of a regulator may reduce or eliminate the value of an asset that has been recorded, such as by reducing or eliminating all or part of a cost from allowable costs, which will affect the carrying amount of any asset recognized in accordance with the above two criteria. Actions of a regulator may also impose a liability on a regulated enterprise, such as by requiring refunds to customers. When an operating asset or an asset under construction of a regulated business-type entity becomes impaired as defined in GASB Statement No. 42 (GASBS 42), *Accounting and Financial Reporting for Impairment of Capital Assets and Insurance Recoveries,* the impairment should be accounted for in accordance with that statement.

These are basic principles underlying regulatory accounting. While a detailed discussion of regulatory accounting is beyond the scope of this guide, readers should be aware of these basic principles for potential application to a government utility's accounting and financial reporting requirements.

SUMMARY

This chapter described the basic accounting and financial reporting requirements for special types of organizations that are governmental entities. There are a number of important differences that financial statement preparers need to be aware of and consider in performing accounting and financial reporting for these entities.

APPENDIX: DISCLOSURE CHECKLIST

This disclosure checklist has been prepared using the accounting and financial reporting guidance contained in pronouncements up to and including GASB Statement 72. Disclosure requirements for more recent statements, most of which are pending their effective date, are contained in the individual chapters. This checklist has been prepared with careful consideration to ensure its accuracy and completeness. However, a checklist does not substitute for professional knowledge and judgment. In addition, this checklist focuses primarily on footnote disclosures for financial statements. For requirements as to the content and format of financial statements themselves, readers should refer to the applicable chapters of this guide. Financial statement preparers and auditors using this checklist should recognize their responsibility to determine the adequacy of disclosures for financial statements. Accordingly, this checklist should be used as only one tool in meeting these responsibilities.

A. Summary of Significant Accounting Policies

1. Does the first note to the financial statements contain a summary of significant accounting policies? ______
2. Does the summary of significant accounting policies include the following? ______

    a. Criteria used to determine the reporting entity (GASBS 14, para 61). ______
    b. Description of the basis of accounting and measurement focus used. ______
    c. Policies with regard to encumbrances (Cod. Sections 2300 and 1700) (not required upon implementation of GASBS 38). ______
    d. The use of the modified accrual basis of accounting for governmental funds (Cod. Section 1600). ______
    e. Description of the use of fund accounting. ______
    f. Effects of component units with different fiscal year-ends (Cod. Section 2300). ______
    g. Policy regarding the capitalization of interest costs incurred during construction of fixed assets (Cod. Section 2300). ______
    h. Whether any fixed asset costs have been estimated and the methods used for the estimation (Cod. Sections 1400 and 2300). ______
    i. Policy regarding the accounting for inventories in governmental funds—purchase or consumption method (Cod. Section 1800). ______
    j. Policy for accounting for vacation and sick leave. ______
    k. Investment policies (I50). ______
    l. Basis of accounting for each fiduciary fund used and a description of the funds in use (SLGA, para 14). ______
    m. Descriptions of the activities accounted for in the major funds, internal service funds, and fiduciary fund types (GASBS 38). ______
    n. Length of time used to define "available" for purposes of revenue recognition in the governmental-fund financial statements (GASBS 38). ______

3. Have the following disclosures been made regarding the government-wide financial statements? (GASBS 34, para 115) ______

    a. A description of the government-wide financial statements, noting that neither fiduciary funds nor component units that are fiduciary in nature are included. ______
    b. The measurement focus and basis of accounting used in the government-wide statements. ______
    c. The policy for eliminating internal activity in the statements of activities. ______
    d. The policy for applying FASB pronouncements issued after November 30, 1989, to business-type activities and to enterprise funds of the primary government. ______
    e. The policy for capitalizing assets and for estimating the useful lives of those assets (used to calculate depreciation expense). Governments that choose to use the modified ______ approach for reporting eligible infrastructure assets should describe that approach. ______
    f. A description of the types of transactions included in program revenues and the policy for allocating indirect expenses to functions in the statements of activities. ______
    g. The government's policy for defining operating and nonoperating revenues of proprietary funds. ______

h. The government's policy regarding whether to first apply restricted or unrestricted resources when an expense is incurred for purposes for which both restricted and unrestricted net position are available. ______

B. Nonmonetary Transactions

1. Do the notes disclose the nature of these transactions, basis of accounting used, and gains or losses recognized on the transfers? ______
2. Are donated fixed assets for general government activities recorded in the general fixed asset account group? (Cod. Section 1400) ______

C. Related-Party Transactions

1. Are the following disclosures made of material related-party transactions, other than compensation agreements, expense allowances, and similar items? (Cod. Section 2300; SLGA, para 17) ______
   a. The nature of the relationship. ______
   b. A description of the transactions, including transactions to which no amounts or nominal amounts have been assigned, and such other information to understand the effects of the transactions on the financial statements. ______
   c. Dollar amounts of the transactions for each period that an operating statement is presented. ______
   d. Amounts due from related parties as of the date of each balance sheet presented (SFAS 57, paras 2–4). ______
2. Is the nature and extent of any leasing transactions with related parties disclosed? (Cod. Section L20) ______

D. Accounting Changes

1. Nature and justification of the change and its effects on the financial statements? ______
2. When applicable, the cumulative effect of an accounting change shown between "extraordinary items" and "excess of revenues over/under expenditures"? ______
3. Material effects of the changes in accounting estimates? ______
4. Disclosures required by APB 20 for change in reporting entity? ______
5. For prior period adjustments: ______
   a. Effects on the excess of revenues over/under expenditures? ______
   b. Disclosure of the effects of a restatement of the beginning fund/net asset balance and on the excess of revenues over/under expenditures for the immediately preceding period? ______
   c. The effects of the adjustment on each period for which financial statements are presented? ______
6. Effects on any historical summaries appropriately disclosed? ______
7. Nature of an error in previously issued financial statements and the effect of the correction of the error on the excess of revenues over/under expenditures before extraordinary items disclosed in the period in which the error is discovered and corrected? ______

E. Disclosures for Defined Benefit Pension Plans (Gasbs 25)

NOTE: The disclosure requirements for defined benefit pension plans and defined contribution plans are described in considerable detail in Chapter 22, including disclosures required by GASBS 67 upon its effectiveness. This chapter should be consulted when preparing these pension plan disclosures.

---

1. If required supplementary information for a cost-sharing or agent plan is not included in the employer's financial statements, do the employer's statements disclose how to obtain the plan's stand-alone reports? ______

2. Is the caption for net position held in trust for pension benefits followed by a parenthetical reference to the plan's schedule of funding progress? ______
3. Do the notes include all of the disclosures in para 32 of GASBS 25 when the financial statements are presented in a stand-alone report or solely in the financial report of an employer? ______
4. If a single-employer plan's financial statements are included in an employer's report, are the following disclosed? ______
   a. Availability of the stand-alone report. ______
   b. Information required for the schedule of funding progress for the three most recent actuarial valuations. ______
5. Do the required disclosures from para 40 of GASBS 25 accompany the schedules of required supplementary information? ______
6. Have the additional disclosures required by GASBS 50, para 4, been provided? (see Chapter 22) ______

F. Disclosures for Defined Contribution Plans

1. Do the notes include all of the required disclosures of para 41 of GASBS 25, as amended by GASBS 50 for item 41b, when the financial statements are presented in a stand-alone report or solely in the financial statements of an employer? ______
2. When a plan's financial statements are presented in both an employer's report and a publicly available stand-alone report and the employer limits its disclosures as permitted by GASBS 25, does the employer disclose how to obtain the stand-alone financial report? ______

G. Disclosures for Postemployment Benefit Other Than Pension (OPEB) Plans (GASBS 43, para 30)

NOTE: The disclosure requirements for OPEB plans are described in considerable detail in Chapter 22, including disclosures required by GASBS 74 upon its effectiveness. This chapter should be consulted when preparing OPEB plan disclosures.

---

1. The notes to the financial statements of a defined benefit OPEB plan should include all disclosures required by this item when the financial statements are presented (a) in a stand-alone plan financial report or (b) *solely* in the financial report of an employer (that is, as another employee benefit trust fund). ______
   a. Plan description: ______
      (1) Identification of the plan as a single-employer, agent multiple-employer, or cost-sharing multiple-employer defined benefit OPEB plan and disclosure of the number of participating employers and other contributing entities. ______
      (2) Classes of employees covered and the number of plan members, including employees in active service, terminated employees who have accumulated benefits but are not yet receiving them, and retired employees and beneficiaries currently receiving benefits. If the plan is closed to new entrants, that fact should be disclosed. ______
      (3) Brief description of benefit provisions, including the types of benefits, the provisions or policies with respect to automatic and ad hoc postretirement benefit increases, and the authority under which benefit provisions are established or may be amended. ______
   b. Summary of significant accounting policies: ______
      (1) Basis of accounting, including the policy with respect to the recognition in the financial statements of contributions, benefits paid, and refunds paid. ______

(2) Brief description of how the fair value of investments is determined, including the methods and significant assumptions used to estimate the fair value of investments, if that fair value is based on other than quoted market prices. ______

c. Contributions and reserves: ______

(1) Authority under which the obligations of the plan members, employer(s), and other contributing entities to contribute to the plan are established or may be amended. ______

(2) Funding policy, including a brief description of how the contributions of the plan members, employer(s), and other contributing entities are determined (for example, by statute, through an actuarial valuation, or in some other manner) and how the costs of administering the plan are financed. Legal or contractual maximum contribution rates should be disclosed, if applicable. ______

(3) Required contribution rate(s) of active or retired plan members, as applicable, in accordance with the funding policy. The required contribution rate(s) should be expressed as a rate (amount) per member or as a percentage of covered payroll. ______

(4) Brief description of the terms of any long-term contracts for contributions to the plan and disclosure of the amounts outstanding at the reporting date. ______

(5) The balances in the plan's legally required reserves at the reporting date. Amounts of net position designated by the plan's board of trustees or other governing body for a specific purpose(s) also may be disclosed but should be captioned designations, rather than reserves. Also include a brief description of the purpose of each reserve and designation disclosed and whether the reserve is fully funded. ______

d. Funded status and funding progress: ______

(1) Information about the funded status of the plan as of the most recent valuation date, including the actuarial valuation date, the actuarial value of assets, the actuarial accrued liability, the total unfunded actuarial accrued liability, the actuarial value of assets as a percentage of the actuarial accrued liability (funded ratio), the annual covered payroll, and the ratio of the unfunded actuarial liability to annual covered payroll (progress). ______

(2) Disclosure of information about actuarial methods and assumptions used in valuations on which reported information about the ARC and the funded status and funding progress of OPEB plans are based, including the following: ______

(a) Disclosure that actuarial valuations involve estimates of the value of reported amounts and assumptions about the probability of events far into the future, and that actuarially determined amounts are subject to continual revision as actual results are compared to past expectations and new estimates are made about the future. ______

(b) Disclosure that the required schedule of funding progress immediately following the notes to the financial statements presents multiyear trend information about whether the actuarial value of plan assets is increasing or decreasing over time relative to the actuarial accrued liability for benefits. ______

(c) Disclosure that calculations are based on the benefits provided under the terms of the substantive plan in effect at the time of each valuation and on the pattern of sharing of costs between the employer and plan members to that point. In addition, if applicable, the plan should disclose that the projection of benefits for financial reporting purposes does not explicitly incorporate the potential effects of legal or contractual funding limitations on the pattern of cost sharing between the employer and plan members in the future. ______

(d) Disclosure that actuarial calculations reflect a long-term perspective. In addition, if applicable, disclosure that, consistent with that perspective, actuarial methods and assumptions used include techniques that are designed to reduce short-term volatility in actuarial accrued liabilities and the actuarial value of assets. ______

(e) Identification of the actuarial methods and significant assumptions used to determine the ARC: ______

i. The actuarial cost method. ______
ii. The method(s) used to determine the actuarial value of assets. ______
iii. The assumptions with respect to the inflation rate, investment return (discount rate) (including the method used to determine a blended rate for a partially funded plan, if applicable), projected salary increases if relevant to determination of the level of benefits, and, for postemployment healthcare plans, the healthcare cost trend rate. If the economic assumptions contemplate different rates for successive years (year-based or select and ultimate rates), the rates that should be disclosed are the initial and ultimate rates. ______
iv. The amortization method (level dollar or level percentage of projected payroll) and the amortization period (equivalent single amortization period, for plans that use multiple periods) for the most recent actuarial valuation and whether the period is closed or open. Plans that use the aggregate actuarial cost method should disclose that because the method does not identify or separately amortize unfunded actuarial accrued liabilities, information about the plan's funded status and funding progress has been prepared using the entry age actuarial cost method for that purpose, and that the information presented is intended to approximate the funding progress of the plan. ______

H. Pension Disclosures for State and Local Governmental Employers (GASBS 27)

1. Is the following information disclosed for each pension plan?

   a. Description of the plan. ______
   b. Funding policy. ______
   c. Sole and agent plans should disclose the information required by GASBS 25, para 21. ______

2. Do sole and agent employers disclose the following information for the most recent actuarial valuation and the two preceding valuations, unless the aggregate actuarial cost method was used? ______

   a. The actuarial valuation date, the actuarial value of plan assets, the actuarial accrued liability, the total unfunded actuarial liability, the actuarial value of assets as a percentage of the actuarial accrued liability, the annual covered payroll, and the ratio of the unfunded actuarial accrued liability to annual covered payroll. ______
   b. Factors that significantly affect the identification of trends in the amount reported. ______
   c. Information about the funded status of the plan as of the most recent valuation date, including the actuarial valuation date, the actuarial value of assets, the actuarial accrued liability, the total unfunded actuarial liability (or funding excess), the actuarial value of assets as a percentage of the actuarial accrued liability (funded ratio), the annual covered payroll, and the ratio of the unfunded actuarial liability

(or funding excess) to annual covered payroll. Employers that use the aggregate actuarial cost method should prepare this information using the entry age actuarial cost method for that purpose only. ______

d. Information about actuarial methods and assumptions used in valuations on which reported information about the ARC, annual pension cost, and the funded status and funding progress of pension plans is based, including the following: ______

(1) Disclosure that the required schedule of funding progress immediately following the notes to the financial statements presents multiyear trend information about whether the actuarial value of plan assets is increasing or decreasing over time relative to the actuarial accrued liability for benefits. ______

(2) Disclosure that the projection of benefits for financial reporting purposes *does not* explicitly incorporate the potential effects of legal or contractual funding limitations, if applicable. ______

(3) In the disclosure of actuarial methods and significant assumptions: ______

(a) If the assumptions used to determine the ARC for the current year contemplate different rates for successive years (year-based or select and ultimate rates), the rates that should be disclosed are the initial and ultimate rates. ______

(b) If the aggregate actuarial cost method is used, disclose that because the method does not identify or separately amortize unfunded actuarial liabilities, information about funded status and funding progress has been prepared using the entry age actuarial cost method for that purpose and that the information presented is intended to serve as a surrogate for the funded status and funding progress of the plan. ______

3. For insured plans, do employers disclose the following? ______

a. Brief description of the insured plan, including the benefit provisions and the authority under which benefit provisions are established or may be amended. ______

b. The fact that the obligation for payment of benefits has been effectively transferred from the employer to one or more insurance companies and whether the employer has guaranteed benefits in the event of the insurance company's insolvency. ______

c. The current year pension expenditures/expense and contributions or premiums paid. ______

4. Does the employer disclose the following information for each defined contribution plan to which it is required to contribute? ______

a. Name of the plan. ______

b. Identification of the public employee retirement system or other entity that administers the plan. ______

c. Brief description of the plan provisions and the authority under which they are established or may be amended. ______

d. Contribution requirements of the plan members, employer, and other contributing entities, and the authority under which the requirements are established or may be amended. ______

e. Contributions actually made by plan members and employees. ______

f. Legal or contractual maximum contribution rate(s) of the employer, if applicable. ______

g. For cost-sharing employers, a description of how the required contribution rate is determined (for example, by statute or by contract, or on an actuarially determined basis) or that the plan is financed on a pay-as-you-go basis. ______

H.(1). Pension Disclosures for State and Local Governmental Employers (GASBS 68)

NOTE: If similar information is required by GASBS 67 and GASBS 68, an employer that includes the pension plan in its financial reporting entity as a pension trust fund or as a fiduciary component unit should present information in a manner that avoids unnecessary duplication.

Single and Agent Employers—Notes to the Financial Statements

1. The following information should be disclosed about the pension plan through which benefits are provided:

   a. The name of the pension plan, identification of the public employee retirement system or other entity that administers the pension plan, and identification of the pension plan as a single-employer or agent pension plan. ______
   b. A brief description of the benefit terms, including (1) the classes of employees covered; (2) the types of benefits; (3) the key elements of the pension formulas; (4) the terms or policies, if any, with respect to automatic postemployment benefit changes, including automatic COLAs, and ad hoc postemployment benefit changes, including ad hoc COLAs; and (5) the authority under which benefit terms are established or may be amended. If the pension plan is closed to new entrants, that fact should be disclosed. ______
   c. The number of employees covered by the benefit terms, separately identifying numbers of the following: ______

      (1) Inactive employees (or their beneficiaries) currently receiving benefits. ______
      (2) Inactive employees entitled to but not yet receiving benefits. ______
      (3) Active employees. ______

   d. A brief description of contribution requirements, including (1) the basis for determining the employer's contributions to the pension plan (for example, statute, contract, an actuarial basis, or some other manner); (2) identification of the authority under which contribution requirements of the employer, nonemployer contributing entities, if any, and employees are established or may be amended; and (3) the contribution rates (in dollars or as a percentage of covered payroll) of those entities for the reporting period. Also, the amount of contributions recognized by the pension plan from the employer during the reporting period (measured as the total of amounts recognized as additions to the pension plan's fiduciary net position resulting from actual contributions and from contributions recognized by the pension plan as current receivables), if not otherwise disclosed. ______
   e. Whether the pension plan issues a stand-alone financial report (or the pension plan is included in the report of a public employee retirement system or another government) that is available to the public and, if so, how to obtain the report (for example, a link to the report on the public employee retirement system's website). ______

Information about the Net Pension Liability

Assumptions and other inputs

1. Significant assumptions and other inputs used to measure the total pension liability, including assumptions about inflation, salary changes, and ad hoc postemployment benefit changes (including ad hoc COLAs) should be disclosed. With regard to mortality assumptions, the source of the assumptions (for example, the published tables on which the assumption is based or that the assumptions are based on a study of the experience of the covered group) should be disclosed. The dates of experience studies on which significant assumptions are based also should be disclosed. If different rates are assumed for different periods, information should be disclosed about what rates are applied to the different periods of the measurement. ______

2. The following information should be disclosed about the discount rate: ______
   a. The discount rate applied in the measurement of the total pension liability and the change in the discount rate since the prior measurement date, if any. ______
   b. Assumptions made about projected cash flows into and out of the pension plan, such as contributions from the employer, nonemployer contributing entities, and employees. ______
   c. The long-term expected rate of return on pension plan investments and a brief description of how it was determined, including significant methods and assumptions used for that purpose. ______
   d. If the discount rate incorporates a municipal bond rate, the municipal bond rate used and the source of that rate. ______
   e. The periods of projected benefit payments to which the long-term expected rate of return and, if used, the municipal bond rate applied to determine the discount rate. ______
   f. The assumed asset allocation of the pension plan's portfolio, the long-term expected real rate of return for each major asset class, and whether the expected rates of return are presented as arithmetic or geometric means, if not otherwise disclosed. ______
   g. Measures of the net pension liability calculated using (1) a discount rate that is 1-percentage-point higher than that required by GASBS 68 and (2) a discount rate that is 1-percentage-point lower than that required by GASBS 68. ______

The Pension Plan's Fiduciary Net Position

1. All information required by this and other financial reporting standards about the elements of the pension plan's basic financial statements (that is, all information about the pension plan's assets, deferred outflows of resources, liabilities, deferred inflows of resources, and fiduciary net position) should be disclosed. However, if (a) a financial report that includes disclosure about the elements of the pension plan's basic financial statements is available on the Internet, either as a stand-alone financial report or included as a fiduciary fund in the financial report of another government, and (b) information is provided about how to obtain the report, reference may instead be made to the other report for these disclosures. In this circumstance, it also should be disclosed that the pension plan's fiduciary net position has been determined on the same basis used by the pension plan, and a brief description of the pension plan's basis of accounting, including the policies with respect to benefit payments (including refunds of employee contributions) and the valuation of pension plan investments, should be included. If significant changes have occurred that indicate that the disclosures included in the pension plan's financial report generally do not reflect the facts and circumstances at the measurement date, information about the substance and magnitude of the changes should be disclosed. ______

Changes in the net pension liability

1. For the current reporting period, a schedule of changes in the net pension liability should be presented. The schedule should separately include the information indicated in subparagraphs (a)–(d), below. If the employer has a special funding situation, the information in subparagraphs (a)–(c) should be presented for the collective net pension liability. ______
   a. The beginning balances of the total pension liability, the pension plan's fiduciary net position, and the net pension liability. ______
   b. The effects during the period of the following items, if applicable, on the balances in subparagraph (a): ______
      (1) Service cost. ______
      (2) Interest on the total pension liability. ______
      (3) Changes of benefit terms. ______

(4) Differences between expected and actual experience in the measurement of the total pension liability. ______
(5) Changes of assumptions or other inputs. ______
(6) Contributions from the employer. ______
(7) Contributions from nonemployer contributing entities. ______
(8) Contributions from employees. ______
(9) Pension plan net investment income. ______
(10) Benefit payments, including refunds of employee contributions. ______
(11) Pension plan administrative expense. ______
(12) Other changes, separately identified if individually significant. ______

c. The ending balances of the total pension liability, the pension plan's fiduciary net position, and the net pension liability. ______
d. If the employer has a special funding situation: ______

(1) The nonemployer contributing entities' total proportionate share of the collective net pension liability. ______
(2) The employer's proportionate share of the collective net pension liability. ______

2. The following additional information should be disclosed, if applicable: ______

a. The measurement date of the net pension liability, the date of the actuarial valuation on which the total pension liability is based, and, if applicable, the fact that update procedures were used to roll forward the total pension liability to the measurement date. ______
b. If the employer has a special funding situation, the employer's proportion (percentage) of the collective net pension liability, the basis on which its proportion was determined, and the change in its proportion since the prior measurement date. ______
c. A brief description of changes of assumptions or other inputs that affected measurement of the total pension liability since the prior measurement date. ______
d. A brief description of changes of benefit terms that affected measurement of the total pension liability since the prior measurement date. ______
e. The amount of benefit payments in the measurement period attributable to the purchase of allocated insurance contracts, a brief description of the benefits for which allocated insurance contracts were purchased in the measurement period, and the fact that the obligation for the payment of benefits covered by allocated insurance contracts has been transferred from the employer to one or more insurance companies. ______
f. A brief description of the nature of changes between the measurement date of the net pension liability and the employer's reporting date that are expected to have a significant effect on the net pension liability, and the amount of the expected resultant change in the net pension liability, if known. ______
g. The amount of pension expense recognized by the employer in the reporting period. ______
h. The employer's balances of deferred outflows of resources and deferred inflows of resources related to pensions, classified as follows, if applicable: ______

(1) Differences between expected and actual experience in the measurement of the total pension liability. ______
(2) Changes of assumptions or other inputs. ______
(3) Net difference between projected and actual earnings on pension plan investments. ______
(4) If the employer has a special funding situation, changes in the employer proportion and differences between the employer's contributions (other than those to separately finance specific liabilities of the individual employer to the pension plan) and the employer's proportionate share of contributions. ______

(5) The employer's contributions to the pension plan subsequent to the measurement date of the net pension liability. ______

i. A schedule presenting the following: ______

(1) For each of the subsequent five years, and in the aggregate thereafter, the net amount of the employer's balances of deferred outflows of resources and deferred inflows of resources in subparagraph (h) that will be recognized in the employer's pension expense. ______

(2) If the employer does not have a special funding situation, the amount of the employer's balance of deferred outflows of resources in subparagraph (h) that will be recognized as a reduction of the net pension liability. ______

(3) If the employer has a special funding situation, the amount of the employer's balance of deferred outflows of resources in subparagraph (h) that will be included as a reduction of the collective net pension liability. ______

j. The amount of revenue recognized for the support provided by nonemployer contributing entities. ______

Required supplementary information—all single and agent employers

1. The required supplementary information identified in subparagraphs (a)–(d), as applicable, should be presented separately for each single-employer and agent pension plan through which pensions are provided. The information indicated in subparagraphs (a) and (b) should be determined as of the measurement date of the net pension liability and may be presented in a single schedule. The information in subparagraphs (c) and (d) should be determined as of the employer's most recent fiscal year-end. If a primary government and one or more of its component units provide pensions through the same single employer or agent pension plan, required supplementary information in the reporting entity's financial statements should present information for the reporting entity as a whole. ______

a. A ten-year schedule of changes in the net pension liability that separately presents the information required by paragraph 44 for each year. ______

b. A ten-year schedule presenting the following for each year: ______

(1) If the employer does not have a special funding situation: ______

(a) The total pension liability. ______

(b) The pension plan's fiduciary net position. ______

(c) The net pension liability. ______

(d) The pension plan's fiduciary net position as a percentage of the total pension liability. ______

(e) The covered-employee payroll. ______

(f) The net pension liability as a percentage of covered-employee payroll. ______

(2) If the employer has a special funding situation, information about the collective net pension liability: ______

(a) The total pension liability. ______

(b) The pension plan's fiduciary net position. ______

(c) The collective net pension liability. ______

(d) The nonemployer contributing entities' total proportionate share (amount) of the collective net pension liability. ______

(e) The employer's proportionate share (amount) of the collective net pension liability. ______

(f) The covered-employee payroll. ______

(g) The employer's proportionate share (amount) of the collective net pension liability as a percentage of covered-employee payroll. ______

(h) The pension plan's fiduciary net position as a percentage of the total pension liability. ______

c. If an actuarially determined contribution is calculated, a ten-year schedule presenting the following for each year: ______

(1) The actuarially determined contribution of the employer. For purposes of this schedule, actuarially determined contributions should exclude amounts, if any, to separately finance specific liabilities of the individual employer to the pension plan. ______
(2) The amount of contributions recognized by the pension plan in relation to the actuarially determined contribution of the employer. For purposes of this schedule, contributions should include only amounts recognized as additions to the pension plan's fiduciary net position during the employer's fiscal year resulting from actual contributions and from contributions recognized by the pension plan as current receivables. ______
(3) The difference between the actuarially determined contribution of the employer and the amount of contributions recognized by the pension plan in relation to the actuarially determined contribution of the employer. ______
(4) The covered-employee payroll. ______
(5) The amount of contributions recognized by the pension plan in relation to the actuarially determined contribution of the employer as a percentage of covered-employee payroll. ______

d. If an actuarially determined contribution is not calculated and the contribution requirements of the employer are statutorily or contractually established, a 10-year schedule presenting the following for each year: ______

(1) The statutorily or contractually required employer contribution. For purposes of this schedule, statutorily or contractually required contributions should exclude amounts, if any, to separately finance specific liabilities of the individual employer to the pension plan. ______
(2) The amount of contributions recognized by the pension plan in relation to the statutorily or contractually required employer contribution. For purposes of this schedule, contributions should include only amounts recognized as additions to the pension plan's fiduciary net position during the employer's fiscal year resulting from actual contributions and from contributions recognized by the pension plan as current receivables. ______
(3) The difference between the statutorily or contractually required employer contribution and the amount of contributions recognized by the pension plan in relation to the statutorily or contractually required employer contribution. ______
(4) The covered-employee payroll. ______
(5) The amount of contributions recognized by the pension plan in relation to the statutorily or contractually required employer contribution as a percentage of covered-employee payroll. ______

Notes to required schedules

Significant methods and assumptions used in calculating the actuarially determined contributions, if any, should be presented as notes to the schedule required by item C in the previous requirement. In addition, for each of the schedules required in the previous requirement, information should be presented about factors that significantly affect trends in the amounts reported (for example, changes of benefit terms, changes in the size or composition of the population covered by the benefit terms, or the use of different assumptions). (The amounts presented for prior years should not be restated for the effects of changes—for example, changes of benefit terms or changes of assumptions—that occurred subsequent to the measurement date of that information.)

Cost-sharing employers—notes to the financial statements

1. The total (aggregate for all pensions, whether provided through cost-sharing, single-employer, or agent pension plans) of the employer's pension liabilities, pension assets, deferred outflows of resources and deferred inflows. If similar information is required by GASBS 68 and GASBS 67, an employer that includes the pension plan in its financial reporting entity as a pension trust fund or as a fiduciary component unit should present information in a manner that avoids unnecessary duplication of resources related to pensions, and pension expense/expenditures for the period associated with net pension liabilities should be disclosed if the total amounts are not otherwise identifiable from information presented in the financial statements. ______
2. The information identified below should be disclosed for benefits provided through each cost-sharing pension plan in which the employer participates. Disclosures related to more than one pension plan should be combined in a manner that avoids unnecessary duplication. ______

Pension plan description

1. The following information should be disclosed about the pension plan through which benefits are provided: ______
   a. The name of the pension plan, identification of the public employee retirement system or other entity that administers the pension plan, and identification of the pension plan as a cost-sharing pension plan. ______
   b. A brief description of the benefit terms, including (1) the classes of employees covered; (2) the types of benefits; (3) the key elements of the pension formulas; the terms or policies, if any, with respect to automatic postemployment benefit changes, including automatic COLAs, and ad hoc postemployment benefit changes, including ad hoc COLAs; and (5) the authority under which benefit terms are established or may be amended. If the pension plan is closed to new entrants, that fact should be disclosed. ______
   c. A brief description of contribution requirements, including (1) the basis for determining the employer's contributions to the pension plan (for example, statute, contract, an actuarial basis, or some other manner); (2) identification of the authority under which contribution requirements of employers, nonemployer contributing entities, if any, and employees are established or may be amended; and (3) the contribution rates (in dollars or as a percentage of covered payroll) of those entities for the reporting period. Also, the amount of contributions recognized by the pension plan from the employer during the reporting period (measured as the total of amounts recognized as additions to the pension plan's fiduciary net position resulting from actual contributions and from contributions recognized by the pension plan as current receivables), if not otherwise disclosed. ______
   d. Whether the pension plan issues a stand-alone financial report (or the pension plan is included in the report of a public employee retirement system or another government) that is available to the public and, if so, how to obtain the report (for example, a link to the report on the public employee retirement system's website). ______

______

Employer's Proportionate Share of Net Pension Liability

Assumptions and other inputs

1. Significant assumptions and other inputs used to measure the total pension liability, including assumptions about inflation, salary changes, and ad hoc postemployment benefit changes (including ad hoc COLAs) should be disclosed. ______
2. With regard to mortality assumptions, the source of the assumptions (for example, the published tables on which the assumption is based or that the assumptions are based on a study of the experience of the covered employees) should be disclosed. ______

3. The dates of experience studies on which significant assumptions are based also should be disclosed. If different rates are assumed for different periods, information should be disclosed about what rates are applied to the different periods of the measurement. ______
4. The following information should be disclosed about the discount rate: ______
   a. The discount rate applied in the measurement of the total pension liability and the change in the discount rate since the prior measurement date, if any. ______
   b. Assumptions made about projected cash flows into and out of the pension plan, such as contributions from employers, nonemployer contributing entities, and employees. ______
   c. The long-term expected rate of return on pension plan investments and a brief description of how it was determined, including significant methods and assumptions used for that purpose. ______
   d. If the discount rate incorporates a municipal bond rate, the municipal bond rate used and the source of that rate. ______
   e. The periods of projected benefit payments to which the long-term expected rate of return and, if used, the municipal bond rate applied to determine the discount rate. ______
   f. The assumed asset allocation of the pension plan's portfolio, the long-term expected real rate of return for each major asset class, and whether the expected rates of return are presented as arithmetic or geometric means, if not otherwise disclosed. ______
   g. Measures of the employer's proportionate share of the collective net pension liability calculated using (1) a discount rate that is 1-percentage-point higher than that required by GASBS 68 and (2) a discount rate that is 1-percentage-point lower than that required by GASBS 68. ______

The Pension Plan's Fiduciary Net Position

1. All information required by this and other financial reporting standards about the elements of the pension plan's basic financial statements (that is, all information about the pension plan's assets, deferred outflows of resources, liabilities, deferred inflows of resources, and fiduciary net position) should be disclosed. However, if (a) a financial report that includes disclosure about the elements of the pension plan's basic financial statements is available on the Internet, either as a stand-alone financial report or included as a fiduciary fund in the financial report of another government, and (b) information is provided about how to obtain the report, reference may instead be made to the other report for these disclosures. In this circumstance, it also should be disclosed that the pension plan's fiduciary net position has been determined on the same basis used by the pension plan, and a brief description of the pension plan's basis of accounting, including the policies with respect to benefit payments (including refunds of employee contributions) and the valuation of pension plan investments should be included. If significant changes have occurred that indicate that the disclosures included in the pension plan's financial report generally do not reflect the facts and circumstances at the measurement date, information about the substance and magnitude of the changes should be disclosed. ______

Other information

1. The following additional information should be disclosed, if applicable:
   a. The employer's proportionate share (amount) of the collective net pension liability and, if an employer has a special funding situation, (1) the portion of the nonemployer contributing entities' total proportionate share (amount) of the collective net pension liability that is associated with the employer and (2) the total of the employer's proportionate share (amount) of the collective net pension liability and the portion of the nonemployer contributing entities' total proportionate share of the collective net pension liability that is associated with the employer. ______

b. The employer's proportion (percentage) of the collective net pension liability, the basis on which its proportion was determined, and the change in its proportion since the prior measurement date. ______
c. The measurement date of the collective net pension liability, the date of the actuarial valuation on which the total pension liability is based, and, if applicable, the fact that update procedures were used to roll forward the total pension liability to the measurement date. ______
d. A brief description of changes of assumptions or other inputs that affected measurement of the total pension liability since the prior measurement date. ______
e. A brief description of changes of benefit terms that affected measurement of the total pension liability since the prior measurement date. ______
f. A brief description of the nature of changes between the measurement date of the collective net pension liability and the employer's reporting date that are expected to have a significant effect on the employer's proportionate share of the collective net pension liability, and the amount of the expected resultant change in the employer's proportionate share of the collective net pension liability, if known. ______
g. The amount of pension expense recognized by the employer in the reporting period. ______
h. The employer's balances of deferred outflows of resources and deferred inflows of resources related to pensions, classified as follows, if applicable: ______

    (1) Differences between expected and actual experience in the measurement of the total pension liability. ______
    (2) Changes of assumptions or other inputs. ______
    (3) Net difference between projected and actual earnings on pension plan investments. ______
    (4) Changes in the employer's proportion and differences between the employer's contributions (other than those to separately finance specific liabilities of the individual employer to the pension plan) and the employer's proportionate share of contributions. ______
    (5) The employer's contributions to the pension plan subsequent to the measurement date of the collective net pension liability. ______

i. A schedule presenting the following: ______

    (1) For each of the subsequent five years and in the aggregate thereafter, the net amount of the employer's balances of deferred outflows of resources and deferred inflows of resources in subparagraph (h) that will be recognized in the employer's pension expense. ______
    (2) The amount of the employer's balance of deferred outflows of resources in subparagraph (h) that will be included as a reduction of the collective net pension liability. ______

j. The amount of revenue recognized for the support provided by nonemployer contributing entities, if any. ______

Required Supplementary Information—All Cost-Sharing Employers

1. The required supplementary information identified in subparagraphs (a) and (b), as applicable, should be presented separately for each cost-sharing pension plan through which pensions are provided. The information indicated in subparagraph (a) should be determined as of the measurement date of the collective net pension liability. The information in subparagraph (b) should be determined as of the employer's most recent fiscal year-end. ______

a. A ten-year schedule presenting the following for each year: ______

   (1) If the employer does not have a special funding situation: ______

      (a) The employer's proportion (percentage) of the collective net pension liability. ______
      (b) The employer's proportionate share (amount) of the collective net pension liability. ______
      (c) The employer's covered-employee payroll. ______
      (d) The employer's proportionate share (amount) of the collective net pension liability as a percentage of the employer's covered-employee payroll. ______
      (e) The pension plan's fiduciary net position as a percentage of the total pension liability. ______

   (2) If the employer has a special funding situation: ______

      (a) The employer's proportion (percentage) of the collective net pension liability. ______
      (b) The employer's proportionate share (amount) of the collective net pension liability. ______
      (c) The portion of the nonemployer contributing entities' total proportionate share (amount) of the collective net pension liability that is associated with the employer. ______
      (d) The total of (b) and (c). ______
      (e) The employer's covered-employee payroll. ______
      (f) The employer's proportionate share (amount) of the collective net pension liability as a percentage of the employer's covered-employee payroll. ______
      (g) The pension plan's fiduciary net position as a percentage of the total pension liability. ______

b. If the contribution requirements of the employer are statutorily or contractually established, a ten-year schedule presenting the following for each year: ______

   (1) The statutorily or contractually required employer contribution. For purposes of this schedule, statutorily or contractually required contributions should exclude amounts, if any, to separately finance specific liabilities of the individual employer to the pension plan. ______
   (2) The amount of contributions recognized by the pension plan in relation to the statutorily or contractually required employer contribution. For purposes of this schedule, contributions should include only amounts recognized as additions to the pension plan's fiduciary net position during the employer's fiscal year resulting from actual contributions and from contributions recognized by the pension plan as current receivables. ______
   (3) The difference between the statutorily or contractually required employer contribution and the amount of contributions recognized by the pension plan in relation to the statutorily or contractually required employer contribution. ______
   (4) The employer's covered-employee payroll. ______
   (5) The amount of contributions recognized by the pension plan in relation to the statutorily or contractually required employer contribution as a percentage of the employer's covered-employee payroll. ______

Notes to required schedules

Information about factors that significantly affect trends in the amounts reported in the schedules required by paragraph 81 (for example, changes of benefit terms, changes in the size or composition of the population covered by the benefit terms, or the use of different assumptions) should be presented as notes to the schedules. (The amounts presented for prior years should not be restated for the effects of changes—for example, changes of benefit terms or changes of assumptions—that occurred subsequent to the measurement date of that information.)

Defined Contribution Plans

Notes to financial statements

1. The following information should be disclosed in notes to financial statements about each defined contribution pension plan to which an employer is required to contribute: ______
   a. The name of the pension plan, identification of the public employee retirement system or other entity that administers the pension plan, and identification of the pension plan as a defined contribution pension plan. ______
   b. A brief description of the benefit terms (including terms, if any, related to vesting and forfeitures and the policy related to the use of forfeited amounts) and the authority under which benefit terms are established or may be amended. ______
   c. The contribution (or crediting) rates (in dollars or as a percentage of salary) for employees, the employer, and nonemployer contributing entities, if any, and the authority under which those rates are established or may be amended. ______
   d. The amount of pension expense recognized by the employer in the reporting period. ______
   e. The amount of forfeitures reflected in pension expense recognized by the employer in the reporting period. ______
   f. The amount of the employer's liability outstanding at the end of the period, if any. ______

Special Funding Situations

GASBS 68 includes disclosure requirements for governments with special funding situations which are based on and are very similar to the disclosure requirements above. GASBS 68 should be consulted for the specifics.

I. Postemployment Benefits Other Than Pensions (OPEBs) for Employers (GASBS 45, paras. 24, 25)

1. Employers should include the following information in the notes to their financial statements for each defined benefit OPEB plan in which they participate, regardless of the type of plan (except as indicated). Disclosures for more than one plan should be combined in a manner that avoids unnecessary duplication. ______
   a. Plan description: ______
      (1) Name of the plan, identification of the public employee retirement system (PERS) or other entity that administers the plan, and identification of the plan as a single-employer, agent multiple-employer, or cost-sharing multiple-employer defined benefit OPEB plan. ______
      (2) Brief description of the types of benefits and the authority under which benefit provisions are established or may be amended. ______

(3) Whether the OPEB plan issues a stand-alone financial report or is included in the report of a PERS or another entity, and, if so, how to obtain the report. ______

b. Funding policy: ______

(1) Authority under which the obligations of the plan members, employer(s), and other contributing entities (for example, state contributions to local government plans) to contribute to the plan are established or may be amended. ______

(2) Required contribution rate(s) of plan members. The required contribution rate(s) could be expressed as a rate (amount) per member or as a percentage of covered payroll. ______

(3) Required contribution rate(s) of the employer in accordance with the funding policy, in dollars or as a percentage of current-year covered payroll, and, if applicable, legal or contractual maximum contribution rates. If the plan is a single-employer or agent plan and the rate differs significantly from the ARC, disclose how the rate is determined (for example, by statute or by contract) or that the plan is financed on a pay-as-you-go basis. If the plan is a cost-sharing plan, disclose the required contributions in dollars and the percentage of that amount contributed for the current year and each of the two preceding years, and how the required contribution rate is determined (for example, by statute or by contract, or on an actuarially determined basis) or that the plan is financed on a pay-as-you-go basis. ______

2. Sole and agent employers should disclose the following information for each plan, in addition to the information in item 1 above: ______

a. For the current year, annual OPEB cost and the dollar amount of contributions made. If the employer has a net OPEB obligation, also disclose the components of annual OPEB cost (ARC, interest on the net OPEB obligation, and adjustment to the ARC), the increase or decrease in the net OPEB obligation, and the net OPEB obligation at the end of the year. ______

b. For the current year and each of the two preceding years, annual OPEB cost, percentage of annual OPEB cost contributed that year, and net OPEB obligation at the end of the year. (For the first two years, the required information should be presented for the transition year, and for the current and transition years, respectively.) ______

c. Information about the funded status of the plan as of the most recent valuation date, including the actuarial valuation date, the actuarial value of assets, the actuarial accrued liability, the total unfunded actuarial liability (or funding excess), the actuarial value of assets as a percentage of the actuarial accrued liability (funded ratio), the annual covered payroll, and the ratio of the unfunded actuarial liability (or funding excess) to annual covered payroll. ______

For sole employers that include the plan in the financial reporting entity (as a trust fund), presentation of information about the plan's funded status and funding progress as required for the plan by GASBS 43 meets the requirements of this item. For agent employers, the requirements of this item apply to the employer's *individual* plan. The information should be presented even if the aggregate multiple-employer plan (all employers) is included as an OPEB trust fund in the employer's report and the required funded status and funding progress information is presented for the aggregate plan. ______

d. Disclosure of information about actuarial methods and assumptions used in valuations on which reported information about the ARC, annual OPEB cost, and the funded status and funding progress of OPEB plans is based, including the following: ______

(1) Disclosure that actuarial valuations involve estimates of the value of reported amounts and assumptions about the probability of events far into the future, and that actuarially determined amounts are subject to continual revision as actual results are compared to past expectations and new estimates are made about the future. ______
(2) Disclosure that the required schedule of funding progress immediately following the notes to the financial statements presents multiyear trend information about whether the actuarial value of plan assets is increasing or decreasing over time relative to the actuarial accrued liability for benefits. ______
(3) Disclosure that calculations are based on the types of benefits provided under the terms of the substantive plan at the time of each valuation and on the pattern of sharing of costs between the employer and plan members to that point. In addition, if applicable, the employer should disclose that the projection of benefits for financial reporting purposes does not explicitly incorporate the potential effects of legal or contractual funding limitations on the pattern of cost sharing between the employer and plan members in the future. ______
(4) Disclosure that actuarial calculations reflect a long-term perspective. In addition, if applicable, disclosure that, consistent with that perspective, actuarial methods and assumptions used include techniques that are designed to reduce short-term volatility in actuarial accrued liabilities and the actuarial value of assets. ______
(5) Identification of the actuarial methods and significant assumptions used to determine the ARC for the current year and the information required by paragraph 25c. The disclosures should include: ______

(a) The actuarial cost method. ______
(b) The method(s) used to determine the actuarial value of assets. ______
(c) The assumptions with respect to the inflation rate, investment return (including the method used to determine a blended rate for a partially funded plan, if applicable), postretirement benefit increases if applicable, projected salary increases if relevant to determination of the level of benefits, and, for postemployment health care plans, the health care cost trend rate. If the economic assumptions contemplate different rates for successive years (year-based or select and ultimate rates), the rates that should be disclosed are the initial and ultimate rates. ______
(d) The amortization method (level dollar or level percentage of projected payroll) and the amortization period (equivalent single amortization period, for plans that use multiple periods) for the most recent actuarial valuation and whether the period is closed or open. Employers that use the aggregate actuarial cost method should disclose that because the method does not identify or separately amortize unfunded actuarial liabilities, information about funded status and funding progress has been prepared using the entry age actuarial cost method for that purpose, and that the information presented is intended to approximate the funding progress of the plan. ______

J. Disclosures Relating to Leases (SFAS 13)

NOTE: The disclosure requirements for leases are described in considerably more detail in Chapter 22. This chapter should be consulted when preparing lease-related disclosure for lessees and lessors.

1. Lessors:

   a. For operating leases, is the following information disclosed?

      (1) Cost and carrying amount of property on lease or held for leasing by major classes and the amount of accumulated depreciation as of the date of the latest balance sheet presented. ______
      (2) Minimum future rentals on noncancelable leases as of the date of the latest balance sheet presented in the aggregate and for each of the five succeeding years and for five-year increments thereafter (amended by GASBS 38). ______
      (3) Total contingent rentals in operations for each period for which a statement of revenues and expenditures is presented. ______

   b. For sales-type and direct financing leases, are the following disclosed?

      (1) Appropriate components of the net investment in the leases as of the date of each balance sheet presented. ______
      (2) Future minimum lease payments to be received for each of the five succeeding fiscal years as of the date of the latest balance sheet presented. ______
      (3) Total contingent rentals included in operations for each period for which a statement of revenues and expenditures is presented. ______

   c. Do the notes provide a general description of the lessor's leasing arrangements? ______

2. Lessees:

   a. For capital leases, are the following disclosed?

      (1) Gross amounts of assets and the accumulated depreciation recorded by major classes as of the date of each balance sheet presented. ______
      (2) The lease obligations classified as current and long-term. ______
      (3) Future minimum lease payments as of the latest balance sheet presented in the aggregate and for each of the five succeeding fiscal years and in five-year increments thereafter, with separate deductions for executory costs and imputed interest. ______
      (4) Total future minimum lease sublease rentals under noncancelable subleases as of the date of the latest balance sheet presented. ______
      (5) Total contingent rentals incurred for each period for which a statement of revenue and expenditures is presented. ______

   b. For operating leases that have initial or remaining noncancelable lease terms in excess of one year, is the following information disclosed?

      (1) Future minimum rental payments required as of the latest balance sheet presented in the aggregate and for each of the five succeeding fiscal years and in five-year increments thereafter. ______
      (2) Total minimum rentals under noncancelable subleases as of the date of the latest balance sheet presented. ______

   c. For all operating leases, is the following information disclosed?

      (1) Rental expense for each period for which an operating statement is presented with separate amounts for minimum rentals, contingent rentals, and sublease rentals. ______
      (2) A general description of the lessee's leasing arrangements, including: ______

         (a) Basis for determining contingent rentals. ______
         (b) Terms of any renewal or purchase options or escalation clauses. ______
         (c) Restrictive covenants. ______

K. Fund Balance

1. Is disclosure made of any deficit fund balance or deficit retained earnings of individual funds and identification of how it will be liquidated? ______
2. Are all changes in fund balance disclosed? ______
3. Are differences between opening fund balances and those previously reported disclosed? ______
4. Are any deficits in internal service funds disclosed? ______

L. Property Taxes

1. Do the notes disclose that property taxes are recorded on the modified accrual basis of accounting in governmental funds? ______
2. If the government excludes some property tax revenues from appropriation to protect cash liquidity, is this restriction disclosed by a designation of fund balance and an appropriate footnote? ______
3. Are the following elements of the government's property tax calendar disclosed? ______
   a. Lien dates. ______
   b. Levy dates. ______
   c. Due dates. ______
   d. Collection dates. ______

M. Grants and Similar Revenues (GASBS 24, NCGAI 6)

1. Is the basis of accounting for recording grants, entitlements, or shared revenues disclosed? ______
2. If grants, entitlements, or shared revenues are held in an agency fund pending determination as to which fund they will be used in, is the amount of the assets so held disclosed in the footnotes? ______
3. Are all cash pass-through grants reported in the financial statements? ______
4. Are amounts recognized for on-behalf payments for fringe benefits and salaries disclosed in the notes? ______
5. For on-behalf payments that are contributions to a pension plan for which the employer government is not legally responsible, is the name of the plan that covers the government's employees and the name of the entity that makes the contributions disclosed? ______
6. If there are two legally separate entities that are the parties to a transaction involving pass-through grants or on-behalf payments or fringe benefits and salaries and they are part of the same governmental reporting entity, are the following disclosed?
   a. Revenue and expenditures/expenses relating to these transactions reclassified as operating transfers. ______
   b. On-behalf payments classified as operating transfer–out by the paying entity. ______
   c. On-behalf payments classified as operating transfer–in by the employer entity. ______
7. Are the following note disclosures included about donor-restricted endowments? (GASBS 34, para 121)
   a. The amounts of net appreciation on investments of donor-restricted endowments that are available for authorization for expenditure by the governing board, and how those amounts are reported in net position. ______
   b. The state law regarding the ability to spend net appreciation. ______
   c. The policy for authorizing and spending investment income, such as a spending-rate or total-return policy. ______

N. Commitments and Contingencies

1. Are the nature and amount of accrued loss contingencies, including total judgments and claims, determined for the year under GASBS 62? ______

2. For loss contingencies not accrued, do the notes disclose the nature of the contingency and an estimate of possible loss, a range of loss, or a statement that such estimate cannot be made? _______
3. Is any no-commitment debt included in the financial statements? _______
4. Are guarantees or any moral obligations assumed by the entity disclosed? _______
5. Are the following disclosures made for unconditional purchase obligations not recorded on the balance sheet?
   a. Nature and term of the obligation. _______
   b. Amount of the fixed and determinable portion of the obligations as of the balance sheet date and for each of the five succeeding fiscal years. _______
   c. Nature of any variable components of the obligation. _______
   d. Amounts purchased for each period for which an operating statement is presented. _______
6. Is disclosure made of conditions that raise a question as to the entity's ability to continue as a going concern and viable plans to overcome this situation? (GASBS 62). _______
7. If appropriations lapse at year-end, are the outstanding encumbrances at year-end disclosed if the government intends to honor them? _______
8. If a government is prohibited by law from budgeting or appropriating property taxes recognized as revenue under the modified accrual basis, is this fact disclosed? _______
9. Are gain contingencies adequately disclosed? _______
10. Are disclosures provided for unused letters of credit and assets pledged for security? _______
11. Are any material violations of legal and contractual provisions disclosed? _______
12. Are loss contingencies disclosed when there is a reasonable possibility that a loss may have been incurred? _______

O. Subsequent Events

1. Are financial statements adjusted for any changes in estimates resulting from subsequent events that provide additional information about evidence existing at the balance sheet date? _______
2. Are events subsequent to the balance sheet date adequately disclosed? _______
3. Are appropriate disclosures made for contingencies arising subsequent to the balance sheet date? _______

P. Reporting Entity (GASBS 14)

1. Does the reporting entity provide information about each major component unit either by including the required combining statements or by presenting condensed financial statements in the notes? _______
2. Is the general fund of a blended component unit presented as a special revenue fund? _______
3. Are appropriate for-profit corporations presented as component units? _______
4. Are amounts due to and from component units for lease transactions reported separately from other lease receivables and payables? _______
5. Where transactions occurring between component units with different fiscal years result in inconsistencies in due to or from amounts or transfers, is the nature of these differences disclosed? _______
6. Are changes in the fiscal years of component units disclosed? _______
7. Do the notes include a brief description of the component units and their relationship to the primary government, including (GASBS 14, para 61):
   a. Discussion of the criteria for including the component units? _______
   b. How the component units are reported? _______
   c. Information about how the separate financial statements of the component units can be obtained? _______

8. Do the notes disclose individual component units considering the unit's significance to the total discretely presented component units and the nature and significance of the relationship to the primary government? (GASBS 14, para 63) ______
9. Do the separate financial statements of a component unit disclose its relationship to the primary government? ______
10. Do the separate financial statements of a component unit disclose its participation in an oversight entity's risk management internal service fund (GASBS 10, paras 77 and 79) and the nature of the participation? ______
11. If the government chooses to present component unit information in the notes, are these details presented, at a minimum? (GASBS 34, para 11)

    a. Condensed statement of net position:

        (1) Total assets—distinguishing between capital assets and other assets. Amounts receivable from the primary government or from other component units should be reported separately. ______
        (2) Total liabilities—distinguishing between long-term debt outstanding and other liabilities. Amounts payable to the primary government or to other component units should be reported separately. ______
        (3) Total net position—distinguishing between restricted, unrestricted, and amounts invested in capital assets, net of related debt. ______

    b. Condensed statement of activities:

        (1) Expenses (by major functions and for depreciation expense, if separately reported). ______
        (2) Program revenues (by type). ______
        (3) Net program (expense) revenue. ______
        (4) Tax revenues. ______
        (5) Other nontax general revenues. ______
        (6) Contributions to endowments and permanent fund principal. ______
        (7) Special and extraordinary items. ______
        (8) Change in net position. ______
        (9) Beginning net position. ______
        (10) Ending net position. ______

Q. Special Assessments (GASBS 6, paras 20 and 21)

1. Are long-term note disclosures provided for special assessment debt if the government is obligated in some manner? ______
2. Do the notes identify and describe any guarantee, reserve, or sinking fund established to cover property owner defaults? ______
3. Is the amount of delinquent special assessment receivables disclosed? ______
4. If the government is not obligated in some manner, do the notes describe the nature of the government's role? ______

R. Public Entity Risk Pools (GASBS 10)

1. If an exposure to loss exists in excess of an accrual or if no accrual is made for an insured event, is a loss contingency disclosed if there is a reasonable possibility that a loss or additional loss will occur? ______
2. Does the disclosure in (1) indicate the nature of the contingency and provide an estimate (or range) of the loss, or state that an estimate cannot be made? ______
3. If it is probable that an unreported claim will be asserted (and there is a reasonable possibility that a loss will be incurred), is disclosure of this assertion made? ______

4. Are the following specific disclosures made about the risk pool?

    a. Description of the risk transfer or pooling agreement. ______
    b. Description of the number and types of entities participating in the pool. ______
    c. Basis for estimating liabilities for unpaid claims and claim adjustment expenses. ______
    d. Indication that liabilities are based on the estimated ultimate cost of settlement, including effects of inflation and other societal and economic factors. ______
    e. Nature of acquisition costs capitalized, including method and amount amortized. ______
    f. Face and carrying amounts of liabilities for unpaid claims and claims adjustment expenses that are presented at present value and the range of discount interest rates. ______
    g. Whether the pool considers anticipated investment income in determining premium deficiencies. ______
    h. Nature and significance of excess or reinsurance transactions, including coverage type, reinsurance premiums ceded, and estimated amounts recoverable. ______
    i. Reconciliation of total claims liabilities in prescribed format. (GASBS 10, para 27) ______
    j. Aggregate amount of liabilities removed from balance sheet for which annuity contracts are purchased. ______

5. Does the entity disclose that it is insured under a retrospectively rated insurance policy and the amount of premiums accrued based on the ultimate cost? ______
6. Are risk pool assessment amounts that are probable but not reasonably estimable disclosed? ______
7. For entities other than risk pools, is the following information disclosed? (GASBS 10, para 74)

    a. Description of risks to which the entity is exposed and ways those risks are handled. ______
    b. Description of the significant reductions in insurance coverage from the prior year, by major categories of risk, and an indication of whether the amount of settlements exceeded insurance coverage for each of the past three fiscal years. ______
    c. If an entity participates in a risk pool, the nature of the participation. ______
    d. If an entity retains the risk of loss:

        (1) Basis for estimating liabilities for unpaid claims, including effects of specific claim adjustment expenses and subrogation, and whether other allocated or unallocated claim adjustment expenses are included (GASBS 30). ______
        (2) Carrying amount of liabilities for unpaid claims that are presented at present value and the range of discount interest rates used. ______
        (3) Aggregate outstanding amount of claims liabilities removed from the balance sheet for which annuity contracts have been purchased. ______
        (4) Reconciliation of changes in aggregate liabilities, in format prescribed by GASBS 10, para 77, as amended by GASBS 30. ______

    e. Is the GASBS 10 required supplementary information presented? ______

S. Landfill Disclosures (GASBS 18, para 17)

1. Is the following information disclosed in the notes?

    a. Nature and source of landfill closure and postclosure costs. ______
    b. That recognition of landfill liability is based on landfill capacity used to date. ______
    c. Amount of the reported liability and the remaining estimated costs to be recognized. ______
    d. How financial assurance requirements are met and any restrictions on assets. ______
    e. The nature of the estimates and potential changes due to inflation or deflation, technology, laws, or regulations. ______

T. Cash, Investments, and Other Assets (GASBS 31 and 40)

1. Are any restrictions on cash and investments disclosed? ______
2. Are the following disclosures made for investments, including repurchase agreements? (GASBS 3, paras 65–80)

   a. Types of investments authorized by legal or contractual provisions, including where differences exist for various funds, fund types, and component units. ______
   b. Significant violations during the period of legal or contractual provisions for deposits and investments. ______
   c. For bank balances or deposits not entirely insured or collateralized the government should provide disclosure of deposits that are subject to custodial credit risk by disclosing the amount of bank balances, the fact that the balances are uninsured, and whether the balances are exposed to custodial credit risk because they are uncollateralized, collateralized with securities held by the pledging financial institution, or collateralized with securities held by the pledging financial institution's trust department or agent but not in the depositor-government's name. ______
   d. For investments exposed to custodial credit risk, the government should provide disclosure of investments that are subject to custodial credit risk by disclosing the investment's type, the reported amount, and how the investments are held. ______
   e. Has the government described its deposit and investment policies that are related to the risks specified in GASBS 40 that are required to be disclosed? If a government has no deposit or investment policy that addresses a specific type of risk that it is exposed to, has this fact been disclosed? ______
   f. Has the government disclosed information about the credit risk associated with its investments by disclosing the credit quality ratings of its investments in debt securities? ______
   g. Has the government disclosed information about concentration of credit risk by disclosing by amount and issuer, investments in any one issuer that represent 5% or more of total investments? (This disclosure does not apply to investments issued or explicitly guaranteed by the U.S. government and investments in mutual funds, external investment pools, and other pooled investments.) ______
   h. Has the government disclosed information about interest rate risk using one of the methodologies prescribed by GASBS 40? ______
   i. Has the government disclosed the terms and fair values of debt instruments whose terms may cause the instrument's fair value to be highly sensitive to interest rate changes? ______
   j. If the government's deposits or investments are exposed to foreign currency risk, has the government disclosed the U.S. dollar balances of such deposits or investments, organized by currency denomination and, if applicable, investment type? ______

3. If unrealized investment losses in one or more component units or funds are not apparent because of unrealized gains in the remaining funds, are the carrying amounts and fair values (where different) for these units disclosed? ______
4. Are outstanding commitments to resell securities under yield maintenance repurchase agreements disclosed? ______
5. Are types of investments made during the reporting period, but not owned at the balance sheet date, disclosed? ______
6. Are losses as a result of default by counterparties (and amounts recovered from prior losses) disclosed? ______
7. Are the following disclosures made for reverse repurchase agreements? ______

   a. For reverse repurchase agreements (other than yield maintenance agreements) outstanding, the credit risk relating to the agreement. ______

b. Commitments to repurchase securities under yield maintenance agreements, including fair value of securities to be repurchased. ______
c. Losses recognized during the period due to default of counterparties and recoveries of losses from prior periods. ______

8. Are the following disclosures relating to investment valuations provided? (GASBS 31, para 15)

   a. The methods and significant assumptions used to estimate the fair value of investments, if that fair value is based on other than quoted market prices. ______
   b. The policy for determining which investments, if any, are reported at amortized cost. ______
   c. For any investments in external investment pools that are not SEC-registered, a brief description of any regulatory oversight for the pool, and whether the fair value of the position in the pool is the same as the value of the pool shares. ______
   d. Any voluntary participation in an external investment pool. ______
   e. If an entity cannot obtain information from a pool sponsor to allow it to determine the fair value of its investment in the pool, the methods used and significant assumptions made in determining that fair value and the reasons for having had to make such an estimate. ______
   f. Any income from investments associated with one fund that is assigned to another fund. ______
   g. Optionally, an entity may disclose realized gains and losses in the notes to the financial statements computed as the difference between the proceeds of the sale and the original cost of the investment sold. ______
   h. External investment pools that elect to report—and other entities that disclose—realized gains and losses should also disclose that: ______

      (1) The calculation of realized gains and losses is independent of a calculation of the net change in fair value of investments. ______
      (2) Realized gains and losses on investments that had been held in more than one fiscal year and sold in the current year were included as a change in the fair value of investment reports in the prior year(s) and the current year. ______

9. Are the following disclosures provided for derivatives? (GASBTB 94-1)

   a. Discussion of relevant accounting policies. ______
   b. Nature of transactions and reason for entering into them, including discussion of credit, market, and legal risk. ______
   c. For proprietary funds implementing FASB Statements, have the disclosure provisions of FASB Statement 119, *Disclosure about Derivative Financial Instruments and Fair Value of Investments*, been provided? ______

10. Are the following disclosures provided for securities lending transactions? (GASBS 28, paras 11–16)

    a. Source of legal or contractual authorization for the use of securities lending transactions. ______
    b. Any significant violations of those provisions occurring during the reporting period. ______
    c. General description of the transactions, including: ______
       (1) Types of securities loaned. ______
       (2) Types of collateral received. ______
       (3) Whether the government has the ability to pledge or sell collateral securities without a borrower default. ______
       (4) Amount by which the value of the collateral provided is required to exceed the value of the underlying securities. ______

(5) Any restriction on the amount of the loans that can be made. ______
(6) Any loss indemnification provided to the entity by its securities lending agents. ______
(7) Carrying amount and market or fair values of underlying securities. ______

d. Whether the maturities of investments made with cash collateral generally match the maturities of the securities loans, and the extent of such matching. ______
e. Amount of credit risk related to securities lending transactions. ______
f. Amount of losses or recoveries of prior losses during the period from securities lending transactions. ______
g. Are appropriate investment disclosures made for collateral received and disclosure made for reverse repurchase agreements? ______

11. Are the following disclosures made for investments carried under the equity method of accounting? (APB 18)
    a. Name of each investee and the percentage of ownership. ______
    b. Accounting policies relative to equity method investments. ______
    c. Difference, if any, between the amount at which the investment is carried and the amount of underlying equity in net position and the accounting treatment for the difference. ______
    d. Aggregate market value of each identified investment for which a market value is available. ______
12. Are the following disclosures made for each joint venture in which the government participates? (GASBS 14, para 75)
    a. Descriptions of the government's ongoing financial interest or financial responsibility in the joint venture. ______
    b. Sufficient information about the joint venture to enable the reader to evaluate whether the joint venture is accumulating financial resources or experiencing financial stress that may result in an additional benefit or burden to the government. ______
    c. Information about the availability of separate financial statements of the joint venture. ______
    d. Disclosure of any information for related-party transactions. ______
13. Are the following disclosures provided for notes and accounts receivable?
    a. Notes and accounts receivable from affiliated organizations disclosed separately. ______
    b. Amounts of interfund receivables and payables, disclosed by fund. ______
14. Are the following disclosures provided for inventories?
    a. Basis for stating the inventories. ______
    b. Substantial or unusual losses from write-downs disclosed separately from other expenditures or expenses. (ARB 43) ______
15. Are the following disclosures provided by major class of asset for capital assets? (GASBS 34, para 117)
    a. Beginning- and end-of-year balances (regardless of whether beginning-of-year balances are presented on the face of the government-wide financial statements), with accumulated depreciation presented separately from historical cost. ______
    b. Capital acquisitions. ______
    c. Sales or other dispositions. ______
    d. Current period depreciation expense, with disclosure of the amounts charged to each of the functions in the statement of activities. ______
16. For collections not capitalized, disclosures should provide a description of the collection and the reasons these assets are not capitalized. For collections that are capitalized, governments should make the disclosures required for all capital assets. ______

17. Are capital assets not being depreciated presented separately from those that are being depreciated? ______
18. Have governments using the modified approach presented the following schedules, derived from asset management systems, as required supplementary information for all eligible infrastructure assets that are reported using the modified approach? (GASBS 34, para 18)
    a. The assessed condition, performed at least every three years, for at least the three most recent complete condition assessments, indicating the dates of the assessments. ______
    b. The estimated annual amount calculated at the beginning of the fiscal year to maintain and preserve at (or above) the condition level established and disclosed by the government compared with the amounts actually expensed for each of the past five reporting periods. ______
19. The following disclosures should accompany the schedules required by item 18:
    a. The basis for the condition measurement and the measurement scale used to assess and report condition. For example, a basis for *condition measurement* could be distresses found in pavement surfaces. A *scale* used to assess and report condition could range from 0 for a failed pavement to 100 for a pavement in perfect condition. ______
    b. The condition level at which the government intends to preserve its eligible infrastructure assets reported using the modified approach. ______
20. The carrying amount of impaired capital assets that are idle at year-end should be disclosed, regardless of whether the impairment is considered permanent or temporary. ______

U. Disclosures Relating to Liabilities (Cod. Section 2300)

1. Do the financial statements disclose the nature of any restrictions on assets relating to outstanding indebtedness? ______
2. Is the following information relating to debt disclosed?
    a. Maturity, interest rates, and annual debt service requirements to maturity for the short-term and long-term issues of outstanding debt. ______
    b. Issuance and payment of debt for the period. ______
    c. Details of capital leases. ______
    d. Amounts of authorized but unissued debt. ______
    e. Existence of any significant bond covenants and liquidity agreements. ______
    f. Violations of bond covenants. ______
    g. Nature and amount of contingent and moral obligations, no-commitment debt, and any actions by the government to extend an obligation to pay. ______
    h. The amount of unpaid debt that has been defeased. ______
    i. Refunding of debt, including the difference between the cash flows to service the old debt and the cash flows to service the new debt, and the economic gains or loss resulting from the transaction. ______
    j. Debt issued subsequent to the balance sheet date but before the financial statements are issued. ______
    k. An existing or anticipated inability to pay debt when due. ______
    l. Terms of interest rate change for variable rate debt. (GASBS 38) ______
    m. Interest requirements for variable-rate debt computed using the rate effective at year-end. (GASBS 38) ______
3. Are amounts payable from restricted assets separately presented in the financial statements, including:
    a. Construction contracts. ______
    b. Revenue bonds. ______

c. Fiscal agent. ______
d. Deposits. ______
e. Accrued interest. ______

4. Are any conversion features of convertible debt disclosed? ______
5. Are the following disclosures made for demand bonds outstanding? (GASBI 1)

    a. General description of the demand bond program. ______
    b. Terms of any letters of credit or other standby liquidity agreements outstanding, commitment fees to obtain letters of credit, and any amounts drawn on them outstanding as of the balance sheet date. ______
    c. Description of the take-out agreement, including its expiration date, commitment fees to obtain the agreement, and the terms of any new obligations under the take-out agreements. ______
    d. Debt service requirements that would result if the take-out agreement were not exercised. ______
    e. If a take-out agreement is exercised converting bonds to an installment loan, the installment loan is reported as debt and included as part of the schedule of debt service requirements to maturity. ______

6. For periods after a troubled debt restructuring, do disclosures include the following?

    a. Extent to which amounts contingently payable are included in the carrying amount of restructured payables. ______
    b. Total amounts contingently payable, when applicable, and conditions under which those amounts would become payable or forgiven. ______

7. If debt is considered extinguished in an in-substance defeasance, do disclosures include a general description of the transaction and the amount of debt that is considered extinguished at the end of the period disclosed for as long as the debt remains outstanding? ______

    a. Do the disclosures in 7 distinguish between the primary government and its discretely presented component units? ______

8. Regardless of where the debt is reported, for a defeasance of debt through an advance refunding, are the following disclosures provided?

    a. General description of the transaction provided in the period of the refunding. ______
    b. The difference between the cash flows required to service the new debt and complete the refunding. ______
    c. Economic gain or loss resulting from the transaction. ______

9. Are any defaults in provisions of security agreements, indentures, or other credit agreements disclosed? ______
10. If a waiver is obtained relating to a debt instrument for a period of time, is the period of time disclosed? ______
11. Are the following conduit debt obligations disclosed? (GASBI 2) ______

    a. General description of the conduit debt transactions. ______
    b. Aggregate amount of all conduit debt obligations outstanding at the balance sheet date. ______
    c. Indication that the issue has no obligation for the debt beyond the resources provided by the related leases and loans. ______

12. Is a schedule of short-term debt and the purpose for short-term debt disclosed? (GASBS 38) ______

13. Debt service requirements to maturity, separately identifying principal and interest for each of the subsequent years and in five-year increments thereafter? ______
14. Is the following information provided about long-term liabilities including both long-term debt (such as bonds, notes, loans, and leases payable) and other long-term liabilities (such as compensated absences, and claims and judgments)? (GASBS 34, para 119) ______
    a. Beginning- and end-of-year balances (regardless of whether prior year data are presented on the face of the government-wide financial statements). ______
    b. Increases and decreases (separately presented). ______
    c. The portions of each item that are due within one year of the statement date. ______
    d. Which governmental funds typically have been used to liquidate other long-term liabilities (such as compensated absences and pension liabilities) in prior years. ______

V. General Disclosure and Financial Statement Presentation Matters

1. Are significant violations of legal or contractual provisions for deposits and investments reported? ______
2. If the combined statements contain a total column, is it captioned "memorandum only" and do the notes describe this as meaning: ______
    a. That the column is for information only?
    b. If interfund balances and transactions have been eliminated? ______
    c. That the column does not present consolidated financial information? ______
3. Are designations and reservations of fund balance that are not evident from the financial statements presented in the notes? ______
    a. If not evident from the financial statements, do the notes disclose material changes in fund balance reserves or designations that are disclosed in the notes?
4. Is the method for recognizing "profits" under construction-type contracts disclosed along with the following other disclosures? ______
    a. If the percentage of completion method of accounting is being used, is the method of measuring the extent of progress toward completion disclosed? ______
    b. Are claims paid in excess of the agreed contract price disclosed? ______
5. Is the method of accounting for expenditures for insurance and similar services that extend over more than one accounting period disclosed? ______
6. Are the following disclosures made relative to budgetary information? (NCGAI 10)
    a. Explanations of differences between the budgetary basis of accounting and GAAP, if any.
    b. The degree to which the reporting entity's financial operations are subject to a comprehensive appropriated budget or nonappropriated budget or are nonbudgeted activities. ______
    c. When a separate budgetary report is issued, do the notes to the general-purpose financial statements make reference to that report? ______
    d. Are any instances where expenditures exceeded appropriation of intended funds disclosed? (Cod. Section 2300) ______
7. Are the following disclosures made relating to extraordinary items: ______
    a. Is a description of the extraordinary event or transaction and the principal items entering into the determination of the extraordinary gain or loss provided? ______
    b. Are the nature, origin, and amount of an adjustment made in the current period to extraordinary items reported in prior periods? ______

c. Have material events or transactions that do not meet the criteria for classification as an extraordinary item been considered for reporting as a separate component of income from continuing operations, with the nature and effect of each transaction disclosed? ______

8. Do the notes disclose the entire amount of interest cost during the period and the amount, if any, that has been capitalized? ______
9. If the entity engages in futures transactions that are accounted for as hedges, is the following information disclosed?

a. Nature of the assets, liabilities, firm commitments, or anticipated transactions that are hedged with futures contracts. ______
b. Method of accounting for the futures contracts, including a description of the events or transactions that result in recognition of income of changes in the value of the contracts. ______

10. Do the notes disclose the total research and development costs charged to expense in each period an income statement is presented by proprietary funds? ______
11. Are the segment disclosure requirements met by providing condensed financial statements in the notes, which include the following? (GASBS 34, para 122) ______

a. Types of goods or services provided by the segment.
b. Condensed statement of net position: ______

(1) Total assets—distinguishing between current assets, capital assets, and other assets. Amounts receivable from other funds or component units should be reported separately. ______
(2) Total liabilities—distinguishing between current and long-term amounts. Amounts payable to other funds or component units should be reported separately. ______
(3) Total net position—distinguishing among restricted (separately reporting expendable and nonexpendable components); unrestricted; and amounts invested in capital assets, net of related debt. ______

c. Condensed statement of revenues, expenses, and changes in net position: ______

(1) Operating revenues (by major source). ______
(2) Operating expenses. Depreciation (including any amortization) should be identified separately. ______
(3) Operating income (loss). ______
(4) Nonoperating revenues (expenses)—with separate reporting of major revenues and expenses. ______
(5) Capital contributions and additions to permanent and term endowments. ______
(6) Special and extraordinary items. ______
(7) Transfers. ______
(8) Change in net position. ______
(9) Beginning net position. ______
(10) Ending net position. ______

d. Condensed statement of cash flows: ______

(1) Net cash provided (used) by: ______

(a) Operating activities. ______
(b) Noncapital financing activities. ______
(c) Capital and related financing activities. ______
(d) Investing activities. ______

(2) Beginning cash and cash equivalent balances. ______
(3) Ending cash and cash equivalent balances. ______

12. For purposes of fund types presenting a statement of cash flows, is the policy disclosed for which short-term investments are considered cash equivalents? ______
13. For interfund transfers, are amounts transferred from other funds by individual major fund, nonmajor governmental funds in the aggregate, nonmajor enterprise funds in the aggregate, internal service funds in the aggregate, and fiduciary fund type disclosed, as well as a general description of the principal purposes of interfund transfers as well as purposes for and amounts of certain transfers? (GASBS 38) ______
14. For interfund balances, are amounts due from other funds by individual major fund, nonmajor governmental funds in the aggregate, nonmajor enterprise funds in the aggregate, internal service funds in the aggregate, and fiduciary fund type disclosed, as well as the purpose for those balances and the amounts that are not expected to be repaid within one year? (GASBS 38) ______

W. Disclosures about Derivatives

GASBS 53 requires governments to include the information in the notes to the financial statements where applicable. Disclosure information for similar derivative instrument types may be provided individually or aggregated. To determine whether derivative instruments are the same type, the commonly known term for the derivative instrument (for example, swaps, swaptions, rate caps, futures contracts, and options written or purchased), the nature of the derivative instrument (for example, receive-fixed or pay-fixed interest rate swaps), the hedged item, if any, and the reference rate should be considered.

1. Has the government provided a summary of their derivative instrument activity during the reporting period and balances at the end of the reporting period? The information disclosed should be organized by governmental activities, business-type activities, and fiduciary funds. The information should then be divided into the following categories—hedging derivative instruments (distinguishing between fair value hedges and cash flow hedges) and investment derivative instruments. Within each category, derivative instruments should be aggregated by type (for example, received-fixed swaps, pay-fixed swaps, swaptions, rate caps, basis swaps, or futures contracts). Information presented in the summary should include:

   a. Notional amount. ______
   b. Changes in fair value during the reporting period and the classification in the financial statements where those changes in fair value are reported. ______
   c. Fair values as of the end of the reporting period and the classification in the financial statements where those fair values are reported. If derivative instrument fair values are based on other than quoted market prices, the methods and significant assumptions used to estimate those fair values should be disclosed. (If a fair value is developed by a pricing service, there is no requirement to disclose significant assumptions if the pricing service considers those assumptions to be proprietary and, after making every reasonable effort, the pricing service declines to make that information available. This fact, however, should be disclosed.) ______
   d. Fair values of derivative instruments reclassified from a hedging derivative instrument to an investment derivative instrument. There also should be disclosure of the deferral amount that was reported within investment revenue upon the reclassification. ______

Disclosure of the information required above may be in a columnar display, narrative form, or a combination of both.

2. Has the government provided the following note disclosures for all hedging derivative instruments?

a. *Objectives*. For hedging derivative instruments, governments should disclose their objectives for entering into those instruments, the context needed to understand those objectives, the strategies for achieving those objectives, and the types of derivative instruments entered into. ______

b. *Terms*. For hedging derivative instruments, governments should disclose significant terms, including: ______

   (1) Notional amount. ______
   (2) Reference rates, such as indexes or interest rates. ______
   (3) Embedded options, such as caps, floors, or collars. ______
   (4) The date when the hedging derivative instrument was entered into and when it is scheduled to terminate or mature. ______
   (5) The amount of cash paid or received, if any, when a forward contract or swap (including swaptions) was entered into. ______

c. *Risks*. For hedging derivative instruments, governments should disclose, if applicable, their exposure to the following risks that could give rise to financial loss. Risk disclosures are limited to hedging derivative instruments that are reported as of the end of the reporting period. Disclosures required by this paragraph may contain information that also is required by other paragraphs. However, these disclosures should be presented in the context of a hedging derivative instrument's risk: ______

   (1) *Credit risk*. If a hedging derivative instrument reported by the government as an asset exposes a government to **credit risk,*** the government should disclose that exposure as credit risk and disclose the following information: ______

   **The credit risk disclosures in this paragraph do not extend to derivatives that are exchange-traded, such as futures contracts. For those derivatives, disclosures for amounts held by broker/dealers are evaluated by applying the custodial credit risk disclosures found in Statements No. 3, Deposits with Financial Institutions, Investments (including Repurchase Agreements), and Reverse Repurchase Agreements, and No. 40, Deposit and Investment Risk Disclosures.*

      (a) The credit quality ratings of counterparties as described by nationally recognized statistical rating organizations—rating agencies—as of the end of the reporting period. If the counterparty is not rated, the disclosure should indicate that fact. ______
      (b) The maximum amount of loss due to credit risk, based on the fair value of the hedging derivative instrument as of the end of the reporting period, that the government would incur if the counterparties to the hedging derivative instrument failed to perform according to the terms of the contract, without respect to any collateral or other security, or netting arrangement. ______
      (c) The government's policy of requiring collateral or other security to support hedging derivative instruments subject to credit risk, a summary description and the aggregate amount of the collateral or other security that reduces credit risk exposure, and information about the government's access to that collateral or other security. ______
      (d) The government's policy of entering into master netting arrangements, including a summary description and the aggregate amount of liabilities included in those arrangements. Master netting arrangements are established when (1) each party owes the other determinable amounts, the government has the right to set off the amount owed with the amount owed by the counterparty, and (3) the right of setoff is legally enforceable. ______

(e) The aggregate fair value of hedging derivative instruments in asset (positive) positions net of collateral posted by the counterparty and the effect of master netting arrangements. ______

(f) Significant concentrations of net exposure to credit risk (gross credit risk reduced by collateral, other security, and setoff) with individual counterparties and groups of counterparties. A concentration of credit risk exposure to an individual counterparty may not require disclosure if its existence is apparent from the disclosures required by other parts of this paragraph, for example, a government has entered into only one interest rate swap. Group concentrations of credit risk exist if a number of counterparties are engaged in similar activities and have similar economic characteristics that would cause their ability to meet contractual obligations to be similarly affected by changes in economic or other conditions. ______

(2) *Interest rate risk.* If a hedging derivative instrument increases a government's exposure to interest rate risk, the government should disclose that increased exposure as interest rate risk and also should disclose the hedging derivative instrument's terms that increase such a risk. The determination of whether a hedging derivative instrument increases interest rate risk should be made after considering, for example, the effects of the hedging derivative instrument and any hedged debt. ______

(3) *Basis risk.* If a hedging derivative instrument exposes a government to basis risk, the government should disclose that exposure as basis risk and also should disclose the hedging derivative instrument's terms and payment terms of the hedged item that creates the basis risk. ______

(4) *Termination risk.* If a hedging derivative instrument exposes a government to **termination risk,** the government should disclose that exposure as termination risk and also the following information, as applicable: ______

(a) Any termination events that have occurred. ______

(b) Dates that the hedging derivative instrument may be terminated. ______

(c) Out-of-the-ordinary termination events contained in contractual documents, such as "additional termination events" contained in the schedule to the International Swap Dealers Association master agreement. ______

(5) *Rollover risk.* If a hedging derivative instrument exposes a government to **rollover risk,** the government should disclose that exposure as rollover risk and also should disclose the maturity of the hedging derivative instrument and the maturity of the hedged item. ______

(6) *Market-access risk.* If a hedging derivative instrument creates **market-access risk,** the government should disclose that exposure as market-access risk. ______

(7) *Foreign currency risk.* If a hedging derivative instrument exposes a government to foreign currency risk, the government should disclose the U.S. dollar balance of the hedging derivative instrument, organized by currency denomination and by type of derivative instrument. ______

d. *Hedged debt.* If the hedged item is a debt obligation, governments should disclose the hedging derivative instrument's net cash flows based on the requirements established by Statement No. 38, *Certain Financial Statement Note Disclosures,* paragraphs 10 and 11. ______

e. *Other quantitative method of evaluating effectiveness.* If effectiveness is evaluated by application of a quantitative method not specifically identified in this Statement (paragraphs 48 and 62), governments should disclose the following information:

(There is no requirement to disclose information that a pricing service considers to be proprietary and after making every reasonable effort the pricing service declines to make available. This fact, however, should be disclosed.) ______

(1) The identity and characteristics of the method used. ______
(2) The range of critical terms the method tolerates. ______
(3) The actual critical terms of the hedge. ______

3. For investment derivative instruments, has the government disclosed their exposure to the following risks that could give rise to financial loss? Risk disclosures are limited to investment derivative instruments that are reported as of the end of the reporting period. Disclosures required by this paragraph may contain information that also is required by other paragraphs. However, these disclosures should be presented in the context of an investment derivative instrument's risk:

   a. *Credit risk.* If an investment derivative instrument exposes a government to credit risk (that is, the government reports the investment derivative instrument as an asset), the government should disclose that exposure. That disclosure should be consistent with the requirements of paragraph 73a. ______
   b. *Interest rate risk.* If an investment derivative instrument exposes a government to interest rate risk, the government should disclose that exposure consistent with the disclosures required by Statement 40, paragraphs 14 and 15. Further, an investment derivative instrument that is an interest rate swap is an additional example of an investment that has a fair value that is highly sensitive to interest rate changes as discussed in Statement 40, paragraph 16. The fair value, notional amount, reference rate, and embedded options should be disclosed. ______
   c. *Foreign currency risk.* If an investment derivative instrument exposes a government to foreign currency risk, the government should disclose that exposure consistent with the disclosures required by Statement 40, paragraph 17. ______

4. Has the government disclosed contingent features that are included in derivative instruments held at the end of the reporting period, such as a government's obligation to post collateral if the credit quality of the government's hedgeable item declines? For derivative instruments with contingent features reported as of the end of the reporting period, disclosure should include:

   a. The existence and nature of contingent features and the circumstances in which the features could be triggered. ______
   b. The aggregate fair value of derivative instruments that contain those features. ______
   c. The aggregate fair value of assets that would be required to be posted as collateral or transferred in accordance with the provisions related to the triggering of the contingent liabilities. ______
   d. The amount, if any, that has been posted as collateral by the government as of the end of the reporting period. ______

5. If a government reports a hybrid instrument, are the disclosures of the companion instrument consistent with disclosures required of similar transactions, for example, disclosures for debt instruments? In that case, the existence of an embedded derivative with the companion instrument should be indicated in the disclosures of the companion instrument. For example, if a government has entered into a hybrid instrument that consists of a borrowing for financial reporting purposes and an interest rate swap, the government's disclosure should indicate the existence of the interest rate swap within the debt disclosure. ______

6. Has the government that reported an SGIC that is fully benefit-responsive, disclosed the following information in the notes to the financial statements as of the end of the reporting period?

   a. A description of the nature of the SGIC. ______
   b. The SGIC's fair value (including separate disclosure of the fair value of the wrap contract and the fair value of the corresponding underlying investments). ______

X. Termination Benefits

1. In the period in which an employer becomes obligated for termination benefits and in any additional period in which employees are required to render future service in order to receive involuntary termination benefits, the employers should disclose a description of the termination arrangement, such as information about the types of benefits provided, the number of employees affected, and the period of time over which benefits are expected to be provided. ______
2. In the period in which an employer becomes obligated for termination benefits, the cost of the termination benefits should be disclosed, if not otherwise identifiable from the financial statements. An employer that provides termination benefits that affect defined benefit pension or OPEB obligations should disclose in the notes the change in the actuarial accrued liability for the pension or OPEB plan attributable to the termination benefits. ______
3. In all periods in which termination benefit liabilities are reported, disclosure should be made of the significant methods (such as whether benefits are measured at the discounted present value of expected future benefit payments) and assumptions (such as the discount rate and health care cost trend rate, if applicable) used to determine liabilities. ______
4. If a termination benefit that otherwise meets the recognition criteria of GASBS 47 is not recognized because the expected benefits are not estimable, that fact should be disclosed. ______

Y. Pledged Revenues

For purposes of the following disclosures, pledged revenues are those specific revenues that have been formally committed to directly collateralize or secure debt of the pledging government, or directly or indirectly collateralize or secure debt of a component unit. The disclosures in this paragraph are not required for legally separate entities that report as stand-alone business-type activities whose operations are financed primarily by a single major revenue source. In an indirect collateralization, the pledged revenue agreement is not directly between the pledging government and the bondholders. That is, the pledging government's revenues do not secure the debt; rather, the debt is secured by its payments to the component units that are financed by that revenue. In essence, the pledging government makes an annual debt service "grant" to the component unit, which in turn pledges that revenue as security for its debt.

1. For each period in which the secured debt remains outstanding, pledging governments should disclose, in the notes to financial statements, information about specific revenues pledged, including (GASBS 48, para 21):

   a. Identification of the specific revenue pledged and the approximate amount of the pledge. Generally, the approximate amount of the pledge would be equal to the remaining principal and interest requirements of the secured debt. ______
   b. Identification of, and general purpose for, the debt secured by the pledged revenue. ______
   c. The term of the commitment—that is, the period during which the revenue will not be available for other purposes. ______

d. The relationship of the pledged amount to the total for that specific revenue, if estimable—that is, the proportion of the specific revenue stream that has been pledged. ______

e. A comparison of the pledged revenues recognized during the period to the principal and interest requirements for the debt directly or indirectly collateralized by those revenues. For this disclosure, pledged revenues recognized during the period may be presented net of specified operating expenses, based on the provisions of the pledge agreement; however, the amounts should not be netted in the financial statements. ______

2. In the year of the sale, governments that sell future revenue streams should disclose in the notes to financial statements information about the specific revenues sold, including (GASBS 48, para 22): ______

 a. Identification of the specific revenue sold, including the approximate amount, and the significant assumptions used in determining the approximate amount. ______
 b. The period to which the sale applies. ______
 c. The relationship of the sold amount to the total for that specific revenue, if estimable—that is, the proportion of the specific revenue stream that has been sold. ______
 d. A comparison of the proceeds of the sale and the present value of the future revenues sold, including the significant assumptions used in determining the present value. ______

Z. Pollution Remediation Obligations

1. For recognized pollution remediation liabilities and recoveries of pollution remediation outlays, has the following been disclosed? (GASBS 49, para 25)

 a. The nature and source of pollution remediation obligations (for example, federal, state, or local laws or regulations). ______
 b. The amount of the estimated liability (if not apparent from the financial statements), the methods and assumptions used for the estimate, and the potential for changes due to, for example, price increases or reductions, technology, or applicable laws or regulations. ______
 c. Estimated recoveries reducing the liability. ______

2. For pollution remediation liabilities, or portions thereof, that are not yet recognized because they are not reasonably estimable, has the government disclosed a general description of the nature of the pollution remediation activities? (GASBS 49, para 26) ______

AA. Going Concern Considerations (GASBS 56)

1. If it is determined that there is substantial doubt about the government's ability to continue as a going concern, do the notes to the financial statements include disclosure of the following, as appropriate:

 a. Pertinent conditions and events giving rise to the assessment of substantial doubt about the government's ability to continue as a going concern for a reasonable period of time. ______
 b. The possible effects of such conditions and events. ______
 c. Government officials' evaluation of the significance of those conditions and events and any mitigating factors. ______
 d. Possible discontinuance of operations. ______
 e. Government officials' plans (including relevant prospective financial information). ______
 f. Information about the recoverability or classification of recorded asset amounts or the amounts or classification of liabilities. ______

BB. Bankruptcy (GASBS 58)

1. If the government has filed for bankruptcy, has the following been disclosed?
   a. Pertinent conditions and events giving rise to the petition for bankruptcy. ______
   b. The expected or known effects of such conditions and events, including: ______
      (1) The principal categories of the claims subject to compromise or that already have been adjusted. ______
      (2) The principal changes in terms and the major features of settlement. ______
      (3) The aggregate gain expected to occur by remeasuring liabilities subject to a proposed Plan of Adjustment, or realized, as appropriate; or a statement that any gain is not yet reasonably estimable and the reasons therefor. ______
      (4) Contingent claims not subject to reasonable estimation, based on the provisions of NCGA Statement. ______
   c. Significance of those conditions and events on the levels of service and operations of the government, and any mitigating factors, such as assumption of services by other governments. ______
   d. Possibility of termination of the government, or any plans to terminate the government, as appropriate. ______
   e. How to obtain a copy of the government's Plan of Adjustment or a statement that a plan is not yet available and an estimate of when it will be completed. ______

CC. Service Concession Arrangements (GASBS 60)

1. Has the following been disclosed in the notes to financial statements of transferors and governmental operators for service concession arrangements?
   a. A general description of the arrangement in effect during the reporting period, including management's objectives for entering into it and, if applicable, the status of the project during the construction period. ______
   b. The nature and amount of assets, liabilities, and deferred inflows of resources related to service concession arrangement that are recognized in the financial statements. ______
   c. The nature and extent of rights retained by the transferor or granted to the governmental operator under the arrangement. ______
2. For each period in which a guarantee or commitment exists, has disclosure been made about the guarantees and commitments, including identification, duration, and significant contract terms of the guarantee or commitment? ______

DD. Nonexchange Financial Guarantees (GASBS 70)

1. A government that extends nonexchange financial guarantees should disclose the following information about the guarantees by type of guarantee:
   a. A description of the obligations that are guaranteed identifying:
      (1) The legal authority and limits for providing financial guarantees. ______
      (2) The relationship to the entity or entities issuing the obligations that are guaranteed. ______
      (3) The length of time of the guarantees. ______
      (4) Arrangements for recovering payments from the issuers of the obligations that are guaranteed. ______
   b. The total amount of all guarantees extended that are outstanding at the reporting date. ______

2. A government that recognizes a nonexchange financial guarantee liability or has made payments during the reporting period on nonexchange financial guarantees extended should disclose the following information:

    a. A brief description of the timing of recognition and measurement of the liabilities and information about the changes in recognized guarantee liabilities, including the following:
        (1) Beginning-of-period balances. ______
        (2) Increases, including initial recognition and adjustments increasing estimates. ______
        (3) Guarantee payments made and adjustments decreasing estimates. ______
        (4) End-of-period balances. ______

    b. Cumulative amounts of indemnification payments that have been made on guarantees extended that are outstanding at the reporting date. ______
    c. Amounts expected to be recovered from indemnification payments that have been made through the reporting date. ______

Governments That Issue Guaranteed Obligations

3. A government that has one or more outstanding obligations at the reporting date that have been guaranteed by another entity as part of a nonexchange transaction should disclose the following information about the guarantee(s) by type of guarantee:

    a. The name of the entity providing the guarantee. ______
    b. The amount of the guarantee. ______
    c. The length of time of the guarantee. ______
    d. The amount paid, if any, by the entity extending the guarantee on obligations of the government during the current reporting period. ______
    e. The cumulative amount paid by the entity extending the guarantee on outstanding obligations of the government. ______
    f. A description of requirements to repay the entity extending the guarantee. ______
    g. The outstanding amounts, if any, required to be repaid to the entity providing the guarantee. ______

4. If a government has issued a guaranteed obligation for which payments have been made during the reporting period by the entity that extended the guarantee and that guaranteed obligation is no longer outstanding at the end of the reporting period, regardless of whether the government has any other outstanding guaranteed obligations at the end of the reporting period, it should disclose:

    a. The amount paid by the entity that extended the guarantee on obligations of the government during the current reporting period. ______
    b. The cumulative amount paid by the entity that extended the guarantee on outstanding obligations of the government. ______
    c. A description of requirements to repay the entity that extended the guarantee. ______
    d. The outstanding amounts, if any, required to be repaid to the entity that provided the guarantee. ______

EE. Mergers, Acquisitions and Transfers of Operations
All Government Combinations

1. For each government combination, the government should include the following information in the notes to financial statements for the period in which the combination occurs:

a. A brief description of the government combination, including identification of the entities involved in the combination and whether the participating entities were included within the same financial reporting entity. _______
b. The date of the combination. _______
c. A brief description of the primary reasons for the combination. _______

Government Mergers and Transfers of Operations

2. The new government or continuing government also should disclose the following information:

   a. The amounts recognized as of the merger date or the effective transfer date as follows: _______

      (1) Total assets—distinguishing between current assets, capital assets, and other assets. _______
      (2) Total deferred outflows of resources. _______
      (3) Total liabilities—distinguishing between current and long-term amounts. _______
      (4) Total deferred inflows of resources. _______
      (5) Total net position by component. _______

   b. A brief description of the nature and amount of significant adjustments made to bring into conformity the individual accounting policies or to adjust for impairment of capital assets resulting from the merger or transfer. _______
   c. The initial amounts recognized by the new or continuing government, if different from the values in (a) and the differences that arise from modifying the carrying values in (a) by the adjustments in (b). _______

Government Acquisitions

3. In the period in which an acquisition occurs, the acquiring government also should disclose the following information:

   a. A brief description of the consideration provided. _______
   b. The total amount of net position acquired as of the date of acquisition. _______
   c. A brief description of contingent consideration arrangements, including the basis for determining the amount of payments that are contingent. _______

Disposals of Government Operations

4. In the period in which operations are transferred or sold, the disposing government should identify the operations and provide a brief description of the facts and circumstances leading to the disposal of those operations. In addition, the disposing government should identify and disclose the following information about the disposed government operations if not separately presented in its financial statements:

   a. Total expenses, distinguishing between operating and nonoperating, if applicable. _______
   b. Total revenues, distinguishing between operating and nonoperating, if applicable. _______
   c. Total governmental fund revenues and expenditures, if applicable. _______

FF. Fair Value Measurements (GASBS 72)

1. GASBS 72 fair value disclosures should be organized by type of asset or liability. The following should be taken into consideration when determining the level of detail and disaggregation and how much emphasis to place on each disclosure requirement: _______

   a. *The nature, characteristics, and risks of an asset or a liability.* Assets and liabilities that share the same nature, characteristics or risks may be aggregated.

For example, U.S. Treasury bills may be aggregated with short-term U.S. Treasury Separate Trading of Registered Interest and Principal Securities (STRIPS) because these investments have similar exposures to interest rate risk. ______

b. *The level of the fair value hierarchy within which the fair value measurement is categorized.* A greater degree of uncertainty and subjectivity suggests that the number of types may need to be greater. For example, fair value measurements categorized within Level 3 of the fair value hierarchy may need greater disaggregation. ______
c. *Whether GASBS 72 or another GASB Statement specifies a type for an asset or a liability.* Disclosures should be disaggregated by type as specified by relevant accounting standards. For example, GASBS 53 requires derivative instrument disclosures that distinguish between hedging derivative instruments and investment derivative instruments. ______
d. *The objective or the mission of the government.* The level of aggregation or disaggregation may differ based upon the objective or mission of the government. For example, the objective of an external investment pool to achieve income or profit suggests greater disaggregation compared to a general purpose government. ______
e. *The characteristics of the government.* A government may be composed of governmental and business-type activities, individual major funds, nonmajor funds in the aggregate, or fiduciary fund types and component units. Additional disclosures may be appropriate if the risk exposure of a particular fund is significantly greater than the deposit and investment risks of the primary government. For example, a primary government's total investments may not be exposed to a concentration of credit risk. However, if the government's capital projects fund (a major fund) has all of its investments in one issuer of corporate bonds, disclosure should be made for the capital projects fund's exposure to a concentration of credit risk. ______
f. *Relative significance of assets and liabilities.* The relative significance of assets and liabilities measured at fair value compared to total assets and liabilities should be evaluated in terms of the government structure as discussed in (e). ______
g. *Whether separately issued financial statements are available.* A government may further aggregate disclosures if a component unit issues its own separate financial statements containing disaggregated information. For example, a state government may consider reduced disclosures of fair value measurements of investments in certain entities that calculate the NAV per share (or its equivalent) if the financial statements of the state's pension plan include that information. ______
h. *Line items presented in the statement of net position.* A type of asset or liability will often require greater disaggregation than the line items presented in the statement of net position. For example, the statement of net position reports "cash and investments" while Statement 3 and Statement No. 40, *Deposit and Investment Risk Disclosures,* require disclosures that focus on deposits and investments. ______

2. A government should disclose the following information for each type of asset or liability measured at fair value in the statement of net position after initial recognition:

   a. For recurring and nonrecurring fair value measurements: ______

      (1) The fair value measurement at the end of the reporting period. ______
      (2) Except for investments that are measured at the NAV per share (or its equivalent), the level of the fair value hierarchy within which the fair value measurements are categorized in their entirety (Level 1, Level 2, or Level 3). ______
      (3) A description of the valuation techniques used in the fair value measurement. ______

(4) If there has been a change in valuation technique that has a significant impact on the result (for example, changing from an expected cash flow technique to a relief from royalty technique or the use of an additional valuation technique), that change and the reason(s) for making it. ______

b. For nonrecurring fair value measurements: the reason(s) for the measurement. ______

Additional disclosures for fair value measurements of investments in certain entities that calculate the net asset value per share

The disclosures listed below apply to investments in entities that meet all of the following criteria: (a) calculate the NAV per share (or its equivalent), regardless of whether the method of determining fair value by using NAV has been applied; (b) do not have a readily determinable fair value; and (c) are measured at fair value on a recurring or nonrecurring basis during the period. A government should disclose information that addresses the nature and risks of the investments and whether the investments are probable of being sold at amounts different from the NAV per share (or its equivalent). A government should disclose the following information for each type of investment:

a. The fair value measurement of the investment type at the measurement date and a description of the significant investment strategies of the investee(s) in that type. ______
b. For each type of investment that includes investments that can never be redeemed with the investees, but a government receives distributions through the liquidation of the underlying assets of the investees: the government's estimate of the period over which the underlying assets are expected to be liquidated by the investees. ______
c. The amount of a government's unfunded commitments related to that investment type. ______
d. A general description of the terms and conditions upon which a government may redeem investments in the type (for example, quarterly redemption with 60 days' notice). ______
e. The circumstances in which an otherwise redeemable investment in the type (or a portion thereof) might not be redeemable (for example, investments subject to a redemption restriction, such as a lockup or gate). ______
f. For those otherwise redeemable investments in (e) that are restricted from redemption as of the government's measurement date: the estimate of when the restriction from redemption might lapse; if an estimate cannot be made, disclose that fact and how long the restriction has been in effect. ______
g. Any other significant restriction on the ability to sell investments in the type at the measurement date. ______
h. If a government determines that it is probable that it will sell an investment(s) for an amount different from the NAV per share (or its equivalent): the total fair value of all investments and any remaining actions required to complete the sale. ______
i. If a group of investments would otherwise meet the criteria in determining whether a sale is probable but the individual investments to be sold have not been identified (for example, if a government decides to sell 20 percent of its investments in private equity funds but the individual investments to be sold have not been identified), such that the investments continue to qualify for the method of determining fair value using NAV: the government's plans to sell and any remaining actions required to complete the sale(s). ______

INDEX

Page references followed by *e* indicate an exhibit